System Quality

System Quality Subgoals	First-Level Characteristics	Second-Level Characteristics
1. Functionality: How well (reliably, clearly, efficiently) does the system function?	Reliability	Completeness Accuracy Robustness/integrity
	Clarity	Consistency Predictability
	Efficiency	Fast turnaround Low memory requirements Nonredundant procedures and processes
2. Ease of maintenance: How easy is it to maintain (understand, modify, and test) the system?	Understandability	Clear documentation Cohesiveness Consistency
	Modifiability	Modular structure Modular independence
	Testability	Clear documentation Modular structure
3. Flexibility: How flexible is the system with respect to changes in its components?	Portability	Site independence Device independence Language independence
	Adaptability	Program-data independence Procedural flexibility

Systems Development

Requirements,
Evaluation, Design,
and Implementation

PWS-KENT Series in Computer Science

Eleanor W. Jordan

University of Texas at Austin

Jefry J. Machesky

KPMG Peat Marwick
Consulting

with

J. B. Matkowski

Capilano College

Systems Development

Requirements,
Evaluation, Design,
and Implementation

 PWS-KENT Publishing Company ∎ Boston

PWS-KENT
Publishing Company

20 Park Plaza
Boston, Massachusetts 02116

Sponsoring Editor: Jonathan Plant
Assistant Editor: Mary Thomas
Production Editor: S. London
Manufacturing Coordinator: Marcia Locke
Interior Designer: Jean Hammond
Cover Designer: S. London
Cover Illustrator: David Biedrzcyki
Typesetter: Pine Tree Composition, Inc.
Cover Printer: Henry N. Sawyer Co., Inc.
Printer and Binder: R. R. Donnelley & Sons Company

PWS-KENT Publishing Company is a division of Wadsworth, Inc.

Library of Congress Cataloging-in-Publication Data

Jordan, Eleanor W.
    Systems development, requirements, evaluation, design,
    and implementation.

    Includes index.
    I. Machesky, Jefry J.   II. Title.
QA403.J458   1989   003   89–97309
ISBN 0-534-92085-3

Printed in the United States of America
90 91 92 93 94—10 9 8 7 6 5 4 3 2 1

Preface

Overview

Today it is likely that anyone working in an organization will be involved in systems development to some extent. The computer hardware and development tools now available have made it possible for employees to be directly responsible for creating their own systems, based on their specific needs. In such an environment it is essential that basic problem-solving skills are learned and applied to the development of an effective system. The goal of *Systems Development* is to give a coherent view of this complex, challenging subject.

Scope of the Book

We have aimed this book at the wide audience of future systems developers, which includes people working or studying in such diverse areas as business, science, engineering, the social sciences, education, and the liberal arts. *Systems Development* provides the basic skills and understanding needed by all those involved with systems development.

This book offers a comprehensive look at systems development from the initial stage of determining user requirements to the final evaluation of installed systems. We feel that the broad scope of the book will help readers see the "big picture" of systems development, thus making analysis and design techniques understandable within the context of the entire systems development process.

Twenty-four minicases and numerous exercises are included to give *Systems Development* a strong pragmatic foundation. Together, the minicases and exercises provide readers with a realistic view of the problems encountered in systems development and the methods by which these problems can be solved.

We expect readers to have some knowledge of computer systems, either from practical experience or from an introductory data processing course. If you are at this basic level, covering all of the text material is best accomplished in two semesters. Those students with a more extensive programming and database background will be able to cover the entire book in one semester.

Learning Features

Systems Development is organized around the premise that three major strategies are necessary to master the subject:

1. We believe in *learning by doing*. Problem-solving skills are nurtured by the use of frequent exercises that test conceptual understanding, rather than simply repeating the text material. The exercise sets are carefully graded. Exercises in

later chapters integrate new material with concepts and techniques presented earlier, so that readers can actively practice patterns of skills.

2. *Management of the process* is stressed throughout the book. Planning development activities and coordinating the developers' tasks are vital to success, and we have been careful to make this clear. Planning techniques are introduced in Chapter 4 and then illustrated in the following eighteen chapters. The link between managing the project and developing the project is an ongoing theme in the book. Numerous planning exercises provide active learning experience for readers.

3. We emphasize *delivery in phases* in this text. This allows readers to master parts of the system mix one-by-one, in an incremental fashion. In practice, this approach allows both developers and users of the system to learn about and modify the parts of the system as the overall systems development project progresses.

Text Organization

The text is organized into six parts: overview, managing activities, and then one part for each of the four stages of the development process: requirements, evaluation, design, and implementation.

Overview

We begin with the big picture. Chapter 1 is an overview of the development process and products. Chapter 2 introduces the conflicting goals of system quality, project management, and organizational relevance that are summarized on the inside front cover of the book. The key balancing act for system developers is to manage the process so the system is produced in a reasonable time, at a justifiable cost, and still meets the specifications of the users, and the goals of the organization. Chapter 3 illustrates how this is accomplished in a case study of a hospital system that is discussed throughout the book.

Managing Activities

Part 2 focuses on management issues for the whole process. Planning is a key part of system delivery; thus the techniques and issues are presented here to allow you to practice planning skills in the exercises throughout the book. Chapter 4 presents guidelines for planning. Chapter 5 outlines three systems delivery approaches, including how to partition systems projects for early delivery of usable subsystems. Also, Chapter 5 presents techniques for graphically developing and illustrating plans. Chapter 6 illustrates a series of estimating techniques to help avoid the unrealistically optimistic estimates of most developers.

Four Stages of Systems Development

Parts 3 through 6 are stage-by-stage discussions of the systems development process. The activities for each stage are summarized on the inside back cover. Chapters 7–12 in Part 3 present techniques for determining requirements, including assessing project risk, context diagrams, critical success factors analysis, interviewing, observing, prototyping, data-flow diagrams, systems flowcharts, data modeling, and documenting requirements. Chapters

13–14 in Part 4 cover evaluation guidelines, matrices, and grids. Chapters 15–18 in Part 5 explain design guidelines and design strategies for user interfaces, data storage, and software. Chapters 19–22 in Part 6 provide guidelines for implementation and strategies for building systems, including coding software, documenting systems and procedures, testing all system components, and finally installing completed systems.

The overview and planning issues introduced in Parts 1 and 2 provide the basis for the guidelines, techniques, examples, and exercises in the later portions of the book. Similarly, such techniques as data flow diagrams and data modeling, which are introduced in Chapters 10 and 11, are integral topics for evaluation, design, and implementation strategies in the following three parts.

The use of real-world examples ensures that no concept remains abstract. Minicases in each chapter illustrate techniques in organizational contexts. In addition to these minicases, episodes from two systems-development project cases run throughout the book. One case is the development of an order tracking system, initially defined in Chapter 8 and then developed in sections throughout Chapter 15–18 to illustrate design strategies. Similarly, the Meadows Hospital Pharmacy System, is first introduced as a system with purchased software in Chapter 3, and used as the basis in later chapters for minicases and exercises on data modeling, data flow diagrams in evaluation, design strategies, construction, testing, and installation.

Supplements

Supplements are available to assist instructors and students in the learning process.

Instructor's Manual with Forms Disk

Chapter-by-chapter suggestions cover recommendations for a variety of formats, including lectures by teachers and guests, class discussions, in-class exercises, and group projects. Transparency masters are provided for lectures, as well as additional discussion questions, exercises, and group projects. Guidelines and sample projects are included for single-class periods, homework, week-long assignments, and half-semester to full-semester projects with real clients. Problem-solving tests may be created from the additional exercises and group projects, all of which have sample answers.

Several semester schedules are provided as models for taking advantage of a variety of classroom formats depending on class interests and the amount of material to be covered in a semester. Our suggested schedules vary with the background of the class and the number of semesters allowed for the systems development course.

Approximately one-third of the exercises have answers in the back of the book. Answers to the remaining exercises are provided in the instructor's manual in large type suitable for transparencies for class discussions and for displaying.

The forms used in the text are provided on a disk, which is included in the instructor's manual. The disk is for use with the IBM-PC, or compatible. A comparable disk for use with the Macintosh is also available through PWS-KENT upon request.

Test Bank Software

Test bank software is available for IBM-PCs and compatible hardware. There are 30 to 60 questions for each chapter in multiple choice, true/false, and fill-in-the-blank format.

Test Item Manual

The hardcopy version of the test bank includes all the questions and answers in the test bank software, plus notes on constructing tests from the instructor's manual supplementary exercises and group projects.

Casebook

A student workbook containing a case study in twenty-one assignments, and forms needed to complete the assignments is available. The workbook was written by Sandra K. Dewitz of the University of Texas at Austin and Robin D. Bier of Coopers & Lybrand, San Francisco. The assignments provide a structured series of exercises that parallel the text topics, beginning with early requirements determination and ending with an installation plan. Completion of the assignments requires the step-by-step development of an integrated system that automates three administrative functions: payroll, accounts payable, and attendance and cost reporting.

Casebook Solutions Manual

Two versions of sample answers to the casebook assignments are available. One version features answers completed with Excelerator, a Computer-Aided Systems Engineering (CASE) tool produced by Index Technology Corporation for IBM-PCs and compatible hardware. The other version features answers completed with SilverrunDFD, a CASE tool produced by XA Systems for Macintosh systems and IBM.

CASE Tool Software

Index Technology Corporation will grant copies of Excelerator to instructors for use with this text. XA Systems will provide Silverrun CASE tools at substantial education reductions. Details are available with the instructor supplements.

Acknowledgements

In the process of writing this book we received encouragement and help from many people.

Sandy Dewitz has improved the book by helping us write clearly and by playing an active role in gathering all the pieces into a coherent whole. It has been a rare privilege to collaborate with such an experienced teacher and creative writer. Thanks also to J.B. Matkowski for many of the minicases taken from her vast consulting experience and for examples and guidelines throughout the book, especially management concerns.

We are indebted to Sirkka Jarvenpaa, a professor at the University of Texas at Austin, who is an amazing source of references, editing, and suggestions about teaching systems development. We are also indebted to several computer artists: Paul Maddock; Newt Jordan; Giao Phan; Khoa Vo; Tony Huang; Ramesh Balwani; Sandra Fletcher; and Martha Smith. They created most of the transparency masters, which have become figures for this book. Paul Maddock and Newt Jordan also suggested presentation formats, which we have incorporated into the artwork. Our sincere thanks to all of you.

In keeping our systems development philosophy of developing and delivering systems in phases, parts of the early drafts of this book have been taught in classes at the National Computer Educators Institute in Edmond, Oklahoma. This book might have become an encyclopedia for systems development for the next century, if our students hadn't helped with much-appreciated reality training. Portions of this book have been used in manuscript form as well by Thom Luce, Ohio University; Dan Stone, University of Illinois; Michael Wolfe, University of West Virginia; and Naveed Saleem, University of Houston at Clear Lake. Thanks for your encouragement and suggestions. We would also like to thank the following reviewers of the manuscript for their comments: Charles P. Bilbrey, James Madison University; Patricia Guinan, Boston University; William L. Harrison, Oregon State University; Cynthia E. Johnson, Bryant College; Paul D. Maxwell, Bentley College; Bernard John Poole, University of Pittsburgh-Johnstown; and Charles Silcox, Widener University.

We would like to name some of the students whose presentations and projects became incorporated into the book in some form, even if we cannot name all of them who helped directly or indirectly. Thanks to Fred Bock, for a lecture on garbage in, garbage out problems; a few slides grew into the Meadows Hospital case. Thanks to Deborah Maddock for her report on post-implementation evaluation, which provided initial drafts for the forms provided in Chapter 22 on that topic. Thanks to Ruben Pinchanski and Murli Nagasundaram for their suggestions about testing strategies and to Delores Gomez and Dan Pendergast for their evaluation examples and exercises. Thanks to Stephen Goldfinger for the first draft of the glossary. Thanks to Barrie Levinson, Dan Samson, Tuulikki Ylostalo, Yogesh Karambaya, Eric Nelson, Khai Tam, Anna Florey, and Susan Bourenane for their contributions to the supplementary materials.

Thanks to Sue Weber of the University of Arizona and David Kroenke of the University of Washington for all their conversations and ideas about systems development. Thanks also to Cynthia Beath of the University of Minnesota for ideas on post-implementation evaluation.

Thanks to PWS-KENT for their project coordination, support, and assistance. Rolfe Janke provided initial encouragement; Mary Thomas has been helpful throughout; and Susan London has been a management miracle.

This is only the beginning of the gratitude owed for a book begun a very long time ago. This book, like our teaching, has been an interactive process in which many have participated. We hope our students know how much we have learned from them. We feel deeply indebted to them for their questions, comments, complaints, projects, and visual metaphors shared over a decade.

E.W.J.
J.J.M.

Contents

CHAPTER 10
Data Flow Diagrams and System Flowcharts   229

CHAPTER 11
Conceptual Data Modeling   262

CHAPTER 12
Requirements Documentation and Management Reviews   301

**Part 5
Design
Specification
Activities**

Systems
and Process
Overview

Information Systems: Product and Process

The Components of an Information System
People
Procedures
Data
Software
Hardware
Component Summary
Minicase: Abby Clark and Her Turnkey System

The REDI Model of Systems Development
Requirements Determination Stage
Evaluation Stage
Design Specification Stage
Implementation Stage
REDI Model Summary
Minicase: Abby Clark's Contract Labor System

The Development Process Matrix
Summary
Key Terms ▪ Note ▪ Exercises ▪ Projects

Overview

What is your experience with information systems? If your main experience with systems is receiving computer-generated payroll checks, reports, or bills, you may imagine an information system as a machine that automatically processes information to create the desired results. You may not realize how many people are involved or how complicated the procedures are for large information systems. If your experience with computer systems includes taking programming classes, you have at least some understanding of the development process. Designing, coding, and debugging assigned homework programs has helped you understand the importance of programs and clear specifications. What you may not realize is that programming is only one part of developing an information system.

This chapter presents a five-component model of an information system, which is the basis of our approach to developing systems. Although an information system is not necessarily centered around a computer, we are concerned here only with computer-based information systems: what they are and how they are developed. Specifically, we plan to

1. Identify the five components of an information system: people, procedures, data, software, and hardware. (Section 1.1)

2. Discuss the REDI model of systems development. (Section 1.2)

3. Introduce the development process matrix, a graphic technique that integrates the components and the system development model. (Section 1.3)

1.1 The Components of an Information System

An **information system** integrates five components—people, procedures, data, software, and hardware—to produce information by accessing and processing data.[1] The five-component model of an information system is represented graphically in Figure 1.1. The components in the figure are arranged symmetrically to denote their equal importance in the systems development process. Data is the center of the system. Notice that the two left-hand components concern people and the two right-hand components concern computers. Both hardware and people are actors—sources of activity. Both software and procedures are sets of instructions; software instructs hardware, whereas procedures instruct people. During systems development, equal attention must be paid to each of these components.

When a system is computerized, many activities formerly performed by people following procedures are instead done by hardware executing software. Nonetheless, both people and procedures are still very important components of the computerized system. The skills the people need and the procedures they perform will change, but both will be very evident in a well-designed information system.

This section introduces the five components of an information system and emphasizes some concerns related to each component.

Figure 1.1

The Five-Component Model of an Information System

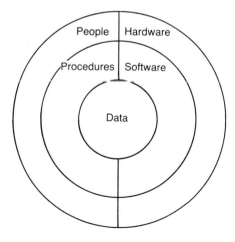

1.1.1 People

The first component of our system model is people. The people involved in an information system assume many different roles. We can classify these roles into three categories: developers, operators, and users.

A systems **developer** works with users to create a system. Developing a system involves understanding the users' needs and building and integrating the five components of a system to meet those needs. Systems development personnel include programmers and systems analysts. The roles and responsibilities of those who may be involved in systems development are summarized in Figure 1.2.

Historically, the first role of the developer was that of a **programmer.** The early systems were straightforward, narrowly defined conversions of existing systems; so once the hardware had been acquired, the only work that remained for the programmer was designing, coding, testing, and documenting programs. Today the first role of many entry-

Figure 1.2
Information Systems
Role Summary

Role	Responsibilities
User	Contributes to requirements determination, alternative evaluation, and project management. Also may document procedures and train other users.
Programmer	Codes, tests, documents, and maintains software.
Analyst	Elicits help from users in order to determine requirements and evaluate alternatives; specifies design and oversees implementation.
End-user consultant	Advises users about any aspect of the development process and managing the process so that end-users can successfully develop their own systems.
Project manager	Plans, monitors, coordinates, and manages the development process.
Trainer	Trains information systems staff or users on any aspect of the development process and managing the process; most frequent training is on development tools.
Database analyst	Advises users and information systems staff about technical and detailed data storage design issues, including maintaining standards for integrated systems. (Also called database administrator or database specialist.)
Fourth generation language consultant	Trains and advises users and information systems staff about fourth generation tools.
Communication specialist	Develops, coordinates, and maintains telecommunication systems accessed by many users.
Office automation specialist	Develops, coordinates, and maintains office automation system; important development responsibilities include evaluating alternatives and user consulting.

level information systems professionals is still programming. In most organizations, however, the duties of the programmer are on-the-job training for becoming an analyst. The entry-level title programmer-analyst reflects the fact that the programmer is expected to accept analyst responsibilities as soon as possible.

The systems **analyst** today is responsible for designing the information system and integrating all five system components. The analyst interacts with users to determine the functions of the system being developed and to evaluate alternative solutions. After the users have selected a solution, the analyst prepares design specifications for the procedures, data, software, and hardware. If new programs are being developed, the analyst serves as a liaison between the users, who determine the functions of the programs, and the programmers, who code and test these programs.

The second category of people is **operators,** who manage, control, service, and maintain computer equipment. Operators run the equipment and perform tasks such as mounting tapes and disks, feeding paper into printers, and ensuring that jobs are run according to a predetermined schedule. Data entry personnel are operators who convert data from handwritten or other formats into electronic form.

The final category, users, includes different people depending on the situation. Since the viewpoint of this text is that of the systems analyst, we will distinguish three user roles:

- end-user (or principal user)
- user-manager
- user-sponsor

The **end-user** interacts directly with the system. The **user-manager** supervises the end-users. The **user-sponsor** is the individual who approves development of the system. Sometimes all three roles are combined; often they are held by different people.

In a savings account system, for example, one end-user is the bank teller who enters transactions and interacts with the bank client. The bank client is also an end-user, since he or she completes the system input forms for deposits or even directly interacts with a remote terminal device to make withdrawals. The user-manager is the head teller or manager of client services. The user-sponsor might be the manager or the bank vice-president who authorized initial work on the savings account system. The responsibilities and some typical business titles for each user category are summarized in Figure 1.3.

Although we have classified people into three categories, you should realize that these categories often overlap. For example, in microcomputer-based information systems, the user is also the operator. And in many systems development efforts, a user is a member of the development team. The team approach to systems development involves users in the development of the system and thereby gains their commitment to the system. Team composition varies with the size and the nature of the system. Small teams may have one user as a team member or leader; larger teams may include several users. Placing the user on the development team to share development responsibilities with the analyst speeds up delivery of a system and improves the system's chances for success.

In the minds of users, the ideal developer (both programmer and analyst) is a team player who

Figure 1.3
Categories of Users

User Category	Typical System Responsibilities	Sample Business Titles
End-user or principal user	Follows procedures critical to system Enters data or oversees data entry Uses detail reports	Payroll Clerk Travel Agent Accountant Hotel Clerk Cashier Benefits Advisor
User-manager	Supervises end-users Reviews summary reports to make decisions	Department Manager Warehouse Director Division Coordinator Chief Clerk
User-sponsor	Approves expenditures for development of system	Vice-President of Finance Director of Marketing Comptroller County Commissioner

- knows all aspects of systems development
- learns the users' language and system requirements thoroughly (functional and organizational knowledge)
- can communicate well, both orally and in writing
- is direct and well organized
- supports the system enthusiastically and consistently
- has no hidden agendas

By the same token, in the minds of developers, the ideal user is a team player who

- knows the system requirements thoroughly
- can communicate well, both orally and in writing
- is direct and well organized
- supports the system enthusiastically and consistently
- has no hidden agendas

Since we do not live in an ideal world, few of us are likely to meet all of these requirements. The techniques in this book are designed to improve the delivery of systems, even with imperfect developers and users.

1.1.2 Procedures

Procedures are instructions for people. One way to categorize procedures is by the kind of people who will follow them. **User procedures** explain how to use software and hardware to obtain desired results and how to enter data and obtain reports. **Operator procedures** explain how the computer operator should run the computer and other equipment. For example, operator procedures explain how to start the system, stop it, back up data for recovery in the event of failure, and so forth.

Historically, operators and users were two completely different groups of people. Operators worked in the computer room and had little interaction with users, who worked in their own departments. In many systems, this is still the case, and thus two sets of procedures are required. Today, however, in many microcomputer-based systems, the user is the operator, in which case the separation of operator and user procedures is superfluous.

The second way to categorize procedures is by the situation in which these procedures will be used: normal versus failure recovery. **Normal procedures** explain how the system is used normally to obtain desired results. **Recovery procedures** explain what to do if the system fails. Recovery procedures encompass procedures to restore the system to operational status as well as procedures to keep backup files so that data can be brought up to date when the system is operating again. The four types of procedures are summarized in Figure 1.4.

The complexity of the procedures is largely dependent on the complexity of the system. That is, an information system that performs more functions and involves more operators and users also requires more detailed procedures. Consider the procedural differences among the three categories of systems, classified by **user access mode:**

- single-user systems
- sequential multi-user systems
- concurrent multi-user systems

A **single-user system** is exactly what its name implies: a system that only one person uses. If you use a microcomputer to write a report, you, your microcomputer, your word processing program, your report data, and your procedures comprise a single-user system. In such a system, procedures explain how to operate the microcomputer, how to run the program, and how to save and print your report. These procedures are quite straightforward, since there is no need to coordinate the activities of several people.

Figure 1.4
Categories
of Procedures

	Users	Operators
Normal	How to use the system to obtain desired results	How to start, stop, and support the system
Failure Recovery	How to proceed when the system is inoperative	How to identify the source of the problem
	How to bring the data model up to date after the system is recovered	How to correct the problem or have it corrected
		How to recover the system

In contrast, consider the same basic system used by multiple users. A **sequential multi-user system** is accessed by more than one user but by only one person at a time. For example, a small office might have a single word processing system that is used by two secretaries. Only one secretary uses the system at any one time, but both use the system to create documents for the business. In this sequential multi-user system environment, procedures become a little more complex, since this system requires coordination among the users. They must establish conventions about naming and backing up documents and picking up a task (e.g., typing a long report) midstream.

The distinctions between single-user systems and sequential multi-user systems are clear when all five components are separate. However, most systems share hardware with other systems. A mainframe computer for a large organization is likely to be the hardware component for hundreds of systems. All these systems, from payroll to marketing analysis, will share some of the same procedures for accessing hardware, but the end-users of many of the systems may never meet. Some of these systems will be single-user systems, but most are likely to be multi-user. Even a microcomputer may be shared by users in an office or a school laboratory. In these environments the office staff and the students must follow the same procedures for operating the microcomputer and the printers, but the systems will be separate, single-user systems unless the sharing of software and data requires coordination of procedures for maintaining data currency and other issues specific to the individual five-component system.

The third category is **concurrent multi-user systems.** These systems allow two or more users to interact with the system, seemingly at the same time. An example of a concurrent multi-user system is a word processing system built around a mini-computer that supports twenty terminals in a centralized word processing department of a large company. Another example is a parts inventory system that allows both the Parts department and the Service department of an auto repair shop to access inventory files.

Concurrent processing poses problems that do not occur with single-user or sequential multi-user systems. Because users of concurrent multi-user systems can share data, the action of one user affects other users. For example, a Service department employee at an auto repair shop might access the parts inventory system, find that there is one 1988 Volvo muffler in stock, and promise a customer one-day service. Meanwhile, a Parts employee might have sold that same muffler! Even worse problems arise when two users change information in the same file.

Because of these and related problems, special procedures are needed in a concurrent processing environment. User procedures must be designed to coordinate user access and to control file updates. For example, employees in the Service department may not be allowed to access the inventory file while a Parts department employee is recording the arrival of new shipments. Similarly, users in both departments may be required to update the inventory file *at the moment* they remove a part from inventory. You can imagine the headaches caused by even one employee's waiting until the end of the day to "subtract" the parts used.

1.1.3 Data

Data is the central component of an information system. **Data** is information that is entered, stored, and accessed to answer questions. People enter data, which is stored on hardware. This stored data is accessed and processed to generate reports, messages, and displays. The three types of data are

- input data—data received by hardware
- data stores—data stored in hardware
- output data—data generated by hardware

Figure 1.5 illustrates the three types of data for a licensing system. The system receives license applications and training certificates (the input data); accesses data stored for licenses and training centers (the data stores); and produces receipts, certificates, and two reports (the output data). Since the purpose of an information system is to answer questions by accessing and processing data, the character and capabilities of the system will be determined by the amount and format of the data. How easy is it to enter data? What reports can be created from the stored data? How helpful are the reports and displays? Because these are critical concerns, the definition of system data is also critical.

Figure 1.5
The Three Types of Data

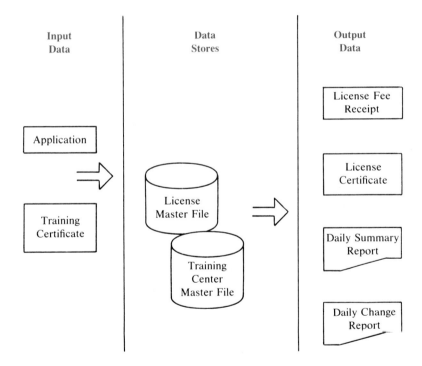

Organized data provides a model of some aspect of reality. A file of employee data, for example, is a model of those employees. In general, the more data that is stored, the more detailed the model is. An employee file with 100 fields, or items, about each employee contains more detail about employees than does a file with 10 fields.

Systems should be designed to store data in sufficient detail that it can be used to answer the questions that will be asked. Ideally, no more data should be gathered than will ever be needed. Consider a company that is designing sales data. For each sale, the company could simply record an invoice number, a customer number, a salesperson number, and an amount. If a customer purchased several items at once, all items could be grouped into one record, as shown in Format A in Figure 1.6. (A record is a group of fields, or items, describing a transaction.)

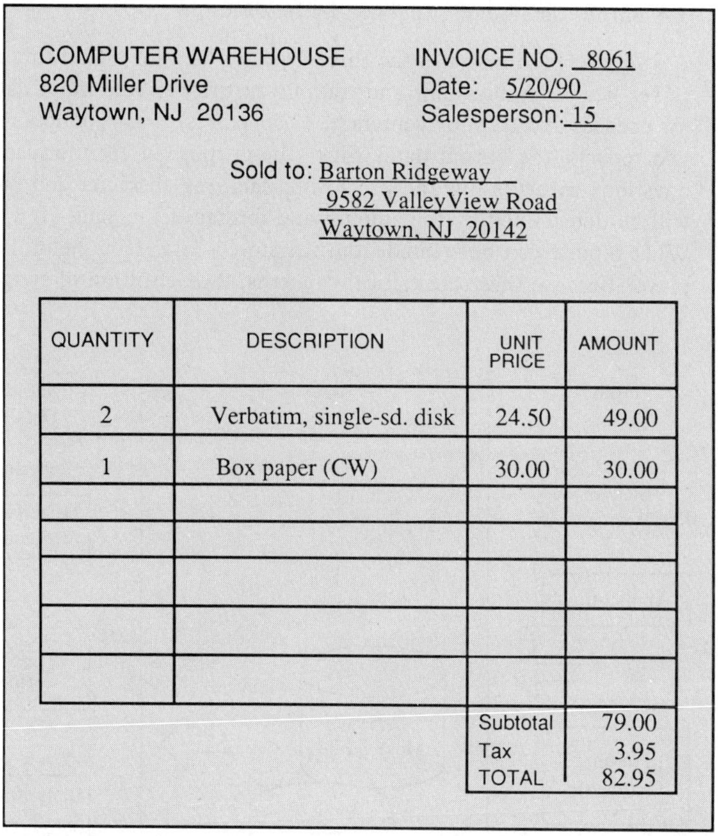

COMPUTER WAREHOUSE	INVOICE NO. _8061_
820 Miller Drive	Date: _5/20/90_
Waytown, NJ 20136	Salesperson: _15_

Sold to: Barton Ridgeway
9582 ValleyView Road
Waytown, NJ 20142

QUANTITY	DESCRIPTION	UNIT PRICE	AMOUNT
2	Verbatim, single-sd. disk	24.50	49.00
1	Box paper (CW)	30.00	30.00
		Subtotal	79.00
		Tax	3.95
		TOTAL	82.95

Format A

Invoice Number	Customer Number	Salesperson Number	Amount
8061	328	15	$79.00

Format B

Invoice Number	Customer Number	Salesperson Number	Item Number	Amount
8061	328	15	1497	$49.00
8061	328	15	0682	$30.00

FIGURE 1.6   Alternative Formats for Sales Records

Is Format A an appropriate design? It may be, depending on the requirements, or the questions likely to be asked. If all you need to know is sales totals by invoice, by customer, and by salesperson, then this design is suitable. If you need to know which items have been ordered by which customers, then this design is not detailed enough. For that information you would need Format B.

If a design includes too much detail, software can be written to compress the data. If there is too little detail in the data design, however, no software or procedure can help. For example, if you need to know total sales by salesperson by day, you can write a program for either Format A or Format B to add the appropriate amounts together. If you need to know the total sales of disks, however, no software can help if you chose Format A, in which data is too highly summarized.

For a data model to be useful, it must be current. Events occur in the outside world that change the condition of the organization. For example, someone takes a widget from inventory. When this happens, the data model must be changed. Otherwise there will be a discrepancy between the data model and reality. If the data model is not kept current, its information, or answers to questions, will be incorrect. The purpose of much of information system processing is to keep the data model current.

In addition to designing data models and procedures for maintaining the models, systems development involves designing all the input and output data forms. These may include manual data entry forms, optical scan codes, magnetic ink characters, voice input and output, data entry screens, and reports of all types (see Figure 1.7).

Figure 1.7
Examples of Forms of
Data Input and
Output

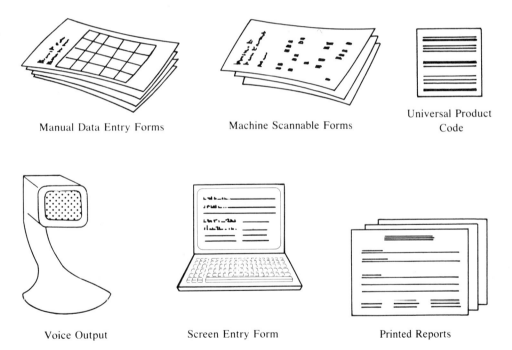

Manual Data Entry Forms   Machine Scannable Forms   Universal Product Code

Voice Output   Screen Entry Form   Printed Reports

1.1.4 Software

Software, often referred to as programs, is the instructions for hardware. Software determines what actions a computer will execute. The Hewlett-Packard 150 is a general-purpose computer. Depending on the application software used, this computer can do word processing, help you learn geometry, or analyze electronic circuits. The choice of software determines what a general-purpose computer will do.

There are three types of software: systems software, application software, and productivity software. **Systems software** controls basic hardware functions or provides a general service. One systems program is the operating system, which controls the computer's resources. Utility programs are a type of systems software that allows you to do such routine tasks as copy or sort files. Special systems software manages networks of microcomputers, controls access to printers, provides communication among microcomputers, and allows for various levels of security for storage space.

Application software performs specific tasks such as inventory, general ledger accounting, or statistical analysis. These tasks may be performed in a variety of situations. The same accounts receivable program, for example, might be purchased by a law firm and a dentist's office, if both organizations needed essentially the same billing and processing procedures.

The third general type of software, **productivity software,** includes spreadsheet software, word processing software, and database management systems. This software increases the user's power to create systems. It is not limited to a specific application, as application software is. Nor does it control basic hardware functions in the way systems software does. For microcomputers, productivity software is the most common development tool, often allowing users to develop their own systems for storing and processing information.

1.1.5 Hardware

Systems developers rarely build **hardware**—the physical components of a system. Instead, they develop specifications and order hardware from vendors. To be an effective systems developer, you need to know the basic types of hardware devices, their capabilities, and their advantages and disadvantages. You also need to know techniques for developing specifications and for dealing, negotiating, and contracting with hardware vendors.

There is a wide variety of computer hardware. Examples of hardware include

microcomputers	disk drives
mini-computers	tape drives
mainframe computers	modems
printers	scanners
emulation boards	disks
graphics boards	tapes

The five basic hardware concerns of the analyst are

- the facility
- the computer
- external storage
- input devices
- output devices

Notice that one hardware concern listed above is the facility. The location of hardware should be planned so that introducing computer hardware does not make the normal procedures more difficult. Adding computer equipment to a business thus can be a complicated task. Sometimes the work area has to be rebuilt to create adequate space for the hardware and to keep cables safely out of walkways. Other times a major concern in choosing hardware is to avoid alteration of the current facilities. Experienced systems analysts will be as concerned with preparing the location, or facility, as they are with choosing the actual hardware devices.

1.1.6 Component Summary

Identifying the components of specific information systems is a good way to check your understanding of the five-component model and the three user access modes of information systems. Figure 1.8 is a brief summary of the components of two single-user systems

Figure 1.8
Components of Two
Single-User Systems
with Shared Hardware

H
The *Hardware* for both systems
is a microcomputer with an
extra disk drive and a printer.

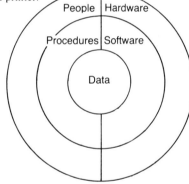

P
Mel Mathews is the developer,
operator, and user.

P
Karen Busk is the
operator and user.

> *P*
> The *Procedures* are operating the
> computer, using the spreadsheet
> package, and backing up and storing
> the spreadsheet disks.

> *P*
> The *Procedures* are operating the
> computer, using the graphics
> program, and storing the disks
> with the poster copies.

> > *D*
> > The *Data* is the initial
> > monthly sales estimate and
> > the spreadsheet report format.

> > *D*
> > The *Data* is the information
> > needed on the posters for the weekly
> > sales staff meetings.

> > > *S*
> > > The *Software* is the operating
> > > system, the spreadsheet package, and
> > > the template spreadsheet of formulas
> > > and labels created by Mel Mathews.

> > > *S*
> > > The *Software* is the
> > > operating
> > > system and the
> > > graphics program.

that have the same combination of hardware. One system, created by Mel Mathews, uses a spreadsheet program. The other system generates posters for Karen Busk; the software component is a graphics program. The two different users follow the same procedures to operate the hardware, but they follow different procedures to operate their own software and manipulate their own data in separate information systems.

Figure 1.9 is an aid to a more detailed analysis of system components. This component summary form lists each of the five components and the subcategories for each component. Figure 1.10 shows a component summary form describing a barber licensing system. The component summary form in Figure 1.9 can be used to complete many of the exercises at the end of this chapter.

In the development of a system, all five components are important. When manual procedures are to be automated, the current system activities of people following these procedures must be understood before software can be designed and coded. In years gone by, many organizations have created disasters by ignoring the data, people, and procedural components of systems development. One example of such a limited system perspective is

Figure 1.9
System Component Summary Form

Component Summary for: _____
(name of system)

_____

1. People
   a. developer
   b. operator
   c. end-user
   d. user-manager
   e. user-sponsor

2. Procedures
   a. user normal procedures
   b. user recovery procedures
   c. operator normal procedures
   d. operator recovery procedures

3. Data
   a. data stores
   b. input
   c. output

4. Software
   a. operating system
   b. application software (or program steps)
   c. productivity software

5. Hardware
   a. facility
   b. computer
   c. external storage
   d. input devices
   e. output devices

_____

Figure 1.10

Sample Identification of System Components from System Description: License Application System

System Description

When a barber wants a hairdresser's license, he or she completes an application at the office of the state board. The application, a training certificate, and $50 are given to the license clerk. The clerk visually checks the documents for completeness and returns them to the applicant if corrections are necessary. If the documents are correct, the clerk enters the application and training certificate data into a VAX 11/780 computer, using a terminal. The system verifies the data, checking it against the license master file and a training center master file. After verification, a receipt and a license certificate are produced and the license master file is updated. The clerk hands the receipt and the license certificate to the applicant.

At the end of each day, the clerk runs a program to create a summary report on the current master file and a detailed list of all added, changed, or deleted license records.

Component Summary for: Barber Licensing System

1. People
   a. developer—not identified
   b. operator—license clerk
   c. end-user—barber, license clerk
   d. user-manager and user-sponsor—not identified

2. Procedures
   a. user normal procedures (barber)—fill out application form
   b. user and operator normal procedures (license clerk)—check application documents, enter application and certificate data, hand receipt to applicant, run daily report program
   c. recovery procedures—not identified

3. Data
   a. data stores—license master file, training center master file
   b. input—application, training certificate
   c. output—receipt, license certificate, daily summary report, daily change report

4. Software
   a. operating system—not identified
   b. application software (or program steps)—verify data, produce receipts, update license master file, generate end-of-day reports
   c. productivity software—none identified

5. Hardware
   a. facility—state board's office
   b. computer—VAX 11/780
   c. external storage—not identified
   d. input devices—terminal
   e. output devices—printer

Notes on Component Section

The component summary here is based directly on the description. When you work the exercises at the end of the chapter, you too should focus only on what is specified in the description for each exercise. Do not make up unspecified parts of the system. If you have experience with systems development, you may be tempted to add your own ideas. The notes below may help you limit your entries for the exercises.

(continued)

Figure 1.10
(Continued)

People: Other personnel might be involved in maintaining this system. For example, some programmer must maintain the programs and a systems programmer might be required for telecommunication support programs. These people should not be added in the exercises, since these additions require you to go beyond the provided system description. It may well be that the clerk uses a purchased program that can be altered only by the software vendor.

Procedures: Additional procedures, such as backing up the master files, would have to be considered in developing a complete licensing system. The component summary, however, names only the procedures referred to in the description.

Data: If more details were provided, fields could be named. However, the description gives only the files and documents. The check for $50 might be included as data, since the clerk probably entered a code for "paid." Also the data entry screen might be added. But then you would logically want to consider menu screens for running programs. Again, the eight data items on the summary form, with or without checks, are most appropriate for the description given.

Software: The four processing steps listed on the summary form could be performed by one or two programs. The objective of this exercise is to identify the main computer program *functions,* not necessarily the particular software modules.

Hardware: The computer and peripherals listed are mentioned directly in the description (VAX and terminal) or are required for data output (printer for reports and receipt). Communication lines might also be added, since clearly the terminal has to be connected to the VAX. But then, what about electrical lines and other cables? Since the purpose of this figure and the exercises is to practice using the five-component model rather than detailing general hardware needs, the three hardware elements (b, d, and e) listed in the example are the best answer.

---

that of the "turnkey system," which consists of only a computer and software. The word *turnkey* is intended to suggest that the user can buy the system, turn the key, and solve the problem. Actually, the problems have just begun. The minicase Abby Clark and Her Turnkey System illustrates some of the problems arising from this limited view.

MINICASE

Abby Clark and Her Turnkey System

Abby Clark bought an eight-unit apartment complex ten years ago. Two years later she sold the complex for a large profit and purchased a sixty-unit complex. Each year after that she purchased additional rental property.

Abby, with the assistance of one receptionist-bookkeeper, managed the financial record keeping herself. The only outside help was an accountant who assisted with taxes at the end of the year. One renter in each complex served as a local property manager, in return for rent credit. This frugality, combined with shrewd purchases, was the basis of Abby's impressive success.

Last year Abby's monthly financial record keeping

reached the point where the new month arrived before the last month's records had been completed. Instead of adding staff, Abby visited a computer store. She announced to the sales clerk that she wanted a computer to help with record keeping for her rental property. "And," Abby added, "I don't want any big, expensive computer with all the frills. Just show me something that works."

Abby managed her clothes budget as carefully as she did her property purchases. So the sales clerk looked Abby over and decided she probably owned a duplex and would not need much in the way of a computer. There was a sale on the Kaypro 4 computer, and Abby was easily convinced it was a bargain with lots of "free software." A software package specifically designed for property management, INVESTMAN, could be bought for the Kaypro 4. So Abby was set. Her total bill came to $3,121.63, as shown in Figure 1.11.

Abby had her own "system" in her own office two hours after she entered the computer store. But, for three months the computer sat in the office untouched by busy Abby or the bookkeeper, who had a severe case of computer phobia. After bickering back and forth with the bookkeeper about who would learn to use the computer and set up INVESTMAN, Abby finally hired her nephew Cecil to do the work.

Cecil, having had a college course in BASIC using a microcomputer, thought this would be a great summer job. In one morning he installed the printer and the computer. Then he settled down to read the INVESTMAN

tutorial. He spent a day working with test files and then asked Abby where the data was. She pointed to two file cabinets. Finally, Cecil started creating the master files.

After two weeks, only a third of the file had been built. (Cecil was a hunt-and-peck typist.) Cecil realized it was going to take another month to convert the remaining folders of data. Also, storing the master file would require eight floppy disks. Inquiries and report generation would be a tedious chore with so many floppy disks.

When Cecil returned to college 500 miles away, the system had been working only four days. No procedures had been documented. Neither Abby nor the bookkeeper knew how to use the computer.

The moral of the story is avoid two-component turnkey systems. The data, people, and procedures components are essential parts of the system. If Abby had planned for the data component, she would have bought

Figure 1.11
The Bill for Abby Clark's Turnkey System

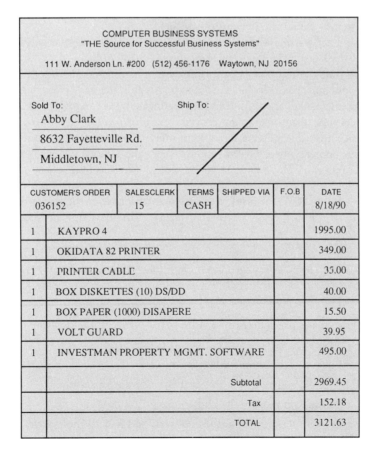

	COMPUTER BUSINESS SYSTEMS					
	"THE Source for Successful Business Systems"					
	111 W. Anderson Ln. #200 (512) 456-1176 Waytown, NJ 20156					

Sold To: **Abby Clark**   8632 Fayetteville Rd.   Middletown, NJ

Ship To:

CUSTOMER'S ORDER	SALESCLERK	TERMS	SHIPPED VIA	F.O.B	DATE
036152	15	CASH			8/18/90

1	KAYPRO 4		1995.00
1	OKIDATA 82 PRINTER		349.00
1	PRINTER CABLE		35.00
1	BOX DISKETTES (10) DS/DD		40.00
1	BOX PAPER (1000) DISAPERE		15.50
1	VOLT GUARD		39.95
1	INVESTMAN PROPERTY MGMT. SOFTWARE		495.00
		Subtotal	2969.45
		Tax	152.18
		TOTAL	3121.63

a Kaypro 10 or other hardware with adequate storage capacity. If Abby had considered the people component, she would have determined her additional personnel needs before acquiring the computer and avoided the loss of income due to failure to take advantage of the capital equipment expenditure (the computer) for three months.

If Cecil had considered procedures and people, he might have recommended that Abby hire a part-time data entry operator, who would have cost three times as much per hour but would have completed the data entry five times faster. While the data entry was being completed by an experienced professional, Cecil could have designed and documented office procedures. Then he could have trained the bookkeeper to operate INVEST-MAN. In this way Cecil would have developed a usable, documented system with a trained end-user before ending his summer employment, leaving Abby with a working five-component system.

1.2 The REDI Model of Systems Development

Now that you're familiar with the components that comprise an information system, we can turn to the process of developing such a system. This section presents an overview of the REDI model of systems development, a model that will be used to organize the rest of this textbook and that will be explained more fully in succeeding chapters.

The **life cycle model** divides the life of a system into two phases: development and production. In the systems **development phase,** the information system is created or revised. After development, the system becomes part of the ongoing process of the business; data is entered and reports are produced. This operational period of an information system is called the **production phase.**

The two phases are depicted in Figure 1.12 as the two halves of a circle. The point at which a system changes from development to production is called **changeover.** At this time the responsibility for the system is transferred from the development team to a production manager. Viewing a system's lifetime as a recurring cycle is helpful, since system changes are as inevitable as organizational changes. A system is first developed and incorporated into company procedures. Then, as the organization improves its business procedures, its information system must be altered to support these changes. So a new development phase begins, ending when the revised system is returned to production. Periods of development and production alternate as long as a system is part of the organization's operations.

In the **REDI model,** the development phase of the life cycle is divided into stages. REDI is an acronym for the four stages of the development model:

R   requirements determination

E   evaluation of alternatives

D   design specification

I   implementation

These stages are labeled in Figure 1.12. Figure 1.13 shows a step diagram of the stage activities:

First, you determine what is required.

Second, you research and evaluate alternative solutions.

Third, you specify the chosen design solution.

Fourth, you implement (build, test, and install) the system.

Let us consider each of these activities in more detail.

Figure 1.12
A Life Cycle Model of
an Information System

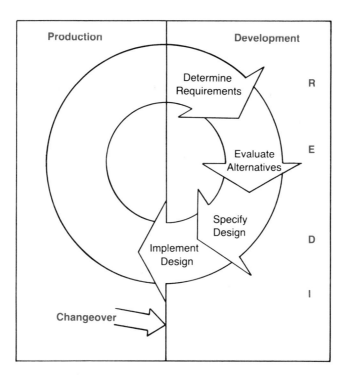

Figure 1.13
The Development
Process Life Cycle

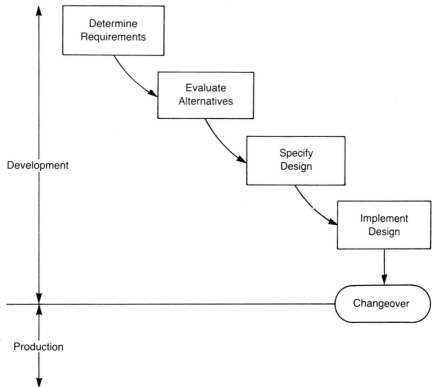

I.2.I Requirements Determination Stage

In **requirements determination,** you first define the **system boundary** or the scope of the systems development effort, and then investigate and state the requirements that the new system must meet. Systems development begins with an opportunity. The opportunity may be to provide a service, improve procedures, or solve a problem. In the requirements stage, you define this opportunity. You need to know what the system should accomplish before you create it, in order to avoid solving the wrong problem or a nonexistent problem.

Figure 1.14 gives examples of requirements-solution boundaries. In Example A the boundary of the system missed the most important requirements entirely. In Example B the solution met only part of the requirements. This is a common occurrence when a system is developed around purchased software; impatient developers often buy software that meets one principal requirement without investigating whether it meets additional requirements. Example C illustrates a solution that was much greater than the requirements called for. The boundary defined in D is the most realistic goal for many business systems. Often you can solve 80 percent of the requirements at 50 or even 20 percent of the cost of fine-tuning the system to meet a full 100 percent of the requirements.

Define the System Boundary   Given an opportunity or need for a system, you define the boundary of the proposed system by performing two complementary activities:

- identifying system objectives
- identifying system constraints

Figure 1.14
Examples of
Requirements-
Solution Boundaries

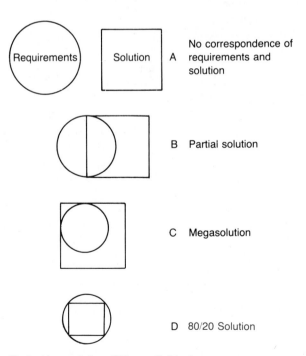

A No correspondence of requirements and solution

B Partial solution

C Megasolution

D 80/20 Solution

Used with permission of Thomas O. Meadows.

System objectives are the goals for the final system. Examples of objectives are reduced labor costs, improved customer service, simplified paperwork, increased accuracy of shipping status reports, and more timely marketing analysis. You should determine and state clear objectives to guide the development process. The development effort needs to be focused on a few, precisely stated objectives. Too many objectives make it difficult for system developers to prioritize tasks. Long wish lists are unrealistic, since projects must compete for limited organizational resources. In contrast, too few objectives or objectives that are imprecisely defined yield the poor requirements fit shown in Figure 1.14.

System constraints are the limits on resources available for development and production. Resources include time, money, personnel, and space. Examples of constraints are the need to use existing hardware, complete the system within six weeks, develop the system for inexperienced users, and respond to queries within ten seconds. Scarcity is a fact of life. Since resources are always limited, you need to determine the limits, or constraints, on what you can deliver before investigating requirements, identifying alternatives, and designing the solution.

Investigate Requirements Requirements are the features of the system components necessary to achieve the system objectives within the constraints. Requirements are statements about data, procedures, and people. Although requirements may describe hardware and software, these components often are not defined until the later stages of identifying alternatives or specifying design.

Requirements are sometimes called **functional requirements** because they state what the system must do—what functions it must perform. Following are some sample functional requirements:

- allow the user to access customer account records and display them on the monitor
- produce summary reports at the end of each business day
- generate a purchase order for an inventory item when its in-stock level falls below a specified level

Screen displays, data entry forms, and report formats may all be defined as functional requirements of a system.

Common strategies for investigating requirements include

- asking users what the system functions should be
- observing users
- reviewing existing systems that meet the stated objectives

These and other strategies will be discussed in Part 3, Requirements Determination Activities.

Requirements can be, and usually are, stated at several levels of detail. At the most general level, the requirements give the basic functions of the proposed system. These functions include generating such reports as depreciation summaries, reorder requests, and order forecasts for an inventory system. The basic contents of the reports are described, and such basic information as the number of inventory items and the frequency of inventory updates is specified.

The amount of information needed in the requirements depends, in part, on what type of software will be used in the system. Requirements should be specified on a general level before you search for existing software in the organization or shop for application software to purchase. If your system requires custom-written software, your specifications must be much more explicit. You should not waste time on design or implementation of software for which requirements are not known in detail. Details required include data specifications for input and output, exact report formats, screen displays, and procedural descriptions.

Figure 1.15 defines and gives examples of the three products of requirements determination: objectives, constraints, and functional requirements. The examples are of general, first-level requirements. Note that if Abby Clark had thought through her needs even this far, she would have purchased a system with greater capacity than the one she bought. Abby's functional requirement of handling records of 1600 rental units is valuable information for determining capacity requirements.

1.2.2 Evaluation Stage

In the **evaluation** stage, you identify and evaluate alternatives for each system component, and then select the best one.

Identify Alternatives Instead of developing the first solution that comes to mind, you should generate a range of alternatives that meet the requirements. To do this, you consider each of the five system components in light of the requirements. Then you create multiple alternatives by specifying appropriate people, procedures, data, software, and hardware.

Developing an alternative is an iterative process. Because the five components are interdependent, a decision about one is likely to affect the others, thus requiring you to reassess the other components. For example, one type of computer hardware might seem feasible until the people component is discussed and the team discovers that this hardware

Figure 1.15
Definition and Examples of Objectives, Constraints, and First-Level Functional Requirements

	Boundary Statements		Functional Requirements
	System Objectives	**System Constraints**	
Definition	Desired goals of the system	Resource limits for development and production	Desired system capabilities; tasks to be performed by the system
Examples (from Abby Clark's Property Management System)	Reduce bookkeeping time for billing from 30 days to 4 days	Initial cost less than $5000 New production costs no greater than current costs Little or no additional office space required No additional personnel required	Process records for 1600 rental units Create monthly bills Generate past due notices

choice requires an operating system specialist to write and maintain unique communication software. An alternative requiring such special personnel might have to be eliminated.

Evaluate Alternatives Once alternatives have been identified, the next step is to evaluate them and select one. Then, you must compare the cost of the best alternative to the value of the problem solution and decide whether to continue. If you decide to continue, the design stage will begin.

Alternatives are evaluated by comparing the benefits to the costs. One benefit might be saving the $15,000 annual salary of a part-time bookkeeper. Another might be reducing air conditioning costs by converting from an old mainframe computer to a mini-computer that produces less heat. Subjective costs and benefits are often included, even though they are difficult to quantify. For example, how much is improved employee morale worth? In later chapters we will discuss several approaches to cost/benefit analysis and provide details on what you must consider when reviewing alternatives.

1.2.3 Design Specification Stage

At this point you have defined the requirements and selected a solution. Next, in the **design specification** stage, you must delineate the design for all five of the components.

First, any changes in the people component must be specified. Job descriptions affected by the new system should be revised, and the impact of the changes should be considered for discussion in training and orientation sessions. The design of reports and screen displays should be tailored to meet the needs of the people who will be using them.

Next, procedures defined in the requirements stage must be verified. Additional procedural details will have to be specified as you design and create training materials. You'll need to plan and organize training sessions for the appropriate production staff and outline user and operator manuals to be completed in the implementation stage.

During the design specification stage, details about system data are decided. Within certain limits, data stores may be designed in different ways and yet the system will perform the same functions; the differences will be in execution speed or data storage requirements. These are design concerns.

Finally, you need to identify appropriate hardware and software. If existing hardware is chosen, you still must test the hardware to determine whether it has adequate capacity to support the new system. If you decide to buy new hardware, you must specify the details for purchasing it, including warranty terms and, in some cases, installation and training. Similar concerns with warranties, installation, and training will dominate software specifications if you elect to purchase commercial software. If custom-written software is required, you need to specify all the details for program coding, training, and documenting.

1.2.4 Implementation Stage

The last stage of the development process is implementing the system as defined, evaluated, and specified. The three **implementation** activities are construction, testing, and installation. If you are developing a system using third generation programming languages, these activities will take longer than the previous three stages combined. Figure 1.16 illustrates the distribution of effort across the stages; these percentages are based on

Figure 1.16

Distribution of Effort
for Systems
Developed with Third
Generation Languages

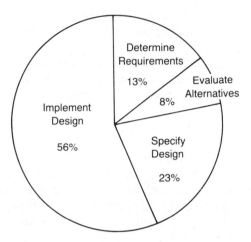

Adapted from Barry Boehm, *Software Engineering Economics* (Englewood Cliffs, N.J.: Prentice-Hall, 1981), p. 92.

experience with systems developed with third generation languages such as COBOL, FORTRAN, and Pascal.

Construction   In the **construction** stage, you build, purchase, and integrate the system components to meet your design specifications. Constructing a system requires different activities, depending on your design decisions. If you are constructing a system that will use custom-written software, you will need to code and document software, establish procedures for system operation and use, and prepare to train system users. No matter what the software source, you will need to build files and make any necessary organizational changes. If you buy software with good documentation, you may be able to eliminate coding and documentation. In addition, you can contract for training, eliminating the need to prepare materials and train users yourself.

Testing   The purpose of **testing** is to make sure all the system components work as they should. Testing is required when imperfect people create systems. So testing is always required, right? We think so, but testing is omitted so often that it seems worthwhile to point out the disastrous consequences of two popular "no-test" strategies.

Abby Clark followed a common two-stage development strategy:

1. Purchase.
2. Install.

After installation, Abby expected to start the production phase. Instead, production was delayed until she hired her nephew, who then had to determine requirements, specify the design, and construct the unpurchased portions of the system. Abby's purchase created major constraints for the second development attempt. Her nephew knew he had to make this particular computer work with the software already purchased.

Few people buy a car without a test drive. Why do people buy computers without a test of any kind? Abby would never have bought an apartment complex without checking the structure, deed restrictions, and occupancy rates. So why did she fail to test this purchase? Actually Abby omitted more than testing. She failed to determine requirements, identify alternatives, and specify design. Note that if she had insisted on a test with her own data, she might have realized that systems development involves more than purchasing and installing. Her belief that a computer could magically improve her business operations was a costly mistake.

A second popular no-test strategy has three stages:

1. Code.
2. Install.
3. Repair the damage.

This strategy results from programmer myopia. A developer with programming skills is sometimes so eager to code that all other activities are omitted. After coding and installing have been completed, the system "test" is conducted by the user. What follows is a series of angry complaints that the system does not perform properly. Each change is coded and the system reinstalled in a rapid-fire succession of development, production, development, production. This strategy is unprofessional and exhausting for everyone involved.

Testing involves all five components. You should test new hardware at the vendor's location or in-house with a warranty that allows you to return unsatisfactory equipment. You should test existing hardware to determine whether it has adequate capacity for the new system. Software that you plan to purchase should be tested following the recommendations of the vendor. After these tests have been conducted, you need to build company-specific test data files and test the software again. Then you build the production data files and test them. Users, especially any new users unfamiliar with the system, should test the procedures, and training materials, and documentation. Finally, after you have tested all the components, you integrate the system and test it as a whole. Testing is a thorough process that must be performed to ensure the integrity of the system.

Installation   System **installation,** the final activity before changeover, is the process of transferring production files and operations from the old system to the new. The key to a successful installation is a phased approach. In the phased approach, you install components one by one so that each component can be verified. Whenever possible, you should design systems so that portions may be installed and operated before the entire system is completed. For example, in installing a multi-site system, you would complete the installation at one site before installing the system at other sites. Similarly, when installing a new system that combines the functions of several old systems, you would install one application of the system, postponing full installation until the first application had proven itself over a period of production.

Changeover   If installation is successful, then changeover is achieved. The manager of the appropriate end-user group assumes responsibility for the system. Although the development team may perform periodic reviews of the system in production, it has no further responsibility. When revisions are required, a new development team is formed and the process is repeated.

1.2.5 REDI Model Summary

The REDI model consists of nine basic activities organized into four stages. These activities are summarized in Figure 1.17. The minicase Abby Clark's Contract Labor System illustrates these activities in the step sequence we have presented in this section.

Stage	Activity	Activity Description
Determine Requirements	R.1 Identify Objectives	• Identify, investigate, and state the objectives of the proposed system.
	R.2 Identify Constraints	• Identify, investigate, and state the constraints of the system in terms of cost and schedule limits.
	R.3 Investigate Requirements	• Investigate, organize, and state the functional requirements of the system, based on the objectives and constraints. The description should include *data, procedures,* and *people.* It may also include hardware and software functions, but specification of these may be postponed until alternative solutions are identified in the next stage.
Evaluate Alternatives	E.1 Identify Alternatives	• Generate potential alternative solutions to meet the requirements for the system, varying *people, procedures, data, software,* and *hardware.*
	E.2 Select Alternative	• Weight, rank, and summarize criteria for selecting alternatives. Then select the alternative that best fits the requirements and justifies the cost.
Specify Design	D.1 Specify Components	• *P* Review job descriptions and *personnel* requirements. Revise as necessary.
		• *P* Review *procedures.* Revise as necessary and design training.
		• *D* Review *data* specifications (input, output, and stores) and revise as necessary.
		• *S* Specify acquisition details or design *software.*
		• *H* Specify purchase details for new *hardware* or verify that existing *hardware* has adequate capacity.
Implement Design	I.1 Construct Components	• Code *software,* build *data* files, document *procedures,* and train *people.*
	I.2 Test Components and System	• *P* Test *users* and *operators* following procedures.
		• *P* Test *procedures,* training, and operation documentation.
	I.3 Install Components and System	• *D* Test preliminary (test) *data* files and production data files.
		• *H* Test new *hardware* with vendor-provided and system-specific routines. Test existing *hardware* for adequate capacity.
		• *S* Test existing *software* with developer-provided data, system-specific data, data designed for thorough *software* testing, and production data. Test custom-developed *software* with data designed for thorough testing and production data.
		• Install the components and system for production use.

Figure 1.17 Development Process Activities Summary

Abby Clark's Contract Labor System

In the previous minicase, Abby Clark bought a property management package and a microcomputer to keep track of bookkeeping for her rental property. Even after her nephew developed the system, neither she nor her bookkeeper spent the time to learn it. Now her book-keeper has resigned and Abby has hired Jennifer, a new bookkeeper who has computer skills.

The property management software that Abby Clark purchased keeps track of all expenditures and re-ceipts for her properties. In addition, Abby must keep track of what she pays to individuals for property mainte-nance. These workers are paid on a contract basis—that is, they are not regular employees.

The Internal Revenue Service (IRS) requires employ-ers to report payments to all individuals paid more than $600 in a year. Abby's property management software does not summarize payments by payees, so even with her new system a tedious search of checks must be made and summarized at the end of each year. To reduce the end-of-the-year bookkeeping, Abby has asked Jennifer to develop a system that will allow month-by-month record-ing. The activities in Figure 1.18 summarize the develop-ment of the new system. Figure 1.19 shows a spread-sheet of the contract labor system.

Source: Newton H. Jordan, Manager of Information Services, Physicians for Social Responsibility, Washington, D.C.

Stage	Activity	Case Problem Action
Determine Requirements	R.1 Identify Objectives	• Abby identifies the need to keep track of contract labor on a monthly basis, in order to (a) reduce the time required at the end of the year for Internal Revenue Service (IRS) reporting, (b) improve procedures for checking the data, and (c) increase the accuracy of the IRS report.
	R.2 Identify Constraints	• Jennifer knows that Abby is unlikely to spend much time or money on this development project. She asks Abby how long the end-of-the-year reporting normally takes. Abby replies that it requires about 10 hours. Jennifer decides that a rea-sonable time for the development of the system would be no more than a half day.
	R.3 Investigate Require-ments	• *P* Jennifer asks Abby what validity checking *procedures* are needed. • *D* Jennifer asks what the IRS report requires (output *data*), the number of contract laborers (*data* store frequency), and how the data is created.
Evaluate Alternatives	E.1 Identify Alternatives	• *P* Jennifer assumes she will be the operator as well as devel-oper and end-user, so there is no variation here.

(continued)

Figure 1.18 Activities Summary for the Contract Labor System

Figure 1.18   (Continued)

Stage	Activity	Case Problem Action
		• *P* Jennifer decides that verification *procedures* will involve comparing the monthly total from the property management software for the contract labor account with each new monthly total. Each month the sum of the totals for each person (the vertical total) and the sum of all the monthly totals to date will be calculated and printed by a spreadsheet. (These totals will then be visually checked by the operator.)
		• *D* Abby's requirements and the IRS requirements narrow the *data* store to twelve columns for months, a name column, and total fields, as shown in Figure 1.19. The *data input* is specified clearly by Abby as gross labor per month, and the *report format* is specified by the IRS.
		• *S* The input and output data is just columns of numbers, so Jennifer decides spreadsheet *software* will meet the objectives and requirements within the time constraints.
		• *H* Jennifer knows that the existing hardware is not being used to capacity, so use of existing hardware is one alternative. However, she also knows that procedures for the current property management system are tedious because of switching floppies, so she lists as another alternative purchasing new hardware.
	E.2 Select Alternative	• Abby eliminates the new hardware alternative. She agrees with all of Jennifer's other decisions except one. Abby says she wants to be able to operate the spreadsheet in case Jennifer is out or too busy at the end of any given month or, more important, at the end of the year.
Specify Design	D.1 Specify People	• *P* Since Jennifer is the developer and end-user, there are no changes to job descriptions or personnel requirements.
	D.2 Specify Procedures	• *P* Jennifer's current *procedures* will be altered slightly with the new system. Instead of waiting until the end of the year to locate and sum the contract labor checks, she will enter the check totals at the end of each month.
	D.3 Specify Data	• *D* IRS instructions specify the basic input and output *data*. For data verification, however, individual monthly totals will also be stored and printed. Jennifer also decides to add a column that will flag rows with "IRS" when the laborer's sheet exceeds $599. The report design is limited by the spreadsheet tool, but various report formats are possible. Jennifer checks with Abby to see if Abby wants anything other than the full spreadsheet as a report.

Figure 1.18 (Continued)

Stage	Activity	Case Problem Action
		Abby verifies that the full spreadsheet is an adequate report format, so Jennifer's only report design is to determine the column arrangements for easy reading as well as easy data entry.
	D.4 Specify Software	• *S* Jennifer plans to use the existing spreadsheet *software* as the development tool. She can "program" this herself, directly from the requirement, so she decides not to write any additional programming specifications.
	D.5 Specify Hardware	• *H* Abby specifies existing *hardware*.
Implement	I.1 Construct Components	• Jennifer creates the spreadsheet and enters two months of data. She writes a short "programmer's guide" documenting the details of the spreadsheet columns and calculations to supplement the requirements list. (This will be helpful for a new bookkeeper or herself, if she forgets some of the details.)
	I.2 Test Components	• Jennifer writes operation instructions for Abby (or a new bookkeeper) to follow.
		• Jennifer checks the totals carefully for two months of data. She then shows the printed spreadsheet to Abby. Abby verifies that it is correct.
		• Abby follows the documented procedures to add data for the next month and creates the end-of-the-year report. Corrections are made to the documentation where errors are found.
	I.3 Install Components and System	• Jennifer brings the spreadsheet up to date by entering the rest of the months in the current year. (Her work is shown in Figure 1.19. She creates a backup copy of the spreadsheet data and marks both disks clearly.

	Jan	Feb	Mar	Apr	May	Jun	Jul	Aug	Sep	Oct	Nov	Dec	Individual Totals	
Jim Dawson	150.00	200.00		300.00									650.00	InS
Alice Roberts		50.00	150.00	50.00									250.00	
Bob Young	75.00	75.00	75.00	75.00									300.00	
Monthly Account Total	225.00	325.00	225.00	425.00										
Crossfoot Test	Horizontal Sum	1200.00												
	Vertical Sum	1200.00	OK											

Figure 1.19 Spreadsheet for the Contract Labor System

1.3 The Development Process Matrix

This chapter has introduced the five components of an information system and has presented an overview of the REDI model of systems development. The **development process matrix**—a two-dimensional model of development activities—will help you better visualize the interrelationships of the components and the REDI model. The columns of the development process matrix are the five components of a system. The rows of the matrix are the four REDI model stages. Each cell represents a development activity or group of activities for a particular component. The 4 × 5 matrix is illustrated in Figure 1.20.

System problems are unique. The matrix provides a simple reference for devising methodologies for each new and unique systems development project. Chapter 5 will explain how this memory aid may be used as the basis for planning.

Figure 1.20
The Development Process Matrix

	People	Procedures	Data	Software	Hardware
Determine Requirements					
Evaluate Alternatives					
Specify Design					
Implement Design					

Summary

An information system is not just hardware and software. A trip to a computer store can provide a tool, but, as Abby learned, it cannot provide a solution. An information system must integrate people, procedures, data, software, and hardware. Data is the central component. Software provides instructions for hardware, and procedures provide instructions for people.

Systems development is a people-intensive process during which developers and users collaborate to create a new information system. The four-stage REDI model is one basis for viewing the development process. The first stage in the REDI model is the determination of requirements. Initially, objectives and constraints for the system are identified, and based on these objectives and constraints, the functional requirements are then investigated and analyzed. During the second stage, various system solutions are proposed, and the alternatives are evaluated in terms of costs and benefits to the organization. The third stage is design, during which the characteristics of each component are specified. The final stage is implementation of the design. The activities of this stage are construction, testing, and installation.

The development of a system is followed by a period of operational use or production. If any revisions are required, the development activities are repeated until the system is ready to go into production again. The cycle of development and production is called the life cycle of an information system. Changeover is the point at which a system goes from development to production.

A development process matrix is a two-dimensional view of development process activities. It is a valuable planning technique for meeting the challenges of each systems development project.

Key Terms

(Section numbers are in parentheses.)

information system (1.1)	**application software (1.1.4)**
developer (1.1.1)	**productivity software (1.1.4)**
programmer (1.1.1)	**hardware (1.1.5)**
analyst (1.1.1)	**life cycle model (1.2)**
operator (1.1.1)	**development phase (1.2)**
end-user (1.1.1)	**production phase (1.2)**
user-manager (1.1.1)	**changeover (1.2)**
user-sponsor (1.1.1)	**REDI model (1.2)**
procedures (1.1.2)	**requirements determination (1.2.1)**
user procedures (1.1.2)	**system boundary (1.2.1)**
operator procedures (1.1.2)	**system objectives (1.2.1)**
normal procedures (1.1.2)	**system constraints (1.2.1)**
recovery procedures (1.1.2)	**functional requirements (1.2.1)**
user access mode (1.1.2)	**evaluation (1.2.2)**
single-user system (1.1.2)	**design specification (1.2.3)**
sequential multi-user system (1.1.2)	**implementation (1.2.4)**
concurrent multi-user system (1.1.2)	**construction (1.2.4)**
data (1.1.3)	**testing (1.2.4)**
software (1.1.4)	**installation (1.2.4)**
systems software (1.1.4)	**development process matrix (1.3)**

Note

1. David M. Kroenke, *Business Computer Systems: An Introduction*, 2nd ed. (Santa Cruz, Calif.: Mitchell Publishing, 1984).

Exercises

(Answers to Exercises 1.1, 1.2, 1.3, 1.7, 1.8, and 1.9 are at the end of the book.)

1.1 Review the minicase Abby Clark and Her Turnkey System. Identify each of the five components of the system, including all the details provided in the case. Use the component summary form presented in Figure 1.9. (Figure 1.10 is an example of a completed form.)

1.2 Georgia Scalo and May Chung share responsibilities as receptionists and stenographers for Franklin Auto Repair. They alternate working the switchboard, handling correspondence, typing, and filing. Each is proficient at using the word processing package WORD, which is installed on the hard disk of the microcomputer in the receptionists' front lobby cubicle.

    a. Assume that Georgia does all the typing for the manager of the Repair division, and May does all the typing for the manager of the Retail division. They keep their stored files on the hard disk. Backup files are on floppy disks; these are kept at their desks. What user access mode are they employing? Why?

    b. Assume that Georgia and May type revisions to each other's documents. Each of them types whatever needs to be done (first draft or revisions). What user access mode are they employing? Why?

1.3 Grocery store checkers at Big Bob's Supermarket use a scanner that reads universal product bar codes (UPC). The bar code for each purchase is translated by the special-purpose computer (the cash register), accessing a product file. This translation triggers a voice output of the price. The product type and the price of each purchase are stored in a file to be used in printing the receipt. After all purchases have been scanned, a receipt is produced and given to the customer.

    a. What is the user access mode for this system?

    b. The hardware for the system just described is a microprocessor, a scanner, and a cash register–terminal. Based on this very limited description, determine the other four components of the system. (Use Figure 1.9 as a model for your answer.)

1.4 When a customer wishes to withdraw cash at a drive-in window at First National Bank, he or she must write a check made out to Cash. The check is sent to the teller office via vacuum tube. One of the four tellers enters the checking account number and the amount on one of the terminals. The amount is subtracted from the proper account balance in the account master file. A transaction slip is then printed with the check amount, updated account balance, and account number. The slip is returned to the customer via the vacuum tube.

    a. What is the user access mode for this system?

    b. The hardware for this system includes vacuum tubes, printer-terminals, and the mainframe computer system at the bank headquarters. Based on this very brief description, determine the other four components. (Use Figure 1.9 as a model for your answer.)

1.5 Experimenters at Fancy Flowers Seed Company record flower colors for new hybrids. The experimenters tally colors on a clipboard while walking down rows of plant boxes. After observations have been completed, each of the three experimenters keys in tally totals on the company's single microcomputer for later analysis. At the end of the day, the senior experimenter runs a program to create a daily experiment report and an updated summary report on the current experimental work. Past information is taken from the hybrid master file for this report; results stored in the file are also updated by the analysis program.

    a. What is the user access mode for this system?

    b. The hardware is a microcomputer with a hard disk, a monitor, and a printer. Based on this limited description, complete a component summary form (Figure 1.9).

1.6 When Software House receives a new computer game from a vendor, manager Peter Sargent creates a one-page word processing file that describes the new game program. He prints a copy to put in his folder of software descriptions. He also merges a copy of the description with a skeleton letter to mail to game buyers. The merged letter (description plus standard announcement information) is edited. Then Peter creates personalized versions of the letter in a merge-print process which accesses his mailing list file of Software House clients. The letters are then mailed to the clients.

    a. What is the user access mode for this system?

    b. The hardware is a microcomputer with a hard disk, a monitor, and a printer. Complete a component summary form (Figure 1.9) for this system.

1.7 A systems development process is described below. For each of the tasks a through i, indicate the code for the development activity from Figure 1.17.

    a. Sam Jones, an auditor for a large insurance agency, wrote a half-page memorandum requesting the creation of a new statistical report as part of the routine quarterly report processing.

    b. Mary spoke to Sam for about 15 minutes and ascertained that the requested report was very similar to another report that was generated as part of the quarterly report system.

    c. Mary created a new program by revising a copy of a similar program.

    d. The new program was tested first on a file of fifty test records and then on all the quarterly data from the last period.

    e. Sam spent an hour with Mary discussing all the changes he wanted and marking them on the test report.

    f. Mary revised the tested version of the program.

    g. The latest revision was then tested on a small file and on the quarterly data.

    h. Mary rewrote the system language to execute the new program as part of the production system. (She did not test this revised production job stream, because the change was so minor that she decided it would not be worth her time or the computer time.)

    i. When the next quarterly reports were run, the job stream with the revised program bombed—that is, failed to complete execution. The operator telephoned Mary. She reviewed a listing of the incomplete execution and quickly found and corrected a misplaced comma in her revised code.

1.8 For the process described in Exercise 1.7, name the individuals who filled the following development team roles:

    a. analyst

    b. programmer

    c. end-user

    d. user-sponsor

1.9 In the development process described in Exercise 1.7, the system failed to complete execution. What omitted activity might have caused this production failure?

1.10 Special Transportation Services (STS), a nonprofit service organization, had been providing bus transportation for the handicapped for three years. The city decided to ask STS for documentation of its services before renewing the city support funds. The only documents kept by the organization were lists of expenditures for such things as gasoline, total fare receipts, and a log of which drivers were out with which of the three vans. The board of directors decided that a computer system should be developed to automate the vehicle logs and generate summary reports. The STS staff consisted of an office manager, a secretary/receptionist, and three drivers. The office manager, Arnie Sklar, agreed to investigate possible systems and report back to the board. The development process activities are described below. Associate each of the tasks a through q with the code for the development activity listed in Figure 1.17.

a. Arnie visited a nearby computer store and told a salesperson what was needed. The sales clerk, Wilma Cohen, listened to Arnie's three or four sentences of explanation and then asked him what volume of data STS had on its logs and what sorts of reports were needed. When Arnie could only guess at the answers, Wilma suggested that he write down everything he could think of that the computer system should do. She also asked him to determine the number of entries in the logs and draft sample reports. During Arnie's next visit to the store, he and Wilma reviewed what he had prepared: copies of typical log pages, estimates of how many trips were made during a year, and a version of a report that would help fill the city's request for summary information.

b. On the basis of Arnie's information, Wilma recommended one of two systems, each with a popular database management package. Arnie presented the costs of Wilma's two recommendations to the board of directors and told them the advantages of each.

c. The directors authorized the purchase of the less expensive hardware and the database management package recommended as the development tool.

d. The system was purchased and installed.

e. Arnie read the manuals and worked the tutorial.

f. Arnie keyed in the parameters to define the files.

g. Finally, he set up the software to create one report.

h. After keying in twenty entries from the log to store in the computer, Arnie figured that it took an average of five minutes to complete one record for a vehicle log entry.

i. Extending that for the 2500 entries from the past year, he realized it would take more than 200 hours to build the file. Neither he nor the secretary had any extra time, so the entire file might not be built for several months.

j. After hearing Arnie's explanation of the time required for file building, the board authorized hiring two data entry specialists on a contract basis.

k. The data entry clerks creted the files in much less time than Arnie had estimated, since they were considerably faster typists than Arnie.

l. After the vehicle log file was built, Arnie tried to produce a report. He was unable to create the report and finally called Wilma for advice.

m. She told him that he needed to create another file of client information and link the two files to create the summaries he wanted. Before this could be done, however, he would need to change how he had organized the log file.

n. At this point Arnie asked the board to hire a consultant who would set up all the files and software to create the reports. They agreed to this after Arnie explained that the database management package he had purchased had required hours of frustrating work so far, and he still was not able to produce the reports the city wanted. If no one was hired, then the money already spent on the system and data entry would be wasted.

o. The consultant wrote the software and built the files for the system.

p. All the reports were reviewed by Arnie to determine their acceptability.

q. The consultant trained each of the van drivers to enter vehicle log data. Arnie was trained to maintain all of the other files. Arnie, as the office manager, paid the consultant after all the reports had been created and reviewed.

1.11 As you might have expected, Arnie (of Special Transportation Services in Exercise 1.10) soon realized that he should have insisted on more information about the data and procedures components. When a file was accidentally deleted one day, there was no backup, because no backup procedures had been written. When a new driver was hired, the experienced drivers had to teach her how to enter data; there were no written data entry procedures. Unfortunately, the difficulties encountered by STS are not uncommon. List activities omitted from the development process that would have been helpful in avoiding these sorts of problems.

Projects

1.12 Visit a user who has developed a system for his or her own use. Carry out the following activities based on your observations and an interview with the user.

    a. Complete a component summary form like the one in Figure 1.9.

    b. Identify the user access mode for the system and explain your choice.

    c. Using Figure 1.17 as a guide, identify the major development activities required to complete the system.

1.13 Visit an analyst in a large organization, such as your school, a company, or a government agency. Ask about a system that he or she has developed recently. Carry out the following activities based on your visit and interview.

    a. Complete a component summary form (Figure 1.9) for this system.

    b. Identify the user access mode for the system and explain your choice.

    c. Using Figure 1.17 as a guide, identify the major development activities required to complete the system.

1.14 Visit or telephone three organizations, each with a different word processing system. Conduct a brief interview with someone in each organization.

    a. Based on your interviews, complete the form shown in Figure 1.21.

Figure 1.21

	Organization Name: _____	Organization Name: _____	Organization Name: _____
Contact person			
Interview date			
Software			
Hardware			
People who use WP software			
Main use			
Person who chose system			
Steps leading to installation			
Strong points of system			
Major problems or regrets			

    b. Write a brief summary statement comparing the approaches of the three companies. How did their approaches facilitate or hinder the successful development of a word processing system?

CHAPTER 2

Managing the Development Process

Overview

Developing a good information system is much like developing an effective textbook. Both processes require that the developer understand the users' needs and be sensitive to the users' level of knowledge and preconceptions. Just as you in your role as developer will create systems for a wide variety of users, we as textbook authors must create a text for a varied student audience.

Our users—you—come to systems development from different backgrounds. Some of you are experienced programmers who have clearly defined views on how a system should be developed. In fact, you may feel that the *real* jobs of systems development are designing and coding software. But, as Figure 2.1 shows, these activities comprise just two of the many cells of the development matrix. In contrast, others of you may have almost no knowledge of the systems development process; you may feel intimidated by the numerous cells of the matrix, wondering how you will ever understand these activities well enough to perform them in your career.

Figure 2.1
A Programmer's Responsibility: Two Cells

	People	Procedures	Data	Software	Hardware
Determine Requirements					
Evaluate Alternatives					
Specify Design				Design software	
Implement Design				Code software	

We feel that the best way to address your varied knowledge and preconceptions is to provide a framework from which all of you can view the systems development process. In much the same way as you will acquaint your users with a new system by showing them flowcharts and sample screens and reports, we will acquaint you with the development process proposed by this textbook by providing an overview of that process.

The responsibilities of a systems developer are numerous and varied. As an information systems professional, you will often be required to manage the process as well as to develop the product. The many options and conflicting goals facing you will make your job both complex and challenging. If you can handle the complexity, you'll find the challenges exciting and rewarding.

The purpose of this chapter is to discuss the management roles of an information systems professional. Specifically, we plan to

1. Discuss the three major goals of the developer—system quality, project management, and organizational relevance—and show the importance of each. (Section 2.1)

2. Identify the management activities of the development team. (Section 2.2)

3. Discuss phased development and software sources as means of addressing these goals and performing these activities. (Sections 2.3 and 2.4)

2.1 Systems Development Goals

The responsibilities for the information systems profession have changed greatly since its inception in the early 1960s. Initial development efforts focused on bread-and-butter accounting applications, such as payroll, customer credit, and accounts payable systems. In these first projects, tedious procedures formerly performed by people were directly transferred to software executed by hardware. The development process for these early systems consisted of writing software to imitate the existing manual procedures. The developer considered only two components of the system: hardware and software. The data component was a direct translation of the old manual forms, reports, and data storage. Developers did not redesign procedures to take advantage of the computer's capabilities, so the production staff of the old manual system could run the automated system with minimal changes in their responsibilities. These staff people did not see procedures as part of the computer system, since the new procedures were essentially the same as the old. The main difference was that tedious calculations and typing were transferred to software and hardware. Thus the computer was viewed as a faster calculator and typewriter.

This limited view of the systems development process, illustrated in Figure 2.2, often worked in early development projects. For example, the manual systems for payroll and personnel were each automated separately, following the approach highlighted in Figure 2.2. This was the fastest way to develop each system, since little time was spent on requirements, evaluation, or design. The major problem was that manual procedures were copied too closely. Redundant manual procedures and data storage were repeated for the various computer systems. Designing information processing for an organization based on

Figure 2.2
The Development Process Matrix for Automating a Single Manual System

	People	Procedures	Data	Software	Hardware
Determine Requirements					Determine facility and equipment require-ments
Evaluate Alternatives					
Specify Design			Copy manual input/ output formats	Design software to imitate existing functions	
Implement Design			Create files	Code, test, and install software	Install hardware, if additional power is needed

the capabilities of typewriters and calculators wasted computer power. Some professionals still hold this narrow view, but their career potential is quite limited. Today the responsibilities of the information systems professional have evolved to include all of the following:

- system quality
- project management
- organizational relevance

2.1.1 System Quality

System quality is a complex goal. Meeting this goal involves developing and interfacing all five system components. **System quality** is judged by the answers to three questions:

- How well does the system function? To be more specific, does the system do what it is supposed to do reliably, easily, and efficiently?
- How easy is the system to maintain?
- How flexible is the system? Can it adapt to changes in its five components?

These questions can be answered by evaluating the system characteristics listed in Figure 2.3.

The first question addresses **functionality.** Does the system meet the requirements? Does it do what it was designed to do? We can investigate system functionality by examining the three first-level characteristics of functionality listed in Figure 2.3: reliability, clarity, and efficiency. Each of these characteristics can be further subdivided into second-level characteristics. **Reliability** means that the system provides accurate, complete answers and its functions are integrated to form one smooth-running system. Not only should a reliable system provide complete and accurate output when correct procedures are followed; it should be robust enough that when errors are made, recovery is easy. Rather than breaking down, leaving the user with a frozen screen, or wildly reproducing erroneous data, a robust system will provide error messages that allow for easy recovery. **Clarity,** or transparency, means that the system is easy to "see into": it interacts with users in a consistent, predictable manner, providing easy-to-learn and easy-to-use instructions, prompts, error messages, and help screens. **Efficiency** means that the system maximizes processing speed and minimizes turnaround time and memory requirements; it avoids repetition and redundancy, both in its user procedures and in its program code.

Fulfilling functional requirements is only one aspect of system quality. Because business systems inevitably change, **ease of maintenance** is also important. Modification of data often has a ripple effect, requiring changes in software, hardware, and procedures. In order to successfully modify a system, the developer must understand the system and be able to test the changes. These three maintenance activities (understanding, modifying, and testing) are the three first-level characteristics of ease of maintenance as shown in Figure 2.3. System maintenance people will be able to understand the system more easily if it is clearly documented and if its programs are developed as single-function, cohesive modules. The system will be easier to test if documentation is so clear that the system can "explain itself" by providing a clear audit trail and precise error messages. Programs will be easier to modify if the modules are fairly independent of one another, so that

Figure 2.3 System Quality	**System Quality Subgoals**	**First-Level Characteristics**	**Second-Level Characteristics**
	1. Functionality: How well (reliably, clearly, efficiently) does the system function?	Reliability	Completeness Accuracy Robustness/integrity
		Clarity	Consistency Predictability
		Efficiency	Fast turnaround Low memory requirements Nonredundant procedures and processes
	2. Ease of maintenance: How easy is it to maintain (understand, modify, and test) the system?	Understandability	Clear documentation Cohesiveness Consistency
		Modifiability	Modular structure Modular independence
		Testability	Clear documentation Modular structure
	3. Flexibility: How flexible is the system with respect to changes in its components?	Portability	Site independence Device independence Language independence
		Adaptability	Program-data independence Procedural flexibility

Adapted from Boehm's software quality tree in Barry W. Boehm, J. R. Brown, and M. Lipow, "Quantitative Evaluation of Software Quality," *Proceedings, 2nd International Conference on Software Engineering* (San Francisco, October, 1976), pp. 592–605.

changing one module does not require changing several others. Designing and implementing systems with these characteristics will be the focus of Parts 5 and 6 of this text.

The fact that organizations change continually makes flexibility the third basic determinant of system quality. Will the system continue to function if the environment changes? Is the system adaptable? The answers depend on the characteristics listed in the lower right-hand section of Figure 2.3. **Flexibility** is based on the independence of each of the five components from system-specific requirements. Under flexibility are two first-level characteristics: portability and adaptability.

A portable system is one that can be moved easily; it can be operated in various environments (site independence) and with various hardware components (device independence and language independence). Microcomputer and mini-computer systems have few special site requirements, whereas mainframes have special temperature restrictions and electrical wiring requirements. Microcomputer systems are therefore much more site independent than mainframe systems. Device independence means that the system has not been written for specific devices, such as a particular disk drive or printer. Some word processing systems support easy selection of a variety of printers from a menu, whereas less device-independent systems require more complex changes to adapt to different devices. A language-independent system can be adapted easily to different operating system software without rewriting the application software. Systems written in a nonstandard program language will require code revisions, whereas systems written in a standard language often can be transferred from one operating system to another with no revisions.

An adaptable system is easy to modify (program-data independence), and its procedures can be molded easily to new users (procedural flexibility). Program-data independence allows data to be changed without changing all the programs that reference the data. For example, data structures defined with a database management system can be altered in one central data definition section without revising all the programs that access the data. Procedural flexibility ensures that standard procedures can be easily adapted by new uses. This flexibility allows an organization to use its existing systems to address various organizational problems.

2.1.2 Project Management

The system quality goals discussed in the preceding section focus on the *product* of development: an information system. This section's topic, **project management,** focuses on the goals of the development *process* itself. In other words, project management goals identify the characteristics of a well-managed project in much the same way that system quality goals identify the characteristics of a well-developed system. To a large degree, users set the quality level for the system being developed; as a systems developer, you just follow their lead. In contrast, as a development team member and especially as a team leader, you set the quality level for the development process; *you* plan, monitor, coordinate, and review. Thus, you are responsible for how well managed the development process is. Managing a project is more than a "minor administrative detail." How well managed the development process is has a great impact on the success of the system developed.

The characteristics of a well-managed project are highlighted by the following three questions:

1. Is the system completed on time?
2. Is the system completed within budget?
3. Are the users (both user-managers and end-users) involved and committed to the success of the system?

A high-quality system will not be a success if it is completed too late to benefit the organization. A long development time, especially one characterized by repeated postponements, frustrates users. Exceeding the development budget is another indication of project management failure.

If changes in system requirements or unforeseen circumstances force schedule or budget overruns, the users should be told about the difficulties so that they can decide whether the scope of the project should be restricted or the schedule or budget expanded. Frequent progress reviews should be held to inform the users of project management issues, as well as to demonstrate system products.

Systems that are technically superb may fail as a result of user dissatisfaction. User involvement during development is necessary to determine what functions are required for a complete, accurate, clear, and efficient system. If the users are part of the development team, they can document their requirements, evaluate alternatives, design user interfaces (reports and screens) and training materials, and implement parts of the system, especially user documentation and training materials. At changeover, their commitment to adjusting to the new system and taking full advantage of all its features will be the key determinant of success.

2.1.3 Organizational Relevance

The fact that an organization has met the goals of system quality and project management does not necessarily mean that it has made effective use of its resources. A high-quality system, completed on time and within budget, is a waste of development effort if it does not contribute to the overall objectives of the organization. Any high-quality system will streamline an organization's operations. Meeting the goal of **organizational relevance,** however, requires more than increased efficiency. In order to contribute to the success of the organization, the system must be relevant to the organization's objectives. The mini-case A High-Quality, Low-Value System illustrates one executive's poor choice of a system to develop.

Figure 2.4
Strategic Decisions for Information Systems Management

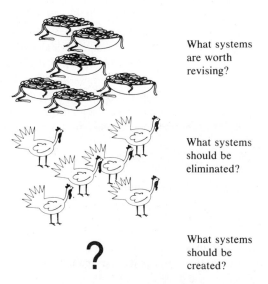

What systems are worth revising?

What systems should be eliminated?

What systems should be created?

The choice of which systems to improve, which to eliminate, and which to initiate should be based on their organizational relevance. The choices are graphically summarized in Figure 2.4. The bowls of spaghetti symbolize unstructured, difficult-to-maintain systems. The turkeys symbolize systems whose value to the organization, relative to costs, is low. These should be eliminated or revised to improve their benefits. You should not

A High-Quality, Low-Value System

Dave, the chief financial officer (CFO) of a prominent wholesale distributor, is just now putting the final touches on his new quarterly financial report. Since coming on board, he's directed a major upgrade of his company's financial reporting systems—which now enable him to produce timely, sophisticated financial reports, including graphic highlights. It wasn't easy. A new computer and months of effort were required to design and install the new system.

Unfortunately, the financial results reported by Dave's new system are most troubling. Sales are significantly off target and investment in inventory is climbing. On top of that, the backlog is at its highest level in years! Top management is beginning to realize that the company's neglected order management and inventory control systems are failing to support the changing demands of the market or the new remote-distribution warehouses.

Dave has just wasted $400,000. His company is losing market share each day.

In retrospect, Dave's mistake is obvious. Giving priority to his financial systems, he ignored the company's (as yet unidentified) critical success factors. A careful examination of what makes his company tick would have resulted in focusing its resources upon improved order and inventory management systems. All too often, as in this case, information technology resources are dedicated to the squeaky wheel—*instead of the broken axle!*

Source: William G. Dauphinais, *Price Waterhouse Review*, vol. 30, no. 2, Summer 1986, pp. 26, 31.

revise a spaghetti system just to improve system quality—you have to consider its benefit to the organization. If the spaghetti system is critical and maintenance costs are high, revise it. Otherwise, if the spaghetti system works and isn't too costly to maintain, you should probably build or revise another system that is more critical to the organization's goals. Because such choices are often difficult, we will consider organizational relevance in greater detail.

A system may help an organization meet its objectives by producing information needed by one or more of the three levels of decision making: *operational, managerial,* and *strategic.*[1] Operational decisions control the hour-to-hour, day-to-day processes. Managerial decisions cover a broader spectrum of issues related to resource allocation and management. Strategic decisions determine the organization's overall strategies for meeting its objectives.

Figure 2.5 lists examples of information systems that support each level of decision making. Systems seldom match the decision-making levels exactly; however, operational systems often produce reports for managerial and strategic level decisions. For example, a well-designed reservation system generates summary reports for management control as well as operational information for clients and reservation clerks. A reservation system can also generate analyses for use in strategic planning. Your job as a project team member is to develop systems that support critical decisions at all three levels. From this perspective, the goal of organizational relevance may be evaluated by answering these questions:

1. Does the system add or improve an operational task critical to the organization's objectives?

2. Does the system support critical management decisions?

3. Does the system have strategic value?

Figure 2.5
Examples of Information System Applications at Each Decision-Making Level

Levels of Decision Making	Focus of Decision Making	Examples of Information Systems Applications
Strategic planning	Strategies for meeting the organization's objectives	Product planning analysis Market planning Research and design planning
Management control	Resource allocation	Budget analysis Salary forecasting Inventory forecasting Production management General ledger
Operational control	Production and staff activities	Payroll Accounts receivable Inventory Reservations Invoicing Order filling Purchase orders

A payroll system is an example of an operational system that is essential to an organization. But the fact that payroll is essential does not automatically make it a top priority for systems development. Dave, the CFO in the preceding minicase, would have been just as foolish to revise the payroll system as he was to build his super financial system. Dave's resources as CFO should have gone into product and sales analysis, which would have revealed more quickly the need for improved order management and inventory control.

The decision as to which systems to improve, eliminate, or initiate should be based on the organization's objectives. Consider the needs of XYZ Construction, a small company that has just bought its first computer system. Automating strategic planning is probably less important to XYZ than the immediate development of an operational system that will improve assets or cash flow. Currently, XYZ is grossing $2 million every year by winning one-fifth of its bids. If an automated bidding system doubled their number of construction bids per year, the potential benefit would be an additional $2 million. Thus, an improved bidding system would directly support the major objectives of this construction firm. A retail business needs systems that increase its client base and ensure timely payments. Government agencies need systems that improve their ability to meet legislative mandates. Figure 2.6 provides additional examples of systems with clear organizational relevance.

In later chapters we will discuss the process of choosing systems with organizational relevance. At this point it is merely important that you understand this vital goal of the information systems profession.

Levels of Decision Making	Examples of Competitive Information System Applications
Strategic planning	A cooperative association of cotton farmers established a communication network with an electronic trading system that allowed buyers to submit blind bids directly to farmers. The increased volume of bids to farmers allowed them to revise their pricing strategy as necessary throughout the buying season.
Management control	A construction firm developed an automated bid system to support management decision making. The effects of last-minute changes by clients could be calculated quickly, helping the construction firm to submit accurate bids by the deadline.
Operational control	An airline used its "frequent flyer" program to identify the target market for an advertising campaign to counteract the effect of a no-frills airline that had hurt market share in one area.
	Oil companies used telecommunication networks to communicate price changes directly to their thousands of distributors, thus gaining the ability to respond more rapidly to changes in the market.

Source: Examples derived from Cynthia M. Beath and Blake Ives, "Competitive Information Systems in Support of Pricing, *MIS Quarterly,* vol. 10, no. 1, March 1986, pp. 85–93.

2.1.4 Balancing Goals

Figure 2.7 summarizes the three goals of systems development:

- system quality
- project management
- organizational relevance

You may be tempted to rank organizational relevance as the most important of the three goals, because draining an organization's resources for nonessential systems may ruin the organization. The potential for organizational relevance, however, will not be realized by a poor-quality system. Nor will this potential be realized if project management is so poor that the system is delivered after the opportunity has passed or when users have become so frustrated with project delays that they are no longer cooperative.

	Goals	Subgoals	Questions to Answer
Figure 2.7 Summary of Information System Goals	System quality	Functionality	1. How well (reliably, clearly, efficiently) does the system function?
		Maintainability	2. How easy is it to maintain (understand, modify, and test) the system?
		Flexibility	3. How flexible is the system with respect to changes in its five components?
	Project management	Timeliness	1. Is the system completed on time?
		Low cost	2. Is the system completed within budget?
		User commitment	3. Are the users (both user-managers and end-users) involved and committed to the success of the system?
	Organizational relevance	Operational control	1. Does the system add or improve an operational task critical to the organization's objectives?
		Management control	2. Does the system support critical management decisions?
		Strategic planning	3. Does the system have strategic value?

Like the legs of a three-legged stool, all three of the goals shown in Figure 2.8 are important to systems development. System quality should be high enough to permit the attainment of system objectives, which should support the organizational objectives. Project management should be adequate to deliver the system on time and within budget and to achieve changeover with the support of management and end-users.

Figure 2.8
Balancing the Three Goals of Systems Development

2.2 Management Activities

Chapter 1 described the life cycle model as a circle with repeating periods of development and production. The development side of the model was depicted as a single series of four clear-cut stages. In actual practice, systems development is not so simple or well structured for a number of reasons, which we will discuss throughout this text. For now we will focus on two major complications:

- Most systems are too large to be developed by one person within a short period of time.
- One user seldom understands the entire system to be developed.

The problem of lengthy development time is addressed by forming a development team to speed up the process. Managing this team requires planning, monitoring, and coordinating of resources. The problem of no single individual's knowing the entire system is addressed through user reviews. Although these four management activities—planning, monitoring, coordinating, and reviewing—do not contribute directly to the systems development product, each is absolutely essential to the system's success. What we see, then, is that every systems development effort produces two streams of activity. One stream focuses on developing the system (creating the product); the other focuses on managing the development process so that the system is developed efficiently and effectively. Figure 2.9 summarizes these two streams of activities.

Figure 2.9
The Two Activity Streams of Systems Development

Development Activities	Management Activities
Determine Requirements	Plan
R.1 Identify Objectives	Monitor
R.2 Identify Constraints	Coordinate
R.3 Investigate Requirements	Review
Evaluate Alternatives	
E.1 Identify Alternatives	
E.2 Select Alternative	
Specify Design	
D.1 Specify Components	
Implement Design	
I.1 Construct	
I.2 Test	
I.3 Install	

2.2.1 Planning

As a project leader, you have four **planning** responsibilities:

- Determine the process activities and sequence.
- Estimate the time required for development.
- Allocate staff and resources.
- Document the schedule.

The schedule for a systems development project summarizes the performance objectives of the development team. The schedule indicates what activities must be performed, when, and by whom. The schedule is the basis for the remaining three management activities: monitoring, coordinating, and reviewing. The existence of a good plan with reasonable time estimates will make monitoring and coordinating much easier. Scheduling frequent review points will ensure that the team develops a system that users and management need.

2.2.2 Monitoring

Project **monitoring** involves tracking individual and team progress. Timely contributions by each team member are critical to the progress of the team as a whole. By comparing current progress to the development schedule, you can make sure that the system will be delivered on schedule. By monitoring at frequent checkpoints, you can identify schedule problems early enough to increase the development staff or change the schedule.

2.2.3 Coordinating

There are three **coordinating** functions:

- Form a development team.
- Coordinate the activities of the development team.
- Coordinate resources for the team.

Form a Development Team   Successful systems development projects are user-driven; that is, the need for the system and the requirements of the system are determined by the potential users of the system. In user-driven development, the choice of users and developers for the team can make or break a project. Usually, a development team consists of one or more users appointed by senior management and several developers appointed by information systems management.

To develop a word processing system for a small law firm, a partner might choose an attorney, the office manager, and a legal secretary to serve as the development team. All of these team members are end-users; one of them may also be the developer and the operator.

To develop a larger system, more developers are needed. For example, a team developing a point-of-sale system for a national franchise should include at least two or three systems analysts. The users on the team should include a cashier who will use the system directly as well as a store manager who will benefit from the reports. Depending on the scope of the point-of-sale system, an inventory manager or buyer might also be on the team.

The principal concern in forming a team is to avoid costly partial solutions by choosing team members who will be able to define the overall requirements, generate and review alternatives, design the solution, and implement it.

Coordinate the Development Team   Coordinating the efforts of a team requires face-to-face contact on an almost daily basis. As a project leader, you need to know the strengths and weaknesses of each team member in order to assign tasks that take advantage of each member's skills. You need to give complete instructions for each task and to review work methods regularly, looking for ways to increase productivity. Coordination of effort is important to working steadily and efficiently as a team.

Coordinate Resources for the Development Team   Coordination of resources is also important to achieving an even and steady flow of work. If a new software development tool is to be used, programmers must be trained before coding can begin. If testing requires communication between computers, communication software should be in place early. Delays that force highly trained people to wait for hardware or software can be extremely expensive. The effectiveness and efficiency of team members depends on their being properly trained and on their having the right tools for each project.

2.2.4 Reviewing

Project **reviewing** requires that you prepare review materials for demonstrations, presentations, and reports, as well as give the presentations and consultations themselves. Your development plan should include frequent reviews with users. The actual products of the development process—reports, menus, data entry screens, procedures, and so forth—should be reviewed by end-users and user-managers as soon and as often as possible. A review point may be scheduled at the end of each stage in the life cycle model of development, or several review points may be scheduled during each stage.

Figure 2.10 summarizes the four management activities.

	Activity	Description
Figure 2.10 Management Activities Summary	Plan	Determine process activities and sequence Estimate time required for activities Allocate staff and resources Document the schedule
	Monitor	Track progress and compare with plan
	Coordinate	Form a development team Coordinate the development team's activities Coordinate resources for the team
	Review	Prepare demonstrations, reports, and presentations Consult users, managers, and technical specialists

2.3 Phased Development

Systems development is a complex problem-solving task. Meeting the three goals of developing and managing the process can be a formidable challenge. Breaking the work into stages and then into activities within stages, as we did in the REDI model life cycle, will simplify the process. The REDI model's clear step-by-step progression is helpful for organizing activities. But you should realize that the actual sequence of activities will vary with every project. In this section we introduce a phased approach to systems development, which emphasizes the importance of user reviews to achieving system quality goals.

In the life cycle approach, the REDI development stages are completed just once. A major problem with this approach is that the user does not review the actual system solution until the entire system is complete. Specification documents may be read and reviewed, but these are seldom read with the attention that the final system receives. Waiting a long time before showing the actual system to the user increases the risk that the user will lose interest in the problem, forget what was originally requested, or identify new problems in the interim.

Phased development is a development strategy in which the REDI stage activities are repeated in several iterations. During each phase, requirements are determined, alternatives are evaluated, solutions are designed, and some portion of the system is implemented and subjected to a user review. Although the activities in each phase will vary depending on the goals of the phase, all the basic activities of the REDI model must be performed to develop a successful system.

The advantage of phased development lies in its frequent user reviews. At the end of each iterative phase, users are shown the system developed so far so that they can provide timely feedback. When users see and respond to a functioning system rather than just ideas on paper, they provide much fuller and more useful feedback. Identifying changes early not only saves time and money but also reduces user frustration. Thus, phased development is an effective strategy for achieving both system quality and project management goals.

Figure 2.11 illustrates phased development in four phases. The activities in the first column complete the first phase, the initial definition of the top-level system interfaces. Some portion of the system, perhaps the major system menus and data entry screens, is designed and implemented. At this point the users can react to the system and provide feedback. In the second phase, the top-level requirements are revised and more detailed requirements are defined. These new specifications are the basis for further development of alternative solutions, design, and implementation. The iteration of stage activities continues until the system is installed and ready for production.

Prototyping is a form of phased development. In **prototyping,** a prototype, or model, of the proposed system is built and shown to the user for feedback. In this text we will use the term *phased development* to refer to a strategy of building and installing *portions* of a system with frequent feedback from the user. We will use the term *prototyping* when the main purpose is to present for feedback a *model,* which may or may not become part of the production system.

The minicase Midtown Bank Trend Analysis illustrates the phased development approach for a trend analysis system.

Figure 2.11
Phased Development

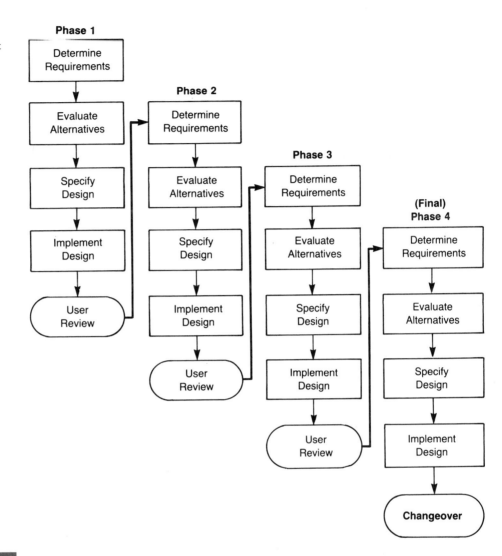

Midtown Bank Trend Analysis

Eric, a new trainee at a large bank, was assigned to automate the loan department's trend analysis system. The trend analysis system collected financial statement data of loan candidates and current customers. The current process, a manual system of recording and storing information for each client on a 3 × 5 trend card, was unsatisfactory for several reasons: updating was awkward and difficult, the paper cards were not very durable, and the reporting procedure was tedious.

The first step for Eric was to get to know the manual system. Then he reviewed current documents, interviewed the loan supervisor, and discussed the procedures with the loan officers, secretaries, and interns. From these investigations Eric determined the general requirements for the people, procedure, and data components.

Next, Eric reviewed the results of his interviews with the loan supervisor to determine the hardware and software components. The department had a PC network and spreadsheet program that was currently being used by loan officers, secretaries, and interns for various projects. Eric thought a database manager would be a better development tool, but retraining the staff would take too long. He decided the network and spreadsheet were sufficient.

Eric then researched the load on the PC system, checking current data memory requirements, future memory requirements for the trend cards data, and response time. Again reviewing his findings with the loan supervisor, Eric offered two data storage alternatives:

1. Raw data alone could be stored for each client.

2. Raw data and trend calculations could be stored for each client.

The first alternative would require more time to generate individual client data displays, because trends would have to be recalculated. The second would require more storage space. The loan supervisor decided that only raw data would be stored, because storage was a more critical constraint than response time.

Eric wanted to show progress as quickly as possible, so he planned the development process in three phases:

1. Create the basic spreadsheet template for data storage.

2. Create templates to calculate trend data for reports and graphs.

3. Design command sequences (macros) for data entry and system control.

Figure 2.12
Overview of Development Deliveries for Midtown Bank Trend Analysis System

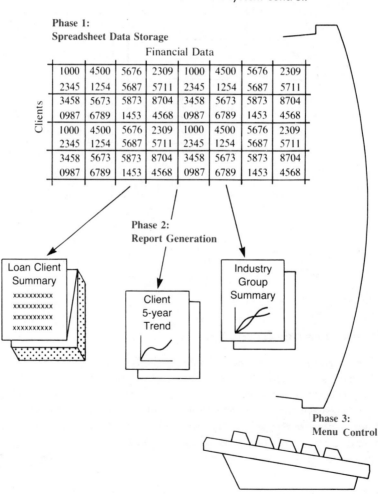

(These phased delivery points are shown in Figures 2.12 and 2.13.)

Eric developed the basic spreadsheet first as the basis for the other development phases. In order to make his system available for use as soon as possible, he delayed creating menu control until phase 3, under the assumption that the more experienced loan officers and secretaries could use the phase 2 system.

The loan supervisor, her secretary, and two loan officers reviewed each phase. Adjustments were made and tested with a small data template until the users and the loan supervisor were satisfied with the system. Interns were then trained to perform data entry. Final installation began with building the production data storage. The results were analyzed and double-checked against the results from the old cards. More adjustments were made, and then the rest of the loan department staff was trained to use the new trend analysis system.

Source: Sherif Nadar, Salomon Brothers Asia Limited, Tokyo.

Development Activities   **Management Activities**

R.1 Identify Constraints

The general objective is to keep borrower financial data without the problems associated with overused 3 × 5 cards.

Approve initiation of development sequence. Set milestones for first stage of investigation.

Review early objectives and alternatives.

R.2 Identify Constraints

Hardware and software components are constrained to the existing PC network and spreadsheet.

R.3 Investigate Requirements

- Identify additional memory and response time requirements.

- Identify further requirements, such as easy-to-learn data entry.

- Create rough report formats for review by the loan officers and supervisor.

E.1 Identify Alternatives

Generate alternatives for meeting added memory and response time requirements of the existing system.

E.2 Select Alternative

INITIAL PLANNING, REQUIREMENTS DETERMINATION, EVALUATION, AND REVIEWS

Review alternatives for meeting requirements. Plan activities and set milestones for development.

Figure 2.13 Summary of Development Phases for the Midtown Bank Trend Analysis System   *(continued)*

Figure 2.13   (Continued)

Review alternatives for meeting requirements. Plan activities and set milestones for development.

D.1 Specify Design (basic template)

Specify template organization and interface with other components.

I.1 Construct Components (basic template)

- Code basic template.

- Document procedures for handling overflow, updating, and backup.

I.2 Test Components (basic template)

Test procedures with template.

I.3 Install (basic template)

**PHASE 1
DESIGN,
IMPLEMENTATION,
AND REVIEW**

Review first iteration. Identify further changes.

D.1 Specify Design (reports and calculations)

Specify report formats and calculation sequences.

I.1 Construct Components (reports and calculations)

- Code calculation template and automated procedures.

- Code report formats.

- Document procedures for generating reports.

I.2 Test Components (reports and calculations)

Test reports and data for accuracy and format.

I.3 Install (reports and calculations)

**PHASE 2
DESIGN,
IMPLEMENTATION,
AND REVIEW**

Review reports and graphs. Identify further changes. Approve system for use by qualified personnel.

Figure 2.13 (Continued)

Review reports and graphs. Identify further changes. Approve system for use by qualified personnel.

PHASE 3 DESIGN, IMPLEMENTATION, AND REVIEW

D.1 Specify Design (macros)

Specify menu format, data entry screens, and control sequences.

I.1 Construct Components (macros)

• Code menu screens.

• Code macros.

• Document procedures for data entry and menu access.

I.2 Test Components (macros)

Test reports with full file.

I.3 Install Components (macros)

Review reports and graphs. Identify further changes. Approve system for training and use.

FINAL INSTALLATION

I.1 Construct Components (final installation)

• Distribute documentation.

• Train personnel for data entry.

• Create full production data file.

I.2 Test Components (final installation)

• Monitor system response with growing file.

• Test reports with full file.

I.3 Install (final installation)

Review tests of data. Approve for use or request further changes.

CHANGEOVER

2.4 Application Software Sources

Achieving the goals of system quality, project management, and organizational relevance requires that systems developers use a variety of methods to build systems. Because software development consumes a large portion of many development efforts, systems developers need to be aware of the various methods of acquiring application software and the relative advantages of each. In most organizations, the demand for new systems is so great that rarely can all new application software be developed by following traditional programming methods. In many small organizations, the cost of developing software in-house is so great that extensive software development simply is not feasible.

This section discusses three sources of application software, in order of cost-effectiveness:

1. existing software (either in-house or commercial)
2. software custom-written by end-users
3. software custom-written by programmers

2.4.1 Existing Software

Why develop software that has already been written? Using existing, well-tested software can eliminate many of the tedious activities and much of the risk of custom development. Furthermore, using existing software is more cost-effective.

You may acquire software from other divisions in your organization, trade associations, bulletin boards, user groups, books, magazines, hardware vendors, or software vendors. Because your main concern in this case is choosing a product that fits your needs, you will emphasize evaluation activities in your development plan. These activities are shaded in the development process matrix in Figure 2.14. As you evaluate software, you should not only look at software functions but also consider training services, vendor support, warranties, and a wide range of system supplements. Remember: Your selection will be the basis for system success or failure.

The ideal way to evaluate existing software is to observe it in use in an organization with similar needs and to interview users. Experienced users in trade associations or user groups can also give you valuable insights into both development and production advantages and disadvantages of various software products. Another approach is to visit computer stores for demonstrations. Or you might have vendors install software on-site so that users and information systems staff can review its performance and documentation.

Acquiring existing software is often a compromise solution. You are looking for the 80/20 solution shown in Figure 1.14—a way of meeting 80 percent of your basic requirements at 20 percent of the cost of the 100 percent solution. If you find a software package that meets most of the requirements identified in the requirements phase and you can afford it, buy it. There is little risk in this approach, as long as you follow a careful selection process. Be sure that the price and the date available are set in the purchase agreement. Sometimes the software is free—then your only risk is the time required to complete the development of the system after the software is acquired.

Although lower price is the major advantage of acquiring existing software, there are many others. One is that all the important users can interact with the software before a large investment is made. Thus any adamant objections to the purchase will be recognized before the system becomes a reality. Another important advantage of acquiring software

Figure 2.14
The Development
Process Matrix for
Development with Ex-
isting Software

	People	Procedures	Data	Software	Hardware
Determine Requirements	Form development team Determine possible users	Determine procedural requirements	Determine I/O and volume requirements	Determine functional requirements	Determine facility and equipment requirements
Evaluate Alternatives	Identify and select users	Identify and select procedures	Identify alternative I/O and storage solutions	Identify and select software	Identify and select hardware
Specify Design	Specify and organize users	Specify procedures and documentation	Specify and organize data	Negotiate contract and order software	Negotiate contract and order hardware
Implement Design	Train people	Test and document procedures	Build test files and production files	Test and install software	Prepare site Install and test hardware

is the time saved. Not only is development time reduced, but the system can be installed earlier, allowing the business to begin taking advantage of whatever profits the system may generate.

The disadvantage of using existing software is that it may not adequately fit the needs of the organization. The mismatch may be caused by the unique features of a particular application or by the lack of compatibility of one of the components with other systems. If your company requires that procedures across software products be compatible, or if it has a highly integrated database, existing software may not serve your needs. These are important issues to evaluate early in your search.

2.4.2 Software Custom-Written by End-Users

In many cases, custom programming may be the only way to obtain the software you need. If your organizational need is great enough, custom programming may be well worth the time and expense. The value of custom-written software depends on how important the system is to the organization.

In the past, custom development has meant that teams of users and computer professionals collaborated on the development of the system. The users would be most active in the requirements determination stage. Once the programmers and analysts understood the requirements and the users selected a solution, the programmers and analysts would design and implement the solution.

There are two problems with this approach. One is that a great deal of time may elapse between the selection of the alternative and the presentation of a working solution. Phased development has been proposed as a solution to this problem. The other problem is that the information systems staff may spend a considerable amount of time trying to understand what the users' requirements are. One way to eliminate this problem is to have the end-users develop their own system, including writing their own software.

Having users write their own software does not eliminate the requirements definition activities, which are shaded in Figure 2.15. This approach does, however, eliminate many communication problems between users and development staff. The development staff does not have to learn the users' functions, nor do the users have to translate their requests into terms that computer experts can understand. Not only can the users write their own software; they can also document procedures in terms appropriate to their area and provide training to fit the background and requirements of their colleagues.

Figure 2.15
The Development Process Matrix for Development with Custom-Written Software

	People	Procedures	Data	Software	Hardware
Determine Requirements	Form development team Determine possible users	Determine procedural requirements	Determine I/O and volume requirements	Determine functional requirements	Determine facility and equipment requirements
Evaluate Alternatives	Identify and select users	Identify and select procedures	Identify alternative I/O and storage design	Identify and select software	Identify and select hardware
Specify Design	Specify and organize users	Specify procedures and documentation	Specify I/O and storage	Specify and design software and testing	Negotiate contract and order hardware
Implement Design	Train people	Test and document procedures	Build test files and production files	Code, test, and install software	Prepare site Install and test hardware

Having users write software is possible only when easy-to-use tools such as microcomputer productivity packages and mainframe query languages are available to users. For mainframe access, the user will be dependent on the information systems staff to provide data, technical support, and tools that allow users to build their own systems. In this case, computer professionals retain responsibility for data, the central component of systems.

The computer professionals assist users in accessing the data, but then the users write the software and develop the procedures.

Fourth generation languages (4GLs), also called fourth generation tools, are one kind of systems development tool available to users. The 4GLs are easier to use and more compact than procedure-oriented **third generation languages** such as COBOL or Pascal, as they require fewer commands to accomplish the same purpose. The 4GLs are ideally suited to developing input/output-oriented systems that primarily accept and re-trieve data with only simple manipulations. They are often inappropriate, however, for systems that perform extensive or complex processing of data. If the system to be devel-oped involves a lot of complex data processing, end-users should ask information systems professionals to design, code, and test programs using a standard third generation lan-guage. Studies have shown that using a 4GL to develop a system that is heavily oriented toward data processing is counterproductive; the system is likely to consume more devel-opment time and effort and perform less efficiently than a similar system developed in COBOL or Pascal.[2] Some examples of fourth generation tools are

> spreadsheets
>
> query languages
>
> nonprocedural languages
>
> screen generators
>
> file managers

The minicase Information Center Consultants at Taco Bell gives an example of how one company supports user development.

2.4.3 Software Custom-Written by Information Systems Professionals

If it is not possible for users to write their own software, then the next most efficient way to develop the software component of a system is to have information systems profession-als develop the system using fourth generation tools. Using fourth generation tools reduces the time spent programming, but the requirements definition and designing activities are as time consuming as in development with third generation languages.

The final and most costly way to develop application software is to have information systems professionals write custom software using third generation languages. Although this method is the least cost-effective, there are many reasons why it is still the prevalent method of development. Following are a few of the reasons:

- Systems already built and running in COBOL are expensive to rebuild, even with faster development methods.

- Fourth generation tools that are compatible with existing COBOL systems may not be available.

- Some programmers resist changing to new, unfamiliar methods.

- High volume or speed requirements for the system may necessitate greater efficiency in production than can be delivered with available fourth generation tools.

MINICASE

Information Center Consultants at Taco Bell

At Taco Bell, the information center consultant contributes from one-fourth to one-third of the effort on a development project: the user does all the rest of the work. These consultants play four important roles in the systems development process:

1. project manager
2. database designer
3. tools expert
4. quality assurance inspector

First, the consultant acts as the *project manager*. Once the user has completed his or her study of the requirements for the new system, the consultant estimates how many hours of work the rest of the project involves. The estimate is based on how much time the user has spent thus far—which is usually 10 percent to 15 percent of the total project time.

From the total project time estimate, the consultant and the user determine how much elapsed time the project will take to complete—which depends on how many hours a week the user plans to spend working on it. And they lay out a schedule for the phases, sometimes using a project management system on a PC.

Once the project is under way, the user and consultant meet at least once a week to review progress. The consultant tracks the user's progress against the initial schedule and sometimes prods the user along. Users have a tendency to want to skimp on analysis and documentation just as programmers do, we are told.

At each weekly progress meeting, the two also agree on the amount of work to be done in the coming week and what milestone will be completed. So projects are tracked weekly. For long projects, the information center consultant writes a weekly memo to the information center manager and the user's manager describing the project's progress.

Second, the consultant is the *database designer*. Taco Bell has discovered that although users can define the data they need, they have a very hard time creating both the logical and the physical database. This takes practice. Therefore, the information center consultant performs this step.

Since the system design—which the user creates—parallels the database design, the consultant must be sure that the user understands the reasoning behind the database design that was chosen. This becomes an iterative process. If the user discovers new data elements, the database design may need to be changed. Users can add additional elements to a branch on the hierarchical design scheme, we are told. But usually only the consultants add new branches to a database design because this may involve shuffling branches.

Third, each information center consultant is a *tools expert*. Users of a tool, such as a fourth generation language (4GL), have one of the center's 4GL experts as their project consultant. Any time they have difficulty using the product, they can get help from their consultant. These consultants also teach end-user courses on the tools they know.

Fourth, the consultants are the quality assurance inspectors for user-developed programs. In this role, a consultant tries to "break" the system by testing its functions. The consultant also checks the code and documentation to see if they comply with the quality assurance manual. This certification step provides both the information center and the user department manager with an inventory of systems being run—and indicates how well each one meets the center's standards.

From this description it is evident that the job of an information center consultant is considerably different from the job of a traditional programmer. The information center consultant's job is to support and help manage the systems development process, not to develop the system itself.

Source: *EDP Analyzer*, vol. 23, no. 4, April 1985, pp. 8–9. Published by United Communications Group, 4550 Montgomery Ave., Suite 700, N. Bethesda, MD 20814.

The time spent evaluating alternatives is likely to be much shorter when software is custom-written rather than purchased. For purchased systems, evaluation activities are the key activities, as emphasized in Figure 2.14. The unique system constraints that force the choice of custom development, however, eliminate many of the options for design alternatives. For example, interfaces with existing systems or information systems policy may so limit the options that there are no alternatives to be evaluated.

In custom development, the emphasis will be on the matrix cells shaded in Figure 2–15. Whether end-users or systems professionals develop the software, requirements determination must be very thorough to avoid wasting time designing and implementing the wrong system. When systems professionals develop software, the frequent interaction with users during system review in a phased development approach reduces the risk of developing an inappropriate system. Whenever third generation languages are used, the design and implementation of programs (represented by the two shaded cells at the bottom of Figure 2.15) will consume more than half of the effort of developing the entire system. This absorption of resources will be discussed in detail in later chapters.

2.4.4 Summary of Software Sources

As fourth generation tools become more popular, user-written software will become more prevalent. In most large organizations, all four types of application software sources will be available:

1. existing
2. user-written
3. custom-written by information systems professionals with fourth generation languages
4. custom-written with third generation languages

Note that the four sources are listed in descending order of efficiency. The most time-consuming and costly option—custom-written with third generation languages—is still prevalent for a variety of reasons, including

- concerns about meeting functional requirements
- lack of training among users and information systems staff in fourth generation tools
- need for efficiency in production

The choice of software tools is likely to remain much the same into the mid-1990s. During the early 1990s there will probably be increasing use of computer-aided system engineering (CASE) tools that generate code from design specifications. Many experts see CASE tools replacing 4GLs as the fastest way to develop systems, but others argue that 4GLs will always be a popular software component. In later chapters we discuss the promise and current state of CASE tools.

Summary

This chapter has focused on the management tasks of the systems development process in order to help you appreciate the importance of managing the process as well as developing the product. Managing the process well is vital to achieving the goals of systems development: system quality, project management, and organizational relevance.

A high-quality system is functional, easy to maintain, and readily adaptable to changing environments. A well-managed development project delivers a system on time, within budget, and with user commitment. Carrying out the four management activities—planning, monitoring, coordinating, and reviewing—requires not only technical skills but also communication and management skills. In addition, the developer must know the organization's goals in order to help it develop and maintain systems relevant to achieving its goals.

Sometimes meeting the goals of systems development requires an approach other than the linear REDI model introduced in Chapter 1. Phased development provides a technique for better addressing system quality and user commitment concerns. By building a system in small increments and gaining user feedback as each increment is developed, a developer is more likely to produce a system that meets user requirements. But to take advantage of the benefits phased development offers, the developer must manage the process closely, planning and coordinating the activities of each phase carefully.

Another consideration in achieving systems development goals is choosing an appropriate software source. The choice will be influenced heavily by project management and organizational relevance goals. Using existing software is ideal if time and budget are vital to system success and if an existing package can fulfill user and organizational needs. Having users develop their own software is especially effective if user commitment to the system is a high priority and if users have the skills and fourth generation tools to do the job. As desirable as these first two options may be, often the only option is to have information systems professionals develop the software using third generation languages. The unique requirements of an organization and high demands for system quality may make any other choice infeasible.

As you can see, systems development involves more than just producing good software and installing the right hardware. Systems development is a balancing act in which you must achieve the right blend of system quality, project management, and organizational relevance to produce a system whose value to the organization outweighs its development and maintenance costs. To be a successful information systems professional, you need not only the technical skills of a programmer and systems analyst but also the management skills and organizational knowledge of a savvy manager.

Key Terms

(Section numbers are in parentheses.)

system quality (2.1.1)

functionality (2.1.1)	**planning (2.2.1)**
reliability (2.1.1)	**monitoring (2.2.2)**
clarity (2.1.1)	**coordinating (2.2.3)**
efficiency (2.1.1)	**reviewing (2.2.4)**
ease of maintenance (2.1.1)	**phased development (2.3)**
flexibility (2.1.1)	**prototyping (2.3)**
project management (2.1.2)	**fourth generation language (2.4.2)**
organizational relevance (2.1.3)	**third generation language (2.4.2)**

Notes

1. Cynthia M. Beath and Blake Ives, "Competitive Information Systems in Support of Pricing," *MIS Quarterly*, vol. 10., no. 1, March 1986, pp. 85–93.

2. Santosh K. Misra and Paul J. Jalics, "Third Generation versus Fourth Generation Software Development," *IEEE Software*, no. 5, July 1988, pp. 8–14.

Exercises

(Answers to Exercises 2.1, 2.3, and 2.8 are at the end of the book.)

2.1 Indicate which systems development goal(s)—system quality (SQ), project management (PM), or organizational relevance (OR)—each of the actions listed below could help achieve. For each goal, tell which subgoals apply. (See Figure 2.7.) For each system quality subgoal, also state which first- and second-level characteristics apply. (See Figure 2.3.)

   a. following structured programming techniques

   b. improving the company's cash flow

   c. reducing data entry errors

   d. using only standard languages to develop custom software

   e. clearly explaining procedures in a users' manual

   f. including milestones in the project schedule

   g. adopting a consistent format for screen design

   h. generating useful reports for management decision making

   i. gaining user acceptance of the system through frequent user reviews

2.2 Indicate the systems development goal(s)—system quality (SQ), project management (PM), or organizational relevance (OR)—each of the actions listed below could help achieve. For each goal, tell which subgoals apply. (See Figure 2.7.) For each system quality subgoal, also state which first- and second-level characteristics apply. (See Figure 2.3.).

   a. documenting each program, its purpose, and the input/output of each module

   b. streamlining user log on/log out procedures

   c. purchasing hardware that requires no special environment

   d. developing an automated mailing system that sends a thank you letter to each new customer

   e. minimizing system downtime

   f. including users on the development team

   g. providing easy-to-access help screens

   h. buying word processing software that is compatible with several popular printers

   i. achieving changeover on time and within budget

2.3 Review the minicase Abby Clark and Her Turnkey System in Chapter 1, keeping in mind the three major responsibilities (or goals) of the systems developer.

   a. What was Abby's dominant goal for systems development?

   b. Explain your answer, describing why each of the three development goals was/was not Abby's dominant goal.

2.4 Review the minicase Abby Clark's Contract Labor System in Chapter 1, keeping in mind the three major responsibilities (or goals) of the systems developer.

    a. What was Abby's dominant goal for systems development?

    b. Explain your answer, describing why each of the three development goals was/was not Abby's dominant goal.

2.5 Like the minicase Abby Clark and Her Turnkey System, Exercise 1.10 in Chapter 1 describes a user-developer who purchases a system to achieve a predefined purpose. After rereading both of these cases, evaluate the actions of the computer salespeople by answering the following questions:

    a. Which systems development goals did each salesperson emphasize?

    b. How well did each salesperson address the individual needs of the user-developer (Abby in Chapter 1; Arnie in Exercise 1.10)?

    c. Critique the behavior of either Abby's or Arnie's salesperson. What could that salesperson have done to help the user-developer achieve the three goals of systems development?

2.6 Harry McKetta was a part-time library clerk at Midtown College. He had learned COBOL at a community college and worked as a COBOL programmer before returning to school to complete a computer science degree.

    The library at Midtown College loaned typewriters as well as books. Checkout data for the fifty typewriters was kept on fifty 3 × 5 index cards. The cards were kept in order by typewriter identification number. This manual system worked well for checking typewriters in and out. It did not work well for notifying students who kept typewriters out past the due date.

    When Harry was given the responsibility for the typewriter loan system, he was horrified by the index card system. Looking up what had happened to typewriter #48 and checking out #32 was easy. Harry, however, did not want to flip through fifty cards every week to see which typewriters were overdue. So Harry wrote a COBOL program that kept track of all fifty typewriters, wrote summary reports, and generated overdue notices. He enjoyed writing the program in "good old COBOL," because his current computer science courses were in Pascal and LISP. Harry wrote the program using the library's terminal access to the college's minicomputer, so there were no initial expenses for the library. The librarians were pleased with the reports and the improved management of the library's typewriters. The old cards and card box were thrown away.

    When Harry graduated, he left behind one well-written, structured COBOL program. But none of the librarians knew how to enter typewriter checkout data or even how to execute Harry's COBOL program. The computer science department had eliminated its only COBOL course years ago, so student helpers who knew COBOL or how to run COBOL programs were rare. There was no procedures list that told how to run Harry's program, or even its name or where it was stored on the college computer. So the new librarian assistant ordered a new index card box and rebuilt the manual system.

    a. What was Harry's dominant goal as a developer?

    b. Explain your answer to a, describing why each of the three systems development goals was/was not Harry's dominant goal.

    c. Evaluate the quality of Harry's system by answering the system quality questions in Figure 2.7.

2.7 Imagine yourself in Harry's situation as described in Exercise 2.6. Knowing what you do about the importance of managing the process and gaining user commitment to the system, how would you go about developing a system for the library?

    a. Identify at least two ways you could involve users in the development of the system.

b. Explain how you would avoid the system quality problems you identified in Exercise 2.6, part c.

2.8 Use the following codes to indicate the approach most appropriate for each situation below. Explain your choice for each situation.

ES   existing software

UWS user-written software

ISWS software written by IS professionals

a. A small law office is developing a word processing system for three secretaries.

b. A manufacturing company is developing a just-in-time resource management system with existing hardware.

c. A finance division of a company is developing a small expense forecasting system on a microcomputer.

2.9 Use the codes from Exercise 2.8 to indicate the approach most appropriate for each situation below. Explain your choice for each situation.

a. A large insurance company is developing a new office automation system, including word processing, telecommunication, and record keeping functions.

b. A mail order company is developing a system to maintain a customer mailing list.

c. A marketing division of an office products company is developing a system to help its sales representatives keep track of customers' names, addresses, and recent orders.

Project

2.10 Visit an organization and evaluate one of its systems on the basis of the three goals of systems development: system quality, project management, and organizational relevance. Using Figure 2.7 as a guide, create an interview form as the basis for your investigation of system quality. Interview at least one developer and one user about the achievement of all three goals, and prepare a report on your findings. Your report should identify the relative importance of each of the three goals in the development of the system, how well each goal was met, the organization's strategies for meeting these goals, and recommendations for future systems development by the organization.

CHAPTER 3

A Prescription System for Meadows Hospital: A Case Study

Overview

The development process activities and responsibilities described in the previous chapters may seem too abstract at this point. To illustrate the basic process, we will describe the experiences of a development team at a large hospital as they implement a new system using purchased software. We will take a life cycle approach rather than a phased development approach, as it is easier to follow and works well for this rather simple application.

Specifically, we plan to

1. Illustrate the development process stage by stage. (Sections 3.2, 3.3, 3.4, and 3.5)

2. Identify the team members' responsibilities for managing the project. (Sections 3.2, 3.3, 3.4, and 3.5)

3.1 Meadows Hospital

Meadows Hospital is a large municipal hospital supported by a metropolitan district. The major responsibility of the hospital is to provide health care services to the community.

One central information systems department supports the entire hospital's administrative and health care functions. Like many information systems departments, the Information Services division, as it is called, has a large backlog of requests. The request we will describe is a Pharmacy division request to automate procedures for keeping records of daily prescriptions.

3.2 The Meadows Requirements Stage

About six months ago, the Pharmacy division completed an Information Services Request for a system to help reduce the paperwork required by the Administrative division. (The request form is shown in Figure 3.1.) Three years earlier the Administrative division had instituted a record-keeping system in the pharmacy to keep track of all drug transactions. Up until recently, the pharmacy staff had managed the required paperwork with one additional pharmacist's assistant. Now, however, the increased workload resulting from a rise in the number of hospital patients and the added demands of a new drug assistance program for city welfare recipients overburdened staff members. Hiring another staff member was not possible because of a city government hiring freeze, so the pharmacy hoped to shift work from its personnel to a computer system.

3.2.1 Form a Development Team

The first task was to form a project team. The Information Services Request in Figure 3.1 provided only a brief problem statement—not enough information to allow Information Services to identify the critical user-manager in order to choose the development team.

To learn more about the scope and urgency of the request, an Information Services supervisor called Tito Hernandez, the assistant manager of the pharmacy, who had written the request. Tito stressed that the difficult work situation created by the paperwork problem was bad for morale and often resulted in overtime.

Next, the Information Services supervisor called the pharmacy manager to verify Tito's request and to choose a development team. Together they decided that Tito would be the best user member for the team. An analyst, Tracy Bell, would serve as project manager. Tracy had good skills and could be counted on to do good technical work, but a long period of maintaining the hospital's on-line inventory system had caused her to lose some of her enthusiasm for her work. Tito's interest would help keep the team going.

Figure 3.1

Information Services
Request by Pharmacy
Division

Meadows Hospital	Information Services Request Form	Page 1 of 1

| System | Pharmacy Record Keeping | Date 1-25-90 |

Service for   Pharmacy   (division)   Supervisor   Tito Hernandez

Extension   283   Authorized Signature   *Tito Hernandez*

Brief Problem Statement

1. Summary reports on drug transactions for Administration (copy attached) require overtime work almost every day.

2. Daily log of drug transactions for Administration interferes with pharmacy operations, especially with recent addition of many welfare clients.

Requested Services

Develop automated log and summary system.

Action by ISD   (ISD use only)

Schedule analyst for requirements determination in May '90; pharmacy manager to choose user for team.

ISD signature   *Tina Sampson*   Date   1-27-90

A new programmer-analyst, Fred Kahn, was the third member of the project team. Just out of school, he was eager to show his talents, so he too would help keep the project moving. Because the project scope was not very large, a team of three members was considered adequate, even though all three had other responsibilities as well.

3.2.2 Determine Functional Requirements

Tracy called a meeting of the project team to define the objectives, investigate the functional specifications, and then determine whether existing software was available for the record-keeping problem.

Because of her recent experience, Tracy focused on an early investigation of existing software. She felt worn down by all the maintenance work she had performed on the inventory system, which had been developed by the Meadows staff. After that system was installed, she had learned that a number of hospitals had purchased well-tested inventory systems incorporating lots of bells and whistles that the in-house system lacked. Documentation on the Meadows inventory system still wasn't complete. Because of her frustration with the custom-developed inventory system, she hoped to solve pharmacy's problem by purchasing a well-documented record-keeping system from a vendor who would provide training for the pharmacy staff. If the vendor also had a help number, Tracy would be through with this project quickly.

The development team devoted two days to investigating the pharmacy problem. Tracy interviewed pharmacists and assistants about their current system for keeping records and their requirements for the new system. Fred talked to the accountant in the Administrative division who handled the pharmacy data sheets and who incorporated them into other hospital record keeping. He also observed the pharmacists and assistants for several hours, both during a peak order period and during a slow period. Tito performed his regular duties managing the pharmacy operations and also identified complaints about the current system.

On the third day, the project team met to discuss their findings. First Tracy presented her problem summary. In her view, the proposed system seemed to be very simple, consisting of two procedures: keying in the drug transactions during the day and running daily summaries at the end of the day (see Figure 3.2). Automating the first step to create a log stored on disk would eliminate the tedious end-of-day work. All of the user requirements could be taken care of by automating this rather straightforward record-keeping system. She thought that by checking the hospital trade magazines and calling a few other hospitals they could easily find out about existing software to automate this record-keeping process.

Figure 3.2
System to Solve
Original Problem

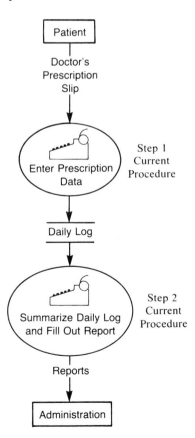

Tracy presented her formal summary of the problem on the Information Services standard problem definition form, which is shown in Figure 3.3. Then she turned to Fred and said, "Well, what did you learn? I hear you've talked to almost everyone in the pharmacy in the last few days."

Figure 3.3

Problem Definition Form for Pharmacy Request

Meadows Hospital	Information Services Problem Definition Form	Page 1 of 1
System Pharmacy Record Keeping System		Date 4-12-90
Analyst Tracy Bell	Signature *Tracy Bell*	

Problem Overview

    1. End-of-day reporting system for daily prescription filling is tedious and error prone.

    2. Tallying for reporting system is done at the end of the day and frequently requires overtime.

    3. Making daily log entries is very time consuming; falling behind on log entries is common and results in complicated catch-up procedures.

Existing System Components   PERSONNEL

    HARDWARE

        none -- manual system   Pharmacist's assistants

    SOFTWARE

        none -- manual system

    DATA   PROCEDURES

      * daily log of 300 to 450   1. log entry for each
         prescriptions   prescription
         (prescription number,
         doctor, patient, drug)   2. tally and prepare end-of-
                                     day report
      * end-of-day report   * COPIES ATTACHED

           ATTACH   NECESSARY   SUPPORTING   DOCUMENTS

Fred shrugged off Tracy's remark. He had been warned by one of the younger programmer-analysts that Tracy might be a rough team leader, but that he could learn a lot from her. In his hours observing the pharmacy staff, he had noticed that the pharmacist's assistant completed two similar processes for each prescription. First, the assistant typed a label with the names of the drug, patient, and doctor from the patient's prescription slip. (This step is shown as step 1a in Figure 3.4.) Then, the same information was entered in a log. (This step is shown as step 1b in Figure 3.4.) Next the assistant clipped the label to the prescription and placed it in a stack of prescriptions waiting to be filled. When the assistant fell behind, which happened frequently, complicated catch-up procedures were required. The assistant typed all the labels so that the pharmacist could keep filling the requests, but each prescription slip not entered in the log was marked with a check so that it could be retrieved later for recording. The label and the corresponding log page shown in Figure 3.5 indicate the extent of data duplication in the two manual procedures.

Figure 3.4
Expanded Target
System

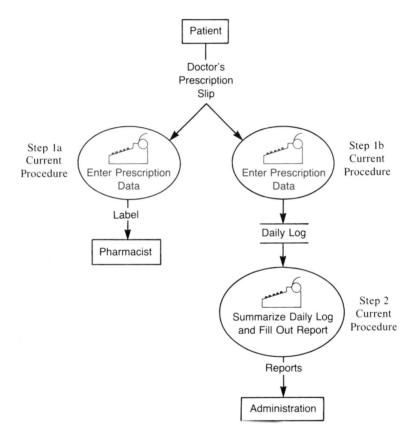

On very busy days the log work had to be delayed until the end of the day. Sometimes a large number of prescriptions would need to be entered before the daily summary report for Administration could be prepared. This problem of unpredictable overtime was one of the main complaints voiced by the pharmacy staff.

Tracy was unaware of this duplication of data entry; neither the pharmacists nor the assistants had mentioned problems with the label-typing process in their discussions with her. All their complaints had dealt with the work done for Administration.

Figure 3.5

Pharmacy Daily Drug
Log and Prescription
Label

| | | | Pharmacy Daily Drug Log | | Sept. 15, 1990 |

Order Number	Patient	Hospital/ Welfare	Doctor	Drug
08793	Alhadad, Hafez	H	Miller, F. G.	Wyamycin
08794	Grena, Emmett	W	Gutierrez, R. T.	Veracillin
08795	Wimberly, Harry	H	Yudof, W. L.	Metaprogesic
08796	Moritz, Evelyn	H	Bounous, P. S.	Malatal

```
Meadows Hospital -- Pharmacy
4508 W. 45th  678-3209  Center City, MI
- - - - - - - - - - - - - - - - - - - - - - - - - - - -
DATE:  Sept. 15, 1990
- - - - - - - - - - - - - - - - - - - - - - - - - - - -
NO. 08793     DR. MILLER, FRED G.
ALHADAD, HAFEZ
TAKE ONE TABLET BY MOUTH  3
TIMES DAILY TILL OUT.
TAKE ON EMPTY STOMACH.
WYAMYCIN   QTY: 21  PHARMACIST: MARY
```

Fred proposed that the new system require only one data entry process, as illustrated in Figure 3.6. In the new system, steps 1a and 1b from Figure 3.4 would be combined in a single step 1, a procedure that created the labels and added them to the log storage file needed for the daily summary. By keying in the label information on a computer instead of typing a label on a typewriter, the assistant could store the data for further processing. At the end of the day, the detailed log information and summary could be generated from the stored data. Fred emphasized that the new key entry process would be faster than the original label-typing process if the full names of doctors were accessed by a three-digit code, thus saving the pharmacist's assistant hundreds of keystrokes every day. For example, instead of typing "Dr. Miller, Fred G." on the prescription label, as shown in Figure 3.5, and "Miller, F. G." on the log, the assistant would use the three-digit code 271 to retrieve Miller's full name. Fred noted that the software should generate the appropriate format for the label and the log when each was printed.

The development team discussed and agreed with Fred's functional requirements. Then Tracy closed the meeting with the presentation of a schedule of work to be done by each team member. The team's next milestone was to have management review the functional specifications and approve the development of a system that would log administrative data, type the labels, and create the daily summary reports as shown in Figure 3.6.

The pharmacy staff assistants and pharmacists were enthusiastic when they heard the team's revised system objectives. With the users' go-ahead, the team prepared the final requirements documentation to reflect the expanded system. The requirements were completed at a general level suitable for a guideline for purchasing software.

Figure 3.6
Proposed New System

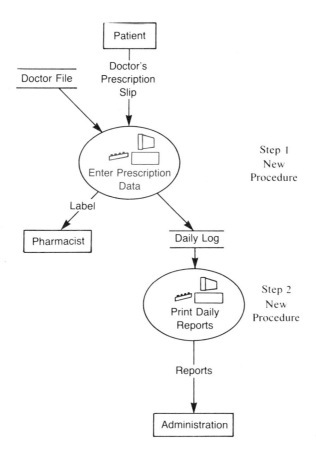

3.2.3 Determine a Software Source

Calls to franchise pharmacies and medical laboratories with similar labeling requirements indicated that a number of pharmacy packages would be candidates for purchase. Nonetheless, Fred suggested that letting the pharmacy staff write their own programs might be a good way to ensure that they supported the new system. Tracy argued that having users custom-write software would not be a timely solution. She pointed out that, although the Meadows Information Services division had fourth generation tools compatible with its database management system, there were *no* pharmacy files established on the database management system, nor had any pharmacy personnel been trained to use it. Also, such a specialized data file was unlikely to receive high priority for database management control.

Although the pharmacy staff would be unable to develop their own system, custom development was well within the capabilities of the hospital's Information Services staff. Tracy thought that she should include custom-written software as a possibility for the management review, but she was confident that the time custom development required would quickly eliminate it from consideration.

The team decided to summarize the costs and benefits of two typical software packages and a custom-designed system. If management chose the custom system, the team would detail specific requirements before proceeding to the design stage. Unless that unexpected decision was made, there was no need to complete full, detailed specifications.

3.2.4 Prepare a Presentation to Management

The three alternatives were summarized in the form shown in Figure 3.7. Rough cost and development time requirements were estimated to be as little as $9,500 and six weeks if the least expensive package compatible with the hospital's current hardware was acceptable. Another alternative, which involved purchasing a microcomputer system and software, would cost approximately $10,500 and would also require about six weeks to implement. If custom-written software was needed, development of documentation and well-tested software would require a total of four and a half months and would cost $15,600.

	Solution Overviews		
	Off-the-Shelf Programs with Microcomputers	**Off-the-Shelf Programs with Current Hardware**	**Custom Programs with Current Hardware**
Initial Hardware Costs	Microcomputer with printer $4,500.00	Terminal $ 900.00 Printer $1,100.00	Terminal $ 900.00 Printer $1,100.00
Program Costs:			
Design	2 wks, 2 staff $2,700.00	2 wks, 2 staff $2,700.00	1 mo, 2 staff $5,600.00
Implementation	2 wks, 1 staff $1,300.00	2 wks, 1 staff $1,300.00	3 mo, 1 staff $8,000.00
Purchase Price	$2,000.00	$3,500.00	0.00
Total Development Cost	$10,500.00	$9,500.00	$15,600.00
Optimum Schedule:			
Evaluation	2 weeks	2 weeks	2 weeks
Design	2 weeks	2 weeks	1 month
Implementation	2 weeks	2 weeks	3 months
Total Post-Requirements Development Time	6 weeks	6 weeks	4.5 months

Figure 3.7   Cost and Schedule Estimates for Three Possible Solutions

3.2.5 Present a Management Review

The project team presented the objectives and functional requirements of the new system to management. The team also presented a summary of the cost estimates of the three alternatives. The managers agreed to the system objectives as presented.

The team discussed the enthusiasm of pharmacy personnel for a microcomputer and possible future acquisition of another micro with additional pharmacy software. On the basis of this discussion, the managers approved the team's plan to proceed with a thorough evaluation of the microcomputer option. The package compatible with the Meadows computer would also be evaluated. Custom-written software would be considered only if the available systems were found to be unacceptable. Because the comparison of costs and time required convinced management of the benefits of existing software, Tracy didn't need to give her prepared speech on the value of having pretested, well-documented existing software as the core of the new system.

3.3 The Meadows Evaluation Stage

At the end of the requirements stage, the team has a general statement of the required functions of the system at the level of detail appropriate for purchasing hardware and software. The goal of the evaluation stage is to identify and select the combinations of components best able to deliver those functions at a reasonable cost.

3.3.1 Identify Alternatives

The first step in the evaluation stage was a full identification of alternative people, procedures, data, software, and hardware. The hardware component was limited to microcomputers and the Meadows Hospital computer. Software options for this limited range of hardware were then considered. Suitable software would be evaluated on the basis of the data, procedures, and personnel requirements.

The earlier list of existing software was expanded as the team called more pharmacies and hospitals. The team also reviewed software catalogues and advertisements in medical and pharmacy trade journals. To find packages compatible with the Meadows current mainframe computer, Tracy contacted the system support representative for assistance.

The investigation of existing software turned up three candidates that met the system objectives. One ran on the Meadows computer and two ran on microcomputers.

3.3.2 Evaluate Alternatives

The development team began its evaluation of the microcomputer software by calling staff at several sites that were currently operating the packages of interest to Meadows Hospital.

Both of the packages sounded acceptable based on these discussions, so the team arranged a visit to observe each package in operation. The three team members, two pharmacists, and a pharmacist's assistant attended both demonstrations.

During each half-day visit, the team noted various characteristics of the system. They asked the users about their experiences learning the system and using it on a day-to-day basis. The quality of the documentation and vendor support were also investigated.

The label-typing portions of the two packages worked well at the user sites. The end-of-day detail listings and summary reports generated by the software, however, were quite different from what the pharmacy was producing currently.

After the visits, Tracy talked to the accountants in Administration about the acceptability of the reports produced by the packages. The summary reports on both packages were acceptable to accounting. In fact, the reports were superior in variety and quality to what was being produced by the manual system.

Data and procedural aspects of the two packages were very different. The Pharmacy Inventory Management package was clearly a mega-solution to the problem. Its main purpose was inventory management, with the labels and reports as a side effect. This system's data entry procedures required basic drug information that had to be coded for later retrieval. Its screens were designed to handle inventory and distribution problems. Although inventory checks could be made very quickly, the label data entry process involved passing through three menus for each label. To bypass the inventory data and complete the label-generating process, dummy codes had to be entered.

The second software alternative, Rapid Pharmacy Package, was more limited. Only three files needed to be maintained. Its doctor file and drug transaction file were the two the Meadows Pharmacy needed. The third file, for customer tax records, did not require any additional data entry, so its inclusion in the system was not a procedural drawback.

The last alternative was Drug Manager, a package for the Meadows Hospital computer. This software was installed on the computer and demonstrated at a terminal in the Administration division. Although the labels and reports this package produced were acceptable, its response time to create the labels was quite slow. Since the original complaint of the pharmacists was lack of time, slow response was considered a major detriment. The vendor of the package assured the team that this slow response time was a hardware problem that could be corrected with communication improvements. Information Services management, however, assured Tracy that there was little chance that those improvements would be made in the coming year.

The last component to be evaluated was hardware. Pharmacy Inventory Management ran on a popular operating system. A wide variety of hardware could be purchased to complete the system. Rapid Pharmacy Package came in three versions, each for a popular microcomputer. Therefore, hardware was not seen as an important limiting criterion for either of these software choices.

3.3.3 Present Alternatives to Management for Review

The team summarized its findings for a presentation to the management in Pharmacy, Administration, and Information Services. A chart detailing the characteristics of each alternative is shown in Figure 3.8. The first two rows of the chart show that the initial cost for buying the software and necessary hardware varied relatively little from system to system. The least costly system, Drug Manager, made the poorest showing on the next two criteria on the chart: response time and downtime. Management decided to eliminate this choice on the basis of its slow speed. Also, given that Meadows' current computer was running near capacity now, adding another on-line system would only increase communication difficulties.

	System Alternatives		
	Rapid Pharmacy Package with Microcomputer X	**Pharmacy Inventory Management with Microcomputer Y**	**Drug Manager with Current Hardware**
Initial Hardware Costs	Microcomputer with printer $4,500.00	Microcomputer with printer $4,200.00	Terminal $ 900.00 Printer $1,100.00
Program Purchase Price	$2,000.00	$4,500.00	$3,500.00
Total Initial Cost	$6,500.00	$8,700.00	$4,700.00
Time Required for Ten Labels*	8 minutes	22 minutes	35 minutes
Downtime Experience**	1.5 days/year	.7 day/year	6.5 days/year

*Average of eight trials at different times of the day; range was 19 to 42 minutes.
**Average of reports from five owners of each micro and average for six months on the Meadows computer.

Figure 3.8 Selected Characteristics of the Three Alternatives

The decision to buy either the Pharmacy Inventory or the Rapid Pharmacy package could not be based on the small difference in their costs. To provide other bases for comparing the alternatives, the team prepared a second chart, which is shown in Figure 3.9. Each of the three columns of this evaluation matrix represented a candidate system. The rows were criteria selected for evaluation, with each candidate rated on the five-point scale explained at the bottom of the matrix.

The cost information from Figure 3.8 was not included in the new chart, but both the label printing time and the downtime were rated. Rapid Pharmacy received a rating of 5 for the fastest label-producing time, with the other two systems receiving much lower ratings. All three systems received high ratings for report quality, based on Tracy's earlier

	Rating of Alternatives*		
	Rapid Pharmacy Package with Microcomputer X	Pharmacy Inventory Management with Microcomputer Y	Drug Manager with Current Hardware
1. Function			
Time for Printing Labels	5	2	1
Report Quality	4	4	5
	9	6	6
2. Human Factors			
Ease of Use	4	2	4
Ease of Learning	5	2	2
	9	4	6
3. Vendor Support			
Documentation	5	5	3
Maintenance	4	4	3
	9	9	6
4. Downtime	4	5	1
Total Ratings	31	24	19

*Rating Key: 5 = excellent, 4 = good, 3 = average, 2 = fair, 1 = unacceptable.

Figure 3.9   Evaluation Matrix for Alternative Pharmacy Systems

discussions with Administration accountants. The human factor and vendor support ratings were based on the team's interviews with experienced users.

Although Rapid Pharmacy had the highest total rating, Tracy encouraged pharmacy managers to seriously consider instituting the full inventory system available with Pharmacy Inventory Management. But the Pharmacy managers were not interested in revising their current manual inventory system. The limited Rapid Pharmacy Package offered them the best solution for reaching their immediate goal: a quick reduction in their record-keeping burden.

3.4 The Meadows Design Stage

The earlier planning for the project had allocated only one Information Services staff member for the design and implementation stages if purchased software was acquired. In line with this plan, Tracy assigned Fred to take over the completion of the project. He would be responsible for the hardware, software, and data components. Tito would be responsible for procedures and personnel. Tracy went on to a new project for another division.

3.4.1 Specify Hardware and Software

Specifications for hardware and software had been completed in the evaluation stage. Fred's next step with respect to these two components was to complete the paperwork the city required for purchases. Although the vendors of Rapid Pharmacy and the chosen microcomputer had promised delivery within three working days, it was important to start the procurement process immediately, since the Meadows purchasing procedures might take the remainder of the two weeks scheduled for design.

Figure 3.10 shows Fred and Tito's design and implementation schedule. The first time line on the schedule shows Fred and Tito's optimistic plan for processing the purchase order through the hospital and city administrations. The asterisk at the top marks the completion of the vendor's delivery and tests. Fred hoped his hand-carrying of the order at key times would speed the process enough that this schedule could be met.

Facility planning was another design problem. Tito wanted to make sure the placement of the microcomputer and printer in the pharmacy area did not disrupt the prescription filling process. He and Fred decided to put the computer where the typewriters had been and to put the printer on a specially built shelf below the counter. Although this placement was not ideal, the pharmacists were adamant that no more counter space could be given up. Tito and Fred reviewed their plans with the pharmacy supervisor, who agreed with the pharmacists' choices. Fred completed a requisition order for the necessary carpentry and electrical work to be performed by the Meadows Maintenance division. The chance of this work's being completed during the design stage was not very good, but the work would be done in time for installation. As a fail-safe measure, Fred and Tito decided to test the new system in the Information Services area.

The second time line in Figure 3.10 indicates the waiting period and construction time necessary. Tito planned to visit the Maintenance division supervisor after the requisition was completed to ensure that the request was not postponed too long.

3.4.2 Specify Data

The pharmacy users and Administration had approved the data entry screen formats and the report layouts for Rapid Pharmacy during the evaluation stage. Data formats were also set. Fred still needed to design the doctor file and customer tax records.

All hospital physicians were to be included in the doctor file. Fred had to decide whether all the other physicians practicing in the city should be included, or just those whose names occurred at least once in the current pharmacy logs. Fred also had to determine the order of the file. The software maintained the file so that the numeric codes for the doctors were kept in order from 001 to 999, but there was no required order for the corresponding names.

Since report summaries by physician could be based on selecting all physicians, a single physician (by numeric code), or a range of numbers, Fred decided to reserve the numbers 001 to 030 for the twelve staff doctors. Grouping them would make it easy to run the summary required by Administration. For the initial file, these names would be arranged in alphabetical order, using every other numeric code. Starting with number 040, all the physicians in the city directory would be listed in alphabetical order. Fred planned to leave some empty code groups so that the list could be kept in approximate

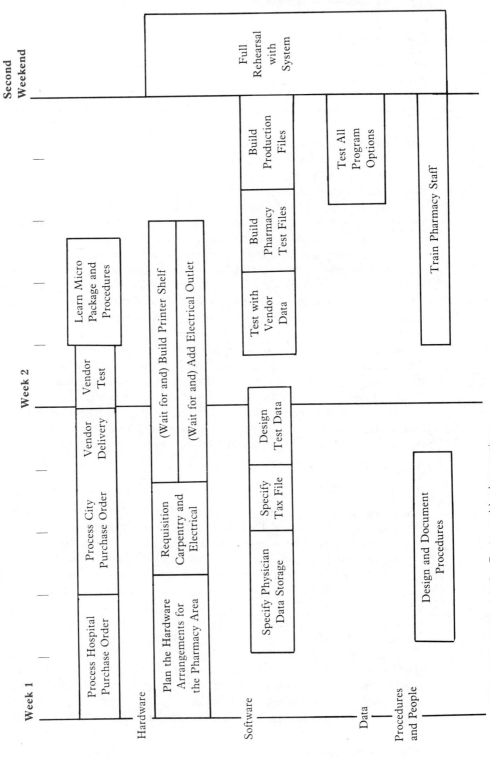

Figure 3.10 Original Schedule for Design and Implementation

alphabetical order as it was updated. Fred thought that this design would ease the daily data entry process, as the pharmacist's assistant would soon memorize the doctor codes used frequently. An alphabetical list posted near the computer could be used to find doctor codes that had not been memorized.

Designing the data for the customer tax file was a simple but necessary activity. Since no customer tax information was going to be kept, Fred designed a dummy file that would not cause operation errors when the customer tax information was ignored in the data entry process.

The final step in the design of the data component was to prepare several test files to be used in the implementation stage to test procedures for normal and recovery operations. Fred also created specific test data for data entry, labels, and summary reports.

3.4.3 Specify Procedures

Fred and Tito worked closely on the procedures design work. Rapid Pharmacy Package had been chosen partly because the operations and user documentation were very thorough. The major additions necessary were specifications about how often the files would be copied for backup security and what procedures would be used to update the doctor file.

3.4.4 Specify Production Staff

No organizational changes were required, since the pharmacist's assistants would have the same responsibilities as before. Only the mechanical procedures had been altered. The microcomputer vendor had included four hours of training in the purchase contract, so training was scheduled to begin as soon as the Meadows procurement paperwork could be completed.

3.5 The Meadows Implementation Stage

Designing procedures had made Fred realize how different implementation is when there is only one computer available. Training, data conversion, and testing could not occur simultaneously as they did on the multi-user Meadows computer. If production were to start on schedule, the microcomputer and software would have to be delivered on schedule and use of the micro for the implementation tasks (construction, testing, and installation) would have to be planned carefully.

3.5.1 Construct a Preliminary System

The hardware was installed in Information Services for construction and testing. (Note: The installation of *hardware* is not the same as the installation of the *system*. All five components must be in place and tested before the system can be installed.) The software was delivered at the same time. Although the design and site construction work could begin before delivery, the testing and training could not begin until after delivery.

Fred built the doctor file and the customer tax file according to procedures developed in the design stage. He examined file listings and test reports to ensure that the file-building procedures were correct. Tito and the pharmacists were also involved in the file construction work, so this activity served as training as well.

3.5.2 Test System Components

Each of the five components had to be tested individually before the full integrated dress rehearsal planned for the second weekend. First, the hardware and the Rapid Pharmacy software were tested by the vendor as soon as they were installed. Then Fred completed the tutorials supplied for the microcomputer operating system and the Rapid Pharmacy Package to test the hardware and software and to learn the system.

The original schedule, shown in the bottom line in Figure 3.10, called for training the pharmacist's assistants on the same days as testing was being conducted. This turned out to be impossible, however, because the tutorials and testing took much longer than Fred had imagined. So Fred decided to postpone the integrated test scheduled for the second week, thus allowing the pharmacist's assistants to complete the tutorials and work with the Meadows Hospital test files before the final test.

Fred and Tito supervised the pharmacist's assistants as they tested the procedures for entering data, preparing labels, and generating summary reports with the test files Fred had constructed. Using small test files with a variety of error situations, they observed each assistant's ability to generate all the reports and labels, to create backup files, and to restart the system from error recovery points.

Tito tested the end-of-day log listing by comparing it to the labels created in the test run. He then checked the summary reports against the log. Tito also checked each test run independently, as did the assistants operating the computer. An accountant in Administration checked several of the summary reports.

Software processing went quite well as far as generating the expected reports from the test prescriptions. The main problems occurred when the assistants formed different interpretations of some of the screen messages and operating procedures. Because of these misinterpretations, several test files were lost, and at one point the vendor had to be called in to help trace the cause of a frozen screen. Each of these problems was solved and documented. The assistants marked the procedures documents provided by the vendor wherever they thought misunderstandings might occur. Then Tito revised the documentation to include necessary warnings and additional explanations.

3.5.3 Construct the Final System

Fred delayed construction of the final production files until he had checked the system and the assistants' ability to use it. After building the production files and creating backup copies, Fred ran several integrated tests using the production files.

3.5.4 Perform the Final Review and Install the System

In the middle of the third week, the pharmacy supervisor and two pharmacists observed a rehearsal test run by the trained pharmacist's assistants in the Information Services test area. Tito summarized the scope and results of their earlier test runs and staff training. Tito and the pharmacy staff discussed the option of installing the system in the pharmacy and keeping the typewriters for a backup system. Such a full parallel implementation would be time-consuming because the assistants would have to type a label on the typewriter as well as enter data on the computer.

Tito pointed out that prescriptions were kept on file as part of normal procedures. The new system could be run alone, and its test log printouts could be examined every two hours. If the log printouts omitted any prescriptions, the manual system could be reinstituted for the logs. Detailed checks of the summary reports could also be made for several days and then once a week for several weeks.

The pharmacy supervisor agreed to this installation strategy, as it provided the security and checking advantages of parallel installation. The tedious duplicating of data entry procedures would be performed only if a check on the log showed that it was necessary. This plan seemed reasonable, since this version of Rapid Pharmacy had been used successfully for millions of prescriptions by six pharmacies that Informations Services had contacted.

Over the weekend the computer was installed in the pharmacy. A short rehearsal on Saturday with the pharmacist's assistants tested the full procedures of typing the labels and clipping them to the prescriptions. Some card files and notebooks had to be relocated on the counters, but otherwise this rehearsal went well. A second rehearsal was held on Sunday to review the system with the pharmacists who had not attended any of the earlier test sessions.

For the first two days of intensive parallel checking, the pharmacists and assistants experienced some stress due to the tedious checking. However, no files were lost or screens frozen. The pharmacist's assistants felt in full control of the computer. Their enthusiastic good-bye to manual log keeping and tallying lessened the pain of having to carefully parallel-check the log printouts.

Summary

Systems development is a time-consuming, people-intensive process, even when off-the-shelf software is used. The case study of the development of an information system for the Meadows Hospital pharmacy illustrates

1. the selection of a project team that includes a user representative
2. thorough requirements determination and evaluation, involving both user interviews and observation
3. the value of taking a broad view of the opportunity to develop a system, rather than a narrow problem-oriented focus
4. the key role that management plays in reviews, especially at the end of the evaluation stage
5. the time required for location-specific testing and documentation of purchased software

Exercises

(Answers to Exercises 3.1 and 3.2 are given at the end of the book.)

3.1 Consider the development goals of the Meadows project team: Tito, Tracy, and Fred. Using Figure 2.7 as a guide, review how well the team considered and met the three major goals of systems development.

3.2 Suppose that Meadows Hospital had chosen a single analyst approach to development of its system rather than the project team approach.

   a. What problems might have arisen if Tracy had assumed full development responsibility, rather than sharing responsibility with Tito and Fred?

   b. What problems might have arisen if Fred had assumed full development responsibility, rather than sharing responsibility with Tito and Tracy?

3.3 What is the main level of decision making supported by the Meadows pharmacy record-keeping system: operational, managerial, or strategic?

3.4 Summarize the development and management activities discussed in the Meadows Hospital case by completing a table in the format shown below. Follow the case page by page, using the codes and labels from Figure 2.9.

Development Activity	Management Participant(s)
R.1 Identify Objectives Complete the Information Services Request	Tito Hernandez

3.5 Suppose Meadows Hospital had completed the pharmacy system with custom-written software written in a third generation language such as COBOL.

   a. What development activities would have been more important (or at least would have taken more time)?

   b. What management activities would have been more important (or at least would have taken more time)?

3.6 Suppose Meadows Hospital had completed the pharmacy system with custom-written software written in a fourth generation language by the pharmacy clerks.

   a. What development activities would have been more important (or at least would have taken more time)?

   b. What management activities would have been more important (or at least would have taken more time)?

2

Management Activities

Planning Overview

Overview

Lack of planning is a major criticism leveled against computer professionals. Overdue, poorly planned projects are common topics in *Computerworld, Datamation,* and other popular trade magazines. Why is planning so often inadequate? This chapter explores answers to that question and provides guidelines for improving planning.

Specifically, we plan to

1. Explain the importance of planning and the common fallacies that lead to omitting the planning process. (Section 4.1)

2. Present guidelines for successful planning. (Section 4.2)

3. Define each of the four planning tasks. (Section 4.3)

4. Discuss various approaches to ordering planning tasks. (Section 4.4)

5. Review products generated throughout the planning process. (Section 4.5)

4.1 Why Don't Analysts Plan?

Planning is omitted so often that it is worthwhile to explore the reasons many analysts fail to plan. We will start, however, with the positive case.

4.1.1 The Value of a Good Plan

Chapter 2 discussed four management activities: planning, monitoring, coordinating, and reviewing. Because a plan is the basis for monitoring, coordinating, and reviewing, planning is absolutely critical to managing the development process. Another reason for planning is that people tend to do more productive work as a deadline approaches. The effects of deadlines on behavior are illustrated in Figure 4.1. The graph in part (a) illustrates the work curve of a project with one deadline; note that weekly productive work increases steadily for the four-month project, with a dramatic increase in the last month. The graph in part (b) shows the effect of multiple deadlines. The same deadline behavior occurs, but the work is spread out more evenly over the life of the project.

Figure 4.1
Example of Four-Month Project Activity

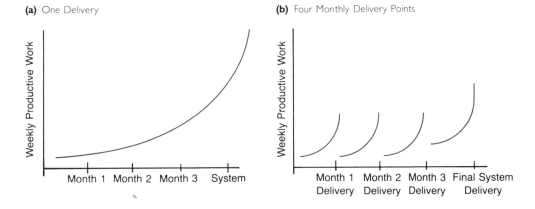

(a) One Delivery

(b) Four Monthly Delivery Points

4.1.2 Common Fallacy 1: System Quality Is All That Matters

Planning is omitted by information systems professionals for a variety of reasons. One argument is that the quality of the system is all that matters for system success. This view is held by some highly creative and technically oriented programmers and analysts whose strengths are in design and programming.

In Chapter 3 we argued that project management is as important as system quality to the success of a system. If a system is completed late, over budget, or in any other way that frustrates users, failure is likely. This argument directly refutes the claim that system quality is all that matters.

In fact, planning is *necessary* for system quality. Intense effort to meet a single deadline under the circumstances illustrated in Figure 4.1(a) leads to fatigue, stress, and morale problems. All of these reduce the quality of work. Developers under severe time pressure are less likely to check their work carefully. They may omit systematic testing in order to deliver a system on time. Training and documentation may also be omitted, since technically oriented analysts often see these as system extras, rather than system necessities. The result is a disaster at changeover. Planning helps systems developers avoid these problems by distributing the work load more evenly across the development period.

4.1.3 Common Fallacy 2: No Estimates Are Better Than Inaccurate Estimates

There are numerous variations on this excuse. Two common ones are

- There are too many variables. The process is too complicated for an accurate estimate to be made, and an incorrect estimate creates more trouble than no estimate.
- I'd rather get started on creating the requested system than spend time on an estimate that won't be correct anyway.

Adopting the philosophy that only perfect estimates are worth the trouble not only leaves you ignorant about project progress; it also does nothing to improve your planning skills. Without a plan you can't monitor progress; you have no way of knowing if you are behind or ahead of schedule. Coordinating the activities of a team without a series of planned deadlines is nearly impossible.

Planning *is* difficult. Perfect planning is impossible. But the solution is *not* to avoid planning! A better solution is to create a rough plan as soon as the initial system objectives and constraints are known. As the functional requirements and design become better defined, you can monitor progress and revise your plan. If the development schedule is flexible, you may be able to postpone the deadline. If the deadline is firm, you must revise the scope of the system to fit the time you have. Either way, the initial plan and revisions to the plan provide the insight needed to make decisions about the schedule and the project boundary.

By following this incremental approach of improving the plan as you learn more about the system, you will become a better planner as systems development proceeds. Your planning expertise will increase from one project to the next. Perfect estimates are not the goal; increasingly *better* estimates are!

4.1.4. Common Fallacy 3: Skip the Planning When You are in a Hurry

Suppose a host decided to skip the division of tasks among three cooks who had to prepare a meal in a hurry. If each cook acted on impulse, together they might prepare a fantastic meal. More likely, though, they'd prepare a meal that was all dessert and no vegetables. If time allowed, these cooks might be able to avoid disaster by quickly preparing other dishes. Time pressure, however, makes good planning absolutely essential, as each dish must be a necessary and timely addition to the meal.

In this respect, systems development planning is like meal planning. The greater the time pressure, the greater the need for planning. Numerous and varied activities must be scheduled so that output from one activity can be used as input to the next activity. You can't test hardware that hasn't been delivered, nor can you code software that hasn't been designed. Given the interdependence of system components, failure to plan effectively increases team conflict and wastes time. If finishing at a particular time is critical, you need to ensure that your team has the resources and skills to meet the deadline. If you have plenty of time, problems can be solved as they arise. For example, a team member who lacks necessary skills can be trained during slack time on a project. Under time pressure, however, having an untrained team member may lead to a disaster.

Whatever the excuse, avoiding the responsibility to plan, monitor, and coordinate systems development projects is foolhardy. The refusal to follow these and other rudimentary management practices has given information systems professionals a poor reputation in the corporate world. James Martin has gone so far as to suggest firing information system managers and replacing them with managers from other departments.[1] Too few information systems professionals, according to Martin, have grown beyond the single goal of creating working third generation language programs.

4.2 Guidelines for Successful Planning

Successful planning requires that you establish milestones. A **milestone** is a planned delivery date for an activity. The delivery may be in the form of a demonstration of the information to users, a requirements summary, an evaluation report, or program specifications. A set of milestones is a major planning product that aids in monitoring, coordinating, and reviewing. Milestones are the key to spreading the work effort evenly. The guidelines presented in this section will be helpful in producing milestones that effectively even out the flow of work.

4.2.1 Keep Deliverable Products Small

In Chapter 2 we discussed the importance of using a phased development approach as a way to obtain frequent feedback from the user. **Phased development,** in which a series of small products are presented to the user, increases the chance that the system, when installed, will be what the user requires. In phased development, subsystems of a larger project are constructed, tested, and installed for production before the entire system project is complete. Strategies for partitioning systems will be explained in Chapter 5. For now, you need only understand that one goal of planning is to avoid monster projects and their difficulties by defining subsystems and implementing them in phases.

In addition to reducing the delay in feedback, partitioning projects reduces management overhead costs. Communication is more difficult with large projects, since they require large development teams. In order to reduce the risk of misunderstanding, within large teams, more meetings must be held, diverting development time to management overhead activities. Partitioning the project keeps team size more manageable and allows the team members to focus on development, not on team communication.

Another reason for partitioning projects is to maintain user interest. The time required for completion of large projects discourages users. As a long project drags on, the enthusiastic sponsor or champion of the project may be transferred to another position. Even if the original users remain on the job, their interest may shift to other concerns. The users may even solve their problems themselves with cost-efficient microcomputer systems. (Having users develop their own systems is often ideal, but it should be a planned strategy. Disgruntled users who are tired of waiting for delivery of a large project are not likely to develop an ideal substitute.)

Yet another reason for partitioning systems is that the chance of changes in requirements increases as time-to-delivery increases. A large system is more likely to be out of date at changeover than is a smaller system that is delivered quickly. Thus, systems should be divided into subsystems that can be delivered to users within a few months. Even with a phased approach, requests for system changes after installation are inevitable, since the user gains a new perspective working with a new system. The key to reducing the number of changes requested is to partition the large system into deliverable subsystems, so that the impact of the revisions is evolutionary rather than revolutionary.

4.2.2 Manage the Product, Not the Process

Monitoring and coordinating systems development requires the measurement of progress. Milestones for measurement should be based on the functions of the system. They should indicate deliverable system products rather than system process steps. For example, the following expressions of **product delivery points** state *what* is to be completed:

- Code the *system control menus.*
- Revise the year-end *summary reports.*
- Demonstrate *control menus* to users.
- Review *summary reports* with users.

In the last two examples, the user-sponsor should approve the system product or note required revisions. Approvals of this type are called **sign-offs.**

Early in the development process, you may feel that delivery of tangible *system products* is not possible. In that case, you may want to identify *process products* instead. The following statements specify processes that must be completed:

- Summarize available accounts receivable packages.
- Interview the three retail store managers.
- Identify and allocate staff to the project activities.

If you take a few moments to review this list of activities, you will realize that these processes can be expressed as products. Applying the product emphasis to "Summarize available . . . packages" yields "Write a *summary report* reviewing available . . . packages." By thinking in terms of products rather than processes, we can transform the list of processes above into this list of process products:

- Write a *summary report* reviewing available accounts receivable packages.
- Prepare *charts documenting current procedures* based on interviews of the three retail store managers.
- Prepare a *Gantt chart* of project activities.

Although these are not system products to be delivered to the user, they are tangible, useful documents that signal the completion of a necessary development activity. As such, they can serve as useful milestones.

Equally important, emphasizing the product of an activity helps you to identify the purpose of the activity. Whereas "Interview the three retail store managers" provides no focus or end goal for this activity, "Prepare charts documenting . . ." explicitly states what this activity contributes to the development project. So, whenever possible, express milestones as system deliverables or process products that will help you monitor your progress.

Monitoring process activities that produce no measurable or tangible products may give you a false sense of security. A milestone such as "Complete half of the requirements investigation" doesn't help you measure your progress, as you can't know what constitutes *half* of the investigation until you've completed the *whole* investigation! By then, your project may be weeks behind schedule. Gauging progress on the basis of hours spent or lines of code produced is similarly ineffective. Early estimates of effort-hours required to complete a project or lines of code required to create a program usually miss their target. And the fact that you've used up half the time allotted for your project doesn't mean that you've completed half the project work! Thus, as a project manager, you must set milestones that effectively measure progress and that alert you to time problems before they get out of hand. System deliverables and process products such as development documents will best serve this function.

The decision table in Figure 4.2 will help you distinguish among system products, process products, and process activities. Figure 4.3 defines relevant terms.

Figure 4.2
Characteristics of Three Types of Delivery Points

	Delivery Becomes Part of Production System	Tangible, Measurable Result
System Product*	Yes	Yes
Process Product	No	Yes
Process Activity	No	No

*This is the best result for an activity, since it directly contributes to the final system delivery.

Figure 4.3
Summary of Planning Terms

Term	Definition
Activity	Any task intended to contribute to developing the system or managing the systems development process.
Delivery point	Completion of a measurable activity that produces a tangible system or process product. *System product delivery points* include activities such as demonstrating data entry screens to users, completing a user's manual, and building test files; *process product delivery points* include activities such as preparing test specifications and writing a report summarizing available application software.
Milestone	A planned delivery date; a measurable activity to be completed at a designated time.
Changeover	Completed installation of a system or subsystem; point at which the user accepts production responsibility for a system or subsystem.

The minicase A Consultant's View of a Project Management Mess reviews the problems in planning large systems and measuring process points instead of system deliveries. As this story proves, better planning is not the entire solution. But accurate planning would have allowed the MIS director to reach the consultant's conclusion without having to pay for the consultant's investigation.

MINICASE

A Consultant's View of a Project Management Mess

We were called in by the MIS director of a technical service company.

"I just transferred over from Engineering a few months ago," he said, "and this software business is really out of hand. In engineering, we knew what a project was and we knew how to manage one. But here we have managers who track gross man-hours, not milestones. We are engaged in a number of major development efforts. The first two just slipped several months within weeks of their scheduled completions. The users already feel they aren't getting anything out of data processing. If this keeps up, I can't be sure we'll make the three-year plan for putting bigger systems into operation. We need better project control, and I want you to train my people so that we get it."

With that, he paused as if to emphasize his conclusion, and then continued in a more reflective tone. "You know what mystifies me? Those two late projects. Until the eleventh hour, they were saying that everything was fine. Then suddenly they slipped four months on a ten-month schedule. When I tried to find out why, they just said that's the way software is. We have good development standards, heavy user involvement, automated project reporting, and thorough requirements analysis. But we don't really track it right. I don't even think they know themselves why the schedules are slipping."

"What are the projects that slipped?" I asked.

"Payroll and transportation," he said. "They are batch, but we are rewriting them to take advantage of a database environment. Transportation includes fleet scheduling and maintenance, on-board parts stocking, material management, order tracking, and time/expense reporting, by the way.

"Frankly, the fact that this particular project is late doesn't bother me a lot," he said, leaning forward, as if

to confide. "What really worries me is the four or five big systems that we have only just started. Take On-line Customer Service, for example. Our current version of that system has hundreds of programs. The preliminary design shows 10 subsystems with almost 200 visible transactions. We think it's going to be at least 400,000 lines of code. They tell me it will be done in a couple of years. But if they are slipping now, how can I believe that estimate? And what do I tell the users?

"No," he finished, "we need much better project control in here. Budget is not the issue and quality will be kept at its current high level. What we need are realistic estimates of schedule and a way to complete them on time. You folks figure out how to do it. Tell me what kind of people we need and what kind of tools to use, and we will go out and get them. Is there anything else you want to know?"

"Just some details," I answered. "In your development standards, what project tasks are tracked and what distinguishes a large project?"

"We sometimes break things into phases," he replied, "but the standard approach is test for feasibility, design, implement, and install. That's what we did for Transportation. We scheduled four months and 182 labor-hours for design, then six months and 494 labor-hours for code and test. Our standards book says that a large project is anything over 20 man-days, but to me a large project is anything over three man-years. We have over 40 people developing and maintaining applications, by the way, so this is important. Let me know how you want to approach it."

With that, he ushered me politely out of his office. My first reaction was disbelief. Why would anyone want to write yet another payroll system from scratch? But I quickly settled down to focus on project planning control. I was, after all, an easy target.

Even before leaving the building, I knew I had two solid leads.

First, they were managing the hours spent, not the results achieved. The MIS director sincerely believes the cost is the measure by which data processing exists within the corporation. Project managers report in those terms because they understand that the director manages resources, not products. Even using earned-value concepts, like percent complete, does not work. When you are keeping track of the hours walked or the number of paces marched, you might easily forget that a milestone is a tangible object along the path.

Second, they were defining as a single project jobs so large as to be unmanageable. Their checklist shows a concern for "schedule, given project size and complexity." But the scope of an individual project is not given.

Whoever defined Transportation as a single project, for example, deserves to go have his ticket punched for good. That system could have been planned as a series of progressive releases. It did not have to be built as one enormous, all-or-nothing project. Why would anyone tackle so much software at once? Why would they promise delivery on such a short schedule? They might have misunderstood software estimating or they might have been under a lot of pressure.

I suspected the worst.

Just solving the project management problems would not be enough to close the case. True, we could set accurate dates for delivery. And the software would be ready very close to schedule. Meeting a schedule is only part of the story, however. "On time" matters, but "what time" matters more.

I had an uneasy sensation that what they really wanted was the software done sooner, a lot sooner. Someone out there was clamoring for applications.

Thinking back, one part of our dialog had bothered me most. Suppose the estimate of 400,000 lines of code in one major application is reasonably accurate. For that size of project, you would expect roughly a three-year effort in which their entire full-time staff would exert over 100 man-years' labor: in other words, this single project would consume the entire development and maintenance staff over the next three years!

Therein lurked the villain. I simple had to deduce that time was the critical factor. The custom development approach, no matter how well managed, would be doomed. When you are faced with a backlog, the traditional programming process is insufficient. Poor planning, focusing on large undoable projects, and measuring the process just keeps firms from admitting their dilemma. Working harder, rather than smarter, is futile in the face of overwhelming demands.

Source: Kenneth E. Schoman, Jr., "The Case of the Applications Backlog," *Datamation*, vol. 30, no. 18, November 1, 1984, pp. 107, 108.

4.2.3 Set Enough Milestones for Good Management

How much planning is enough? The answer is "It depends." The right amount of planning depends on the size of the project, the size of the development team, and the purpose of the plan. Plans are made at a number of points in a development project for varying reasons. The first plan may include a list of four activities or five subsystems, with a rough estimate of how long each should take. This first plan would be part of an initial investigation to determine whether the project was worth pursuing. A rough estimate like this one might be all a manager needed to decide whether the scope and costs were reasonable or ridiculous. Spending more time on planning at this early stage would not be worth the resources expended.

Plans that are created for reviews with users should be simple enough to be communicated easily. The 7 ± 2 rule is a good one to follow for graphic presentations to groups.

According to this rule, five to nine activities is all that should be presented on one chart, because seven figures, objects, or numbers is about all that most people remember easily from each page in a presentation. If details are important, they should be distributed to the reviewers as a handout. Another way to comply with the 7 ± 2 rule is to divide up your material so that each chart contains a limited portion of the plan.

After a project has been approved and the systems development team is ready to begin work, a plan should be constructed with enough measurable activities (milestones) that the team's work can be monitored and coordinated. As a rule of thumb, we suggest a minimum of one milestone per team member per week. For example, let's say that a three-member team has been assigned to complete a project that is estimated to take four months:

```
Number of weeks = 4.3 weeks/months × 4 months
                = 17 weeks (approximately)
Number of milestones = 17 weeks × 3 team members
                = 51 milestones
```

These milestones could be presented in the form of a one-page, single-spaced list of activities.

The milestone rule of thumb should not be extended literally to projects of every size. If there were six project team members and development was expected to last a year, the formula method would lead to a minimum of 312 milestones. It would be foolish for the project leader to plan the full year in such detail. Instead, several major milestones should be set, based on five to twelve delivery points. Then, a few weeks before the next phase begins, the leader should plan that phase in detail, following the milestone rule of thumb.

Our purpose in this section has been to provide general rules on how much planning is enough. These are summarized in Figure 4.4. In Section 4.3 we will suggest formats for activity lists. In Chapter 5 we will explain in detail the procedures for identifying activities.

Figure 4.4
How Much Planning Is Enough?

Purpose of the Plan	Stage of Development	Planning Rule of Thumb
Quick check for feasibility	Early	Major milestones as needed for rough estimate
Presentation for review	Anytime	7 ± 2 activities per page or chart in graphic form
Monitoring and coordinating	After development team has been formed or team size is known	Current and next phase: 1 measurable activity per team member per week (minimum) Later phases: 1 or 2 activities per week

4.2.4 Involve the Right People

Whether the planner is a user or an information systems specialist, plans should be reviewed with the users, including the end-users, the user-manager, and the user-sponsor. A complete understanding on the part of the users of the milestones, delivery points, and changeover dates is important in involving them in the project and in preventing unpleasant surprises later. Approval of each of the major delivery points and the changeover should be obtained from representative users, including the user-sponsor.

Plans for a large system that interfaces with other systems should be reviewed with the maintenance teams of those systems. Changes in the interfaces are likely to necessitate a series of modifications of related systems. These changes need to be coordinated. Likewise, any technical support that will be required during the project needs to be scheduled and reviewed early in development. Operations and information systems management should review the plans for all systems that require significant technical resources.

This section has offered four guidelines to successful planning:

- Keep deliverable products small.
- Manage the product, not the process.
- Set enough milestones for good management.
- Involve the right people.

Keep these guidelines in mind as you read the next section on the tasks of planning systems development.

4.3 Planning Tasks

Planning the systems development process means determining *what* must be done to create an installed working system, *who* will accomplish this work, and *when* the work will be done. Specifically, planning involves four tasks:

1. Determine the required process activities and sequence.
2. Estimate the time required for each activity and for the total development.
3. Allocate staff and resources.
4. Document the schedule, including milestones.

In Figure 4.5 these four tasks are illustrated as the four planning activities that precede monitoring, coordinating, and reviewing.

4.3.1 Determine Process Activities and Sequence

Process activities are all the tasks required to develop a system and to manage the development process. You should list these activities as a starting point for your plan. Be sure to state them as product delivery points whenever possible.

If your project is a short one, your activity list may be your final planning document. In this case, you simply add times and staff to your list and set the sequence of activities with your time schedule.

Figure 4.5

Management Activities
and Planning Products

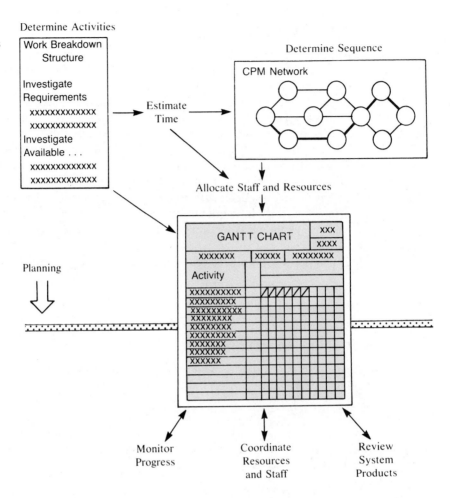

For longer projects, listing activities and determining their sequence will require more work. If you are the only developer working on the project, your list will give a sequence of tasks, to be accomplished one after another. If a development team is working on the project, many of the activities listed will be scheduled simultaneously. In that case, close attention is required to make sure that tasks A and B are both completed on schedule if both are critical for task C to begin on time. The **critical path method (CPM) network** in the upper right-hand corner of Figure 4.5 is an example of a graphic tool for determining the sequence and time requirements of development activities. Constructing the critical path method is a good technique for expanding and sequencing a list of activities. The steps in determining activities and their sequence will be discussed in detail in Chapter 5.

4.3.2 Estimate Time

Estimating the time required for each task is difficult, even for experienced analysts. Numerous studies have been conducted on estimating total completion times for projects based on lines of code and other characteristics of systems development. No published guidelines, however, are available for estimating the time required for such diverse tasks as writing user manuals and investigating existing programs.

Chapter 6 will present several methods for estimating project time. For the purposes of this overview chapter, let us assume that planning is a two-step process in which you estimate the time required for each individual activity and then sum these times to arrive at the total time required. For large projects, an intermediate step will be required. In order to know which times to sum, you will need to draw a CPM network showing which activities must follow other activities and which can be completed simultaneously.

4.3.3 Allocate Staff and Resources

As a project manager, once you have determined what activities need to be done when, you need to assign team members with the required skills to each activity. In the ideal situation, all the needed team members are available at the necessary times. As you can imagine, this ideal situation seldom occurs. Because other priorities may limit the selection of staff and some team members may need training, you should expect to revise your preliminary time estimates and schedule.

No matter how much staff flexibility you have, you must take the time to specifically allocate staff. Allocating staff is more than just forming a group of people; it involves matching team members' skills with development activities, even if you need to train a team member to create the matching skill.

Resources too must be allocated. Does each team member have adequate access to development tools? Do the team members know which organizational resources might be helpful and how to obtain them? Are there any constraints on their use of organizational resources, computer time, staff time, and so forth? All of these questions must be answered for project work to flow smoothly.

4.3.4 Document the Schedule

In the center of Figure 4.5 is a Gantt chart. **A Gantt chart** lists project activities, shows each activity's starting and ending time, and indicates the person assigned to each activity. As a project manager, first you will use a CPM network to estimate the time and sequence of tasks; then you will use a Gantt chart to plan and monitor the details of starting and ending dates and resource allocation.

Critical path method networks and Gantt charts are the principal tools for documenting schedules. These graphic planning techniques may show only general details, as would be appropriate for management reviews or initial project orientation meetings with the development staff. Or they may be extremely detailed schedules that show individual responsibilities and the milestones appropriate for controlling the project. These techniques will be explained and illustrated in detail in Chapter 5.

No matter what form you use to document the schedule, you will need clear milestones to monitor progress. If early milestones are missed, you must consider revising later deadlines. Either productivity must be examined and improved or the functional requirements of the system must be reduced or the completion deadline must be extended. Without the early warning provided by monitoring milestones, no one is likely to know that project delivery time is slipping until it is too late to remedy the difficulties.

4.4 Timing of Planning Tasks

The order of the four planning tasks depends on what limits are set and what decisions are made before planning begins. The next two sections will discuss two common approaches to planning.

4.4.1 Starting from the Beginning

In the ideal situation, the project manager determines requirements before planning. The more you know about the functional requirements, the more assurance you have that your plan will be accurate. After you have determined project activities, you estimate time, allocate staff, and document the schedule. Then you review your plan. Is the schedule acceptable? Do the requirements of the system justify the allocated resources?

If the answers to these questions are positive, fine. Your team can start work according to the plan. If the answers are negative, you need to revise the requirements and then revise your plan to meet the modified requirements. These revisions return you to the planning loop, in which you re-estimate time, reallocate staff if necessary, and document the revised schedule. Again you check your plan against the requirements. Depending on the results of your review and the reaction of management, you either proceed with development or reenter the planning loop yet another time. This approach is shown in part (a) of Figure 4.6.

(a) Requirements Known and No Schedule of Staff Constraints

(b) Planning Constraints Set Early

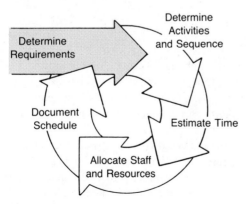
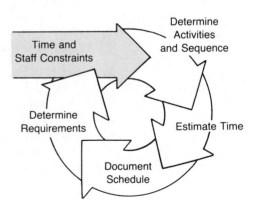

Figure 4.6 Two Orders of Planning Activities

4.4.2 Starting with the Answer

Sometimes project constraints include a time deadline and limited staff resources. This situation is illustrated in part (b) of Figure 4.6. In this situation, the estimation and allocation activities have already been done. So your job is to determine what activities are necessary, given the time and staff constraints. An advantage of this approach is that you can estimate time for individual activities based on the known skills of the people assigned to the project. After you've determined the details, you document the schedule and, again, check the schedule against the requirements. But in this case, the time constraint is given priority.

If the time allowed to complete the project is short, your only option may be to implement existing software. In that case, verifying your plan against requirements means investigating whether acceptable software exists. If none exists, then you may argue for revising the time or staff constraint or both. If your revision is approved, you return to the planning loop to make the necessary time, resource, and activity revisions.

As these two planning sequences show, the planning approach depends on what you know when you create your plan. In every situation, however, planning starts with the known factors and then progresses through the remaining planning activities until all the project milestones have been set. As a project manager, you must adapt to difficult constraints. For example, a legislative mandate may impose a rigid time deadline, allowing no flexibility in project completion time. Or a powerful executive may argue for a deadline so forcibly that your career depends on meeting the schedule, no matter how unrealistic it appears to be. In these cases, you should review the schedule difficulties with the user-sponsor. If the deadline cannot be extended to allow time to meet system requirements, the scope of the system should be narrowed so that the deadline can be met.

4.4.3 Quick Planning for a Small Project

For an uncomplicated, well-defined project, planning may be so informal and spontaneous that it may appear to have been skipped entirely. The minicase Ledger Summary Revision for Meadows Hospital provides an example of quick planning.

Note that the first three planning activities—determining activities, estimating time, and allocating resources—have been completed by the end of the telephone exchange between Mr. Yarrow and Fred Kahn. Staffing was a given; the team will include only Fred, the programmer-analyst, and Mr. Yarrow, the accountant who made the request. Fred has listed a series of process activities and their sequence. He has also estimated a time for each delivery point and for the changeover.

1. Check functional requirements (the next day)
2. Review test output (early next week)
3. Install revised program (by the end of next week)
4. Test system with revised program (by the end of next week)
5. Changeover (for the next production run, which is the following week)

Ledger Summary Revision for Meadows Hospital

Mr. Yarrow is an accountant in the Administration division of Meadows Hospital. One of his responsibilities is the general ledger system, which was automated about ten years ago. A recent policy change in how the state subsidizes hospital expenses for welfare recipients has necessitated changes to several of the financial systems, including general ledger processing. To initiate the system modification, Mr. Yarrow calls programmer-analyst Fred Kahn. Fred has been maintaining the ledger system for about a year.

"Fred, can you revise the current ledger program to accumulate some of the pharmacy and service charges differently? The state rules have changed, so the reimbursements will be different. I would also like to revise the final one-page summary so that it just lists the debit and credit totals for each of the twenty-two ledger accounts."

"Sure, Mr. Yarrow," Fred replies. "I'll bring over a copy of the current ledger printout and see what format changes you want for the summary and discuss the codes that will need to be accumulated differently. I can do that tomorrow, and if there aren't too many differences from the current summary lines and accumulations, I think I can have a test version for you to review by early next week. If that meets with your approval, I can install the changed program and run a quick system test before the regular monthly production run of the ledger occurs the following week. Of course, if there are many changes, the new system won't be ready for the regular ledger production run."

This type of planning and verbal commitment is appropriate for an experienced analyst and a small, well-defined project. When information systems professionals apply this same quick judgment to large, complicated development projects, however, they give the field a poor reputation. A problem inexperienced analysts have is that they do not possess Fred's mental checklist. Scheduling, estimating, and establishing milestones, even for a very small project, requires a series of activities that seems easy only after experience has made it habitual. Beginners, and all analysts on large projects, should proceed deliberately through a series of planning activities to meet the goals of scheduling, estimating, and providing milestones for control.

Whether the planning process is long or short, the last step—documentation—should not be skipped. We know from the case study in Chapter 3 that Meadows Hospital has an Information Services Request form. After his phone conversation with Fred, Mr. Yarrow should complete this form and ask the appropriate managers to sign it. Fred's delivery points should be listed and attached to the Information Services Request, and a copy of these documents should be given to both team members and management.

4.5 Planning Products

Planning activities generate reports that directly support the three major goals of systems development. Figure 4.7 is a list of the planning products that support each goal.

Summary

Planning is a critical part of the systems development process. Many professionals neglect planning for a variety of reasons. But none of the reasons justifies the increased likelihood of failure that results from neglecting to plan.

Development Goals	Planning Products
Organizational relevance	Guidelines for monitoring and coordinating development—can be a list of milestones, Gantt chart, or CPM network.
Project management	Enumeration of activities required to create a complete system that meets all system requirements—can be a list of activities, Gantt chart, or CPM network.
System quality	Staff allocation needed to ensure adequate technical expertise and good relations with users—can be a list of activities with responsible staff noted, Gantt chart, or CPM network.
	Schedule estimates for determining whether a project justifies its development expense.

Figure 4.7
Planning Products That Serve Development Goals

Guidelines for planning are

1. Keep deliverable products small.
2. Manage the product, not the process.
3. Set enough milestones for good management.
4. Involve the right people.

All of these must be considered when you attempt to commit a schedule to paper.

The four planning tasks are (1) determining process activities and sequence; (2) estimating time; (3) allocating staff and resources; and (4) documenting the schedule. The sequence of the four tasks may vary, but all should be completed before you proceed too far with any development project.

The timing of planning tasks will depend on the organizational environment and the nature of the particular project. In the ideal situation, the project begins with requirements determination and continues through completion of the four standard planning tasks. In some cases, the total time available for development is a preset constraint. In others, the assignment of staff to the project may be determined by organizational constraints that are unchangeable. Whatever the starting point, the final product of planning must be a documented schedule, with milestones that can be used to monitor and coordinate the process until changeover is achieved.

Key Terms

(Section numbers are in parentheses.)

milestone (4.2)	sign-offs (4.2.2)
phased development (4.2.1)	critical path method (CPM) network (4.3.1)
product delivery points (4.2.2)	Gantt chart (4.3.4)

Note

1. James Martin, *Information Systems Manifesto* (Englewood Cliffs, N.J.: Prentice-Hall, 1982).

Exercises   (Answers to Exercises 4.1, 4.2, and 4.3 are at the end of the book.)

4.1 Identify each of the following milestones as a system product delivery point, a process product delivery point, or a process activity with no measurable product. For each system or process product delivery point, specify what is delivered.

    a. Complete a CPM overview chart.

    b. Review planning details with sponsor.

    c. Complete user's manual.

    d. Complete a specific program module.

    e. Finish the first week of evaluation work.

4.2 Assume that you have been asked to manage a six-month project. The requirements determination has been completed in the first two months. You are to plan the remaining four months of activity for a six-member team.

    a. What is the minimum number of milestones you should have in a detailed four-month plan?

    b. What alternative planning strategy might you use, rather than complete a detailed four-month plan? Be specific about the number of milestones.

    c. Explain your answer to part b.

    d. Assume that you are presenting your four-month plan to the six-member team. What form will your presentation take? Be specific about the level of detail of your planning presentation.

4.3 Each of the statements below specifies a process activity with no measurable product. Convert these statements into either system or process product delivery points.

    a. Design a program to facilitate user access.

    b. Identify project activities and schedule time for each.

    c. Test purchased software.

    d. Interview the computer operator about current operations.

    e. Complete the initial investigation.

4.4 Each of the statements below specifies a process activity with no measurable product. Convert these statements into either system or process product delivery points.

    a. Determine the failure recovery process for data entry.

    b. Prepare to train users.

    c. Plan to redesign the work site to accommodate new hardware.

    d. Contact vendors about existing software.

    e. Identify data elements for the accounts payable file.

4.5 Identify each of the following milestones as a system product delivery point, a process product delivery point, or a process activity with no measurable product. For each system or process product delivery point, specify what is delivered.

    a. Complete the requirements determination report.

    b. Complete 100 effort-hours of work on the display screens.

    c. Demonstrate the system for the client.

    d. Update the project schedule with the sponsor.

4.6 A systems development project is estimated to require twenty-four team members on a two-year schedule.

    a. What is the minimum number of milestones that you should have, according to the standard rule of thumb?

    b. What is the problem with following the rule of thumb in this case?

    c. What is an alternative planning strategy? Be specific about the number of milestones in the alternative plan.

4.7 How many milestones are required for a seven-week project involving three team members?

Projects

4.8 In Chapter 3 of *Controlling Software Projects* (New York: Yourdon Press, 1982), Tom DeMarco argues that there should be a separate information systems group that specializes in planning and controlling projects. Some organizations have official project managers who specialize in planning and controlling; others have project leaders who are responsible for planning and controlling projects. Which approach do you think is better? Prepare a presentation or paper stating your views, DeMarco's, and those of at least two additional sources.

4.9 The discussion in Section 4.2.3 about how much planning is enough is very brief. For a longer and more sophisticated discussion of this topic, read Section 20.10 of Barry Boehm's *Software Engineering Economics* (Englewood Cliffs, N.J.: Prentice-Hall, 1981). Write a paper or organize a class presentation on how Boehm's guidelines apply to the question of how much planning is enough. Based on Boehm's guidelines, provide examples of systems that require elaborate planning and those that require little planning. Make your connections between the examples and the guidelines clear.

CHAPTER 5

Planning Techniques

Work Breakdown Structure
The Checklist Approach
The Matrix Approach
The Product Delivery Approach
Choosing the Best Approach

Critical Path Method (CPM) Networks
CPM Network Definition and Goals
CPM Network Rules
PERT Charts

Gantt Charts
Gantt Chart Definitions and Goals
Gantt Chart Rules
Minicase: Word Processing Systems for *Outerspace* Magazine

Planning Software
Summary
Key Terms ▪ **Note** ▪ **Exercises** ▪ **Project**

Overview

The last chapter presented guidelines for successful project planning, monitoring, and coordinating. This chapter focuses on two major planning tools: critical path method (CPM) networks and Gantt charts. First we discuss how to create a work breakdown structure for a project. Then we define each technique, explain its goals, and discuss the rules and drawing procedures. We conclude with comments about project management software.

Specifically, we plan to

1. Present methods for arriving at a work breakdown structure. (Section 5.1)

2. Discuss the management goals of critical path method (CPM) networks and Gantt charts. (Sections 5.2.1 and 5.3.1)

3. Explain how to read and create CPM networks and Gantt charts. (Sections 5.2.2 and 5.3.2)

4. Describe and provide examples of computer tools for planning. (Section 5.4)

5.1 Work Breakdown Structure

A **work breakdown structure** is a hierarchical list of the activities required to complete a system. It is a task list in outline form, with a coding scheme to identify each activity. To determine the activities for a work breakdown structure, you may follow one of three approaches:

- the checklist approach
- the matrix approach
- the product delivery approach

These planning approaches can be combined or used alone as the basis for creating a work breakdown structure. Examples of these approaches are given in Figure 5.1.

Figure 5.1
Three Approaches to Determining Activities

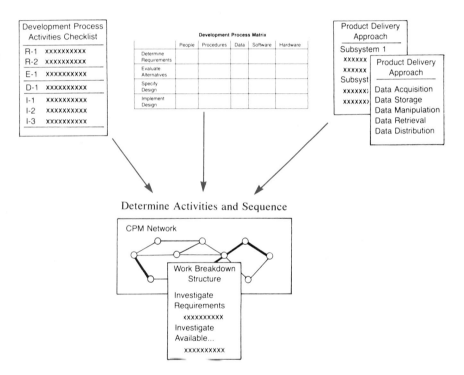

5.1.1 The Checklist Approach

The **checklist approach** is a planning method used to identify activities for a development schedule. A checklist of development and management activities is shown in Figure 5.2. (Refer to Figures 1.17 and 2.10 for definitions of these activities.) The development activities are classified under one of the four stages of the REDI life cycle, and each activity is assigned a code based on its REDI stage initial and a numeric designator. As an analyst, you must identify the necessary management activities, such as planning and reviewing, and schedule them among the development activities. The number and order of these activities will depend on the size and type of the system you are developing.

Figure 5.2
Activity Checklist

Development Activities	Management Activities
Determine Requirements	Plan
R.1 Identify Objectives	Monitor
R.2 Identify Constraints	Coordinate
R.3 Investigate Requirements	Review
Evaluate Alternatives	
E.1 Identify Alternatives	
E.2 Evaluate Alternatives	
E.3 Document Alternatives	
E.4 Obtain Management Decision	
Specify Design	
D.1 Specify People	
D.2 Specify Procedures	
D.3 Specify Data	
D.4 Specify Software	
D.5 Specify Hardware	
Implement Design	
I.1 Construct	
I.2 Test	
I.3 Install	

The advantage of the checklist approach is that it requires little work. Figure 5.2—the basic checklist augmented with management activities—can be used exactly as it is for the development of small, low-risk systems. Figure 5.3 is an example of a more detailed checklist that incorporates specific management activities. Note that the second and fifth activities, R.2 and R.5, are to form the project team (a coordinating activity) and to plan the overall schedule (a planning activity). Planning is included again as the first step in design, D.1. The management activities of reviewing and preparing for reviews are included at the end of every stage.

Figure 5.3
Expanded Checklist
for Custom Development

R—Requirements Stage

R.1 Identify Problem or Opportunity
R.2 Form Project Team
R.3 Identify Objectives
R.4 Identify Constraints
R.5 Plan Overall Schedule: Gantt Chart or CPM Network
R.6 Determine Functional Requirements
  R.6.1 Define Current System (DFDs, I/O Summaries)
  R.6.2 Define Physical Model (System Flowcharts, Context Diagrams)
  R.6.3 List Functional Requirements
R.7 Determine Source of Software
R.8 Assess Feasibility (In Depth to Justify Further Requirements Work): Initial Feasibility Report
  R.8.1 Assess Technical Feasibility
  R.8.2 Assess Cost Feasibility
  R.8.3 Assess Schedule Feasibility
R.9 Determine Specific Requirements
  R.9.1 Draw Logical Model
  R.9.2 Complete System Definition
  R.9.3 Determine Problem Specifications
  R.9.4 Complete Specific Requirements
R.10 Assess Feasibility (In Depth to Justify Evaluation Stage): Revised Feasibility Report
  R.10.1 Assess Technical Feasibility
  R.10.2 Assess Cost Feasibility
  R.10.3 Assess Schedule Feasibility
R.11 Prepare Management Review Package
R.12 Obtain Management Approval

E—Evaluation Stage

E.1 Generate Alternatives
  E.1.1 Identify Alternative Components
  E.1.2 Identify Alternative Solutions
E.2 Evaluate Alternative Solutions
  E.2.1 Determine Criteria
  E.2.2 Rank and Weight Criteria
  E.2.3 Rate Alternatives
  E.2.4 Compute Composite Ratings
  E.2.5 Select One or Two Alternatives
E.3 Document or Demonstrate Each Chosen Alternative
  E.3.1 Expand Cost and Schedule Details
  E.3.2 Summarize Solution-Problem Fit
E.4 Obtain Management Approval

D—Design Stage

D.1 Plan Design and Implementation Stage Schedule and Resources
D.2 Design User Interfaces

(continued)

Figure 5.3
(Continued)

D—Design Stage

	D.2.1	Specify System Testing
	D.2.2	Specify Installation Procedures
	D.2.3	Specify Changeover Procedures
D.3	Specify or Design Programs	
D.4	Specify Database	
D.5	Specify Hardware	
D.6	Specify Procedures	
	D.6.1	Specify User Procedures for Installation
	D.6.2	Specify User Procedures for Production
	D.6.3	Specify Operation Procedures
D.7	Design People Component	
	D.7.1	Write Job Descriptions
	D.7.2	Determine Organization's Structure
	D.7.3	Design Training Materials
D.8	Document or Demonstrate Design	
	D.8.1	Update Cost and Schedule Details
	D.8.2	Summarize Solution-Problem Fit
D.9	Obtain Approval	
	D.9.1	Obtain Technical Approval
	D.9.2	Obtain Management Approval

I—Implementation Stage

I.1	Preliminary Construction	
	I.1.1	Prepare Site
	I.1.2	Install Hardware
	I.1.3	Code Programs
	I.1.4	Build Test Files
I.2	Preliminary Test	
	I.2.1	Test Components
	I.2.2	Test System
I.3	Final Construction	
	I.3.1	Revise Programs
	I.3.2	Build Production Files
	I.3.3	Write Procedures Manuals
	I.3.4	Hire and Train Personnel
I.4	Test	
	I.4.1	Test Subsystems
	I.4.2	Test System
I.5	Install System	
I.6	Obtain Management Approval (of Completion)	
I.7	Changeover	

Some organizations use prescribed checklists that include several hundred activities. These standardized lists are especially helpful if developers are transferred from one project to another.

The disadvantage of the checklist approach is the delay in feedback. Because this approach adheres to a rigid life cycle model, the user doesn't see any part of the system until the implementation stage. If you go through lengthy requirements, evaluation, and design stages before demonstrating some portion of the system to the users, you are likely to lose their attention and interest. A second disadvantage is that this approach emphasizes process over product. As you learned in Chapter 4, managing the product, not the process, is a key to effective systems development. So as you list the activities to be performed, try to phrase them as system and process product delivery points. Including tangible milestones compensates for the heavy process orientation of the checklist approach. Using the matrix or product delivery approach in combination with the planning checklist will also achieve this focus.

5.1.2 The Matrix Approach

You are already somewhat familiar with the matrix approach. You've seen the development process matrix, a two-dimensional checklist, in preceding chapters. The row headings are the four REDI stages; the column headings are the five system components. The row dimension defines the process; the column dimension defines the product. A matrix is depicted at the top of Figure 5.1. Detailed versions of the process matrix are presented in Figures 2.14 and 2.15.

One advantage of the matrix approach is that the system component dimension of the matrix focuses attention on the system and process product delivery points necessary to build a complete system. A second potential advantage of the matrix approach is that it doesn't prescribe a predefined sequence of activities. You can sequence the activities in each cell according to the objectives of your project. The resulting flexibility is an advantage to an experienced analyst, but may make the matrix a confusing or insufficient planning tool for a beginning analyst.

5.1.3 The Product Delivery Approach

The **product delivery approach** is a planning method in which large projects are broken down into several phases. The phases of a project may be based on subsystems or data capabilities, which are delivered separately to the user before the entire project is completed.

In Chapter 4 we discussed the importance of phased development for large projects. The reasons given for partitioning systems into phases were

- Requests for system changes after installation are inevitable, as the user gains a new perspective from working with the system. This learning process is likely to have a greater impact on a large system than on a small system.

- Partitioning projects reduces management overhead costs by simplifying communication.

- The frequent installations of a partitioned project's subsystems maintain user interest.
- The probability of changes in requirements increases as time-to-delivery increases. Partitioning a large system reduces time-to-delivery, thereby diminishing the number of post-installation changes.

What is a large project? The MIS director in the Chapter 4 minicase A Consultant's View of a Project Management Mess said that his company's definition of a large project was "anything over 20 man-days." But the director's own definition was anything over three man-years. This second definition is the equivalent of 720 effort-days, almost forty times the company definition! As you can see, there is no standard definition in the field of an unacceptably large project; but the minicase consultant's horror of large projects is a common reaction of experienced developers. Our own rule of thumb is that any project requiring more than six months to the first installation should be partitioned for phased development. You need to have very good reasons for extending delivery time beyond six months, in view of all the problems associated with large projects.

How you partition a large system will depend on the project itself. When multiple systems are being purchased or revised, the easiest way to partition is on the basis of subsystems. For example, a small business automating for the first time would first need to examine broad organizational needs in order to define and evaluate its requirements. The goal of this preliminary review would be an overall plan for the project. The next major work breakdown activity would be to purchase and develop one subsystem, such as payroll. Developing the first subsystem will provide valuable insights for the development of subsequent subsystems.

Suppose a manufacturing company plans to purchase systems for customer invoicing, accounts receivable, and customer cash receipts. As shown in Figure 5.4, the first activities are a review of general requirements for all three systems, because all three are part of the company's procedures to manage customer payments. If the customer invoicing system was considered the most crucial, that system would be the focus of the early investigation and the first to be purchased. Keeping in mind the overall plan, the analyst would make one of the constraints for the purchase of the invoicing system the availability of compatible accounts receivable and customer cash receipts systems. If the invoicing system was a success, the purchase and development of the other subsystems would follow.

Now suppose this manufacturing company already has three working, stand-alone systems for customer invoicing, accounts receivable, and customer cash receipts. But management wants a new integrated system to reduce repetitive and error-prone data entry. The new system is to perform all the functions of the original three systems. If you treated this task as one large project and followed a strict life cycle checklist approach, you would be courting disaster. Instead, you should follow a phased development approach for each of the subsystems. The major categories of this work breakdown structure are the same as those in Figure 5.4. Again, your initial job is to determine an overall plan and general requirements for the entire integrated system. Then you develop the customer invoicing system as the first subsystem, allowing the users to begin working with part of the new integrated system. User feedback will help you revise this portion of the integrated system before the details of the other subsystems are determined. This approach will save development time, since you solve design problems for one subsystem before the entire system is constructed and tested.

Figure 5.4
Gantt Chart Based on the Product Delivery Approach

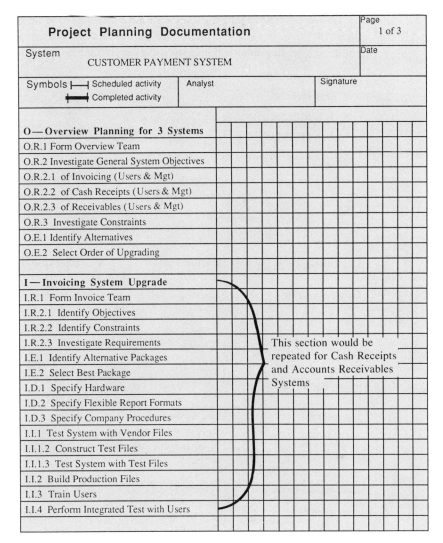

Partitioning this project into subsystems creates two problems. The first is that special programs must be designed, written, and tested to interface the new portion of the system with the old stand-alone systems. Generally, the smoothness of the transition from the old to the new system more than justifies this additional time and effort. A second problem is that the boundaries of many old systems are based on the capabilities of people using typewriters and calculators. If you follow these old guidelines, you're unlikely to create a system that takes full advantage of the power of computers. You need to be alert to this possible drawback and to design a system that builds on, but is not limited by, the old system's capabilities.

A second way to partition a system for a series of product deliveries is based on the view that data is the basic product of an information system.[1] With this approach, you subdivide development activities to successively deliver the capabilities for

- data acquisition
- data storage
- data manipulation
- data retrieval
- data distribution

Each of these data capabilities is defined in Figure 5.5. Your choice of which data capability to deliver first depends on the system.

Figure 5.5
Definitions and Examples of Five Basic Data Capabilities

Capability	Definition	Example
Data acquisition	Entering data	• Scanning UPC codes in a point-of-sale system • Clerk's keying in data in the blank fields on a data entry screen • Students' filling in the squares for social security number and course numbers at registration
Data storage	Storing data on disk, tape, drum, microfiche, or other form for later access	• Storing data in a form easily accessed with a fourth generation tool • Storing backup files on tape to be kept off-site
Data manipulation	Processing data	• Calculating financial ratios
Data retrieval	Extracting data for manipulation and distribution (creating reports, screens, floppy disks, etc.)	• Retrieving monthly sales data • Retrieving product information from main storage to manipulate with a spreadsheet on a microcomputer
Data distribution	Sending data in any form (reports, screen displays, floppy disks, etc.)—usually refers to sending data off-site using communications or mail systems rather than directing delivery to a single end user	• Establishing procedures for nationwide data access • Selling address lists on tapes • Selling data on floppy disks for further analysis • Establishing access to all client records in all the retail outlets of a company

Following this phased development approach for the manufacturing company mentioned above would require a new plan. Suppose that one major complaint had led management to decide to integrate the three systems. The company's financial analysts had complained repeatedly about the detailed reports provided by the three current systems. They argued that analysis of the customer payment patterns was unnecessarily difficult. Because the data needed was organized in three stand-alone systems, revising the current reports would be time consuming. The ideal way to deliver the revised reports quickly would be to create the data storage for the new integrated system (thus making progress toward that goal), but to allow the financial analysts to retrieve and manipulate their own data with user-oriented fourth generation tools.

Following this rationale, you would plan the design and implementation of new data storage first, as shown in the second major category (DS) in Figure 5.6. The next major

Figure 5.6
Page 1 of an Early Gantt Chart Based on the Data Capabilities Approach to Product Delivery

Project Planning Documentation																	Page 1 of 3
System Integration of 3 Customer Payment Systems																	Date
Symbols ⊢—⊣ Scheduled activity ▬▬ Completed activity						Analyst						Signature					
						Week											
Activity*	1	2	3	4	5	6	7	8	9	10	11	12	13	14			
O – System Planning																	
O.R Determine Requirements	⊢—⊣																
O.E Evaluate Alternative Plans			⊢—⊣														
O.D Prepare Design Specifications					⊢—⊣												
DS – Develop Data Storage																	
DS.R Determine Requirements							⊢—⊣										
DS.E Evaluate Alternative Structures								⊢—⊣									
DS.D Design Data Structures and Interfaces									⊢—⊣								
DS.I.1 Build Test Database										⊢—⊣							
DS.I.2 Code and Test Interfaces										⊢—⊣							
DS.I.3 Build Production Database												⊢—⊣					
DR-- Develop Data Retrieval																	
DR.I.1 Train on 4th Generation Tools								⊢—⊣									
DR.I.2 Code Programs											⊢—⊣						
DR.I.3 Test with Test Database											⊢—⊣						
DR.I.4 Test with Production Database													⊢—⊣				
DA – Data Acquisition																	
DA.R Determine Requirements																	
DA.E Evaluate Alternatives																	
DA.D Design Screens and Procedures																	
DA.I.1 Code Programs																	
DA.I.2 Write Procedures Manual																	
DA.I.3 Train End Users																	
DA.I.4 Test Data Entry																	
DA.I.5 Install Data Entry Capability																	

*Not shown: Weekly team reviews on Friday

activity (DR) would be to develop and deliver the data retrieval capability. By training end-users in the eighth week, you could make your first delivery quickly. With training and available tools, the end-users could generate their own reports by accessing the integrated data storage. Meanwhile your project team would continue to work on the next section of the integrated system: data acquisition. The suggestions and complaints of end-users of the data storage and retrieval sections would provide valuable information for your work.

5.1.4 Choosing the Best Approach

The project characteristics that determine which approach is best for defining a work breakdown structure are

- project size
- project risk
- development team experience

Small projects with little risk of failure can be planned easily and safely by following the checklist approach. If the objectives, constraints, and functional requirements are likely to be the same when the project is finished as when it was started, going from R.1 straight through to I.3 on the checklist in Figure 5.2 should be sufficient. Either small size or stability of requirements ensures that the checklist approach is an acceptable choice for a particular project.

An inexperienced development team will want to follow a checklist/matrix approach. Beginners seldom have the confidence to partition a project during the early planning stages, unless there is an obvious partitioning into subsystems. In this situation, develop the subsystem with a clear user payoff and low risk first. If the project is difficult to partition, and large or risky, you should allow considerable slack time for revisions after the first installation.

Large projects and risky projects should be planned with a product delivery approach. The activities leading to each delivery may be derived from a checklist or a matrix. Either way, frequent deliveries reduce the problems and post-installation revisions associated with long development cycles.

5.2 Critical Path Method (CPM) Networks

After you've identified the project activities, you're ready to plan the project schedule. This section discusses an important tool for project planning: the CPM network.

5.2.1 CPM Network Definition and Goals

A **critical path method (CPM) network** is a graphic tool that shows the sequence of tasks, simultaneous activities, and time requirements for a project. The **critical path** is the sequence of activities requiring the longest amount of time. The only way to decrease project schedule time is to reduce the time required for an activity on the critical path.

A CPM network can help you to

- determine task sequence
- identify simultaneous development activities

- allocate staff
- calculate total project effort and schedule

Better execution of the above tasks in turn helps you to meet your project management goals by improving your planning, monitoring, and coordinating efforts.

The level of detail of a CPM network depends on the purpose of the network. When a development team is discussing the necessary steps in a project, team members may draw a CPM network that covers several blackboards or large charts. In reports, however, CPM networks should be restricted to ten or fewer activities per page, for readability. For large projects, more detail is required to monitor and coordinate individual activities. In these cases, a Gantt chart, described later in this chapter, may be more appropriate.

5.2.2 CPM Network Rules

The symbols and labeling conventions for CPM networks are summarized in Figure 5.7. Lines (or arrows) and circles are the only two symbols. The lines of a CPM network indicate tasks. Small circles, or nodes, indicate the completion of tasks. Any tasks that precede a node must be completed before the task following the node may be started.

Figure 5.7
Symbols for Critical Path Method (CPM) Networks

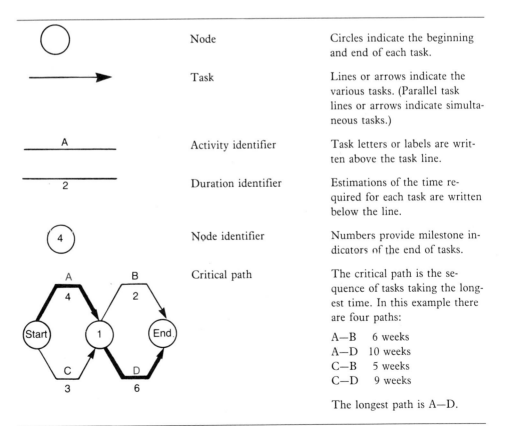

	Node	Circles indicate the beginning and end of each task.
	Task	Lines or arrows indicate the various tasks. (Parallel task lines or arrows indicate simultaneous tasks.)
A	Activity identifier	Task letters or labels are written above the task line.
2	Duration identifier	Estimations of the time required for each task are written below the line.
4	Node identifier	Numbers provide milestone indicators of the end of tasks.
	Critical path	The critical path is the sequence of tasks taking the longest time. In this example there are four paths:

A—B	6 weeks
A—D	10 weeks
C—B	5 weeks
C—D	9 weeks

The longest path is A—D.

The easiest way to construct a CPM network is to complete a development process matrix and then use the matrix as a beginning point. An alternative beginning point is a generic detailed checklist like the one in Figure 5.3. Start your CPM chart in the upper left-hand corner of a large blackboard or flip chart, drawing arrows for all the earliest tasks. As you draw in later tasks, you will remember predecessor tasks that should be inserted between nodes. The network is likely to become quite messy and require several redrawings, but this brainstorming approach is excellent, especially for helping a team to remember all the important tasks. A CPM software package may help with this process, although you should expect to revise your effort several times, just as you would on the blackboard.

One important concept emphasized by CPM networks is the difference between total project effort and minimum project schedule. The simple CPM network at the bottom of Figure 5.7 contains four tasks that must be completed to reach the end of the project. The **total project effort** is the sum of the times required for each task. In this example the total effort is the sum of the times for the four tasks:

$$4 + 2 + 3 + 6 = 15 \text{ weeks}$$

Total project effort is commonly measured in man-weeks or man-months. In this text, we use the terms effort-weeks and effort-months, both to avoid chauvinism and to clearly distinguish the total effort from schedule or calendar time. The number of **effort months** will be the same as schedule time only when all tasks are performed sequentially and only *one* person is assigned to the project.

In the example in Figure 5.7, tasks A and C can be completed concurrently, as can tasks B and D, so the minimum project schedule is *less* than the total project effort. The **minimum project schedule** is the sum of the times required for the tasks on the critical path. Assuming that staff are available when needed, the minimum project schedule for this example is

$$4 + 6 = 10 \text{ weeks}$$

We have adopted the terms schedule-weeks and schedule-months to distinguish this measure of time from effort-weeks and effort-months. The number of **schedule-months,** or calendar months required to complete a project, is almost always lower than the number of effort-months, since some tasks usually can be performed concurrently if two or more people are assigned to the project. (We'll discuss this difference again in Chapter 6.)

Sometimes two activities (A and B) occur simultaneously, and both must be completed before another (C) can start. If A takes four days and B takes two days, there are two days of slack time in B's path. **Slack time** occurs whenever one path or portion of a path is shorter than a simultaneous path.

The rules for drawing CPM networks are listed in Figure 5.8. Figure 5.9 illustrates how the sequence of tasks and critical path are determined. Figure 5.10 shows correct and incorrect CPM networks for the same task list.

5.2.3 PERT Charts

A popular extension of the CPM network is the PERT chart. PERT is an acronym for Program Evaluation and Review Technique. Instead of a single time estimate for each

Figure 5.8
Rules for CPM
Networks

1. Identify each task using an arrow or line.

2. Identify the beginning and end of tasks with a circle or node indicator.

3. Show the sequencing of tasks by having each task follow all immediate predecessors.

4. Put the name of the task or the task letter above each task arrow or line.

5. Put a number representing estimated time to completion below each task arrow or line.

6. Include a footnote identifying the unit used for time estimations (days, weeks, or months).

7. Number nodes from left to right. (Otherwise numbering choices are arbitrary.)

8. Use a dark or colored line to indicate the critical path. (The critical path is the sequence of tasks requiring the longest time.)

Figure 5.9
CPM Example

CPM Task List

Activity	Immediate Predecessors	Effort-Days
A	Start	2
B	A	1
C	B	1
D	A	3
E	D	2
F	A	2
G	F	1
Completion	E, C, G	Total Effort 12

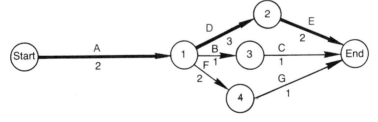

Possible Paths	Effort-Days Required
A—B—C	4
A—D—E	7
A—F—G	5

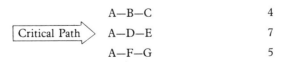

Minimum Schedule = Time Required for Critical Path
= 7 schedule-days

Figure 5.10
Alternative Network
Solutions to the
CPM Task List in
Figure 5.9.

Same Paths, Different Node Numbers (Correct Equivalent)

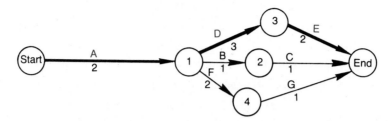

Different Path Layout (Correct Equivalent)

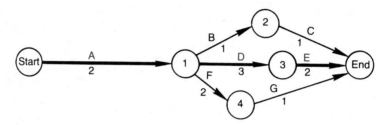

Inclusion of Nonexistent Activity (Incorrect)

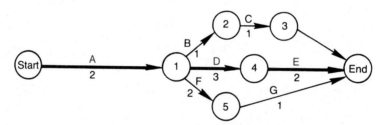

task, in a **PERT chart** you have three estimates: shortest possible time, most likely time, and longest possible time. These three time estimates provide a range of total required times. A formula may then be applied to come up with a single PERT estimate. Computer software is available to reduce the tediousness of this process. The time estimate derived from a PERT chart tends to be more accurate than a best-guess estimate.

5.3 Gantt Charts

Like a CPM network, a **Gantt chart** is a graphic tool for planning, monitoring, and coordinating.

5.3.1 Gantt Chart Definitions and Goals

The columns of a Gantt chart are labeled with dates. The duration of each activity is shown by a horizontal bar covering the allotted time period. Figures 5.4 and 5.6 are both

Gantt charts. You may copy the blank Gantt chart in Figure 5.11 to use for exercises and projects.

Figure 5.11
Gantt Chart Form

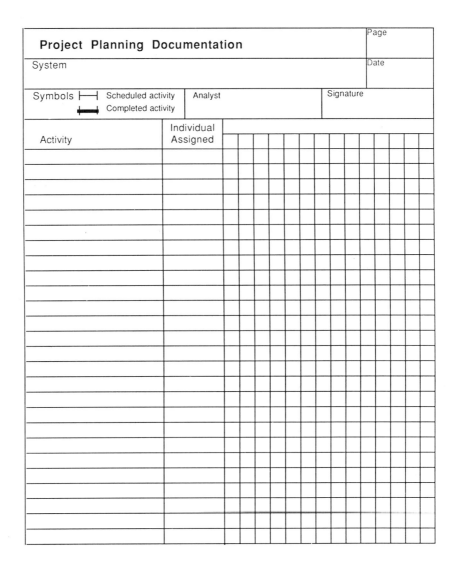

A Gantt chart shows detailed tasks more clearly than a CPM network does and includes a column for noting individual assignments. These additional details make the Gantt chart especially useful in allocating personnel resources and in monitoring completion schedules.

5.3.2 Gantt Chart Rules

The rules for constructing Gantt charts are summarized in Figure 5.12. Gantt chart symbols that distinguish scheduled activities from completed activities can help you to monitor projects. In Figure 5.13, a darkened scheduled activity line indicates completion of that task. By updating this chart each week, you can see whether activities are completed on schedule.

The uses of CPM networks and Gantt charts are illustrated in the minicase Word Processing Systems for *Outerspace* Magazine.

Figure 5.12
Rules for Gantt
Charts

1. Identify all tasks in the first vertical column.

2. For long task lists, use an outline format (work breakdown structure) and lettering sequence such as that shown in Figure 5.13.

3. Identify time periods (days, weeks) for each of the date columns, including dates whenever possible.

4. Use a time bar to show the time allotted for each task. (See the symbols in Figures 5.6 and 5.13.)

5. Darken the time bar as each task is completed. (For tasks that are past the projected time period, this may mean extending a dark bar, as illustrated in Figure 5.13.)

6. Identify individuals responsible for each task, when possible.

7. To improve your monitoring and coordinating efforts, list at least one measurable activity (milestone) per team member per week.

Figure 5.13
Gantt Chart Indicating
Progress

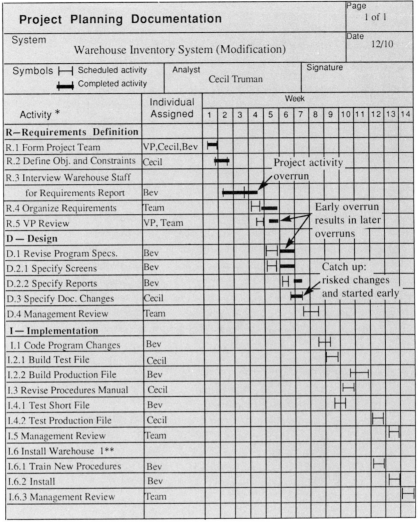

Project Planning Documentation		Page 1 of 1														
System Warehouse Inventory System (Modification)		Date 12/10														
Symbols ⊢⊣ Scheduled activity ▬ Completed activity	Analyst Cecil Truman	Signature														
Activity *	Individual Assigned	Week													
		1	2	3	4	5	6	7	8	9	10	11	12	13	14
R—Requirements Definition															
R.1 Form Project Team	VP,Cecil,Bev	⊢■													
R.2 Define Obj. and Constraints	Cecil		⊢■												
R.3 Interview Warehouse Staff															
for Requirements Report	Bev			⊢■⊣											
R.4 Organize Requirements	Team					⊢■									
R.5 VP Review	VP, Team					⊢■									
D — Design															
D.1 Revise Program Specs.	Bev						⊢■								
D.2.1 Specify Screens	Bev						⊢■								
D.2.2 Specify Reports	Bev						⊢■								
D.3 Specify Doc. Changes	Cecil						⊢■								
D.4 Management Review	Team								⊢⊣						
I — Implementation															
I.1 Code Program Changes	Bev								⊢⊣						
I.2.1 Build Test File	Cecil								⊢⊣						
I.2.2 Build Production File	Bev									⊢⊣					
I.3 Revise Procedures Manual	Cecil									⊢⊣					
I.4.1 Test Short File	Bev									⊢⊣					
I.4.2 Test Production File	Cecil											⊢⊣			
I.5 Management Review	Team												⊢⊣		
I.6 Install Warehouse 1**															
I.6.1 Train New Procedures	Bev												⊢⊣		
I.6.2 Install	Bev													⊢⊣	
I.6.3 Management Review	Team														⊢⊣

Project activity overrun

Early overrun results in later overruns

Catch up: risked changes and started early

* Weekly team reviews not shown here
** Repeat for warehouses 2 through 5

Word Processing Systems for *Outerspace* Magazine

Outerspace magazine is a monthly publication that specializes in science fiction with a technological bent. Scientific articles are also published. The magazine was founded by Bert Johnson and Doug Samson. The company now has a staff of seventeen employees, who are loyal and enthusiastic. The employees are proud to be producing a high-quality magazine without the fancy trappings of a big company.

As one of two fiction editors, Sheila Lee reviews twenty-five stories a week, and she is falling steadily behind. Reviewing twenty-five stories means dictating and proofing twenty-five letters: rejection, acceptance, or agreement to consider a revised submission. In past years she enjoyed writing encouraging letters, but now time pressure means curt letters: "Your story is rejected," "Your story is accepted," or "You can try again." Sheila

decided that she needed a word processing (WP) system. She met with Doug, the co-owner and business manager, to discuss her problem.

Sheila brought a computer advertisement to the meeting. "Doug, here's a $2,199 solution to some of my frustrations. What do you think?" Doug was skeptical of the price. How could a computer sell for only $2,199 when a new heavy-duty typewriter costs $1,000?

Doug knew that marketing had problems keeping up with the correspondence and that the circulation staff had complained about slow turnaround from secretaries. These problems seemed to indicate company growing pains. Neither Doug nor his partner, Bert, the editor-in-chief, wanted to hire additional staff. The building was already overcrowded with editors, marketing personnel, subscription services staff, and clerical support staff.

Figure 5.14

Results of Telephone Research on Word Processors (May 1989)

	Store			
	Business Computer Store	**Hi-Tech Center**	**Computer Technology**	**Advanced Solutions**
System Price with WP, Printer	$2199 (Special sale)	$1300	$3675	$3673
Computer	Tandy 3000 NL with UGA adaptor, UGM 200 monitor	Commodore Amiga	Macintosh SE	Macintosh SE 20 with standard keyboard
WP Program and Cost	WordPerfect 5.0 $449.00	Scribble $80.00	Microsoft Word $225.00	Microsoft Word $299.00
Printer Type and Cost	DMP 132 $219.95	Stan NX 1000 $250.00	Image Writer II $475.00	Image Writer II with cable $479
Comments	Desktop publishing, hard drive	Color monitor, excellent graphics, desktop publishing	Extended keyboard, hard drive, desktop publishing, graphics	Compact, hard drive, floppy

Figure 5.15
Project Team
Selection for the
Outerspace Magazine
WP Systems

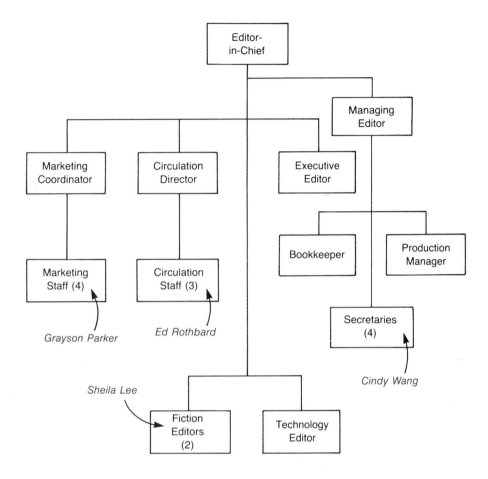

Word processing systems might prove beneficial to each of these groups.

Doug asked Sheila to do a market survey of microcomputer prices as an initial investigative step. The results of her market survey are summarized in Figure 5.14. Sheila admitted that the selection of word processing systems for the entire company seemed much more complicated than she had thought. She still felt that a computer was the answer, but she didn't feel confident about buying microcomputers and WP software for the entire company.

After talking with his partner, Doug decided that the investigation of WP systems should proceed. One of the marketing people, Grayson Parker, had worked as a systems analyst for a government agency before deciding that graphics design was a more rewarding profession. Doug asked Grayson to head the project team, with Sheila representing the editorial staff, Ed Rothbard representing circulation, and secretary Cindy Wang representing the clerical staff, as shown in Figure 5.15.

Grayson's knowledge of systems and the limited scope of WP systems meant he could plan fairly well early in the project. He constructed a CPM network of tasks and added time estimates for each of the tasks, as shown in Figure 5.16. The fourteen-week critical path is shown by the dark line. When Grayson met with the team to discuss their tasks, he said that the basic strategy would be to define the company's requirements and then go shopping. After they knew what their alternatives were, they would evaluate them and select the best one for *Outerspace*. They would design a company-specific solution around their purchases and then implement the systems for each staff member.

When the development team saw Grayson's CPM

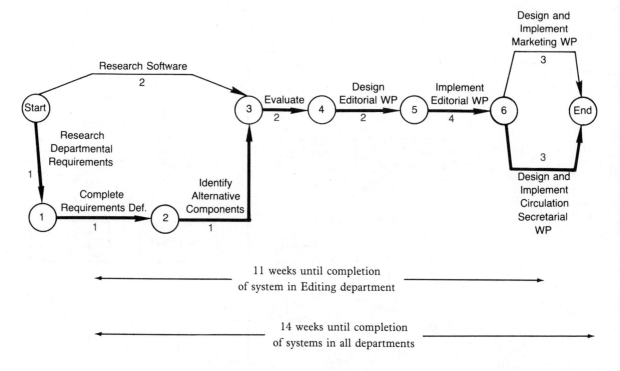

Figure 5.16 Critical Path Method Network for the *Outerspace* Magazine WP Systems

Time in weeks (very rough estimates; assumes part-time work, when other work allows break)

	People	**Procedures**	**Data**	**Software**	**Hardware**
Determine Requirements	Check interest at all staff levels	Research current correspondence procedures, esp. mass mailing	Research volume of typing dept.-by-dept.	WP package with good track record	Wait until WP package chosen
Evaluate Alternatives	Try for ease-of-use for all staff	Look for easy letter procedures and mail-merge	Have all this fit our publishing business	Identify top 2 to 5 and evaluate carefully	Identify types and capacity for top 1 or 2 choices

Figure 5.17
Example of Development Process Matrix for Early Planning for the *Outerspace* Magazine WP Systems

	People	Procedures	Data	Software	Hardware
Specify Design	Determine initial users	Investigate outside contractor to train and set co. procedures or design themselves	Organize drafts for basic letters to boiler plate, also addresses	Try warranty on hardware and software from single vendor	
Implement Design	Send 4 to 6 people to a local training class	Document naming procedures, file backup and recovery	Build boiler plates	Install and test For all basic letters	Prepare work spaces early install and test

Install and completely test for editorial, staff before implementing in other departments.

network, they protested that fourteen weeks seemed too long. Grayson explained the importance of doing a good job determining requirements before approaching the vendors. Since the fourteen-week estimate was based on immediate delivery, it might take even longer to install the systems.

Grayson explained the CPM network to the team members. The first machine was to go to Sheila at node 4 on the chart (Figure 5.16). He expected the editorial systems to be up and running smoothly for the editors at the eleven-week point (node 6). At that time they would introduce systems for the marketing and circulation departments. The systems would be phased in slowly so that mistakes would not be duplicated. At the end of the meeting, Grayson assigned Ed to do further research on word processing packages.

Figure 5.18
Checklist for Early Planning for the *Outerspace* Magazine WP Systems

Checklist of Activities for Development with Purchased Software

R—Requirements Stage

R.1 Identify Problem or Opportunity ◄——— set by Doug already
R.2 Form Project Team
R.3 Identify Objectives
R.4 Identify Constraints
R.5 Determine Functional Requirements ◄——— do department-by-department
    R.5.1 Define Current System (DFDs, I/O Summaries)
    R.5.2 List Functional Requirements of New System
R.6 Prepare Management Review Package ◄——— start by middle of second week
R.7 Obtain Management Approval ◄——— by end of third week

(continued)

E—Evaluation Stage

E.1   Identify Alternatives
    E.1.1   Identify Alternative Components ←——— Ed start now on calling people
    E.1.2   Identify Alternative Solutions   with WP systems they like
E.2   Evaluate Alternative Solutions
    E.2.1   Determine Criteria
    E.2.2   Rank and Weight Criteria
    E.2.3   Rate Alternatives
    E.2.4   Compute Composite Ratings
    E.2.5   Select One or Two Alternatives
E.3   Negotiate Purchase Agreement (with demonstration or warranty period)
E.4   Assess Feasibility of Chosen Alternatives
    E.4.1   Expand Cost and Schedule Details
    E.4.2   Summarize Solution-Problem Fit
    E.4.3   Document or Demonstrate Each Chosen Alternative
E.5   Obtain Management Approval ←——————— by end of fifth week

Project Planning Documentation		Page 1 of 3														
System Word Processing -- Phase I		Date 7/27														
Symbols ⊢⊣ Scheduled activity ⊢■⊣ Completed activity	Analyst Grayson	Signature														
Activity	Individual Assigned	Weeks													
		1	2	3	4	5	6	7	8	9	10	11	12	13	14
R—Requirements Definition															
R.1 Identify Objectives	Grayson	H													
R.2 Identify Constraints	Grayson	H													
R.3 Investigate Department Req.															
R.3.1 Marketing	Grayson	H													
R.3.2 Circulation	Ed	H													
R.3.3 Editors	Sheila	H													
R.3.4 Administration	Cindy	H													
R.4 Prepare Summary Report	Grayson		H												
R.5 Management Review															
R.5.1 Prepare Posters	Grayson	⊢—⊣													
R.5.2 Team Review	Team		H												
R.5.3 Management Review	Team, Owners			H											
E—Evaluate Alternatives															
E.1 Identify Alternatives															
E.1.1 Draw Chart of Alternatives	Ed				H										
E.1.2 Identify Best 3 to 5	Grayson					H									
E.2 Investigate Alternatives															
E.2.1 Visit User Sites	Team					H⊣									
E.2.2 Visit Vendors	Team					H⊣									
E.2.3 Negotiate Contracts	Ed, Grayson						H								
E.3 Management Review															
E.3.1 Prepare Summary Report	Team						H								
E.3.2 Present Best	Team, Owners							H							
2 or 3 Contracts								H							

Detail to this point corresponds to node 4 on Figure 5.16

Figure 5.19   Page I of Grayson's Gantt Chart

After the meeting, Grayson developed the matrix shown in Figure 5.17 to determine the activities for the project. He also used a basic checklist, which is shown in Figure 5.18. These planning work notes led to the Gantt chart in Figure 5.19.

The project team at *Outerspace* magazine was ready to begin development work. The team alternated between planning activities and early problem definition work until the plans were detailed enough for the four team members to proceed individually.

5.4 Planning Software

Many computer packages are available to reduce the tediousness of project planning. The principles we've discussed for drawing and reading CPM networks and Gantt charts apply directly to most computer versions of these planning aids. In some cases, data will be entered into a task list like the one shown at the top of Figure 5.9. An alternative is the graphic approach taken by Apple's project planning package MacProject. In MacProject, the first step is to draw a network, as shown in Figure 5.20. Tasks, drawn as nodes, are labeled with the starting date and the time required, and lines are drawn to identify task predecessors. From this network MacProject creates a table on which you enter the beginning project date, the duration of each task, and the individual assigned to each activity. MacProject then creates a Gantt chart, as shown in Figure 5.21. The *Outerspace* minicase project has been used as the basis for the graphics in Figures 5.20 and 5.21.

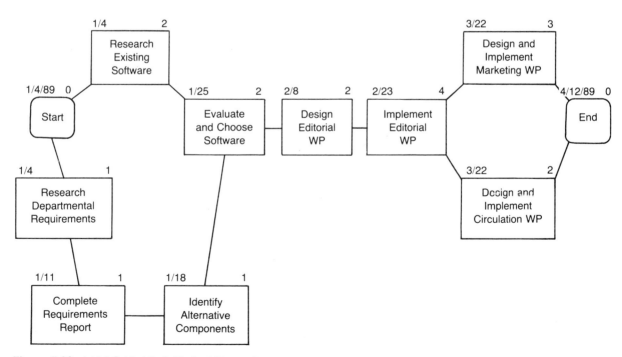

Figure 5.20 Initial Critical Path Method Network

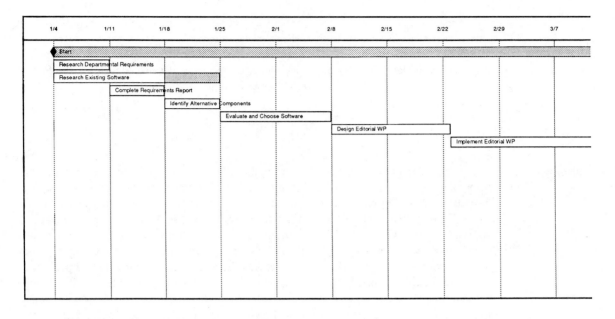

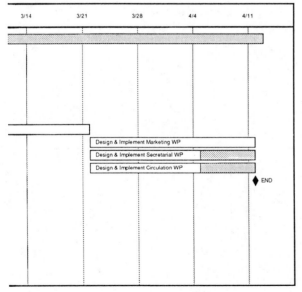

Figure 5.21   MacProject Gantt Chart for *Outerspace* Magazine Project (Shaded areas indicate slack time)

Summary

Planning is an integral part of the systems development process. CPM networks and Gantt charts are tools commonly used in the planning process. There are many computer programs available to help you create CPM networks and Gantt charts.

The first step in planning is creating a work breakdown structure, a hierarchical list of activities required to complete a system. Three approaches to structuring work activities are the checklist approach, the matrix approach, and the product delivery approach.

The CPM network is a graphic tool that shows task predecessors, simultaneous activities, and time requirements for projects. The objective of the critical path method is to determine the minimum time to project completion, which is the time required by the critical path. A CPM network is useful for determining activities for projects of any size. It is less helpful than a Gantt chart, however, for monitoring and coordinating these activities.

The Gantt chart is a graphic tool for project planning, monitoring, and coordinating. The Gantt chart communicates task details such as schedule and team assignments clearly and thus is better than a CPM network for managing large projects.

Key Terms

(Section numbers are in parentheses.)

work breakdown structure (5.1)	effort-months (5.2.2)
checklist approach (5.1.1)	minimum project schedule (5.2.2)
product delivery approach (5.1.3)	schedule-months (5.2.2)
critical path method (CPM) network (5.2.1)	slack time (5.2.2)
critical path (5.2.1)	PERT chart (5.2.3)
total project effort (5.2.2)	Gantt chart (5.3)

Note

1. Daniel S. Appleton, "Information Asset Management," *Datamation*, vol. 32, no. 3, February 1, 1986, pp. 71–76.

Exercises

(Answers to Exercises 5.1, 5.2, 5.9, and 5.10 are at the end of the book.)

5.1 Several tasks, their immediate predecessors, and the time in weeks (five-day work weeks) required for their completion are provided in Figure 5.22.

Figure 5.22

Task	Immediate Predecessor	Weeks
A	Start	2
B	A	1.5
C	B	2
D	C, G, H	3
E	A	4
F	B	3
G	E, F	1
H	A	4
Completion	D	

a. Draw a CPM network.

b. State the critical path as a list of activities, and draw the path on the network using a heavy or colored line.

c. What is the minimum project schedule (in schedule-weeks)?

    d. What is the total project effort (in effort-weeks)?

    e. Assume that work is started on Monday, January 10. Draw a Gantt chart to keep track of progress.

    f. Assume that any employee involved with the project can work on any activity. How could schedule project time be reduced?

5.2 Several tasks, their immediate predecessors, and the time in effort-days required for their completion are provided in Figure 5.23.

Figure 5.23

Task	Immediate Predecessor	Days
A	Start	2
B	A	3
C	B	1
D	Start	3
E	Start	2
F	E	2
G	D, F	1
H	D, F	1
I	H	2
Completion	C, G, I	

    a. Draw a CPM network.

    b. State the critical path as a list of activities, and draw the path on the network using a heavy or colored line.

    c. What is the minimum project schedule (in schedule-days)?

    d. What is the total project effort (in effort-days)?

    e. Draw a Gantt chart using Day 1, Day 2, and so forth, as header dates.

    f. Assume that any employee involved with the project can work on any activity. How could schedule project time be reduced?

5.3 Several tasks, their immediate predecessors, and the time in effort-days required for their completion are provided in Figure 5.24.

    a. Draw a CPM network.

    b. State the critical path as a list of activities, and draw the path on the network using a heavy or colored line.

    c. What is the minimum project schedule (in schedule-days)?

    d. What is the total project effort (in effort-days)?

    e. Draw a Gantt chart using Day 1, Day 2, and so forth, as header dates.

    f. Assume that any employee involved with the project can work on any activity. How could total project schedule time be reduced?

Figure 5.24

Task	Immediate Predecessor	Days
A	Start	2
B	A	3
C	A	1
D	C	3
E	Start	2
F	E, B	2
G	Start	1
H	G	1
Completion	D, H, F	

5.4 Several tasks, their immediate predecessors, and the time in effort-weeks (five-day work weeks) required for their completion are provided in Figure 5.25.

Figure 5.25

Task	Immediate Predecessor	Weeks
A	Start	2
B	Start	6
C	Start	2
D	C	3
E	A	4
F	B, D	3
G	B, D	1
H	G	4
Completion	E, F, H	

    a. Draw a CPM network.

    b. State the critical path as a list of activities, and draw the path on the network using a heavy or colored line.

    c. What is the minimum project schedule (in schedule-weeks)?

    d. What is the total project effort (in effort-weeks)?

    e. Assume that work is started on Monday, February 3. Draw a Gantt chart to keep track of progress.

    f. Assume that any employee involved with the project can work on any activity. How could total project schedule time be reduced?

5.5 In order to complete a client display center, three components have to be built, tested, and combined as outlined in Figure 5.26.

Figure 5.26

Task	Description	Immediate Predecessor	Days
A	General design	Start	9
B	Detailed design of component 1	A	5
C	Fabrication of component 1	B	4
D	Testing of component 1	C	2
E	Detailed design of component 2	A	7
F	Fabrication of component 2	E	4
G	Testing of component 2	F	0.2
H	Detailed design of component 3	A	8
I	Fabrication of component 3	H	4
J	Testing of component 3	I	2
K	Combined testing of 1 with 2	D, G	2
L	Combined testing of 1 and 2 with 3	J, K	2
	Completion	L	

a. Draw a CPM network for the construction project.

b. What is the critical path? Mark it on your network with a heavy or colored line.

c. What is the minimum project schedule (in schedule-days)?

d. What is the total project effort (in effort-days)?

e. Draw a Gantt chart using Day 1, Day 2, and so forth, as header dates.

f. Assume that any employee involved with the project can work on any activity. How could total project time be reduced?

5.6 Figure 5.27 gives the tasks, predecessor tasks, and estimated time requirements for the requirements definition stage of an effort to revise payroll processing.

a. Draw a CPM network.

b. What is the critical path? Mark it on your network with a heavy or colored line.

c. What is the minimum project schedule for the requirements stage, according to this estimate?

d. What is the total project effort?

e. Draw a Gantt chart using Day 1, Day 2, and so forth, as header dates.

f. Assume that any employee involved with the project can work on any activity. (1) How could total project time be reduced? (2) Is this realistic? (3) Why or why not?

Figure 5.27

Task	Description	Immediate Predecessor	Days
S	Start study phase		
A	Finance Division completes description of present system	S	10
B	Each division completes division objectives	S	4
C	Information Systems Division (ISD) completes constraints	S	5
D	Preliminary meeting arranged	A, B, C	2
E	Preliminary meeting held	D	1
F	ISD summarizes functional requirements	E	2
G	Finance reviews functional requirements	F	3
H	ISD researches off-the-shelf software	F	5
I	ISD completes feasibility study	H	3
J	Administrative review period	G, I	3
K	Revisions completed by ISD and Finance	J	7
L	Final presentation arranged	J	2
M	Management review held	K, L	1
	Completion	M	

5.7 The activity list in Figure 5.28 has been organized according to a work breakdown structure.

   a. Draw a CPM network.

   b. What is the critical path? Mark it on your network with a heavy or colored line.

   c. What is the minimum project schedule (in schedule-months)?

   d. What is the total project effort (in effort-months)?

   e. How could project time be reduced? The same programmer-analyst personnel can work on tasks under S and H plus D.1, D.3, and D.4. Data entry clerks will do D.2, and users will do all tasks under P.

   f. Draw a Gantt chart for development and implementation. Assume the project will begin Monday, October 1.

5.8 Assume that purchased software is available for the project described in Exercise 5.7.

   a. Redraw the network with the S—Software Development section revised as shown in Figure 5.29.

   b. List the activities on the critical path for the revised activity list.

   c. What is the minimum project schedule?

   d. What is the total project effort?

Figure 5.28

Task Description	Immediate Predecessor	Months
S—Software Development		
S.1 Program specifications	Start	2
S.2 Program coding	S.1	3
S.3 Program testing	S.2	2
S.4 Application testing	S.3, H.3, D.4, P.3	1
H—Hardware Development		
H.1 Equipment specifications	Start	1
H.2 Vendor selection	H.1	0.5
H.3 Equipment installation and testing	H.2	1.5
D—Data Development		
D.1 Data file specification	Start	1
D.2 Test files created	S.1, H.1, D.1	0.5
D.3 File conversion	D.1, D.2	3
D.4 Production file testing	D.3	1
P—Procedures Development		
P.1 Work procedure specifications	Start	2
P.2 Training specifications	P.1	2
P.3 Pre-installation training	P.2	2
Completion	S.4	

Figure 5.29

Task Description	Immediate Predecessor	Months
S—Software Development		
S.1 Alterations specified	Start	0.5
S.2 Alterations coded	S.1	0.5
S.3 Program testing	S.2	1.0
S.4 Application testing	S.3, H.3, D.4, P.3	0.5

5.9 Figure 5.30 describes the implementation of a point-of-sale system. This task table is for a five-day work week except for final installation tasks.

  a. Draw a critical path network.

  b. What is the critical path? Use a heavy or colored line to indicate it on the network.

Figure 5.30

Task Description	Immediate Predecessor	Effort
S—Software Development		
S.1 Write software	Start	14 weeks
S.2 Test software	S.1	4 weeks
P—Personnel Development		
P.1 Write user specifications	Start	1 week
P.2 Prepare training sessions	P.1	1 week
P.3 Train sales clerk user	P.2	1 week
D—Data Development		
D.1 Build new master files	Start	3 weeks
D.2 Test validity of master files	D.1	1 week
C—Customer Interface		
C.1 Write customer advertisements	Start	3 weeks
C.2 Print customer advertisements	C.1	3 days
C.3 Mailing time allowed	C.2	1 week
I—Systems Installation		
I.1 Weekend simulation	S.2, P.3, D.2	Sat. 8 A.M.–Sun. 8 P.M.
I.2 Changeover	C.3, I.1	Sun. 9 P.M.–Mon. 2 A.M.
Completion	I.2	

    c. What is the minimum project schedule?

    d. What is the total project effort?

    e. How could project time be reduced? Refer to specific tasks. Programming staff will be responsible for S, D, and I. The users will work on P and C.

    f. Draw a Gantt chart to keep track of progress. Plan the project for a starting date of Monday, February 4.

5.10 For the problem described in Exercise 5.9, assume that programs were purchased in the design stage and program development was limited to one week, as shown in Figure 5.31.

    a. Revise the critical path.

    b. List the activities on the critical path for the revised activities list.

    c. What is the minimum project schedule?

    d. What is the total project effort?

Figure 5.31

Task Description	Immediate Predecessor	Effort
S—Software Development		
S.1 Install software	Start	1 day
S.2 Build test files	Start	1 day
S.3 Test software	S.1, S.2	1 week

5.11 Consider the Gantt chart in Figure 5.6.

    a. Which activities are system product delivery points?

    b. Which activities are process delivery points?

    c. Which activities will be difficult to measure?

    d. Assume that a five-member team will work on the integration of the receivables system. Does this plan satisfy the Chapter 4 rule of thumb for the minimum number of milestones? Explain your answer.

    e. What justification could you offer for a below-minimum number of milestones?

5.12 Consider the Gantt chart in Figure 5.13. The project is for two team members, Cecil and Bev.

    a. Which activities are system product delivery points?

    b. Which activities are process delivery points?

    c. Which activities will be difficult to measure?

    d. Does this plan satisfy the Chapter 4 rule of thumb for the minimum number of milestones? Explain your answer.

    e. How adequate do you think the plan will be for the first fourteen weeks of the project? Justify your answer.

5.13 Consider the CPM network in Figure 5.16. This network was drawn to be used in a presentation to team members and management. Does this network satisfy the Chapter 4 rule of thumb for the number of activities on presentation displays? Explain your answer.

5.14 Consider Grayson's Gantt chart in Figure 5.19.

    a. Which activities are system product delivery points?

    b. Which activities are process delivery points?

    c. Which activities will be difficult to measure?

    d. Does this plan satisfy the Chapter 4 rule of thumb for the minimum number of milestones? Explain your answer.

    e. How adequate do you think the plan will be? Justify your answer.

5.15 Review the minicase Midtown Bank Trend Analysis in Chapter 2 and answer the following questions:

    a. Are Eric's phases based on subsystems or data capabilities?

b. Identify the data capability completed in each of Eric's three phases.

c. Is Eric's development process phased installation or just phased development? Explain your answer.

Project

5.16 Assume that you are to carry out the project in Exercise 1.14 with two other students. Assume that, in addition to creating the table and report for parts a and b, the three of you are to give a polished half-hour presentation on your findings. Complete the following tasks in order to *plan* these group activities as a two-week project.

a. Construct a task list using a work breakdown structure. Indicate the predecessor tasks and the time in effort-days required to complete each task. (Use a format like that of the activity lists in Figures 5.28 and 5.30.)

b. Draw a CPM network to show that you are making good use of the time of all three team members.

c. Complete a Gantt chart, giving the name of the team member responsible for each task and dates for the full two weeks. (Make up names and dates, unless your instructor has made this a group project and you have real partners and deadlines.)

Estimating Techniques

Overview

Estimating the effort required to develop a system is difficult. Even an imperfect estimate, however, is better than no estimate. This chapter discusses the goals for estimating and presents five estimating methods. For each method we specify what procedures to follow, when you should use the method, and what its limitations are.

Specifically, we plan to

1. Discuss guidelines for estimating. (Section 6.1)

2. Explain the procedures, appropriateness, and limitations of five estimating methods:

   the sum-of-tasks method (Section 6.2)

   the 3-times-programming rule (Section 6.3)

   the lines-of-code model (Section 6.4)

   the function point model (Section 6.5)

   the life cycle stage model (Section 6.7)

3. Alert you to some problems in developing a project schedule. (Section 6.6)

6.1 The Goals of Estimating Effort

In Chapters 2 and 5 we argued that a good plan is a necessary part of project management. An essential element of a good plan is a reasonable estimate for the completion of major milestones and changeover.

Estimating the effort required for a project is difficult because there are always many unknowns. You usually have to make early estimates without knowing the detailed requirements. Your project team members and their abilities may also be unknown. Effort estimates are, therefore, usually best guesses based on a series of best guesses about the project and staff resources.

In this chapter we provide several strategies for arriving at best-guess estimates. These methods are very simple, because using more complicated methods in the early part of a project would be a waste of time. Nonetheless, these simple methods can prevent a disaster of the magnitude of the one in the following minicase. In the minicase, the first time-to-completion estimate for a new system combining payroll and personnel functions was six months. As it turned out, changeover occurred two years later. This overrun represents a fourfold error in the time estimate; the budget estimate was off by a factor of more than five. The methods in this chapter would have provided a much better estimate of the effort and therefore the time required for this project, as well as a better basis for budget estimation.

A Payroll/Personnel System for Smith County

Smith County, with a payroll of 6000 employees, distributes paychecks every two weeks. In 1982 the Finance department staff decided that their present payroll system was inadequate to meet the county's evolving needs. The old system was entirely batch, having been written in the 1960s in COBOL. The Payroll staff decided that an on-line system providing easy access to personnel records would be a logical replacement.

A consulting firm, hired by Smith County to develop the system, tried to modify a canned payroll package. Well into the project, the consultants realized the impossibility of their task. The county's eight unions required so many exceptions to payment procedures that a canned software approach could not solve the problem. The project was abandoned for two years (Bubble A in Figure 6.1).

The next attempt began in 1984. The county's own Information Services department reviewed the scope of the task and estimated that the project could be completed in six months at a cost of $185,000, using a fourth generation database management system with its own language. After further requirements determination, however, the county analysts decided that their estimate was too optimistic. They upped the cost to $365,000 and the time to 10 months (Bubble B on Figure 6.1).

On the basis of the second estimate, the delivery target date was set for January 1, 1986. By September 1985, the requirements had been defined in detail; however, programming specifications had not even been started. Clearly, the January 1 deadline could not be met without additional staff. So a second consulting firm was hired to help the county's Information Services department complete the project (Bubble C in Figure 6.1). Although only 3½ months remained, the Payroll staff thought that the consultants could still complete the system by the January 1 target. The users' opinion of their own IS department was very low, and the relationship was quite strained. The users claimed, "The analysts are too slow. They're egotistical and can't communicate."

The consultants soon discovered that many design requirements had not been considered or even scheduled. There had been no file design, no test plan, no system architecture. There wasn't even a hierarchy chart for the on-line system menu control. The county analysts seemed to have little understanding of the capabilities or demands of an on-line system.

Programming finally began in November 1985 (Bubble D in Figure 6.1). At this point, the project was turned over entirely to the consultants, one county analyst, and five county programmers. The consultants and county staff worked together very little, however, which caused problems at installation, since the county staff did not know how to operate the system.

By January 1, much of the programming had been finished, but the system was far from completion. The installation date was extended to April 1, as indicated by Bubble E in Figure 6.1. The consultants began working sixty- to eighty-hour weeks in order to meet the new

Figure 6.1
Estimates and Final Cost for the Smith County Payroll/ Personnel System

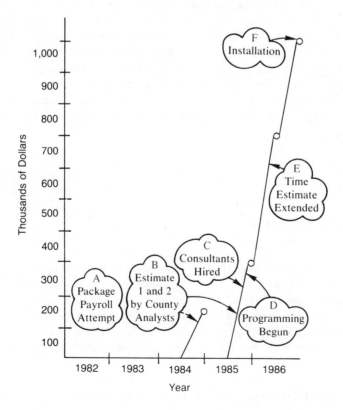

deadline. By April 1, 150 on-line programs and 50 batch programs had been written and individually tested, but all documentation had been postponed until after installation.

Integrated testing was the most poorly planned part of the project. The users had decided that the new system must deliver the same results as the old system, even if the old system was wrong. So the testing phase of the project consisted of running both systems in parallel and then comparing the results. After several parallel runs, the two systems were in unison. The users decided that the system should be installed on July 1, the first day of Smith County's fiscal year.

Although the parallel runs verified the accuracy of the new system, they did not test any of the hundreds of new system features. This testing was left for production. During the first four months of production use, debugging the system was a constant headache.

The system was finally completed and installed in July 1986, with a total development time of approximately two years and a price tag of over $1 million. Also, because of the limited involvement of the county analysts and programmers, the county was forced to pay two outside consultants for ten months of post-installation maintenance.

Source: Cary Peele, consultant, Austin, Texas. (This is a true story. The county name and a few details have been changed, but the scope of the project, estimates, and problems are all based on the consultant's experience.)

Estimating correctly would certainly not have prevented all the headaches for the users, county IS staff, and consultants in the Smith County minicase. The county probably would have developed a new payroll system even if the million-dollar price tag and two-year development time had been known in advance. But a reasonable initial estimate would have provided the basis for better resource planning.

The most costly errors in the payroll/personnel system project resulted from overlooking steps during planning. The county analysts assigned to this project simply did not know all the activities required to develop an on-line, integrated system. Any estimate of total project effort is bound to be wrong if important tasks are left out. Even extraordinarily careful estimating, however, cannot prevent system failure if the development process itself is inadequate. Good estimation is a predecessor to, not a substitute for, thorough requirements determination, evaluation, design specification, and implementation.

Estimating seems to be a step that either is not done at all or is overemphasized. Once again we stress the complementary nature of project management and systems development. Estimating project effort and schedule is essential for project management. The amount of time devoted to estimating should be commensurate with the project. You need to estimate the time and effort required by a project as reasonably as possible, without sacrificing system quality for estimating quality.

6.2 The Sum-of-Tasks Method

The **sum-of-tasks method** is a straightforward estimation method. Its procedures are implied by its name:

1. Determine all the tasks.
2. Estimate effort for each task.
3. Sum the individual estimates to arrive at an estimate for the total project.
4. Stick with the total, no matter how high it seems.

6.2.1 Procedures for the Sum-of-Tasks Method

Chapter 5 provided three approaches to the first step, determining the tasks:

- the checklist approach
- the matrix approach
- the product delivery approach

If your activities list is complete, much of your work is done. Often the greatest errors are caused by omitting steps, as the Smith County analysts did when they failed to schedule many of the basic design specification activities required in any large systems development project.

The second step, estimating individual task effort, requires experience. We recommend that inexperienced developers seek the advice of a reliable vendor, an experienced analyst, or an end-user consultant to complete this step. Otherwise, you must base your guesses on the most relevant experience you have.

The third step is one of simple addition: sum the individual effort estimates to calculate the total effort required for the project. Remember that although the schedule may be collapsed somewhat by having a team of developers work on multiple tasks simultaneously, many steps (such as the delivery of hardware or software) cannot be collapsed no matter how many people are on the team.

The last step may be the hardest: stick with the total, no matter how high it seems. If the estimated time is unacceptable and cannot be reduced by adding staff, then reduce the scope of the project. Do not reduce the total estimate to something "more reasonable" because of management pressure. Tom DeMarco talks about this problem of negotiating project length:

> I have sat through sessions in which estimates were haggled as at a bazaar: "Fifteen months." "No more than nine." "I can't do it in less than a year, no matter what." "My final offer is eleven months." "You got it." I have trouble keeping a straight face at such sessions. But I'm usually the only one; all others are deadly serious. They think that what they're doing is "estimating," and probably believe it helps them to hone their abilities. I think it is low comedy.[1]

6.2.2 When to Use the Sum-of-Tasks Method

You need to exercise caution when using the sum-of-tasks method to estimate effort for a custom development project. For these projects, estimating the effort required to complete each task is very difficult because it will depend on the nature of the project and the skill level of the team members. Furthermore, we know of no published guidelines to help you make these estimates. For these reasons, we recommend that only experienced developers use the sum-of-tasks method for custom development projects.

When developing systems based on existing software, even inexperienced developers can use the sum-of-tasks method effectively. By observing a few guidelines, you can minimize the risks of estimation. For example, if the software you need is not available at the time you select it, stipulate in your contract with the vendor that payment is contingent on the software's being available by a specified date. If the software has to be modified, make payment contingent on a bug-free installation. You should take advantage of the fact that software vendors, with their experience customizing and installing software, can estimate the effort required more accurately than you can.

The main problem that arises in planning for development with existing software is the failure to include necessary steps. The minicase Abby Clark and Her Turnkey System in Chapter 1 described a system that failed because the purchaser did not plan any evaluation, design, or implementation activities (training, file building, and so forth). Abby could have gone to a business systems vendor who would have helped her estimate her needs. Even better, if she had attended a trade association meeting for rental property managers, she might have had a chance to discuss systems with entrepreneurs who had similar problems and experience with different systems. One of her trade association contacts might have referred her to a consultant who had satisfactorily developed a system for another property manager facing the same constraints that Abby did.

An end-user experienced with a fourth generation tool may feel comfortable using the sum-of-tasks method to plan for a single-user system that uses the same 4GL tool. The end-user's estimates are likely to be fairly accurate. Even if they aren't, the risk is usually low, since such systems are relatively inexpensive.

For multi-user systems with programs developed with fourth generation tools, estimation with the sum-of-tasks method can be as difficult as for any multi-user system developed with a third generation language. Using a fourth generation tool will speed programming and allow incremental development, thus decreasing the risk of unpleasant surprises for users at changeover. Nonetheless, estimating effort for tasks such as designing files, constructing and validating software, and designing procedures for updating files will be very difficult. Similarly, the effort involved in designing and implementing procedures to ensure security, data integrity, and quick response time will be difficult to estimate. Unfortunately, there are no references to help you estimate effort for these activities, as far as we know. The solution for some organizations, as described for Taco Bell in the minicase in Chapter 2, is to have end-user consultants available at an information center. These consultants have gained expertise in estimating for a variety of end-user-developed systems as part of their project management role in the center.

6.2.3 An Example of Estimating with the Sum-of-Tasks Method

In Chapter 5 we provided several examples of detailed task lists: Figures 5.4, 5.6, 5.13, and 5.19. In this section we will employ an unrealistically short list, since our goal is to illustrate the procedures for this method, rather than to focus on the first step of arriving at a complete list. Let us return to Meadows Hospital to examine a smaller system than the prescription processing system developed in Chapter 3.

MINICASE

Developing a Spreadsheet Application for Meadows Pharmacy

Tito Hernandez, the assistant manager of the pharmacy at Meadows Hospital, was interested in installing a spreadsheet on the microcomputer that the pharmacy had acquired. He visited Tracy Bell, the analyst who had worked with him on the administrative system, and requested her advice. After asking Tito about his requirements for a spreadsheet, Tracy began to draw the rough CPM chart in Figure 6.2.

Tracy talked as she drew. "Okay, Tito, I know you have one specific use for a spreadsheet, and that sounds

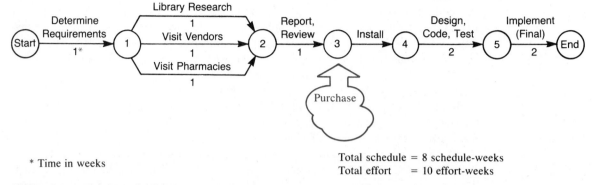

* Time in weeks

Total schedule = 8 schedule-weeks
Total effort = 10 effort-weeks

Figure 6.2 Rough Draft of Critical Path Method Network

like a valid requirement to me. Still, I think it would be wise to interview others in the pharmacy about their interests. I think we ought to spend a week interviewing other staff members to determine their requirements. If no one else is interested, I recommend the spreadsheet supported by our Microcomputer User Services group, which you can begin installing, designing, coding, and testing immediately. But if there is interest in several spreadsheet applications, we should at least investigate other spreadsheets. Maybe our standard spreadsheet has templates for pharmacy problems, or maybe some other spreadsheet would be better."

Drawing in three lines from node 1 to node 2 on Figure 6.2, Tracy continued: "If staff members have a variety of uses for spreadsheet applications, I recommend

spending a week looking into alternatives. Someone can check the library, someone else can talk to vendors, and a third staff member can visit some other pharmacies. All this evaluation work can take place simultaneously.

"Then we ought to allow a week to organize and report the results. Being optimistic, I'll include the review meeting and decision in the same week." Tracy drew a line from node 2 to node 3.

"Being even more optimistic," Tracy said as she drew in a line for a week from node 3 to node 4, "I'll assume that the spreadsheet you decide on is the one we already have in the hospital or one that we can purchase immediately, so installing and vendor testing can be completed in a week.

"Finally, let's leave two weeks for you to design,

		Effort		Schedule	
Task	**Weeks**	**Percent**	**Weeks**	**Percent**
Determine Requirements	1	10	1	12.5
Evaluate Alternatives	3	30	1	12.5
Purchase				
Report, Review	1	10	1	12.5
Install, Vendor Tests	1	10	1	12.5
Design, Code, Test	2	20	2	25
Implement Final System (Retest, Train, Document)	2	20	2	25
Totals	10	100	8	100

Figure 6.3 Effort and Schedule Summary for System, Developed Using the Sum-of-Tasks Method

code, and test the spreadsheet template and another two weeks for the final implementation, which will include your training the staff to update the spreadsheet regularly.''

At the end of the discussion, Tracy had a rough estimate for the development schedule, as shown in Figure 6.2. The minimum project schedule would be eight weeks, based on adding the rough estimates Tracy had

made for each individual activity. The total project effort would be ten weeks, which would also be the minimum schedule if only one person worked on the project. The total project effort and the minimum schedule for this example are compared in Figure 6.3. Notice that evaluating alternatives consumes three effort-weeks but only one schedule-week, because three people will work on this task simultaneously.

Tracy's on-the-spot sketch of a CPM network worked well to identify tasks and estimate effort and schedule for this simple project. Another method she could have used is a checklist, like the one in Figure 5.3, stored in a microcomputer as a spreadsheet or word processing template and altered for specific development projects. The process would still have been basically the same as in this example—determining all the individual tasks and summing them to arrive at an estimate of total project effort.

6.2.4 Limitations of the Sum-of-Tasks Method

The value of the sum-of-tasks method depends on your ability to determine all the activities required to develop a system and then assign a realistic effort estimate to each activity. After Tracy had made her optimistic rough guess for Tito, she would have been wise to draw another quick chart that included steps for such activities as waiting for a spreadsheet to be purchased. She also could have included the time it would take Tito to learn the spreadsheet before designing his own particular use. This more detailed plan of work could be completed immediately, or after the week of requirements determination had improved Tracy's knowledge of the system's scope.

A major limitation of the sum-of-tasks method is that it is only as good as your individual estimates. If you're a beginner working on a custom-developed system, one of the following methods may be more helpful.

6.3 The 3-Times-Programming Rule

Most analysts are former programmers. One of the problems with this career path is that the time you spend programming may narrow your vision so that you see an assignment as a programming task, rather than a project involving the development of all five components. On the other hand, one of the advantages of this route is that you gain a good sense of how much effort is required to develop particular programs.

One rule of thumb that has been in use for a long time is the **3-times-programming rule.**[2] With this method, you estimate how long it would take you to program the system and then multiply by 3 to estimate how much effort it will take to deliver a tested, documented system.

6.3.1 Procedures for the 3-Times-Programming Rule

The steps in the 3-times-programming rule are

1. Estimate the number of programs and their difficulty.
2. Estimate the effort required to complete the programs, including coding and debugging.

3. Multiply the time calculated in Step 2 by 3. This product represents an estimate of the total effort for a system developed with a third generation language.

4. If the system will be developed with a fourth generation tool, divide the programming effort calculated in Step 2 (*not* the total effort) by the factor by which programming productivity is improved. Subtract this amount from the original estimate calculated in Step 2 to derive the amount of programming time saving. Then subtract the amount saved programming from the total effort derived in Step 3 to estimate the total effort for the system.

The first step, estimating the number and difficulty of the programs, requires some knowledge of the application system to be developed, which may be provided by an area expert. The second step, estimating programming effort, is based on your own knowledge of how long coding and debugging programs takes. The third step, multiplying the estimate from Step 2 by 3, gives the best guess for the total system development effort using a third generation language. The fourth step adjusts your estimate for a system being developed with a fourth generation tool.

To illustrate the process, we will use the 3-times-programming rule to calculate an estimate for the system in the Smith County minicase. Let's say that a count of the programs in the existing payroll and personnel systems shows that there are 75 payroll programs and 32 personnel programs, for a total of 107 programs. Although the integration of the system will reduce that number somewhat, the new features desired will necessitate adding some new programs. A reasonable guess for Step 1 might be 110 programs. (The actual number turned out to be 200 programs because many on-line reports were added, but we are making these estimates from the perspective of a planner in the early stages of development.)

For Step 2, we might estimate that it would take three programmer-analysts a year to code and debug 110 programs in COBOL, for a total of three effort-years. (That would be three programs per programmer per month, which is pretty optimistic for creating debugged programs. But then programmers are usually optimistic about programming effort.)

The multiplication in Step 3 yields

```
3 programming effort-years × 3 = 9 development effort-years
```

Because the Smith County payroll/personnel system is to be developed with a fourth generation tool, however, the estimate needs to be adjusted. This estimate based on reprogramming the system in COBOL presumably overestimates the development effort, as there should be some gain in productivity with the database language. Assuming that productivity will increase by a factor of 3, we reduce the three effort-years of programming to 1 effort-year. Subtracting the one year programming effort with the 46L from the 3 year effort with COBOL, we have a saving of 2-effort-years. Subtracting 2 effort-years from 9 effort-years, we arrive at an estimate of 7 effort-years. Note that two-thirds the *programming* effort is saved, not two-thirds the *total* development effort.

6.3.2 When to Use the 3-Times-Programming Rule

The 3-times-programming rule is useful when you have little expertise in systems development but considerable experience in programming. All that is required beyond this expertise is enough information about the project to guess how many programs will be required and how complex they will be.

6.3.3 Limitations of the 3-Times-Programming Rule

One limitation of the 3-times-programming rule is that it provides only a rough guess. But that rough guess is better than a wild guess or no guess.

The estimate for the Smith County project derived from the 3-times-programming rule is much better than the Smith County analysts' first estimate of six months and second estimate of ten months. It would be almost impossible to compress a 7 effort-year project into a year, even with eight developers on the team. The time required to coordinate such a large full-time team would be too great. What the estimate should have been is hard to know, since the two-year delivery time in the minicase was based on the delivery of a system that was only partially tested and largely undocumented.

Another limitation of the 3-times-programming rule is that it is helpful only to experienced programmers who can estimate programming time fairly accurately. It provides little aid to the end-user developer.

6.4 The Lines-of-Code Model

The most common basis for estimation is lines of code. The best-documented and -researched lines-of-code model was developed by Barry Boehm.[3]

6.4.1 Procedures for the Lines-of-Code Model

There are two steps in effort estimation using the **lines-of-code model:**

1. Estimate the number of lines of code.
2. Calculate the total number of effort-months (EM) by solving the equation

   $$EM = 2.4 \ (KDSI)^{1.05}$$

   where KDSI is the number of thousands (K) of delivered source instructions.

   For example, assume that a system will require 10,000 lines of code, 10 KDSI. Completing the formula, we have

   $$EM = 2.4(10)^{1.05} = 2.4(11.22) = 26.9 \ or \ 27 \ effort\text{-}months$$

6.4.2 When to Use the Lines-of-Code Model

As its name implies, the lines-of-code model is useful only when you can estimate the total number of lines of code required to develop a system. The Boehm model and others in the literature were developed from studies of systems built with third generation languages, so their application is limited to third generation language systems. To obtain a rough estimate for systems built with fourth generation tools, you could follow the adjustment step suggested in the 3-times-programming rule.

6.4.3 Limitations of the Lines-of-Code Model

The main limitation of the lines-of-code model is that it depends on the accuracy of the lines-of-code estimate. If you have a poor estimate of the number of lines of code needed, you will have a poor estimate of the total effort for the project. Another problem with the lines-of-code model is that it does not take into account the resources available to the team (such as software tools) and the skills of the team itself (such as functional area experience). Experiments indicate that programmer productivity varies greatly. Boehm's own research on the lines-of-code model showed that the capability of the development team was the single biggest factor affecting completion time. (You should realize, however, that the sum-of-tasks and 3-times-programming methods are also limited by some theoretical and often very rough estimate of average performance. The people factor is always extremely difficult to estimate.) This factor and others, and their relative impact on project completion, are listed in Figure 6.4 in order of their effect on development time. For example, a high-quality team can complete a system about four times as fast as a very poor team. Modern programming practices, however, were found to be only $1\frac{1}{2}$ times faster than traditional methods.

Figure 6.4
Factors That Affect Completion Time for System Development

System Cost Driver	Relative Effect on System Cost
Personnel/team capability	4.18
Product complexity	2.36
Required reliability	1.87
Timing constraint	1.66
Applications experience	1.57
Storage constraint	1.56
Modern programming practices	1.51
Software tools	1.49
Virtual machine volatility	1.49
Virtual machine experience	1.34
Turnaround time	1.32
Database size	1.23
Schedule constraint	1.23
Language experience	1.20

6.5 The Function Point Model

An alternative method for estimating system development time is based on the functional requirements of a proposed system. The **function point model** is intuitively appealing in that the number and complexity of the functions that must be delivered are used to estimate the development effort.[4] (The complexity of each function is used as a weight in determining the time to be allotted to the function.) The best approach to using the function point model is to first build a record of projects at your organization and then develop a model specific to the experiences of your organization. To illustrate the use of a function point model, we will use historical data already accumulated.[5] Our purpose in using the particular items and values in this function point model is to provide concrete examples; the model should be tailored to the organization in which it will be used.

6.5.1 Procedures for the Function Point Model

There are five steps in estimating the total function points and the total project effort:

1. Categorize the functions according to type and complexity, and then estimate the number of functions in each category. (Categories might include simple input functions, complex input functions, simple output functions, and so on.)

2. Multiply the number of functions in each category by the appropriate complexity weight to calculate the number of function points for each category. Figure 6.5 is an example of a complexity weight scale for various categories of functions.

Figure 6.5
Complexity Weight
Scale

	Weight				
Function	**Simple**	**Moderate**	**Average**	**Complex**	**Highly Complex**
Input	2	3	4	5	6
Output	3	4	5	6	7
Master File	5	7	10	13	15
Inquiry	2	3	4	5	6
Interface	4	5	7	9	10

Source: Adapted from Steve Drummond, "Measuring Applications Development Performance," *Datamation*, vol. 31, no. 4, February 15, 1985, p. 104.

3. Total the number of function points for all categories.

4. Assign values to the project influencing factors and total them. Project influencing factors are factors that may contribute to the difficulty of the overall project.

5. Compute the effort-months by solving an equation reflecting the relationship of effort-months to function points and project influencing factors.

These steps are illustrated for a sample project in Figure 6.6.

The first two steps build a table which you can use to total the unadjusted function points. Column 3 of the table in Figure 6.6 gives the number of functions of each type and level of complexity. These numbers may be rough guesses or counts based on a review of a complete requirements document. Column 4 gives the appropriate complexity weight for each type of function, based on the weight scale provided in Figure 6.5. Multiplying the weight in column 4 by the number of functions in column 3 gives the function points for each type. Totaling these yields the total unadjusted function points.

The fourth step is to determine and quantify the effect of factors that influence the complexity of the entire system. Figure 6.6 lists the project influencing factors used by one organization.[6] (Some other factors that might be considered are presented in Figure 6.4.) Each of these project influencing factors can affect the difficulty of the overall project. For example, the more complicated the communication requirements are, the greater

Figure 6.6
Example of Function
Point Estimation

Steps 1, 2, and 3: Determine the type, complexity, and number of functions (columns 1, 2, and 3); multiply column 3 by the complexity weight (column 4) to obtain the function points (column 5); and total the function points.

(1) Function	(2) Difficulty Level	(3) Number	(4) Complexity Weight	(5) Function Points
Inputs	Moderate	2	3	6
Inputs	Complex	4	5	20
Outputs	Simple	3	3	9
Outputs	Average	6	5	30
Master files	Average	2	10	20
Inquiries	Simple	12	2	24
Interfaces	Moderate	4	5	20
Interfaces	Complex	18	9	162
			Total Unadjusted Function Points (FP)	291

Step 4: Evaluate project influencing factors (0 = little or no difficulty, 3 = average difficulty, 5 = great difficulty).

Communication facilities	0
Distributed processing	1
On-line processing	3
Data volumes and performance objectives	2
Complex processing logic	0
Multiple sites	5
Conversion difficulty	3
System flexibility	3
Total Project Influencing Factor Value (PIF)	17

Step 5: Calculate effort-months.

```
EM = .036 × FP × PIF
   = .036 × 291 × 17
   = 178.092 or 178 effort-months
```

the project effort. If no communication were needed between computers, you would assign the first factor a rating of 0, as was done in the example problem. If some data communication were required, but you expected the current communication facilities to be able to handle it with few or no changes, you might assign the factor a 1. Similarly, the other factors would be assigned values based on the likelihood that complications associated with them would extend the project effort. Once all the factors have been assigned values, these values are totaled.

The final step is to insert the computed values for total unadjusted function points and total project influencing factors into the following equation and solve it:

EM = .036 × FP × PIF

where EM is the number of effort-months, .036 is a constant, FP is the total unadjusted function points, and PIF is the total project influencing factor value. This particular equation is most accurate for projects in the four to six effort-year range. Estimates for longer projects were found to underestimate the actual effort at the organization where this equation was developed.[7] Shorter projects tended to be completed faster than estimates indicated.

6.5.2 When to Use the Function Point Model

An advantage of the function point model is that it makes intuitive sense to users. Whether the estimate is based on an early rough guess about the functions or a later, careful investigation of required functions, users can accept that a system with twenty screens will take longer to develop than one with fifteen screens. Comparing function point calculations is an effective way to quantify the difference. So long as the users are not misled about the precision of the estimates generated, function point models can improve communication between users and analysts.

The precision of the effort estimate derived from a function point model depends on how well the model fits the circumstances of a particular project. If an organization is converting a series of systems from one hardware environment to another, a function point model may be developed based on the first few systems and then used to estimate the time required for later systems. In this case, a very accurate estimate of the functions of the systems to be converted can be derived from the existing systems. In the more general case, an organization develops a function point model (similar to that given in Figures 6.5 and 6.6) based on its own methodology and a particular development tool. Once requirements have been determined, this model serves as the basis for an effort estimate.

If requirements have not been fully determined, a rough estimate of the functional requirements will yield only a very rough estimate of total effort, much as a rough estimate of the number of lines of code will provide only a very rough estimate of total effort. The accuracy of the estimates will improve steadily as requirements determination progresses. If data flow diagrams have been completed, then functions can be tallied fairly accurately from the diagrams and the estimates may be very accurate. (Data flow diagrams are explained in Chapter 10.)

6.5.3 Limitations of the Function Point Model

The model details presented here were derived from one organization's experience with twenty-nine projects.[8] The purpose of the model was to measure productivity, not to estimate a project schedule, so no claims are made for the accuracy of this specific model beyond those made for the 3-times-programming rule: any well-considered estimate is better than a wild guess or no estimate at all.

Although there are a number of computer programs available for estimating effort based on functional requirements, most of the published research examines function point models only as measures of productivity. This research shows that a function point model is clearly more appropriate than a lines-of-code model to compare the productivity of a team developing systems using a 4GL to that of a team using a third generation language.

The articles and books listed in the Notes section at the end of the chapter provide information on

- measuring productivity with function point models (Drummond, Leslie)
- building organization-specific models for estimating project schedules (DeMarco)
- additional references on function point estimation (Leslie)

Before you use a particular methodology to estimate the effort required to develop a system with a particular language, it is important to determine that the model is valid and has a reasonable range of accuracy.

6.6 The Life Cycle Stage Model

The research-based **life cycle stage model** allocates percentages of effort to the various stages for the average project.[9] The percentages used in this simple model, adapted to fit the REDI model stages, are depicted in the top pie chart of Figure 6.7. The bottom pie chart shows how the percentage for implementation is divided among three major implementation activities: construction, testing, and installation.

6.6.1 Procedures for the Life Cycle Stage Model

The life cycle model can be applied in conjunction with one of the other methods we have suggested to estimate the total project effort. After calculating a total effort estimate using the sum-of-tasks, 3-times-programming, or lines-of-code model, you determine an estimate for each stage by multiplying the total effort estimate by the percentage for that stage in the model. Consider a project estimated to require two effort-years. To estimate the duration of the requirements determination stage, you would multiply the total estimated effort (24 months) by the average percentage for that stage from the pie chart (13%):

```
24 months × 13% = 24 × .13 = 3.12 or 3 effort-months
```

Once a project is under way, the model can be used to estimate the effort required to complete the remaining tasks. Consider a project that has taken ten months from initiation to the end of program debugging. The amount of effort required to integrate, test, and install the system can be calculated from the model in a number of ways. One way is to set the ratio of months needed to percentage of system effort equal to a known ratio, and then solve for the unknown value. Following this procedure, you would calculate

$$\frac{X \text{ months}}{15\% + 5\%} = \frac{10 \text{ months}}{13\% + 8\% + 23\% + 36\%}$$

To solve for the unknown, multiply each side by 20 percent:

$$X = \frac{10(20)}{80} = 2.5 \text{ more effort-months}$$

Figure 6.7
Distribution of Effort
for Systems
Development with
Third Generation
Tools

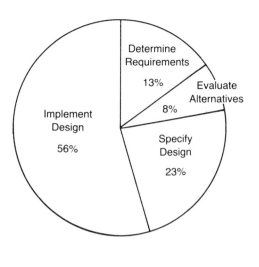

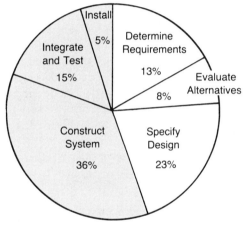

An alternative method for solving this same problem would be to first determine the total percentage completed:

```
13% + 8% + 23% + 36% = 80%
```

Since it took 10 months to complete 80%, each "percentage point" of the project required 10 months/80%, or .125 month. Multiplying this historically based estimate of months per percentage point by the percentage of the project remaining, we arrive at the same answer as above:

```
.125 month/% × 20% = 2.5 more effort-months
```

6.6.2 When to Use the Life Cycle Stage Model

The life cycle stage model is based on the percentage of effort expended at each stage. For this information to be useful to you as a project planner, you have to translate it into an estimate of schedule, given the characteristics of your project. For example, if the design stage normally consumes 23 percent of a project's effort, what does that mean in terms of time in your project schedule? How would that time change if two or more analysts were assigned to the design task? Any estimation based on this model will be only as good as your answers to these questions.

As its name suggests, this model is best suited to use with a sequential, life cycle approach. It can be used to estimate project effort under phased development, but the calculations will be more difficult; you will need to sum the sequences of REDI activities several times, since they are iterated. Estimating the effort required for integration and testing after the individual components have been constructed is still possible.

The main value of this method, like the others presented in this chapter, is preventing excessive optimism, an amazingly prevalent trait among systems developers. Perhaps we would never have chosen to be systems developers if we admitted to ourselves how much time development, particularly testing and revising, takes. Imagining that each new system will be completed without unpleasant surprises is perhaps only human nature.

6.6.3 Limitations of the Life Cycle Stage Model

Because the life cycle stage model is used in conjunction with one of the previous estimation techniques, the limitations on usefulness that apply to those techniques apply here as well. For example, whereas the life cycle stage model combined with the sum-of-tasks model invites disaster when used by an inexperienced developer, this combination can produce good estimates in the hands of an experienced developer estimating total effort for a routine project. When using the life cycle model, be sure to consider the potential drawbacks of the technique used to estimate total effort. After you calculate this total estimate, check your effort allotments to see if your stage activities roughly conform to this model. If they do not, you may want to consider whether you have underestimated or overestimated some of the individual activities.

6.7 Developing a Project Schedule

Now that you've seen how to determine total project effort using estimating techniques, you need to be able to map these estimations on a Gantt chart or CPM network, as discussed in Chapter 5. If you've estimated effort using the sum-of-tasks method, you already have a fairly detailed schedule, especially if, like Tracy in the Adding a Spreadsheet to the Pharmacy System minicase earlier in this chapter, you drew a rough draft of a CPM network as you planned your effort. You have already decided how much time each activity requires, so to develop your project schedule, you just need to identify concurrent tasks and determine how many people to assign to each task; then you'll have a good estimate of the project's schedule. If you're working from one of the rougher estimates of project effort, however, you first need to decide how much time to allot to each activity.

In contrast to the total effort consumed by an activity (effort-months), the total schedule time devoted to an activity (schedule-months) can be manipulated by concentrating personnel and other resources to complete that activity more quickly. For example, if coding and testing software for a new system requires twenty-four effort-months, it will also require twenty-four schedule-months if only one programmer is assigned to this task. But if two or more programmers can work on this task concurrently, you can substantially reduce the number of schedule-months required. Similarly, if you invest in a productivity tool to speed the coding or testing process, you may be able to reduce the number of schedule-months as well as effort-months.

Several difficulties arise when you go to plan a detailed project schedule based on your estimate of total effort-months. How do you convert from effort-months to schedule-months? Very optimistic systems developers just divide the number of effort-months by the number of people on the team. If a project is estimated to require fifty effort-months and five people will work on it, a total of ten schedule-months will be required, right? Not likely! Unfortunately, estimating a project schedule is not that easy.

In his classic book *The Mythical Man-Month,* Frederick Brooks points out several characteristics of systems development projects that make estimating schedule time more than a matter of simple division.[10] One of these factors, the probability of multiple events, is relevant to any plan that requires the completion of multiple tasks. Assume that the probability of your team's completing each task on schedule is .9. Assume also that ten tasks (a pitifully low estimate) must be completed to achieve changeover and that beginning one task is not dependent on completing a previous task. The statistical laws of probability tell us that the likelihood that all ten will be completed on time is $.9^{10} = .35$. Not exactly the kind of odds you'd want to bet on! So you must develop the habit of overestimating the amount of schedule time needed, to compensate for the likelihood that at least some tasks will overrun their allotted time. Estimate at least fourteen to sixteen schedule-months for the fifty-effort-months/five-people project mentioned earlier.

A second factor to consider is that many tasks must be completed sequentially, so no matter how many people work on a project, not all tasks can be performed at the same time. These sequential tasks form the critical path on a CPM network. If the CPM network for our fifty-effort-month project has a critical path of fifteen effort-months, the project will require at least fifteen schedule-months. The estimate of project schedule can be reduced further only if assigning more developers to one of the sequential tasks will speed its completion. For example, if the task of writing user documentation can be subdivided into writing the procedures manual and writing a reference manual, the project schedule can be reduced by assigning two people to work on these tasks simultaneously. The ability to recognize which tasks can be subdivided is a useful skill for a project planner.

The CPM network can also help you apply another Brooks rule of thumb: the maximum number of people that should be assigned to a project is equal to the maximum number of concurrent, independent tasks. Thus, in our hypothetical example, if at most only three tasks are concurrent and independent, we should assign three, not five, people to our project and increase our estimate of time to a minimum of eighteen schedule-months.

The last of Brooks's factors we will discuss is one of the most important and least recognized facts about development projects. Contrary to common belief, the relationship between the number of people assigned to a project and the amount of time a project requires is *not* linear. Figure 6.8 shows two line graphs. Graph (a) illustrates the "mythical man-month" relationship; graph (b) approximates the relationship between team size and project schedule. Notice two features of the second graph:

1. Project time is *not* reduced in direction proportion to increases in team size.

2. As team size grows larger, the proportion of time saved becomes incrementally

Figure 6.8

The Relationship between Team Size and Schedule Time

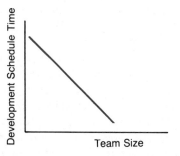

(a) The myth: The minimum schedule drops linearly as team size increases.

(b) The reality: Schedule time drops curvilinearly as team size increases.

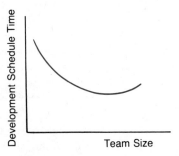

smaller, until adding another team member actually *increases* the amount of time required.

What accounts for this relationship? **Management overhead.** As the team increases in size, the amount of time needed for the management overhead activities of coordinating, monitoring, planning, and reviewing increases. When adding another team member increases management time more than it decreases development time, a net increase in project time results. Among experienced systems developers, a team size of four or five full-time developers is considered optimal; adding more team members often seems to be at least as much of a hindrance as a help!

In spite of all the difficulties involved, there are many times when it is necessary to make a rough estimate of a minimum schedule. Let's say two experienced programmer-analysts will be working on a project that you have estimated will take twenty-one effort-months. You might estimate the minimum schedule by first estimating the effort division between programming and other tasks.

```
Programming effort  =   7 months
Remaining effort    =  14 months
Total effort        =  21 months
```

Note that programming effort was estimated at one-third of the total effort, in keeping with both the 3-times-programming rule and the life cycle stage model. (The total of 56 percent for implementation in the life cycle stage model includes testing, documenting, building data files, installing, and so forth, as well as programming.)

The next step would be to estimate a reduction for each type of effort. The programming part of the schedule is where you can usually count on the most gains. You might estimate the minimum programming schedule by dividing the seven months of effort in half for the two people: $7 \div 2 = 3.5$. Then add extra time for necessary coordination of efforts:

```
3.5 + .5 = 4 months
```

You might decide that the schedule for the remaining effort could not be reduced by half, since there would be a greater need for coordination during the decision-making stages of determining requirements, evaluating, and designing. Also, there would be more nonsequential waiting, especially for user reviews and management decisions. Thus you might expect the remaining schedule to take 75 percent as long, rather than the 50 percent (factor of 2) used for programming:

```
14 × .75 = 10.5 or 11 months
```

The resulting minimum schedule estimate would be

```
4 + 11 = 15 schedule-months
```

If you had three experienced programmer-analysts, you might estimate the steps this way:

```
(7 months programming ÷ 3) + overhead = 2.33 + .67 =  3
(14 months remaining × .50) + overhead=   7 +   1 =  8
                        Total Schedule Estimate = 11
```

What if one of the team members was inexperienced and could help only with programming and minor tasks? In that case you might calculate the nonprogramming schedule at 75 percent, as we did for two experienced programmers:

```
3 months programming + 11 months remaining = 14 months
```

What if all three developers needed training in the programming language? Or none of the development team had experience in the application area? The answers to these types of questions will affect your estimates.

Ideally you will have time to apply the sum-of-tasks method and to create a CPM network and Gantt chart in order to make accurate effort and schedule estimates. When you just need rough estimates at the early stage of a project, however, these rules of thumb may provide better estimates than your quick optimistic first guess.

Summary

Estimating task effort is an important part of the planning process. This chapter presented five techniques for estimating total project effort. Which method is appropriate depends on the situation.

The sum-of-tasks method is useful to an experienced analyst or project leader. With this technique, you list all the tasks and then estimate the effort required for each. Finally, you add the effort estimates to determine the total effort for the project. If some of the activities can be performed simultaneously, the minimum project schedule will be less than the total project effort.

The 3-times-programming rule is valuable if you have extensive programming experience and can estimate the effort required for programming the system. The first step is to list the necessary program modules. Next you estimate how much effort will be needed to code and debug the programs. Finally, you multiply the programming effort by three to determine the estimated total project effort.

The lines-of-code model is the most common estimation technique. First, you estimate the number of lines of code required for the system. Then you calculate the total project effort using the formula provided in this chapter or another formula that has been developed by your organization based on its experience with previous projects.

The function point model provides an intuitively appealing method for estimating development effort, since it is based on the complexity and number of functions that must be delivered. First, you determine the type and complexity of each required function. Then you calculate the total project effort using the weighting factors provided in this chapter or weights determined from a historical study of projects completed by your organization.

The life cycle stage model allows you to estimate the effort required for each stage of the development process. If the sum-of-tasks method has been used to arrive at an estimate of total effort, then the baseline percentages from the life cycle stage model can be used to check the effort allocated to various development stages in the estimating process. If the 3-times-programming or lines-of-code technique has been used, the life cycle stage model percentages can be used to derive effort estimates for the various stages from the total estimate.

Estimating is an important but difficult task. The tools presented here are by no means perfect, but the estimates they generate are much better than no guess at all or a guess based on myths about team size and project schedule. Once you have finished your estimation, document your planned schedule and use it to monitor, coordinate, and review your team's progress. Unreasonably short estimates produce unreasonable stress. Unreasonably long estimates waste resources. Knowing how to make reasonable estimates is crucial for success in systems development.

Key Terms

(Section numbers are in parentheses.)

sum-of-tasks method (6.2)	function point model (6.5)
3-times-programming rule (6.3)	life cycle stage model (6.6)
lines-of-code model (6.4)	management overhead (6.7)

Notes

1. Tom DeMarco, *Controlling Software Projects* (New York: Yourdon Press, 1982), p. 12.

2. Barry Boehm, *Software Engineering Economics* (Englewood Cliffs, N.J.: Prentice-Hall, 1981), p. 64.

3. Ibid.

4. Steve Drummond, "Measuring Applications Development Performance," *Datamation*, vol.

31, no. 4, February 15, 1985, pp. 102–108. See also Robert E. Leslie, *Systems Analysis and Design: Method and Invention* (Englewood Cliffs, N.J.: Prentice-Hall, 1986).

5. Drummond, "Measuring Applications."

6. Ibid., p. 104.

7. Ibid., p. 108.

8. Ibid., pp. 102–108.

9. Boehm, *Software Engineering*, p. 65.

10. Frederick P. Brooks, Jr., *The Mythical Man-Month* (Reading, Mass.: Addison-Wesley Publishing, 1982), pp. 14–26.

Exercises

(Answers to Exercises 6.1, 6.2, 6.3, 6.7, and 6.8 are at the end of the book.)

6.1 Ann A., a programmer-analyst, estimates that she will need ten months to code and debug the COBOL programs for a cash receipts and point-of-sale processing system to interface with the current invoicing system. Her ten-month coding estimate is based on a short statement of the functional requirements and an assumption that she can complete the system without any requests for revisions by users.

    a. How many effort-months will the total project require?

    b. What is the basis of your answer?

    c. Assume that a second experienced developer is assigned to this project. What is your best estimate of the minimum project schedule time?

    d. Justify your answer to part c.

6.2 a. If Ann A. (in Exercise 6.1) guesses that the cash receipts and point-of-sale system will require twenty-two COBOL programs, for a total of 13,000 lines of code, what is your best estimate of the effort required for system development?

    b. What is the basis of your answer?

    c. Assume that two experienced developers are assigned to help Ann on this project. What is your best estimate of the minimum project schedule time?

    d. Explain your answer to part c.

    e. Assume that a 4GL is to be used to complete this system instead of COBOL. If coding with this 4GL is supposed to be four times as fast as coding with COBOL and Ann knows the 4GL well, what is your best estimate of the total number of effort-months required to develop the system?

    f. Explain your answer to part e.

    g. What is your best estimate of the number of schedule-months required for Ann and the two experienced developers to complete the system with the 4GL described in part e? Assume that all three developers are experts in this 4GL.

    h. Explain your answer to part g.

6.3 A programmer-analyst has worked ten months to plan, define, and complete a detailed design for a transaction processing system.

a. Assuming only the task of implementation remains, use the life cycle approach to determine how many more effort-months are likely to be required until completion.

b. What is the basis of your answer?

c. Assume that a second experienced developer is assigned to this project. What is your best estimate of the minimum project schedule time?

d. Explain your answer to part c.

e. Assume that two experienced developers join the original programmer-analyst to complete the system. What is your best estimate of the minimum schedule time required to complete the system?

f. Explain your answer to part e.

6.4 Bob B., a programmer-analyst, estimates that he will need four months to code and debug the COBOL programs for a customer order-entry system. His four-month coding estimate is based on a short statement of the functional requirements and the assumption that he can complete the entire system with little or no user interaction.

a. How many months of effort is it likely to take Bob from project initiation until changeover is completed?

b. What is the basis of your answer?

c. Assume that a second experienced developer is assigned to this project. What is your best estimate of the minimum project schedule time?

d. Explain your answer to part c.

e. Assume that two experienced developers join the original programmer-analyst to complete the system. What is your best estimate of the minimum schedule time required to complete the system?

f. Explain your answer to part e.

6.5 a. If Bob B. (in Exercise 6.4) guesses that the customer order-entry system will require seven COBOL programs, for a total of 8000 lines of code, what is your best estimate of the effort required for system development?

b. What is the basis of your answer?

c. Assume that two experienced developers are assigned to help Bob with this project. What is your best estimate of the minimum project schedule time?

d. Explain your answer to part c.

e. Assume that a 4GL is to be used to complete this system instead of COBOL. If coding with this 4GL is supposed to be three times as fast as coding with COBOL and Bob knows the 4GL well, what is your best estimate of the total number of effort-months required to develop the system?

f. Explain your answer to part e.

g. What is your best estimate of the number of schedule-months required for the three experienced developers to complete the system with the 4GL described in part e? Assume that all three developers are experts in this 4GL.

h. Explain your answer to part g.

6.6 A programmer-analyst has worked nine months on a COBOL system. The programs are debugged. The integrated system is about to be tested.

    a. How much more effort (in months) is likely to be required for testing and installation?

    b. What is the basis of your answer?

    c. Assume that another developer is assigned to this project. What is your best estimate of the minimum project schedule time?

    d. Explain your answer to part c.

6.7 Imagine that you are a systems analyst in the Information Services department of a state agency that regularly handles a variety of requests. The department has received the following request from a user:

We need an automated system to handle licensing of pet stores. I have been responsible for licensing barbers, and now my boss has asked me to take responsibility for licensing pet stores also. We have six months to get this up and running before the new state law is in effect.

Assume that you will alter copies of your COBOL barber licensing programs for this system. Based on this limited information, complete a Gantt chart that includes *at least* fifteen activities. Assume that you will begin on May 15. Use columns representing half-months or weeks. Schedule times for each activity in order to meet the six-month deadline.

6.8 Read the following case study on planning for the development of a marketing analysis system, and then answer the questions at the end.

Situation The vice-president for Marketing of Stafford Plastics, Inc. has requested that the Information Services division (ISD) develop a marketing analysis system to help with decisions about product development and advertising. The current sales analysis system provides a wealth of information on the sales force and customers in each region. The VP envisions a system that uses this data plus external information about manufacturing areas that are heavy users of plastic products. The ISD director has assigned a project team to look into the costs and benefits of such a system.

Team Members

Tom A.: MBA graduate who has worked in the Stafford marketing R&D group for three years: the marketing analysis system request is actually an outgrowth of suggestions he made to his boss, the R&D director.

Mo F.: Programmer-analyst responsible for maintaining the sales analysis system; has six years of experience in ISD.

May H.: Programmer-analyst who has been with ISD six months.

Constraints The core of the system (that is, the basic processing programs) should be in COBOL, since Stafford's DBMS has query and report generation capabilities but no full-service 4GL. Also, the sales analysis system is in COBOL.

Additional Information on the System and Stafford Plastics There are sixteen regional offices. Each has its own sales force and some autonomy over product choices and sales goals. Tom wants a system flexible enough to vary somewhat across regions.

    The sales analysis system consists of thirty-two COBOL programs with interactive data entry, some query capability, and both weekly and monthly batch report runs. Mo guesses (based on just a fifteen-minute talk last week with Tom about his idea) that the core of the proposed system will be about half this size, but a greater variety of report runs will be required. Her best guess is that the average program will have about fifteen to seventeen pages of source code, or about 1,000 lines.

a. Make a rough estimate of the total effort and schedule required for this project and state the basis for your estimate. (Do this quickly, based on just the information given.)

b. Create a three-column table that explains your strategy for meeting each of the information systems goals and subgoals for the proposed marketing analysis system. The first column lists the goals (system quality, project management, and organizational relevance) and subgoals (functionality, etc.) as summarized in Figure 2.7. The second column is a fact from the case study that justifies your concern or lack of concern for the particular subgoal. The third column is a list of activities to meet each of the subgoals. The table is started below

Information System Goal and Subgoal	Relevant Case Issue	Activity Planned to Meet Subgoal
SQ — Functionality	Determining all the desired functions to meet Tom and the VP's goals here is likely to be tricky, since this is a strategic system that cannot be based on any existing systems at Stafford Plastics.	Allow time for interviews and as much research as possible to determine the functions that will meet the system objectives.
SQ — Maintainability	etc.	etc.

c. Complete a development process matrix to aid in planning and requirements definition. It should be based on the very limited information you have.

d. Assume that the team has $3\frac{1}{2}$ work days to prepare for a management review of costs and benefits. Complete a Gantt chart listing the tasks for the Stafford project team for these $3\frac{1}{2}$ days. This chart should show the name of the member assigned to each task. The afternoon of the fourth day will be divided between a team review and the presentation to management. Include these activities in the Gantt chart also.

e. Complete a one-page CPM network that illustrates your plan for completing the *entire* system. It should be suitable for presentation to management.

(Note: Part d involves detailed planning for an early management review. Part e calls for general planning for the entire project.)

6.9 If all you have to go on is a best guess that a system will require about 12,000 lines of PL/1 (a third generation language), what is your best guess for the required effort for total system development?

6.10 a. If all you know is that it took you three months to revise a COBOL oil and gas package for your first client, and two months to revise it for your second client, what is your best guess for your third client?

b. Justify your answer to part a.

6.11 The only task you have left is integrated testing. It has taken a year to get to this point. How much more effort will be required to reach changeover?

6.12 You think you could program a menu-driven grading system for yourself in twenty to thirty hours. What is your best guess for the effort required to prepare this system for distribution to six other faculty members? Explain your answer.

6.13 Reread the minicase A Consultant's View of a Project Management Mess in Chapter 4, and then answer the following questions.

   a. Estimate the total project effort for the on-line customer service system ("10 subsystems . . . at least 400,000 lines of code")>

   b. Use the MIS director's figures on labor-hours (what we call effort-hours) scheduled for the transportation system to estimate the total project effort required to develop the transportation system.

   c. Discuss this minicase in terms of the difficulties of project scheduling. Consider problems caused by tasks that must be completed sequentially and the "costs" (in development time) of management overhead.

   d. Given that the customer service system can be partitioned into ten subsystems, what is the minimum number of members you would assign to its development team? How would use of a team of this size affect the minimum project time? (Use your total project effort estimate from part a and your knowledge of scheduling problems to make this estimate.)

6.14 Estimate the effort-months required for a proposed forecasting system that will have a total of six data input forms (half are complex, half simple), fourteen reports (all average), and three master files (one complex, two average). The performance of this very high volume batch processing system must be consistently efficient. The logic is highly complex.

6.15 Estimate the effort-months needed for a proposed transaction processing system that will have a total of sixteen data entry screens forms (roughly a quarter of them simple, the rest complex), twelve basic inquiry formats, eighteen reports (two complex, the rest average), and one main master file, which is complex. The involvement of eight different sites is expected to create numerous complications, as will the enhancement of communication facilities. The system needs to be very flexible, since changes are likely to be frequent.

3

Requirements
Determination
Activities

Requirements Determination Overview

Overview

One characteristic of a good systems analyst is the ability to shift from one perspective to another and, in the process, to construct an adequate view of the total system and its five components. This ability is especially important in requirements determination. If we think of a problem as the difference between what is and what ought to be, we see that requirements determination is basically the process of determining what the current information system does and what users think it ought to do.

The tasks of synthesizing the many user perspectives and defining the current and proposed systems place many demands on an analyst. The analyst must have very good interpersonal and communication skills in order to learn from users what the current system does and what functions the proposed system must perform. In addition, the analyst must understand the organization and the role played by the proposed information system. As the job title implies, the analyst must also have excellent analytical skills. Finally, the analyst must be a bit of a juggler, capable of balancing the goals of systems development and the multiple, often conflicting viewpoints of users.

Chapter 7 is an overview chapter in which we acquaint you with the basic activities of requirements determination and alert you to some of the concerns an analyst must address during this stage. Specifically, we plan to

1. Define requirements determination and relate it to the three goals of systems development. (Section 7.1)

2. Introduce the tools and structured techniques of requirements determination: context diagrams, data flow diagrams, data models, and process specifications. (Section 7.2)

3. Discuss the activities of requirements determination. (Section 7.3)

4. Present strategies for managing the requirements determination process and provide guidelines for choosing a good strategy mix. (Section 7.4)

7.1 The Importance of Requirements Determination

Requirements determination is the set of activities performed to gain an understanding of a problem. It provides a systematic way of structuring a definition of the current and required systems and identifying the objectives of and constraints on its development. These activities are managed so as to support the three goals of systems development: system quality, project management, and organizational relevance.

7.1.1 System Quality

Requirements determination supports the goal of system quality by defining the characteristics and functions of the required system. Understanding these requirements fully and accurately is vital to the development of a high-quality system. In many ways, this first stage of requirements determination is the foundation on which the system is built; misperceptions and ill-defined needs now will yield a poor system later. Many studies have shown that the number one cause of project failure is inadequate determination of requirements: you can't design or implement a high-quality system if you don't know what is required!

As you perform the requirements determination activities, you need to keep in mind the three characteristics of a quality system: functionality, ease of maintenance, and flexibility. Review the detailed definitions given in Figure 2.3, and plan to address all these characteristics as you define the requirements of the proposed system. The guidelines and techniques offered in this chapter and in Chapters 8 through 11 will help you achieve the goal of system quality.

7.1.2 Project Management

If the requirements determination stage is poorly managed, the system will likely be late and over budget and will not satisfy its objectives. Good management of this stage requires attention to the information gathered as well as coordination of the activities performed.

The requirements determination activities support the goal of project management by identifying the objectives and constraints of the systems development project and by involving the user in the development process. **System objectives** are the goals or end results that you hope to achieve as you develop a system; **system constraints** are the limits placed on resources for the development and production of the system. Your task as a systems analyst is to achieve as many of the objectives as possible within the constraints that you face.

A well-managed requirements determination stage provides a good foundation for the rest of the development activities. You can build a good foundation by

1. Establishing a good development team
2. Building a positive relationship with users and increasing their commitment to system success
3. Defining the expected costs and benefits of the development effort
4. Presenting the requirements effectively in both oral and written reports

The guidelines and techniques offered throughout Part 3, especially Section 7.4 of this chapter and all of Chapter 12, will help you perform these management tasks effectively.

In addition to building a good foundation, you need to establish milestones for delivering requirements process products. As you'll see later, many documents and graphic representations are generated in this stage. You'll want to avoid dumping all these documents on the users at one time; instead, keep your process product deliveries small and use them to educate users. Schedule frequent user reviews, perhaps on a one-to-one basis, to verify your understanding and to build each user's trust. Then culminate your requirements determination activities with a full-scale user and management review at which you summarize your findings. Setting milestones for the completion of process products will also help you define a schedule and decide when to stop your investigation. Without a schedule, your requirements determination activities may drag on forever, for there's always another piece of information that could be gathered and another requirement that could be clarified further.

The obvious consequence of poor requirements determination is a system that fails to meet the users' needs. A less obvious but more serious consequence is loss of the users' trust. To build trust, communicate clearly, correctly, and comprehensively with users and try to meet their needs within a reasonable amount of time. If the requirements determination activities are incomplete or inaccurate, users will lose confidence in the development team and in the development process. This loss of trust will affect not only the current, short-term development activities, but also the users' long-term attitude toward information systems technology and personnel. In extreme cases, users may become hostile or may isolate the information systems group from the mainstream of organizational activities; sometimes users will even sabotage the information system itself. Thus, one cannot overestimate the importance of getting off to a good start in the requirements determination stage.

7.1.3 Organizational Relevance

The activities of requirements determination support the goal of organizational relevance by clarifying both organizational and system objectives. By placing the information system in the wider context of the organization, the analyst can align the system's objectives, constraints, and requirements with those of the organization. This orientation is known as the **top-down approach** to requirements determination.

The top-down approach recognizes that there are at least three levels of requirements in an organization, as illustrated in Figure 7.1. You begin by investigating the objectives, constraints, and requirements at the highest level—the whole organization. At this level, strategic management sets the organization's goals and defines the constraints placed on reaching these goals. Many organizations define specific organizational information requirements that must be considered before detailed information requirements are determined.[1] For example, an organization may have an overall information systems plan that stipulates the use of microcomputers rather than mainframes, the brand of hardware to be purchased, or the database management system to be used. These organizational information requirements not only define some of the system-level objectives but also become system-level constraints.

Figure 7.1
Three Levels of
Requirements within
an Organization

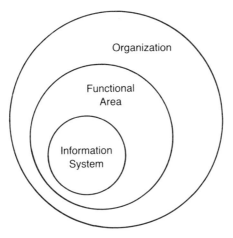

At the second level are the organization's functional divisions, headed by tactical managers. Any functional area information requirements and constraints must fit the wider organizational requirements and constraints. For example, if strategic management has set for the organization a goal of increasing profits 15 percent, the Marketing division will be interested in information systems that help improve sales or that monitor the company's sales performance. Similarly, the Manufacturing division will be interested in information systems that cut manufacturing costs.

At the lowest level is the individual information system. Within the Marketing division, there will be several information systems, only one of which may be the focus of a particular development effort. Each individual system can be viewed as a subsystem of the organization-wide information system; thus, information system requirements must also conform to organizational information requirements. The objectives, constraints, and requirements of this level must be defined accurately and precisely to ensure system success.

Using the top-down approach will help you to meet the goal of organizational relevance. This approach focuses your attention on organizational needs and goals as you define the system. As you develop the system, you can then align system-level objectives with organizational objectives and keep an eye on resource constraints.

7.2 The Techniques of Requirements Determination

Because system requirements tend to evolve over time, we need techniques to manage the complex process of developing a system in a changing organizational environment. One way to deal with the shifting nature of requirements is to use structured tools and techniques, such as context diagrams, data flow diagrams, conceptual data models, and process specifications, to illustrate the requirements of the system.

In traditional requirements documentation, an earlier approach to system documentation, the analyst develops a written summary of all the functional requirements of the system. The problem with this approach is that these detailed specifications often are difficult to read. Users may simply refuse to read a long, dense narrative description of requirements. Even if users do read and comment on the requirements, making the inevitable changes in the narrative is time consuming and tedious.[2]

Structured techniques are designed to reduce the amount of time spent reacting to change requests during and after systems development. System documentation created using automated structured techniques is easier to modify, because it consists mainly of graphics that illustrate the proposed system. In keeping with the top-down approach to requirements determination, the first graphic produced using structured techniques is the **context diagram,** which gives a broad overview of the information system environment, including data flows into and out of the system. The **data flow diagram (DFD),** the next product in this top-down process, moves from general requirements to more specific requirements, illustrating the processes, movement, and storage of data in the system. A detailed definition of data and relationships is provided by the **conceptual data model.** The **process specifications** provide a detailed definition of the processes performed. Figure 7.2 summarizes these structured techniques, which will be discussed more fully in later chapters.

Figure 7.2
Summary of Graphic Techniques for a Structured Approach to Requirements Determination

Technique	Definition	Purpose
Context diagram	Chart that illustrates the immediate environment of an information system, including the external sources of data, the external destinations of data, and the data that flows into and out of the system.	1. Defines the boundaries of the old and new systems. 2. Documents early interviews with users.
Data flow diagram (DFD)	Chart that shows the movement of data between processes and storage areas within a system, as well as from external sources and to external destinations.	1. Aids the analyst in developing insights about the problem and opportunity. 2. Provides an overview of data flow, data storage, and processes.
Conceptual data model	Diagram that describes data storage.	1. Provides an overview and details about data storage.
Process specifications	Description of system processes.	1. Provides details about processes.

Structured requirements determination provides a valuable summary of requirements that becomes the foundation for choosing acceptable existing software or for designing a system with custom-developed software. As Figure 7.3 shows, these tools are used throughout the systems development process. Additional structured techniques such as structure charts and module specifications are used during the design stage. Structured techniques also yield systems that are modular, hierarchically organized, and easy to maintain.

Figure 7.3
Summary of
Structured Techniques

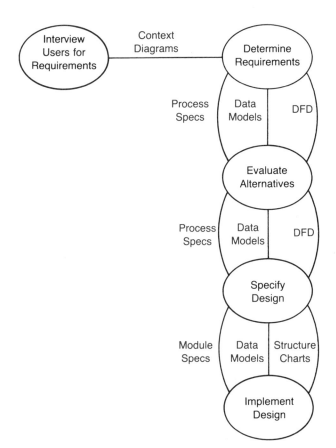

A potential drawback of using structured techniques is the amount of manual labor required to draw and redraw the graphics as a definition of the system emerges.[3] Automated tools have been developed to overcome this liability and to maintain consistency among the various structured techniques. These tools, called **CASE tools** (Computer Aided System Engineering), provide graphics capabilities that greatly reduce the effort required to create and modify DFDs and data models; they also provide consistency-checking functions that help developers use the structured techniques correctly. In addition, many CASE tools facilitate the creation and maintenance of a **design repository**—an automated storage facility for systems development information such as data element definitions and report and screen descriptions. For example, Silverrun-DFD,[4] the CASE tool used to generate many of the figures in this text, not only helps the analyst develop DFDs but also maintains a design repository.

A few CASE tools also generate executable code from system specifications. At the time this book was published, there were only a few of these code-generating CASE tools in production. They were confined to specific hardware and software and offered limited assistance with the early, unstructured activities of requirements determination. In the future CASE tools may be available for automating many of the requirements determination activities. Once the requirements were defined in the CASE tool format, they would then be compiled and debugged in the same way source code is now. When the system specifications were error-free, the CASE tool would then generate the system software, greatly reducing the time required for design and implementation activities.

7.3 The Activities of Requirements Determination

Requirements determination involves three basic activities:

R.1 Identify Objectives

R.2 Identify Constraints

R.3 Investigate and Specify Requirements

Although these activities are listed as three separate steps, they are interrelated; the definition of one element affects the definition of the others. Thus, the process of requirements determination is iterative, cycling back and forth between problem and solution. Here is where the analytical and balancing skills of the analyst come into play. As an analyst, you must keep objectives, constraints, and requirements in mind almost simultaneously in order to analyze the current system and to propose an effective new system.

The process of requirements determination begins when a user identifies a problem or opportunity that can be addressed by an information system. Usually the user completes an Information Services Request as we saw in the Meadows Hospital case (see Figure 3.1). Although the user may begin work on the problem without an analyst's help, we will assume that an analyst is consulted.

7.3.1 Identify System Objectives

The first activity of requirements determination is identifying system objectives. How broad are the objectives for the proposed system? To determine the general system objectives, you must first define the boundaries of the proposed system. As Figure 7.4 shows, these boundaries include the three levels described in the top-down approach to requirements determination (organizational, functional area, and system plus a fourth level—the geographical boundaries.

The **organizational boundaries** define the scope of the system as it interacts with entities outside the organization. Consider a small business's personnel record-keeping system, which generates reports on the percentages of minorities interviewed and hired. These reports must be submitted to the Equal Employment Opportunity Commission; thus the boundaries of this system extend beyond the organization itself. In this case the objectives, constraints, and requirements of the external commission will have to be investigated so that the business delivers the required reports. Similarly, a hospital billing

Figure 7.4

Requirements Boundaries

Information Levels	Requirements Boundaries	Basic Question
Organizational	Organizational	Do the system boundaries extend outside the organization?
Functional area	Functional area	Do the system boundaries cross functional areas or divisions of the organization?
Information system	Information system	Does the proposed system incorporate more than one old system (manual or automated)?
	Geographical	What physical areas (floors of a building, branch sites, or organizations) do the system boundaries encompass?

system may access charge rates from a Medicare/Medicaid federal data repository; thus its boundaries also encompass part of another organization. The complexity of requirements determination increases when a system must access data from or provide information to an external source. Interacting with an external entity often means conforming to its standards, so these standards must be identified and understood as part of the requirements determination process. Obviously, a system that does not extend beyond the organization is easier to investigate than one that does.

The **functional area boundaries** define the major organizational divisions or subunits affected by the system. For example, an order entry system will probably affect the Sales, Distribution, Inventory, Accounting, and Production divisions. In the Chapter 3 case study, developing a new prescription labeling and logging system affected not only the Pharmacy division but also Accounting and Administration, since these divisions used the new reports. Although systems often bridge several functional areas, the fewer functional areas involved, the easier the job of determining requirements will be.

The **information system boundaries** define the extent of the activities the proposed system will perform, thus limiting the scope of the tasks encompassed by the system. Will the new system incorporate more than one existing system? Again referring to the Meadows Pharmacy case, remember that the initial request targeted a system to automate administrative reporting tasks (a single manual system). Fred's observations showed that, while automating the reporting task, they could also easily automate the prescription logging and label generating task (a second manual system). Tracy suggested that the pharmacy's drug inventory management system (a third manual system) also be automated. Incorporating this third manual task, however, would have extended the system boundaries further than pharmacy staff members were willing to go; thus, the final system incorporated just the first two formerly manual, formerly separate (and redundant!) systems. The staff's unwillingness to incorporate the third task area illustrates the importance of defining system boundaries that reflect the users' priorities and that don't introduce more complexity than the users—or the project team—can bear. As with organizational and functional area boundaries, the job of determining requirements will be easier if the system boundaries encompass just one task. It's also important that system boundaries not exceed the time and money constraints placed on the project.

The **geographical boundaries** define the physical area encompassed by the system. Geographical boundaries may be floors within a building, buildings within a complex, or branch offices within an organization. For example, a bank may decide to develop an automated teller system at only one of its several branches, planning to introduce the same service at all other branches if the system is successful. Or a manufacturer may decide to automate one production line within its factory. Geographical boundaries determine not only the physical space affected by the system but also the difficulty of interviewing users. Traveling to six sites, for example, complicates investigating requirements, even if the proposed system will serve only one organization and functional area.

The purpose of stating boundaries is to ensure that you have accurately defined the scope of the development project. Just as you determine the scope of a report before you begin researching and writing about the topic, you must determine the scope of the development project before you begin defining objectives. Ignoring this step wastes resources and may yield mega systems that overshoot their real target or inadequate systems that fall short of their intended goal. (You may want to refresh your memory of requirements-solution fit by referring to Figure 1.14.) Context diagrams, discussed in Chapter 8, are a structured tool that will help you to investigate and specify these boundaries.

Once you have defined boundaries, you can state the goals of the system. The goal of an order processing system may be to *improve customer service* by speeding up delivery of customer orders; that of an image processing system may be to *reduce the volume of paper accessed, manipulated, and stored.* System objectives should

1. Support organizational and functional area objectives.
2. Define measurable standards for the project.
3. Be realistic goals that are likely to be achieved.

If the organizational and functional area objectives are not clear, you may need to investigate them before you can state system objectives. The following are examples of measurable system objectives:

- Reduce the error rate on customer billing from the current 2 percent to less than .5 percent while maintaining a processing rate of four transactions per minute.
- Reduce response time for personnel records to less than 5 seconds.

Whether a particular goal is realistic depends in part on the constraints imposed on development.

7.3.2 Identify System Constraints

Scarcity is a fact of life in all organizations, since each has a limited supply of resources with which to achieve its objectives. Money, time, people, space—all must be budgeted effectively if the organization is to survive. Thus, all systems development projects are constrained by factors such as budget, schedule, and personnel availability; these **management constraints** are requirements stipulated by management to control the expenditure of organizational resources. In addition, the kind of system to be developed may be constrained by predefined factors such as the need to maintain compatibility with the current hardware configuration, to keep production costs under $1000 per month, or to avoid hiring additional production staff.

Constraints can determine the boundaries of a proposed system. For example, the preliminary objective may be to install point-of-sale terminals at all store sites, but resource constraints may limit initial planning and development to the two stores with the largest sales volume. This boundary decision may be included as a system constraint: "Initial development and installation will be limited to the Houston and Phoenix stores."

Constraints make "wish list" objectives infeasible and often demand that the system developed be something less than the system desired. Part of your job as an analyst is to help users differentiate between needs and wants; you must help them realize that needs are a subset of wants. To develop a system within the imposed constraints, you will have to curb those users who want every piece of information a system can provide, even though they actually need only a small, well-defined subset of that information. You will find that systems development is much easier if you define specific objectives and focus project resources on achieving these objectives.

7.3.3 Investigate System Requirements

System requirements describe the features of each system component necessary to achieve the objectives within the stated constraints. Requirements often specify how to access data, how to process it to produce the required information, or how to control a business process such as inventory management or payroll processing. These requirements are sometimes called **functional requirements** because they state the functions the system must perform. Identifying and summarizing these requirements is best done using structured techniques such as DFDs and conceptual data models. Because you're not yet familiar with these techniques, the following examples of system requirements are presented as written specifications:

- Allow the user to alter, add, or delete records from the supplier account file.
- Generate prescription labels and maintain a prescription log using data entered by the pharmacist's assistant.
- Maintain accounts receivable records by allowing users to update customer accounts and by generating bills and past-due notices.

Figure 7.5 presents the development process matrix overview of requirements determination. Notice that requirements determination involves investigating and stipulating the features of all five system components. Your job as a systems analyst is to

1. Identify the production staff.
2. Describe the procedures that these staff members must follow.
3. Describe input and output and determine the data to be accessed and stored.

Figure 7.5
Requirements Deter-
mination Overview

	People	Procedures	Data	Software	Hardware
Determine Requirements	Form development team Determine users	Determine procedural requirements	Determine storage and I/O requirements	Determine functional requirements	Determine facility and equipment requirements
Evaluate Alternatives					
Specify Design					
Implement Design					

4. State the general functions to be performed by software.

5. Describe the environmental conditions and types of hardware needed.

Remember that these tasks are seldom performed in one sequential pass; instead, requirements are refined through multiple iterations of these tasks. You should also keep in mind that no single user knows everything about the current system or understands all the requirements of the new system.

7.4 Strategies for Requirements Determination

The naive view of requirements determination is that all the analyst has to do is to ask what users want, document their needs, and get their approval of the documented requirements. Unfortunately, the process isn't usually that simple; fortunately, we can offer several suggestions to help you overcome the most common problems. Some specific problems and their solutions are summarized in Figure 7.6. The following subsections deal with more general strategies for evaluating and dealing with project risk.

7.4.1 The Measures of Project Risk

Associated with every project are uncertainties that influence its potential for success. **Project risk measures** are factors that determine the degree of risk associated with developing a system. We will examine four factors that affect risk: the characteristics of the system environment, the proposed system, the users, and the development team.[5]

Characteristics of the System Environment Environmental characteristics affecting project risk are the stability of the organization and the functional area, the clarity of their objectives, and the degree of structure in their procedures. If the organization or functional area is in a precarious position or is in the midst of changing objectives, then determining organizational and functional area objectives will be a tricky or impossible

Figure 7.6	**Problem**	**Possible Solutions**
Suggested Solutions to Common Requirements Determination Problems	1. Difficulty eliciting details from users because they don't know what they want, think the system is obvious and simple, or fear that the system they really need will be too costly or will take too long to develop.	1a. Derive requirements by studying the existing system. b. Derive requirements from solutions that succeeded in a similar organization. c. Include users on the development team to educate them and gain their commitment. d. Ask users what they don't want in the new system or dislike about the current system. e. Use prototyping to educate users and to allow users to provide feedback.
	2. Difficulty communicating because user and analyst perspectives are very different.	2a. Avoid computer jargon. b. Use graphics, visual aids, or a prototype to illustrate the system. c. Assign a functional area specialist to be project leader, or assign an analyst who knows business functions well. d. Encourage end-user development.
	3. Difficulty predicting future requirements because they are likely to change.	3a. Study the organization and similar organizations in order to predict changes you're likely to encounter. b. Use easy-to-modify techniques during analysis and design. c. Adopt phased development as your overall strategy.
	4. Difficulty working with users because they resent the interruption or fear the impending change.	4a. Educate users about the benefits of the system through frequent reviews. b. Choose a strategy that doesn't rely heavily on user input. c. Use prototyping to educate users and to allow users to provide feedback. d. Assign only committed users to the development team.
	5. Difficulty defining system boundaries and prioritizing requirements because users have unrealistic expectations.	5a. Define the system in phases and complete only the highest-priority phase first. b. Delineate rough costs (time and money) of any unrealistic user requirements and ask the users to decide if the benefits justify the cost. c. Assign users with realistic expectations to the development team and make them responsible for educating other users about costs and benefits.

task. Likewise, if current organizational or functional area procedures are unstructured and poorly defined, then automation is likely to be risky. The need to redesign procedures for an organization greatly increases the difficulty and risk of systems development. Any organization or functional area that has experienced a recent upheaval (for example, a major restructuring, a new division head, or substantial growth) or that shows signs of poor management (for example, high turnover or low morale) is a poor candidate for systems development. Defining the boundaries and the requirements of a system in an unstable organization or functional area may be impossible, because it is unclear where procedures start and stop.

Characteristics of the Proposed System   The stability and clarity of system objectives and the degree of structure in system procedures also affect risk. Systems that have standard procedures, such as word processing, billing, and many accounting applications, have a low project risk because the functions are fairly simple and routine. Most activities at the operational level involve repetitive processing of transactions whose inputs and outputs are usually quite stable; thus, requirements are unlikely to change as the system is developed.[6] In contrast, systems developed for managerial and strategic applications tend to be more risky. Procedures at these levels are often less well defined and more susceptible to changes caused by factors in the environment. As a result, user requirements may change before the system can be implemented.

Additional characteristics of the system that may affect project risk are its size and scope. In the Chapter 4 minicase A Consultant's View of a Project Management Mess, we saw that most developers are wary of taking on large projects. Some criteria for measuring project size are

1. The number of systems being replaced or modified
2. The number of interfaces with existing systems
3. The expected development time required
4. The complexity of system requirements[7]

Any project that modifies more than one existing system, interfaces with more than one other system, or requires more than twelve months to develop should probably be considered a large project. The larger the project, the higher the project risk. A database management system project that combines the files of several divisions into a large organizational database is very risky. Its scope encompasses several divisions, and its requirement that all the separate, differently named files and data fields be merged into one common database is highly complex. Furthermore, the complexity of this project suggests that it will require a long schedule, thereby increasing the chances that user requirements will have changed by the time the system is implemented.

Characteristics of the Users   How experienced are the users in running the current application? How well do they understand the organization, its objectives, and its procedures? Are they receptive to the project? How many people will use the system? How knowledgeable are they? The users' knowledge level is a good indicator of how well they will be able to recognize and state the system requirements. Their attitude toward the new system will determine how cooperative they will be in sharing their knowledge with the development team. Thus it is extremely important to involve users so that the project benefits from their expertise and gains their commitment. The more knowledgeable, experienced, and cooperative the users are, the greater the likelihood of completing the project successfully.

Characteristics of the Development Team The knowledge, experience, and attitudes of the development team are just as critical to project success as are those of the users. If the proposed system requires a new technology (for example, new hardware, a new operating system, or a new programming language) that the development team has no experience with, project risk increases.[8] Also important are the analysts' communication skills. How well the analysts elicit user requirements and listen to user needs greatly influences their ability to identify a complete, accurate set of requirements.

7.4.2 The Evaluation of Project Risk

Figure 7.7 is a form for evaluating and summarizing the risk of a project. (The strategies in Figure 7.7 will be discussed in the next section.) Two to four questions are listed for each of the four risk factors. Responding "yes" to all the questions will yield a total score of 11 points, indicating very little risk. Responding "no" to all the questions will yield a total score of −11 points, indicating the maximum risk. The total for most projects will fall between these two extremes.

Keep in mind that you may be able to reduce project risk in several ways. If the system affects more than one functional area, you may be able to reduce project risk by segmenting development to address the primary requirements of the functional areas sequentially. Phased development may be useful in this situation to reduce project risk if the project, as originally defined, is too large. The phases may be based on subsystems or data capabilities; both of these methods of determining phases were discussed in Chapter 5. If the development team lacks experience with the technology, you may be able to reduce project risk by hiring a consultant well versed in that technology to lead the development team.

The numerous strategies, tools, and techniques of systems development provide a "bag of tricks" that you can employ to reduce the level of project risk. If these tricks fail to reduce risk substantially, you can compensate by choosing a requirements determination strategy mix appropriate to your project.

7.4.3 The Choice of a Strategy Mix

Adopting one or more of the following strategies can make the task of determining system requirements easier[9]:

1. **Asking strategy:** interview the intended users of the system.

2. **Deriving strategy:** investigate current systems in your own or a similar organization.

3. **Analyzing strategy:** closely study the activities of the functional area to determine the area's inputs and outputs, objectives, critical success factors, decision-making procedures, and interactions with other parts of the organization.

Figure 7.7

Worksheet for
Choosing a Strategy
Mix for Requirements
Determination

STEP 1: Evaluate project risk.

FACTORS AFFECTING PROJECT RISK	+1 yes 0 maybe -1 no	FACTOR RATING (+1, 0, -1)
1. Characteristics of the system environment		
A. Stable, well-defined objectives?		_____
B. Structured, clear procedures?		_____
2. Characteristics of the information system		
A. Model available or requirements stable and readily specifiable?		_____
B. Procedures addressed are routine and well-structured?		_____
C. Only one existing system affected by proposed system?		_____
D. Project can be completed within one year?		_____
3. Characteristics of the users		
A. Users have functional expertise?		_____
B. Users have experience developing systems?		_____
C. Users are committed to project?		_____
4. Characteristics of the development team		
A. Analysts have experience developing similar systems?		_____
B. Analysts are skilled at eliciting requirements?		_____
TOTAL POINTS		_____

STEP 2: Convert total points to rating of project risk.

POINTS	PROJECT RISK	STRATEGY
8 - 11	Low	Asking
5 - 7	Medium	Deriving
Less than 5	High	Analyzing
		Prototyping

STEPS 3 and 4: Determine mix of requirements determination strategies.

STRATEGY	PERCENT OF REQUIREMENTS DETERMINATION INVESTIGATION
Asking	_____ %
Deriving from an existing system	_____ %
Analyzing/researching	_____ %
Prototyping	_____ %
TOTAL	100 %

4. **Prototyping strategy:** develop a working model of the system to help users identify requirements.

Generally, no single strategy provides a complete view of the information system requirements. Thus analysts often combine these strategies, perhaps beginning with the asking strategy and then gleaning more detailed information by investigating a similar system (deriving) or by analyzing the functional area.

Your selection of a strategy mix should be based on the total points for overall risk as well as the individual risk measures associated with characteristics of the system environments, the proposed system, the users, and the development team. The lower the overall risk, the larger the percentage of requirements determination effort that can be spent on asking. The more risk increases, as shown in step 2 of Figure 7.7, the less you can rely on the asking strategy and the more you must depend on the deriving, analyzing, and prototyping strategies. For example, a project in which an expert programmer-analyst is creating a system for a single expert user that will replace a few well-defined manual procedures will have a very low total risk. Assuming that the expert is cooperative, simply asking the expert user what is required is likely to be the most efficient strategy and involve little risk of unpleasant surprises. The overall risk would be higher with more users and a greater functional scope. Likewise, the total risk would be higher if environment or system characteristics were unstable or unclear. In either case, more time would need to be planned for following deriving, analyzing, and prototyping strategies.

Individual risk measures also affect the time that should be allotted to each of the four requirements determination strategies. For example, if the proposed system requirements were unstable or very difficult to specify, the analyzing and prototyping strategies would be most useful, even if the total project risk was low or medium, because the environment was stable and structured and both users and developers were excellent.

Each of the four strategies works better in some situations than in others. The asking and deriving strategies are best followed when system complexity is low and user knowledge is high. The asking strategy works best for very stable systems whose users have a clear understanding of the system's functions. To use the asking strategy effectively, you must be able to rely on the knowledge and experience of the users. The deriving strategy is most successful for systems that perform standard functions, such as payroll processing, where the emphasis is on manipulating the data, not on altering or improving the content of the information produced. In such cases, familiarity with existing systems, whether automated or manual, in the user organization or in similar organizations can help both developers and users to identify requirements. Whether or not you end up purchasing the software, deriving requirements from an existing system speeds up requirements determination.

The analyzing and prototyping strategies help analysts determine the requirements of complex systems about which users have little knowledge and for which no existing systems can serve as models. A development team needs knowledge and experience to successfully follow the analyzing and prototyping strategies. The analyzing strategy is most useful when an existing system is being altered to perform new or extended functions (for example, a payroll system is being altered to comply with new federal reporting requirements) or when the system being developed will perform nonstandard functions (for example, an image processing system is being developed to allow users to display a computer image of customer correspondence on their monitors). To analyze an old system in order to produce a new one, analysts must be very familiar with structured techniques and possess very good analytical skills. The prototyping strategy is appropriate when the system is so new or so unusual that no models exist that can help users visualize what the requirements of the new system will be.

We propose a three-step procedure for choosing a strategy mix:

1. Evaluate the effects on the project of the characteristics of the system environment, the system, the users, and the development team, assigning point values as in Figure 7.7.

2. Determine the level of project risk by totaling the points.

3. Choose a primary strategy based on the level of project risk and individual risk measures.

4. Choose a secondary strategy that complements your primary strategy.

Figure 7.7 is an evaluation form that you can use to perform these steps. The minicase Sydney Productions' Materials Handling Simulation Project takes you through an example of assessing project risk and choosing a strategy mix.

MINICASE

Sydney Productions' Materials Handling Simulation Project

Abel, a chief programmer with Sydney Productions Inc (SPI), was very interested in new technologies and new methodologies; thus, his life as an information systems professional was quite exciting. Abel had just discovered simulation, a useful tool that new sophisticated software and faster hardware had made even more attractive. Abel felt that using simulation in the Production division would give SPI a competitive edge and enhance its corporate image. Abel also felt that developing a simulation project would improve his chances of being promoted.

Abel embarked on a campaign to sell simulation to the managers at SPI. Although he had no experience in simulation, he was experienced in project development and felt that he could do the job.

The Information Services division (ISD) had had a slow year. Most of SPI's systems were old but functional, and upper management did not want to rock the boat with unnecessary upgrades. ISD management wanted an increase in their budget, however, and to justify the desired increase they needed something new. So when Abel suggested simulation, they embraced his proposal with open arms.

ISD management and Abel proposed a simulation project to the senior managers of the Production division. These managers initially received the proposal with some ambivalence. But Production was in the throes of expansion, and the materials handling group needed a way to increase throughput. After some thought, Production's senior management designated Eric, the materials handling manager, to evaluate the feasibility of using simulation to achieve this objective.

Eric was a good choice. A professional engineer with ten years of experience in materials handling, Eric had a solid track record of excellence and innovation at SPI. Thus, senior management trusted his opinion. A friend of his in the grain industry had told Eric about the successful use of simulation to model grain terminal operations. So Eric invited his friend—and the consultant who had installed the simulation model—to view the materials handling operation at SPI. The consultant felt that although an elaborate simulation model was not needed, materials handling could be improved by using simulation.

Eric reported his findings to Production management. He suggested that they hire the consultant, who also had a good understanding of materials handling, but senior management wanted to keep the project in-house and to have Abel lead it. Eric was not completely comfortable with their decision, but he understood the need for in-house expertise and respected Abel's development skills. Nonetheless, Eric persuaded the Production and Information Services managers to agree to call in the consultant if any problems occurred during development.

The consultant had been emphatic that the quality of the specifications describing the materials handling operations would determine the quality of the simulation system. Both Abel and Eric knew the value of thorough requirements determination. When senior management gave Abel and Eric the go-ahead for the project, Abel could hardly wait to get started by determining his primary approach to requirements determination.

Using the project evaluation form in Figure 7.8, Abel began his analysis of project risk. The boundaries of the

Figure 7.8

Abel's Assessment of
Project Risk and
Choice of a Strategy
Mix

STEP 1: Evaluate project risk.

FACTORS AFFECTING PROJECT RISK	+1 yes 0 maybe -1 no	FACTOR RATING (+1, 0, -1)
1. Characteristics of the system environment		
A. Stable, well-defined objectives?		+ 1
B. Structured, clear procedures?		+ 1
2. Characteristics of the information system		
A. Model available or requirements stable and readily specifiable?		+ 1
B. Procedures addressed are routine and well-structured?		+ 1
C. Only one existing system affected by proposed system?		+ 1
D. Project can be completed within one year?		+ 1
3. Characteristics of the users		
A. Users have functional expertise?		+ 1
B. Users have experience developing systems?		- 1
C. Users are committed to project?		+ 1
4. Characteristics of the development team		
A. Analysts have experience developing similar systems?		- 1
B. Analysts are skilled at eliciting requirements?		+1
TOTAL POINTS		7

STEP 2: Convert total points to rating of project risk.

POINTS	PROJECT RISK	STRATEGY
8 - 11	Low	Asking
5 - 7	Medium	Deriving
Less than 5	High	Analyzing
		Prototyping

STEPS 3 and 4: Determine mix of requirements determination strategies.

STRATEGY	PERCENT OF REQUIREMENTS DETERMINATION INVESTIGATION
Asking	45 %
Deriving from an existing system	20 %
Analyzing/researching	10 %
Prototyping	25 %
TOTAL	100 %

new system were quite clear: the system would simulate the materials handling function at Sydney Productions. From past experience, Abel knew that the Production division had well-defined operational procedures. He also felt comfortable that the usual well-defined approach for which SPI management was known would be appropriate for this project. So Abel assigned a +1 rating to questions 1A and 1B. The availability of a similar model (and an experienced consultant) led Abel to give a +1 rating to question 2A. And because the materials handling system was a well-structured, single-purpose system, he felt confident assigning a +1 rating to the other questions about the system.

Eric, his key user, had a solid performance record, a good attitude toward the project, and an excellent understanding of materials handling. Therefore, Abel rated Eric +1 on functional expertise and on project commitment; Eric's lack of development experience yielded a −1 on that characteristic. Abel had no experience with

simulation, but he felt that his own experience as a project leader and chief programmer would be an asset, so he rated himself −1 on 4A and +1 on 4B.

Because his analysis yielded a project risk score toward the low end of the medium range, Abel chose asking as his primary strategy for requirements determination. Since simulation was unfamiliar to both users and developers, he selected prototyping as a secondary approach for modeling the materials handling process. This approach would reduce the risk associated with the users' and his lack of experience with simulation. He and Eric would work closely on the operational model throughout the project, thus compensating for Eric's lack of systems development experience. And if Abel encountered problems, he would call in the consultant. Abel would also derive many of the preliminary requirements by analyzing existing system documents and observing the day-to-day materials handling functions.

Summary

Requirements determination is the most important yet the most difficult of the four stages of systems development. It is difficult because it depends so heavily on the human ability to communicate, analyze, remember, understand, and synthesize information needs.

The activities of requirements determination are (1) identifying system objectives, (2) identifying system constraints, and (3) investigating system requirements. To identify system objectives, you must first define the four boundaries of the system: organizational, functional area, information system, and geographical. Then you can determine the objectives of the system; these objectives must be realistic statements that define measurable standards and that support organization-wide objectives. These objectives must also be achievable, given system constraints such as budget, schedule, and staff resources.

One approach to requirements determination is the top-down approach. The top-down approach begins with the organization-wide picture and progresses to more concrete levels of detail. It helps to ensure project consistency, because strategic management, the group with the greatest understanding of the organization, sets the organizational requirements that each system must comply with as information system requirements are determined.

To position a project for success, you need to evaluate project risk and select a requirements determination strategy mix that helps you cope with that risk. Factors affecting project risk include characteristics of (1) the system environment, (2) the proposed system, (3) the users, and (4) the developers. The four basic strategies are asking, deriving from an existing system, analyzing an existing system, and prototyping. The asking and deriving strategies are best when project risk is low and users are able to specify requirements. The analyzing and prototyping strategies are most appropriate when project risk is high and users can't specify requirements easily.

Key Terms

(Section numbers are in parentheses.)

system objectives (7.1.2)

information system boundaries (7.3.1)

system constraints (7.1.2)

geographical boundaries (7.3.1)

top-down approach (7.1.3)

management constraints (7.3.2)

context diagram (7.2)

system requirements (7.3.3)

data flow diagram (DFD) (7.2)

functional requirements (7.3.3)

conceptual data model (7.2)

project risk measures (7.4.1)

process specifications (7.2)

asking strategy (7.4.3)

CASE tools (7.2)

deriving strategy (7.4.3)

design repository (7.2)

analyzing strategy (7.4.3)

organizational boundaries (7.3.1)

prototyping strategy (7.4.3)

functional area boundaries (7.3.1)

Notes

1. Gordon Davis, "Strategies for Information Requirements Determination," *IBM Systems Journal,* vol. 21, no. 1, 1982, pp. 4–30.

2. Edward Yourdon, *Managing the Structured Techniques,* 2nd ed. (Englewood Cliffs, N.J.: Prentice-Hall, 1979).

3. Edward Yourdon, "What Ever Happened to Structured Analysis?" *Datamation,* vol. 32, no. 11, June 1, 1986, pp. 133–138.

4. Silverrun-DFD, version 1.00 (1987), is made by XA Systems Corporation, Quebec, Canada. It was programmed by Serge Lessard and Christian Gauthier.

5. See James I. Cash et al., *Corporate Information Systems Management: Text and Cases,* 2nd ed. (Homewood, Ill.: Irwin, 1988) and Davis, "Strategies."

6. Cash, *Corporate Information Systems Management,* p. 432.

7. Daniel S. Appleton, "Very Large Projects," *Datamation,* vol. 32, no. 2, January 15, 1986, pp. 63–68.

8. Cash, *Corporate Information Systems Management,* p. 431.

9. Davis, "Strategies," p. 12.

Exercises

(Answers to Exercises 7.1, 7.2, and 7.5 are at the end of the book.)

7.1 The administrative staff of the Engineering Research division (ERD) of Applied Research, Inc. wants a system to create special reports from the division's payroll data. Currently, the ERD administrative staff produces three or four reports each month for the business manager of the ERD. The ERD staff would like a microcomputer system that would create the two reports they run every month and make it easy for them to generate the additional reports that are required less frequently. In addition to preparing these reports, the ERD administrative staff compiles, enters, runs, and distributes reports on the payroll system for all ERD staff.

a. Who are the users of the proposed system?

b. What organizational levels would be affected by the proposed system?

7.2 The list below is a mixture of objectives, constraints, and requirements for the proposed reporting system in Exercise 7.1. Identify each item as an objective, constraint, or requirement.

a. The system must run on the current ERD staff microcomputers.

b. The current five to ten hours required for special monthly payroll reports should be reduced to two hours.

c. Duplicate data entry and manual calculations should be eliminated.

d. The system should generate the ERD Payroll Client summary and the ERD Salary and Wages Subaccounts summary report.

7.3 The vice-president of the Information Systems division and the manager of Systems Development at Applied Research, Inc. have decided that the centralized payroll system used by all divisions of Applied Research, Inc. should be re-created. The major agitators for this re-creation have been the payroll unit clerks of the Administrative Services division. They are continually frustrated by the awkward procedures and the frequent problems caused by the patched and repatched payroll system which is now twenty years old.

a. Based on this brief problem statement, determine the users of the proposed system.

b. What organizational levels would be affected by the proposed system?

7.4 The list below is a mixture of objectives, constraints, and requirements for the proposed payroll system in Exercise 7.3. Identify each item as an objective, constraint, or requirement.

a. Data entry will be completed in each of the divisions of the company, not in the Administrative Services division.

b. Validity checking and revisions will be completed in each of the divisions of the company, not in the Administrative Services division.

c. Manual data entry and transportation of input data will be minimized.

d. The system will be completed in one year.

7.5 Use the evaluation form in Figure 7.7 to evaluate project risk and choose a strategy mix for the Chapter 1 minicase Abby Clark and Her Turnkey System. For this evaluation, assume that you are a thoughtful store clerk, rather than the careless clerk in the story. Evaluate the risk based on what you would have known *if* you had questioned Abby about her objectives, constraints, and requirements *before* suggesting purchases.

7.6 a. Use the evaluation form in Figure 7.7 to evaluate project risk and choose a strategy mix for the marketing analysis system in Exercise 6.8. Make educated guesses about any missing details.

b. Explain what you could do to reduce the risk of this project.

7.7 Indicate the requirements determination strategy that would be best in each of the following circumstances, and justify your answer. In each case, identify the single strategy to follow most often, rather than a strategy mix.

a. You are implementing a new manufacturing system. Although the users are quite knowledgeable about manufacturing, the new system will be based on leading-edge manufacturing concepts that your company has never used before.

b. You are developing Phase IV of a planned corporate database expansion. Implementation is becoming easier for each phase, as users and developers gain experience in the development process. Phase III implementation was very successful.

c. You are planning to revise the existing accounting system. This system was implemented seven years ago using third generation technology. The system is delivering exactly what the users need, but the software is becoming obsolete and is not compatible with the current technology used by the firm for more recently developed systems.

d. You are designing a sales forecasting system. Sales forecasting is currently done by the vice-president of the Marketing division once a month. Senior management wants to develop an accurate but flexible system to replace the manual system. It is important that the computerized system accurately reflect the activities performed by the vice-president. Management is willing to provide you with the time and budget that a thorough investigation requires.

7.8 Refer to the Chapter 3 case study of Meadows Hospital. Assume that you are a member of the steering committee that must decide which projects to fund. Use the evaluation form given in Figure 7.7 to evaluate project risk and to choose a strategy mix for these two situations:

a. The system to be developed will generate labels and maintain a prescription log as well as produce summary reports for management (current situation).

b. The system to be developed will *only* generate labels; no log or management reports will be produced (hypothetical situation).

7.9 Review your evaluations of the project situations given in Exercise 7.8. Which project has the lower risk? Why? Discuss what could be done to reduce the risk of the higher-risk project.

Projects

7.10 Read Alexander Wolfe's article "Software Productivity Moves Upstream," *Electronics,* July 10, 1986, pp. 80–86. Then prepare a short oral or written report in which you discuss some of the attempts to improve software productivity by automating requirements determination.

7.11 In his article "What Ever Happened to Structured Analysis" (*Datamation,* June 1, 1986, pp. 133–138), Edward Yourdon discusses some of the problems with structured techniques and suggests that CASE tools will alleviate these problems. Read the article and prepare a short oral or written report in which you detail the problems and explain how CASE tools can solve them.

7.12 The following articles discuss the benefits of using CASE tools during the early stages of systems development and describe some of the CASE tools currently available. After consulting these articles, prepare a short oral or written report in which you either (a) identify eight to ten of the most important criteria in choosing a CASE tool for requirements determination or (b) compare and contrast three to four CASE tools in terms of how well each supports requirements determination activities.

Thomas A. Bruce, "CASE Brought Down to Earth," *Database Programming and Design,* October 1988, pp. 22–39.

Michael L. Gibson, "A Guide to Selecting CASE Tools," *Datamation,* vol. 34, no. 13, July 1, 1988, pp. 65–66.

Giovanni Perrone, "Low-Cost CASE: Tomorrow's Promise Emerging Today," *Computer,* November 1987, pp. 104–110.

7.13 On pages 7 through 11 of his article "Strategies for Information Requirements Determination" (*IBM Systems Journal,* vol. 21, no. 1, 1982, pp. 4–30), Gordon Davis discusses three limitations that make using *only* the asking strategy a poor choice for requirements determination. Read this discussion and then prepare an oral report in which you explain these limitations to your classmates.

Understanding the Organizational Context

Overview

Chapter 7 stressed the importance of a top-down approach to requirements determination. We stated that a top-down approach involves first looking at the big picture—the organization—and then progressing to increasingly smaller snapshots or levels of detailed requirements. Taking a top-down approach is important, because users complain all too frequently that information systems professionals lack sensitivity to the organization and its objectives, constraints, and requirements. As an analyst, you need to understand the organization before you attempt to determine the requirements for an individual information system.

In this chapter we provide you with two techniques for understanding the organizational environment of systems: critical success factors (CSFs) and context diagrams. Specifically, we plan to

1. Discuss how to use the Critical Success Factors method to learn about the organization and its requirements. (Section 8.1)

2. Explain how to prepare and use a context diagram to learn about the role of the proposed information system within the organization. (Section 8.2)

These techniques will aid you in identifying a preliminary set of requirements and in determining boundaries.

8.1 Critical Success Factors

Most of your attention during requirements determination will focus on the individual information system. First, however, you need to understand the organization's objectives and constraints. Organizational requirements are based on the organization's (1) objectives and goals, (2) strategies and policies, (3) structure, and (4) critical success factors. In this section, we discuss the first three of these concerns in the context of the fourth; that is, we describe the **Critical Success Factors (CSF) method** as a technique for identifying organizational information requirements.[1] This method is designed to determine the organization's **critical success factors:** the few factors that are critical to the organization's success and that must be attained if the organization is to survive. The following basic steps in the CSF method are discussed in this section:

1. Study the organization by examining its objectives, goals, strategies, and policies.
2. Identify key managers to interview about their critical success factors.
3. Plan and conduct the interviews.
4. Analyze the information collected, preparing a list of organization-wide critical success factors to be considered as the individual information system is designed.

8.1.1 Studying the Organization

Every level of management—in fact, every industry—has critical tasks that must be performed correctly if its objectives are to be attained.[2] The first step in determining these critical success factors is to identify the organization's objectives and its guidelines for achieving them.

Organizational objectives are the organization's reason for existing; they state the long-term purpose of the organization. The major objective of most organizations is to deliver a product or service in a cost-effective manner. To support this objective, the organization sets goals that state specific tasks to be achieved within a specified time: for example, to lower production costs 15 percent over the next two years, or to increase market share to 30 percent within the next fiscal year.

Figure 8.1 lists some of the objectives and goals of Meadows Hospital; it also illustrates how organizational objectives are reflected in the objectives of the functional area (the pharmacy) and the information system (the pharmacy's prescription system). Because organizational information requirements filter down to these more detailed levels, knowing the organization's requirements is a logical first step in learning about the information requirements of the functional area and of the system itself.

To further understand the organization, you need to know the guidelines it has established for meeting its objectives. These guidelines, commonly called strategies, state how the organization will commit its resources to accomplish its objectives. As we've emphasized throughout this text, all organizations have limited resources; how they choose to use these resources indicates what they think is important or what critical areas most need to be supported. Thus, an organization's strategies provide insights to its critical success factors.

Figure 8.1

Examples of Objectives and Goals at All Three Managerial Levels for Meadows Hospital

Organizational objective	Provide health care service to the community.
Organizational goal (related to pharmacy system)	Improve pharmacy services for clients by optimizing pharmacy procedures within the next year.
Pharmacy division objective (functional area)	Provide pharmacy services to clients. Keep track of all drug transactions.
Pharmacy division goal	Improve the efficiency of the division within the next year by implementing a computer system to handle paperwork generated by drug transactions.
Prescription system objective	Improve the efficiency of the Pharmacy division by automating drug transaction record keeping.
Prescription system goal	Schedule an analyst for requirements determination within a month.

Strategies are implemented as organizational policies, the guidelines for everyday business operations. These policies provide a framework for addressing the problems encountered as the organization pursues its objectives. As an information system is developed, many of the organization's strategies and policies become information requirements. Figure 8.2 gives examples of strategies and policies that became requirements for the pharmacy's prescription system in the Chapter 3 case study.

Figure 8.2

Meadows Hospital Strategies and Policies That Affect System Objectives

Pharmacy division strategy	Track and report all drug transactions.
Pharmacy division policies	Enter prescription data in daily log on pharmacy data sheets. Prepare end-of-day summary of daily log. Send summary report to Administration.
Information system requirements	Automate daily logging of prescription data. Produce end-of-day summary report for Administration.

To some extent you can learn an organization's objectives, goals, strategies, and policies by talking with one or two key people. To gain a fuller understanding of requirements, you may need to interview several managers at different levels of the organization. Therefore, your next step is to identify the people who can tell you more about the organization and its critical success factors.

8.1.2 Choosing People to Interview

As we explained in Chapter 2, decision making in an organization occurs on three levels: the strategic level, which determines the organization's objectives and strategies; the managerial level, which controls the broader decision making of a functional area and allocates resources to meet the organization's objectives; and the operational level, which controls the hour-to-hour, day-to-day operations of the organization. A graphical technique for representing these levels is an **organization chart.** An organization chart gives the names of the functional areas and managers at all three levels.

Figure 8.3 lists the components of a good organization chart, and Figure 8.4 shows an organization chart for Meadows Hospital. In Figure 8.5 the Meadows Hospital chart has been altered to reflect the preliminary boundaries for the pharmacy prescription system. The user-sponsor division—the pharmacy—is circled. Other areas that may use the system are connected to the pharmacy by labeled arrows, which indicate the direction and nature of the interfaces. For example, patients come to the pharmacy from the Emergency and In-Patient divisions; reports from the pharmacy are sent to Administration and Finance.

Figure 8.3

Characteristics of a Good Organization Chart

1. Clearly structured divisions of functions.

2. Obvious lines of command between the strategic, managerial, and operational areas.

3. Appropriately titled functional areas.

4. Titles that explain the area of responsibility.

5. Names of key decision makers.

6. Telephone extension numbers and office numbers of key decision makers.

Figure 8.4

Organization Chart for Meadows Hospital (Simplified)

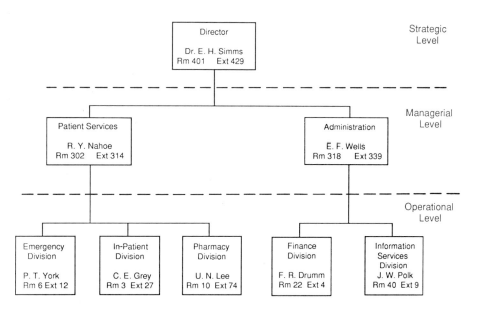

Figure 8.5
Organization Chart
Showing Preliminary
Boundaries and
Requirements for
Meadows Hospital

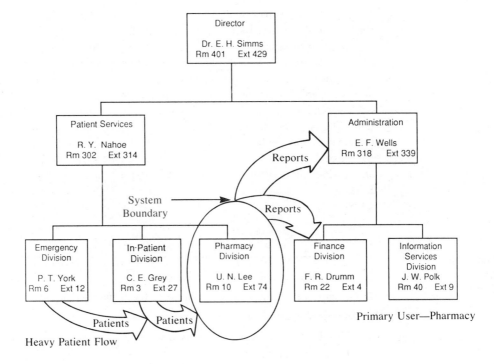

From this preliminary overview of the organization and the proposed information system, you could determine people to interview. Obviously you would eventually focus on people in the Pharmacy division. But at this stage, you would need to maintain a broader view and plan to talk with all the managers whose areas would be affected by the system—those in Administration, Finance, and so forth. If the organization and directly affected functional areas had clear objectives and policies and if the proposed system had a well-defined boundary and clear objectives, these would be the only interviews needed for this broad investigation of objectives. If the project seemed risky, however, you might also want to interview at least one or two managers at each level (for example, Dr. Simms and R. Y. Nahoe), even though they were not directly affected by the system.

8.1.3 Planning and Conducting the Interviews

Once you have some knowledge of the organization's objectives and guidelines and have identified key people, you need to plan and schedule interviews. As you prepare for your interviews, you should keep in mind the reasons for conducting them. Your goals in conducting the interviews are

1. To understand the organization and the interviewee's role in it.
2. To understand the interviewee's goals and objectives.

3. To learn the interviewee's critical success factors.

4. To help the interviewee more thoroughly consider information needs.[5]

We've already discussed Reasons 1 and 2 in some detail. To better understand Reason 3, you need to consider the four sources of critical success factors:

1. *The industry to which the organization belongs.* Each type of organization has its own set of CSFs, relating to such concerns as product mix, market share, pricing, and cost control. For example, no matter what its size or location, every hospital is concerned about cost containment.

2. *The organization's competitive strategy, industry position, and geographical location.* There are factors specific to each organization that determine its place in the industry and how it must respond to competitors. If all the other hospital pharmacies keep computer accounts of their customers' prescriptions, Meadows Hospital's pharmacy may have to do the same to remain competitive.

3. *Environmental factors.* Government regulations and requirements, economic conditions, and demographics all affect how well an organization performs and what its most pressing needs are. Meadows Hospital may be very concerned about developing an automated billing system if the Health and Human Services department will soon implement a new Medicare/Medicaid reimbursement system.

4. *Temporal factors.* Certain concerns may be of particular importance to an organization at a particular time. The director of Meadows Hospital may be very concerned about reducing short-term operating costs if the number of patients served is expected to decline over the next few months.

As you prepare for your interviews, you need to plan to include questions that will help the interviewee think about all these sources. You may want to send a memo to each person to be interviewed, outlining the purpose of the interview and briefly discussing CSFs. Send this memo at least two or three days before the interview so that the manager has time to think about the critical success factors. Figure 8.6 lists several questions you may want to ask during your interviews. Chapter 9 provides more information on planning and conducting interviews.

8.1.4 Analyzing the Organization's CSFs

After you've conducted all your interviews, you're ready to compile a list of organizational critical success factors. Begin by reviewing each interviewee's CSFs and assigning them to one of the four source categories. Then aggregate the CSFs within each category to eliminate redundancy and determine whether a pattern emerges; several managers may have mentioned the same CSF or variations on the same CSF. For example, interviews with Meadows Hospital managers may have revealed that one of the director's CSFs is providing on-site pharmaceutical services to hospital patients. At a lower managerial level, this concern may have appeared as a need for timely and accurate data about prescriptions. This same CSF may have appeared at the operational level as a concern for efficient entry of prescription data and generation of summary reports. Although stated differently at each managerial level, a single organizational CSF emerges: providing, managing, and

Figure 8.6

Examples of Questions for CSF Interview

1. How would you describe your role within this organization?

2. What is your primary mission as [job title]?

3. What are the formal and informal goals of your functional area? What information do you need to achieve these goals?

4. What aspects of your job require the most attention?

5. What aspects of your job are most critical to the success of your division? To the success of the organization as a whole? How do you gather information about them?

6. How would you prioritize your critical success factors—that is, those factors that are critical to your division and to the organization as a whole?

7. In what areas are failures most likely to hurt your division? Your organization?

8. If you could have access to only three pieces of information about your division (organization), what three pieces of information would you most want?

9. What environmental factors most affect how you do business?

10. Describe something a competitor might do that would directly affect your division (organization).

11. What are your most pressing short-term concerns? Long-term concerns?

12. How do you know when you've achieved your objectives? What are your measures of success?

13. How well does your division (organization) attain each critical success factor?

efficiently operating an on-site pharmacy. Figure 8.7 shows examples of critical success factors derived from the Meadows Hospital case.

Knowing an organization's critical success factors facilitates information systems planning in several ways. First, because you know what the organization as a whole values most, you can better align system objectives with organizational objectives. Second, you can more effectively match system requirements to organizational information requirements, perhaps revealing to users a means of satisfying both their own needs and the organization's overall needs. For example, in the Meadows Hospital case, Fred discovered a way not only to provide the reports that the Administrative division required but also to reduce the pharmacy assistants' workload by eliminating redundant data entry procedures. Because Fred kept in mind the critical success factors of both the hospital administrators (timely and accurate data about prescriptions) and the pharmacy operational staff (efficient entry of prescription data), the team was able to develop a single system to address the requirements of both. Third, your knowledge of CSFs will help you form a preliminary evaluation of the system's likely benefits. A system that addresses the critical success of factors of several managers (as the pharmacy system did in the Meadows Hospital case) probably justifies its costs and should be given priority for development.

The minicase Lite's Production Management System emphasizes the importance of knowing the organization before developing an information system.

Figure 8.7
Examples of Critical
Success Factors for
the Pharmacy System

Organizational critical success factors	24 hour emergency service Extended stay in-patient service On-site psychiatric service On-site pharmaceutical services
Functional area critical success factors (related to system)	
Administrative division	Comprehensive record keeping
Pharmacy division	Timely service to clients Minimal paperwork Daily log of all drug transactions Summary reports to Administration
Information system critical success factors	
Pharmacy division	Patient information keyed only once Label data stored for further processing End-of-day detailed log information and summary report generated

MINICASE

Lite's Production Management System

George had been an analyst with Trecor Manufacturing for two years when Lite Manufacturing offered him a senior analyst position developing a production management system. George gladly accepted, confident that he could implement the system since he had worked on a similar project at Trecor.

Although the people at Lite seemed friendly, everyone was busy and didn't have much time to talk to George when he arrived. Being new to the company, George wanted to create a favorable impression. So, rather than interrupt the Production managers, who always seemed to be involved in some urgent activity, George decided to draw on his experience at Trecor to start the requirements determination for the project. How much could one production management system differ from another?

George found it difficult to track down documents, since Lite had few well-documented procedures. Most job procedures were "inherited" by word of mouth, with little or no documentation and little understanding about why things were done the way they were. George discovered that few of the Production managers were really interested in having a computerized system. Management by crisis seemed to be the order of the day, and the managers did not welcome the thought of fitting work with a computer system into their already hectic days. Given the difficulty of gathering information and the managers' lack of interest, George questioned the feasibility of the project, but decided to give it his best shot.

Before long Information Services management began pressuring George to complete requirements determination. It seemed that the Production managers had complained to Information Services that they hadn't seen anything on this project to indicate that work was in progress. With the first quarter drawing to a close, Production had to report to senior management on the status of their first-quarter objective of optimizing production performance. George, feeling overwhelmed, decided to produce some sort of a summary document, with the intention of fixing any problems such as missing or incorrect information later.

Production management was relieved to have a document in hand so that they could report to senior management that the solution to Production's problems was on the way. The Production managers didn't have time to read the document; they were too busy with daily problems. So they simply gave George a verbal go-ahead on the system. They would worry about George's actual delivery only when money or time ran out.

Months went by, and George became concerned. The system wasn't coming together quite as he had hoped. He had tried to show Production parts of the new system, but the only feedback he had received was on the screen display layouts that he had sent through interoffice mail. These comments and corrections he diligently tried to accommodate. When he tried to speak to his Information Services manager about his problems, he was assured that this was the way it was at Lite. He was not to worry; his system would probably be just fine.

Finally George tested his system and prepared it for installation. Production management was called in to review the project.

The review was a disaster. Production had not inspected earlier parts of George's system because they had been in the midst of a major divisional reorganization. Because Lite's production policies were significantly different from Trecor's, George had designed a system that was totally inappropriate for its users.

How could George have prevented the disaster? Let's retrace George's actions to see what he could have done differently, given what we have learned about understanding the organization.

Rather than worrying about creating a favorable impression, George should have taken a broader view. First, he should have considered the organization's objectives. Because Lite is a manufacturing company, the profitable, efficient, and timely operation of its production area is a primary organizational critical success factor. To learn more about Lite's structure and its objectives, policies, and critical success factors, George should have studied the organization chart (Figure 8.8) to identify managers to interview.

From the organization chart, George could have determined that he needed to talk with all the managers listed under the Production division as well as the highest-level managers in Marketing/Sales and Finance/Administration. From his most senior user, Production manager Oliver James, George should have solicited a commitment to the project. James's endorsement of the interviews would have eased George's access to Production managers.

From his interviews George would have learned that Production was in the middle of a major reorganization that was likely to negate any work that he might do. He also would have learned how different Lite was from his old firm, Trecor.

Alerted to the upheaval in Production, George should have requested a brief meeting with the CEO to find out the major organizational goals for the coming year. These organizational goals were likely to affect Production's policies and strategies and thus also the production management system George was supposed to implement. From the CEO, George would have learned that Lite intended to reorganize Production within the next six months, to increase the sales staff by 15 percent by the end of the year, to buy a new inventory management package within two months, to replace the old inventory

Figure 8.8

Organization Chart
for Lite Manufacturing

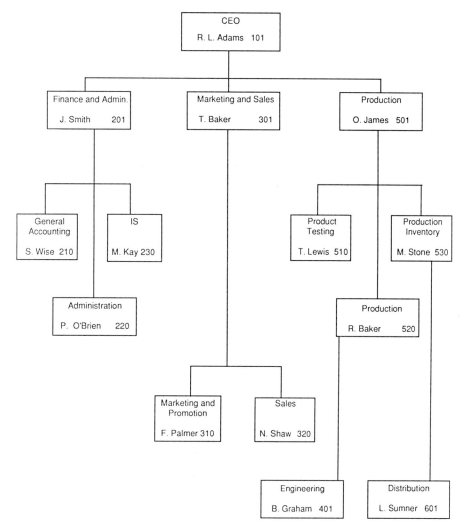

management system, and to create more comprehensive financial management within the next eighteen months.

Knowing about these objectives would have alerted George that some of the indirect users of the proposed system—in particular, inventory management—were undergoing changes. George would have realized that, with this many major changes happening at Lite, a number of the strategies and policies would change, including the critical success factors for Production.

If George had followed the CSF method, our story would have had a very different ending, as detailed in the New Ending for Requirements Determination at Lite minicase.

A New Ending for Requirements Determination at Lite

George prepared a report to IS management and Production management, stating the organizational goals for the next eighteen months and recommending that the development of the production system be delayed until the reorganization of Production had been completed. He also suggested that his experience in production systems at Trecor might be useful in helping Production define new procedures. In addition to assisting Production during its reorganization, George would get a head start in understanding the requirements of the new production system.

Senior management approved George's report and assigned him to help the Production managers identify critical success factors. The Information Services managers were pleased to be part of a major reorganization, and the Production managers were pleased to have George's assistance. Furthermore, George was pleased because his reorganization recommendations were accepted, so the future for system evaluation, design, and implementation was promising. Everyone won, and no time, effort, or money was wasted creating a system that could not serve the organization's purposes.

8.2 Context Diagrams

Information systems never stand alone; they serve the objectives of the entire organization and of one or more functional areas. Understanding the role of a proposed system within the organization gives you a context, allowing you to view the system not as an island by itself, but as one link in an information chain that serves the needs of the whole organization. A **context diagram** is a structured graphical tool for identifying the organization's functional areas and the processes that are performed within and between these areas and between the organization and the outside world.[4] A context diagram can be used to determine the boundaries and general objectives of a system. It also can be used to begin investigating proposed procedures and data requirements.

8.2.1 Context Diagram Symbols

Three symbols are used in context diagrams to represent external entities, internal entities, and data flows. An **external entity** is an agency, business, or person outside the organization, such as the Equal Employment Opportunity Commission, the United Way, or a customer or supplier. An **internal entity** is a person, place, or functional area within the organization. A **data flow** is a transfer of data between two entities; for example, a customer (external entity) places an order (data flow) with the order processing department (internal entity).

The symbols for context diagrams are shown in Figure 8.9. A shadowed or unshadowed square indicates an external entity. Either a rounded rectangle or a circle indicates an internal entity. If a rounded rectangle is used, the internal entity is labeled in the bottom of the rectangle. Both of these notations are common. The simple square and circle are commonly drawn for manual diagrams, whereas the shadowed square and rounded rectangle are common computer-generated symbols. A data flow is always shown as an arrow, with a label accompanying it.

Figure 8.9
Symbols for Context
Diagrams

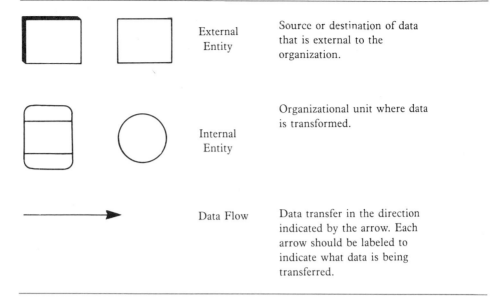

External Entity	Source or destination of data that is external to the organization.
Internal Entity	Organizational unit where data is transformed.
Data Flow	Data transfer in the direction indicated by the arrow. Each arrow should be labeled to indicate what data is being transferred.

8.2.2 The Three Levels of Context Diagrams

There are three levels of context diagrams:

1. A user-level diagram describes one functional area's operational activity.
2. A combined user-level diagram provides an overall view of the activities of related user groups.
3. An organization-level diagram reflects a consolidated view of the activities of the organization.

The first context diagrams to be drawn are those at the user level. You begin by interviewing a user in each functional area in order to identify the data flows between that area and other entities inside or outside the organization. As you interview each user, you can draw a context diagram to help the user visualize the entities and data flows and to verify your understanding of the functional area's role in the organization.

After you've drawn a context diagram for each functional area, you're ready to consolidate these user-level diagrams into a single combined user–level diagram. During this process, your main concern is that the individual user-level views are consistent with one another. You may have to talk with some users again if discrepancies arise as you compile the combined user–level context diagram.

Once consistency has been achieved, you can simplify the combined user–level context diagram by focusing on only those entities and data flows affected by the proposed system. So your next step is to draw a system boundary line around all the internal entities that will use the proposed system. (An example is shown in Figure 8.17.) It's important that the users verify this boundary, since it defines the scope of your investigation and the scope of the proposed system. The internal entities can then be collapsed into a single entity—the organization—to form the organization-level context diagram. From this diagram you can identify the general requirements of the organization, many of which may become general requirements of the proposed system.

The steps in preparing the three levels of context diagrams are given in Figure 8.10. The minicase Context Diagrams for Universal, Inc. takes you through these steps.

Figure 8.10

Steps in Creating Context Diagrams

Step 1	Title the diagram with the names of the organization and user division, the systems development project, and the date of the interview.
Step 2	a. Identify the major internal entities of the organization by using the organization chart and drawing the functional areas as internal entities.
	b. Remember to include external entities such as customers, suppliers, or government agencies.
Step 3	a. Use the organization chart to identify the manager responsible for each major entity.
	b. Interview each manager to identify the data flows between entities.
Step 4	a. Document the information gathered from each manager in a user-level context diagram.
	b. Place the name of the functional area in the symbol used to represent the internal entity, and number symbols from top to bottom and left to right.
	c. Label the lines indicating data flows between entities with the name of the transferred data.
Step 5	Repeat Step 4 until all users have been interviewed and the information from each interview has been represented in a user-level context diagram.
Step 6	Verify the completeness and consistency of the user-level context diagrams by comparing data flows into and out of each entity. Conduct second interviews as needed to resolve any discrepancies.
Step 7	Consolidate the user-level context diagrams to create a combined user–level context diagram.
Step 8	Draw a line on the combined user–level context diagram to show the system boundary.
Step 9	Collapse the entities within the system boundary into a single entity that represents the organization, thus creating the organization-level context diagram.
Step 10	Use the organization-level context diagram to identify the general organizational requirements.

Context Diagrams for Universal, Inc.

Universal, Inc. is a retailing and distribution company that has grown rapidly in the past few years. Its current manual processes for tracking orders are inadequate for its growing business. After determining that a new system was needed, top managers at Universal hired a consultant to investigate the current process and recommend steps to create an automated system.

Jayne Ingerson, the consultant, began her investigation with the organization chart in Figure 8.11 and documents that explained the organization's objectives, goals, strategies, and policies for the next year. After analyzing the documents, Jayne scheduled an interview with the manager of each functional area.

Figure 8.11
A Simplified
Organization Chart
for Universal, Inc.

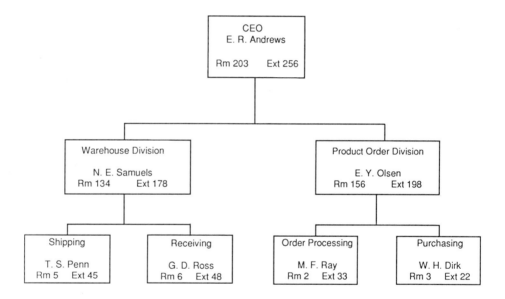

During Jayne's first interview, M. F. Ray described how the Order Processing department interacts with the customer (an external entity) and Warehouse Shipping (an internal entity) to process an order. First, the customer places an order with the Order Processing department. The Order Processing department then requests that Warehouse Shipping ship the product to the customer. The Warehouse ships the product to the customer and notifies Order Processing that the shipment has been made. The Order Processing department then prepares an invoice and sends it to the customer. Jayne summarized the interview with Ray by quickly drawing the context diagram shown in Figure 8.12. (Note that this context diagram is drawn by hand. The rest of the

context diagrams in this minicase were created using Silverrun-DFD, a CASE tool.[5]

In the next interview, the Warehouse Shipping manager, T. S. Penn, confirmed Ray's statements. Penn added that the Warehouse Shipping department is responsible for inventory management. When stock is low, Shipping notifies Order Processing, which keeps a copy of the Low Inventory Notice and sends another copy to Purchasing. Purchasing places an order with the product supplier (an external entity). When the product is received from the supplier, Warehouse Receiving confirms receipt to Purchasing. Jayne represented Penn's information with the context diagram shown in Figure 8.13. (Note that filing a copy of the Low Inventory Notice is not shown

Figure 8.12
User-Level Context
Diagram after
Interview with Ray

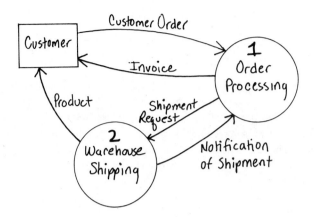

Figure 8.13
User-Level Context
Diagram after
Interview with Penn

Order Tracking System for Universal, Inc.
Warehouse Shipping   December 11, 1990

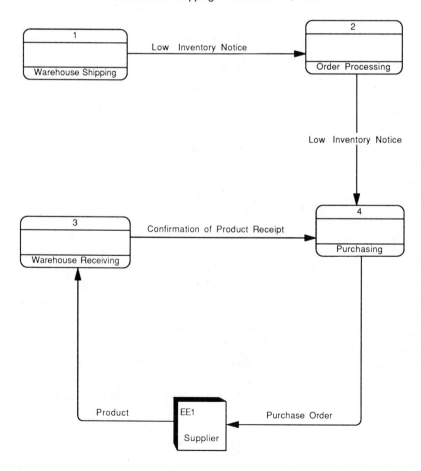

Figure 8.14
User-Level Context
Diagram after
Interview with Dirk

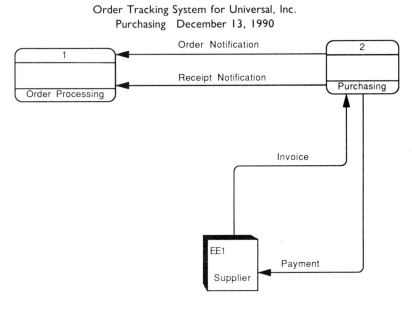

Order Tracking System for Universal, Inc.
Purchasing   December 13, 1990

Figure 8.15
Combined User–Level
Context Diagram for
Universal, Inc.

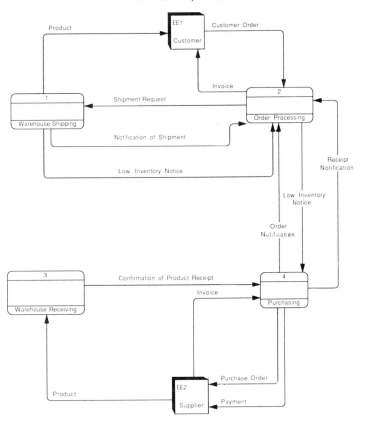

Order Tracking System for Universal, Inc.
December 14, 1990

on the context diagram; only data flows *between* entities are shown.)

To obtain a more detailed view of these procedures, Jayne next interviewed W. H. Dirk, head of Purchasing. Dirk explained that Purchasing notifies Order Processing when a product has been ordered and again when the product is received. Purchasing awaits confirmation of product receipt before processing and paying any invoices from the supplier. Jayne drew the context diagram shown in Figure 8.14 to reflect this information.

Jayne's interview with G. D. Ross, head of Warehouse Receiving, simply confirmed the details she had already learned. So Jayne was ready to consolidate the three user-level context diagrams into the single combined user–level context diagram shown in Figure 8.15. Then Jayne collapsed all internal entities to form the organization-level context diagram shown in Figure 8.16. From this diagram, Jayne was able to make a preliminary list of basic procedures included in the order tracking system:

1. Receive orders from customers.
2. Send invoices to customers.
3. Send products to customers.
4. Send orders to suppliers.
5. Receive invoices from suppliers.
6. Send payments to suppliers.
7. Receive products from suppliers.

Jayne presented her organization-level context diagram and this preliminary list of procedures to Olsen and Samuels for their approval. Looking over the diagram, Olsen laughed. "Well, Jayne, everything looks great, except that there seems to be one thing missing. The customer places an order," Olsen said, pointing to the customer order data flow, "and we send an invoice and the products. But Universal won't last long if we never receive payment from the customer!" Jayne quickly added the payment data flow to her diagrams.

Figure 8.16
Organization-Level
Context Diagram for
Universal, Inc.

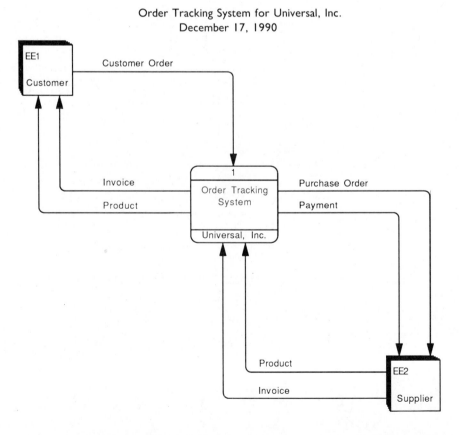

Order Tracking System for Universal, Inc.
December 17, 1990

Figure 8.17

Combined User–Level
Context Diagram for
Universal, Inc.

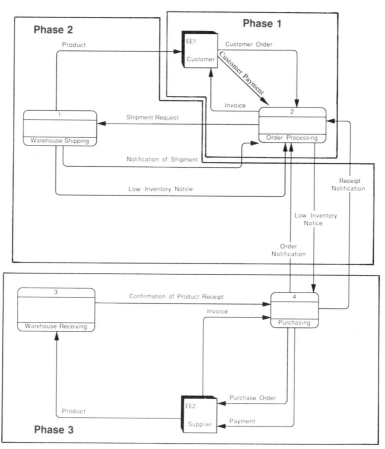

Order Tracking System for Universal, Inc.
December 14, 1990

Jayne then asked Olsen and Samuels to consider the system boundary. Developing a system that automated all the data flows in the user-level context diagram in Figure 8.15 would significantly improve the operations of the company, but the final system would take more than a year to complete in-house. Olsen was mainly concerned with improving the processes that directly affected the customer, since these had a clear impact on Universal's profit. He asked Jayne to plan to complete this work as soon as possible. She suggested that this work be considered the first phase of the project and marked the Phase 1

boundary shown on Figure 8.17. (Jane's addition of the customer payment is also shown in Figure 8.17.) Phase 2 would be the customer shipment data flows, and Phase 3 would be the supplier and receiving data flows.

Both managers approved the requirements documents Jane presented, including the revised context diagrams and preliminary plans for system development phases. Jayne proceeded with her investigation to develop a recommendation for revising the order tracking system.

8.2.3 The Value of Context Diagrams

Context diagrams serve three important purposes as you determine preliminary requirements:

1. Context diagrams support a data-oriented approach to system design.
2. Context diagrams help you investigate the output and process requirements of the organization.
3. Context diagrams help you define the boundaries of the proposed system.

Context diagrams help you view data as a shared organizational resource—a resource that belongs to and may be used by the whole organization, not just one functional area or system. Thus, context diagrams support a data-oriented approach to requirements determination. They facilitate a phased development approach based on data capabilities, as explained in Chapter 5.

Early in the process, making rough drawings of entities and data flows is an excellent way to elicit data requirements from users. For example, to learn about an existing system you might say, "Okay, you receive payments from the customer," and start to draw a data flow from the customer entity to the Shipping department. But your user would quickly say, "No, we never receive payments directly. Actually, the customer first must. . . ." In such situations, a context diagram helps you obtain an accurate, complete description of procedures.

In Chapter 10 you'll learn about a more detailed version of a context diagram called a data flow diagram (DFD). A DFD is a structured tool that can help you determine the specific input, output, and processing requirements of a system. A context diagram, which in essence is the highest level of a data flow diagram, provides the organization-wide perspective you need to apply the top-down approach to requirements determination. Like CSFs, context diagrams emphasize the role the system plays in the organization, thus promoting the sharing of data and the elimination of redundant procedures.

Summary

This chapter introduced two techniques for learning about an organization's objectives and requirements: the Critical Success Factors (CSF) method and the context diagram.

The CSF method enhances your understanding of organizational requirements by helping you identify those factors that are critical to the organization's success. Critical success factors are derived from four sources: the organization's industry, its competitors, its environment, and temporal factors that affect the organization for only a short time. By referring to an organization chart—a graphic representation of the organization's structure and levels of management—you can determine the operational, managerial, and strategic people whom you will need to interview in order to compile a list of the organization's CSFs. This list of CSFs represents the most pressing requirements of the organization, which the proposed system should in some way address so as to maximize its organizational relevance and value.

The context diagram is a structured tool that focuses more specifically on system requirements and boundaries. Composed of three symbols representing internal entities, external entities, and data flows, context diagrams provide a graphic representation of the organization's output and processing requirements. They help you identify the functional areas and the entities outside the organization that will use the proposed system. Drawing a user-level context diagram for each functional area gives you a chance to learn about the role each area plays in accomplishing the organization's objectives. Consolidating the user-level diagrams to form one combined user–level context diagram provides a consistent, verified overview of organizational inputs, outputs, and processes. Based on this diagram you can determine the boundaries of the system and limit the scope of your requirements determination activities. Finally, by collapsing all internal entities to form an organization–level context diagram, you can identify necessary organizational requirements.

Key Terms

(Section numbers are in parentheses.)

Critical Success Factors (CSF) method (8.1)
critical success factors (8.1)
organization chart (8.1.2)
context diagram (8.2)

external entity (8.2.1)
internal entity (8.2.1)
data flow (8.2.1)

Notes

1. See C. V. Bullen and J. F. Rockart, "A Primer on Critical Success Factors," *Center for Information Systems Research Working Paper No. 69* (Cambridge, Mass.: Sloan School of Management, MIT, June 1981), pp. 383–423, and John F. Rockart, "Chief Executives Define Their Own Data Needs," *Harvard Business Review*, vol. 7, no.2, March–April 1979.

2. Rockart, "Executives Define Data Needs," p. 86.

3. Bullen and Rockart, "Primer on CSF."

4. Ken Orr, *Structured Requirements Definition* (Topeka, Kan.: Ken Orr and Associates, 1981).

5. Silverrun-DFD, version 1.00 (1987), is a product of XA Systems Corporation, Quebec, Canada.

Exercises

(Answers to Exercises 8.1 and 8.3 are at the end of the book.)

8.1 Quality Beverages has been a supplier of speciality beverages to a loyal group of customers for over thirty years. Ellis Fletcher, the owner of Quality Beverages, is very particular about how his products are manufactured. He demands that products be as fresh as possible for his customers. To ensure freshness, the Inventory Management department orders only from suppliers who grow the raw product locally. This local order process is a unique feature of Quality Beverages, since the companies that have the greatest market share place orders much too large to be filled locally. Inventory Management limits the time the raw product sits on the shelf waiting for processing to one week. The raw product is processed in batches, the number of which is determined by monthly sales forecasts which are adjusted by the actual orders placed. Following industry standards, beverages not sold within two weeks are destroyed.

Identify the critical success factors for Quality Beverages. Indicate from which of the four sources each CSF is derived.

8.2 Review the Chapter 1 minicase Abby Clark and Her Turnkey System. Identify the critical success factors in Abby's property management system, and indicate from which of the four sources each is derived.

8.3 List the errors in the user-level context diagram in Figure 8.18. Draw a corrected version of the diagram.

Figure 8.18

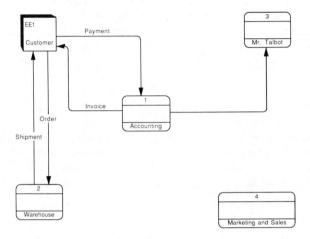

8.4 List the errors in the organization-level context diagram in Figure 8.19.

Figure 8.19 ABC Manufacturing Accounts Receivable System Organizational–Level Context Diagram

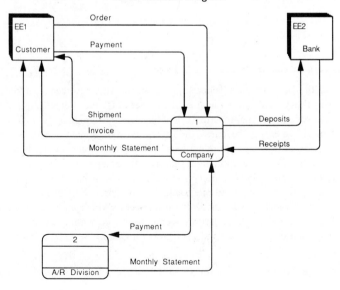

8.5 Bob's Auto Supply is a small business specializing in the wholesale distribution of auto parts to area auto repair businesses. Bob Murray, the owner, is thinking about installing an inventory and sales management system to help him keep track of sales to the forty-six auto repair services in his area and manage his inventory better. Currently he tracks sales and maintains inventory records manually.

Bob hired John Gonzales, a small business computer systems consultant, to investigate the requirements of the proposed system. John's first step was to interview the sales and shipping clerks in order to learn more about the organization and its way of doing business.

John began by interviewing Beth Daniels, the sales clerk, to learn how sales are processed. Bob's Auto Supply services its regular accounts on an as-needed basis. As-needed sales involve the customer's calling to place an order for parts needed within forty-eight hours. When a customer calls, Beth fills out an order form in triplicate and gives all three copies to the shipping clerk for immediate processing. If shipping is out of stock, Beth calls the suppliers to try to arrange immediate delivery of any out-of-stock parts. If any part of the order cannot be filled within forty-eight hours, she calls the customer. Beth keeps one copy of the order form for her sales records and places the other in a file drawer for the part-time accountant to process.

Next John interviewed the shipping clerk, Paul Webster. When Paul receives an order form from the Sales department, he fills the order, noting any items not in stock on the order form. Then Paul places one copy of the order form in the box with the parts and puts the box on the to-be-delivered dock, where the delivery truck driver picks it up for his next round of deliveries. Paul returns the other two copies of the order form to Beth.

a. Prepare a user-level context diagram for John's interview of Beth Daniels.

b. Prepare a user-level context diagram for John's interview of Paul Webster.

c. Consolidate these diagrams to create a combined user–level context diagram.

d. Prepare an organizational level context diagram including all appropriate details from part c.

8.6 Ben Freedman is the owner of Video Corner, Inc. His firm rents and sells educational videos both to the general public and to educational institutions. Ben decided to install a sales reporting system for the movement of video tapes. He hired Fran Alexander to set up the system. Fran began her investigation of the requirements by interviewing each area staff member and recording the information on context diagrams.

First, Fran interviewed the sales desk clerk, who is responsible for serving walk-in customers. When a customer requests a video, the sales desk clerk prepares the order, collects the fee, and sends the customer to the inventory clerk, who fills the order. The customer returns rented video tapes to the sales desk clerk, who then gives them to the inventory clerk to be restocked. The sales desk clerk sends copies of all customer invoices to the Accounting department.

Next Fran interviewed the special orders desk clerk. Educational institutions and other customers who make bulk orders for videos place their orders with the special orders desk clerk, who sends these requests to the inventory clerk. The customers pick up filled orders from the inventory clerk or request that the tapes be delivered. The special orders desk clerk sends a copy of the customer order to the Accounting department, which invoices the customer. Customer payment is due within thirty days of pickup or delivery.

a. Prepare a user-level context diagram for Fran's interview with the sales desk clerk.

b. Prepare a user-level context diagram for Fran's interview with the special orders desk clerk.

c. Prepare a combined user–level context diagram that summarizes the information Fran has collected.

    d. Prepare an organization–level context diagram including all the appropriate details from part c.

Project

8.7 Visit an organization, and conduct a critical success factors investigation by interviewing employees in at least two different functional areas. Complete a report based on your interviews, in which you include all of these sections:

    a. An executive summary of the interview process and your conclusions

    b. A table of contents

    c. A discussion section that identifies the critical success factors of the organization as a whole and at least two functional areas and points out the strengths and weaknesses of the organization in attaining its objectives

    d. Summary lists and tables of objectives and critical success factors to accompany the discussion section

    e. An appendix of your interview agendas and notes

CHAPTER 9

Requirements Determination Strategies

Overview

Chapter 7 introduced four strategies for determining requirements: asking, deriving, analyzing, and prototyping. In this chapter we discuss each strategy in more detail and provide guidelines for using these strategies as you investigate the requirements of a proposed information system. Although we will discuss these strategies separately, you should remember that usually these strategies are used in combination.

9.1 The Asking Strategy

Asking is *always* part of the strategy mix. Although the degree to which you can rely on the asking strategy will vary with the level of project risk, you should always consult the users to learn their views of system requirements. Given such problems as busy users, differences in perceptions, and the many others identified in Chapter 7, doing a good job of soliciting user input can be difficult.

9.1.1 Guidelines for Using the Asking Strategy

Following three basic guidelines will help you use the asking strategy effectively:

1. Always have an agenda.
2. Use a graphic technique to solicit and verify information.
3. Ask specific questions.

The first guideline emphasizes preparation. Before you interview one or more users, you need to prepare an agenda listing the meeting participants and the key issues to be discussed. Your agenda should include any questions about the requirements of the system that were raised during your preliminary study of the organization (see Chapter 8). Your investigation may have revealed inconsistencies or conflicting objectives, or it may have alerted you to a critical success factor that the proposed system can support. Perhaps your context diagrams showed that a procedure needed to be clarified before you could understand how the current system functions. These and numerous other issues should be identified *before* you interview users. Always be prepared; always know the objective of the interview or meeting. Share your agenda with the meeting participants so that they come to meetings ready to discuss these issues. Figure 9.1 is an example of a memo distributed to announce a meeting's agenda.

Figure 9.1
An Example of a
Meeting Agenda
Memo

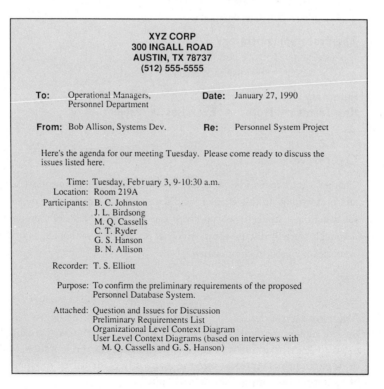

XYZ CORP
300 INGALL ROAD
AUSTIN, TX 78737
(512) 555-5555

To: Operational Managers,   **Date:**   January 27, 1990
          Personnel Department

From: Bob Allison, Systems Dev.   **Re:**   Personnel System Project

Here's the agenda for our meeting Tuesday. Please come ready to discuss the
issues listed here.

         Time: Tuesday, February 3, 9-10:30 a.m.
     Location: Room 219A
 Participants: B. C. Johnston
                J. L. Birdsong
                M. Q. Cassells
                C. T. Ryder
                G. S. Hanson
                B. N. Allison

     Recorder: T. S. Elliott

      Purpose: To confirm the preliminary requirements of the proposed
                Personnel Database System.

     Attached: Question and Issues for Discussion
                Preliminary Requirements List
                Organizational Level Context Diagram
                User Level Context Diagrams (based on interviews with
                    M. Q. Cassells and G. S. Hanson)

The second guideline focuses on soliciting complete and accurate information. As students you spend a lot of time trying to follow detailed discussions of complex ideas (your typical college lecture!), so you know the value of visual aids in conveying complex material. Graphic techniques can also be used in discussing requirements with users. In one-to-one interviews, use a small flip chart for creating lists and drawing diagrams (for example, context diagrams and data flow diagrams). These graphic aids help the interviewee to visualize ideas and relationships and alert you to redundancies, inconsistencies, and missing information. They also help you verify details, as well as serving as useful summaries of your interview. At larger meetings, you can use chalkboards, large flip charts, or overhead transparencies to get the group's attention and to illustrate the group's ideas.

The third guideline helps you elicit information from users who are so busy that they are eager for the interview to end. By asking specific questions, you facilitate communication and guide the users to quickly provide the information you need. The more clearly you formulate your questions, the more useful the users' responses will be. Different kinds of questions yield different kinds of responses. Open questions, which begin with phrases such as "Tell me about . . ." or "What is the purpose of . . . ," tend to encourage descriptive responses and to elicit the users' feelings. Closed questions—those requiring a yes/no or predefined response—help you verify information. Use leading questions to encourage users to consider how the current system can be improved. For example, by pointing at a context diagram and asking "What do you actually do with this report from Shipping?" or "What is the most important data flow on this diagram?" you help the user think about the system's functions and shortcomings. If you are demonstrating a prototype or early version of a system, you will find that even the busiest user is likely to look carefully and respond thoughtfully to any questions you ask. You should continue asking questions until you have collected and understood the information you need.

9.1.2 Choosing People to Interview

If an organization has a formal procedure for initiating projects, the commitment of senior management will already have been provided in writing when you begin the interview process. If no formal procedure is required, you will always want to interview the appropriate senior person in the organization first, to gain senior management's commitment to the project.

Generally speaking, you will need to interview two groups of people: (1) all functional area managers whose divisions will use the system and (2) a representative sample of users who currently perform procedures to be automated or will use the proposed system. (If the system is small, it may be possible to interview all users.) Choosing people to interview will be easier if you have already completed the preliminary investigation outlined in Chapter 8. From your organization charts and context diagrams, you can easily identify the key functional areas and key users of the proposed system. Then you can list these people, categorized by functional area and job function, and schedule individual and group interviews.

Your interview schedule should be planned so that you proceed from the bottom up; that is, you should begin by interviewing users who perform day-to-day operations. This user information is verified by interviewing the users' supervisor or manager—first alone and then in a group meeting with the users. After you have completed interviews in a particular area of operations, you repeat this process with another group of users and their manager. To verify information about each functional area, you interview the functional area manager alone and then in a group meeting with the operational managers who work in that functional area. Figure 9.2 lists the steps in the interview process.

Figure 9.2
The Steps in
Interviewing

1. Choose a functional area based on the priorities suggested by your preliminary study.
   a. List all personnel, from the most senior to the individuals who perform the day-to-day tasks.
   b. Schedule interviews from the bottom up, starting with individual users and then proceeding in turn to supervisors, section heads, operational managers, functional area managers, and the strategic managers.
2. Begin by interviewing individuals responsible for the day-to-day operations.
3. After individual interviews have been completed, interview the operational manager to verify the information collected from individuals and to collect further information.
4. Interview the operational manager and his or her subordinates together in a group session.
5. Repeat Steps 1 through 4 until all operational managers in that functional area have been interviewed individually and in group sessions with the staff.
6. Interview each functional area manager individually and in a group session with his or her operational managers.
7. Interview each strategic manager individually and in a group session with his or her functional area managers.
8. Review all requirements with a representative group of users to ensure the correctness of the functions and objectives.

9.1.3 Interviewing Groups: The Nominal Group Technique

Suppose the concerned users at a meeting you convened could not agree on the most important requirements for a proposed system. How would you handle each user's concerns without compromising system quality or creating antagonism? The first step might be to have each user list ideas on paper. Then all the users' ideas could be listed on a blackboard and discussed by the group. Finally, each group member could prioritize the ideas discussed, and the individual rankings could be compiled to form a group ranking.

The group discussion method described in the preceding paragraph is called the Nominal Group Technique.[1] The **Nominal Group Technique (NGT)** is a group interview technique developed to facilitate meeting procedures and to maximize individual contributions by minimizing the inhibitions caused by pressures from peers or superiors. NGT aids idea generation and discussion by separating ideas from specific personalities. It focuses the group's attention on the problem and encourages tolerance of conflicting ideas. NGT also encourages participation and brainstorming by discouraging censure and promoting freewheeling thinking. It assumes that the more ideas generated, the greater the likelihood that superior ideas will surface. Figure 9.3 lists the six steps in the Nominal Group Technique.

Figure 9.3
The Nominal Group Technique

The Six Steps in the Nominal Group Technique

1. Individuals generate ideas during or before the meeting.
2. Individuals' ideas are listed in round-robin fashion.
3. The group discusses the ideas, possibly adding ideas to the list.
4. Each group member ranks the listed ideas.
5. Individual rankings are compiled to form a group ranking.
6. The group ranking of ideas is discussed. If the group ranking is unacceptable, Steps 3 through 5 are repeated.

When used to elicit requirements, NGT stimulates the group to discuss system objectives and constraints and to resolve individual differences in perceptions of the system in order to form a group consensus. NGT can also be used to prioritize the objectives and requirements that guide systems development within the specified constraints. In addition, NGT can be used to explore problems, generate alternative solutions, and select a solution or a project to be developed. The minicase Using NGT for Systems Planning at Woods, Inc. illustrates the use of this technique in information systems planning.

MINICASE

Using NGT for Systems Planning at Woods, Inc.

Woods, Inc., a major supplier of wood products, became successful because of its commitment to service. Woods is headquartered in the Southeast and has subsidiaries across the country. Despite its size, Woods is a tight organization that prides itself on its efficient customer delivery and its timely reports to the home office. To maintain these strengths, Woods needs to develop a more efficient sales reporting and communication system.

Lana McRae, a consultant, has been hired by Woods to plan the communication network and sales reporting project. In an early meeting, users chose phased implementation as the development strategy. Now Lana needs to know Woods's priority for implementing the system at

its various subsidiaries, so she has scheduled a meeting to discuss this issue with users. Lana's memo announcing the meeting time, participants, and agenda is shown in Figure 9.4. Because she plans to use the Nominal Group Technique to establish implementation priorities, her memo asks each meeting participant to give her a prioritized list of subsidiaries before the meeting.

Lana begins the meeting by reminding the group of their earlier discussions and briefly describing NGT. Then she distributes an ordered list of subsidiaries (Figure 9.5), which she prepared before the meeting to save time. Following the name of each subsidiary are the individual rankings (highest priority = 15 points, second-highest priority

Figure 9.4

Lana's Agenda Memo

Woods, Inc.
39870 Ben Franklin Blvd
Burlington, AL 68023
(205) 672-8906

To:	Project Planning Team	**Date:**	October 9, 1990
From:	Lana McRae, Consultant	**Re:**	Priority List

Here's the agenda for our meeting next week. I've attached a list of the Woods offices, including the head office and fourteen subsidiaries. Please rank these fifteen offices in the order of their priority for implementation (assign 15 pts for your top choice, 14 to your second,...and 1 to your last choice). Return your ranked list to me no later than Tuesday, October 15 so that I can summarize the rankings for our meeting. We'll determine a final priority list by using the Nominal Group Technique that worked so well at our last meeting.

Time: Thursday, October 17, 10-11:30 a.m.

Location: Conference Room 386

Participants: Harding Jones, CEO
Hilda Erikson, VP-Finance
Allen Cartwright, VP-MIS
Mike Spalding, VP-Marketing

Recorder: Pat Brown

Purpose: To determine the priority for implementing the proposed communication network and sales reporting system at the Woods head office and subsidiaries.

Attached: Office List for Priority Assignments

= 14 points, and so forth) and the total number of points for that subsidiary. Lana explains the numeric rating system and invites discussion of the rankings.

Harding Jones, chief executive officer, notes his relief that everyone ranked the home office in Alabama as the number one priority. But he is dismayed to see so little agreement among subsequent rankings. Hilda Erikson, senior vice-president of Finance, suggests that rankings may have varied so greatly because no criteria for prioritizing were identified. Soon everyone begins offering reasons for the differences, and the meeting is reduced to chaos.

Lana reins in the group members by suggesting that they each take five minutes to list criteria for prioritizing subsidiaries for implementation. This five-minute respite restores order and allows Lana to regain control of the meeting.

Next Lana goes around the conference table, re-

questing that each participant give one criterion, which Lana writes on the blackboard in the front of the room. After all of the criteria have been listed (Figure 9.6), she leads a discussion of these criteria and then requests that the participants write the five most important criteria on their notepads. Lana gives the group a few minutes to make their choices. Meanwhile she copies the twelve criteria on another blackboard, leaving room to tally the votes.

Lana calls on the participants one by one. They each vote for the five criteria they consider most important, ranking the most important as 5, the second most important as 4, and so forth. When the voting has been completed, Lana totals the rankings and announces the top five criteria (Figure 9.7). The group discusses the criteria briefly and decides to re-evaluate the individual priority lists of subsidiaries based on these criteria.

Lana uses NGT again to conduct the ranking, discus-

Figure 9.5
Results of the First
Round: Prioritized List
of Subsidiaries

Office	Rankings				Total Points
	1	2	3	4	
Woods, Inc. (Head office), Alabama	15	15	15	15	60
Millworks, Inc., Arkansas	9	12	14	13	48
Aurora Wood Products, Georgia	10	11	13	11	45
Woods Service Company, Connecticut	11	9	11	14	45
Woodruff Products, Tennessee	6	14	8	10	38
Construction Distributors, New Hampshire	12	13	1	12	38
King Builders, Texas	14	7	9	8	38
Redwood Distributors, Washington	13	10	12	1	36
Woods Warehousing, Massachusetts	8	3	10	9	30
Anchor Tree Corp., New York	7	8	6	6	27
Alaska Wood Products, Alaska	4	6	5	7	22
Fox Valley Woods, California	2	4	7	2	15
Pacific Wood Products, Oregon	3	5	2	4	14
Ace Product Corp., Maine	1	2	4	5	12
Naper Woods Inc., Maine	5	1	3	3	12

Figure 9.6
List of Twelve Criteria (unranked)

- Profit margin
- Average monthly sales (past six months)
- Subsidiary's reporting record (i.e., timeliness)
- Size (number of employees)
- Annual sales over the past three years
- Number of sales representatives
- Contribution to Woods's net profit
- Proximity to the home office
- Frequency of communication with the home office
- Date of inception (starting with the oldest subsidiary)
- Quality of IS resources
- Contribution to Woods's total sales

Figure 9.7
Top Five Criteria
(unranked)

- Proximity to the home office

- Contribution to Woods's total sales

- Number of sales representatives

- Frequency of communication with the home office

- Average monthly sales (past six months)

---

sion, and reranking of subsidiaries. Assigning priority to the subsidiaries is quite easy now that the group has agreed on its criteria. As the meeting ends, Lana can't help smiling to herself. She hadn't expected to use NGT *twice* in this meeting. But knowing how effectively it achieves consensus, she had used it both to avoid chaos and to help the group establish a priority list that all could accept.

9.2 The Deriving Strategy

The deriving strategy assumes that the requirements of the proposed system can be *derived* by studying an existing system. Thus for the deriving strategy to be used, a system comparable to the proposed system must already exist either in the user organization or in a similar organization. This strategy is helpful when, no matter how well you interview users, they still provide little insight into the system requirements. It's also effective when high turnover among users has eroded the base of user expertise on which the asking strategy relies. If the existing system has severe procedural problems that the proposed system must eliminate, the deriving strategy is especially valuable as a complement to the analyzing or asking strategy. Techniques used in the deriving strategy include studying a proprietary system or package; observing users as they perform the tasks of the current system; and researching textbooks, business periodicals, and industry studies for descriptions of similar systems.

9.2.1 Guidelines for Using the Deriving Strategy

To use the deriving strategy well, you must be able to compare the existing system to the proposed system.[2] If the organization's existing system functions poorly or has been plagued by problems, you may not be able to—or want to!—derive requirements by studying its operation. Instead, you should study a successful system in another organization or research similar systems in textbooks or business periodicals.

To derive requirements, you must identify the features that the existing system and the proposed system share. For example, all payroll systems require similar inputs (hours worked, wage per hour, federal income tax deduction, etc.), processing (calculating gross and net salary), and outputs (paychecks). By identifying these similarities, you confirm that the existing system is an appropriate model for the proposed system. Next you need to establish how the proposed system will differ from the existing system. Perhaps the existing payroll system has no inputs for state income tax, life insurance, or charitable deductions—all of which are required by the proposed system. Recognizing these differences will help you derive expanded requirements of the existing system to more accurately for the proposed system. Creating data flow diagrams and other graphics will help you identify these similarities and differences.

How much time should you spend studying an existing system? Estimates vary widely depending on the size and complexity of the system being studied. A rough guideline is to limit the time spent investigating the current system to no more than half of the total requirements determination time. The key is to spend only as much time as is needed to identify the main requirements of the new system; in other words, look backward to the existing system just long enough to build a map to guide you as you move forward to the new system.

9.2.2 Techniques of the Deriving Strategy

One way to derive requirements is to collect and review documents about the organization, the functional area, and the existing system. Whether the existing system is manual or automated, documents that explain the system and its role in the organization are often a good starting point. Job descriptions and operations manuals can provide excellent descriptions of manual systems, just as program listings and system specifications can describe automated systems. Functional area and organizational objectives, policies, and procedures also help to identify requirements. For example, if an organizational policy requires that all purchases exceeding $250 be approved by a division manager, one requirement of a proposed accounts payable system would be to verify that a purchase was approved before payment was made.

Figure 9.8 lists documents that you will want to review as you study an existing system. These documents may be found in the information services library or in the users' functional area. Some organizations have central libraries or archives that contain

Figure 9.8
Summary of Documents for Deriving Requirements

Documents for Any Existing System	Documents for an Existing Computerized System
Procedures documentation	Requirements document
User training manuals	Context diagrams
Sample reports	Data flow diagrams
Sample documents and forms	Data structure charts
Job descriptions for all users	Input and output report formats
Organizational documents	Design repository
Preliminary context diagram of the organization	Software manuals
	Hardware manuals
Project risk evaluation form	Database operating procedures
	Operations manuals
	Facilities layout

important organizational documents catalogued for easy access. Other organizations store documents in the relevant functional areas. Still others maintain extensive system libraries, which catalog all the documentation generated as a system is developed and maintained. Your main question as you review these documents is "Are they current, accurate, and complete?" Too often a division's formally stated objectives and written procedures don't reflect what's really considered important and how things are really done.

When very little documentation exists or when its accuracy is questionable, observing the operations of an existing system can help you derive requirements. Remember that in the Meadows Hospital case, it was Fred's observation of the pharmacist's assistants that revealed the redundancy in the manual prescription system and exposed the need to streamline procedures. Everyone knew that the current system was too time consuming and labor intensive, but only Fred's observation of pharmacy operations revealed that the data used to generate a prescription label could be posted automatically to the daily log.

If used correctly, observation can be a powerful technique for deriving requirements. Often you will need to design an observation instrument before you conduct your observations. An **observation instrument** is a guidesheet for collecting observations; it prompts the observer to provide all the information needed, such as date, time, location, person performing the task, task performed, duration, and so forth. To use the observation technique successfully, you must have a clear sense of what is to be observed. Developing an observation instrument helps you define the activity and collect reliable and accurate information.

Two major concerns in using the observation technique are unobtrusiveness and timing. Whenever you observe users, your presence should be unobtrusive. Obviously your observations won't be very accurate if your presence changes how users perform their tasks. Similarly, your observations will be inaccurate if they are not carefully timed. A single observation on a Tuesday morning will not reflect the beginning-of-week, end-of-day, end-of-week, or end-of-month processing of the current system, nor will it uncover problems that arise during peak periods. Observation of a department store's credit sales approval system on a Monday morning in July will present a very different view of transactions than would the same observation on a weekend before Christmas. Thus you may need to conduct several observations to capture a total, accurate view of a system.

A third technique for deriving requirements is researching secondary sources for descriptions of similar systems. Textbooks about systems development, manufacturing, and business functions such as accounting, finance, and marketing may describe systems that resemble the one you are developing. Studying the descriptions of these systems will help you determine the requirements for your system. Similarly, business periodicals and industry studies may provide useful information. For example, a study of automated manufacturing systems may help you understand the minimum functional requirements of a system to lower production costs.

9.3 The Analyzing Strategy

The analyzing strategy is a good choice when the existing system is being changed so significantly or is so poor that deriving useful requirements from it would be impossible. The analyzing strategy is also particularly effective for determining the requirements for a new system being developed to take advantage of an opportunity. For example, if an organization wanted to develop a customer service network in order to increase its market share, the Nominal Group Technique could be used to surface and prioritize customer needs and to match those needs to system requirements.

Developers often must identify requirements by analyzing the functional areas that will use the proposed system. This analysis can take one of several forms. The Critical Success Factors method and context diagrams are two techniques commonly used.

9.3.1 Guidelines for Using the Analyzing Strategy

Although the analyzing strategy is less well defined than the other strategies, there are some guidelines you can follow as you analyze the organization and functional area(s):

1. Be sure you understand the organizational and functional area objectives and critical success factors.
2. Study carefully the inputs, processing, and outputs of the functional area(s) using the system.
3. Focus on decision processes as much as possible.[3]

Assuming that you've already conducted the preliminary investigation of the organization outlined in Chapter 8, you should have a clear picture of what's really important to the organization and the functional area. You should also have a fairly good sense of the data flows between the internal and external entities. You may need to analyze these data flows and the processes that act on them more closely to develop a complete and detailed picture of how a functional area can fulfill its objectives. For example, creating detailed data flow diagrams of the inputs, processing, and outputs of a Purchasing department will help you understand its operations. Keep in mind that if the current system is poor or is to be substantially altered, you will need to build your understanding from an analysis of how things *should* be done, not necessarily from how they *are* done. Consult with users, focusing on the requirements of the proposed system and using data flow diagrams to illustrate, verify, and document the proposed system's inputs, processing, and outputs.

Focusing on the users' decision processes will help you maintain your emphasis on the proposed system and avoid anchoring on a poorly functioning current system. If you analyze the kinds of decisions the users make and the procedures they follow to make those decisions, you can identify the inputs (data needed to make a decision), processing (how data is manipulated to generate a decision), and outputs (reports and other information that communicate a decision or that serve as the basis for making a decision). Focusing on the decision process is especially effective if that process is fairly well structured. Investigating ad hoc decision is much more difficult, but it is necessary to provide insight into the system requirements for new managerial and strategic systems.

9.3.2 Analyzing Procedures and Decisions

In Chapter 1 we defined procedures as instructions for people; procedures explain how to use a system to achieve a desired result. Using a system may involve performing many tasks—some entirely manual, such as completing an application form, and others requiring interaction with system hardware, such as keying in data or loading a tape on a tape drive.

The procedures for performing these tasks must be described clearly and accurately as requirements are determined.

An effective way to analyze and summarize procedures is by constructing a procedures table. By drawing attention to the actors, objects, conditions, and actions of a process, a procedures table can help you identify the details and problems of current decision-making processes. The steps in constructing a procedures table are as follows:

1. Working from users' descriptions of the process, identify objects, actions, and ambiguities.
2. Complete a preliminary procedures table corresponding to the process.
3. Clear up any ambiguities by reviewing the preliminary table with the user.
4. Draw a final version of the procedures table to include in the requirements document.

In the narrative analysis in Figure 9.9, *actions* are enclosed in boxes and *objects* of the actions are underlined. Circles indicate conditions ("if"s) and multiple actions on objects. Ambiguities are marked with question marks to remind the analyst to clarify these points with the user.

Figure 9.9
Narrative Analysis of a
User's Process
Description

When a barber wants a state hairdresser's license he or she completes an application at the state board office. The application, a training certificate, and $50 are given to the license clerk.

Define?

The clerk visually checks the documents for completeness and returns them to the applicant if corrections are necessary. The clerk then enters the application and training certificate data into a

How?

VAX 11/780 computer using a terminal; the system verifies the data, checking it against the license master file and a training center master file. After verification, a receipt and license certificate are produced and the master file is updated. The clerk hands the receipt and certificate to the applicant.

more specific?

At the end of each day the clerk runs a program to create a summary report on the current

☐ = action
___ = item

master file and a detailed list of all added, changed, or deleted license records.

The procedures table in Figure 9.10 summarizes the information from Figure 9.9. Notice that this table emphasizes who does what to which object. The "if"'s make clear the *conditions* in the process. The table separates the normal process from the end-of-day process.

Procedures tables are useful in the asking and deriving strategies as well as the analyzing strategy. When the descriptions of processes elicited from users are very complex, analyzing the processes and decisions may capture the procedure better than simply listing the steps or drawing a diagram. If the users are knowledgeable or an existing system can be studied, however, these simpler techniques are usually sufficient.

	Actor and Action	**Upon**	**Conditions and Action**
Figure 9.10 Procedures Table for the Barber Licensing System	*Procedures for Each Applicant*		
	Applicant completes	Application Training certificate $50 check	
	Clerk verifies	Application Training certificate $50 check	If error—return to applicant If correct—continue
	System verifies	Application license and license code on license master file Training certificate and training code on training center master file	If error—return to applicant If correct—continue
	System produces	Receipt License certificate	
	System updates	Master file	
	Clerk returns	Receipt License certificate	
	End-of-Day Procedures		
	Clerk runs	Summary report of current master file Detailed list of adds, changes, and deletes	

9.4 The Prototyping Strategy

Sometimes a proposed system is so unlike any system the users know that they're unable to specify its requirements. They can't say for sure what the new system should look like, but they'll know it when they see it. In this situation, users need a prototype to help them decipher requirements. Only in the last decade has prototyping become a feasible option. The advent of fourth generation tools, such as application generators, has reduced the cost of "know it when I see it" requirements determination, making prototyping a viable and valuable strategy.

Prototyping differs from phased development in a fundamental way. Prototyping, as we discuss it here, is a strategy for requirements determination, the first stage of the REDI development model. Prototyping involves *building a model* that users can refer to in order to identify system functions. In contrast, phased development is a strategy for *developing a system*. In phased development, all four of the REDI stages are repeated in several iterations in order to deliver working segments of the final system as quickly as possible. In prototyping, once requirements have been identified, the final three stages—evaluation, design, and implementation—may be completed sequentially in a single iteration or may be carried out at different times for different portions of the system, following a phased development strategy.

Both prototyping and phased development are effective because they provide an excellent method of getting user feedback. The strategy of modeling user interfaces early in system development is helpful even when users are clear about their needs. When users aren't clear or won't cooperate, prototypes are absolutely essential.

9.4.1 Guidelines for Using the Prototyping Strategy

Because prototyping is a fairly new strategy, we don't have the final word yet on its effectiveness. Investigations of its benefits and shortcomings, however, suggest some guidelines for using prototyping effectively during requirements determination.[4]

One of the major benefits of prototyping is that it involves users and strengthens the user-analyst relationship. To realize this benefit, you need to form a partnership with the users and to encourage and support their enthusiastic, thoughtful review of the prototype. The prototype itself is an excellent attention-getter; allowing users to interact with the working model and see their suggestions direct its development tends to ensure a high degree of user enthusiasm, involvement, and commitment. Being receptive to users' suggestions and cheerfully implementing them in the prototype will earn you a more favorable user evaluation of both the development process and its product.

A second benefit of the prototyping strategy is that its flexibility tends to permit the resolution of user interface issues that might jeopardize the success of the project. Prototyping is most commonly used to develop interactive systems in which the user interface is a critical component. Because prototypes, especially those built with fourth generation tools, are easy to modify, you are better able to develop a system that users find easy to learn and easy to use. Our guidelines for designing an effective user interface, which are presented in Chapter 16, will also help you achieve this benefit.

The greatest shortcoming of the prototyping strategy is its potential lack of structure and control. Systems whose requirements have been determined through prototyping are often more difficult to integrate with other systems and exhibit a less coherent design. They also tend to use hardware capabilities less efficiently and to undergo less rigorous implementation-stage testing. To avoid these shortcomings, you need to carefully control and coordinate the prototyping process. Remember that the prototype is just a means of eliciting requirements; it is *not* the system itself. You need to complete all the REDI stage activities as diligently as usual and to plan carefully, being sure to set explicit cost, effort, and time limits. Also be sure to set cut-off dates for experimenting with each aspect of the prototype and to define procedures for documenting and testing (including the final tests discussed in Chapter 21).

By following these guidelines, you should be able to profit from prototyping's benefits and avoid its shortcomings.

9.4.2 Techniques of the Prototyping Strategy

With the prototyping strategy, the analyst builds software to match the users' requirements for reports, screen manipulation, and database queries. Users actually work with the prototype, suggesting modifications and additional features. In essence, the prototyping strategy elicits requirements through repeated iterations of the analysts' building the prototype and the users' suggesting revisions. These iterations continue until both the users and the analysts believe that they've determined the major requirements.

The initial prototype is the analysts' best guess of requirements based on the preliminary investigation. The initial prototype serves as a starting point—an anchor—for the users' and the analysts' shared model. As this model evolves and is refined, the requirements it uncovers must be documented and verified. A description of the final version of the prototype serves as part of the requirements document that analysts and programmers use to develop the fully operational system. The description should include printouts of all the screens and reports, as well as procedural details and hierarchy charts showing the sequence of menus and control statements.

Summary

A variety of strategies, guidelines, and techniques can be used to determine the requirements of a proposed system. The appropriate mix of the four strategies outlined in this chapter—asking, deriving, analyzing, and prototyping—is contingent on the nature of the development project. When the users are knowledgeable and the proposed system is similar to the users' current system, you can usually rely on the asking and deriving strategies to elicit a complete and accurate set of requirements. When the users are unfamiliar with the features of the proposed system or when the existing system is very poor, you usually will need to rely more on the analyzing and prototyping strategies. Prototyping is an effective, even necessary strategy if the user interface is critical to system success.

The techniques used in connection with the four strategies include all those introduced in Chapters 7 and 8: context diagrams, data flow diagrams, and the Critical Success Factors method. This chapter introduced two additional techniques: the Nominal Group Technique, useful for interviewing groups, and procedures tables, useful for illustrating and verifying the functional area decision processes. Although these formal techniques are quite effective, other less formal techniques can be equally effective. For example, when a decision process is very simple, just listing the steps in the process may be adequate. Thus you should not feel constrained by the structured techniques; experience will teach you to use whatever works best.

Key Terms

(Section numbers are in parentheses.)
Nominal Group Technique (9.1.3)
observation instrument (9.2.2)

Notes

1. George Huber, *Managerial Decision Making* (Glenview, Ill.: Scott, Foresman, and Co., 1980).

2. G. B. Davis, "Strategies for Information Requirements Determination," *IBM Systems Journal*, vol. 21, no. 1, 1982, pp. 4–29.

3. Ibid.

4. See Maryam Alavi, "An Assessment of the Prototyping Approach to Information Systems Development," *Communications of the ACM*, vol. 27, no. 6, June 1984, pp. 556–563, and Barry W. Boehm, Terence E. Gray, and Thomas Seewaldt, "Prototyping Versus Specifying: A Multiproject Experiment," *IEEE Transactions on Software Engineering*, vol. SE-10, no. 3, 1984, pp. 290–302.

Exercises

(Answers to Exercises 9.1, 9.2, 9.4, and 9.8 are at the end of the book.)

9.1 Review Tracy and Fred's requirements determination activities in the Chapter 3 case study.

    a. What are the users' overall needs?

    b. How will the new system facilitate communication within the organization?

9.2 What types of documents could Tracy and Fred have collected during their initial investigation of requirements in the Chapter 3 case study? What information could they have derived from each document?

9.3 Ron Evans just designed and implemented a state-of-the-art sales forecasting system for the regional sales manager. The regional manager thought it was great and promptly sent a report generated by this forecasting system to his boss, the vice-president of Sales and Marketing. The VP had been reframing organizational policies and strategies for the Sales and Marketing division for the last three months to support the CEO's six-month plan for expansion. The expansion will result in a major change in operating and reporting procedures within Sales and Marketing. The VP thanked the regional manager, but returned the report along with a copy of the new organizational policies for the Sales division and an example of a forecasting report that would be more consistent with the new policies.

a. What important step in information gathering did Ron forget?

b. Discuss how Ron could have avoided this problem.

9.4 Referring to the Chapter 3 case study, prepare an interview schedule for Tracy and Fred to follow during requirements determination.

9.5 Referring to the Chapter 3 case study, prepare an agenda memo for the project team meeting to discuss the findings from the team's two-day investigation of the current system. Use Figure 9.1 as a guide in formatting your agenda memo.

9.6 Referring to the minicase Using NGT for Systems Planning at Woods, Inc., discuss how Lana used the Nominal Group Technique. Outline the events in the minicase that correspond to NGT's six steps.

9.7 Referring to the Chapter 3 case study, discuss how Tracy could have used the Nominal Group Technique in her interviews with the pharmacists and assistants.

9.8 When a teller at Central Bank receives a completed request form for a cash withdrawal from a client, the teller enters the client's checking account number and the amount of the withdrawal into the computer system. The system verifies the account number. If the account number is correct, the system checks the account balance to ensure that there are sufficient funds to process the withdrawal. If there are sufficient funds, the amount is subtracted from the account balance and an account transaction is created and added to the daily transaction log. A cash withdrawal receipt is printed, which the teller hands to the client along with the requested cash.

Complete (a) a narrative analysis of the procedures and (b) a tabular analysis of the procedures and decisions for the cash withdrawal procedures.

9.9 The following information about an organization's inventory procedures is gained from an interview with a warehouse supervisor:

A complete shipment is made immediately if the amount on hand is at least as large as the amount ordered. If the amount on hand is inadequate and additional goods are expected within a week, the order is held until the goods arrive.

A partial shipment of goods is made when there is some available inventory and no additional goods are expected for at least a week.

A back-order shipment is made when inventory is completely gone or when a partial shipment was made previously.

An out-of-stock notice is sent immediately in the case of either a partial shipment or a back order. No out-of-stock notice is sent when the order is held for a shipment expected within a week.

Prepare a procedures table that indicates the correct inventory action for incoming orders.

9.10 An interview with the assistant dean of a university reveals that the College of Business Administration has instituted a grade point average (GPA) requirement for admission into business college major programs for juniors and seniors. Freshman and sophomore prebusiness majors who are unlikely to meet these requirements are sent warning letters. A warning letter is sent when a prebusiness major has taken at least six required freshman and sophomore courses and has a GPA of below 2.5 for the required courses or an overall GPA of below 2.5. Letters are not sent to students who have already applied for a major. Nor are letters sent to any prebusiness students who have a GPA of above 2.5 for both their required coursework and their overall work.

Prepare a procedures table that shows when warning letters are sent to business students who have grade point problems.

Project

9.11 Read R. E. A. Mason and T. T. Carey, "Prototyping Interactive Information Systems," *Communications of the ACM,* vol. 26, no. 3, May 1983, pp. 347–354. Prepare a short oral presentation in which you discuss the prototyping methodology described. Compare this methodology to the REDI methodology taught in this text.

CHAPTER 10

Data Flow Diagrams and System Flowcharts

Overview

English is a rich language for writing novels, but it is a poor tool for describing systems. Chapter 8 introduced the context diagram, a graphic tool for identifying data flows and defining the boundaries of a system as part of the initial investigation of requirements. In this chapter we explain the procedures for another structured technique: the data flow diagram (DFD). We also provide detailed instructions for drawing system flowcharts.

Specifically, we plan to

1. Explain the use of each DFD symbol. (Section 10.1)

2. Provide rules and step-by-step illustrations on drawing DFDs. (Section 10.2)

3. Present the symbols for and explain the construction of system flowcharts. (Section 10.3)

4. Summarize the differences among system flowcharts, program flowcharts, and DFDs. (Section 10.4)

10.1 Data Flow Diagram Symbols

Preparing a context diagram is a preliminary step in creating a **data flow diagram (DFD)**. Data flow diagrams identify the major data flows within the system boundaries, the processes (procedures and software), and the storage areas for data.

Data flow diagrams use only four symbols. Three of these are used in context diagrams: the shadowed or unshadowed square, the rounded rectangle or circle, and the arrow. The fourth symbol—a pair of horizontal lines with or without two vertical connectors on the left side—designates a data store. The symbols are defined in Figure 10.1; examples of their use appear in Figure 10.2. Because the DFD identifies processes as well as internal entities, the symbol for an internal entity in the context diagram becomes a process box in the DFD.

Figure 10.1
Symbols for Data Flow Diagrams

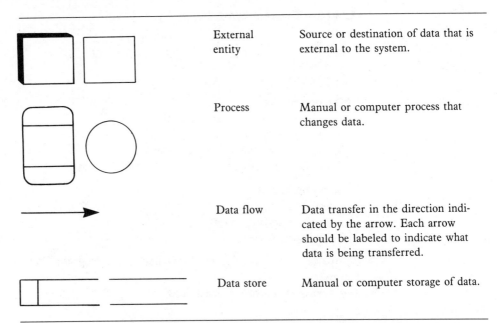

	External entity	Source or destination of data that is external to the system.
	Process	Manual or computer process that changes data.
	Data flow	Data transfer in the direction indicated by the arrow. Each arrow should be labeled to indicate what data is being transferred.
	Data store	Manual or computer storage of data.

The DFD symbols used in this text are the first ones shown in Figure 10.1. These symbols are standard in references on systems development[1]; they are also the ones created with the CASE tool Silverrun-DFD.[2] The second set of symbols was presented in two of the earliest books using data flow diagrams.[3] Both sets of symbols are common. Since the variations are slight, you should have no problem reading and creating DFDs with either symbol set.

10.1.1 Process Boxes

Each **process box** in a DFD describes an action on data. The box should have three labels, as illustrated in Figure 10.3. The *identifier* is a number indicating the process's place in the sequence. The *action* is identified by a predicate phrase specifying an act and the data on which it is performed. The *actor* or *place* is defined by a noun indicating who performs the action or where the action is performed. Using active verbs to label the action makes it easier to identify transformations of data in the system. Figure 10.4 is a

Figure 10.2
DFD with Symbols
Labeled

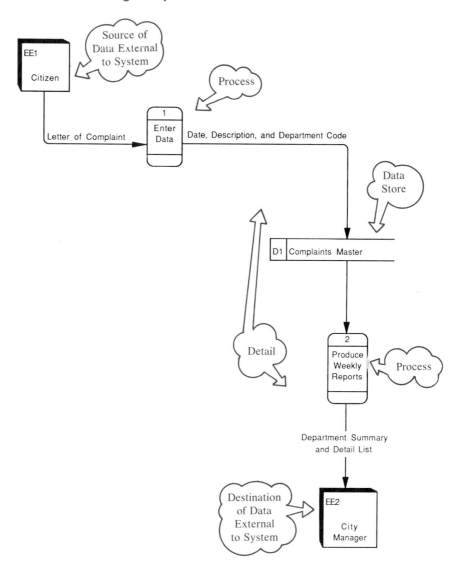

Figure 10.3
Process Symbol with
Labels

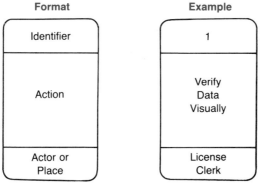

Figure 10.4
Examples of Common
Active Verbs for DFD
Labels

Valid Verbs	Invalid Verbs (do not transform data)
Add	Display
Build	Get
Calculate	Input (The verb is "enter.")
Change	Inquire
Check	Open
Compute	Output
Create	Print
Delete	Read
Determine	Report
Distribute	Store
Edit	Write
Enroll	
Enter	
Examine	
Find	
Format	
Initialize	
Insert	
List	
Merge	
Perform	
Post	
Produce	
Record	
Reformat	
Register	
Sort	
Subtract	
Terminate	
Test	
Update	
Validate	

action makes it easier to identify transformations of data in the system. Figure 10.4 is a list of verbs commonly used in process boxes.

DFDs are read as a series of actions on data. Reading the DFD in Figure 10.2, we obtain the following system description:

> Letters of complaint received from citizens are *entered* into a complaints master file. The date, department code, and a complaint description are stored for each letter. Weekly reports are *produced* from the complaints master file and given to the City Manager. Two weekly reports are produced: a department summary and a detail list.

A process step is required for any transfer of data from or to a data store—data moves from one place to another only by and for processing. Thus, a process box must *always* appear between a data store and an external user. Figure 10.5 illustrates three errors caused by omitting the processes of entering and retrieving data from stores. You may be interested to know that Silverrun-DFD, the system documentation software used to produce the DFDs in this text, would not allow us to make these errors, so we had to draw the lines in by hand.

Figure 10.5
Missing Process Boxes

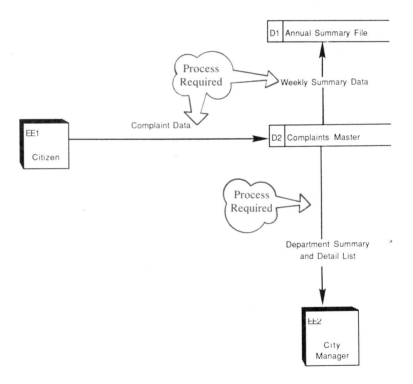

DFDs do not provide information about whether a process is performed by a manual procedure or a computer program. Nor do they provide control information. There is no notation for "if" conditions, because conditions are not processes; they do not transform data. This information may be given in the process specifications, which explain any details required for each process box, as shown in Process 1 in Figure 10.9.

10.1.2 Data Flow Arrows

Data flow arrows link all the process boxes and data stores in DFDs. In general, data flow arrows should be identified. In his classic reference on data flow diagrams,[4] Tom DeMarco makes one exception to this labeling rule—data flows into and out of simple files. Since the data model (which we'll discuss in Chapter 11) describes the structure of each data store, listing the details of a data flow that is simply the records of a file would be redundant. For the exercises in this chapter, you may choose to label all arrows or to omit labels for a record update or report generation from a file.

DFDs show the flow of data, not materials. In a distribution system, an invoice is often attached to a package of goods. The invoice is noted on the data flow diagram, but the package of goods is not. The level of detail of the labels on data flow arrows will depend on the available information and the purpose of the DFD.

10.1.3 Data Store Rectangles

A pair of horizontal lines, with or without two vertical connectors on the left side, marks a data store. **Data stores** can be manual files (folders, file cabinets, in-baskets, and so forth) or computer files (disks, tape, cards). The type of file is not indicated on the DFD. Instead, all details about the nature of the data store are included in the data model.

When data flows into a data store, the data store is transformed. An addition of a record, a deletion, or a change in fields is indicated as an input data flow, which alters the data store. A simple access of a file is not indicated as a data flow. For example, querying the complaints master file in Figure 10.2 for either the date of the letter or the department code would not be shown as an input data flow, because simply accessing a data store does not change it.

A data store is *never* the direct recipient of unprocessed data from external sources or from other data stores. Nor is data from a data store ever directly delivered to an external destination or another data store. There must be a process step in between. Because the needed process steps were omitted, the DFD in Figure 10.5 erroneously suggests that the citizens themselves directly store complaint data in the city's files and that reports are created directly by the complaint master file.

10.1.4 External Entity Squares

The processes and data flows shown on a DFD are *internal* to the specified system or subsystem. Just as in context diagrams, it is helpful to identify the external sources of data and the external destinations of data created by the system. A shadowed or unshadowed square is used to identify these external data sources and destinations, which represent the immediate interfaces of the system with the external world.

When an external source of data is also a destination for data, a loop may be used, like the one in Figure 10.6. Another approach is to repeat the square, as shown in Figure 10.7. When an external entity is repeated, its occurrence number is noted in parentheses, (1/2 means first occurrence of two). In this example the input/output connection is simple enough that either approach is acceptable. In more complicated DFDs, a loop may be

Figure 10.6
Source and
Destination Loop
Showing System
Feedback to External
Entity

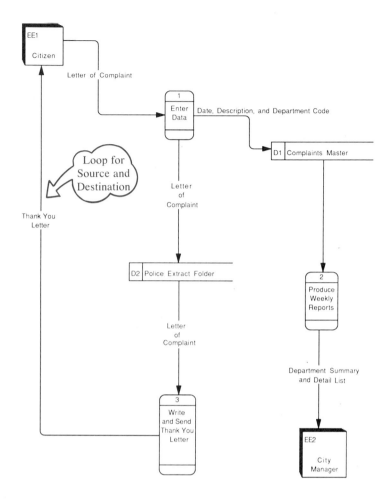

hard to read and may detract from the top-to-bottom and left-to-right organization of the DFD.

The destinations or uses of data created by the system are not always known at the time a DFD is drawn. In these cases the data flows go nowhere; that is, they point outside the system, with no square to indicate the receiver of the report or other output data. Similarly, data flows may originate from nowhere.

A frequent error among beginning students is to confuse places with processes. If a letter is sent to the City Clerk's office and an assistant clerk enters data from the letter, the process of data entry is shown as a process box, *not* the square illustrated in Figure 10.8. A similar mistake is to indicate both the process and its internal location, as shown in Figure 10.9. The location of a process internal to the system is not shown as a source box. The purpose of DFDs is to illustrate data flows and processes *internal* to the system; the place in the system where a process occurs can be indicated in the bottom third of the process box, as shown in Process 1 in Figure 10.9.

Figure 10.7
External Entity Square
Repeated as Source
and Destination for
Improved Readability

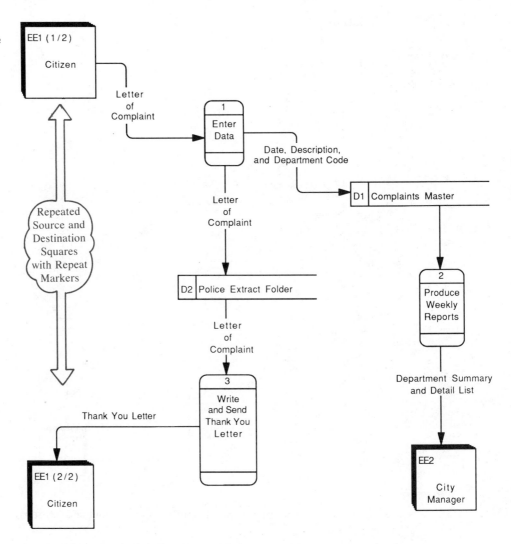

10.2 DFD Construction

The level of detail included in a DFD depends on the purpose of the diagram. If the purpose is to verify all the steps taken by end-users, detailed process steps should be included. If the purpose is to communicate with managers, a simple overview DFD may be most appropriate. For now we will not consider the decision as to level of detail. We will concentrate on the task of translating English into a DFD, including *all* details appropriate for DFDs. In the early development process, analysts practice a similar myopia in order to concentrate on data flow, postponing determining details until they have a better understanding of the system.

For readability, data flow diagrams should be organized to read from left to right and top to bottom. This recommendation applies to the overall organization of the diagram,

Figure 10.8
Mistaken Use of
Square and Location
for Internal Process

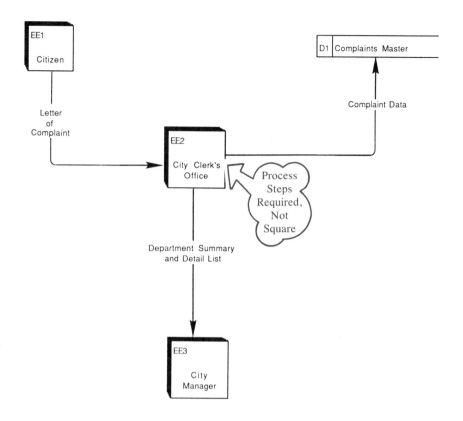

not to each data transformation. In interactive processes, for example, an action will quite often be a response to an earlier action, in which case the data flow will return to the original external source. Sometimes readability can be improved by placing an input data store below a process. One way to achieve overall left-to-right and top-to-bottom organization is to place the key external source or initial process in the top left-hand corner of the page and work down and to the right.

The above-mentioned DFD rules are summarized in Figure 10.10. Rules of this type can be specified as company standards for documentation, much as programming standards are specified.

10.2.1 DFD Construction from an Ordered Example

The minicase Step-by-Step Construction of the License System DFD illustrates the development of a data flow diagram process by process. The system diagrammed is the licensing application system described in Figure 1.10, which is repeated as Figure 10.11 for easy reference. In the following figures, each English sentence of the description is converted into the appropriate DFD symbols.

Figure 10.9
Erroneous Inclusion of
Location of Internal
Process

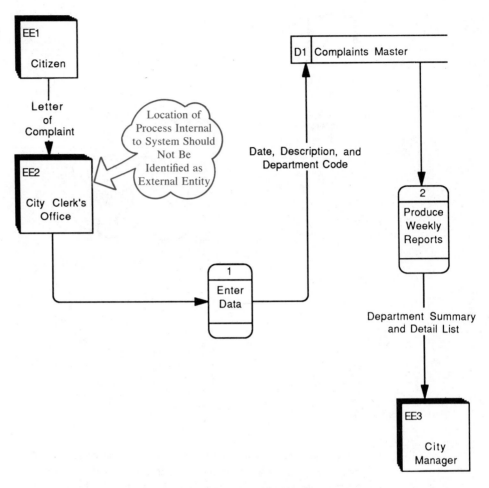

Figure 10.10
Rules for Data Flow
Diagrams

Overall

1. Know the purpose of the DFD. It determines the level of detail to be included in the diagram.

2. Organize the DFD so that the main sequence of actions reads left to right and top to bottom.

Processes

3. Identify all manual and computer processes (internal to the system) with rounded rectangles or circles.

4. Label each process symbol with an active verb and the data involved.

5. A process is required for all data transformations and transfers. Therefore, never connect a data store to a data source or destination or another data store with just a data flow arrow.

6. Do not indicate hardware or whether a process is manual or computerized.

7. Ignore control information ("if"s, "and"s, "or"s).

Figure 10.10
(Continued)

Data flows

8. Identify all data flows for each process step, except simple record retrievals.

9. Label data flows on each arrow.

10. Use data flow arrows to indicate data movement, not nondata physical transfers.

Data stores

11. Do not indicate file types for data stores.

12. Draw data flows into data stores only if the data store will be changed.

External entities

13. Indicate external sources and destinations of data, when known, with squares.

14. Number each occurrence of repeated external entities.

15. Do not indicate actors or places as entity squares when the process is internal to the system.

Figure 10.11
Description of License
Application System

System Description

When a barber wants a hairdresser's license, he or she completes an application at the office of the state board. The application, a training certificate, and $50 are given to the license clerk. The clerk visually checks the documents for completeness and returns them to the applicant if corrections are necessary. If the documents are correct, the clerk enters the application and training certificate data into a VAX 11/780 computer, using a terminal. The system verifies the data, checking it against the license master file and a training center master file. After verification, a receipt and a license certificate are produced and the license master file is updated. The clerk hands the receipt and the license certificate to the applicant.

At the end of each day, the clerk runs a program to create a summary report on the current master file and a detailed list of all added, changed, or deleted license records.

Component Summary for: Barber Licensing System

1. People
   a. developer—not identified
   b. operator—license clerk
   c. end-user—barber, license clerk
   d. manager and user-sponsor—not identified

2. Procedures
   a. user normal procedures (barber)—fill out application form
   b. user and operator normal procedures (license clerk)—check application documents, enter application and certificate data, hand receipt to applicant, run daily report program
   c. recovery procedures—not identified

3. Data
   a. data stores—license master file, training center master file
   b. input—application, training certificate
   c. output—receipt, license certificate, daily summary report, daily change report

(continued)

Figure 10.11
(Continued)

4. Software
   a. operating system—not identified
   b. application software (or program steps)—verify data, produce receipts, update license master file, generate end-of-day reports
5. Hardware
   a. facility—state board's office
   b. computer—VAX 11/780
   c. external storage—not identified
   d. input devices—terminal
   e. output devices—printer

Note that the description omits many process details. For example, how does the clerk run the end-of-the-day reports? DFDs state *what* the processes are, not *how* the processes are completed. The process specifications explain how the processes are performed. If all the process information were packed into this one graph, the DFD would no longer be simple, and its value in providing a quick visual overview would be lost.

MINICASE

Step-by-Step Construction of the License System DFD

The first entry in Figure 10.12 is a square for the barber as an external source of data. The process of filling out the application is not included as a process box on the chart, because the barber's action is external to the system. If the application were mailed in, the same result would be achieved as far as the targeted information system process is concerned.

In Figure 10.13 details are added to the data flow arrow. The training certificate and the $50 check are completed by processes external to the system. The procedures for completing these input documents are set by the barber's school and the bank, not by the licensing board.

The third sentence in the English narrative provides information about a manual process step. In Figure 10.14 a data flow is added to show the possibility of returning the certificate and the check to the barber if they are incomplete. Also, items on the application form may have to be redone. No information about the conditional nature of this action is provided. Data flow arrows simply indicate all possible flows.

In Figure 10.15 a data flow arrow is added to show the flow of the verified data. No process box is added for the clerk's action of entering the data in this DFD it is implied by the flow arrow. The hardware is also omitted for this process-oriented DFD, but it could be in-

Figure 10.12
Step 1 in Construction
of the DFD

Sentence Description	DFD Equivalent
When a barber wants a hairdresser's license, he or she completes an application at the office of the state board.	

Figure 10.13
Step 2 in Construction
of the DFD

Sentence Description	DFD Equivalent
The application, a training certificate, and $50 are given to the license clerk.	

Figure 10.14
Step 3 in Construction
of the DFD

Sentence Description	DFD Equipment
The clerk visually checks the documents for completeness and returns them to the applicant if corrections are necessary.	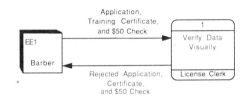

Figure 10.15
Step 4 in Construction
of the DFD

Sentence Description	DFD Equivalent
If the documents are correct, the clerk enters the application and training certificate data into a VAX 11/780 computer, using a terminal.	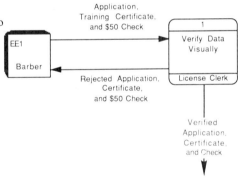

cluded as the "actor" if the purpose of the DFD was a detailed summary of the existing system.

The fifth sentence in the narrative identifies two data stores: the license master file and a training center master file. Notice that in Figure 10.16 the data flow is indicated as output *from* each data store *to* the verification process. No input is shown to either data store, because neither file is updated. Exactly what is checked on each master file is not specified in the English narrative, so the data labels on the arrows are logical guesses.

The additions for the sixth and seventh sentences are shown in Figure 10.17. The sixth sentence results in the addition of a third process box to the DFD: Produce Receipt. The license record is a logical guess for the updated master file, since the English language description is not explicit.

It seems reasonable for verification, file update, and receipt production to occur in the same program step. When drawing DFDs, however, we are not concerned with program steps—our aim is to identify all the known

Sentence Description   **DFD Equivalent**

The system verifies the data, checking
it against the license master file and a
training center master file.

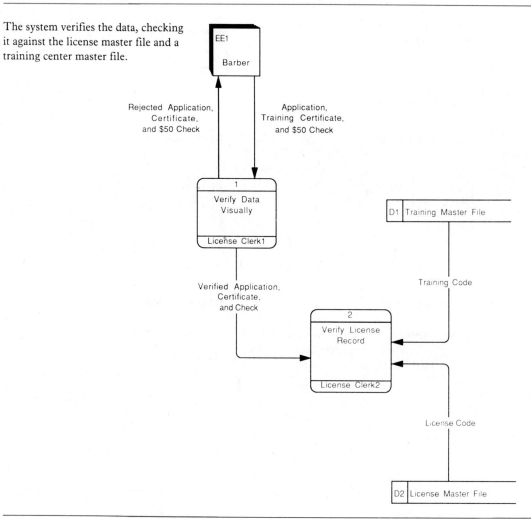

Figure 10.16   Step 5 in Construction of DFD

Sentence Description	DFD Equivalent

After verification, a receipt and a license are produced and the license master file is updated.
The clerk hands the receipt and the license certificate to the applicant.

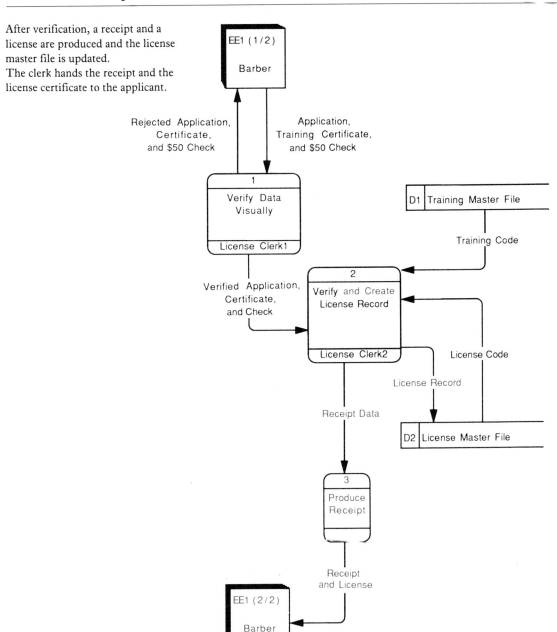

Figure 10.17 Steps 6 and 7 in Construction of the DFD

Sentence Description	DFD Equivalent

At the end of each day, the clerk runs a program to create a summary report on the current master file and a detailed list of all added, changed, or deleted license records.

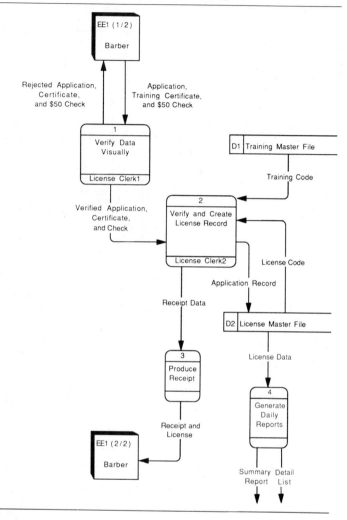

Figure 10.18 Step 8 in Construction of the DFD

process steps. Defining program steps is a computer detail that is postponed until later in development. The label for the second process box, however, is changed to show the full process.

The seventh sentence provides the information that the receipt and the license certificate are given to the applicant. The act of handing the two documents to the barber is such a trivial one that it is not included as a process box. The delivery of the documents is represented by a data flow arrow and destination. The square for the barber is repeated at this point.

Figure 10.18 shows the completion of the data flow diagram. The process step Generate Daily Reports is added, with data flow input from the license master file data store. Since no information is provided about the destination of the reports, the data flow arrows point outside the system rather than to any specific destination.

The figures in this minicase have shown how to construct a **logical data flow diagram,** an abstract version of system requirements that details the functions of a system without specifying the people or places involved.

10.2.2 DFD Construction from an Unordered Example

The English narrative in Figure 10.11 was tailored for a DFD exercise. So are Exercises 10.3 through 10.8 at the end of this chapter. It is important to remember, however, that a user will seldom provide the needed information in the correct order for a DFD. For example, the preceding information about the licensing application system might have been gathered in an interview with the manager of the license application office, who might have explained the process as follows:

> I get two reports at the end of every day. Or almost every day. One is the detail list of all the changes that were made on that day. You know, whoever came in for a license or mailed in an application. Sometimes we run the update program to delete people with expired licenses as well. The other report is a summary that covers all the licenses that are still active. That all works fine. I mean, those reports are okay. But keeping track of training schools is a problem. It isn't that there are many new ones. It's just that the Education department which accredits new schools seldom lets us know about the new ones. You can imagine how angry newly graduated barbers are when we tell them their school doesn't exist. Yesterday, someone came in and. . . .

You might have to take pages of notes just to find out the information needed to diagram the license application process being investigated!

We recommend that you start by making a user-oriented context diagram. This preliminary diagram will help you understand the existing system before you complete detailed data flow diagrams, the data models, and process specifications.

Whether you create a context diagram or a DFD as a first step, the following reminders will help you develop a model of a system for a DFD:

1. Be prepared to do several drafts of your DFDs.

2. Start by extracting external sources and destinations of data. Place the external sources on the top and left side of the page and the destinations on the bottom and right side of the page. Fill in the processes and data stores required to connect the sources to the destinations.

3. Verify your process boxes by listing the processes (software and procedures) as shown in the component summary of Figure 10.11. Do the same with data and people.

10.2.3 Leveling Data Flow Diagrams

The data flow diagram for a complicated system may fill one or more large sheets of paper. Packing one diagram with too many details will cause confusion. To make your DFD more readable, you should create an overview data flow diagram from context diagrams and then decompose the overview into more detailed DFDs.

Structured decomposition, or **leveling,** is the process of organizing DFDs into a hierarchy of increasingly detailed views of processes. The overview, or parent, data flow diagram shows only the main processes. It is the level 0 diagram. Each **parent process** is composed of more detailed processes, call **child processes.** The most detailed processes, which cannot be subdivided any further, are known as **functional primitives.** Process specifications are written for each of the functional primitives in a process.

Figure 10.19 illustrates two levels of data flow diagrams. The system overview DFD, diagram 0, has only four processes. Each is numbered for later reference. Although only diagram 2 and diagram 4 are shown, there would be four pages of level 1 DFDs, one for each of the four major processes. Processes 2.1, 2.2, and 2.3 are detailed, or child, processes for the parent process 2. Depending on the complexity of the system, you might want to further decompose these processes, creating the level 2 diagrams 2.1, 2.2, and 2.3.

The input and output data shown should be consistent from one level to the next. The external sources and destinations for a parent should also be included for the child

Figure 10.19
Structured Decomposition of DFDs

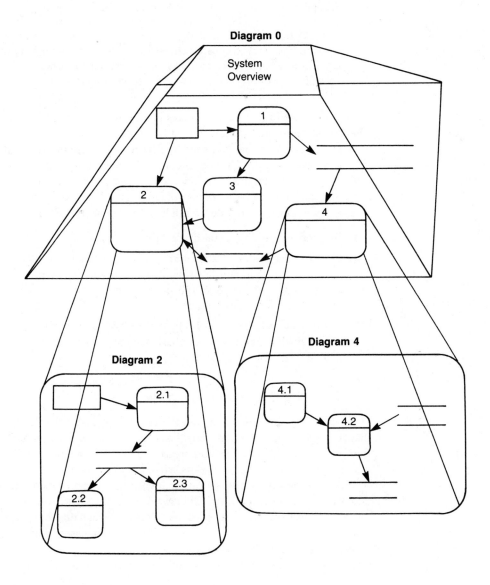

processes. Note that diagram 4 in Figure 10.19 shows the same input and output data stores as does the overview.

Another example of structured decomposition is shown in Figures 10.20 through 10.22. Figure 10.20 is a level 0 DFD for the order tracking system discussed in the Chapter 8 minicase Context Diagrams for Universal, Inc. This diagram is similar to the combined user-level context diagram in Figure 8.15, but the focus is now on three processes. The internal entities Warehouse Shipping and Warehouse Receiving have been combined user–level context diagram in Figure 8.15, but the focus is now on three processes. The internal entities Warehouse Shipping and Warehouse Receiving have been leveled to create diagrams 1, 2, and 3. Diagram 2 is shown in Figure 10.21. Process 2.3 has been leveled further; the level 2 diagram is shown in Figure 10.22. Each parent process is marked with an asterisk to show that it has been leveled in another diagram.

Figure 10.20
Level 0 DFD Diagram

Diagram 0: Proposed Order Tracking System for Universal, Inc.
January 16, 1991

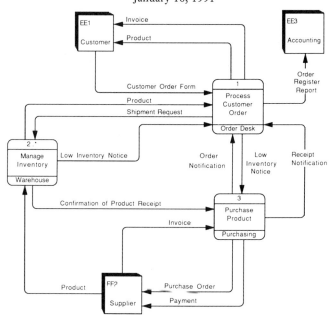

10.3 System Flowcharts

A **system flowchart** is a graphic tool for depicting hardware, programs, and data at the file level.

The two major purposes of system flowcharts are

- documenting existing hardware, programs, and file processing
- communicating proposed hardware, program, and file interface designs

Figure 10.21
Level 1 DFD Diagram

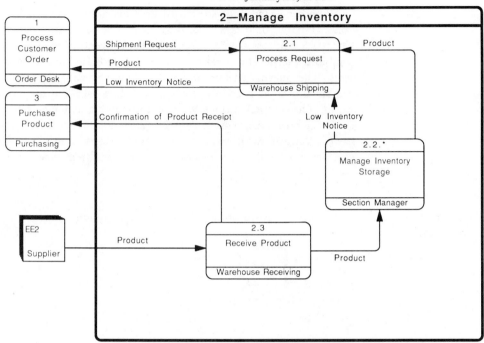

Diagram 2: Proposed Order Tracking System for Universal, Inc.
January 16, 1991

Figure 10.22
Level 2 DFD Diagram

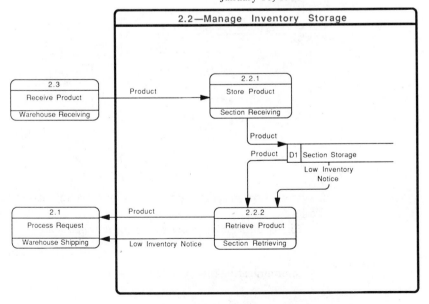

Diagram 2.3: Proposed Order Tracking System for Universal, Inc.
January 16, 1991

You are probably familiar with program flowcharts and with the system flowcharts that illustrate file handling in programming textbooks. Several of the program flowcharting symbols are used in system flowcharts, and both program and system flowcharts use the same stepwise, top-to-bottom organization. System flowcharts, however, serve different purposes than do program flowcharts. They illustrate *what files are processed*, rather than *how data fields are processed*. Even at its most detailed level, a system flowchart indicates a program as one process rectangle. At a higher level, one process rectangle may indicate a system of many programs.

System flowcharts are included in technical documentation to show the hardware and program modules for existing systems. The example in Figure 10.23 is from a programmer's system documentation manual. The process and file labels are specific to the particular installation.

Analysts use system flowcharts to communicate with other analysts and programmers on the project development team. The system flowcharts used as a basis for discussion during the development process are less specific than the one in Figure 10.23. Often program and file names have not yet been established, so labels are merely descriptive of the proposed activities and contents.

10.3.1 System Flowchart Symbols

The various system flowchart symbols provide information about hardware. The three process symbols shown in Figure 10.24 distinguish among processes at a general level. A rectangle indicates a computer process. A square indicates a process performed by auxiliary equipment such as a printer, and a trapezoid indicates a manual process.

Symbols for the different storage devices provide more explicit information about hardware. Figure 10.25 illustrates the symbols for tape, direct access, punch card, and punch tape storage. The storage media shown in Figure 10.25 are also input and output media. Figure 10.26 summarizes other hardware symbols that distinguish among types of inputs and outputs: documents, screen display, manual (keyboard) input, and voice input and output. The symbols in Figure 10.26 represent only input and output media, not storage media. Data from these input media must be transformed into a computer-readable form before it can be stored. Similarly, data for these output media must be created by some process on the system flowchart. In contrast, storage media symbols can indicate either input for or output from flowchart processes.

The hardware details in system flowcharts provide a basis for discussing very specific system trade-offs. Figures 10.27 and 10.28 illustrate two ways of processing students' answers to tests, whether the scanner uses punch cards or tape for storage. In Figure 10.27 the scanning process (shown as an auxiliary equipment square) creates cards. In order to avoid repetition of the relatively slow card reading process, the data on the cards is copied to a disk prior to computer processing. In Figure 10.28 this copying step is eliminated because the scanning process creates a tape rather than cards.

The symbol for a communication link and the flow lines for specific types of file access (input, output, or both input and output) are shown in Figure 10.29. Like data flow diagrams, system flowcharts indicate file input only when data in the file is changed. Neither an input arrow nor an input/output arrow should be used to show simple file

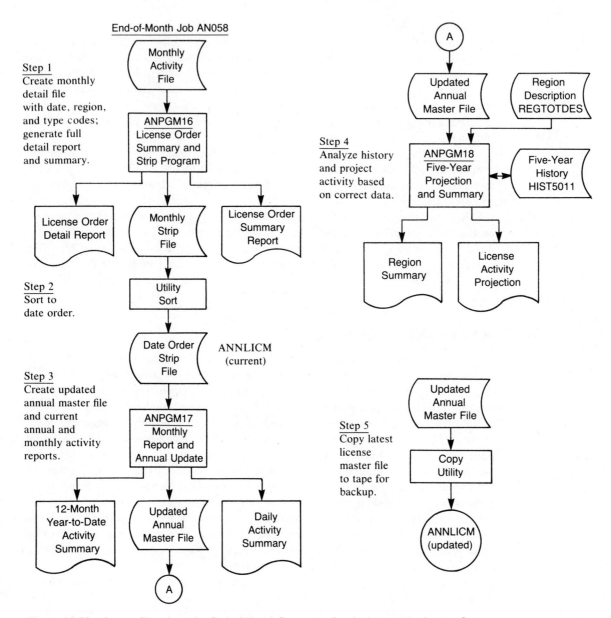

Figure 10.23   System Flowcharts for End-of-Month Processing for the License Application System

Figure 10.24
System Flowchart
Symbols for Process
Steps

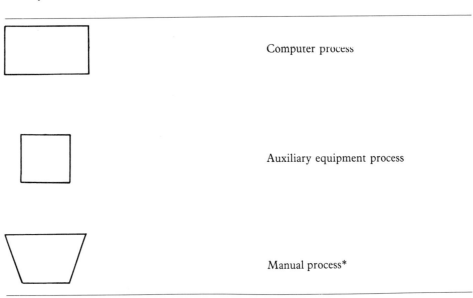

Computer process

Auxiliary equipment process

Manual process*

*A manual process is shown on system flowcharts only when it is an integral step in the continuation of a computer sequence. The filling out of forms and other manual processes typically shown in DFDs do not appear in system flowcharts.

Figure 10.25
System Flowchart
Symbols for Hardware
Storage

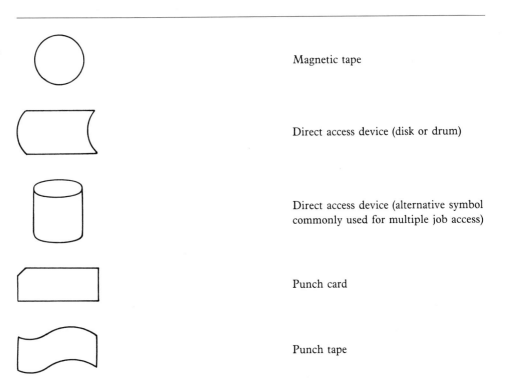

Magnetic tape

Direct access device (disk or drum)

Direct access device (alternative symbol commonly used for multiple job access)

Punch card

Punch tape

Figure 10.26
System Flowchart
Symbols for Input and
Output

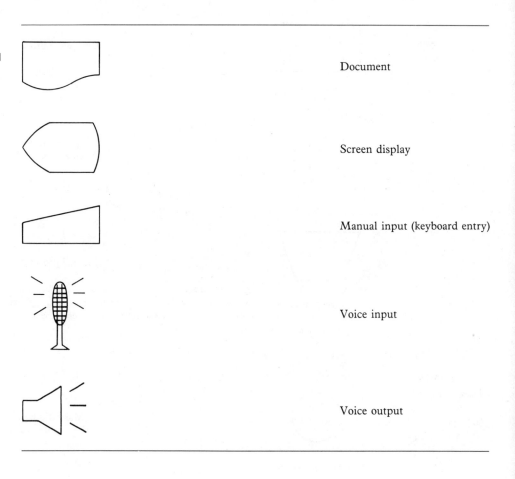

Document

Screen display

Manual input (keyboard entry)

Voice input

Voice output

access. Only direct access files may be both input and output media for the same process blocks.

10.3.2 System Flowchart Organization

System flowcharts are normally organized in columns. If a system flowchart is too long to fit in one sequence on a page, a circle is used to connect column sequences on the same page. A blocked arrow is used to indicate continuation on another page. These two symbols are shown in Figure 10.30.

System flowcharts were originally developed for batch processing systems. Their sequential, top-to-bottom organization is appropriate for these systems. Columnar organization, however, is less appropriate for system overview flowcharts, like the one shown in

Figure 10.27
System Flowchart of
the Scanning Process
with Cards

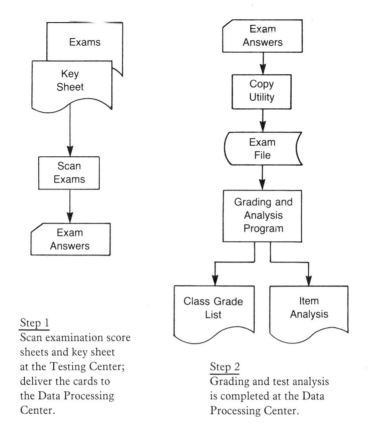

Step 1
Scan examination score
sheets and key sheet
at the Testing Center;
deliver the cards to
the Data Processing
Center.

Step 2
Grading and test analysis
is completed at the Data
Processing Center.

Figure 10.31, and interactive processing flowcharts, like the one shown in Figure 10.32. The organization of such flowcharts centers around a major process block (Figure 10.31) or main file (Figure 10.32). These charts may be read from left to right rather than from top to bottom.

10.3.3 System Flowchart Levels

System flowcharts have two basic levels of detail. The most detailed level shows commands for a run or job. Examples of **job-level system flowcharts** appear in Figures 10.23, 10.27, 10.28, and 10.32. In this type of chart, each process block represents a program.

The second type is an overview flowchart like the one in Figure 10.31. **Overview** (that is, more global) **system flowcharts** depict multiple tasks. Their process blocks represent several programs or entire applications. The flowchart in Figure 10.31 is an overview of the licensing system. It illustrates the major files and reports for the daily processing of applications illustrated in the Figure 10.18 data flow diagram and the end-of-month processing shown in detail in Figure 10.23.

Figure 10.28
System Flowchart of
the Scanning Process
with Tape Storage

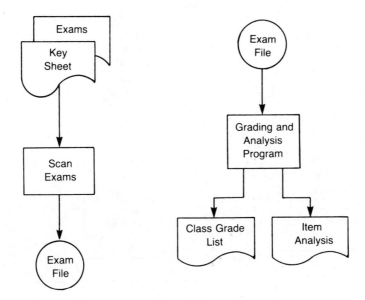

Figure 10.29
System Flowchart Indi-
cators for Interfaces

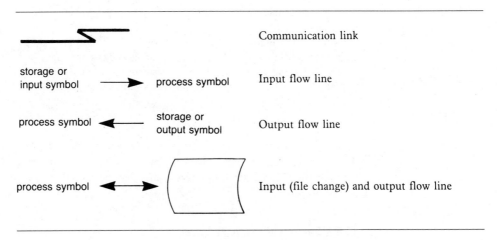

Figure 10.30
System Flowchart
Connector Symbols

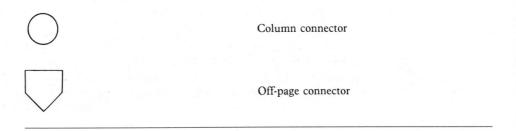

Figure 10.31
Higher-Level System
Flowchart for the
Licensing System

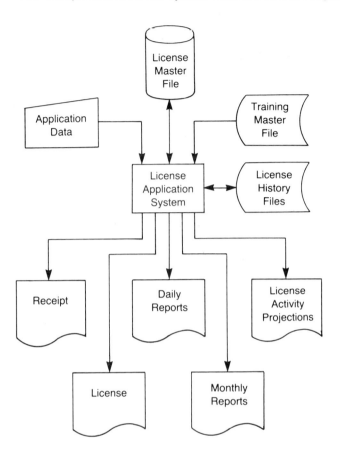

Note that not all reports and files shown in Figure 10.23 are repeated in the overview flowchart in Figure 10.31. The purpose of an overview flowchart is to present the basic task or tasks of a system rather than specific details. The system flowchart in Figure 10.32 is at the same level of detail as the flow diagram in Figure 10.18. The rules for constructing system flowcharts are summarized in Figure 10.33.

10.4 Comparison of DFDs, System Flowcharts, and Program Flowcharts

System flowcharts, program flowcharts, and data flow diagrams all serve different purposes. Construction difficulties arise when one type of chart is drawn to serve multiple purposes or to achieve a goal inappropriate to the technique.

Figure 10.34 contrasts the three types of charts. A comparison of the data flow diagram in Figure 10.18 and the system flowchart in Figure 10.32, both of which describe the same process, provides a more dramatic illustration of the differences. The DFD has four process boxes. The system flowchart has three computer program process blocks,

Figure 10.32
Job-Level System
Flowchart for the
Licensing System

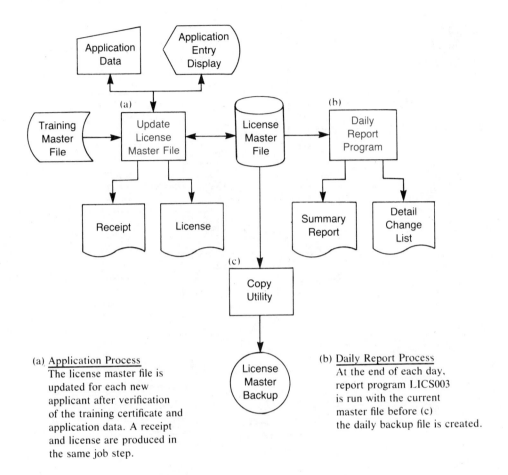

(a) <u>Application Process</u>
The license master file is
updated for each new
applicant after verification
of the training certificate and
application data. A receipt
and license are produced in
the same job step.

(b) <u>Daily Report Process</u>
At the end of each day,
report program LICS003
is run with the current
master file before (c)
the daily backup file is created.

including a copy utility for file backup that is omitted in the DFD. Note also the differences in the representation of data entry in Figures 10.18 and 10.32. In the data flow diagram, the document flow is shown for the first three process steps, which are all manual. On the system flowchart, key entry and data display are represented by hardware symbols, with the processing indicated only by one program that accepts the data and creates the screen display. Although both of these charts are correct descriptions, because they serve different purposes they highlight different aspects of the system.

Figure 10.33

Rules and Recommendations for Constructing System Flowcharts

1. Know the purpose of the system flowchart. It determines the level of detail presented. For example, system overview flowcharts and charts for visual presentations should show less detail than procedures documentation.

2. Identify all process blocks appropriate to the purpose of the chart.

3. Identify the inputs and outputs for each process with the appropriate symbols.

4. Label all symbols.

5. For lower-level flowcharts, use narrative descriptions for documentation detail.

6. Each output must be generated by a process. Therefore, do not link outputs directly with input or storage symbols.

Figure 10.34

Comparison of DFDs, System Flowcharts, and Program Flowcharts

	System Flowcharts	Program Flowcharts	Data Flow Diagrams
Original purpose	Development of batch processing computer systems	Program design	Investigation of system requirements
Hardware	Storage devices shown	None shown	None shown
Programs	Process blocks typically shown as programs or commands	Subprogram detail given	Not mapped to program steps
Data	Files only	Full detail, all levels	Explicit with respect to storage of files and flow of fields
Procedures	Mainly computer, auxiliary equipment	Computer only (internal to program)	Manual and computer
People, places	None shown	None shown	Data sources and destinations external to the system shown

Summary

A data flow diagram is a graphic tool used to illustrate the manual and computer processes of a computer system. It is one of four structured tools for requirements determination: context diagrams, data flow diagrams, data models, and process specifications. These techniques were designed to handle the evolutionary nature of requirements for systems in changing organizational environments.

Data flow diagrams focus on the data component of a system and the processes that transform data. DFD symbols are kept simple in order to convey information to the user in an unintimidating way—only process boxes, external entity squares, data store rectangles, and data flow arrows are used. Computer hardware and other technical details are avoided in order to simplify the system presentation and to postpone decisions about the physical implementation of revised or new components.

A system flowchart is a hardware-oriented system description. The many symbols used with this graphic technique identify specific storage devices and program steps of automated systems. Such flowcharts are necessary for technical documentation of systems.

Unlike system flowcharts and data flow diagrams, program flowcharts focus on program-specific details of *how* data is to be processed. Although program flowcharts employ many of the same symbols as system flowcharts, system flowcharts provide a higher-level view of systems than do program flowcharts. Whereas program flowcharts focus on data at the field level, system flowcharts focus on data at the file level. Data flow diagrams offer an even higher-level view of the system, providing information on file-level transformations of data as well as field-level transformations when appropriate.

Key Terms

(Section numbers are in parentheses.)

data flow diagram (DFD) (10.1)	**parent process (10.2.3)**
process box (10.1.1)	**child processes (10.2.3)**
data stores (10.1.3)	**functional primitives (10.2.3)**
logical data flow diagram (10.2.1)	**system flowchart (10.3)**
structured decomposition (10.2.3)	**job-level system flowcharts (10.3.3)**
leveling (10.2.3)	**overview system flowcharts (10.3.3)**

Notes

1. See David B. Brown and Jeffrey A. Herbanek, *Systems Analysis for Applications Software Design* (Oakland, Calif.: Holden-Day, 1984), and Chris Gane and Trish Sarson, *Structured System Analysis: Tools and Techniques* (Englewood Cliffs, N.J.: Prentice-Hall, 1982).

2. Silverrun-DFD, version 1.0 (1987), is a product of XA Systems, Corporation, Quebec, Canada.

3. Tom DeMarco, *Structured Analysis and System Specification* (Englewood Cliffs, N.J.: Prentice-Hall, 1978), and Edward Yourdon, *Managing the Structured Techniques,* 2nd ed. (Englewood Cliffs, N.J.: Prentice-Hall, 1976).

4. DeMarco, Tom, *Structured Analysis and System Specification.*

Exercises

(Answers to Exercises 10.1, 10.3, 10.4, 10.5, and 10.9 are at the end of the book.)

10.1 List all the errors in the data flow diagram in Figure 10.35.

10.2 List all the errors in the data flow diagram in Figure 10.36.

10.3 Draw a data flow diagram for the grocery store checkout system in Chapter 1, Exercise 1.3, showing all the appropriate details.

10.4 A fifth-grade class uses a simple word processing program to create the class newspaper. Every month the teacher makes a list of different topics. Each student writes an article on one of the topics and stores it on his or her own floppy disk. Students read and edit one another's article files. A final version of each of the articles is then created. These individual

Figure 10.35

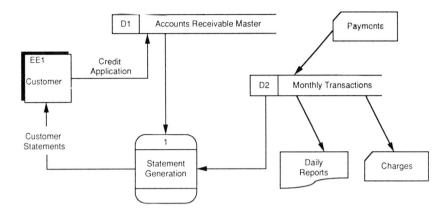

Figure 10.36

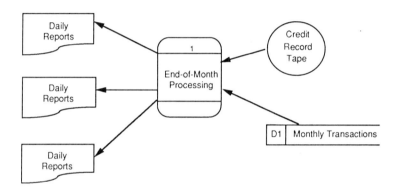

master copies are cut and pasted by the newspaper editor to produce the paper. Copies are then made and distributed to the entire school.

Draw a data flow diagram for the production of the class newspaper, showing all the appropriate details.

10.5 Draw a data flow diagram for the check cashing process in Chapter 1, Exercise 1.4, showing all the appropriate details.

10.6 Draw a data flow diagram for recording, analyzing, and reporting the experimental work with flowers described in Chapter 1, Exercise 1.5. Show all the appropriate details.

10.7 Draw a data flow diagram for Peter Sargent's game advertisements in Chapter 1, Exercise 1.6, showing all the appropriate details.

10.8 After a school orders copies of educational software, Peter Sargent's first step is to update his school client master file. Once the updating is complete, he runs a program to create a summary report of the updated school client master. His summary report goes in his business records folder. Draw a data flow diagram for Peter's record-keeping process for educational software, showing all the appropriate details.

Note: Exercises 10.9 through 10.14 ask you to draw system flowcharts for the processes diagrammed in the preceding exercises. Because data flow diagrams and system flowcharts have different purposes and characteristics, the following descriptions differ from those provided for drawing DFDs. Some details have been added, and others have been omitted. Your system flowcharts should inlcude all the *appropriate* details provided.

10.9 Draw a system flowchart for the following process steps in the point-of-sales system at Big Bob's Supermarket.

For each item purchased, the entry program converts bar code information into an abbreviated product name and price. The conversion requires accessing disk storage of a product master. The name and price are shown on the cash register display. They are also stored on a disk. The price is "spoken" by the computer.

The internally stored item information is used to generate the customer receipt and update the disk file on daily sales activity.

10.10 Draw two system flowcharts for work on a class paper, one for each of the two processes described below.

Student newspaper writers in a fifth-grade class create articles on floppy disks, using a simple word processing program. They make hard copies of their articles for other student writers to review.

Students revise their own articles and create final hard copy versions based on colleague recommendations.

10.11 When a teller at First National Bank receives a check for cash from a client, the client's checking account number and the amount of the check are entered in the computer. The amount is subtracted from the account balance in the disk account master storage file, and a transaction (check number and amount) record is added to the account master. A transaction slip is printed with the check amount, updated account balance, and account number.
Draw a system flowchart for a cash withdrawal from a checking account.

10.12 Researchers at Fancy Flower Seed Company manually enter their experimental results, using a data management program that stores their daily records on a single disk file called DAILYNEW. This file is one of two input files for a statistical analysis program that creates a daily experimental record and an updated summary report. The other file accessed by the analysis program is the current experimental master file, PASTHIST. The analysis program also updates PASTHIST. A third process step each day is to copy PASTHIST to a tape cassette backup file.
Draw a system flowchart for data collection and analysis at Fancy Flower Seed Company.

10.13 Peter Sargent is the manager of Software House, a retail store that specializes in computer programs. When a new game program is received, Peter announces its availability to all game buyers on the Software House mailing list. His announcements are personalized letters created by word processing. The process is as follows:

Peter first creates a file that describes the new game and then prints a copy of the file for his games folder.

The description of the game and a boilerplate letter addressed to game buyers are then copied to a new file, which is edited to create a new announcement file.

Finally, announcement letters are printed with the specific names and addresses of the game buyers.

Draw a system flowchart for the word processing work Peter does to create the mailer.

10.14 Software House keeps computer records on schools that purchase educational programs.

When a school orders ten copies of a program, Peter Sargent, the manager, takes the following steps:

First he copies his current school master file to a new file.

Then he updates the new copy of the school file to show that ten more copies of that program have been sold to the school.

Finally, he runs a report program that prints a summary of programs sold for each of his current "active" educational programs and schools on the school master file.

Draw a system flowchart for Software House's computer processing.

Conceptual Data Modeling

Overview

The data flow diagram (DFD) introduced in Chapter 10 is a model that describes data as it is transformed by the processes of a system. A DFD, however, is not a complete description of data. For the data-oriented approach to systems development discussed in Chapter 8, data must be described independently of the processes that use it. We will use a conceptual data model* to describe data independently of processes. Specifically, in this chapter we plan to

1. Provide an overview of data modeling. (Section 11.1)

2. Explain the constructs used for data modeling. (Section 11.2)

3. Explain how a data flow diagram can help validate a data model. (Section 11.3)

4. Provide rules and step-by-step illustrations for constructing a data model. (Section 11.4)

5. Explain how phased development, or prototyping, can be used in constructing a data model. (Section 11.4.3)

---

*In this chapter we will often shorten the term "conceptual data model" to just "data model." Chapter 17 will explain why the distinction between a conceptual data model and other types of data models is important.

11.1 Introduction to Data Modeling

Conceptual data modeling is a technique for analyzing and describing the data needed by the users of a system. In analyzing the data, you focus on understanding the conceptual structure of the data. In describing the data, you make concise, accurate, and readable statements about the nature of the data. The data description has to be readable by users, programmers, and other technical specialists, because it is a blueprint for database design (see Chapter 17).

Describing the data for a system is difficult. Not only does a typical system have many users who employ many different inputs and outputs, but the analyst is usually not familiar with the system and must learn about it as he or she analyzes and describes the data. The description of data must be detailed, to satisfy the processing needs of the system. Yet the description must also be general so that it results in a database that satisfies the overall data needs of the organization. As if the task were not difficult enough already, the analyst must produce the data description within the time and budget constraints for the project.

Why is a data flow diagram not a complete data description? A DFD shows only how data is used by the processes of a system. A DFD does not represent the relationships an organization needs among the data entities. Thus a database based on a DFD would fall short of meeting the criterion of organizational relevance.

A data model, on the other hand, encourages the analyst to base the analysis of data on the needs of the organization and on the way the users view, or conceptualize, the data. The detailed data needs of the system processes, such as outputs and screens, are added to the model later. Because the data model describes data from the perspective of the organization—not from the perspective of the detailed system processes—it leads to a database that is more adaptable to the data needs of the organization.

Describing data using a data model requires

1. A set of constructs (entity, relationship, attribute, identifier, and dependency) for defining data
2. Rules controlling how the constructs are drawn to form a data model
3. A method for constructing the data model using the constructs and rules

To illustrate the constructs, rules, and method for data modeling, we will continue the development of an order tracking system for Universal, Inc. This case problem was introduced in Chapters 8 and 10. Jill Anderson, a data analyst, has summarized the data necessary for an order tracking system at Universal, Inc.; her summary appears in Figure 11.1. The top bubble in Figure 11.1 is based on the following description of order tracking by Margaret Ray, the manager of the Order Processing department:

Customers place *orders* for Universal *products*. Orders are filled in the Order Processing department by order processing clerks. In the Order Processing department, an *order number* is assigned to each order for identification and an *invoice* with the *cost* of the products for the order is produced. When the invoice is sent to the customer, a *shipment* is also made to the customer. Shipments are made in the Shipping department by shipping clerks.*

---

*Note that information about suppliers was not included in Margaret's explanation. We left out supplier information to simplify the data model.

Figure 11.1
Data Modeling

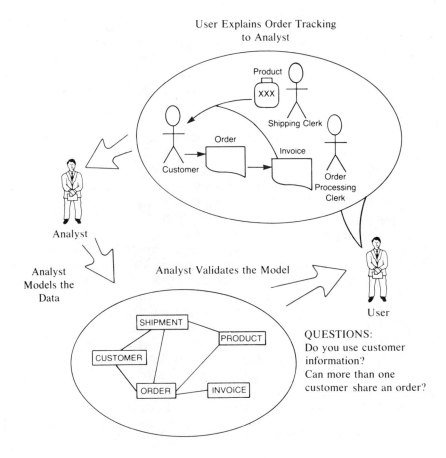

As the first step in modeling the data, Jill identified the departments that would use data from the system—the Order Processing department and the Shipping department. She defined the departments as subsystems of the order tracking system. Defining subsystems would allow Jill to analyze and describe the data needs of each department separately, which would simplify her analysis. After the subsystems were defined, Jill identified and defined the next level of detail—entities and relationships—for each subsystem. Entities are designated by boxes in Figure 11.1: SHIPMENT, CUSTOMER, ORDER, INVOICE, and PRODUCT. Relationships are designated by lines between entities: CUSTOMER:ORDER, ORDER:INVOICE, and so forth. Jill validated the accuracy of the data model by formulating questions to ask Margaret, such as "Do you use customer information?" "Can more than one customer share an order?" After validating the model with Margaret, Jill put the entities and relationships into the data model, as shown in Figure 11.2. The data model in Figure 11.2 represents the order tracking data from the organization's perspective. Next, from an analysis of the input screens needed for the system, Jill defined attributes and grouped them under the entities of the data model. As a final step, Jill reviewed the system's output screens and reports to validate the attributes of the data model. The data model in Figure 11.3 includes the attributes needed to produce the outputs of the order tracking system.

Figure 11.2
Universal's Order
Tracking Data Model

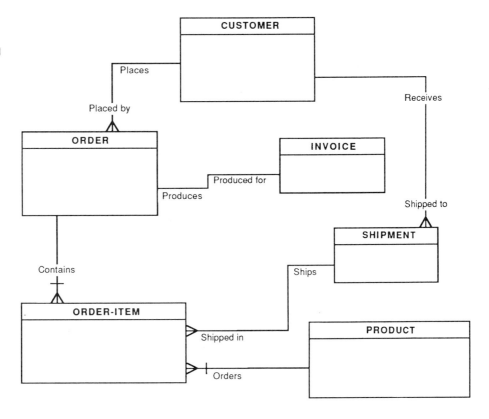

Now that we have introduced the constructs, rules, and method of data modeling, we will look at the data modeling constructs in greater detail. In Section 11.3 we will explain how a data flow diagram can help validate a data model, and in Section 11.4 we will provide a detailed example of constructing a data model.

11.2 Data Modeling Constructs

The six constructs of a data model are entity, attribute, identifier, relationship, dependency, and role. For each one we will

1. Introduce a symbol to represent the construct.
2. Define the construct.

3. Illustrate the construct with an example from the order tracking data models in Figures 11.2 and 11.3.

4. Define rules for using the construct.

Figure 11.3
Universal's Order
Tracking Data Model
with Attributes

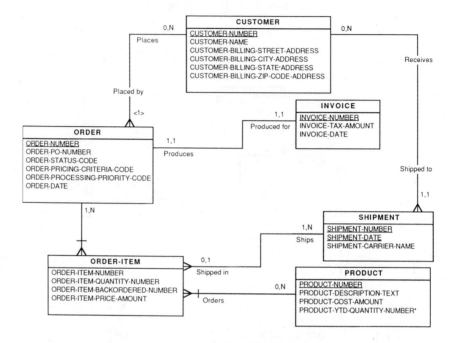

The last part of this section illustrates alternative data modeling symbols.

11.2.1 Entity

Boxes denote entities (see Figure 11.4). An **entity** is any type of thing about which data is collected—an object, person, abstract concept, or event. In the data model for order tracking in Figure 11.2, CUSTOMER and PRODUCT are entities about which data is collected.

Figure 11.4
The Entity Symbol

Entity definitions should stress the meaning of the entity to the user. For example, the definition of the CUSTOMER entity would be "A company or person that has ordered, or might order, a product from Universal." Each definition should include an example, such as "XYZ Inc., XXX Inc., and John Doe are customers of Universal." Definitions of entities are maintained in the design respository (see Chapter 12).

Because they stand for an abstraction rather than a collection of things, entities are labeled with singular nouns. For example, the CUSTOMER entity represents a single abstract object called customer. It does not represent all of the individual instances of companies and people that are the customers of Universal. Hence, the name is the *singular* noun CUSTOMER, rather than the plural CUSTOMERS.

The rules for constructing entities are as follows:

1. An entity name can appear only once in a data model.

2. Each entity must be assigned a unique identifier (identifiers will be discussed later in this section).

3. No instances of entities are included in the data model (instances will be explained next).

The abstract object defined as the PRODUCT entity in Figure 11.2 is not the physical product that can be felt or seen. The actual product is referred to as an instance of the entity. An **instance** is defined as a unique set of values for the attributes of an entity. Figure 11.5 shows two instances of the PRODUCT entity.

Figure 11.5
Two Instances of the
PRODUCT Entity

Product Number	Product Description Text	Product Cost Amount	Product Ytd Quantity Number
250	printer ribbons	5.00	20200
4567	std. computer forms	20.00	14500

11.2.2 Attribute

Names within an entity box denote attributes (see Figure 11.6). An **attribute** is a characteristic of interest or fact about an entity. For the order tracking system, the customer's name and billing address (street, city, zip code) must be known in order to bill a customer. In Figure 11.3, CUSTOMER-NAME and CUSTOMER-BILLING-CITY-ADDRESS are characteristics of a customer, and thus they are attributes of the CUSTOMER entity.

Figure 11.6
Entities with
Attributes

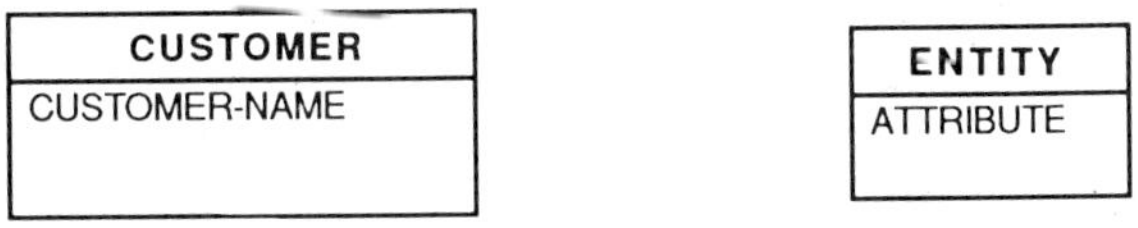

CUSTOMER
CUSTOMER-NAME

ENTITY
ATTRIBUTE

The definition of an attribute will include information about

- the meaning of the attribute to the users
- the technical characteristics of the attribute when it is implemented as part of the database for the system

Included in the meaning of the attribute should be an explanation of why the attribute is a characteristic of the entity. For example, the attribute CUSTOMER-BILLING-

CITY-ADDRESS is defined as "The city portion of the address for a customer. Bills or invoices are sent to the customer's billing address." Definitions should be designed to be meaningful to the users of the system. The technical characteristics of the attribute should include

- the length in characters of the attribute
- the type of data: alphanumeric, numeric, or alphabetic

Definitions of attributes are maintained in the design repository.

The name of an attribute is composed of an entity prefix, qualifier words that define the characteristic of the entity, and a classword that defines the purpose or use of the data. For example, the attribute CUSTOMER-BILLING-CITY-ADDRESS belongs to the entity CUSTOMER, represents the characteristic BILLING-CITY, and is used as an ADDRESS. Guidelines for naming attributes are provided in Figure 11.7.

The rules for constructing attributes are as follows:

1. An attribute name can appear only once in a data model.
2. An attribute must be associated with, or grouped onto, an entity.
3. No values for attributes are included in the data model (values will be explained next).

The data stored in the database for an attribute is called a value. In Figure 11.5, two values are shown for each of the four product attributes listed. The value of an attribute describes something about the instance of a single entity. For example, the value "std. computer forms" for the attribute Product Description Text is part of the description for an instance of the PRODUCT entity with product number 4567.

Values, like instances, are not explicitly included in the data model. This is because the data model is used to represent a *description* of data, not the data actually stored in the database at any particular time.

In addition to attributes, there are derived attributes. **Derived attributes** are attributes whose values are derived from the values of other attributes. In Figure 11.5, the value Product Ytd Quantity Number for product number 4567 describes how many products have been ordered since the beginning of the year. In Figure 11.3, the value PRODUCT-YTD-QUANTITY-NUMBER for the PRODUCT entity is derived by adding up the values of ORDER-ITEM-QUANTITY-NUMBER for all ORDER-ITEM instances having the product number 4567. If derived attributes are placed in the data model, they are denoted by an asterisk at the end of the attribute name (see the PRODUCT entity in Figure 11.3). It is not necessary to place derived attributes in the data model, because they can be determined from attributes already in the data model. Users, however, may need to see the derived attributes to be convinced that all data of interest to them will be provided by the system. Recognizing when an attribute is derived is important, because during database design you will decide whether the values of derived attributes will be stored in the database or calculated by programs.

11.2.3 Relationship

Besides data on orders, customers, and products, order tracking at Universal requires information about which customers ordered which products. Hence, the description of

An attribute name is structured using the following scheme:

ENTITY-QUALIFIER(S)-CLASSWORD

as in the attribute name PATIENT-PHONE-NUMBER. The classword, qualifier, and entity components of an attribute name are described below:

Definition	Examples	Sample Attribute Names
The *classword* designates the purpose or use of the attribute. It is the most general category of data. Some classwords can be abbreviated.	ADDRESS (ADDR)—Data referring to location. AMOUNT (AMT)—Numerical unit representing a sum or total of money. CODE—Combination of letters and/or numbers that represents other data. CONDITION (COND)—Represents on/off, true/false, or yes/no. DATE—Data indicating time. NAME—One or more words designating a person, place, organization, idea, etc. NUMBER (NBR)—Quantity or numerical unit other than money upon which mathematical functions can be performed. PERCENT (PCT)—Numerical unit representing a portion of another value. TEXT—One or more words other than names.	PATIENT-CITY-ADDRESS PATIENT-CITY-ADDR DRUG-BRAND-COST-AMOUNT DRUG-BRAND-COST-AMT
The *qualifier* defines further the exact meaning of the attribute. Qualifiers can be almost any word and they are commonly abbreviated.	IDENTIFIER (ID) LABEL STREET USAGE YEAR-TO-DATE (YTD)	EMPLOYEE-ID-NUMBER PRESCRIPTION-LABEL-TEXT PATIENT-STREET-ADDRESS DRUG-BRAND-YTD-USAGE-NBR
The *entity* is the name of the entity onto which the attribute is grouped. Entity names are often abbreviated when used in attribute names.	PRESCRIPTION (PRESCT)	PRESCT-LABEL-TEXT

Figure 11.7 Guidelines for Naming Attributes

data must include the relationships between CUSTOMER and ORDER and between ORDER and PRODUCT. Each of these relationships must be defined in the data model.

Lines denote relationships (see Figures 11.8 and 11.9). A **relationship** is a correspondence, or association, among one or more entities.* In Figure 11.2, for example, the line connecting CUSTOMER with ORDER designates that the two entities are related. Relationships are bidirectional: CUSTOMER is related to ORDER, and ORDER is related to CUSTOMER.

Figure 11.8
Relationship Symbols
and Examples

Figure 11.9
Many-to-Many
Relationships and
Intersection Entity

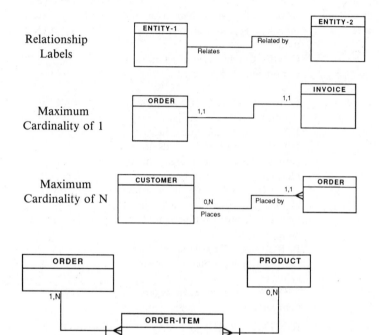

Relationships are defined by referring to instances of the entities that participate in the relationship. For example, the relationship between CUSTOMER and ORDER is defined as "A *single* customer places *many* orders, but a *single* order is placed by a *single* customer." To help readers interpret the definition of a relationship in the data model, labels are sometimes attached to the relationship line. For example, the label "Places" between CUSTOMER and ORDER tells us that a customer places orders. Relationship labels are illustrated in Figure 11.8.

Relationships are named by combining the names of the two entities. For example, the relationship between CUSTOMER and SHIPMENT is named CUSTOMER: SHIPMENT. Each relationship is named and defined in the design repository. Note that the names and the labels of a relationship are not the same thing.

---

*Relationships among more than two entities are possible, but in this book we will address only relationships between two entities.

An important part of the definition of a relationship is its cardinality. **Cardinality** specifies how many instances of one entity can describe one instance of the other entity in the relationship. Cardinality has both a minimum and a maximum value, specified as {min,max} on the relationship line. To define the minimum and maximum cardinality of a relationship, you must answer two questions. The first question determines minimum cardinality: How many instances of the related entity *must* the entity be related to? The answer is either 0 or 1. The second question determines maximum cardinality: How many instances of the related entity *can* the entity be related to? The answer is 1, many (denoted as N), or a number greater than 1. In the CUSTOMER:ORDER relationship in Figure 11.8, the cardinality of the CUSTOMER to ORDER relationship is {0,N} and of the ORDER to CUSTOMER relationship is {1,1}. That is, a customer can place a minimum of zero orders and a maximum of *many* orders. An order must be placed by both a minimum and a maximum of one customer.

After information about the cardinality of a relationship has been obtained from users, it is often possible to validate assumptions about cardinality by reviewing a report or screen. For example, the Order Register report in Figure 11.10 shows that one instance of CUSTOMER (the customer with the number 123) is associated with two instances of ORDER (numbers 1234234 and 1234500).

Report date: 8/28/90

INVOICE NUMBER	ORDER PO NUMBER	CUSTOMER NUMBER	NAME AND ADDRESS	TOTAL ORDER COST	------PRODUCT------		------QUANTITY------		ITEM COST
					NO.	DESCRIPTION	ORDER TOTAL	BACK-ORDERED	
1568	1234234	123	XYZ Inc. PO Box 23 Austin, TX	$60.00	4567	std. computer forms	3	0	$60.00
1569	345690	145	Don's Food 16 Wood Ave. Austin, TX	$225.00	4567	std. computer forms	10	0	$200.00
					250	printer ribbons	5	0	$25.00
1570	1234500	123	XYZ Inc. PO Box 23 Austin, TX	$475.00	4390	special forms	4	1	$160.00
					250	printer ribbons	3	0	$15.00
					4567	std. computer forms	15	0	$300.00
				TOTAL AMOUNT:	$760.00				

Figure 11.10   Order Register Report

In order to make data models easy to understand, the maximum cardinality of a relationship is represented graphically. When the maximum cardinality of a relationship between two entities is one, a simple line is drawn between the two entities (see Figure 11.8). In Figure 11.3, the cardinality of the relationship between ORDER and INVOICE is {1,1}, and the cardinality of the relationship between INVOICE and ORDER is {1,1}. Universal has a policy that only one invoice can be issued for each order and each order can have only one invoice. When the maximum cardinality of a relationship is many, a three-prong connector is attached to the relationship line on the multiple-instance end of the relationship (see Figure 11.8). In Figure 11.3, the cardinality of the relationship between CUSTOMER and ORDER is {0,N}. Since a single customer can place many orders, the three-prong connector is attached to ORDER.

When the two entities in a relationship have a maximum cardinality of N to each other (often referred to as a many-to-many, or N:M, relationship), a new entity, called an **intersection entity,** is created between them (see Figure 11.9). The cardinality between each related entity and the intersection entity is always {0,N}, or {1,N}. The cardinality between the intersection entity and each related entity is always {1,1}.

Intersection entities are necessary because N:M relationships can have attributes and the data model allows attributes only for entities. In Figure 11.3, the relationship between ORDER and PRODUCT is {N,M}. A single order can have many products, and a single product can be a part of many orders. The intersection entity for the ORDER: PRODUCT relationship is ORDER-ITEM. One attribute of ORDER-ITEM is ORDER-ITEM-QUANTITY-NUMBER. Notice that ORDER-ITEM-QUANTITY-NUMBER is not a characteristic of either the ORDER or the PRODUCT entity. ORDER-ITEM-QUANTITY-NUMBER is a characteristic of a product that has been ordered—that is, the relationship between the ORDER and PRODUCT entity.

An intersection entity is named with a noun. The name can be either a meaningful description of the relationship, such as ORDER-ITEM or LINE-ITEM, or a combination of the names of the entities that participate in the relationship. For example, the ORDER-ITEM relationship could have been named simply ORDER-PRODUCT.

All rules that apply to entities also apply to intersection entities. The name used for an intersection entity must be unique in the data model. The intersection entity must have an identifier (see the following section). The identifier for an intersection entity is composed of identifiers for the two related entities and any other attributes necessary to create a unique identifier. For example, ORDER-ITEM is identified by ORDER-NUMBER and PRODUCT-NUMBER. If the combination of ORDER-NUMBER and PRODUCT-NUMBER were not unique, a compound identifier that included ORDER-ITEM-NUMBER could be used.

Rules for constructing relationships include the following:

1. Each relationship should be labeled.
2. If possible, the line for one relationship should not cross the line for another relationship. (A data model with crossed lines is hard to read.)
3. Minimum and maximum cardinalities should be established for each relationship.
4. Each relationship must be part of a unique path between two entities (paths will be explained next).

A path is a series of one or more relationships that can be followed between two entities. In Figure 11.3, there are two paths between CUSTOMER and SHIPMENT. The first path is CUSTOMER:SHIPMENT, which provides information about customers receiving shipments (and shipments sent to customers). The second path is a combination of relationships providing the same information. First, CUSTOMER:ORDER shows that a customer can place many orders. Next, ORDER:PRODUCT shows that an order can have many order items. Finally, ORDER-ITEM:SHIPMENT shows that an order item will be shipped in a shipment. The second path also shows that a customer can receive many shipments, because a customer can place many orders and each order can have one or more shipments of order items.

A data model should be as simple as possible; that is, the model should not provide the same information more than once. Thus, when paths between the same two entities provide the same information, one path should be deleted. In the Universal data model, the path defined by the CUSTOMER:SHIPMENT relationship could *probably* be deleted without the loss of any information about order tracking data. We must qualify this statement, however, because Universal might allow an order to be shipped to a customer different from the customer who placed the order. Note that the relationship between SHIPMENT and ORDER-ITEM cannot be deleted, because the information about the order items contained in a shipment would be lost.

11.2.4 Identifier

The underlining of an attribute denotes an identifier (see Figure 11.11). An **identifier** is an attribute or a set of attributes that has a unique value for each instance of an entity. Each entity needs to have at least one unique identifier so that each instance of the entity can be referenced without being confused with another instance. Uniqueness implies that for all possible instances of the entity, no two values of the identifier will be the same. In Figure 11.3, for example, no two customers should have the same CUSTOMER-NUMBER. The Order Register report in Figure 11.10 confirms that the customer number for XYZ Inc. is 123 and the customer number for Don's Food is 145. Notice that the attribute CUSTOMER-BILLING-CITY-ADDRESS in Figure 11.3 is not unique, because the customers Don's Food and XYZ Inc. in Figure 11.10 are both located in Austin. Thus, although identifiers and attributes are both characteristics of customers, attributes can have the same values whereas identifiers cannot.

When a single attribute cannot guarantee a unique identifier, it is necessary to create a compound identifier by combining the values of several attributes. In Figure 11.3, the SHIPMENT entity requires a compound identifier composed of SHIPMENT-

Figure 11.11
Entity with Identifier

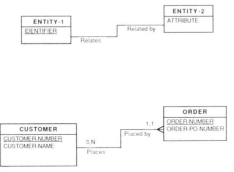

NUMBER and SHIPMENT-DATE. The compound identifier is needed because the four-digit SHIPMENT-NUMBER used by Universal is not guaranteed to have unique values for all possible shipments. Universal ships 10,000 orders in six months, but because the SHIPMENT-NUMBER has only four digits, its maximum value is 9999. Therefore, each value of SHIPMENT-NUMBER occurs about twice each year. In order to create a unique identifier for the SHIPMENT entity, SHIPMENT-DATE and SHIPMENT-NUMBER are combined.

When an entity has more than one identifier, each alternative identifier is denoted by a number. The ORDER entity in Figure 11.3 has two identifiers: the ORDER-NUMBER, denoted with an underline, and the combination identifier composed of ORDER-PO-NUMBER and CUSTOMER-NUMBER, denoted with a <1>. The <1> on the CUSTOMER:ORDER relationship indicates that the alternative identifier for ORDER has been formed by combining the CUSTOMER identifier (CUSTOMER-NUMBER) and the ORDER-PO-NUMBER. Note that <1> implies a 1,1 cardinality.

Identifiers are defined and named in the same way as attributes. Definitions of identifiers are maintained in the design respository.

The rules for constructing identifiers are as follows:

1. An identifier name can appear only once in a data model.

2. An identifier must be associated with, or grouped onto, an entity.

3. No values for an identifier are included in the data model.

4. An identifier has a unique value for every instance of the entity.

11.2.5 Existence and Identifier Dependency

Often, when two entities are related, the instances of one entity will owe their existence to instances of the other entity in the relationship. For example, it is difficult to conceive of an order without a customer. Hence, there is an **existence dependency** between ORDER and CUSTOMER. Existence dependency is represented in the data model by specifying a minimum cardinality of one for a relationship. In Figure 11.3, the relationship between ORDER and CUSTOMER has a minimum cardinality of one.

Entities that depend on another entity for their existence often depend on that same entity for a part of their identifier. An **identifier dependency** exists when the instances of an entity cannot be uniquely identified by the values of its attributes. The dependent entity, therefore, must use the identifier of a related entity or entities or its identifier.* In Figure 11.3, ORDER-ITEM does not have an attribute that can uniquely identify its instances. The ORDER-ITEM-NUMBER cannot be used as an identifier, because its values will repeat for every order. Therefore, ORDER-ITEM must use the identifiers of ORDER and PRODUCT to identify its instances. Identifier dependency is denoted by placing a small line perpendicular to the relationship line near the dependent entity. Note that the line implies a 1,1 cardinality. In Figure 11.3, the lines placed next to the ORDER-ITEM entity mean that the identfier for ORDER-ITEM is a combination of ORDER-NUMBER and PRODUCT-NUMBER.

When an alternative identifier is dependent, an identifier number is placed on the

*The dependent entity is also referred to as the "weak" entity in the relationship.

relationship line. In Figure 11.3, the < 1 > next to the ORDER entity specifies that an alternative identifier for ORDER is CUSTOMER-NUMBER plus ORDER-PO-NUMBER.

11.2.6 Role

The relationship construct discussed in Section 11.2.3 associates different types of entities. For example, the entity CUSTOMER is associated with the entity ORDER. In contrast, the **role** construct associates similar entities. For example, in Figure 11.12, the CUSTOMER-TYPE role associates the entities RETAIL-CUSTOMER and WHOLESALE-CUSTOMER. Roles are important, because users often think of entities in terms of specific roles. For example, the manager of the retail store at Universal would think of customers as retail, rather than wholesale, customers.

Figure 11.12
Customer-Type Role

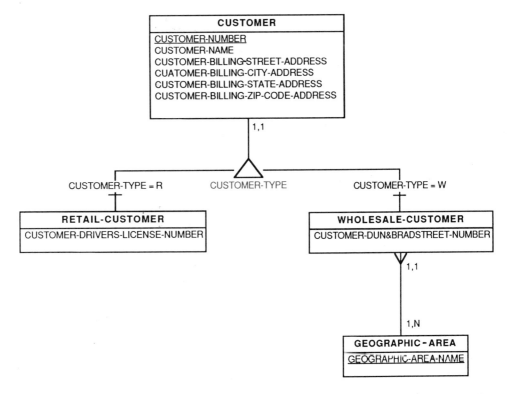

A triangle that connects two or more entities denotes a role. Roles represent categories or types of a generic entity such as CUSTOMER.

There are two rules for constructing roles:

1. Each role must have a role discriminator, identifier, and minimum and maximum cardinality.

2. Each role of an entity must have at least one attribute or relationship that is not shared by the entity's other roles. (In Figure 11.12, RETAIL-CUSTOMER

includes the attribute CUSTOMER-DRIVERS-LICENSE-NUMBER, but WHOLESALE-CUSTOMER does not. Also, WHOLESALE-CUSTOMER has a relationship with GEOGRAPHIC-AREA, but RETAIL-CUSTOMER does not.)

The role discriminator is the attribute that determines which role applies to an instance of the generic entity. In Figure 11.12, CUSTOMER-TYPE is the role discriminator. When CUSTOMER-TYPE = W, the customer is a wholesale customer. When CUSTOMER-TYPE = R, the customer is a retail customer.

Figure 11.13
Summary of Data
Modeling Symbols

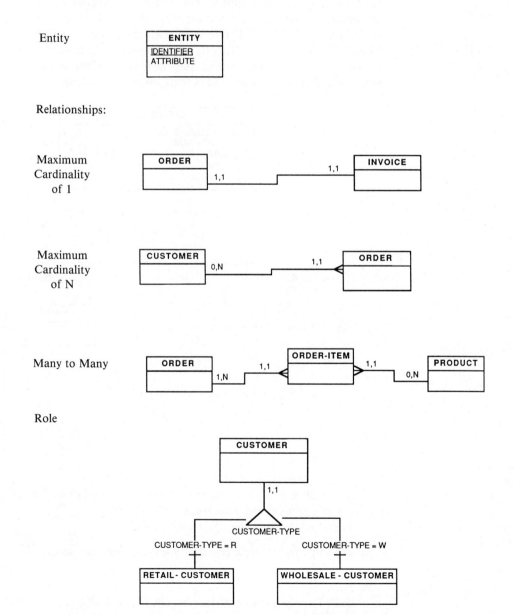

The identifier of a role can be the same as or different from the identifier of the generic entity. In Figure 11.12, the identifier dependency symbol above each role entity indicates that the identifiers of the RETAIL-CUSTOMER and WHOLESALE-CUSTOMER entities are the same as that of the CUSTOMER entity. It is possible, however, for the identifier of a role to be different from that of the generic entity. For example, Universal might use the CUSTOMER-DUN&BRADSTREET-NUMBER as the identifier of the WHOLESALE-CUSTOMER entity.

The cardinality of a role specifies the minimum and maximum number of role instances that can exist at one time. In Figure 11.12, a customer must have a minimum of one role (a customer must be either a retail or a wholesale customer), and a customer can have a maximum of one role (a customer cannot be both a retail and a wholesale customer).

Figure 11.13 provides a summary of the data modeling symbols, and Figure 11.14 provides a summary of the rules used to represent the constructs presented in this section.

Figure 11.14
Rules for Data
Modeling

Entity	1. An entity name can appear only once in a data model.
	2. Each entity must be assigned a unique identifier.
	3. No instances of entities are included in the data model.
Attribute	1. An attribute name can appear only once in a data model.
	2. An attribute must be grouped onto an entity.
	3. No values for attributes are included in the data model.
Intersection entity	1. The name of an intersection entity can appear only once in a data model.
	2. Each intersection entity must have a unique identifier.
	3. No instances of intersection entites are included in the data model.
Relationship	1. Each relationship should be labeled.
	2. If possible, the line for one relationship should not cross the line for another relationship.
	3. Minimum and maximum cardinalities should be established for each relationship.
	4. Each relationship must be part of a unique path between two entities.
Identifier	1. An identifier name can appear only once in a data model.
	2. An identifier must be grouped onto an entity.
	3. No values for an identifier are included in the data model.
	4. An identifier has a unique value for every instance of the entity.
Role	1. Each role must have a role discriminator, identifier, and minimum and maximum cardinality.
	2. Each role of an entity must have at least one attribute or relationship that is not shared by the entity's other roles.

Note that this chapter uses CAPITAL letters to refer to objects in a data model or a data flow diagram. For example, the word ORDER refers to the entity ORDER in the order tracking data model. In contrast, the word "order" (in lowercase letters) is used to signify an instance of the ORDER entity. For example, we would say that a customer can place many orders.

11.2.7 Alternative Symbols for Data Modeling

The set of data modeling symbols shown in Figure 11.13 is only one of many possible notations for constructing data models. Other notations are also used widely.[1]

The alternative notation shown in Figure 11.15 is called **entity-relationship (ER) notation**.[2] The rectangular symbol used in this book to represent an entity is also used in ER notation. In several other respects, however, ER notation differs from the system employed in this book.

1. ER notation represents attributes with a line and identifiers with a dot placed on the attribute line.

2. ER notation uses a diamond symbol instead of a line for a relationship.

3. ER notation specifies the maximum cardinality of a relationship on a relationship line, and it does not use three-prong connectors to indicate cardinality.

4. No special intersection entities are used in ER notation—the diamond symbol can represent either a relationship or an intersection entity.

5. ER notation uses a double box symbol and an arrow pointing at the double box to represent existence dependency. The dependent entity is placed within the double box. For example, in Figure 11.15 ORDER is dependent on CUSTOMER.

Figure 11.15
ER Notation

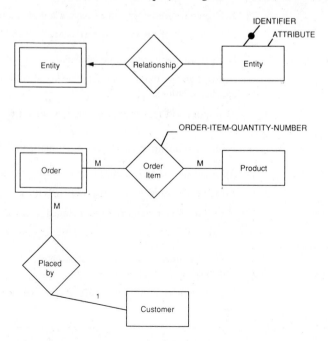

11.3 Validating Data Models Using Data Flow Diagrams

A data flow diagram can be used to validate the entities, relationships, and attributes in a data model. In addition, the data flows in a data flow diagram can be used to derive attributes for a data model. In this section we will illustrate these processes using the Track Orders data flow diagram* in Figure 11.16 and the order tracking data model in Figure 11.3.

Figure 11.16
Track Orders Data Flow Diagram

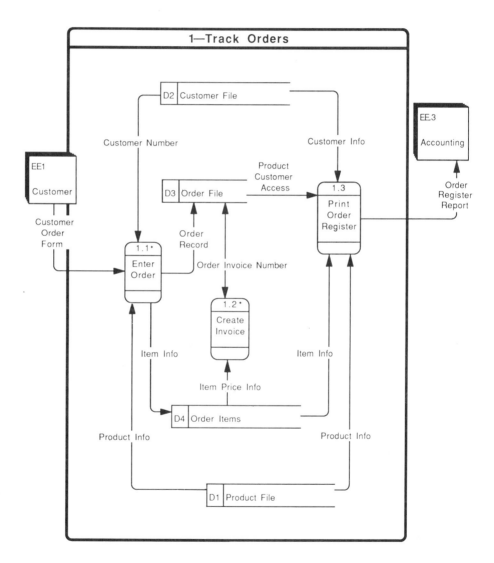

*The Track Orders DFD is a decomposition of the Process Customer Order process on the Order Tracking System DFD in Figure 10.20. The name of the process has been changed to Track Orders and some data flows have been eliminated to simplify this example.

To validate entities in the data model in Figure 11.3, we can compare them with the data stores in Figure 11.16. The data stores for products, customers, orders, and order items should correspond to entities in the data model. The data model in Figure 11.2 has entities for each of these data stores, plus two other entities, SHIPMENT and INVOICE. The analyst who developed the Track Orders data flow diagram should be asked why SHIPMENT and INVOICE data stores are not included in it.

To validate relationships in the data model, we can note the data stores that are used together in the same process. For example, the PRODUCT, CUSTOMER, and ORDER files are all used by the Enter Order process. Relationships, therefore, must exist among PRODUCT, CUSTOMER, and ORDER. The data model in Figure 11.3 shows that CUSTOMER is related to PRODUCT through ORDER.

To validate dependencies in the data model, we can note how data is created in the data flow diagram. For example, in the Enter Order process, both the PRODUCT-NUMBER and the CUSTOMER-NUMBER must be acquired before an ORDER record can be created in the ORDER file. An existence dependency, therefore, must exist between ORDER and CUSTOMER and between ORDER and PRODUCT.

To derive attributes for the data model, we can look at the data that comprises the data flows in the data flow diagram. For example, one data flow listed in Figure 11.16 is Order Register Report. Looking at this report (see Figure 11.10), we can see that it contains 12 attributes. Each attribute is grouped onto an entity in the order tracking data model.

11.4 Data Model Construction

The top-down approach discussed in Chapter 8 can be applied to the construction of a data model. The process of writing a report is analogous to that of analyzing and describing data in top-down fashion. Your first step in writing a report is to decide on a topic and develop an outline that defines what will be included in the report. Then, as you write the report, you make changes to the outline as you learn new information about the topic. You revise the report until you are satisfied that it is accurate and concise. This top-down method helps manage the difficult writing process and helps ensure that the finished report is of good quality.

You construct a data model using a similar method. The steps in constructing a data model for a system are

1. Construct a high-level data model that shows how the data from the system relates to other data in the organization, and partition the data model into subsystems.

2. Construct a data model for each subsystem.

    2.1. Identify and define the general groups of entities and relationships between entities.

    2.2. Validate the entities, identifiers, relationships, and dependencies.

    2.3. Define the attributes, and group the attributes onto the entities.

    2.4. Validate the attributes in the data model.

3. Integrate the subsystem data models into one data model for the system.

Figure 11.17
Procedure for Data
Modeling

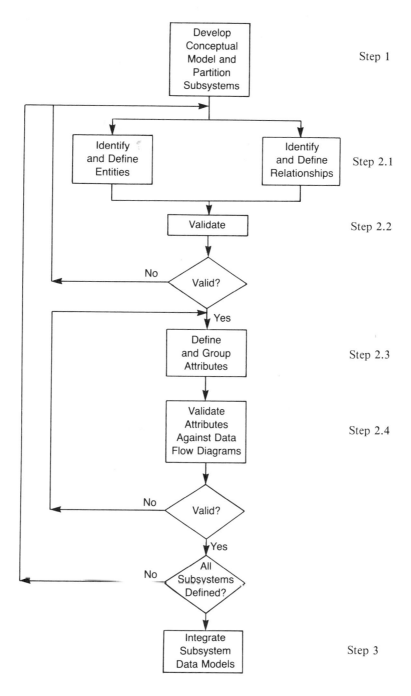

The procedure for data modeling is shown as a flowchart in Figure 11.17. When construction is complete, the deliverables will include the data model, a design repository containing the name and definition of each object in the data model, and a log of the assumptions that were made in constructing the data model. Each of these deliverables will be illustrated in the minicase Return to Meadows Hospital.

Two techniques that can substantially simplify model construction are starting from a central entity and using a comment log. The presence of a **central entity** makes it easier to define the relationships between the other entities in the data model. A **comment log** provides documentation that can be used to validate the data model. For example, a comment in the log for the order tracking data model might be "Ask Margaret Ray if customers can share an order." Note, however, that when possible you should ask the user about the assumption at the time the assumption is made.

11.4.1 Data Model Construction from an Ordered Example

In the following minicase, the Meadows Pharmacy case introduced in Chapter 3 has been expanded to illustrate the data modeling techniques discussed in Chapters 8 through 11. This expansion focuses on the data requirements phase and the development of a data model to describe the data needed for the pharmacy system. For purposes of illustration, we have expanded the development team. In addition to Tito Hernandez, the assistant pharmacy manager, Fred Kahn, the programmer/analyst assigned to the project, and Tracy Bell, the project leader, the team now includes Mary Henderson, the pharmacy manager and senior pharmacist, and Jayne Ingerson, a data analyst.

MINICASE

Return to Meadows Hospital

In Chapter 3 the Information Services request was general and vague, as is typical in many installations. To speed this minicase along so that we can concentrate on data modeling, we will assume that Mary Henderson and Tito Hernandez, the pharmacy manager and assistant manager, completed the much more detailed Information Services request shown in Figure 11.18. Let us now follow Jayne Ingerson, the data analyst, through the various steps in constructing a data model.

1. Developing a High-level Data Model and Partitioning It into Subsystems

Jayne started by identifying the major entities and relationships of the pharmacy system. At the highest level the pharmacy system uses data about four types of things: drugs, prescriptions, patients, and physicians. The overview data flow diagram (level 0) developed by Fred (Figure 11.19) identified for her the major subsystems for the phar-

macy system: Pharmacy, Inventory, and Administration. Jayne partitioned the pharmacy system entities into subsystems by determining which subsystems were responsible for creating instances of the entities. She acquired this information from the description of the pharmacy system in Figure 11.18 and from talking with Mary and Tito: instances of PRESCRIPTION are created in the Pharmacy department (pharmacy subsystem), instances of DRUG are created in the Inventory department (inventory subsystem), and instances of PHYSICIAN and PATIENT are established by the Hospital Administration department (administration subsystem). Jayne denoted the subsystems on the data model by drawing boundaries around the entities, as shown in Figure 11.20.

Next, Jayne had to decide the order in which the subsystems would be modeled in more detail. She asked Mary Henderson to assign a priority to each subsystem, and Mary assigned the highest priority to the pharmacy

Figure 11.18
Information Services
Request by Pharmacy
Division

Meadows Hospital	Information Services Request Form	Page 1 of 1
System Pharmacy Record Keeping		Date 1-25-89

Service for   Pharmacy   (division)   Supervisor   Tito Hernandez

Extension   283   Authorized Signature   *Tito Hernandez*

Requested Services

1. Develop automated summary reports, logs, and prescription labels.

2. Integrate all master files used by the Pharmacy, Inventory, and Administrative departments.

System Description

Prescription slips for patients at the hospital are filled out by doctors. Normally, the patient brings the slip to the pharmacy where the prescription is processed. Processing a prescription requires:

1. Verifying the existence of the physician who ordered the prescription.
2. Assigning a number to the prescription and establishing the prescription in the prescription file.
3. Filling of the prescription by the pharmacist. The pharmacist:
   3.1 Displays the prescription information on the CRT.
   3.2 Uses the information to fill the prescription with drugs from inventory.
   3.3 Updates the prescription record with the brand of the drug and the pharmacist identification number.
   3.4 Prints the prescription label with the name of the patient.
   3.5 Attaches the label to the prescription container and gives the container to the patient.

Daily reports are generated using information from the "filled" records of the prescription file. Two reports are printed: (1) Drug Supplier Report and (2) Daily Drug Report.
1. The Drug Supplier Report is used for inventory control. The report uses the drug supplier information in the supplier file and drug information in the drug file.
2. The Daily Drug Report is sent to Administration. It contains only information from the prescription file.
    ISD Signature   *Gloria Gratel*   Date 1-28-89

---

subsystem. Jayne decided that PRESCRIPTION was probably a central entity, because it had relationships with all of the other entities in the data flow model in Figure 11.20. Therefore, Jayne started the modeling of entities and relationships with PRESCRIPTION.

2.1. Modeling Entities and Relationships

Figure 11.21 shows Jayne's first draft of the pharmacy data model. The focus is on data required to support the pharmacy subsystem. Although only PRESCRIPTION was

totally within the boundary of the pharmacy subsystem, Jayne knew that data from DRUG, PATIENT, and PHYSICIAN would be used by the subsystem and, hence, had to be modeled also. Jayne placed PRESCRIPTION, identified as the central entity during the high-level modeling, in the center of the model. She defined and documented each entity in the preliminary design repository (see Figure 11.22).

Jayne used the system description provided in Figure 11.18 to analyze identifiers for the entities. She noticed

Figure 11.19
Context Diagram for
the Pharmacy System

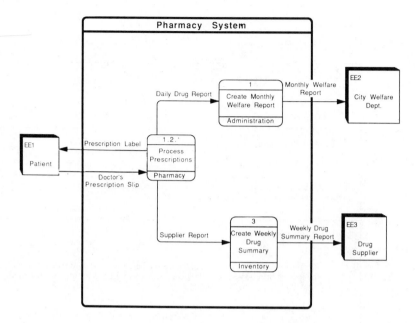

Figure 11.20
Data Model with
Subsystem Boundaries

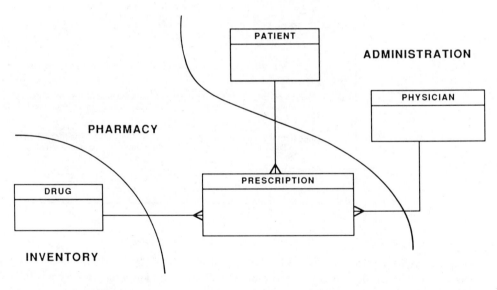

that DRUG-NAME and PATIENT-NUMBER are used on the DOCTORS-PRESCRIPTION-SLIP to identify the patient and the drug, that a unique PRESCRIPTION-NUMBER is assigned to each prescription in the pharmacy department, and that physicians are identified by their last name (PHYSICIAN-LAST-NAME). Next, Jayne defined and named the identifiers. Using the naming guide-

lines in Figure 11.7, she changed PATIENT-NUMBER to PATIENT-ID-NUMBER and PRESCRIPTION-NUMBER to PRESCRIPTION-ID-NUMBER. The identifiers were then documented in the preliminary design repository (see Figure 11.22).

Jayne used an analogy to determine the cardinalities of the relationships on the first draft of the data model.

Figure 11.21
First Draft Pharmacy
Data Model

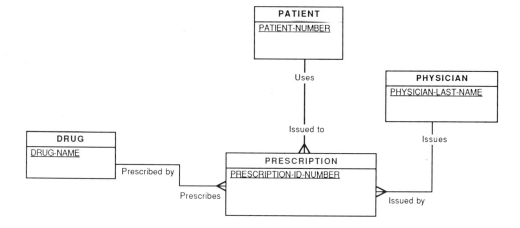

She thought of a prescription as an order and a drug as a product and used the Universal data model in Figure 11.3 for guidance: the relationship between the CUSTOMER and the ORDER entity is {0,N}, and between the ORDER and the PRODUCT entity is {N,M}. She assumed, however, that at the Meadows Pharmacy a prescription would not be issued for more than one drug, so she defined the relationship between DRUG and PRESCRIP-TION as {0,N}. She documented the assumption in the comment log as a reminder to ask Mary Henderson about the relationship during validation of the model. Jayne later changed the relationship from DRUG to DRUG-BRAND. The cardinality of the relationship between PHYSICIAN and PRESCRIPTION appeared straightforward: one physician can prescribe many prescriptions, but one prescription can be prescribed by only one physican.

To define existence dependencies, Jayne again used the Universal analogy. She noted that the existence of an order is dependent on the existence of a customer. Similarly, the existence of a prescription must be dependent on the existence of a patient. That is, a prescription cannot exist without a patient. She also hypothesized that a prescription could not exist without a drug and, probably, without a physician. Minimum cardinalities of one were created to specify the dependencies. She again documented her assumptions about dependencies in the comment log.

After defining existence dependencies, Jayne decided to add a second identifier for PRESCRIPTION. She thought that a patient probably would not receive two prescriptions from a physician for the same drug on the same day. PRESCRIPTION-DATE was added as a second identifier for PRESCRIPTION. She placed a < 1 > on the PRESCRIPTION-DATE identifier to distinguish it from the PRESCRIPTION-ID-NUMBER identifier. PRESCRIP-TION-DATE was combined with the identifiers of the entities on which PRESCRIPTION is dependent to form the second identifier for PRESCRIPTION: DRUG-NAME + PATIENT-ID-NUMBER + PHYSICIAN-LAST-NAME + PRESCRIPTION-DATE. A < 1 > was placed on the PRESCRIPTION:DRUG relationship line near the PRE-SCRIPTION entity to denote the identifier dependency. Now that Jayne had identified and defined the entities, identifiers, relationships, and dependencies, her next step was to refine and validate the data model.

2.2. Validating the Entities and Relationships
Before Jayne talked with Mary and Tito to validate the model, she wanted to ensure that it was as complete as possible. She also wanted to give Tracy and Fred the opportunity to critique the data model. Jayne's first validation step, therefore, was to review the data model and the Process Prescription data flow diagram with Tracy and Fred. First, they compared the data stores in the data flow diagram with the entities in the data model. They noticed that the PHARMACIST and DRUG SUPPLIER files were not represented in the data model. Consequently, these were added as entities (see Figure 11.23). Because the pharmacist must be an employee of

Figure 11.22
Preliminary Design Repository for the Pharmacy Data Model

Entities

DRUG	Description:	A chemical substance that is used by a patient for a medical reason. A drug can be either prescription or nonprescription: Wyamycin and aspirin are drugs.
PATIENT	Description:	A person who is receiving treatment and/or drugs at Meadows Hospital. Example: Steve Mack is a patient.
PHYSICIAN	Description:	A person licensed by the state of Michigan to practice medicine (includes prescribing drugs). Example: F.G. Miller is a physician.

Relationships

PATIENT: PRESCRIP-TION	Cardinality:	
	Description:	A patient uses many prescriptions, but a prescription can be issued to only one patient. A prescription cannot exist without a patient.
PHYSICIAN: PRESCRIP-TION	Cardinality:	
	Description:	A physician can issue many prescriptions, but a prescription can be issued by only one physician. A prescription cannot exist without a valid physician.
DRUG: PRESCRIP-TION	Cardinality:	
	Description:	A drug can be prescribed by many prescriptions, but a prescription can prescribe only one drug. A prescription cannot exist without a drug.

Attributes and Identifiers

DRUG-NAME

PATIENT-ID-NUMBER

PHYSICIAN-LAST-NAME

PRESCRIP-TION-ID-NUMBER

Meadows Hospital, the identifier for the PHARMACIST entity was defined as PHARMACIST-EMP-ID-NUMBER. However, Jayne was not sure how drug supplier should be identified. She asked Tito Hernandez, who said he thought that the names of the suppliers were unique. Hence, DRUG-SUPPLIER-NAME was designated as the identifier. Jayne made a note in her comment log to ask someone in the Inventory department how they identified suppliers. Figure 11.24 shows the revised data model.

In Figure 11.24, the relationship between DRUG-SUPPLIER and DRUG is {N,M}. DRUG-BRAND is the intersection entity for the relationship. Using the SUPPLIER report shown in Figure 11.25, the three analysts employed the instances of entities represented on

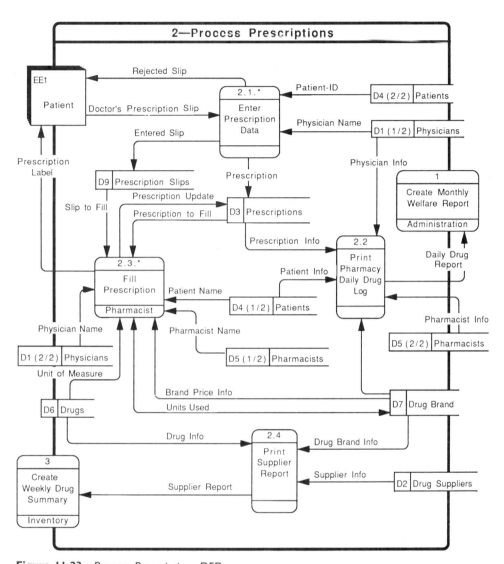

Figure 11.23 Process Prescriptions DFD

the report to validate the DRUG:DRUG-SUPPLIER relationship. The report shows that both Acme Drug and Super Drug supply the drug Wyamycin (one drug has many drug suppliers) and that Acme Drug has supplied two different drugs (one drug supplier can have many drugs). Hence, the cardinality of DRUG:DRUG-SUPPLIER is {N,M}.

Next Jayne, Fred, and Tracy reviewed the data flow diagram to validate the existence dependency for the PHARMACIST:PRESCRIPTION relationship. The data model in Figure 11.24 specifies a minimum cardinality of 0 for the PRESCRIPTION:PHARMACIST relationship. That is, PRESCRIPTION is not dependent on PHARMACIST. The data flow diagram in Figure 11.23 shows that

Figure 11.24
First Draft Pharmacy
Data Model with
Entities and
Relationships

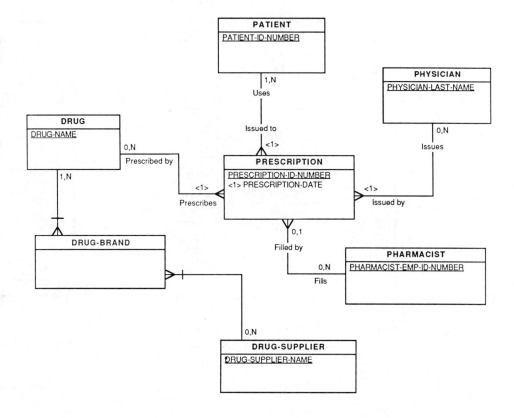

Figure 11.25
Supplier Report

Report Date: 09/15/90

Supplier Number	Supplier Name	Drug Name	Brand	U.O.M.	YTD Usage	Quantity Available
0067	Acme Drug, Inc.	Wyamycin	Wyam-Plus	Cap	1500	7500
		Veracillin	Veracillin	Cap	120	500
0125	Super Drug	Meprogesic	Meprog-Plus	Cap	3000	250
		Wyamycin	Wyam-Delux	Cap	1250	1300
0129	Mega Drug, Inc.	Malatal	Malatal	Cap	100	500
		Brosymin	Mega-Bromo	10 ml	230	1200
0340	SEB Ltd.	Brosymin	SEB-Bromo	10 ml	680	500
		Loprocil	Loprocil	10 cc	300	3400

a prescription is filled in the Fill Prescription process *after* it has already been established in the Enter Prescription Data process. The pharmacist, therefore, fills an existing prescription, but does not establish a prescription. Thus, PRESCRIPTION is not dependent on PHARMACIST.

As the final step in validating the data model, Jayne reviewed, or walked through, the model with Tito Hernandez and Mary Henderson. Tito and Mary validated the model and answered the questions that Jayne had noted

in her comment log. Mary argued against Tito's earlier suggestion of using DRUG-SUPPLIER-NAME to identify DRUG-SUPPLIER. Mary told Jayne that vendor numbers are used to identify suppliers in the Inventory and Hospital Administration departments. Jayne changed the identifier for DRUG-SUPPLIER to DRUG-SUPPLIER-VENDOR-ID-NUMBER and updated the data model to reflect the new identifier (see Figures 11.26 and 11.27).

Figure 11.26
Revision of Drug-Supplier Identifier

Figure 11.27
Pharmacy Data Model with Entities and Relationships

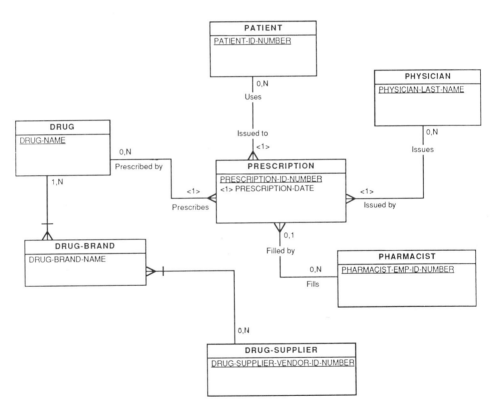

2.3. Defining and Grouping Attributes

Jayne's next task was to define and group attributes on the data model in Figure 11.27. She decided to start by decomposing the data flow for prescription label. Jayne ex-

amined a prescription label (see Figure 11.28) to identify potential attributes. Figure 11.29 shows Jayne's analysis of the prescription label data to identify attributes.

Next, she defined the attributes that had been identi-

Figure 11.28
Sample Prescription
Label

```
Meadows Hospital -- Pharmacy
4508 W. 45th  678-3209  Center City, MI
- - - - - - - - - - - - - - - - - - - - - - - - - -
DATE: Sept. 15, 1990
NO. 08793    DR. MILLER, FRED G.
ALHADAD, HAFEZ
TAKE ONE TABLET BY MOUTH  3
TIMES DAILY TILL OUT.
TAKE ON EMPTY STOMACH.
WYAMYCIN  QTY: 21  PHARMACIST: MARY
```

Figure 11.29
Decomposition of
Prescription Label
Data

Prescription label
↳ (1) Date, (2) Prescription number, (3) Physician name, (4) Patient name, (5) Dosage instructions, (6) Drug name, (7) Drug quantity, (8) Pharmacist name

1. Date ⟶ PRESCRIPTION-DATE

2. Prescription number ⟶ PRESCRIPTION-ID-NUMBER

3. Physician name ⟶ PHYSICIAN-FIRST-NAME
PHYSICIAN-MIDDLE-INITIAL-NAME
PHYSICIAN-LAST-NAME

4. Patient name ⟶ PATIENT-FIRST-NAME
PATIENT-LAST-NAME

5. Dosage instructions ⟶ PRESCRIPTION-DOSAGE-INST-TEXT

6. Drug name ⟶ DRUG-NAME

7. Drug quantity ⟶ PRESCRIPTION-DRUG-QTY-NUMBER

8. Pharmacist name ⟶ PHARMACIST-FIRST-NAME

fied and documented the definitions in the design repository. Jayne was careful to define attributes according to how users would view and use them. Some of the attributes, such as PRESCRIPTION-ID-NUMBER and PHYSICIAN-LAST-NAME, had already been defined as identifiers.

To create the following definition for the attribute prescription dosage instruction, for example, Jayne consulted a pharmacist.

Definition: The dosage instruction specifies the number of units of a drug (determined by the unit of measure) that the patient will use at one time, as well as any special methods for taking the dosage. Example: An instruction might be "take *one* tablet three times a day."

The technical characteristics of the prescription dosage instruction were defined to ensure that it could be satisfactorily produced as an output by the system. On the basis of her discussion with the pharmacist, Jayne determined that the dosage instructions would be a 90-character text field.

Next, Jayne grouped the attribute dosage instruction onto an entity. Dosage instruction is a characteristic of PRESCRIPTION.

Finally, she named the dosage instruction attribute using the guidelines in Figure 11.7. Since the dosage instruction is a text field, the classword is TEXT. To further define the attribute, Jayne added the qualifying words DOSAGE and INSTRUCTION. Adding PRESCRIPTION as the entity for the name resulted in PRESCRIPTION-DOSAGE-INSTRUCTION-TEXT. The entity for the dosage instruction is PRESCRIPTION-DOSAGE-IN-STRUCTION-TEXT. She abbreviated the attribute name as PRESCRIPTION-DOSAGE-INST-TEXT.

Jayne continued defining attributes, using the Supplier Report data flow (see Figure 11.25). While defining the attribute for YTD Usage from the Drug Supplier report, Jayne discovered a problem with the pharmacy data model.

Jayne knew that the attribute for YTD Usage was derived. She defined and grouped the attribute to validate that it could be derived from attributes in the data model. The definition for YTD Usage was a formula for deriving the attribute: "For a given brand of drug (identified by DRUG-BRAND-NAME), find prescriptions that have a PRESCRIPTION-DATE greater than or equal to the first day of the year and less than or equal to the date of the report; sum the values of PRESCRIPTION-DRUG-QTY-

NUMBER for each prescription found." The technical definition for the attribute was "7 numeric digits, no decimal places." She named the attribute DRUG-BRAND-YTD-USAGE-NUMBER*.

Reviewing the data model shown in Figure 11.30, Jayne saw that the PRESCRIPTION entity would have to be related to the DRUG-BRAND entity to allow the values of PRESCRIPTION-DRUG-QTY-NUMBER to be summed for a value of DRUG-BRAND. She added a relationship from PRESCRIPTION to DRUG-BRAND. The relationship between DRUG and PRESCRIPTION was deleted, because the new PRESCRIPTION:DRUG-BRAND rela-

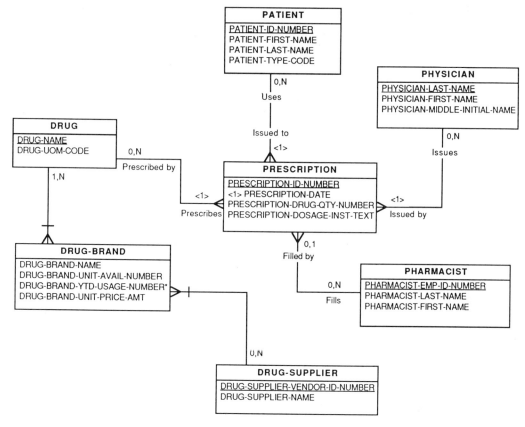

Figure 11.30 Pharmacy Data Model

tionship created a new path, through DRUG-BRAND, between PRESCRIPTION and DRUG. The final data model for the pharmacy subsystem is shown in Figure 11.31. The final design repository for the data model is shown in Figure 11.32.

2.4. Validate Attributes Against Output Reports and Screens

After she finished defining and grouping the attributes onto entities in the data model, Jayne validated the data model against the outputs of the system. The final validation was conducted to ensure that all attributes had been defined and grouped.

The data model shown in Figure 11.31 contains all the attributes needed for the pharmacy subsystem. It is not always desirable, though, to include all of the attributes in the data model, because the model can become difficult to read. An alternative is to maintain a list of the attributes sorted by entity prefix (see the design repository in Figure 11.32). Identifiers, however, should always be shown on the data model.

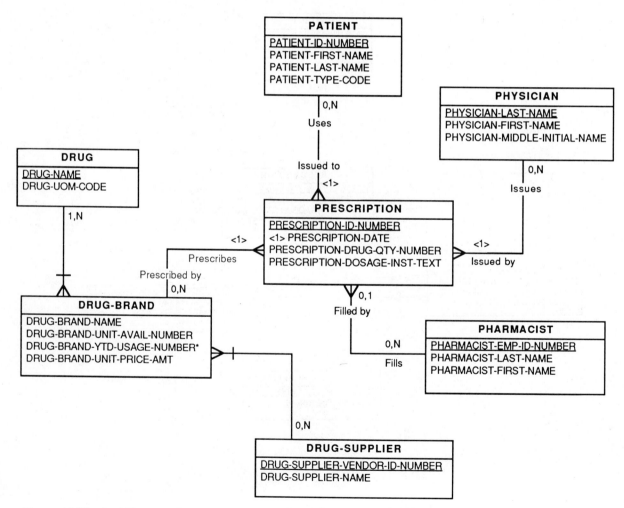

Figure 11.31 Final Pharmacy Data Model with Attributes

Figure 11.32

Design Repository for
the Pharmacy Data
Model

	Entities
DRUG	Description: A chemical substance that is used by a patient for a medical reason. A drug can be either prescription or nonprescription. Example: Wyamycin and aspirin are drugs.
DRUG-BRAND	Description: A specific drug that is supplied by a drug supplier under a brand name. Example: Acme Drug Wyamycin Plus. DRUG-BRAND is the combination of DRUG and DRUG-SUPPLIER.
DRUG-SUPPLIER	Description: An organization that is licensed in the state of Michigan to sell drugs to pharmacies. The organization can be a manufacturer, wholesaler, hospital, etc. Example: SEB Ltd. is a drug supplier.
PATIENT	Description: A person who is receiving treatment and/or drugs at Meadows Hospital. Example: Steve Mack is a patient.
PHARMACIST	Description: A person employed by Meadows Hospital who is licensed by the state of Michigan to fill prescriptions. Example: Mary Henderson is a pharmacist.
PHYSICIAN	Description: A person licensed by the state of Michigan to practice medicine (includes prescribing drugs). Example: F. G. Miller is a physician.
PRESCRIPTION	Description: An order for a drug. A prescription is for a drug that is prescribed by a physician and used by a patient. Example: Prescription No. 08793 for Wyamycin, prescribed by Dr. Fred Miller for patient Hafez Alhadad, is a prescription.

Relationships

PATIENT: PRESCRIPTION	Cardinality: 0, N and 1, 1
	Description: A patient can use no or many prescriptions, but a prescription can be issued to only one patient. A prescription cannot exist without a patient.
PHARMACIST: PRESCRIPTION	Cardinality: 0, N and 0, 1
	Description: A pharmacist can fill no or many prescriptions, but a prescription can be filled by only one pharmacist. A prescription may exist without a pharmacist because a physician writes a prescription before it is filled.
PHYSICIAN: PRESCRIPTION	Cardinality: 0, N and 1, 1
	Description: A physician can issue many prescriptions, but a prescription can be issued by only one physician. A prescription cannot exist without a valid physician.
DRUG-BRAND: PRESCRIPTION	Cardinality: 0, N and 1, 1
	Description: A drug brand can be prescribed by many prescriptions, but a prescription can prescribe only one drug brand. A prescription cannot exist without a drug brand.

(continued)

Figure 11.32
(Continued)

DRUG:DRUG-
SUPPLIER

Cardinality: many to many
Description: A drug can be supplied by many drug suppliers, and a drug supplier can supply many drugs. The DRUG-BRAND entity is the combination of drug and drug supplier.

Attributes and Identifiers

Note: Definitions are not provided for attributes and identifiers.

DRUG-BRAND-NAME

DRUG-BRAND-UNIT-AVAIL-NUMBER

DRUG-BRAND-UNIT-PRICE-AMT

DRUG-BRAND-YTD-USAGE-NUMBER* (derived)

DRUG-NAME

DRUG-SUPPLIER-NAME

DRUG-SUPPLIER-VENDOR-ID-NUMBER

DRUG-UOM-CODE

PATIENT-FIRST-NAME

PATIENT-ID-NUMBER

PATIENT-LAST-NAME

PATIENT-TYPE-CODE

PHARMACIST-EMP-ID-NUMBER

PHARMACIST-FIRST-NAME

PHARMACIST-LAST-NAME

PHYSICIAN-FIRST-NAME

PHYSICIAN-LAST-NAME

PHYSICIAN-MIDDLE-INITIAL-NAME

PRESCRIPTION-DATE

PRESCRIPTION-DOSAGE-INST-TEXT

PRESCRIPTION-DRUG-QTY-NUMBER

PRESCRIPTION-ID-NUMBER

3. Integrating the Subsystem Data Models

The objective of subsystem integration is to resolve any discrepancies between the subsystem models so that a single database can be designed that will best serve the data requirements of all subsystems. Subsystem integration is important because any discrepancies remaining after the subsystems are integrated must be resolved by technical database specialists who may not have a good understanding of user requirements. Subsystem integra-

tion is necessary because subsystem data models can differ with respect to relationships, identifiers, dependencies, and attributes.

During the integration of subsystems, Jayne combined the pharmacy, administration, and inventory data models into one data model for the system. While she was integrating the administration and pharmacy data models, she found that the DRUG-BRAND:PRESCRIPTION relationship was used by the pharmacy data model and the DRUG:PRESCRIPTION relationship was used by the administration data model.

Jayne determined that the relationship between PRESCRIPTION and DRUG was a duplicate path. Although the Administration had to report on drugs, not brands of drugs, Jayne knew that the relationship between PRESCRIPTION and DRUG-BRAND would provide the DRUG-NAME for a prescription. A value for DRUG-NAME could always be determined from a value for DRUG-BRAND-NAME, because although the relationship between DRUG and DRUG-BRAND was {1,N}, the relationship between DRUG-BRAND and DRUG was {1,1}. That is, one instance of DRUG-BRAND was related to just one instance of DRUG. Hence, the relationship PRESCRIPTION:DRUG was deleted.

11.4.2 Data Model Construction from an Unordered Example

The pharmacy data model in the minicase was developed from user interviews, a simple system description, a data flow diagram, and screens and reports. It is important to remember, however, that you will never be provided with all of the information needed to construct a data model. For example, creating the data model for the administrative subsystem of the pharmacy system would likely require an interview with the manager of the Administration department. The information gathered during the interview might include the following:

> Administration receives the Daily Drug Report from the clerk in the Pharmacy department. The report is manually checked against the patient's record to determine if the patient is a regular or a welfare patient. From the daily reports, a monthly report is generated that breaks down the prescriptions issued for welfare patients. The list of welfare patients and their prescriptions, the dollar amounts of the drugs, and the year-to-date drug costs for the patients is sent to the City Welfare department. Along with the Welfare report, a report is sent that shows the types of drugs prescribed during the past year by physician, including the total quantities and dollar amounts for drugs. The welfare clerk for the city reviews the reports and sends a check to reimburse the hospital for the welfare patient prescriptions.

11.4.3 Data Model Construction Using Prototyping

Chapter 7 explained that the probability of success of the requirements phase is greatly influenced by the risk of the system project. One way to reduce risk is to refine the model using the phased development, or prototyping, strategy discussed in Chapter 2. Prototyping can reduce the risks associated with an unknown scope of work, unclear goals for the organization and the application area, inexperienced users, and inexperienced developers. Prototyping reduces these risks by allowing users and developers to refine and validate data requirements through a trial-and-error process while gaining experience with the system. The data model is refined as output reports and screens are designed for the system. Through working with outputs and screens, users refine and validate the entities, relationships, identifiers, dependencies, and attributes needed by the system. The risk of poor communication is also reduced.

Prototyping requires a relational database system with an easy-to-use query language. These advanced tools are needed to permit rapid changes to the outputs and screens (or prototype system). In general, the prototyping procedure is as follows:

1. Construct the data model with entities, relationships, identifiers, dependencies, roles, and attributes.

2. Transform the data model into tables in the relational database (we will discuss this process in Chapter 17).

3. Gather samples of currently used data and enter the data into the relational database.

4. Develop screen formats and output reports based on the entities and relationships of the data model, using the query language of the database.

5. Train users to use the new system and give them time to interact with the system. The users will think of many potential improvements to the system while they interact with it. This step provides a more complete set of information requirements.

6. Review the information gathered in Step 5, and revise the entities, relationships, identifiers, dependencies, and attributes needed to support the new system.

7. Repeat the previous two steps until the system revisions stabilize.

The prototyping technique complements, rather than replaces, the data modeling method presented earlier. High-level data modeling, modeling of entities and relationships, and attribute definition and grouping are still necessary. With prototyping, however, the validation step is more thorough than with the normal data modeling method. The initial data model with entities, identifiers, relationships, roles, and attributes is implemented as a set of files, using the relational database system. The validation of the data model is accomplished by users and designers working with the prototype system.

Summary

Conceptual data modeling consists of analyzing and describing the data needed by the users of a system. To complete a data model, you need (1) a set of constructs for defining data, (2) rules to control how the constructs are combined to form a data model, and (3) a method for constructing the data model using the constructs and rules. The constructs of a data model are entity, attribute, identifier, relationship, dependency, and role.

The data modeling method starts with construction of a high-level model that is partitioned into subsystems. Next, entities and relationships are defined. Attributes are then defined and grouped onto entities. After all subsystem data models have been constructed, the subsystem models are integrated into one data model for the entire system.

In the data modeling notation used in this book, a name within an entity rectangle denotes an attribute and a line designates a relationship. An alternative to this data modeling notation is ER notation. ER notation uses a line for an attribute and a diamond symbol for a relationship.

A data flow diagram can be used to help validate entities, relationships, and dependencies in a data model. In addition, the data flows of a data flow diagram can be used to derive attributes for a data model.

Prototyping can be used to refine a data model. The prototyping technique complements, rather than replaces, the data modeling method. The major steps in constructing a data model are still necessary with prototyping.

Key Terms

(Section numbers are in parentheses.)

entity (11.2.1)	**identifier (11.2.4)**
instance (11.2.1)	**existence dependency (11.2.5)**
attribute (11.2.2)	**identifier dependency (11.2.5)**
derived attributes (11.2.2)	**role (11.2.6)**
relationship (11.2.3)	**entity-relationship (ER) notation (11.2.7)**
cardinality (11.2.3)	**central entity (11.4)**
intersection entity (11.2.3)	**comment log (11.4)**

Notes

1. See J. V. Carlis, "Logical Data Structures," Computer Science Dept., University of Minnesota, TR 85-21, 1985; and Mary E. S. Loomis, *The Database Book* (New York: Macmillan, 1987).

2. P. P. S. Chen, "The Entity-Relationship Model: Toward a Unified View of Data," *ACM Transactions on Database Systems*, vol. 1, no. 1, March 1976, pp. 9–36.

Exercises

(Answers to Exercises 11.1 through 11.6 are at the end of the book.)

11.1 Refer to the pharmacy data model (Figure 11.31) and the Pharmacy Daily Drug Log (Figure 11.33) to complete the following.

a. List all the attributes of the entity PRESCRIPTION.

b. List all the identifiers of the entity PRESCRIPTION.

Figure 11.33
Pharmacy Daily Drug Log

Report date: 09/15/90

Number	Patient	H/W	Physician	Pharmacist	Drug	Brand
08793	Alhadad, Hafez	H	Miller, F. G.	Henderson, M.	Wyamy-cin	WyamPlus
08794	Grena, Emmett	W	Gutierrez, R. T.	Henderson, M.	Veracillin	Veracillin
08795	Wimberly, Harry	H	Yudof, W. L.	Murphy, R.	Mepro-gesic	MeprogPlus
08796	Mortiz, Evelyn	H	Bounous, P. S.	Gordon, M.	Malatal	Malatal
08797	Mack, Steve	H	Miller, F. G.	Henderson, M.	Brosymin	SEB-Bromo
08798	Mack, Steve	H	Miller, F. G.	Murphy, R.	Loprocil	Loprocil
08799	Wiser, Pete	W	Yudof, W. L.	Gordon, M.	Brosymin	MegaBromo

c. What is the cardinality of the relationship between the entity PHARMACIST and the entity PRESCRIPTION?

d. Is DRUG-BRAND an entity or a relationship? Explain your answer.

e. State one instance of the entity DRUG.

f. State a value of the attribute PRESCRIPTION-DATE.

11.2 Refer to the data model in Figure 11.34 to complete the following.

    a. List all the entities in the data model.

    b. List all the attributes in the data model.

    c. List all the identifiers in the data model.

    d. List all the relationships in the data model and their cardinalities.

    e. List all the existence dependencies in the data model.

Figure 11.34

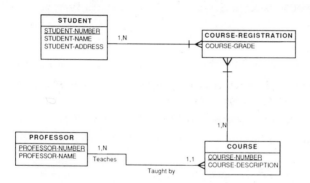

11.3 Redraw the pharmacy data model in Figure 11.31 using ER notation.

11.4 List all the errors in the data model in Figure 11.35.

Figure 11.35

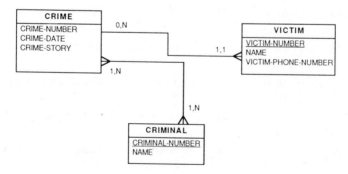

11.5 List all the errors in the data model in Figure 11.36.

11.6 Write a description for the data model in Exercise 11.4. Be sure to write something about each construct (entity, attribute, identifier, relationship, and dependency) in the data model.

11.7 Write a description for the data model in Exercise 11.5.

Figure 11.36

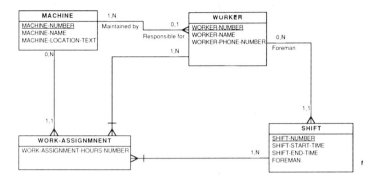

11.8 Write the questions that you would have to ask in order to validate the data model in Figure 11.37.

Figure 11.37

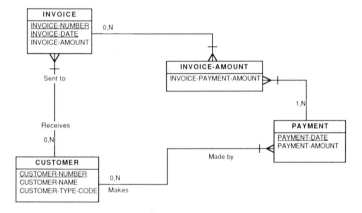

11.9 Provide names for the following attributes (abbreviate the name if it exceeds thirty-one characters):

   a. the amount that is charged for a drug

   b. the number of prescriptions that a pharmacist fills in one year

   c. the home phone number of a doctor

   d. the birth date of a patient

   e. the ethnic category of a patient

   f. a number that identifies a physician

11.10 Assume that the attribute PATIENT-TYPE-CODE in the pharmacy data model in Figure 11.31 can have a value of either H or W (hospital or welfare patient).

   a. How could the definition of PATIENT-TYPE-CODE be changed to allow for a patient who is both a hospital and a welfare patient? Why might this change be necessary?

   b. Assume that the Monthly Welfare Report (Figure 11.19) lists every prescription issued to welfare patients during the month. Would the data model provide the correct information for the report if your new definition for PATIENT-TYPE-CODE were used? Explain your answer.

c. Change the pharmacy data model so that it will provide the correct information for the Monthly Welfare Report if a patient is both a welfare and a regular hospital patient. State any assumptions you make in order to draw the new data model.

11.11 Explain how the pharmacy data model (Figure 11.31) supports the generation of the Supplier report shown in Figure 11.25.

11.12 In the pharmacy data model, the cardinality of the relationship between drug and drug supplier is many to many. Suppose Meadows Pharmacy designated one supplier as the primary supplier for a drug, but also used other suppliers when necessary. Change the pharmacy data model to reflect this fact. Define any new entities or relationships that you create and state any assumptions you make in order to draw the new model.

CHAPTER 12

Requirements Documentation and Management Reviews

Overview

Each phase of the systems development process requires planning and management. Project planning was introduced in Chapter 1, where we emphasized managing the *process* rather than the product, setting milestones, and documenting results. In this chapter we explain how to document the information gathered during requirements determination and how to present it effectively to management and users.

Specifically we plan to

1. Discuss management strategies for documenting requirements. (Section 12.1)

2. Describe the organization and format of the requirements document. (Section 12.2)

3. Give techniques for documenting the five system components. (Section 12.3)

4. Provide guidelines for conducting walkthroughs and management reviews. (Section 12.4)

12.1 Management Strategies for Requirements Documentation

Determining and documenting requirements can be an overwhelming task, even for small projects. It seems that there is always another form to study or another procedure to clarify.

Developers investigating current and proposed systems are generally deluged with information. Nonetheless, they often feel uncertain about whether they have identified all the users' concerns. The comprehensiveness of the information collected by developers is critical, since the requirements provide the basis for evaluating the project. The requirements determination activities culminate in the **requirements document,** a formal written report that brings together the developers' findings about the current system and the requirements of the proposed system. If the project is accepted, the requirements document becomes the foundation for the evaluation, design, and implementation stages. Because this document serves as the official resource manual for the development project, it must be clearly written, and its information must be accurate and complete.

Using one of the following three strategies to manage requirements documentation will ensure that the requirements document constitutes a solid foundation on which to build the development project:

1. Form a team to share responsibility for preparing the document.
2. Assign an information center consultant to oversee users' requirement determination activities.
3. Hire a technical writer to coordinate and edit the actual requirements document.

With the team strategy, each person on the development team gathers and documents requirements for a particular area. The divison of responsibility might be as follows.

- Users—coordinate requirements determination within their functional areas.
- Analysts—compile and coordinate all information gathered.
- Database specialist—specify database requirements.
- Communications specialist—specify communications requirements

Each team member is responsible for the correct and comprehensive collection and documentation of requirements for the assigned functional area.

An alternative is to appoint an information center consultant to oversee users, who investigate the requirements themselves. The consultant meets with the users to review progress, provide assistance, and monitor the information gathered. The consultant acts as project manager, designer, tools expert, and quality assurance inspector for the users. This strategy is particularly effective when users have some knowledge of systems development. Even when information systems professionals will actually develop the system, having users determine requirements and document the current system is a good idea.

Following the third management strategy, the development team investigates and documents the requirements, but the project manager assigns a technical writer to compose the report and to be responsible for the organization, readability, and completeness of the requirements document. For this strategy to be successful, the technical writer must be experienced in systems development.

Whatever strategy is followed, the end product is the requirements document. Because this document is such an important management product of the systems development process, most of this chapter is devoted to discussing its contents and providing guidelines for documenting requirements effectively.

12.2 The Requirements Document

The requirements document is the process product delivery of the requirements determination stage. It represents the tangible culmination of all your efforts to learn about the users' current system and their requirements for the proposed system. Compiled as you perform the activities of requirements determination, the requirements document embodies your knowledge of the organization, the users, their current system, and their needs and expectations for the proposed system. This document should synthesize your analysis of the many user perspectives and system facets, expressing clearly and completely what individual users could only half-express. You hope that the users will think "Ah, yes—that's what I meant" or "Yes, that's just the way we do things" as they read the requirements document. Remember that the project will be accepted or rejected largely on the basis of the ideas expressed in this document.

12.2.1 Guidelines for Preparing the Requirements Document

As a formal business report, the requirements document has many characteristics of other business reports. If you haven't studied business report writing, you may want to review some reference books on the subject.[1] Many organizations have their own report writing manuals, which dictate the format, style, and organization of all company reports. If your employer has such a manual, be sure to study it carefully, since it will be your best guide to writing a report for your particular audience.

We offer four general guidelines to help you prepare an effective requirements document:

1. *Make your report user friendly.* Just as a good user interface is tailored to the system users, a good report is tailored to the report readers. Consider your audience: What do they know? What do they need to know? How can you present the information they need so as to make it easy for them to access and to understand?

2. *Compose your report so that it is easy to read.* Don't buy into the nonsense that a report must be a dense, monolithic document in which you impress your readers by using eight-syllable words. A good report uses the vocabulary of its readers, not the jargon of its writers. It is divided into logical, clearly labeled sections that help the readers find information quickly. Your report should emphasize the results of your study; it should *not* be a step-by-step replay of the investigation process.

3. *Use graphics effectively to illustrate ideas.* Graphics are especially important in the requirements document, but they are not the whole story. You need to provide text that describes the purpose of the diagrams, models, tables, and drawings you include. Generally, interspersing text with graphics works well. That is, you may want to briefly describe a procedure and then provide a simple graphic that illustrates it. Whatever you do, *don't* prepare a requirements document composed *only* of graphics. Always provide text that explains the purpose of each graphic.

4. Keep in mind the 5C's of business writing:

Clear: Ideas are expressed in ordinary language and short to medium-length sentences.

Concise: Main points are stated directly, often in numbered or bulleted lists.

Concrete: All ideas are fully developed and illustrated so that readers will understand them completely.

Coherent: The parts are well organized, and the sentences flow logically.

Conversational: A good report "talks" to its readers as though writer and readers were in the same room.

Remember that the success of the development project rests on your communicating the requirements clearly in this document. As you package the information you've gathered and the graphics you've drawn, keep these guidelines in mind.

12.2.2 Organization of the Requirements Document

Figure 12.1 provides a model of a requirements document; it lists the parts of the document in the order in which they are usually presented. Depending on the nature of your project, your document may include fewer or more parts and may present them in a somewhat different order. Nonetheless, this outline is a good model from which to work.

The document begins with an executive summary. The executive summary condenses the most important information for busy readers who can't study the whole report. You should present only major points here; if the readers want a more detailed analysis, they can refer to the report itself. The idea is to summarize in one or two pages the information that managerial readers must know in order to evaluate the project for further development. This summary includes

- the project problem statement
- the user benefits
- the major objectives
- the constraints
- the date of the initial request for development
- the expected completion date and estimated cost for the system

The executive summary should also list the participants—at minimum, the project manager and the user-sponsor.

The **project authorization form,** which follows the table of contents, lists the acceptance criteria for system installation. This document will be signed by the project manager and the user-sponsor. The sign-off indicates agreement with the contents and provides the go-ahead to commence the next phase of the project. An example of a project authorization form is given in Figure 12.2.

The first section of the body of the report presents the information of most interest to the readers: conclusions and recommendations. Here you enumerate the major requirements your study has uncovered and state your recommendations concerning the proposed system. For example, you might conclude that the functional area's needs will continue to evolve rapidly over the next few years. You might recommend that the proposed system

Figure 12.1

Model of a Requirements Document

Preliminary parts	1. Executive Summary
	2. Table of Contents
	3. Project Authorization Form or for Information Services Request
Report body	4. Conclusions and Recommendations

5. Project Environment
   5.1 Boundary Statement
   5.2 Project Objectives and Constraints
   5.3 Evaluation of Project Risk
   5.4 Acceptance Criteria

6. Organizational Context (optional)
   6.1 Objectives, Goals, Strategies, Critical Success Factors, and Policies (as needed)
   6.2 Organization Chart
   6.3 Context Diagram

7. Existing System Environment
   7.1 Functional Area Objectives, Goals, Strategies, Critical Success Factors, and Policies (as needed)
   7.2 People
   7.3 Procedures (Focus only on those factors and details of concern in the proposed system)
   7.4 Data
   7.5 Software
   7.6 Hardware

8. Requirements of the Proposed System
   8.1 People
      8.1.1 Job Descriptions of New Positions
      8.1.2 Revised Job Descriptions of Current Positions
   8.2 Procedures
      8.2.1 Normal, Backup, and Error Recovery—Illustrated with Structured Techniques
         Context Diagrams
         Data Flow Diagrams
         Procedures Tables
      8.2.2 Processing Cycles and Deadlines
      8.2.3 Report Formats
   8.3 Data
      8.3.1 Data Model
      8.3.2 Data Volume
      8.3.3 Data Definition
   8.4 Software
      8.4.1 Specification of Functions to Be Automated
      8.4.2 Constraints on Development or Purchase
   8.5 Hardware
      8.5.1 Hardware Capacity
      8.5.2 Facility Requirements

Supplements

9. Appendixes
   9.1 Existing System Documentation
   9.2 Supplementary Charts, Diagrams, etc.

10. Glossary of Terms (optional)

Figure 12.2
Project Authorization
Form for User Sign-off

Project Authorization		Page
System		Date
Analyst	Signature	

Stages to be   Requirements
Authorized: Determination _____ Evaluation _____ Design _____ Implementation _____

Approval
Approval of this document authorizes work to begin on the stage(s) checked here. Work is limited to the value covered by the most recent cost/benefit evaluation (attached).

Name		Division		Signature		Date

Documentation Attached or Authorization Details

Project Details (for Checked Stages only)

Estimated Start Date.. _____
Estimated Changeover Date.................................... _____
Estimated Schedule-hours (or -months)................... _____
Estimated Rate of Return on Total Costs................. _____

be based on standard software (for example, programming language) and hardware so that compatibility and expandability do not become problems later on. The purpose of this section is to give the readers information they can act on. The rest of the report serves to support the conclusions and recommendations stated here.

The project environment section presents the objectives and constraints of the project and evaluates project risk. It verifies the boundaries determined during the preliminary investigation, clearly delineating the scope of the project. The project risk evaluation form is often included in this section.

The organizational context section summarizes the information gathered during the preliminary investigation. The purpose of this section is to place the project within the context of the organization. Here you discuss organizational objectives, strategies, policies, structure, and critical success factors related to the project. A list of organizational information requirements, an organization chart, and an organization-level context diagram are often presented. In some cases this section may be omitted if the information is not vital to project success.

The existing system environment section gives an overview both of the functional areas using the existing manual or automated system and of the system's components. It identifies the functional area's requirements and the problems of the existing system. Although the outline in Figure 12.1 lists numerous topics to be covered in this section, use you own judgment in deciding which topics to address and at what level of detail to address them.

The requirements of the proposed system section is the most important part of the document and deserves most of your attention. Here you discuss the requirements in detail, addressing each system component in turn. Because this section is the "meat" of the requirements document, all of Section 12.3 is devoted to techniques to help you document these system requirements.

Often the requirements document is supplemented with appendixes and a comprehensive glossary of terms. The appendixes may include procedures manuals, job descriptions, sample reports, screen layouts, and other elements of the existing or proposed system. If information is vital to the readers' understanding of the report, it should be given in the report, *not* in the appendixes. Appendixes are optional, as is the glossary of terms. Generally speaking, a glossary should be included only to ensure the consistent use of terms throughout the project. Unfamiliar terms should be defined as they occur in the document.

12.3 Documentation Techniques

The structured tools used to elicit and verify requirements also serve as documentation in the requirements document. In this section we provide some supplementary techniques to ensure that requirements documentation is thorough. Although these techniques apply to documenting both the existing system and the requirements of the proposed system, our emphasis here is on the requirements of the proposed system.

12.3.1 Documenting People Requirements

A useful graphic for documenting people and their roles is the organization chart. This chart identifies managers whose input is necessary for the success of the project. It also gives a snapshot of the organization's structure and the functional areas affected by the system.

Job descriptions are an excellent source of information about users' duties and responsibilities. This information maps people to processes (who does what) and can be used to clarify development team roles and to assign tasks to specific people. The people and roles to be identified include

- the user-sponsor and user functional areas
- the IS development team
- the IS operations staff
- any external consultants and specialists

12.3.2 Documenting Procedures Requirements

The structured techniques introduced earlier in this text are excellent for documenting the procedures of existing and proposed systems. Data flow diagrams and procedures tables are especially useful—as long as they are simple enough for readers to understand. Technical graphics often can be simplified and transformed into nontechnical graphics such as those given in Figures 3.2, 3.4, and 3.6. Fred created these simple graphics to illustrate how the redundant procedures of the pharmacy's existing manual system could be streamlined in the proposed automated system. Using icons, as Fred did in these figures, makes graphics easier for users to understand. Figure 12.3 shows two versions of simple, graphic documentation of the same procedures for creating customer-specified data files in several forms. One is a graphic iconic drawing, and the other is a simplified data flow diagram.

Figure 12.3
Graphic Process
Specifications

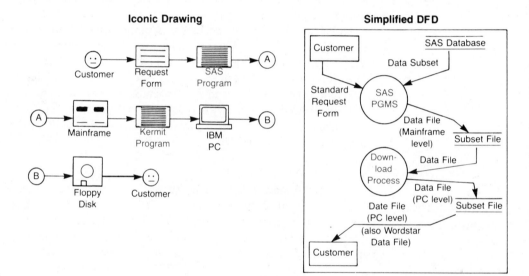

Depending on the complexity of the procedures and the necessity of precise definitions, the development team may need to use **process specifications** to supplement structured and graphic techniques. Process specifications are concise descriptions of procedures. Figure 12.4 shows two examples of process specifications for the procedures that are graphically illustrated in Figure 12.3. One is a decision table. The left column lists conditions, and the right column gives the corresponding procedures for each possible condition. The second example in Figure 12.4 is a sequential list of procedures, in which only the basic actions are specified. Decisions tables are created when alternative procedures are necessary and difficult to clarify in a simple sequential list.

Similarly, numbered lists often effectively capture the steps in a sequential process. We have used simple lists frequently in this text to describe procedures such as drawing a data flow diagram or planning an interview schedule. The key to creating good lists is using active verbs that focus on the task. For example, "Verify the log by comparing the

Figure 12.4
Table and List
Process Specifications

Decision Table		Sequential List	
If a Customer Requests . . .	**Then You Will Need To . . .**	**Manual**	**Automated**
A. A Mainframe Data File	A1. Retrieve data subset from SAS database. A2. Create data file. A3. Save data file to customer account.	Secretary logs request form ① Send request form to ② Data Control	③ Retrieve data subset (SAS Database) ④ Create data file (mainframe level)
B. A PC-Level Data File	B1. Perform A1 and A2. B2. User Kermit to download file to PC. B3. Save file to floppy disk. B4. Mail floppy disk to customer.		⑤ Download data file to PC ⑥ Copy data to floppy disk data file ⑦ Import data file to Wordstar as non-document file (if requested)
C. A Wordstar Data File	C1. Perform steps B1 through B3. C2. Import data file to Wordstar as a nondocument file. C3. Mail floppy disk with Wordstar file to customer.	Mail data file to customer (floppy disk) ⑧	

information on the prescription to its entry on the log" is an active sentence that focuses on *how* the task is performed. In contrast, the sentence "The prescription is compared to its entry on the log to verify its accuracy" focuses on *what is processed*, not how the process works. Always focus on the process rather than what is being processed.

12.3.3 Documenting Data Requirements

Data is one of the most valuable organizational resources, second only to people. Because the accuracy of the data is so important to the success of the system, all system data must be documented fully. During the requirements determination stage, however, you will probably be able to create only a conceptual data model. The conceptual data model, discussed in Chapter 11, provides an overview of the data that the system will process and store. From this overview, you can roughly estimate the **data volume**—the amount of data the system must be able to process and store. Data volume is estimated by determining the size (number of characters or bytes) of each record and multiplying by the number of records. For example, if each employee record consists of 200 characters and there are 500 employee records, the employee file will require at least 100,000 bytes, or about 100K, of memory. If the system consists of several files, you repeat this estimation process for each file and then sum the estimates to determine the total data volume. Knowing the data volume will help you estimate hardware requirements.

If you are in a position to document data requirements only at a very abstract level, a good technique for conveying these requirements to users is to create simple graphics that link the input data to the report generated. For example, Figure 3.5 in the Meadows Hospital case shows a simple graphic that relates the data on a prescription label to its report line on the pharmacy's Daily Drug Log. If the prototyping strategy is being used, however, you may already have a clear and detailed picture of the data and may be able to include a preliminary version of the design repository.

The design repository, which supplements the visual information provided by the data model, is a catalog of all data within the organization. It contains a detailed definition of the data, including

- Name and description of each data element or data group
- Valid ranges of values for the element or group
- Uses and sources of the data
- User or user group responsible for the data
- Programs and systems that access the data
- People authorized to access the data
- Location of the data

The design repository is used to manage the data resources of an organization. It cross-references data sources and definitions so that integrity of meaning and use can be maintained. Chapters 16 and 17 will more fully discuss data definition as system design activities.

12.3.4 Documenting Software Requirements

Part of the requirements determination effort focuses on identifying the functions to be performed by software. When the development team anticipates using existing software, these functions can be outlined in rather general terms. But when custom-written software is required, the development team may need to use process specifications to represent these functions. When detailed logic is important to a full specification of software requirements, each process bubble on the data flow diagram should be documented as a process specification. The process specifications may have a table or list format, like the examples shown in Figure 12.4 for documenting procedures. More detailed process specifications for software may be written in Program Definition Language (PDL), a specification language that describes actions and conditions in a process specification. Chapter 18 provides a full discussion of when and how to use PDL.

12.3.5 Documenting Hardware Requirements

Documenting a proposed system's hardware requirements generally involves addressing two concerns: system capacity and facility layout. The purpose of **capacity planning** is to estimate the processing requirements for the proposed system. Estimating the system's processing requirements can be as simple as estimating the data volume and noting that the system requires at least 40 megabytes of on-line storage, or it can be as complex as considering not only secondary storage needs but also processing speeds, the number of terminals to be supported, on-line versus batch processing, and numerous other hardware issues.

To estimate the proposed system's processing requirements, you may need to research similar organizations that have implemented systems of the same type and scale. Noting their hardware specifications and configurations will give you a good estimate of your input, output, and processing requirements. This strategy is especially useful when the existing system is largely a manual system. When you are upgrading an existing computerized system, identifying hardware requirements is somewhat easier because you can use the current installation as a starting point. In either case, you need to accurately estimate processing requirements in order to ensure that the hardware will meet system needs at changeover and beyond. Too many organizations have underestimated their hardware requirements, and thus have developed systems that were already too small at changeover to meet the organization's expanded needs. Figure 12.5 lists some of the hardware capacity planning concerns that your requirements document might address.

Specifying the facility layout for the proposed system involves describing the system's environmental requirements. Will the user area have to be redesigned to accommodate

Figure 12.5

Hardware and Facility Requirements to Document

Inventory of existing system (when replacing an automated system)	List and describe the current hardware components and their capacity (for example, three 1600 bpi tape drives, five PCs with 640K CPUs and dual floppy drives)
CPU requirements	Provide a rough estimate of CPU capacity required Estimate processing speed required (if important) Estimate main memory needs
Data I/O and storage requirements	Estimate access speed requirements (direct or sequential access) Estimate amount of storage needed based on data volume and backup needs Give a preliminary list of peripherals needed (for example, number and type of printers)
Communication requirements	Describe any changes in the physical layout Specify air conditioning, special wiring, or fire protection needs Consider changes in users' current work environment—lighting, noise reduction, increased work space
Facility requirements	Present an overview of networking and telecommunication needs (if applicable)—type of network required, number of terminals, communications controller

special electrical or air-conditioning needs of the system hardware? If the plan is to replace all the secretaries' typewriters with terminals or microcomputers, will the secretaries' work area need to be enlarged? Will the lighting that was appropriate for using typewriters be appropriate for viewing video display terminals? Your purpose at this point is *not* to create a detailed physical layout—you *can't*, since you don't know which hardware components will be part of the chosen solution. Instead, your purpose is to list the *likely* requirements of the facility so that the cost of meeting these requirements can be evaluated as part of the cost of the proposed system.

12.4 Walkthroughs and Management Reviews

Throughout requirements determination and the other stages of development, you will need to encourage users to review and verify your work as often as possible. As we discussed the techniques for eliciting user requirements, we emphasized the importance of having users verify data flow and context diagrams, report formats, and so forth, as they are drawn. These informal reviews, called walkthroughs, take very little time, yet they provide one of the most effective ways to gain user trust and commitment and to ensure that the system developed is the system required. Management reviews are more formal reviews that are held less frequently and cover a wider range of material.

In this section we give some guidelines on when and how to conduct walkthroughs and management reviews. Figure 12.6 is a matrix designed to help you decide whether a walkthrough or a management review, with either an individual user or a group of users, will better serve your purposes.

Figure 12.6
Types of User Reviews

	Individual	**Group**
Informal Walkthrough	Important for verifying detailed requirements and building good user-developer relations.	Important for generating ideas and building a group consensus.
Formal Management Review	Important for gaining approval at each management level and for securing user-sponsor's acceptance.	Important for gaining user and management approval of products at each milestone and for obtaining approval to commence the next stage of activities.

12.4.1 Walkthroughs

Walkthroughs are conducted to obtain user feedback and to encourage communication among users and developers. Tracing the processes and objects acted upon as you discuss a context diagram, procedures table, or data flow diagram with users is an excellent way to verify requirements. A walkthrough also helps identify inconsistencies, uncover problems, and secure user approval of the information gathered so far.

Requirements walkthroughs bring together developers and users, often in small groups or one to one, for short, informal meetings which are usually conducted on the users' turf.[2] These meetings, which may last less than fifteen minutes, provide a relatively painless way of eliminating conceptual errors during this critical stage. Holding frequent short walkthroughs allows the users to focus on smaller system chunks, thus avoiding the overload users often experience when confronted with everything all at once.

Later in the project, users and developers will conduct design, code, and testing walkthroughs. These walkthroughs focus on the users' verification of design assumptions and on the developers' validation of program design, coding, and test plans. In these later stages, walkthroughs encourage cohesion among developers, helping them to function as an "egoless team."[3] Walkthroughs make both users and developers responsible for the accepted requirements and design specifications.

Figures 12.7 and 12.8 give examples of forms that may be used to document walk-

Figure 12.7
Walkthrough Action
List Form

Walkthrough Action List	Page
System	Date

Analyst	Type of Walkthrough
Questions	Resolution

Figure 12.8
Walkthrough
Confirmation Form

Walkthrough Confirmation Form		Page
System		Date
Analyst	Signature	Meeting Date

Walkthrough Team		Acceptance	
Name	Present	Date	Initials

Walkthrough Objectives

Documentation
   List materials attached to this form.

Confirmation Date	Signature

throughs. The walkthrough action list is used to record questions raised during a walk-through; this form also documents how questions were resolved. The walkthrough confirmation form can be used to document any walkthrough; it serves as a kind of "mini sign-off," indicating the users' acceptance of the information studied.

12.4.2 Management Reviews

Management reviews are longer, more formal meetings conducted after each major milestone to gain user acceptance (sign-off) and to review the project schedule. They are presented to a select group of users, the user-manager, the user-sponsor, and any information systems personnel responsible for overseeing the project.

During requirements determination, management reviews are held to gain user acceptance of

- Project boundaries, objectives, and constraints
- Organization and system requirements

Depending on the scope and complexity of the project, these issues may be discussed and resolved at one or more meetings. Generally speaking, it's a good idea to gain management approval of the development team's understanding of boundaries, objectives, and constraints as early in the requirements determination stage as possible. Gaining this approval right away increases the team's confidence and ensures that members' focus is correct as they investigate requirements.

The guidelines given earlier for preparing the requirements document are just as relevant to conducting a management review. The biggest challenge is deciding what information to present. You don't want to overwhelm the audience by presenting too much information in too much detail. Yet you need to give the highlights of your investigation. The quality of your presentation will establish the credibility of the requirements document and will influence the likelihood of user acceptance and management approval of the project.

Summary

One of three strategies may be followed to ensure that the requirements document is clearly written and accurate: (1) form a team to share responsibility for preparing the document, (2) assign an information center consultant to oversee the process, or (3) hire a technical writer experienced in systems development to collate and edit the team's findings.

Creating a complete and thorough requirements document requires much preparation and organization. When preparing the document, follow the guidelines for report writing provided by your organization. Your document should be user friendly and readable, should make effective use of graphics, and should adhere to the 5C's of business report writing.

The number of sections and amount of detail in the requirements document will depend on the nature of the project. The document begins with an executive summary, followed by a table of contents. Conclusions and recommendations are given in the first section. A description of the project environment, organizational context, and existing system follows. Next the requirements of the proposed system are addressed in detail with information on people and their roles, procedures, data (including data volume), software, and hardware concerns such as system capacity and facility layout. If existing software is to be used, documentation may be somewhat general; custom-written software requires concise descriptions of procedures known as process specifications.

Walkthroughs and management reviews verify your understanding of user requirements. Walkthroughs should be conducted frequently to allow users to review and verify your work. Management reviews are more formal meetings involving a select group of users, the user-manager, the user-sponsor, and any information systems personnel responsible for overseeing the project.

Key Terms   (Section numbers are in parentheses.)

requirements document (12.1)	capacity planning (12.3.5)
project authorization form (12.2.2)	walkthroughs (12.4.1)
process specifications (12.3.2)	management reviews (12.4.2)
data volume (12.3.3)	

Notes

1. See John S. Fielden and Ronald E. Dulek, *Bottom Line Business Writing* (Englewood Cliffs, N.J.: Prentice-Hall, 1984); and William Strunk and E. B. White, *The Elements of Style* (New York: Macmillan, 1972).

2. Tom DeMarco, *Structured Analysis and System Specification* (Englewood Cliffs, N.J.: Prentice-Hall, 1980), p. 112.

3. Edward Yourdon, *Managing the Structured Techniques* (Englewood Cliffs, N.J.: Prentice-Hall, 1976), pp. 188–191.

Exercises   (Answers to Exercises 12.1 and 12.9 are at the end of the book.)

12.1 Refer to the Meadows Hospital case in Chapter 3 to complete the following.

   a. What requirements strategy did Tracy use to manage the requirements determination phase? Give examples from the case to support your answer.

   b. Give examples of the types of walkthroughs and management reviews (formal/informal, group/individual) that Tracy and Fred conducted with the users in the requirements determination stage.

12.2 Create a simple, nontechnical graphic to illustrate the procedure shown in Figure 10.18.

12.3 Discuss how the following could have affected the outcome of Lite's production management system in the Chapter 8 minicase:

   a. a comprehensive requirements document

   b. each of the three strategies for managing requirements determination

   c. walkthroughs and management reviews

12.4 Reread the Chapter 3 case study, especially Sections 3.1 and 3.2. Then write a one-page executive summary, suitable for inclusion in a requirements document, that presents the development team's findings, conclusions, and recommendations.

12.5 Create a simple, nontechnical graphic to illustrate the procedure shown in Figure 11–16.

12.6 After reviewing the Chapter 3 case study and Figures 8.1, 8.2, 8.5, and 8.7, prepare a two- or three-page project environment section for the Meadows Hospital pharmacy system requirements document. Discuss (1) the project objectives and constraints, (2) the project boundaries, and (3) the acceptance criteria.

12.7 After reviewing the Chapter 3 case study, prepare a one- or two-page report in which you discuss the hardware and facility requirements for the Meadows Hospital pharmacy system.

12.8 Discuss how the requirements document addresses each of the goals of systems development: system quality, project management, and organizational relevance.

12.9 Review the cash withdrawal procedures described in Exercise 9.8.

a. Create a simple, nontechnical graphic, like the iconic drawing in Figure 12.3, to summarize the cash withdrawal procedures.

b. Create a simple DFD, like the one in Figure 12.3, to illustrate the cash withdrawal procedures.

c. Create a sequential list summary of manual and automated procedures for the cash withdrawal processes, following the format shown in Figure 12.4.

12.10 Review the inventory procedures described in Exercise 9.9.

a. Create a simple, nontechnical graphic, like the iconic drawing in Figure 12.3, to summarize the inventory procedures.

b. Create a simple DFD, like the one in Figure 12.3, to illustrate the inventory procedures.

c. Create a decision table to illustrate the inventory procedures, following the format shown in Figure 12.4.

d. Create a sequential list summary of manual and automated procedures for inventory actions, following the format shown in Figure 12.4.

12.11 Review the procedures described in Exercise 9.10 for sending warning letters to business students.

a. Create a simple, nontechnical graphic, like the iconic drawing in Figure 12.3, to summarize the warning letter procedures.

b. Create a simple DFD, like the one in Figure 12.3, to illustrate the warning letter procedures.

c. Create a decision table to illustrate the warning letter procedures, following the format shown in Figure 12.4.

d. Create a sequential list summary of manual and automated procedures for sending warning letters, following the format shown in Figure 12.4.

Projects

12.12 Obtain a copy of the requirements documentation for two different projects. If possible, obtain one document that you think is excellent or at least good and one that you consider poor. Critique the two documents and write a report explaining your evaluation of the strengths and weaknesses of each document.

12.13 Interview developers in two different organizations about their policies and actual documentation practices. Write a report summarizing what you learn.

4

Evaluation Activities

Evaluation Overview

Overview

The main goal of requirements determination activities is to learn *what* the users want. The goal of evaluation activities is to determine whether the benefits of what the users want justify the costs. The process is an iterative one of determining *what* the system function will be and then, if necessary, revising the scope of the system to increase the benefits or decrease the costs. Part 4 focuses on the evaluation activities part of this iteration. We present criteria for evaluating systems (Chapter 13) and explain two basic evaluation techniques (Chapter 14). Specifically, in this chapter we plan to

1. Define the evaluation process. (Section 13.1)

2. Explain how to choose criteria for proposed projects. (Section 13.2)

3. Provide guidelines for successful evaluation. (Section 13.3)

4. Discuss two quick evaluation methods—the rough pass and payback analysis. (Section 13.4)

5. Discuss the limits of evaluation. (Section 13.5)

6. Provide guidelines for sequencing evaluation activities. (Section 13.6)

7. Give an example of a good evaluation report. (Section 13.7)

13.1 What Is Evaluation?

Evaluation, in systems development terms, refers to the broad range of activities leading to the choice of a system from a range of alternatives. The place of evaluation within the systems development process is illustrated in Figure 13.1. Evaluation involves more than comparing benefits and costs; evaluation stage activities also include generating alternatives and then deciding which alternative is best. Sometimes the decision may be to think of better alternatives, to revise one or more alternatives, or to abandon the project.

Figure 13.1
The Systems Development Process: Overview DFD

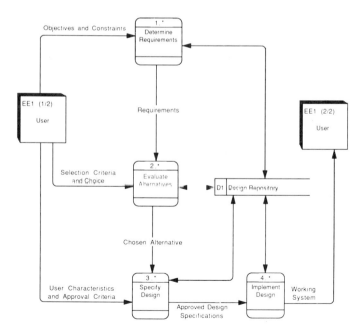

Figure 13.2 provides a data flow diagram of the evaluation stage activities. The evaluation activities in the development process matrix are highlighted in Figure 13.3.

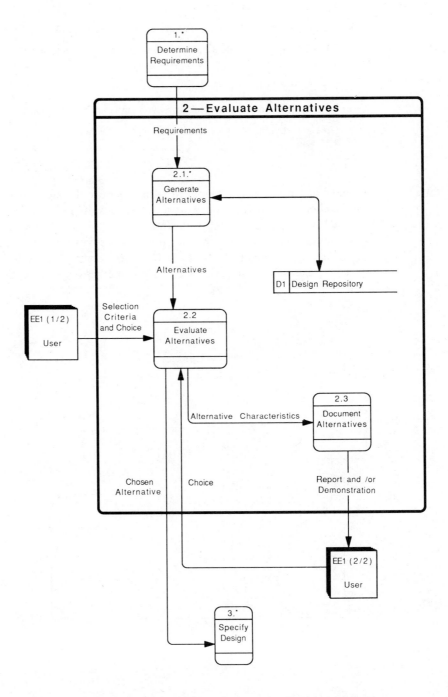

Figure 13.2
Evaluation Stage
Activities: Overview
DFD

Figure 13.3

A Summary of Evaluation Activities

	People	Procedures	Data	Software	Hardware
Determine Requirements					
Evaluate Alternatives	Identify and select users	Identify and select procedures	Identify alternative I/O and storage solutions	Identify and select software	Identify and select hardware
Specify Design					
Implement Design					

13.1.1 The Full Evaluation Process

The basic activities in evaluation are

E.1 Generate alternatives

E.2 Evaluate alternatives

E.3 Document alternatives

E.4 Obtain management decision

The detailed steps in these four activities are listed below. Although all of these activities are completed for most projects, the exact order shown here is seldom followed.

E.1 Generate alternatives
   E.1.1 Identify alternative users
   E.1.2 Generate alternative procedures
   E.1.3 Generate data designs
   E.1.4 Generate software and hardware alternatives

E.2 Evaluate alternatives
   E.2.1 Determine criteria
   E.2.2 Rank and weight criteria
   E.2.3 Determine criteria values
   E.2.4 Rate alternatives
   E.2.5 Compute composite ratings
   E.2.6 Select one or two alternatives

E.3 Document or demonstrate chosen alternatives
   E.3.1 Expand cost and schedule details
   E.3.2 Summarize solution-problem fit

E.4 Obtain management decision

13.1.2 Evaluation of Alternatives: Evaluation or Feasibility Analysis?

So far, we've been discussing evaluation procedures in terms of multiple alternatives. But you need to realize that you will often be required to evaluate just one solution. *Evaluation* is the term generally used to refer to comparing two or more alternatives in order to choose the best one. A second term, **feasibility analysis,** is often used to refer to the same process when only one solution is being evaluated in order to decide whether to pursue that solution, revise it, or abandon it. Figure 13.4 highlights the similarities and differences between the two types of evaluation.

Figure 13.4
Two Types of
Evaluation

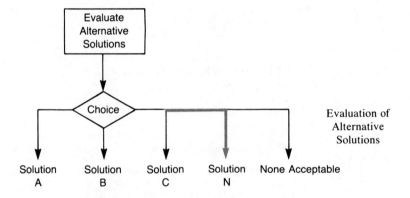

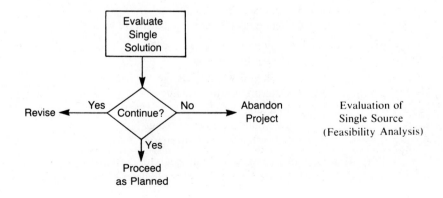

In this text, we use the term *evaluation* to describe both situations, since in either case you may need to abandon the project or generate new or revised solutions. Also, any single project should be evaluated in terms of its value to the organization in relation to alternative projects. Thus, even if your project has an excellent cost/benefit ratio, management may decide to pursue another project that better serves the objectives of the organization.

No matter how many solutions are being assessed, evaluation is more than just choosing the best alternative; sometimes it involves choosing to abandon the project or to revise the alternatives and then re-evaluate them. It's important that you remember that systems development is not an inevitable progression from determining requirements to implementing a system.

13.2 Guidelines for Successful Evaluation

Whether you are dealing with multiple solutions or a single solution, the following guidelines can help you to conduct a successful evaluation.

1. Be creative.
2. Consider all five components.
3. Look for the best solution, not the perfect solution.

13.2.1 Be Creative

One of the attributes of an effective systems developer is creativity: the flexibility of mind that allows you to generate innovative ideas by viewing old problems in new ways. One of the keys to effective systems development is coming up with new and better ways to address old problems or to take advantage of new opportunities. The more creative you are, the more alternatives you're likely to generate. The more alternatives you generate, the more likely you are to identify the best solution, given your requirements and constraints.

But how do you become creative? Such advice is easy to give but not so easy to follow. One technique for encouraging creativity is brainstorming. You and the other development team members could meet during the evaluation stage to conduct a free-form alternative-generating session or follow the structured brainstorming method presented in Chapter 9, the Nominal Group Technique. During this session, you would present whatever ideas came to mind, withholding criticism and discussion until the members' idea pool had been exhausted. The key to a successful brainstorming session is creating an accepting, nonjudgmental atmosphere in which self- and group-censorship is discouraged. One of your responsibilities as project leader would be to maintain such an atmosphere.

Another way to encourage creativity is to expose yourself to varied, even conflicting ideas and to keep up with current systems development techniques and design alternatives. As a new graduate, you may be more familiar with the many options available than your more seasoned colleagues are. You may be more open to developing systems around existing software or to using fourth generation tools. In that case, you can encourage creativity among your colleagues by pointing out these alternatives. They, in turn, can provide you with insights into how they and others have dealt with situations similar to yours. In addition, reading professional journals and participating in professional organizations will help you stay current and keep your mind active. Most of all, you want to avoid a closed mind-set in which you've "seen it all" and have a too-ready solution for every problem.

Reviewing DFDs is another way to encourage yourself to consider a variety of alternatives, rather than focus on one quickly conceived solution. Use of a graphic tool such as a DFD also has the added advantages of helping users better understand their options and ensuring that developers are really communicating with the users. For an example of the use of a DFD to generate and evaluate alternative solutions, we will return to the Meadows Pharmacy case.

MINICASE

An Alternative for Reducing Paper Clutter at Meadows Hospital

Inventory managers at Meadows had recently expressed concern about the stacks of reports they received from Order Processing. The reports were often out of date and added clutter to the Inventory department's already messy desks. The development team thought that an on-line Supplier report would be a good alternative to the hard-copy Supplier report sent to the Inventory department every week. The alternative would be creating a Supplier Report file that could be accessed on-line via CRTs in the Inventory department.

The development team evaluated the on-line report alternative by updating the Process Prescriptions DFD in Figure 11.23. The resulting DFD is shown in Figure 13.5. Process 2.4, which was Print Supplier Report in Figure 11.23, has been changed to Update Supplier Report File, with a data storage output rather than a hard-copy report. The developers explained the impact of the change by listing the effects of the alternative on the five information system components:

1. *People.* Inventory managers would have to be trained to use CRTs and to access the on-line report programs. The training of operators to create and distribute the Supplier report would no longer be necessary.

2. *Procedures.* Operator procedures for printing and distributing the Supplier reports would no longer be necessary.

3. *Data.* A new Supplier Report file would have to be designed and maintained.

4. *Software.* Programs would have to be developed for updating the Supplier Report file. Programs would also have to be developed for the Supplier report screens.

5. *Hardware.* Three CRTs would have to be purchased for Inventory management.

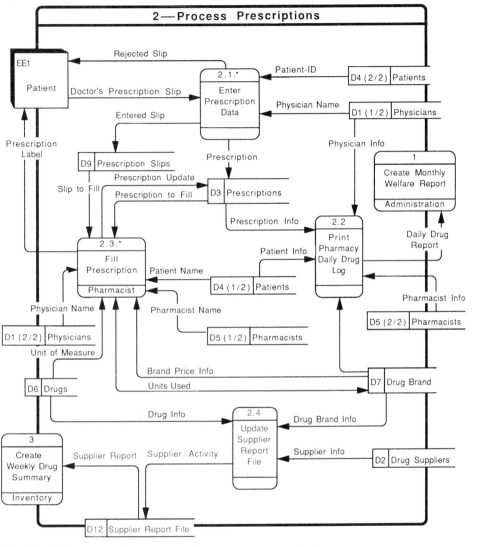

Figure 13.5 Data Flow Diagram for Generating Alternative Systems

Finally, you can encourage creativity by *really* listening to users. When you only half-listen, you tend to develop a closed mind-set. But when you listen carefully to users' concerns, needs, and ideas, you're more likely to see the uniqueness of their situation and to think of new and better ways of addressing that situation. Also, the alternatives you generate will more fully address the users' needs and concerns.

13.2.2 Consider All Five Components

One common error in systems development is to consider only software and hardware solutions. As the development process matrix in Figure 13.3 shows, all five components must be considered during evaluation. Sometimes only changes in personnel or procedures are needed to solve a problem or take advantage of an opportunity. Thus, overemphasizing hardware and software alternatives can mean developing more system than the situation warrants.

Evaluating Personnel Alternatives   One of the scarcest and most costly organizational resources is people. This is especially true of information systems personnel. Therefore, the best solution often hinges on the availability of trained user and support personnel. For example, you would want to think twice before choosing a new word processing system for a pool of 100 typists. The software might be relatively inexpensive, but the training costs might be astronomical! You would need to weigh the expected gains against the expected training costs, reduced productivity, and potentially lower employee morale. It's no coincidence that large organizations tend to stay with a product, at most converting to that product's upgrades. In the same vein, you should hesitate before choosing a database solution that requires your small company to hire a database specialist. On the other hand, in a larger organization, hiring that same database specialist may so reduce problems with the current database system that the additional personnel costs are justified by productivity and employee morale gains.

Evaluating Procedures Alternatives   As you evaluate hardware, software, and data solutions, you must consider the procedures required to use the hardware and software and to enter and access the data. You may reject an existing software package—even though it meets all user requirements—simply because its user procedures are too complex. What good is a terrific program that no one wants to use? From another standpoint, you need to identify procedural changes to the current system that may reduce time and effort expended, thus reducing production costs without generating new development costs. For example, if users complain that the current system's response time is too slow, you may be able to solve the problem by shifting CPU-intensive processing to nonpeak hours. Considering a hardware upgrade would be premature if you had not first considered less complex and less costly alternatives.

Evaluating Data Alternatives   Data alternatives include input, output, and storage formats. What should the data entry screens look like? In what format should reports be printed? Does the system require an integrated database? What file access mode is most appropriate? Even more fundamental, what data items must be entered, processed, and stored? The answers to these and related questions will help you not only to understand the data requirements but also to choose hardware and software compatible with these requirements. By carefully considering data alternatives, you may discover that new hardware and software are not needed; revising current programs to accept new data or to format reports differently may be all that's required.

Evaluating Software and Hardware Alternatives Throughout the text we have emphasized the importance of having people and procedures concerns drive development process decisions. Different alternatives for the people and procedures components lead to variations in the data, software, and hardware components. In the Meadows Hospital minicase, changing procedures in order to reduce paper clutter required data and program revisions and additional hardware.

The major software alternatives were presented in Chapter 2: existing software versus software custom developed by users or information systems professionals. The Chapter 3 case study involved choosing between existing software and a custom-developed pharmacy system for Meadows Hospital. Chapter 14 illustrates more sophisticated evaluation techniques with a case in which developers must select a database management system to purchase. Within the custom-developed category, the minicase in the previous section introduced a particular software alternative for the order processing system at Meadows Hospital.

The major hardware alternatives are managing with existing hardware and purchasing new hardware. The Generating Alternative Solutions for Environmental Research Associates minicase in Chapter 14 will show how this decision drives evaluation activities when hardware is the first component considered.

13.2.3 Look for the Best Solution, Not Perfection

Remember that the best solution is the one that justifies the expense of development and maintenance. In Chapter 1, you learned that the 80/20 solution is often most feasible—the 100 percent solution is likely to cost more than it is worth to the organization. The best solution is the alternative that meets the necessary requirements at a justifiable cost and within a reasonable time.

13.3 Choosing Evaluation Criteria

The major evaluation criteria for a system will be the system objectives. Everything in Chapters 1 and 7 about objectives applies to evaluation criteria. In fact, for a small new system or a minor system revision, we recommend that you follow a life cycle approach and identify and evaluate alternatives based on the system objectives. For larger systems, we recommend that you follow a phased approach to development. In phased development, you identify major objectives and constraints in the first iteration of requirements determination activities. The next stage is to evaluate one or more aspects of the system, choosing more precise evaluation criteria, on the basis of the guidelines in this section. When management has selected one of the alternatives you presented, you continue with design or return to requirements activities to further refine the system objectives and constraints.

13.3.1 Importance of Criteria

Choosing objectives or criteria on which to evaluate a system or a phase of a system is a critical step, because an objective viewed as critical in one situation may be inappropriate in another. For instance, ease of use is a common objective or criterion for most systems. When security is important, however, gaining access may require difficult steps that are not at all user friendly. Thus, banks and police agencies may choose to make access very difficult for some systems and yet have easy, menu-driven access for others systems.

The criteria you identify for evaluating alternatives should have several characteristics. First, the criteria should address the specific primary requirements identified by users in the requirements determination stage. A long wish list is confusing and distracting. You'll find that evaluation is easier when you have a clear prioritized list of criteria. System objectives established early in requirements determination guide the selection and priority ordering of criteria, but are too general to provide a complete list of criteria for evaluating every one of the numerous alternatives identified throughout a large project. Second, the criteria should be independent. That is, one criterion should not be a redundant rephrasing of another. Third, the criteria should state functional requirements, not design specifications. For example, "the system is easy to use" is an evaluation criterion; "the system is menu driven" is a design specification. Fourth, the criteria should define factors by which the success of the system can be measured.

In Chapter 7 we stressed that objectives and requirements should be distinguished from constraints. Criteria should also be distinguished from constraints. Following are some examples of criteria and constraints.

Criteria	Constraints
Easy access to system.	System installed within 13 weeks.
No extensive relearning required for infrequent users.	Development costs under $20,000.
	Production costs not to exceed current costs.

The examples of criteria above might have been taken directly from a list of objectives for a project involving a small revision to a system. Or they might have been selected from a longer requirements list for a larger system, as the criteria appropriate for the selection of the interface design for one phase of the system.

Criteria and constraints are both important in the evaluation process. As we will discuss in more detail later, constraints often eliminate alternatives from further evaluation. The merits of each remaining alternative are then measured on a criterion-by-criterion basis.

There are three types of criteria, based on the three goals of systems development presented in Chapter 2:

- System quality
- Project management
- Organizational relevance

Keeping these goals in mind will help you to generate questions for interviews with users and managers and to determine criteria specific to the particular system being developed.

13.3.2 System Quality Criteria

System quality depends on three system characteristics:

- Functionality
- Ease of maintenance
- Flexibility

System functionality criteria describe the required capabilities of the system. Does the system perform all the necessary functions? Are backup procedures explained? Is the system easy to use? Should it be easy to use? Is the system fast? Should it be faster? What are the incremental costs of achieving faster response time? Does the system provide adequate storage? Should the system be on-line? How will customers perceive the system? How much do their perceptions matter?

System maintenance criteria relate to the ease with which the system can be modified. Is the system easy to understand? Is the system well documented? Does the structure of the system make modification and testing easy? Because system maintenance consumes a tremendous amount of time and effort over the system life cycle, ease of maintenance is often a criterion for measuring system success.

System flexibility criteria ask whether a system can be used in many different situations without modifications. Can the hardware be changed? Is the software language a common one known by staff members? Are the procedures documented? The system must be able to adapt to the rapidly shifting needs of the organization.

Although the questions above are by no means exhaustive, the answers to these questions will help you to generate criteria for evaluation. You may find that the Nominal Group Technique, presented in Chapter 9, is an effective way to generate and prioritize these criteria.

13.3.3 Project Management Criteria

A successful system is

1. On time
2. Within budget
3. User-driven

The first two goals are actually constraints which limit the time and money that can be devoted to meeting user requirements. These constraints help you to ground your system quality criteria in reality so that, instead of choosing criteria that describe the ideal system, you choose criteria that describe the best system you can reasonably develop given your time and money constraints. The third goal serves as a reminder that your job is to develop a system that meets the users' requirements. Therefore, you should choose criteria that directly address users' requirements, and you should consult with users as you establish these criteria.

The goals of meeting time deadlines and budget limits may be included as criteria or constraints in the evaluation process. If a system had to be completed within a year to meet a government requirement, for example, all alternatives that would require more than a year would be eliminated of this goal or constraint. If a system was designed to increase cash flow, timeliness would be an important goal and a heavily weighted criterion in the evaluation process. The criterion of timeliness, however, might be no more important than a system quality criterion such as ease of use or secure access, and therefore it would be just one of several criteria investigated in the identification of alternatives and selection.

13.3.4 Organizational Relevance Criteria

Organizational relevance criteria address not the specific capabilities of the system but the system's contribution to the organization's stability or growth. Thus, many organizational relevance criteria are the dominant criteria. For example, an accounts receivable system would be designed to meet the system quality criterion of improving billing procedures in order to improve cash flow, thereby serving the great organizational relevance goal of increasing financial stability. Or a customer order system would be designed to meet the system quality criterion of being easy to use in order to also increase market share, thereby strengthening the organization's competitive edge.

On a larger scale, managers use organizational relevance criteria to determine which projects to approve. Just as you as a systems developer focus on identifying which alternative best addresses a specific project goal, managers must identify which projects best address the organization's goals. It is management's job to review the time and money savings, increased productivity, or improved security each project offers and to choose projects to approve. Should the current payroll system be revised to provide better reports, or should a new telecommunications system be developed to improve the organization's marketing efforts? Since time, money, and personnel are scarce resources, managers must focus systems development efforts in areas where the marginal benefit is likely to be the greatest. Thus, projects will be considered and implemented in accordance with their worth to the organization.

13.4 Quick Evaluation Methods

This section presents two quick, or rough, evaluation methods. More detailed evaluation techniques are introduced in Chapter 14.

13.4.1 A Rough First Pass

As you begin the evaluation stage, your **rough first pass**, or early evaluation of ideas for systems solutions, is likely to follow the six steps below. The identifiers in parentheses are from the detailed checklist in Section 13.1.1.

Step 1 (E.1)   Generate alternatives

Step 2 (E.2.3) Determine rough estimates of cost and development time for each alternative

Step 3 (E.2.6) Compare alternatives

Step 4 (E.2.6) Eliminate alternatives outside of constraints

Step 5 (E.3) Document chosen alternatives

Step 6 (E.4) Obtain management decision

Assume that your development team has generated four alternatives: Solutions A, B, C, and D. This is the Step 1, or E.1. The second step is to estimate the cost and time associated with developing each alternative. Let us say these estimates are as follows:

	Rough Estimates	
	Cost	Development Time
Solution A	$100,000	6 months
Solution B	100,000	2 years
Solution C	250,000	9 months
Solution D	400,000	$2\frac{1}{2}$ years

Step 3 is to compare these results. Ranking the solutions by their costs and time constraints suggests that the best solution is A.

Rank	Cost	Time
1	A, B	A
2	—	C
3	C	B
4	D	D

On this rough first pass, however, you want to avoid deciding that Solution A is *the best* alternative. You need to consider other factors before choosing one alternative.

In Step 4, you eliminate any solutions that are outside the constraints set by management. For example, managers may believe that this system is urgently needed—a competitive opportunity exists that may disappear. Depending on their definition of "urgent," two, three, or all of the alternatives may be eliminated.

Steps 5 and 6 are to present a summary of these comparisons to management. Afterward you follow management's decision as to which solutions you should examine in further detail. Management may decide that, although solution A is the least expensive and will be finished the soonest, B or C has features that make it the better solution.

13.4.2 Payback Analysis

Payback analysis is an evaluation technique in which the costs and benefits of a system are compared by determining the time period required to recoup costs. This model is a popular technique for analyzing capital investments of less than $10 million. Simulations of capital budgeting models have shown that the payback analysis model closely approximates more sophisticated models in uncertain environments. Because of its popularity and its ease of use, this model is presented here. You should be aware of its drawbacks, however.

The payback analysis model suffers from several well-known deficiencies. The model ignores the time value of money—in other words, money received in the future is considered as valuable as money received today. Also, benefits received from an investment beyond the payback point are not considered, which creates a bias in favor of projects with a short-term payoff. Finally, the model does not consider the overall profitability of an investment, since only benefits received up to the payback point are considered. For a more robust treatment of this issue, consult Sundem and Fremgen.[1]

The four steps in payback analysis are

1. Determine benefits (from objectives).
2. Determine costs of the proposed solution.
3. Calculate the payback point.
4. Decide whether the payback point is soon enough for a likely payoff.

Let us consider the first three steps in more detail.

Step 1—Determining Benefits   The first step is to state all quantifiable benefits that will result from the development of the system. Although these benefits will always be based to some extent on guesswork, you should try to provide the most accurate estimates possible. There are two categories of benefits:

1. **Tangible benefits** are those that can be physically observed and quantified. Examples are reductions in cost per transaction, response time, labor costs, and storage rental; increased sales; and increased interest earnings resulting from faster receipts processing.
2. **Intangible benefits** are those that cannot be quantified easily. Examples are improved company image, better customer service, and higher employee morale.

Always quantify (make tangible) the benefits of the system, unless the feasibility analysis is only a formality being completed after the decision to develop the system has already been made. For example, you might quantify better customer service in terms of more repeat customers. If the average customer purchase was $68 and you estimated that the new system would result in a 10 percent increase in repeat customers, the value of the improvement would be $68,000 for a current customer base of 100,000 customers. To place a value on improved employee morale, you might first determine the employee retention rate and the cost of training each new employee affected by the system being evaluated. If the company was spending $150,000 a year to train new clerks to replace those who quit and the retention rate was only 60 percent, a system that increased the retention rate to 80 percent would be worth $75,000 per year.

Step 2—Determining Costs The second step is to state all relevant costs. There are two categories of costs:

1. **Development costs** are expenses incurred during the systems development process. Examples are salaries and overhead for programmers and analysts and expenditures for purchases of hardware, software, and materials.

2. **Production costs** are expenses incurred during the production phase of the system life cycle. Examples are maintenance fees, labor costs for data entry and computer operators, and expenditures for materials such as processing forms and printer paper, and rental fees.

A complication in most installations is that some costs involve "real money" and others do not. In all installations certain costs are the main drivers of decisions.

Step 3—Calculting the Payback Point The **payback point** is the time required to re-cover the costs of developing the system. For example, assume the estimated benefits and costs for a hypothetical system have been calculated as follows:

```
Expected annual savings (labor)      $20,000
Expected annual savings (storage)    $10,000
Expected annual net sales increase   $10,000
               Total benefits        $40,000


Labor (analyst, users, etc.)                  $10,000
Material (software, hardware)                  $90,000
Variable overhead (clerical help, etc.)       $ 5,000
                       Total costs            $105,000
```

If we assume there are no ongoing production costs beyond the initial cost of the system, then

$$\text{Payback} = \frac{\text{Costs/yr}}{\text{Benefits/yr}} = \frac{\$105,000}{\$40,000} = 2.625 \text{ years}$$

The expected payback point is 2.625 years. Note, however, that this formula works *only* when costs and benefits are expressed in annual terms and ongoing production costs are ignored.

We will now consider another example that requires more analysis—one for a system with ongoing production costs. Assume that the benefits and costs are to be calculated from these figures:

Benefits. Additional net sales revenue during the first production year is expected to be $20,000. Additional annual net revenue for the second and following years is estimated at $30,000.

Costs. A team of three people (two IS, one user) will work half-time (on the average) for 12 months. The monthly *full-time* cost of direct labor and employee benefits for the team is $8,000. An overhead cost of $1,000 per month is to be allocated for each half-time employee.

Total production costs for the system are estimated to be $430 a month for the life of the system.

Based on this information, we first determine the yearly benefits, as shown in Step 1 in Figure 13.6. Then we determine costs, as shown in Step 2 in Figure 13.6. Finally, the payback point is graphically determined, as shown in Step 3 in Figure 13.6.

In this problem the payback point is reached in four years. If this system is likely to be obsolete by then, the decision should be to revise or abandon the project. If the system's life is likely to extend past five years, then development should proceed.

13.5 The Role of the Evaluation Process

The time required to conduct a thorough evaluation of system solutions constitutes only a small portion of the total time required for systems development. Nonetheless, formal reviews are not undertaken in many information systems projects. Given that evaluation analysis is an important process in information systems development, why do so many project teams omit this step as they develop information systems?

One reason people tend to avoid evaluation is the difficulty of the task. Evaluations require that the costs and benefits of an information system be identified and quantified in monetary terms. Identifying the costs and benefits of an information system requires great effort. Typically this information must be pieced together by consulting many different sources. Once the costs and benefits of the system have been identified, quantifying this information in monetary terms is still a complex (some say impossible!) task. Because of the difficulty of acquiring and analyzing information, some organizations see little value in conducting formal evaluations.

In many cases, no evaluation is required, since it is obvious that the information system under consideration is necessary and will be developed. In cases where there is no doubt about the need for a system, conducting a formal evaluation makes little sense. Nevertheless, some organizations have a policy requiring formal evaluations of all information systems. If the need for a system is obvious, formal evaluation can become an irrelevant exercise in completing forms, which erodes the developers' appreciation for the value of other, more relevant evaluations.

Sometimes information systems are requested by high-level executives within an organization. In these cases evaluation is rarely conducted, because high-level executives are not constrained by the procedures mandated within the Information Services department. Ideally, the executive's ability to obtain information systems upon demand is based on a recognition of the extensive knowledge and expertise required to obtain a high-level management position in an organization.

Figure 13.6
Payback Analysis
Example

Step 1:

Cumulative Benefits

Year 1	Year 2	Year 3	Year 4	Year 5
0	$20,000	$50,000	$80,000	$110,000

Step 2:

Cumulative Costs

	Month 1	. . .	Month 12	Year 2	Year 3	Year 4	Year 5
Direct labor	$4,000		$48,000	$48,000	$48,000	$48,000	$48,000
Overhead	3,000		36,000	36,000	36,000	36,000	36,000
Supplies	430		5,160	10,320	15,480	20,640	25,800
Total	7,540		89,160	94,320	99,480	104,640	109,800

Step 3:

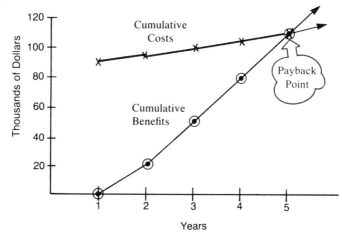

Given the preceding information, you may wonder why a discussion of evaluation is even necessary. If evaluation is a difficult task, which in many cases is not performed, why does this book devote two chapters to it? You need to know how to evaluate systems in the many situations in which evaluation is worthwhile and important to information systems development. The detail level and timing of evaluation will be determined by factors discussed in the next section.

13.6 Timing and Sequence

A dilemma inevitably arises when we try to determine the timing of the evaluation of alternatives. The sooner we make the assessment, the less likely the organization is to waste resources on a risky or worthless project or a poor alternative. But the sooner we make the assessment, the less we know about possible solutions and thus the less reliable the estimate is.

A rule of thumb for dealing with this dilemma is to make rough estimates frequently, but postpone a thorough, well-documented analysis until enough is known to make fairly reliable estimates. If rough estimates show that the cost of the project is obviously out of line with the benefits, further analysis is unnecessary.

An experienced developer can usually identify a low benefit/high cost project without performing a tediously thorough analysis. Similarly, in many circumstances a high-benefit system will so obviously justify its cost that the additional expense of performing a complete feasibility analysis would be wasted. The projects that must be analyzed carefully are those with no obvious cost/benefit ratios and those with such high costs that the risk of a costly failure is great.

Determining the sequence of evaluation activities requires similar judgment. We recommend that alternatives be identified for every project except those where the constraints essentially determine the solution. System enhancements (often called maintenance) are the most common examples of projects in which constraints are so set and so pervasive that there is little choice in solutions.

Alternatives should be generated, documented, and evaluated for all projects that are costly or that affect many people or procedures. The alternatives should be presented to a representative group of end-users and managers. These presentations should be scheduled as frequently as necessary for the development team and management to make informed decisions.

13.6.1 Sequence of Evaluation Activities for Custom Development

The sequence most often recommended for custom development under the life cycle approach is outlined below and illustrated by the flowchart in Figure 13.7.

1. Determine requirements.
2. Analyze feasibility based on a rough outline of one possible solution.
3. Decide whether to continue with the proposed project.
4. If you decide to continue, proceed with development by completing evaluation of alternative solutions, design specification and implementation, and changeover.
5. If you decide not to continue with the project as proposed, either drop the project or redefine it to include lower costs or greater benefits.

Figure 13.7
Evaluation Sequence
for Custom
Development

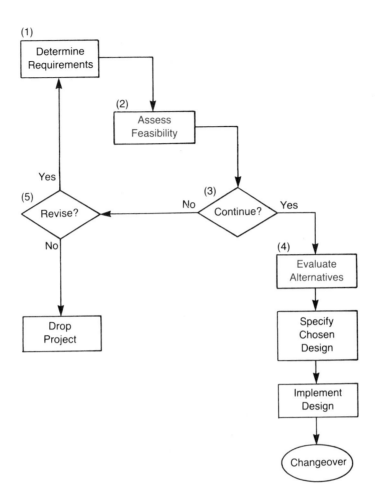

13.6.2 Sequence of Evaluation Activities for Purchased Software

Selecting software is a very common evaluation activity. The steps we recommend are diagrammed in Figure 13.8 and outlined below.

1. Determine requirements.
2. Identify alternative system components, and identify alternative software packages compatible with these system components.

Figure 13.8
Evaluation Sequence
for Purchased
Software

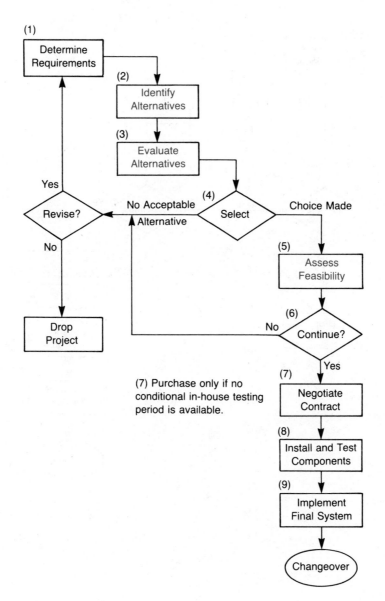

3. Determine, rank, and rate criteria; evaluate products on the chosen criteria.

4. Select the best alternative. If one is acceptable, go to Step 5; otherwise, revise or drop the project.

5. Assess the feasibility of the chosen package in greater detail, comparing its costs and benefits. (This may be a quick analysis, depending on the relative costs and benefits.)

6. If the purchase is feasible, proceed with the remaining development steps. Otherwise, revise requirements or abandon the project.

7. Negotiate a pre-purchase contract that includes appropriate training, support, testing, and guarantees. Purchase the program at this point *if* no conditional, in-house testing period is available. (Avoid making a final purchase until after testing, if at all possible.)

8. Install and test system components thoroughly before continuing with final implementation. Test data should include vendor-provided data, a small portion of production data, and a designed subset of data with errors.

9. Complete implementation for the production system.

13.7 Evaluation Reports

No matter how well you research an evaluation question, your work is likely to be unappreciated by managers unless you communicate your results well. Guidelines for reporting evaluations are listed in Figure 13.9. The minicase Evaluating Word Processors for School Administrators is an example of a professional evaluation report of word processing software available at the time the report was written.

Figure 13.9

Guidelines for Writing Evaluation Reports

1. If the report is more than two or three pages, provide an outline and an executive summary.

2. State the objectives of the evaluation and the intended audience in the introduction to the report.

3. State the evaluation criteria clearly.

4. Include details in tables so that the narrative reads like a story rather than like a list of numbers.

5. Use graphic summaries where possible. (Chapter 14 will explain how to ceate evaluation matrices and grids.)

6. Make recommendations where possible and appropriate, being clear about the relevant conditions or contingencies.

Evaluating Word Processors for School Administrators

A high performance word processor should be easy to learn, but powerful enough to take on the tasks of school administrators and their staffs. Those tasks include: letters, reports, newsletters, budgets, purchase orders, curriculum proposals, and form letters.

With these criteria in mind, we reviewed five word processors: WORD PERFECT 4.1, Microsoft WORD 3.1, VOLKSWRITER 3, WORDSTAR 2000 R2, and MULTIMATE 3.31. We chose these word processors because they have a large share of the marketplace, they all have good reputations for company support (with well thought out updates), and they are readily available nationwide. Then we rated each program for its ease of use and its functional capabilities. (See Figure 13.10.)

Five Basics for an Easy But Powerful Processor   When you are evaluating a professional word processor, there are five basic requirements we think administrators should look for:

1. *A short learning curve.* A professional word processor should allow administrators to work with it productively in less than a hour. Two of the programs, WORD PERFECT and Microsoft WORD, provide well-planned tutorials that teach specific skills, starting with the easiest and then building on what has been learned previously with objectives and goals for every step.

2. *WYSIWYG screen display.* The screen display of a word processor should be as close to printed output as possible, so that "what you see is what you get" (WYSIWYG). All of the programs, except VOLKSWRITER, make good use of the various graphic cards available. However, none do a good job of dealing with superscripts, subscripts, italics, or scientific notation.

3. *Function key commands.* Function keys should control commands as much as possible; and the package should contain templates that fit on the keyboard so that you can see which key is for what command.

The command keys should act as toggle switches (the same key that turns underlining on turns it off when pressed again). WORD PERFECT does this particularly well, allowing even levels of commands to be turned easily on or off. There should be a command line displayed on the screen that shows which commands are active. Microsoft WORD really shines here, almost overwhelming you with information. Very quickly you get used to being able to know at a glance what commands are operational.

4. *Two-part documentation.* The documentation should be divided into two parts, a reference and a tutorial. The reference manual should include a glossary and index as well as a table of contents.

5. *Help.* The user should be able to access a help sequence from anywhere in the program; and help should "know" that you want information about the last command given. WORDSTAR invented the context sensitive help screen and has developed it into an almost uncanny artificial intelligence. When all else fails, there should be a "help line" phone number to the company (preferably an 800-number) staffed by knowledgeable people who can answer your questions. Both Microsoft and Word Perfect Corporation excel in this area—although both require that you pay a small annual fee to continue this support after a warranty period is up.

Power Means a Large Range of Functions   Power in a word processor means the operator can perform common tasks with minimal mechanical or manual setup. An example would be merging a form letter with a mailing list. A person could print the mailing list and manually insert the appropriate data into the letter; or the word processing program could do it all automatically.

Power users require that a good program help them in a number of ways:

Source: Lanny Hertzberg and Jan Caston, *Electronic Learning*, vol. 6, no. 6, March 1987, pp. 29, 30.

Figure 13.10

Ratings Summary for
Word Processors

How the Word Processors Compare

The features of these words processors were rated on a scale of 0–5 (0 = completely unsatisfactory, 1 = unsatisfactory, 2 = average, 3 = good, 4 = very good, 5 = excellent).

Function	Word Perfect 4.1	Microsoft Word 3.1	Volks-Writer 3	Wordstar 2000R2	Multimate 3.31
WYSIWYG*	4	3	4	4	4
Function Keys	4	3	4	2	3
Show Commands	3	5	3	4	3
Smart Help	4	3	3	4	3
Tutorial Manual	4	4	2	3	3
Auto Merge	4	4	3	4	3
Math Capable	4	4	3	4	2
Control Columns	4	3	3	4	4
Define Forms	4	3	2	3	2
Footnotes	4	4	2	4	2
Index	4	4	1	1	1
Bibliography	1	1	1	1	1
Outline	4	4	1	1	1
Speller choices	5	2	3	4	4
Cut & Paste two documents	3	4	1	3	1
Print any page	3	4	1	4	3
Use DOS	4	3	4	3	3
Use Macros	4	3	0	4	3

*What You See Is What You Get

Math capable. A program should have full arithmetic capability. All of these packages are math capable; however, MULTIMATE scored lowest for these functions.

Forms. The user should be able to define forms, and then simply fill in the form either manually or by merging with another document. None of these programs did this very well.

Report essentials. The user should, while doing a report, be able to automatically generate a table of contents, footnotes, an index, and a bibliography. No program does bibliographies yet, and I am not sure why, since it should not be difficult to do.

Speller. The popular high-performance word processors usually contain a speller. The speller should provide a list of choices of possible misspelled words; those choices should include phonetic equivalents. All of the programs included spellers, but WORD PERFECT and WORDSTAR had the fastest and most expandable.

Windows. A word processor should have the ability to display more than one document at the same time (usually called windows) and allow the user to cut and paste from one to another. Here Microsoft WORD was excellent, but requires the use of a mouse. The user should be able to load and save different formats and insert them at any place within a document.

Printer selection. Printer selection should be a matter of simply choosing a printer by name the first time and then that should be the default printer until the user chooses a new one. MULTIMATE and WORD PERFECT let you easily select a printer as well as change from one to another. The user should be able to search a document either backward or forward and print selected pages in any order. None of the programs did this well.

Macros. The programs should allow macros or glossaries; i.e., the user should be able to save commonly used keystrokes (whether it be words or commands) in files that can allow the user to invoke the "macro" with a maximum of two keystrokes. WORDSTAR and WORD PERFECT were judged to have the easiest to use macros.

WORD PERFECT Comes Out on Top   Overall we preferred WORD PERFECT in more categories than any other. All of the programs reviewed lacked one or more of the above characteristics. That doesn't mean that they are bad word processors, for you may not need all the functions we have listed. The best way to buy is to carefully review the kinds of tasks that you commonly do, ranking them by order of importance. Then determine what you need to perform those tasks and make sure your word processor has those capabilities.

The minicase is a well-written evaluation from an educator's magazine, *Electronic Learning*. The objectives of the software evaluation are identified early, with a clear reference to the intended user. The very first paragraph gives a common-task list so that readers can determine immediately whether the evaluator understands their needs. The major criteria also are given in the first paragraph: "easy to learn" and "powerful enough" for the necessary tasks of the target user. The more specific criteria under each of these major criteria are given in the table and discussed in detail in the body of the report. In addition to the evaluation criteria, three minimum criteria are mentioned: large market share; reputation for good company support, including updates; and ready availability nationwide. **Minimum (first cut) criteria** like these were used to narrow the range of products before evaluation.

The table in the minicase is an example of an evaluation matrix, a tool that will be discussed in Chapter 14. The table would be easier to read if the criteria were organized into several categories. The table assigns equal value to all criteria, which is reasonable for an evaluation for a large general audience. For an organization-specific evaluation, however, the criteria should be weighted to show the priorities of the users.

The criteria are well explained so that readers can consider whether their needs match the interests of the evaluator. Finally, a clear recommendation is made, but the author is careful to state that the weights for criteria will differ for each user. Different weights might lead to different selections.

Summary

Evaluation activities encompass the tasks of generating and selecting alternative system components. Data flow diagrams provide a technique for exploring alternatives and documenting the choice. The criteria for evaluation are based on the goals of system quality, project management, and organizational relevance.

Payback analysis is a quick method for making an early guess about whether a project is worth pursuing. More thorough analyses may be made as the project continues and requirements are detailed.

Key Terms

(Section numbers are in parentheses.)

feasibility analysis (13.1.2)   **development costs (13.4.2)**
rough first pass (13.4.1)   **production costs (13.4.2)**
payback analysis (13.4.2)   **payback point (13.4.2)**
tangible benefits (13.4.2)   **minimum (first cut) criteria (13.7)**
intangible benefits (13.4.2)

Note

1. See G. Sundem, "Evaluating Capital Budgeting Models in Simulated Environments," *The Journal of Finance,* September 1975, pp. 977–992; and J. Fremgen, "Capital Budgeting Practices: A Survey," *Management Accounting,* May 1973, pp. 19–25.

Exercises

(Answers to Exercises 13.1 through 13.4 are at the end of the book.)

13.1 The criteria for an inventory system are listed below. Specify whether each criterion is good, poor, or not an evaluation criterion. Explain your answers.

  a. System runs well.

  b. System has hard disk storage.

  c. System costs less than $10,000.

  d. System is used by our competitors.

13.2 Reread the minicase Abby Clark and Her Turnkey System in Chapter 1. Now suppose that Abby is dissatisfied with her Kaypro 4 system and has asked her nephew, Cecil, to prepare a list of criteria and constraints to assist her in purchasing a new system. Cecil, after some consideration, has provided Abby with the lists shown in Figure 13.11. Critique Cecil's choice of criteria and constraints.

13.3 The Rightway Corporation is a retail sales business. Rightway buys various products wholesale and sells them to retail customers. Rightway is experiencing too many delays due to its

Figure 13.11

Criteria	Constraints
1. Usage—the system will be used daily by the bookkeeper.	1. Total hardware and software cost under $4,000.
2. User satisfaction—the bookkeeper will enjoy using the new system.	2. Training and other costs under $1,000.
3. Operational efficiency (in terms of resources)— fast response time, efficient use of disk space, smooth-running system, lack of errors in computer operations context.	3. System operational within six weeks.

current system for documenting sales. Management has commissioned an investigation of a new system, setting three management constraints on development:

1. Total development costs cannot exceed $50,000.

2. Annual production costs cannot exceed $22,000.

3. The plan must be implemented by the start of the next quarter (within three months).

Three proposals have been introduced to the IS development team. These three proposals are called the Phone Plan, the Patch Plan, and the Motivate Plan.

Phone Plan   This plan calls for immediate purchase of car phones for all the salespeople. Then all the salespeople would have to do after a sale is call a preset number and give the details of the sale. A unique benefit of this method is that the salespeople could call in their sales while in transit, therefore reserving more time for selling. Currently, Rightway has twenty salespeople. The purchasing agent has called several vendors of cellular phones and all promise delivery within thirty days at an average price of $800 per phone. The accounting department estimates that the plan would increase each salesperson's monthly phone bill by about $150. The Accounting department does not anticipate any increased workload with the Phone Plan.

Patch Plan   This plan calls for hiring another bookkeeping employee to document sales. Rightway does not have a Personnel department and anticipates spending about $200 searching for this employee. The search should take a month, and training should take two weeks. The employee is expected to work forty hours per week for fifty weeks and have two weeks of paid vacation. Rightway plans to pay the new employee $10/hour.

Motivate Plan   This plan calls for paying overtime to the existing employees. The employees would be paid at time and one-half for any hours over eight per day or forty hours per week. Only the hourly employees in the Bookkeeping department would be eligible for this overtime. Currently, there are five such employees, who work on average fifty weeks per year at $10 per hour. The Accounting department has estimated that each employee in the bookkeeping department would average five hours of overtime per week.

To develop your answers to the following questions, refer to the rough first pass presented in Section 13.4.1.

   a. Create a table showing the rough estimates of all costs for each plan.

   b. Rank the alternatives on the bases of cost and development time.

   c. Which plans, if any, fail to meet management constraints?

   d. Can any arguments be made for considering any plan eliminated in part c?

13.4 Big State University is considering purchasing a set of off-the-shelf programs to improve its time-consuming registration process. The university has sufficient capacity on its IBM mainframe system to run the programs with no change in hardware configuration.

It is estimated that currently fifty-five clerks in various departments throughout the university each work an average of forty hours each semester to complete the registration process. These clerks are paid $8 per hour. There are three semesters each year (fall, spring, and summer). It is estimated that the new software for registration will save two-thirds of the time required for clerical processing. Two additional intangible benefits are expected. First, the software will provide university administrators with more complete statistics on the registration process. Second, students will spend less time standing in lines.

The costs of the new system are as follows. The software package itself costs $20,000. Five data-entry operators will have to be hired and trained by the university to input data into the new programs. Each operator (paid $12 per hour) will work eighty hours each semester. The university will pay $1000 to train each new operator. In addition, it is estimated that using the new software will increase paper and supply costs by $2000 per semester. Finally, the cost of converting data to the new system is expected to be $3000.

Based on this background information, answer the following questions:

a. What is the payback point?

b. Would you recommend purchasing the proposed software?

c. What information, in addition to the payback point, would be important to this decision?

13.5 Place each of the evaluation criteria listed below into one of the following system quality (SQ) or project management (PM) categories:

```
Functional Criteria (SQ-Fu)
Maintenance Criteria (SQ-M)
Flexibility Criteria (SQ-Fl)
Project Management Criteria or Constraints (PM)
```

a. ease of use

b. basic functions

c. documentation

d. memory requirements

e. vendor support

f. compatibility with existing hardware

g. access time

h. printing speed

i. fonts supported

j. cost of updates

k. warranty

l. ability to be implemented within four months

m. ease of file update

n. peripherals supported

o. low production cost

p. tutorials

13.6 Place each of the evaluation criteria listed below into the category SQ–Fu, SQ–M, SQ–Fl, or PM, based on the definitions given in Exercise 13.5.

   a. leveled menus for novice and expert users

   b. ability to customize

   c. number of records allowed

   d. field length and number

   e. ability to integrate with other systems

   f. security controls provided

   g. languages supported

   h. site requirements

   i. memory expansion capability

   j. availability

   k. help screens

   l. error recovery procedures

   m. system downtime

13.7 You are a new member of the property evaluation board of Longworth and Associates, a company that acquires undervalued companies, improves their management, and then sells them at a healthy profit. Of the seven board members, you are the only one with a systems design background. The other members have accounting, finance, and general management backgrounds.

   Longworth and Associates wants to develop a new bidding acquisition system to replace its current Bid Analysis System (BAS). BAS is a very limited system that requires special coding for each investigation of a new property. In the process of identifying an undervalued company, a property analyst gathers a large amount of data and then works with one of the financial clerks to calculate a bid using BAS.

   The Research department has offered three systems development projects, A, B, and C, to replace BAS. The Finance department has estimated the expected return on investment (ROI) for each of the three proposed systems development projects. The evaluation board has chosen seven other criteria in addition to ROI and has assigned a value of 0 to 5 to each criterion, 5 being the most favorable or greatest value. After careful consideration, the board has assigned a weight to each of the eight criteria, the total weight equaling 100 percent. A summary table of the board's evaluation results is provided in Figure 13.12.

   a. Is plan C with a weighted average of 4.0 considerably better than the current system, BAS? Does it warrant immediate development?

   b. Do the eight evaluation criteria represent the criteria you would consider to be primary for the project? What additions or deletions would you make? Does independence of criteria matter?

   c. Why does criterion 7 have a negative weight? Do you think the organization of this company is top-down or decentralized? Why?

   d. Add and delete criteria as you deem appropriate. Explain your changes and recalculate scores.

   e. What is your recommendation based on the revisions you made in part d? Explain your choice.

Evaluation Criteria	Criteria Weights	Current BAS		Replacement Plan A		Replacement Plan B		Replacement Plan C	
		Raw Rate*	Weighted Rate	Raw Rate	Weighted Rate	Raw Rate	Weighted Rate	Raw Rate	Weighted Rate
1. Return on investment	.25	1	.250	2	.500	3	.750	5	1.250
2. Ability to keep workers employed	.10	4	.400	3	.300	2	.200	1	.100
3. Benefit to the user (e.g., easy to operate and understand)	.10	5	.500	4	.400	4	.400	2	.200
4. C.E.O.'s rating of system	.15	2	.300	3	.450	4	.600	5	.750
5. Quality of report	.15	3	.450	3	.450	3	.450	5	.750
6. Frequency of use	.20	5	1.000	4	.800	4	.800	3	.600
7. Interaction required between the analyst and the user	−.10	5	−.500	4	−.400	3	−.300	1	−.100
8. Ability to meet functional requirements	.15	5	.750	4	.600	4	.600	3	.450
Total weighted average	1.00		3.15		3.10		3.50		4.00

*Raw rates: From 1 = least value to 5 = greatest value

Figure 13.12

13.8 Standard University wants to acquire a multiple-microprocessor energy management system to better regulate and conserve the university's energy expenditures. Three vendors, Energy, Inc., Micro Controls, and Econetics, have passed the rough first pass and have proposed systems with roughly the same life-cycle costs for acquisition and basic maintenance. Figure 13.13 shows the results of an evaluation of the proposed systems on a number of criteria.

a. Separate the ten evaluation criteria into constraints and criteria.

b. Consider the criteria for any overlaps; condense these evaluation criteria into a list of nonredundant criteria.

Figure 13.13

| | Vendor | | |
Criteria	Energy, Inc.	Micro Controls	Econetics
1. Steady-state energy savings	10%	8%	12%
2. Controls	Adequate	Very good	Marginal
3. Ease of operation	Adequate	Good	Adequate
4. Diagnostics	Adequate	Good	Poor
5. Availability	0.990	0.995	0.975
6. Growth/update capability	Adequate	Good	Adequate
7. Safety features	Very good	Good	Adequate
8. Accounting functions	Good	Good	Very good
9. Vendor reliability and support	Very good	Good	Very good
10. Savings analysis package	Good	None	None

13.9 Refer to Exercise 13.8. Assume that the following criteria are designed as minimum standards to be used as constraints in the rough first pass.

```
Criterion 1: Steady-state energy savings
Criterion 5: Availability
Criterion 9: Vendor reliability and support
```

Vendor reliability and support are assigned raw values as follows: very good = 10, good = 8, adequate = 6, marginal = 4, and poor = 2. Steady-state energy savings are assigned raw values as shown in Figure 13.14.

Figure 13.14

Parameters	Raw Value
$0\% \leq$ savings $< 3\%$	2
$3\% \leq$ savings $< 6\%$	4
$6\% \leq$ savings $< 9\%$	6
$9\% \leq$ savings $< 12\%$	8
$12\% \leq$ savings $< 15\%$	10

Availability is assigned raw values as shown in Figure 13.15.

a. Calculate the raw values of the three constraints for each system.

b. What raw value total must a system have achieved to pass the rough first pass?

c. What system appears the best in terms of raw values of the three constraints? Will this always be the case?

Figure 13.1!

Parameters	Raw Value
.970 ≤ availability < .975	2
.975 ≤ availability < .980	4
.980 ≤ availability < .985	6
.985 ≤ availability < .990	8
.990 ≤ availability < .995	10
.995 ≤ availability < 1	12

13.10 Reread Exercise 2.6 about Harry McKetta, the COBOL whiz. Now suppose the head librarian of Midtown College library has approved the new clerk's suggestion that they return to the manual card system.

    a. List criteria and constraints to support the librarian's decision to return to the manual system. In your analysis consider why a new system written in either Pascal or Lisp, both of which are taught in the Computer Science department, was not her final decision.

    b. Did the chief librarian make the correct decision? If so, why? If not, explain the correct solution.

13.11 Whirling Dervish Wholesalers imports wicker and bamboo products from around the world for sale to retailers in the United States. Whirling keeps large inventories of products in various countries and therefore has unique inventory management problems. After extensive evaluation of existing inventory management software, the company has determined that no existing package would meet its needs. The DP department of Whirling has proposed developing an inventory management system using a relational database package called RELD-BASE. The details of the proposal follow.

    The initial cost for RELDBASE is $18,000. In addition, there is a $6,500 annual fee for updates and information on RELDBASE. A team of three programmer-analysts would require four months of development time to create the new system. Each programmer-analyst is paid $24,000 per year. Costs of converting to the new system are expected to be $6,000.

    The major benefit of the system would be a reduction in the inventory carrying costs of the company. It is expected that the company would be able to reduce the financing costs of carrying inventory by $1,000 per month for the first year that the system was in operation. In the second year, inventory carrying costs would decrease by $1,200 per month. In remaining years, inventory carrying costs would decrease by $800 per month. In addition, the sales department anticipates a reduction in long distance telephone costs of $700 per month due to the improved communication of inventory information that would result from the new system.

    a. What is the payback point?

    b. Would you recommend purchasing the proposed software?

    c. What information, in addition to payback point, would be important to this decision?

13.12 The Standard University Psychology Laboratory is acquiring a mini-computer to perform experiment monitoring and data reduction functions. Three mini-computer vendors—

Associated Minicomputers, Inc., Amalgamated Minicomputers, Inc., and Consolidated Minicomputers, Inc.—have proposed systems, each at a total cost of about $100,000 and a basic hardware speed of 1 million ops/sec. Figure 13.16 shows the results of the Psychology Lab's evaluation of the proposed systems.

Figure 13.16

	Vendor		
Criteria	**Associated**	**Amalgamated**	**Consolidated**
Hardware features	Very good	Good	Good
Operating system features	Good	Outstanding	Good
Data management features	Good	Outstanding	Adequate
Language support	Adequate	Good	Good
Programming support	Good	Very good	Good
Ease of conversion	Very good	Adequate	Good
Vendor reliability support	Good	Good	Very good
Application package	Adequate	Very good	Good
Operation system overhead	10%	50%	5%
System availability	75%	90%	95%

Assume that the descriptions of outstanding, very good, good, and adequate have been assigned raw values of 20, 18, 15, and 10, respectively. Also assume that the criteria of vendor reliability, operation system overhead, and system availability are management constraints used only for the rough first pass, not for the final decision process. The three vendors have all successfully passed the rough first pass.

a. Given the weights shown in Figure 13.17, which vendor should be chosen? (Hint: Construct a decision grid as shown in Figure 13.12.)

Figure 13.17

Criteria	**Weight**
Hardware features	.20
Operating system features	.20
Data management features	.10
Language support	.20
Programming support	.05
Ease of conversion	.10
Application package	.15
	1.00

b. Assuming the evaluation criteria and weights used in part a are correct, is the choice in part a necessarily correct?

c. Are there any additions or deletions you would make to the seven evaluation criteria given?

Project

13.13 Read the article by J. L. King and E. L. Schrens, "Cost Benefit Analysis in Information Systems Development and Operation," *Computing Surveys,* vol. 10, no. 1, March 1978, pp. 19–34. Then do *one* of the following

a. In the article, the authors describe a five-step process for conducting cost/benefit analyses. Prepare an outline of the steps and their subtasks that you can distribute to your classmates. In a short, informal presentation, explain the highlights of this process and be ready to answer your classmates' questions about it.

b. In Section 3 of the article, the authors discuss several problems in performing a cost/benefit analysis. Prepare an oral or written summary of these problems. Tailor your report to an audience composed of your classmates.

CHAPTER 14

Evaluation Techniques

Evaluation Matrices
    Definition
    Matrix Construction

Evaluation Grids
    Definition
    Grid Construction
    Minicase: Selecting a Database for *Outerspace* Magazine

Evaluation Activities
    Generating Alternatives
    Minicase: Generating Alternative Solutions for Environmental Research Associates
    Evaluating Software
    Evaluating Alternative Projects

Summary
Key Terms ▪ Exercises ▪ Projects

Overview

The last chapter presented steps and guidelines to help you evaluate alternatives. This chapter focuses on two evaluation tools: evaluation matrices and grids. For each tool, we present the definition, goals, and rules for making effective use of the technique. Then we review the identification and evaluation process activities for identifying alternative components, system solutions, and projects.

Specifically we plan to

1. Explain what an evaluation matrix is and how to construct it. (Section 14.1)

2. Explain what an evaluation grid is and how to construct it. (Section 14.2)

3. Illustrate the use of these techniques. (Section 14.2)

4. Discuss the use of these techniques to generate alternatives, evaluate software, and evaluate alternative projects. (Section 14.3)

14.1 Evaluation Matrices

Thorough evaluations of system alternatives frequently lead to a confusing mass of details. An evaluation matrix is a valuable aid in organizing the details for analysis, documentation, and management reviews.

14.1.1 Definition

An **evaluation matrix** is a summary table showing the criteria, weights, and ratings for two or more alternatives being evaluated. The criteria usually are placed on the rows of the matrix and the alternatives on the columns. The order may be switched if there are few criteria and many alternatives.

The purposes of an evaluation matrix are to

- Summarize the details relevant to evaluation
- Provide a basis for discussing and selecting alternatives

14.1.2 Matrix Construction

Before you can begin to construct a matrix, you must choose the evaluation criteria and complete your investigation. When you have completed your investigation, you will have an organized set of notes that needs to be summarized for the team members and managers. The evaluation matrix is one tool for summarizing these details and presenting the highlights of your research to others.

The steps in constructing a matrix are outlined in Figure 14.1. Although many of the steps are clerical, there are several decisions to be made. Steps 2a and 3a require you to choose criteria and alternatives to include in the matrix. Depending on the purpose of the matrix, you may choose to list all or only a limited number of the criteria considered in researching alternatives. You might list all criteria in an early evaluation so that your

Figure 14.1

Steps in Constructing Evaluation Matrices

Step 1	Title the matrix with the name of the organization, the purpose of the evaluation, and the date of the evaluation.
Step 2	a. Choose criteria for the evaluation matrix based on the system requirements and the purpose of the matrix.
	b. Organize the criteria on the matrix for easy review.
	c. Determine a weighting scale and the weight for each criterion, based on the priorities determined in the investigation of requirements.
Step 3	a. Select alternatives to be evaluated at this stage in the process. These may be all known possibilities or two or more possibilities selected on the basis of minimum criteria or constraints.
	b. Make each alternative a column heading.
Step 4	a. Determine a rating scale and the raw rating for each alternative on each criterion.
	b. Calculate the weighted rating for each alternative on each criterion by multiplying the weight by the raw rating for that criterion.
Step 5	Calculate the total weighted rating for each alternative by summing the entries in the weighted rating column.
Step 6	Clearly mark the scales for the weights and the ratings.

team members can consider the detailed investigation results. For a presentation to management, however, you would probably choose a more limited set of criteria for the matrix. (The detailed matrix might be used as a report appendix or as a handout to supplement an oral presentation.) Similarly, the number of alternatives on the matrix will be greater in the early stages of investigation than later, when only the top choices are presented.

The steps in matrix construction will be illustrated after we explain another technique, the evaluation grid. For an example of an evaluation matrix, see Figure 14.3.

14.2 Evaluation Grids

Evaluation grids provide a graphic distillation of the organized details presented in evaluation matrices. They are particularly helpful for management reviews.

14.2.1 Definition

An **evaluation grid** is a graphic summary of the ratings of alternatives on two criteria. The grid is a two-dimensional graph that is divided into four quadrants (see Figure 14.4). Quadrant I, the lower left-hand quadrant, represents a low rating on both criteria. Quadrants II and III, the lower right-hand and upper left-hand quadrants, represent a mixed rating: low on one criterion, high on the other. Quadrant IV, the upper right-hand quadrant, represents a high rating on both criteria.

The purpose of an evaluation grid is to illustrate important differences among alternatives. A grid is especially helpful for reviewing a large number of alternatives; its graphic representation captures the comparative ratings of alternatives better than the detail included in a tabular evaluation matrix.

14.2.2 Grid Construction

A grid is a simplified graphic representation of a matrix. Once an evaluation matrix has been completed, only the three steps in Figure 14.2 are required to construct a grid. The grid uses two criteria from the matrix as axes. These criteria may be **composite criteria**—standards that combine two or more related criteria under one label. For example, one of the axes might be Ease of Use, which might be computed by summing the scores

Figure 14.2
Steps in Constructing
Evaluation Grids

Step 1	Title the grid with the name of the organization, the purpose of the evaluation, and the date of the evaluation.
Step 2	a. Choose two major evaluation criteria for the two axes. If you choose composite criteria as axes, then you must average the weighted scores to calculate each composite score.
	b. Label each of the axes with one of the criteria.
	c. Label each of the axes with an appropriate numeric scale.
	d. Divide the graph space into four quadrants.
Step 3	Plot each of the alternatives based on its total weighted score for each criterion.

for ease of learning, ease of use, and documentation quality. The alternatives are placed on the grid according to their scores on the two criteria.

Step-by-step illustrations of how to draw grids and create matrices are provided in the minicase Selecting a Database for *Outerspace* Magazine. Note that Alex Tuttle, the researcher in the minicase, is *not* a very thorough evaluator. This minicase's purpose is to explain the two evaluation techniques presented in this chapter, not to provide a thorough account of evaluation procedures.

MINICASE

Selecting a Database for *Outerspace* Magazine

You may remember *Outerspace* magazine's search for a word processor, which was described in a minicase in Chapter 5. After Outerspace installed a microcomputer and word processing system for the entire company, Alex Tuttle was hired to be the information systems staff. It was Alex's job to provide training and support.

Doug Samson, a co-owner and the business manager, was unhappy with the outside service firm that processed Outerspace's subscriptions. He asked Alex what other options might be available. Alex suggested that doing the work in-house with a database package would provide greater flexibility and more timely service. Because of the company's limited IS staff, Alex recommended that Outerspace consider only easy-to-learn and easy-to-use database packages. The only training required should be a thorough on-line tutorial. Doug wanted the database to be used to generate monthly reports for different departments, as well as to process subscriptions. The only advanced function that users might require would be a sort function. Doug asked Alex to research the possibilities.

Alex started his preliminary review of available databases in the library. He found a series of *Datapro* articles that evaluated popular databases very thoroughly. (Datapro is a research and publishing firm that evaluates computer hardware and software products.) In order to summarize the information on the top six recommended databases, Alex created the matrix shown in Figure 14.3. He used the criteria and ratings given in the *Datapro* articles, because Datapro has a reputation for being unbiased. Alex would eventually use the matrix in Figure 14.3 to create an evaluation matrix weighting the important criteria on the basis of Outerspace's needs. Rather than

do this detail work for all six databases, however, Alex decided to narrow the number of alternative databases to the two or three that appeared to best meet Outerspace's specific needs.

Alex created the evaluation grids in Figures 14.4 and 14.5 to help him eliminate some alternatives. The business manager's primary concerns were ease of learning (tutorial quality) and ease of use, so these were chosen as the evaluation criteria on the axes of the grid in Figure 14.4. Alex scaled the X and Y axes based on the ranges of ratings found in his matrix. Then he plotted the ratings of each database. Alex used the same technique to create the grid in Figure 14.5. But this time he chose Basic Functions and Sorting/Indexing Capability as the evaluation criteria.

Comparing the two grids, Alex noted that the databases in the best quadrant (IV) differed only slightly:

Grid 1 (Figure 14.4)	Grid 2 (Figure 14.5)
R:base	R:base
Revelation	Revelation
Unify	dBase III
Data Ease	Unify

R:base, Revelation, and Unify all fell in the fourth quadrant on both evaluation grids. Therefore, Alex eliminated Data Ease, dBase III, and PC/Focus from the alternatives list.

Having reduced the number of alternatives to three databases (R:base, Revelation, and Unify), Alex con-

	Database System (month/year reviewed)					
Performance Criteria	R:base System V (September '86)	Revelation (August '85)	Data Ease 2.5 (May '86)	dBase III Plus (April '86)	Unify (May '86)	PC/Focus (March '86)
Basic Functions						
Installation and Setup	8.5	8.2	8.0	7.3	6.0	6.0
User Interface	8.5	7.5	7.7	6.0	8.0	7.0
Forms Design	9.0	8.6	8.5	8.0	7.5	5.5
Data Entry	8.3	8.0	8.0	9.0	8.0	7.0
Data Retrieval	8.2	9.0	7.7	7.5	8.5	7.0
Report Generation	8.5	8.3	8.0	8.3	6.5	9.0
Print Functions	6.0	5.0	6.0	5.0	7.0	5.5
Average	8.1	7.8	7.7	7.3	7.4	6.7
Documentation						
Tutorial	8.5	8.0	6.5	5.5	7.5	4.0
Help Screens	8.0	6.5	3.0	7.0	8.0	6.5
Printed Documentation	8.3	7.2	8.0	7.7	7.7	6.0
Average	8.3	7.2	5.8	6.7	7.7	5.5
Advanced Functions						
Security	7.0	4.0	8.5	8.0	8.5	9.5
File Modification	8.1	9.5	8.8	8.5	7.5	5.0
Math Functions	8.7	7.0	8.6	8.5	7.0	8.7
Data Transfer	8.0	7.0	8.0	8.3	6.5	7.0
Sorting/Indexing	8.0	8.0	7.7	8.5	8.5	8.0
Relational Capabilities	8.4	9.5	8.8	8.0	8.0	8.5
Programming Language	9.5	NA	6.0	9.0	8.5	7.5
Average	8.2	7.5	8.1	8.4	7.8	7.7
Vendor Support						
Telephone Support	6.0	6.0	7.2	7.5	7.5	7.5
Vendor Response	8.0	6.0	6.8	9.0	7.5	8.0
Updates	9.0	8.0	8.0	8.0	8.0	8.0
Newsletters, Mailings, etc.	8.0	7.0	7.5	9.5	7.5	8.0
Training Aids	NA	NA	8.0	9.0	NA	7.0
Average	7.8	6.8	7.5	8.6	7.6	7.7
Ease of Use						
Novice Proficiency	8.4	7.5	8.0	7.0	7.0	7.5
Experienced User Proficiency	8.7	9.0	8.4	8.0	8.5	7.0
Data I/O	8.0	9.0	6.8	8.5	8.0	7.0

Figure 14.3   Benchmark Test Results (Datapro Research Corporation)

	Database System (month/year reviewed)					
Performance Criteria	R:base System V (September '86)	Revelation (August '85)	Data Ease 2.5 (May '86)	dBase III Plus (April '86)	Unify (May '86)	PC/Focus (March '86)
Ease of Interaction w/Other Appli:	8.2	6.5	8.0	7.5	7.7	7.0
Average (Ease of Use)	8.3	8.0	7.8	7.7	7.8	7.1
Training Time						
Novice Proficiency	8.3	6.0	8.0	6.5	6.5	6.5
Experienced User Proficiency	8.4	8.5	8.4	7.0	7.5	6.0
Average	8.4	7.3	8.2	6.8	7.0	6.3

Source: Datapro *Directory of Microcomputer Software,* August, 1985; March, 1986; April, 1986; May, 1986; and September, 1986. Ratings represent Datapro editors' evaluations during benchmark testing. The scale is from 1 = poor to 10 = excellent.

Figure 14.3 (Continued)

Figure 14.4
A Comparison Grid
for Ease of Use and
Tutorial Quality

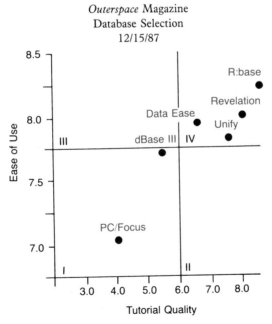

Outerspace Magazine
Database Selection
12/15/87

Quadrant	
I	Poor
II, III	Fair–Good
IV	Very Good

Figure 14.5
A Comparison Grid
for Functionality

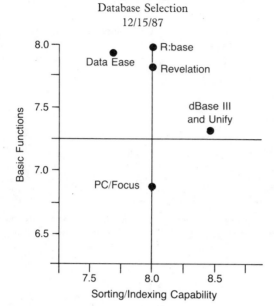

structed an evaluation matrix to summarize the Datapro ratings and to further evaluate the three selected packages on Outerspace's criteria.

Step 1 Alex titled the matrix with the organization's name (*Outerspace* Magazine), the evaluation purpose (Database Selection), and the evaluation date (12/15/87), as shown in Figure 14.6.

Step 2 a. Alex chose the evaluation criteria (1) Basic Functions, (2) Ease of Use, (3) Tutorial, and (4) Sorting/Indexing. Alex's reason for choosing Basic Functions was that a database's function rating is a basic measure of its functionality. He chose Ease of Use and Tutorial because management wanted a database that would be easy to learn and use. Sorting/Indexing was the only advanced function needed, so he included it as an evaluation criterion.

b. Alex organized the four criteria on the matrix for easy review, as shown in Figure 14.6.

c. Alex established a weighting scale with 1 = least important and 5 = most important. He assigned weights based on the system priorit-

ies identified by management and users. Ease of Use and Tutorial were given weights of 5 because management preferred an easy-to-use and easy-to-learn database over all others. Basic Functions was given a high weight of 4 because functionality is important to ease of use. Sorting/Indexing was given a low weight of 2 because users weren't certain that it was a necessary function.

Step 3 a. Alex selected the alternatives based on his earlier grid work.

b. He made each of the three databases a column heading, as shown in Figure 14.7.

Step 4 a. Alex used the Datapro rating scale of 1 = poor to 10 = excellent, since he had used their data.

b. By multiplying the weight by the raw rating from Datapro for each alternative, Alex calculated the weighted ratings. These are listed in Figure 14.7.

Step 5 Alex calculated the total weighted rating for each alternative by summing the entries in the weighted rating column, producing the totals in Figure 14.8.

Outerspace Magazine
Database Selection
12/15/87

Criteria	Weight
1. Basic Functions	4
2. Ease of Use	5
3. Tutorial	5
4. Sorting/Indexing	2

Step 1 Title the matrix with the organization's name, the evaluation purpose, and the evaluation date.

Step 2 a. Choose evaluation criteria, as discussed in Chapter 13.
     b. Organize the criteria for easy review.
     c. Determine a weighting scale:

```
1 = least important  5 = most important
```

     Assign criterion weights based on system priorities.

Figure 14.6 Evaluation Matrix Construction: Steps 1 and 2

Outerspace Magazine
Database Selection
12/15/87

Criteria	Weight	R:base		Unify		Revelation	
		Raw Rating	Weighted Rating	Raw Rating	Weighted Rating	Raw Rating	Weighted Rating
1. Basic Functions	4	8.1	32.4	7.4	29.6	7.9	31.6
2. Ease of Use	5	8.3	41.5	7.8	39.0	8.0	40.0
3. Tutorial	5	8.5	42.5	7 5	37.5	8.0	40.0
4. Sorting/Indexing	2	8.0	16.0	8.5	17.0	8.0	16.0

Step 3 a. Select alternatives to be evaluated.
     b. Make each alternative a column heading.

Step 4 a. Determine a rating scale:

```
1 = poor  10 = excellent
```

     b. Calculate the weighted rating by multiplying the weight by the raw rating for each alternative.

Figure 14.7 Evaluation Matrix Construction: Steps 3 and 4

Outerspace Magazine
Database Selection
12/15/87

| Criteria | Weight* | R:base | | Unify | | Revelation | |
		Raw Rating**	Weighted Rating	Raw Rating	Weighted Rating	Raw Rating	Weighted Rating
1. Basic Functions	4	8.1	32.4	7.4	29.6	7.9	31.6
2. Ease of Use	5	8.3	41.5	7.8	39.0	8.0	40.0
3. Tutorial	5	8.5	42.5	7.5	37.5	8.0	40.0
4. Sorting/Indexing	2	8.0	16.0	8.5	17.0	8.0	16.0
Total Weighted Rating			132.4		123.1		127.6

*Weighting scale: 1 = least important; 5 = most important
**Rating scale: 1 = poor; 10 = excellent

Step 5   Calculate the total weighted rating for each alternative by summing the weighted rating column.

Step 6   Clearly mark the scales for the weights and the ratings.

Figure 14.8   Evaluation Matrix Construction: Steps 5 and 6

Step 6   Alex marked the scales used for the weights and ratings at the bottom of the matrix in Figure 14.8. The evaluation matrix was now ready for management review.

To summarize the detailed matrix for management, Alex drew an evaluation grid.

Step 1   Alex titled the grid with the organization's name (*Outerspace* Magazine), the evaluation purpose (Database Selection), and the date (12/15/87), as shown in Figure 14.9.

Step 2   a. Alex chose Ease of Use and Tutorial as the two major criteria for evaluation because they had the highest weights in the matrix.

b. He then labeled the axes as shown in Figure 14.10.

c. Based on the ranges of weighted ratings found in the matrix, he determined the appropriate numeric scales and placed them on the axes.

d. He marked quadrant lines at 40.5 for Ease of Use and 39.5 for Tutorial rating.

Step 3   Alex plotted each of the alternatives based on its weighted score for each criterion, as shown in Figure 14.11.

Alex then organized and copied his tables and grids for a meeting of Outerspace managers to discuss the available alternatives and make the final selection.

Figure 14.9
Evaluation Grid Con-
struction: Step 1

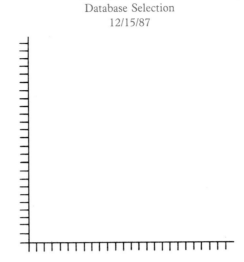

Outerspace Magazine
Database Selection
12/15/87

Step 1   Title the grid with the organization's name, the evaluation purpose, and the date.

Figure 14.10
Evaluation Grid Con-
struction: Step 2

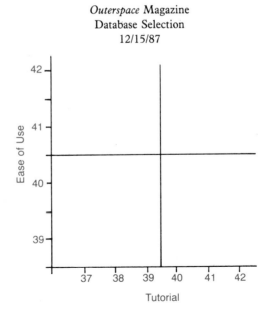

Outerspace Magazine
Database Selection
12/15/87

Step 2   a. Choose two major criteria for evaluation, based on the system requirements.
   b. Label each of the axes with one of the criteria.
   c. Label each of the axes with an appropriate numeric scale.
   d. Divide the graph space into four quadrants.

Figure 14.11
Evaluation Grid Con-
struction: Step 3

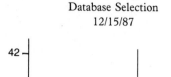

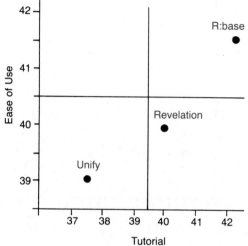

Step 3   Plot each of the alternatives based on its weighted score for each criterion:

	Tutorial	Ease of Use
R:base	42.5	41.5
Unify	37.5	39.0
Revelation	40.0	40.0

14.3 Evaluation Activities

Chapter 13 discussed the wide variety of evaluation activites that occur at different points in the systems development process. In this section we will discuss how matrices and grids can be used in three different evaluation activities.

14.3.1 Generating Alternatives

Generating alternatives is the first step in the evaluation process. The steps you need to follow to generate alternatives are outlined in the level 2 data flow diagram (DFD) in Figure 14.12. Figure 14.13 is a components identification matrix, a development process matrix adapted for alternatives generation. Thinking of necessary characteristics on a component-by-component basis helps you to generate ideas about objectives and constraints, as well as to identify evaluation criteria and guidelines for evaluation research.

As you generate alternatives, your ideas will be "driven" by the component whose alternatives are generated first. These alternatives will tend to determine possible alternatives for the other four components. In Chapter 2 you learned about the alternative sources

Figure 14.12

DFD Summary for Generating Alternatives

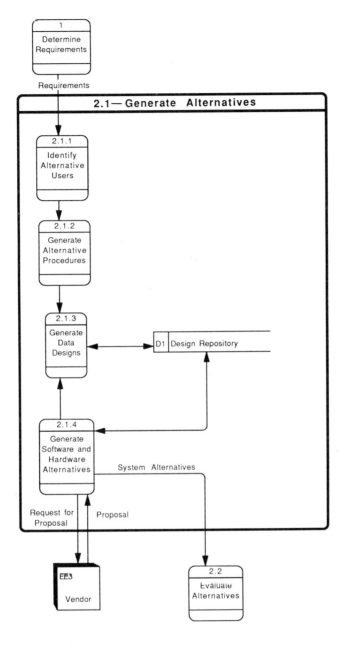

of software and how the choice of a source (existing, custom developed by end-users using 4GLs, or custom developed by IS professionals using 3GLs or 4GLs) constrained the choice of the other components. You've also seen how data requirements determine possible alternatives for the other components. In the following minicase, a matrix is used to illustrate two other approaches to alternatives generation: hardware-driven and people-driven.

Figure 14.13
Components Identification Matrix

Components	Alternative 1	Alternative 2	Alternative 3
People			
Procedures			
Data			
Software			
Hardware			

MINICASE

Generating Alternative Solutions for Environmental Research Associates

Environmental Research Associates is an engineering research firm. The firm has grown from three founding engineers to a staff of forty-seven professionals (engineers, statisticians, and computer experts) and twelve support people (clerks, data entry operators, and secretaries). Maintaining their company's client base and its high level of revenue depends on high-quality reports. Currently reports are produced by secretaries from the engineers' handwritten drafts using dedicated word processors. (These are machines used only for word processing. They do not have a range of capabilities as a microcomputer does.) The firm is considering developing a report processing system that could incorporate graphs and other materials generated by the data analysis, thus saving retyping and pasting work.

Hardware-Driven Approach   One of the senior engineers wants to purchase microcomputers so that he can analyze his own data. The business manager, on the other hand, is more concerned about money, so she recommends using the existing mini-computer as the hardware component. The matrix in Figure 14.14 outlines the implications of these two alternatives for each of the other components.

Notice that the two hardware alternatives limit the selection of alternatives for the other components. Because the mini-computer is relatively difficult to use, a system in which it was the hardware component would be accessible only to frequent users who had received extensive training, eliminating the engineers as users. The hardware similarly constrains the number of feasible software alternatives and the capabilities that can be supported.

A potentially disastrous disadvantage of using the hardware-driven approach is that the hardware, rather than user requirements, determines the system's capabilities. The hardware-driven approach violates the analyst's rule of thumb about identifying user requirements *before* identifying suitable hardware. The DFD in Figure 14.12 shows the first step as identifying users, *not* reviewing alternative hardware choices. Nonetheless, in the real world systems development often is hardware driven, largely because of real constraints (organizational resources) that limit the organization to implementing a *feasible* system, not an *ideal* system. If your organization can't afford new hardware, you must develop the best system you can with the hardware available. In these situations, the hardware-driven approach is appropriate.

People-Driven Approach   At a meeting of department managers, Environmental Research Associates' head engineer requested that the engineers be given greater control over the report generation process.

The word processing staff do the best they can with their dedicated equipment, but those machines aren't capable of

Component	Alternative 1: Microcomputer	Alternative 2: Existing Mini
Hardware	Purchase new microcomputers—consider compatibility with the existing mini.	Use the existing mini-computer.
Software	There are lots of WP programs available that support text and graphics—integrated WP, graphics, and spreadsheet.	The current system is compatible with only one WP program.
Data	It should be possible to find a program to support symbols crossing three lines.	The mini WP program supports only one-line symbols.
Procedures	Micros are easy to use; little training is required. Procedures need to be developed for downloading data from the mini.	The mini is difficult to use; extensive training will be required. Procedures suitable for secretarial use need to be developed.
People	Secretaries and engineers—ease of use makes it feasible to have the system available to engineers, thus reducing the secretarial workload	Secretaries only—difficulty of learning makes it necessary for users to use the system frequently in order to maintain skill

Figure 14.14 Hardware-Driven Approach to Alternatives Generation

Component	Alternative 1	Alternative 2
People	Engineers and secretaries	Secretaries only
Procedures	Procedures need to be clearly documented for infrequent users (engineers).	Training is probably more important than documentation, though a good users' manual is always a plus.
Data	The system should handle text, graphics, and numeric data; be able to do statistical analysis; and allow multi-line characters.	The system should have good text-handling capabilities and an easy-to-use graphics generator; it should allow multi-line characters.
Software	The software needs to be easy to learn but also support advanced features for secretarial use; it must support graphics and data manipulation.	Same here, plus it must support other secretarial WP requirements (memos, letters, schedules, etc.).
Hardware	Micros of desktop publishing quality, networked to laser printer	Here too, or use current mini and customize WP program to support extra features.

Figure 14.15 People-Driven Approach to Alternatives Generation

producing the kinds of reports we need, so we end up doing everything at least twice. My engineers feel caught in
the middle—between reams of data supplied by the statis-
tics division, data that we have to condense and make sense
out of, and the limited capabilities of the WP program that
can't reproduce the sense that we've made! The engineers
want more control over this process. They want a system
that can take the data from stats and condense it into
meaningful graphs and tables for their reports.

The supervisor of word processing agreed and suggested that a new system be developed that involved both
the engineers and the secretaries—or at least made the
secretaries' jobs easier. The matrix in Figure 14.15 identifies the components for these two alternatives. The second matrix leads to a different selection. Comparing the
matrices allows the environmental research associates
staff to insure that they make the right choice.

Figure 14.16

Issues in Alternatives
Generation

Component	Issues

People	1. In development:
	   a. Project team composition (for requirements definition and re-view at all stages): in-house versus consulting mix; groups re-quiring user representation; skills of DP members
	   b. Documentation writers: end-users or DP or contract writers
	   c. Program developers: end-users or DP or contract programmers
	2. In production:
	   a. Types of users (training, frequency of use)
	   b. Number of users
	   c. Geographical dispersion of users
	   d. Attitudes of users

Procedures	1. End-user interface: menu- or command-driven 2. Data entry: query, template, or formatted string 3. End-user procedures for normal processing and failure recovery 4. Operation procedures (data control procedures) for normal process-ing and failure recovery
Data	1. Types of data allowed (numeric, textual, graphic), flexibility of storage 2. Storage types for production and backup files 3. Organization of data: files, records, and so forth (discussed in Chapter 17)
Software	1. In purchasing off-the-shelf software: alternatives that meet func-tional requirements and are compatible with existing systems 2. In developing software for end-user computing: alternative tools, people, and data control procedures 3. In developing software with 4GL tools: need for fast development and production efficiency; compatibility with existing systems 4. In developing software with a second or third generation language: whether production efficiency or special requirements justify slower development; compatibility with existing systems
Hardware	1. In using existing hardware: available configurations and current ca-pacity 2. In purchasing hardware: alternatives that meet program and data requirements (Note: Program and data alternatives usually must be evaluated first.)

Notice that in the people-driven approach to alternatives generation, the needs of the primary system users determine the characteristics of the other components. The solutions described are similar to those generated by the hardware-driven approach, but the emphasis is on what the users need, not on what the hardware can do. Throughout this text, we have emphasized the people-driven approach as a key to successful systems development. In earlier chapters we used the term "user-driven" to highlight the importance of developing systems that meet the requirements of the users.

No matter which component you emphasize, the table in Figure 14.16 highlights some of the factors you need to consider as you generate alternatives.

14.3.2 Evaluating Software

You've already seen numerous examples of software evaluation, including the selection of both a word processing program and a database program for *Outerspace* magazine. The exercises at the end of this chapter will give you more practice in performing this very common evaluation stage activity. In this section we will discuss resources for information about existing software and categorize the criteria used in software evaluation.

Resources for Software Information   Figure 14.17 lists twelve valuable sources of information about software. Given the wealth of resources about existing software, there's no reason your evaluation should be hindered by a lack of information.

Figure 14.17
Resources for Software Information

1. Other companies with similar needs—best resource on all five components

2. Computer magazines, such as *Computerworld, Datamation,* and *The Information Center*

3. Computer review periodicals, such as *Application Software Reports, Datapro Directory of Microcomputer Software* (and others inn Datapro Series), *Minicomputer Software Quarterly,* and *Software Buyer's Guide*

4. Books on software—check your library's subject index

5. Software search services, such as Searchmart Corporation, *The Micro Exchange,* Sofsearch, and PC Telemart, Inc.

6. Newsletters available for many popular microcomputers, applications, and interest groups

7. Literature indexes, such as *Computer Literature Index* and *Business Periodicals Index*

8. Trade magazines—industry-specific trade journals often run articles and advertisements on software designed to meet their industry's needs

9. Computer conventions—excellent for exposure to up-to-date products

10. User groups—great sources of public-domain software and of users' opinions of software products; check computer journals or Yellow Pages for groups in your area

11. Consultants—insist on references or choose a consultant based on other users' recommendations

12. Short computer courses offered by colleges, some vendors, and many large businesses–course instructors are good source of users' opinions of software

Companies that have solved, or attempted to solve, similar problems are probably the best source of information about software. Try to get permission to visit their sites to interview users and technical people. (Chapter 8 includes a list of questions for on-site and telephone interviews.) You can learn about companies to visit from trade organizations (for example, the local AMA chapter for doctors or the local real estate board for realtors) or from vendors. Vendors should always be able to provide a list of current users of the software product you are considering.

User groups are a helpful source of information that is not available elsewhere. Members can save you time and money by giving you an evaluation of the software you are considering. You should be able to get the addresses of user groups in your area from computer-specific magazines or from local computer vendors. Most user groups are for specific microcomputers or mainframes. IBM's SHARE is probably the best-known user group.

Your library also can provide numerous sources of information about software. Computer review periodicals are devoted exclusively to evaluations, comparisons, and lists of names and addresses for specific programs. A few of them also carry general interest articles. These periodicals give more review space to specific packages than do most computer magazines. You'll also find your library's card catalog a useful source of books, and its reference guides will provide easy access to numerous articles. These reference guides identify magazine articles written about specific subjects in the computer field. Independent review articles are particularly valuable guides in choosing programs. Even review articles written by biased sources can be helpful, so long as you are aware of the author's bias. Advertisements can also be valuable. Some offer inexpensive demonstration disks that can help you evaluate alternative products.

Criteria in Software Evaluation   Because software can be evaluated on the basis of so many criteria, it is helpful to identify major categories of criteria. These categories permit you to group several criteria into one composite criterion, simplifying your graphic presentations.

In Chapter 13, we discussed system quality criteria in terms of the three major characteristics of a successful system: functionality, ease of maintenance, and flexibility.

In the case of software, **functional criteria** relate to the capabilities of the software. Does the software support all the necessary functions with the required reliability, clarity, and efficiency? **Maintenance criteria** focus on how easily the software can be modified, maintained, and tested. **Flexibility criteria** address the issues of portability and adaptability: Is the software compatible with the organization's current equipment? Does it conform with company procedures to ensure security and data integrity? Figure 14.18 provides a breakdown of these categories and suggests some criteria in each category.

You'll also need to consider **constraints** stipulated by management to limit costs, schedule, and staff requirements. Issues in this category include development and production costs and availability of software.

14.3.3 Evaluating Alternative Projects

So far we've emphasized one aspect of your role as a systems developer—evaluating alternatives within a single project. You'll need to shift focus and maybe change hats to appreciate this section's topic: how to evaluate a project's value to the company. Here you need

Figure 14.18
Categories of System
Quality Evaluation
Criteria

Functionality	Reliability	Completeness Reputation for accuracy and dependability Quality of vendor support
	Clarity	Quality of tutorials Error recovery procedures Quality of user interface (easy to learn and use) Quality of user documentation Need for and availability of training
	Efficiency	Ease of access to most commonly used features Turnaround time Retrieval speed Memory requirements
Maintainability	Modifiability	Availability of 4GL interface Provisions for updating data structures Quality of system documentation
	Maintainability	Cost of updates Compatibility of revised versions with old version
	Testability	Possibility of prepurchase test Availability of vendor test Compatibility with current hardware
Flexibility	Portability	Requirements for special devices (e.g., graphics printer)
	Adaptability	Interfaces with other programs Support of multiple users Ability to adjust to needs of beginning and advanced users

to see yourself in a management role, facing twenty proposed projects, only a few of which you can afford to develop. What criteria should you use to evaluate alternative projects?

In Chapter 8 you learned about organizational objectives and critical success factors. That knowledge, combined with the brief discussion of organizational relevance criteria in Chapter 13, should help you identify criteria for project evaluation. Two types of criteria are used in project evaluation. Organizational relevance factors determine the project's contribution to organizational goals and profitability and include such criteria as criticality to delivery of organization services and return on investment. Success factors determine the probability of the project's being completed successfully. Among these factors are user commitment, the IS staff's experience with similar systems, and estimated time to completion. (These are a shorter version of the Chapter 7 risk factors.) You should note that an evaluation of these factors is a vital part of a complete analysis of a project's feasibility.

In Figure 14.19, an evaluation matrix is used to evaluate four systems competing for development resources. This matrix was constructed by following the steps outlined ear-

	Weight*	Revised Payroll		Accounts Receivable		Purchase Order		Investment Analysis	
		Raw Rating**	Weighted Rating	Raw Rating	Weighted Rating	Raw Rating	Weighted Rating	Raw Rating	Weighted Rating
Organizational Relevance Factors									
Criticality to delivery of current corporate services	.3	2	.6	3	.9	3	.9	1	.3
Criticality to delivery of future corporate services	.2	1	.2	4	.8	5	1.0	2	.4
Importance to providing decision support aid	.1	1	.1	3	.3	3	.3	2	.2
Importance to providing future decision support aid	.2	1	.2	3	.6	4	.8	2	.4
Return on investment	.2 / 1.0	2	.4 / 1.5	2	.4 / 3.0	4	.8 / 3.8	5	1.0 / 2.3
Risk Factors									
Stability of IS development staff	.2	3	.6	3	.6	1	.2	1	.2
Knowledge of users	.2	1	.2	2	.4	1	.2	1	.2
Commitment of users	.5	2	1.0	1	.5	3	1.5	2	1.0
Stability of process	.2	1	.2	2	.4	1	.2	1	.2
Number of user sites (more = higher risk)	.3 / 1.4	2	.6 / 2.6	1	.3 / 2.2	2	.6 / 2.7	1	.3 / 1.9

*Weights: From .1 = unimportant to .5 = highly critical
**Raw rating values for relevance factors: From 1 = unimportant to 5 = highly critical
Raw rating values for risk factors: From 1 = high risk to 5 = low risk

Figure 14.19 Evaluation Matrix for Alternative Projects

lier in this chapter. The main differences between this matrix and the other matrices you've seen are that (1) all criteria are organizational relevance criteria, (2) alternative solutions have been replaced by alternative projects, and (3) organizational relevance and risk criteria have been grouped into factors for easy translation to an evaluation grid. Projects that achieve high scores on both factors are the most attractive prospects for development, since they contribute the most to the organization and involve low or acceptable risk. The purchase order system in Figure 14.19 is an example of such a system—it has the highest organizational relevance score (3.8) and the closest to optimal (lowest) total risk score (2.7). Projects that score well on relevance factors and poorly on risk factors should not be automatically ruled out; their importance to the organization may justify taking a chance on their high risk. Projects that score poorly on both relevance and risk factors can safely be set aside, reducing the development backlog that every organization faces. Even rejected projects should be reviewed annually, however, as an organization's priorities, personnel, and resources are likely to change.

Summary

This chapter introduced two techniques to help you evaluate alternative solutions or projects. The evaluation matrix is a tabular representation of the weighted criteria used to evaluate two or more alternatives. This matrix is especially useful for prompting discussion of alternatives and generating a numeric rating of each alternative on several criteria. The evaluation grid is a graphic representation of the numeric ratings of alternatives on two criteria. By providing a summary of the data from the evaluation matrix on a clear, easy-to-interpret graph, the grid simplifies comparison of a large number of alternatives.

Before you can construct an evaluation matrix or grid, you must generate alternatives to evaluate. The generation of alternatives can be facilitated by using a components identification matrix to identify feasible alternatives for each system component. The component whose alternatives are identified first tends to "drive" the alternatives generation process. Two approaches—the hardware-driven approach and the people-driven approach—were illustrated in this chapter.

Evaluating software is one of the most common evaluation stage activities. Sources of information about software include other companies, software review indexes and journals, and numerous library resources. The criteria for evaluating software are derived primarily from system quality criteria and management constraints.

In evaluating alternative projects for development, you need to focus on organizational relevance criteria in order to determine which projects can contribute most to the organization's growth and stability. Also important are success factors, the criteria that measure the project's likelihood of being completed successfully.

Your ability to generate creative, feasible alternatives and to identify and weight the criteria most relevant to the selection of system components or projects will make you a valuable development team member, a successful analyst, and an astute manager.

Key Terms

(Section numbers are in parentheses.)

evaluation matrix (14.1.1)   **maintenance criteria (14.3.2)**
evaluation grid (14.2.1)   **flexibility criteria (14.3.2)**
composite criteria (14.2.2)   **constraints (14.3.2)**
functional criteria (14.3.2)

Exercises   (Answers to Exercises 14.1, 14.2, and 14.5 are at the end of the book.)

14.1 Walker and Sons is an accounting firm that prepares tax returns for small businesses and individuals. An investigation of two accounting packages capable of handling much of the firm's work has resulted in the matrix in Figure 14.20. Create an evaluation grid for the two accounting packages, ACCM and TAX. For the vertical axis, use the composite criterion Functional Capabilities, which consists of Ability to Meet Clients' Reporting Requirements (#1) and Job Costing Capabilities (#8). For the horizontal axis, use the composite criterion Support, which combines Vendor Support and Services (#2) and Installation and Training (#3). Use the homework due date for the grid date.

		ACCM		TAX	
Criteria	Weight*	Raw Rating**	Weighted Rating	Raw Rating	Weighted Rating
1. Ability to Meet Clients' Reporting Requirements	5	4	20	5	25
2. Vendor Support and Services	4	5	20	3	12
3. Installation and Training	5	5	25	3	15
4. Data Availability	4	5	20	5	20
5. Flexibility	3	4	12	5	15
6. Ease of Use/Learnability	3	4	12	3.5	10.5
7. Documentation	3	3	9	3	9
8. Job Costing Capabilities	2	4	8	2	4
Total Weighted Rating	140		126		110.5

*Weight Key: From 1 = least important to 5 = most important
**Raw Rating Key: From 1 = unacceptable to 5 = excellent

Figure 14.20

14.2 Create an evaluation grid for the five word processing packages in the Chapter 13 minicase Evaluating Word Processors for School Administrators. For the vertical axis, use the composite criterion Manuscript Capabilities, defined as the ability to provide footnotes, indexes, bibliographies, and outlines. For the horizontal axis, use the composite criterion Support, defined as a combination of show commands, smart help, and a good tutorial manual.

14.3 Snack Vending Company (SVC) wants to establish a database containing information on its products, machines, and product movements. SVC handles more than 200 machines located on a university campus. Each of these machines holds twenty to forty snack products, depending on the machine capacity and location. SVC carries a line of fifty snack products. SVC management wants to know which products and machines are the most and least profitable.

The proposed database will hold all product information (price, cost, description, etc.) and all machine information (machine number, location, capacity, etc.), as well as product movement information (product, machine, daily movement, etc.). Daily movement is a count of the number of products of each type that were not sold by day's end. This count is taken every morning as the vendor refills a machine. From this information, weekly movement and profit reports will be generated for management.

Your job as an analyst is to choose the best database for this system. Assume that you are obliged to use one of the company's microcomputers. Use the evaluation matrix in Figure 14.3 (Datapro's database matrix) to create your own matrix. Choose the criteria most useful for this database selection. Can you think of any other important criteria? Weight the criteria according to SVC's needs. From the completed evaluation matrix, create one or two evaluation grids. Finally, recommend a database package to SVC management.

14.4 What other research strategies could Alex Tuttle have used in this chapter's first minicase to investigate databases for *Outerspace* magazine?

14.5 You have been selected by the school advisory committee to suggest ways to supplement classroom instruction. You have decided to recommend computer-based training in authoring software packages. From the data in Figure 14.21, create an evaluation grid for the seven authoring packages analyzed. For the vertical axis, use Functional Capabilities (criteria 1–5); for the horizontal axis, use Support (criteria 6–8).

14.6 Pratt and Sons is a small brokerage firm located in the Southwest. A primary component of success in the brokerage industry is brief, high-quality research of the underlying industries. Joe Pratt Jr. has recommended that a quality laser printer, which costs between $3,000 and $5,000 be purchased. The high-quality image of the laser type will complement the written research. Joe has gathered information about seven laser printers. Given the criteria and weights in Figure 14.22, create an evaluation grid for the seven printers. For the vertical axis, use the Functional Capabilities (criteria 1–6); for the horizontal axis, use the Support Capabilities (criteria 6–9).

14.7 Reread the Chapter 5 minicase Word Processing Systems for *Outerspace* Magazine, paying particular attention to user requirements and to Sheila's Figure 5.14 summary of WP alternatives.

    a. Develop a components identification matrix, assuming that Outerspace's management insists on purchasing IBM or IBM-compatible hardware.

    b. How does this hardware-driven approach alter or restrict the alternatives Sheila generated?

14.8 Assume that neither the WP in the Chapter 5 minicase nor the DB system in this chapter's minicase Selecting a Database for *Outerspace* Magazine has been implemented yet.

    a. Develop an alternative projects evaluation matrix to help Doug Samson decide which project to fund.

    b. Briefly explain your choice of organizational relevance and risk factors and the weight assigned to each.

    c. Which project should be funded? Why?

14.9 Review the project evaluation matrix in Figure 14.19.

    a. Which two projects would be the poorest choices?

    b. Explain your answer to part a.

    c. How would you decide which project to eliminate if you could complete only three of the four projects?

Criteria	Weight	Clas		TEL		ICON/AUTHOR*	
		Raw Rating	Weighted Rating	Raw Rating	Weighted Rating	Raw Rating	Weighted Rating
1. Text Control	10	4	40	4	40	4	40
2. Graphics/Type Control	20	3	60	4	80	5	100
3. Screen Control	20	3	60	4	80	4.5	90
4. Sound Control	10	5	50	0	0	4.5	45
5. Access Levels/Reports	15	3	45	4.5	68	4.4	66
6. Help and Error Messages	10	4	40	3	30	3	30
7. Peripheral Support	5	3	15	4.5	23	4.5	23
8. Documentation	10	4	40	3.8	38	3.5	35
Total Weighted Rating			350		359		429

*Formerly called Maestro/PC
Source: "Authoring Packages: One Way to Supplement Classroom Instruction," *Electronic Learning,* February, 1988, pp. 38–40.

Figure 14.21

Criteria	Weight	Apple		Digital		Facit	
		Raw Rating	Weighted Rating	Raw Rating	Weighted Rating	Raw Rating	Weighted Rating
1. Speed (page/min.)	15	4	60	4	60	4	60
2. Stand. RAM	5	5	25	4	20	5	25
3. Interface*	5	2	10	3	15	2	10
4. Input (bins/sheets)	10	3.5	35	4	40	4	40
5. Resident Fonts	20	5	100	3	60	1	20
6. Graphics Capability	20	4.5	90	3.5	70	4	80
7. Toner Life	5	3	15	3	15	5	25
8. Duty Cycle**	10	2.5	25	3.5	35	3.5	35
9. Warranty	10	3	30	5	50	5	50
Total Weighted Rating			390		365		345

*RS-232 or Parallel or Appletalk, or a combination
**Recommended pages per month the laser printer is capable of handling before premature wear can be expected.
Source: "Laser Printers Are Quiet and Fast, But They Do Have Limitations," *Electronic Learning,* March, 1988, pp. 34–37.

Figure 14.22

PC PILOT		TENCORE		CAMELOT		LOGOWRITER	
Raw Rating	Weighted Rating	Raw Rating	Weighted Rating	Raw Rating	Weighted Rating	Raw Rating	Weighted Rating
4	40	4	40	3	30	4	40
5	100	5	100	3	60	2	40
5	100	4.2	84	3	60	5	100
4.5	45	0	0	0	0	4.5	45
3.5	53	4.5	68	5	75	3.5	53
3	30	3	30	4	40	3	30
4.5	23	5	25	4	20	4	20
4.5	45	5	50	3.8	38	4.5	45
	436		397		323		373

Figure 14.21   (Continued)

Hewlett-Packard		NCR		Qume		Toshiba	
Raw Rating	Weighted Rating	Raw Rating	Weighted Rating	Raw Rating	Weighted Rating	Raw Rating	Weighted Rating
4	60	4	60	4.5	68	5	75
2	10	1	5	4	20	2	10
2	10	4	20	1	5	2	10
5	50	3	30	4	40	4	40
1	20	1	20	5	100	1	20
2	40	1.5	30	4	80	1	20
5	25	3	15	4.5	23	4.5	23
2.5	25	2	20	3	30	5	50
3	30	3	30	4	40	5	50
	270		230		406		298

Figure 14.22   (Continued)

Projects

14.10 Using the resources available at your library, research spreadsheet packages. Identify eight to ten criteria valuable in the evaluation of these packages, and use these criteria to evaluate three to five packages. Prepare a written or oral report summarizing your research results for a management audience.

14.11 Interview an information services staff member at a local company. Focus your interview questions on *one* or *two* of the following topics. Then prepare an oral or written report summarizing information that would be useful to your classmates.

Techniques used to generate alternatives
Evaluation criteria important to the selection of hardware
Effects of management constraints on the alternatives generation and evaluation processes
Management criteria for evaluating alternative projects
Emphasis placed on people/procedures during alternatives generation and evaluation

5

Design
Specification
Activities

CHAPTER 15

Design Specification Overview

Purpose and Goals of Design Specification
System Quality
Project Management
Organizational Relevance

Design Specification Activities
Designing the User Interface
Designing the Database
Designing Programs
Designing Procedures
Negotiating Hardware and Software Contracts
Review and Approval of the Design

Managing the Design Specification Process
Summary
Key Terms ▪ Note ▪ Exercises

Overview

Design is the process of creating the specification, or blueprint, used to implement an information system. The blueprint must realize equally important objectives: (1) it must completely and accurately satisfy users' requirements, and (2) it must clearly communicate to the programmers of the system how the users' requirements will be implemented. Part 5 focuses on the design specification activities of the systems development process. Specifically, we address

- The goals and activities of design specification (Chapter 15)
- User-interface design activities (Chapter 16)
- Database design activities (Chapter 17)
- Program design activities (Chapter 18)

In this overview chapter, we plan to

1. Identify the purpose and goals of design specification. (Section 15.1)

2. Introduce the design specification activities. (Section 15.2)

3. Provide some insights into managing the steps in the design specification process. (Section 15.3)

15.1 Purpose and Goals of Design Specification

The purpose of systems design is to specify how the requirements for an information system will be implemented. As Figure 15.1 shows, in your role as designer you address all five components of an information system: people, procedures, data, software, and hardware. Often, however, one or more of these components will be emphasized depending on the type of user access and the source of application software for the system. Designing multiple-user systems will generally require greater attention to procedures and data than designing single-user systems will. Utilizing existing (packaged) software will greatly reduce the time and effort your team will need to devote to designing the software components.

Figure 15.1

A Summary of Design Specification Activities

	People	Procedures	Data	Software	Hardware
Determine Requirements					
Evaluate Alternatives					
Specify Design	Specify and organize production users	Specify procedures and documentation	Specify and organize data or design I/O and database	Negotiate contract and order programs or design programs and test	Negotiate contract and order hardware
Implement Design					

The emphasis of Part 5 is on designing custom-written software. Developers of custom-written software are guided by the three information system goals introduced in Chapter 2: system quality, project management, and organizational relevance. Figure 2.7 provided a summary of design goals; it is repeated here as Figure 15.2 for easy reference.

15.1.1 System Quality

The quality of a system is measured by its functionality, ease of maintenance, and flexibility. System quality is the characteristic most visible to the user of the system. Consequently, the user as well as the designer evaluates the quality of a system. It is the skills and priorities of the systems developers, however, that largely determine whether the quality goal is achieved.

Systems developers are very goal directed people. Studies have shown that when developers are directed to satisfy quality criteria such as ease of maintenance, their designs do indeed produce systems that are easy to maintain.[1] On the other hand, when developers

Goals	Subgoals	Questions to Answer
System quality	Functionality	1. How well (reliably, clearly, efficiently) does the system function?
	Maintainability	2. How easy is it to maintain (understand, modify, and test) the system?
	Flexibility	3. How flexible is the system with respect to changes in its five components?
Project management	Timeliness	1. Is the system completed on time?
	Low cost	2. Is the system completed within budget?
	User commitment	3. Are the users (both user-managers and end-users) involved and committed to the success of the system?
Organizational relevance	Operational control	1. Does the system add or improve an operational task critical to the organization's objectives?
	Management control	2. Does the system support critical management decisions?
	Strategic planning	3. Does the system have strategic value?

are told to achieve narrow quality criteria such as efficiency, their designs produce very efficient systems, whose programs use a minimum amount of computer memory or whose databases use a minimum amount of storage space. Unfortunately, such narrow design criteria often result in efficient systems that do not meet the other important quality criteria of ease of maintenance and flexibility. Rather than concentrating on a single quality criterion, developers should strive to achieve the proper mix of functionality, ease of maintenance, and flexibility during the design process.

15.1.2 Project Management

You achieve project management objectives by completing design activities on time and within budget. Particularly for complex projects, the project manager and team members must identify and then carefully plan, monitor, coordinate, and review the critical components (the products) of the design. In addition, designers must keep the project sponsor and users informed about the status of a project in relation to time and cost objectives.

Managing a technically complex project that involves new telecommunications and relational database technology will require particular attention to the design of the hardware, programs, and database. In addition to being technically complex, a project may be politically complex. Managing any system involving multiple departments or shared databases will require great attention to the design of procedures, documentation, and training. Obviously the project sponsor and users are assuming a great deal of risk in undertaking such a complex project. It is necessary, therefore, to hold regularly scheduled reviews during the design stage so that users are not surprised by schedule and cost over-runs.

15.1.3 Organizational Relevance

Your system will be relevant to the organization if its design contributes to realizing the objectives of the organization. If an organizational objective is to implement databases that can be shared by application systems and departments, for example, then special attention should be devoted to designing the database so as to meet this objective.

15.2 Design Specification Activities

What are the specific activities and deliverables that comprise the design stage? To gain a perspective on these activities, you first need to see how the design stage fits into the total systems development process. The data flow diagram in Figure 15.3 shows all four stages of the systems development process. Notice that the input for the design stage is the requirements specification for an alternative chosen in the evaluation stage. The major output, or deliverable, of the design stage is a design specification approved by the users of the system. The approved design specification guides the construction, testing, and

Figure 15.3
The Systems
Development
Process: Overview
DFD

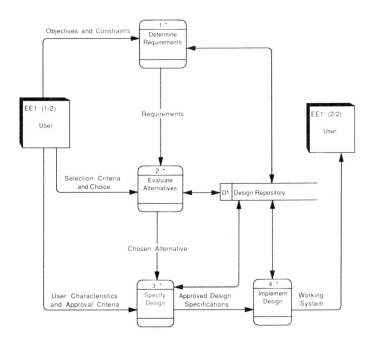

installation of the working system (that is, programs, documentation, and training) during the implementation stage.

Figure 15.4 shows the specific steps required to develop the components of the approved design specification. There are six steps in the design specification stage: (1) designing the user interface, (2) designing the database, (3) designing programs, (4) designing

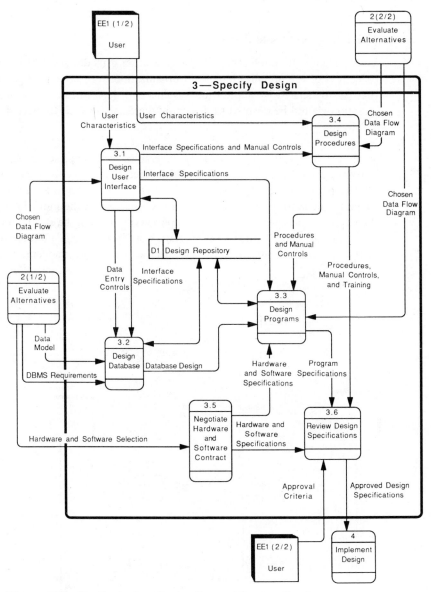

Figure 15.4 The Design Specification Stage of Systems Development

procedures and training, (5) negotiating hardware and software contracts, and (6) review and approval of the design. These steps are discussed in more detail below.

15.2.1 Designing the User Interface

During **user-interface design,** the first step in the design process, you specify how the system will appear to the users through its reports, screens, menus, and other control mechanisms. Because the user accesses the system via the interface, designing an effective user interface is crucial to meeting the ease-of-use and ease-of-learning objectives of system quality. To achieve these objectives, you must involve users in the design process and have the users approve each report, screen, and menu before it is implemented as part of the system. You can enhance your systems design skills by following general design guidelines that have been proven to produce quality interfaces. A quality interface is simple, clear, and consistent and provides adequate feedback to the user. Interface design guidelines are presented in Chapter 16.

Inputs to the interface design process are the design repository, the chosen data flow diagram, and the user characteristics. The outputs, or deliverables, of the interface design process are the updated design repository, interface specifications, and the manual and data entry controls. The **interface specifications** are the design layouts and characteristics of the external documents, internal reports, report screens, data entry screens, and dialogues (that is, menus, questions and answers, and commands). The **data entry controls** are standards designed to ensure the accuracy, integrity, and confidentiality of the data that is entered and accessed through the interface.

15.2.2 Designing the Database

Database design, the second step in the design stage, is the process of specifying how the data requirements for a system will be implemented as a database. Your objective as you design a database is to ensure that it satisfies the data requirements of the users, including their requirements for reports and screens. Another objective of database design is to satisfy the system quality criteria of functionality, maintainability, and flexibility. Transforming a data model into a database design is a complex process. The logical and physical design guidelines given in Chapter 17 will help you to manage this complicated process.

Inputs to database design are the design repository, data entry controls, interface specifications, the conceptual data model, and the database management system (DBMS) requirements. The conceptual data model describes user data requirements. The interface specifications explain how the data in the database will be accessed. Data entry controls define the sensitivity of the data. Finally, the DBMS requirements specify the type of database system that will be used to implement the database.

The deliverables of the database design step are an updated design repository and the database specifications. **Database specifications** describe the logical and physical structures of the database. These structures include data elements, records, keys, relationships, file organizations, physical records, and indexes of the database.

15.2.3 Designing Programs

Program design is the process of packaging the interface, procedure, and database specifications into specifications for programs. Your objective during program design is to specify programs that are adaptable and easy to maintain. You can accomplish this objective by designing programs that are composed of small, independent modules. The information on cohesion and coupling in Chapter 18 will help you to design program modules.

Inputs to the program design step are the design repository, the chosen data flow diagram, procedures and manual controls, interface specifications, the database design, and the hardware and software specifications. The deliverables of the program design step are the updated design repository and the **program specifications,** which include program structure charts and a test plan. The program specifications will guide computer programmers during the implementation stage.

15.2.4 Designing Procedures

Procedure design, the fourth step in design specification, involves describing the flow of work for the new system. Normal and failure recovery procedures must be designed for both the user and the computer operator. You also design and create training materials during this step.

The inputs to procedure design are the chosen data flow diagram, user characteristics such as work procedures, interface specifications, and manual controls. The main deliverables of procedure design are the procedures, manual controls, and the training materials for the system. The procedures and controls specify all the normal production and failure recovery procedures required to run the system effectively. They must state how often the database will be backed up, who will back up the database, who will run daily reports, and so on. Training materials include user and computer operator manuals, tutorials, and outlines of training courses.

15.2.5 Negotiating Hardware and Software Contracts

While the other design steps are being performed, you will also be negotiating with vendors for any additional hardware and purchased software required for the new system. The inputs to this step are specifications for the hardware and software chosen during the evaluation stage. Often, these specifications will be stated formally in proposals received from hardware and software vendors. Vendors will propose hardware and software solutions that satisfy system requirements, and they will also indicate the cost of purchasing and implementing each solution. Based on these proposals, you negotiate delivery schedules and prices that meet the schedule and budget constraints for the development project. The hardware and software specifications for the selected proposal are the output of this step in the design stage.

If you were designing a system that required several microcomputers, for example, you would first solicit proposals and bids from several vendors. During the evaluation stage, you would evaluate these proposals to select the configuration that best fulfilled your requirements, given the amount of money budgeted for this purchase. Then, during the design stage, you would negotiate with the chosen vendor to obtain the most favorable price and delivery schedule for the microcomputers. You would follow the same process to solicit bid proposals and negotiate terms for software purchases.

15.2.6 Review and Approval of the Design

The review and, one hopes, approval of your design is the last step in the design stage. During this step, the users—in particular, the user-managers—re-evaluate the feasibility of the project and of the schedule in light of economic, technical, operational, and human factors. The inputs to this step are the approval criteria of management (for example, is the cost of the new system still within the original budgeted amount?), hardware and software specifications, program specifications, procedures, manual controls, and training materials. The deliverables of the review and approval step are the approved design specifications. If approved, the design specifications then become the input for the implementation stage.

In summary, the design stage includes six distinct steps, starting with user-interface design and ending with design review and approval. Each step creates design information that is then used in other design steps. The data flow diagram in Figure 15.4 illustrates the steps as processes and the design information as process inputs and outputs. Figure 15.5 provides a summary of the inputs and outputs for each design step.

15.3 Managing the Design Specification Process

Although the six design activities have been presented as distinct steps, they are, in fact, interrelated in a number of ways. First, the steps are iterative. That is, each design step will result in changes to the deliverables of the previous design steps. For example, while designing a program for a screen, the designer might decide that the screen was too complicated. The screen would then be changed to simplify the program. The changed screen, of course, would have to be approved by the user of the application.

Second, different design steps will be emphasized depending on the type of system you are developing. For example, if the system has a single user and is being developed with existing software, then your emphasis will be on specifying adequate hardware and procedures for training. If the acquired software has little or no flexibility, the design stage will include only three steps: (1) design procedures, (2) negotiate hardware and software contracts, and (3) review design specifications. If the acquired software has variable reports and parameters, then you may have to do some work on interface and program design, but not nearly so much as is required to design a multi-user system using custom-written software. In the case of custom-written software, although all six design steps must be performed, the emphasis will be on designing the user interface, database, programs, and procedures.

Third, the same data flow diagrams and design repository will be used throughout the design phase to coordinate the efforts of individual designers. For example, during the design of an order tracking system, the data flow diagram used by one designer to identify an order entry screen will be used by another designer to identify the manual procedures needed to process order forms that are entered using the order entry screen. If the designer of the program for the order entry screen discovered a new data element, that designer would simply place the element in the design repository, thereby making it available to

	Inputs	Outputs
3.1 Design User Interface	Design repository Chosen data flow diagram User characteristics	Updated design repository Manual and data entry controls Interface specifications
3.2 Design Database	Design repository Data entry controls Interface specifications Conceptual data model DBMS requirements	Updated design repository Database design
3.3 Design Programs	Design repository Chosen data flow diagram Procedures and manual controls Interface specifications Database design Hardware and software specifications	Updated design repository Program specifications
3.4 Design Procedures	Chosen data flow diagram User characteristics Interface specifications and manual controls	Procedures and manual controls Training materials
3.5 Negotiate Hardware and Software Contracts	Hardware and software selection	Hardware and software specifications
3.6 Review Design Specifications	Approval criteria Hardware and software specifications Program specifications Procedures, manual controls, and training materials	Approved design specifications

the database designer, who could then add the element to the appropriate file in the database.

Summary

Design is the process of creating a specification, or blueprint, for the implementation of an information system. Design involves the specification of hardware, software, data, procedures, and people. The three goals of system quality, project management, and organizational relevance guide the design process. The steps in the design process are (1) design the user interface, (2) design the database, (3) design the programs, (4) design procedures and training, (5) negotiate the hardware and software contract, and (6) review and approve the design.

Key Terms
(Section numbers are in parentheses.)

user-interface design (15.2.1)	database specifications (15.2.2)
interface specifications (15.2.1)	program design (15.2.3)
data entry controls (15.2.1)	program specifications (15.2.3)
database design (15.2.2)	procedure design (15.2.4)

Note

1. Gerald M. Weinberg and E. L. Schulman, "Goals and Performance in Computer Programming, *Human Factors,* vol. 16, no. 1, pp 70–77.

Exercises

(Answers to Exercises 15.1 through 15.5 are at the end of the book.)

15.1 Explain the role of the DFD and design repository in the design specification process.

15.2 List and explain the three goals that guide the design process.

15.3 List and explain the six activities in the design specification process.

15.4 Explain how the type of user access and the software source influence the emphasis placed on design activities.

15.5 The Gantt chart in Figure 15.6 shows the breakdown of design activities for development of an information system that will use custom-written software. What general concerns do you have regarding the scheduling of design activities for the system?

Figure 15.6

Activity / Document	Oct	Nov	Dec	Jan	Feb	Mar	Apr	May	
Design User Interfaces	⊢———⊣								
Negotiate Hardware and									
Software Contract	⊢——⊣								
Design Procedures	⊢—⊣								
Design Training		⊢—⊣							
Design Database		⊢———————⊣							
Design Programs		⊢———————————————⊣							
Review Design					⊢————⊣				

15.6 A general contractor in the construction industry has hired you to develop an information system using existing software. The system is to be an integrated database application composed of general ledger, accounts payable, accounts receivable, billing, payroll, job costing, and inventory modules. Every department in the contractor's organization will use the new system. The contractor will also be implementing new accounting procedures as the system is implemented. These new procedures are likely to be met with some resistance from the user departments. What design activities will require special emphasis for this project? Why?

CHAPTER 16

User-Interface Design

Interface Design Activities
Minicase: Return to Universal, Inc.

Types of Interfaces
External Documents
Internal Reports
Report Screens
Data Entry Screens
Human-Computer Dialogues

Guidelines for Interface Design
External Documents
Internal Reports
Report Screens
Data Entry Screens
Human-Computer Dialogues

Designing Interfaces
Interface Design from an Ordered Example
Minicase: Return to Meadows Hospital

Summary
Key Terms ▪ **Exercises** ▪ **Project**

Overview

The documents, reports, and screens of a system are the user interface. The user interface is the only part of the system that the user sees. The rest is invisible. The user interface, therefore, is the most important part of the system for the user. It must be designed to be both usable and learnable. In this chapter we plan to

1. Provide an overview of interface design activities. (Section 16.1)

2. Explain the types of interfaces. (Section 16.2)

3. Provide guidelines for designing interfaces. (Section 16.3)

4. Provide a step-by-step illustration of designing an interface. (Section 16.4)

16.1 Interface Design Activities

Figure 16.1 highlights the interface design process. The inputs to the design process are the user characteristics, the data flow diagram, and the design repository. The outputs of the design process are the data entry controls and the detailed interface specifications for external documents, internal reports, report and data entry screens, and human-computer dialogues.

Figure 16.1
Inputs and Outputs for Interface Design

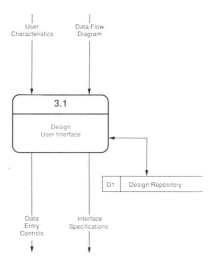

Designing usable and learnable interfaces requires an understanding of (1) the general types of interfaces, (2) the guidelines for designing each type of interface, and (3) the method for designing the user interface. We will illustrate interface design by returning to the Universal case.

Return to Universal, Inc.

Llisa Finn, an experienced systems analyst, has been assigned to design the user interface for the Universal order tracking system. The design process steps Liisa will follow are shown in Figure 16.2.

As the first step in interface design, Liisa uses the human-computer boundary on the data flow diagram shown in Figure 16.3 to identify the types of interfaces required by the system. The human-computer boundary separates human from computer processes. Every data flow that is within or crosses the boundary represents a potential document, screen, or report. In this example

there are three interfaces, which Liisa lists in Figure 16.4, identifying them by number, name, and type of interface. To complete this interface summary table, she extracts the data elements for each interface from the repository of design information.

Next, Liisa designs the human-computer dialogue using menus that will allow the users to retrieve the order tracking reports and screens (see Figure 16.5). As a final step, she designs the documents, reports, and screens of the order tracking system. An example data entry screen is shown in Figure 16.6.

Figure 16.2
Interface Design
Activities

Review the
Human-Computer
Boundary

Create an
Interface
Summary Table

Design Documents,
Reports, and Screens

Design the
Dialogue

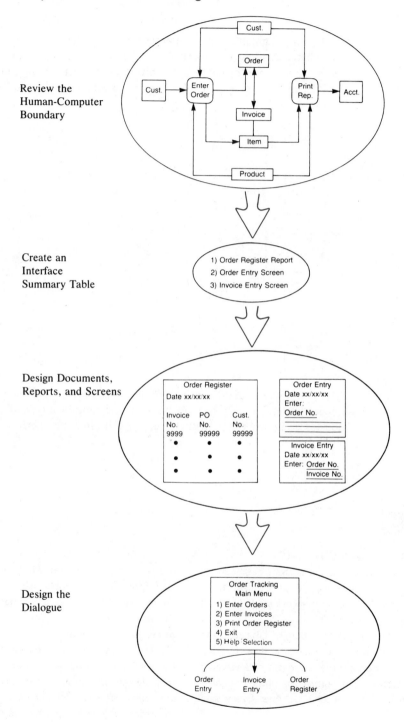

Figure 16.3
Order Tracking Data
Flow Diagram

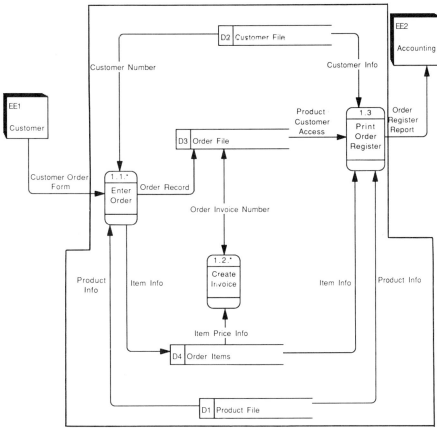

Human-Computer Boundary

Figure 16.4
Interface Summary
Table for the Order
Tracking System

Number	Name	Type	Data Elements
1	Order Entry Screen	Data entry screen	ORDER-NBR, ORDER-DATE, ORDER-STATUS-CODE, ORDER-PRICING-CRITERIA-CODE, CUST-NBR, ORDER-PO-NBR, {1,N} PROD-NBR, ITEM-QUANTITY-NBR, ITEM-BACK-ORDERED-NBR
2	Invoice Entry Screen	Data entry screen	ORDER-NBR, INVOICE-NBR, INVOICE-TAX-AMT, INVOICE-DATE
3	Order Register Report	Internal report	INVOICE-NBR, ORDER-PO-NBR, CUST-NBR, CUST-NAME, CUST-BILLING-STREET-ADDR, CUST-BILLING-CITY-ADDR, CUST-BILLING-STATE-ADDR, CUST-BILLING-ZIP-CODE-ADDR, PROD-NBR, PROD-DESC-TEXT, ITEM-QUANTITY-NBR, ITEM-BACK-ORDERED-NBR, PROD-COST-AMT

```
TODAY'S DATE XX/XX/XX   INVOICE ENTRY SCREEN              SCREEN 003


    ENTER:


        ORDER NUMBER
        INVOICE DATE (MM/DD/YY)
        INVOICE TAX AMOUNT   $

        INVOICE NUMBER         999999999



    PRESS F1 or ENTER key to update
    PRESS F3 to exit without update
    PRESS F8 to return to previous screen
    PRESS F10 for HELP
```

```
                   ORDER TRACKING MAIN MENU              MENU 005

    1) Enter Orders

    2) Enter Invoices

    3) Print Order Register Report

    4) Exit to Main UNIVERSAL Menu

    5) HELP

    SELECTION: _____

    Enter number of selection and press enter
```

16.2 Types of Interfaces

There are five types of interfaces: external documents, internal reports, report screens, data entry screens, and human-computer dialogues, which may take the form of menus, prompts, or commands. The types of interfaces are illustrated in Figure 16.7. For each type of interface, we will

1. Define the interface.
2. Illustrate the interface with an example.
3. List the components of the format.
4. Discuss any important design issues.

16.2.1 External Documents

An **external document** provides information to, or requests an action from, people outside of the system, such as customers, suppliers, stockholders, or employees. For example, the invoice in Figure 16.8 is a form that is sent to customers. Other types of external

Figure 16.7

Summary of Interface Types

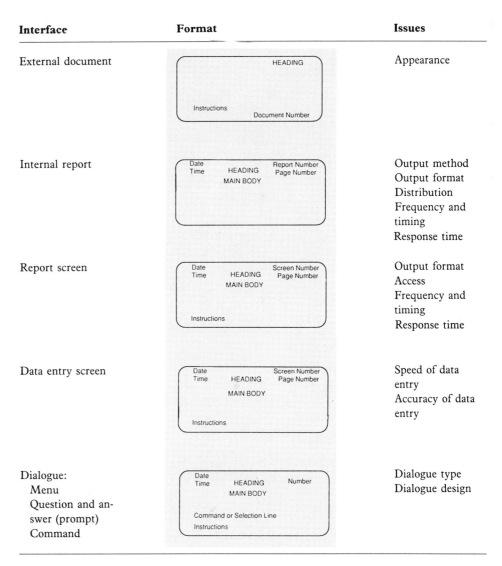

Interface	Format	Issues
External document		Appearance
Internal report		Output method Output format Distribution Frequency and timing Response time
Report screen		Output format Access Frequency and timing Response time
Data entry screen		Speed of data entry Accuracy of data entry

Dialogue:
  Menu
  Question and an-
  swer (prompt)
  Command
		Dialogue type
		Dialogue design

documents include purchase orders and paychecks. The purpose of external documents is often to elicit an action from the recipient of the document (for example, an invoice is designed to elicit a payment from a customer).

The format of an external document includes a heading (for example, Sales Order), main body (such as products ordered and prices), and instructions (for example, payment due on receipt of invoice). The heading identifies the document, provides column headings that define the information in the main body, and supplies information about the sender and the recipient of the document. The main body provides detailed information, such as products that have been ordered and prices. The instructions convey information about using or responding to the document.

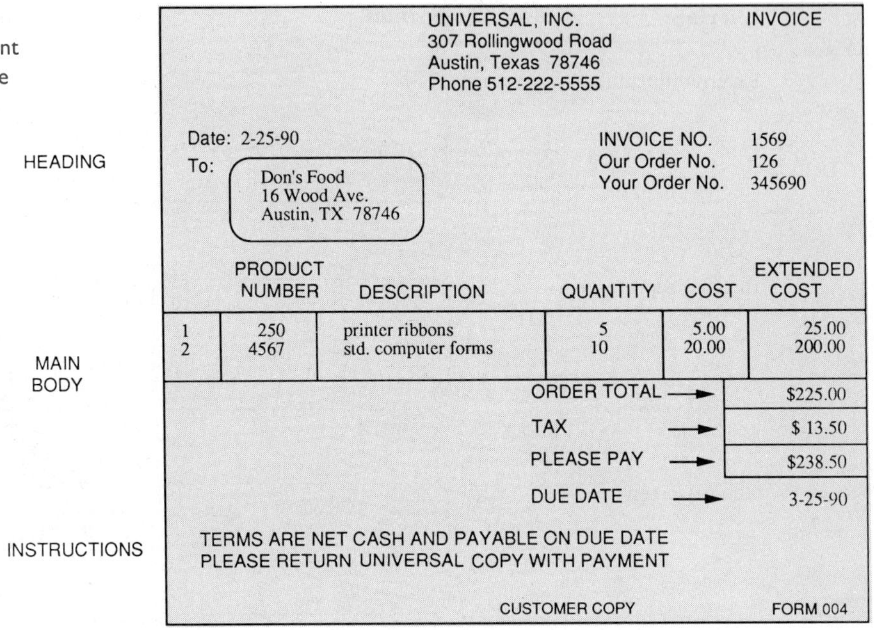

Figure 16.8
External Document
Layout for Invoice
Example

HEADING

MAIN
BODY

INSTRUCTIONS

		UNIVERSAL, INC.			INVOICE
		307 Rollingwood Road			
		Austin, Texas 78746			
		Phone 512-222-5555			

Date: 2-25-90

To:
> Don's Food
> 16 Wood Ave.
> Austin, TX 78746

INVOICE NO.   1569
Our Order No.   126
Your Order No.   345690

	PRODUCT NUMBER	DESCRIPTION	QUANTITY	COST	EXTENDED COST
1	250	printer ribbons	5	5.00	25.00
2	4567	std. computer forms	10	20.00	200.00

ORDER TOTAL ⟶ $225.00

TAX   ⟶ $ 13.50

PLEASE PAY   ⟶ $238.50

DUE DATE   ⟶   3-25-90

TERMS ARE NET CASH AND PAYABLE ON DUE DATE
PLEASE RETURN UNIVERSAL COPY WITH PAYMENT

CUSTOMER COPY   FORM 004

Because external documents are often used by customers, suppliers, and shareholders, the appearance of the documents is an important design issue. The documents have to be carefully designed to give the organization a "quality" image.

16.2.2 Internal Reports

An **internal report** supplies information to personnel within an organization. For example, the Order Register report in Figure 16.9 supplies information about invoices and

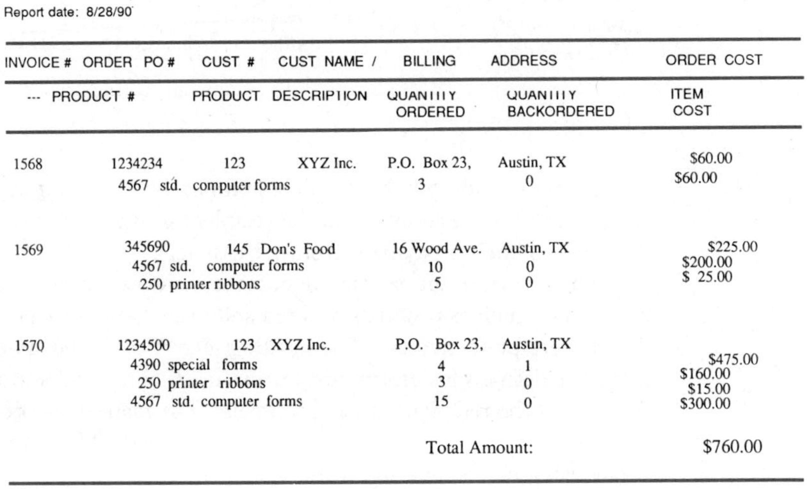

Figure 16.9
Order Register
Report

Report date: 8/28/90

INVOICE #	ORDER PO #	CUST #	CUST NAME /	BILLING	ADDRESS	ORDER COST
--- PRODUCT #		PRODUCT DESCRIPTION	QUANTITY ORDERED	QUANTITY BACKORDERED		ITEM COST
1568	1234234	123	XYZ Inc.	P.O. Box 23,	Austin, TX	$60.00
	4567 std. computer forms		3	0		$60.00
1569	345690	145	Don's Food	16 Wood Ave.	Austin, TX	$225.00
	4567 std. computer forms		10	0		$200.00
	250 printer ribbons		5	0		$ 25.00
1570	1234500	123	XYZ Inc.	P.O. Box 23,	Austin, TX	
	4390 special forms		4	1		$475.00
	250 printer ribbons		3	0		$160.00
	4567 std. computer forms		15	0		$15.00
						$300.00
				Total Amount:		$760.00

orders to personnel in the Accounting department. The Order Register report is a report in hard-copy (printed) form. A hard-copy report is normally printed on paper that can accommodate 132 or 80 columns.

A printed internal report is composed of a heading and a main body. The heading identifies the report with a name and a report number and provides column headings that define the information reported in the main body. Unlike external documents, internal reports typically do not contain instructions.

The main issues in designing internal reports are

1. *Output method*—whether the report will be printed using a printer or displayed via a CRT. Guidelines for selecting an output method are provided in Figure 16.10.

Figure 16.10
Guidelines for Determining Output Method

	A CRT Is Recommended If the Answer Is	A Printer Is Recommended If the Answer Is
1. How many people will use the report?	Few	Many
2. When is the report needed?	Immediately on demand	At fixed times
3. How often is the same report used?	Seldom	Often
4. How long is the information from the report useful?	A short time	A long time
5. Where is the report used?	At the main office	Away from the main office
6. How many people are there per CRT in the users' working area?	Less than 10	More than 10

2. *Output format*—whether the report will be tabular, graphic (for example, bar charts, line graphs), or a combination of the two.

3. *Distribution*—who will receive the report.

4. *Frequency and timing*—how often the report will be printed and when exactly (for example, 8 A.M.) it is needed.

5. *Response time*—the acceptable printing time for the report (for example, the report must be printed in one hour).

Maintaining the design documentation for large systems with many reports can become tedious, and thus errors are likely to occur. To keep track of the documentation, we use the Report/Screen Specification sheet shown in Figure 16.11.

16.2.3 Report Screens

A **report screen** is an output method in which a report is displayed via a CRT. The Invoice Inquiry screen in Figure 16.12 supplies information similar to that provided by the Order Register report.

Figure 16.11
Report/Screen
Specification Form

Report/Screen Documentation	Page
System:	Date

Purpose:

Analyst

Frequency

Distribution or Access:

1.
2.
3.
4.
5.
6.

Layout (or Attach form):

A report screen is composed of a heading, main body, and instruction window. The heading and main body contain the same types of information as they do in an internal report. The instruction window provides information on operating the screen, including

- Accessing help screens
- Scrolling (displaying more screens of information)
- Exiting to different screens

The operation of the screen is controlled through the use of function keys. The instruction window also provides a line for messages informing the user of any mistakes made in using the function keys and how to correct those mistakes.

Figure 16.12
Invoice Inquiry Screen

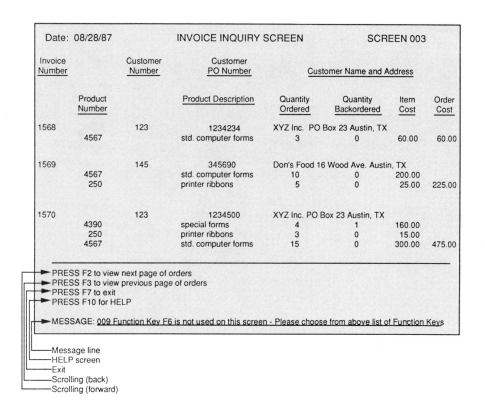

In addition to the design issues discussed in conjunction with hard-copy reports, screen design must address the limitation of a CRT. The issues in screen design are

1. *Output format*—whether the output will be tabular, graphic, or both. A potential disadvantage of using CRTs is that a computer display screen can usually accommodate a maximum of 80 columns and 20 to 24 lines of information. Reports, in contrast, may contain 132 columns and 50 lines of information. In addition, with screens the user can view only one page of information at a time.

2. *Access*—who will access the screen. A limitation of report screens is that a user must have access to a CRT in order to view any information.

3. *Frequency and timing*—how often the information for the screen will be updated and at what time the information is needed.

4. *Response time*—the acceptable display time for the screen (for example, the screen should display in three seconds).

16.2.4 Data Entry Screens

A **data entry screen** is used to enter data into computer files from source documents or reports, as well as to update data. The Order Entry screen in Figure 16.13 is used to enter information from the Customer Order form (see Figure 16.19).

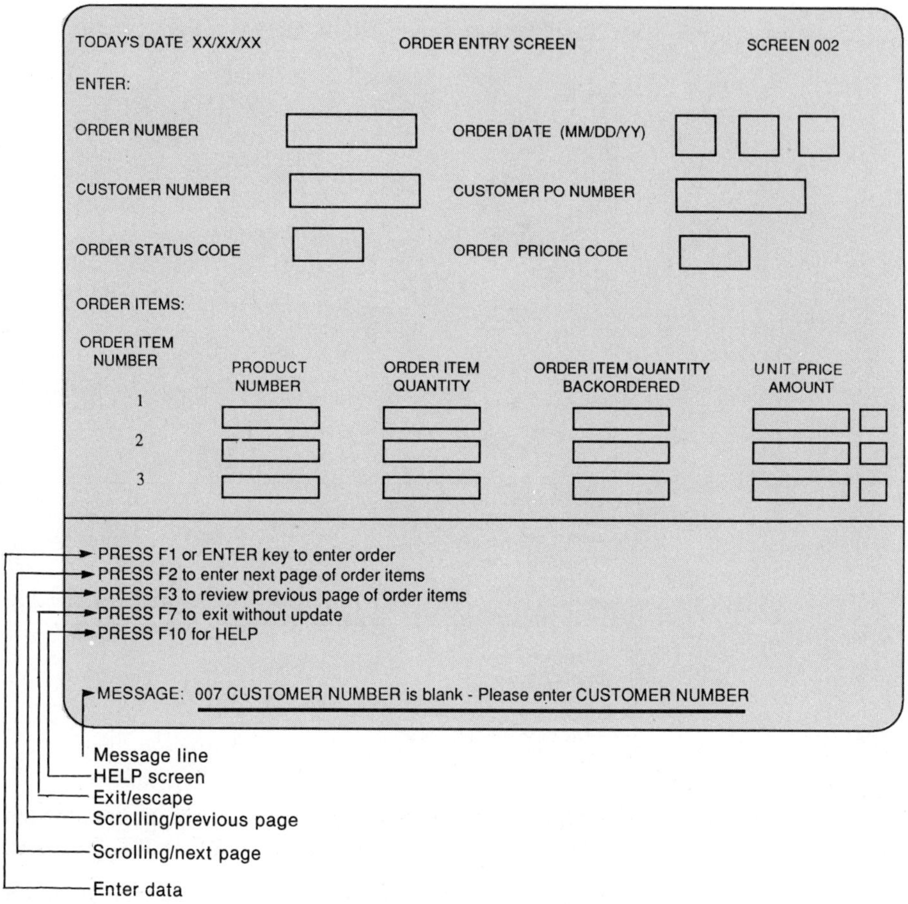

Figure 16.13
Order Data Entry
Screen

The data entry screen has the same components as the report screen: a heading, main body, and instruction window. The instruction window is similar to that of a report screen.

Two issues are important in designing data entry screens:

1. *Speed of data entry*—screens should be designed to make the entry of data as fast as possible.

2. *Accuracy of data entry*—screens should be designed to protect the accuracy of the data that is entered into files.

16.2.5 Human-Computer Dialogues

The **human-computer dialogue** defines how the interaction between the user and the computer takes place. For example, the Order Tracking menu in Figure 16.6 defines the valid screen and report selections for a user of the system.

There are three common types of dialogues: (1) menu, (2) question and answer, or prompt, and (3) command. These three types of dialogues are illustrated in Figure 16.14.

1. With a menu dialogue, a **menu** displays a list of alternative selections. The user makes a selection by choosing the number or letter of the desired alternative. Menu dialogues are the most common type, because they are appropriate for both frequent and infrequent users of a system.

2. With a **question and answer,** or prompt, dialogue, questions and alternative answers are presented. The user selects the alternative that best answers the question. For example, after an order was entered on the Order Entry screen, the system might ask if the user would like to create an invoice and offer two answers—yes or no. Question and answer dialogues are most appropriate for intermediate (between frequent and infrequent) users of a system.

Figure 16.14
Types of Dialogues

1) MENU

```
ORDER TRACKING MAIN MENU        MENU 005


1) Enter Orders
2) Enter Invoices
3) Print Order Register Report
4) Exit To Main UNIVERSAL Menu
5) HELP
```

2) QUESTION AND ANSWER

Do you want to enter orders (Y/N)?
Do you need help making a selection (Y/N)?

3) COMMAND

```
LEGEND

_____ (underline) = mandatory
__ , __ = either/or
{ } = available selections
```

E\ENTER   ⎰ ORDERS   ⎱
          ⎱ INVOICES   ⎰

P\PRINT   {ORDER REGISTER REPORT   }

H\HELP

X\EXIT

C\CALL   ⎧ MENU 001 ⎫
          ⎨ MENU 002 ⎬
          ⎩ MENU 003 ⎭
            MENU 004

3. A **command** dialogue requires the user to issue commands (either by entering text or by pressing special function keys) in order to make selections. For example, the user might type the command "ENTER ORDERS" to start the Order Entry screen. Command dialogues are appropriate for frequent users of a system, who can memorize the correct commands.

Typically, a specific dialogue will be composed of more than one type of dialogue. For example, a menu will often be combined with a command dialogue (using a command line or function keys). Such a combination is appropriate for both frequent and infrequent users of a system.

The major issues in designing dialogues are

1. *Dialogue type*—given the frequency of user access to the system, what type of dialogue is the most usable and learnable?

2. *Dialogue design*—how should the specific dialogue be designed?

16.3 Guidelines for Interface Design

Users require interfaces that are usable (that is, easy to use and helpful to them in their work) and learnable. If you are thinking that usable and learnable are very subjective criteria, you are right. How good a user interface is depends very much on the user of the interface. A data entry clerk who must enter 100 purchase orders each day will care most about the speed of data entry. A usable interface would require a minimum number of keystrokes to enter an order. On the other hand, a company president who needs to check on the status of a shipment once or twice a week will care most about the ease with which the system can be used and learned. A learnable interface would not require the president to remember what to do to look up an order.

To design a good user interface, you must determine the usability and learnability requirements of all known and potential users of the system. This makes interface design a complex process. Fortunately, there are general design guidelines to help you manage the design process.

The general guidelines for designing interfaces are summarized in Figure 16.15. They are organized on the basis of five criteria used to evaluate the usability and learnability of the user interface: (1) quality, (2) simplicity, (3) clarity, (4) consistency, and (5) feedback. A short discussion of the criteria and guidelines follows.

1. *Quality.* The interface should be aesthetically pleasing.

2. *Simplicity.* A simple report or screen provides information that is logically connected to only one thought or idea. General-purpose reports and screens that are employed by many users for different activities (for example, a screen that displays every field of a file) are not simple. A good way to determine whether a screen or report is simple is to try to give it a title or name. If you cannot think of a good title, the report or screen is probably not simple.

3. *Clarity.* A clear report or screen is easy to read and interpret. Clarity is enhanced when abbreviations are minimized, every field is labeled, and white (blank) space is used to separate fields.

Figure 16.15

General Guidelines for
Interface Design

Quality	1. Design reports, screens, and documents that are aesthetically pleasing—reports, screens, and documents should be symmetrical and uncluttered.
Simplicity	1. Design reports, screens, and documents to provide information that is logically connected to only one thought or idea.
	2. Design data entry screens so that the user can "escape" without updating the file.
	3. Minimize the number and length of keywords used for commands.
	4. Try to limit menus to a maximum of nine selections.
Clarity	1. Design reports, screens, and documents to be easy to read and interpret.
	a. Use functional terms (no technical jargon).
	b. Minimize abbreviations.
	c. Standardize abbreviations.
	d. Label every field.
	e. Left-justify fields on screens.
	f. Use upper-case letters for field labels.
	2. Provide a title and number for every report, screen, document, and menu. Center the title and use upper-case letters. Place the number in the top righthand corner.
	3. Use blank space (instead of lines or dashes) to separate areas on a screen or report.
	4. Place a page indicator in the upper righthand corner of a document, report, or screen. Number each page relative to the other pages (page 1 of 10).
	5. Order instructions in the instruction window of a screen from most to least used (for example, ENTER is first, HELP is last).
	6. Use upper- and lower-case letters for instructions, when possible.
	7. Design menu dialogues in a hierarchical structure.
	8. Order menu selections from most to least used (for example, ENTER ORDERS is first, HELP is last).
Consistency	1. Design reports, screens, and documents so that similar functions are always in the same relative location (for example, the title is always at the top and is centered, the instructions are always at the bottom).
	2. Be sure that individual function keys always serve the same purpose (for example, F10 for HELP).
Feedback	1. Design screens so that users are always aware of the status of an action:
	a. Use error messages to provide feedback on mistakes.
	b. Use confirmation messages to provide feedback on updates or general actions.
	c. Use status messages to provide feedback when a long wait is possible, as when a file is being updated.
	2. Never leave a screen blank—at least acknowledge receipt.
	3. Make error messages polite and informative—the message should explain the error and tell the user how to correct it.
	4. Allow the user to reverse an action when possible, or query the user when actions are far-reaching (for example, "Do you really want to delete?").

4. *Consistency.* The same areas of reports and screens should always be used for the same functions. For example, the instruction window should always be on the bottom of the screen. In addition, function keys should always serve the same purpose. Figure 16.16 provides suggestions for function keys.

Figure 16.16
Suggested Function
Keys

Key	Command
F1	ENTER
F2	Request next page of information (scroll forward)
F3	Request previous page of information (scroll back)
F4	
F5	Restore all fields on screen to original values
F6	Restore one field to its original value
F7	Exit screen without updating
F8	Return to previous screen
F9	
F10	HELP

5. *Feedback.* Feedback provides the user of a screen with information about the status of an action. When the user makes a mistake, an error message should tell the user what caused the error and how to correct it. Figure 16.17 provides guidelines for error messages.

Which of the above criteria will be most important in a particular situation will depend on the type of interface.

16.3.1 External Documents

The most important criteria for external documents are quality and clarity. Quality is important because external documents are a reflection of the organization that sends them. The documents should look professional; for this reason many external documents are preprinted by forms manufacturers, rather than printed in-house. Clarity is important because the recipient usually relies on the document for guidance in taking action. For example, the recipient of an invoice will need to verify that the items on the invoice were, in fact, received and then pay for the items according to the terms of the invoice. Clearly printed order numbers, item descriptions, and terms of payment (for example, "Terms are net cash and payable on presentation") will expedite proper payment.

16.3.2 Internal Reports

Internal reports should be simple and clear. A simple report communicates only the information needed by a user. A clear report identifies and distinguishes the information that is presented in the main body. A clear report avoids abbreviations and jargon, has prominent

Figure 16.17
Guidelines for Error
Messages

1. A message should contain enough information to allow a user to correct a problem without referring to additional documentation.

2. Messages should be consistently presented:
   Use few auxiliary verbs, few articles.
   Use affirmative statements.
   Use complete sentences.
   Do not ask questions.
   Do not use contractions (e.g., *it is,* not *it's*).
   Do not use "power words" (e.g., ILLEGAL, INVALID).
   Use upper and lower case, if possible.
   Use upper case for keywords and acronyms (e.g., ZIP code).
   Capitalize values a user may enter (e.g., enter CUSTOMER NAME).
   Capitalize keys a user may press (e.g., PRESS ENTER).
   Do not refer to other messages (e.g., see message XYZ).
   Try to avoid the use of blinking fields.

3. Do not attempt to be humorous.

4. Do not threaten punishment.

5. Do not use jargon.

6. In general, messages should answer:
   How serious the problem is
   What value(s) are in error
   What the permissible values are

7. Messages should be numbered.

Source: D. E. Peterson, "Screen Design Guidelines," *Small Systems World,* vol. 6, no. 8, February 1979.

column headings, and includes white space between the items of information in the main body.

The Order Register report in Figure 16.9 is an example of a report that is simple, but not clear. The report is simple because it provides the Accounting department with information that is used to document invoices sent to customers. Information such as the invoice number and the customer number is included in the report. Extraneous information, such as the order number (a number only used in the Order Tracking department), is not included. The Order Register report is not designed clearly, however. The information in the main body is not easy to read and is not easily associated with the column headings in the heading. Abbreviations such as "ORDER PO #" and "CUST #" make the column headings awkward. An improved Order Register report is shown in Figure 16.18.

16.3.3 Report Screens

The important criteria for report screens are simplicity, clarity, consistency, and feedback. Like internal reports, screens should be simple. They should communicate only the information that the user requires to perform a job.

Figure 16.18
Improved Order
Register Report

Report date: 8/28/90

INVOICE NUMBER	ORDER PO NUMBER	CUSTOMER NUMBER	NAME AND ADDRESS	TOTAL ORDER COST	------PRODUCT------ NO. DESCRIPTION		------QUANTITY------ ORDER TOTAL BACK-ORDERED		ITEM COST
1568	1234234	123	XYZ Inc. PO Box 23 Austin, TX	$60.00	4567	std. computer forms	3	0	$60.00
1569	345690	145	Don's Food 16 Wood Ave. Austin, TX	$225.00	4567 std. computer forms 250 printer ribbons		10 5	0 0	$200.00 $25.00
1570	1234500	123	XYZ Inc. PO Box 23 Austin, TX	$475.00	4390 special forms 250 printer ribbons 4567 std. computer forms		4 3 15	1 0 0	$160.00 $15.00 $300.00
			TOTAL AMOUNT:	$760.00					

For the sake of clarity, column headings should be distinguished from the information presented on the screen, and abbreviations should be avoided. Special features like blinking fields and reverse video and color should be used with discretion. Rather than help a user to use the screen, these types of features often prove distracting.

Consistency requires that the same function key be used to exit all the screens in an application system. The Invoice Inquiry screen in Figure 16.12 and the Invoice Entry screen in Figure 16.5 are examples of inconsistent screens. The Invoice Entry screen uses function key F3 to exit the screen, and the Invoice Inquiry screen uses function key F7.

The feedback provided to the user by the instruction window should be clear. If a mistake is made, the error message should clearly state the error and how to correct the problem. For example, if the user used function key F6 when it was not defined for that screen, an appropriate error message would read: "009 Function Key F6 not used for this screen — Please choose from the above list of Function Keys."

16.3.4 Data Entry Screens

The criteria that are important in the design of report screens are also important in data entry screen design: simplicity, clarity, consistency, and feedback. The objective is to make data entry fast and accurate. Following are some guidelines for achieving fast data entry.

1. *Simplicity.* Values that can be or retrieved from the database calculated should not be entered. For example, if the UNIT PRICE AMOUNT on the Order Entry screen in Figure 16.13 is always the PRODUCT-COST-AMOUNT (from the PRODUCT record), the system should retrieve the amount from the database.

On the other hand, if Universal provided special prices to some customers, a separate field for ITEM PRICE AMOUNT would be necessary.

2. *Clarity.* The data entry screen should read from left to right and top to bottom. The layout of the Order Entry screen in Figure 16.13 facilitates the entry of order information because the data values are arranged from left to right and top to bottom. Part a of Figure 16.20 shows the flow of data entry for the screen in Figure 16.13. If the sequence of fields on the screen were such that data entry flowed as shown in part b, the data entry process would be much slower.
3. *Consistency.* The fields of the screen should be in an order consistent with that of the fields of the source form. The Order Entry screen in Figure 16.13 is similar to the Customer Order form in Figure 16.19. Both the screen and the form present the Order Number first and the Order Date second.

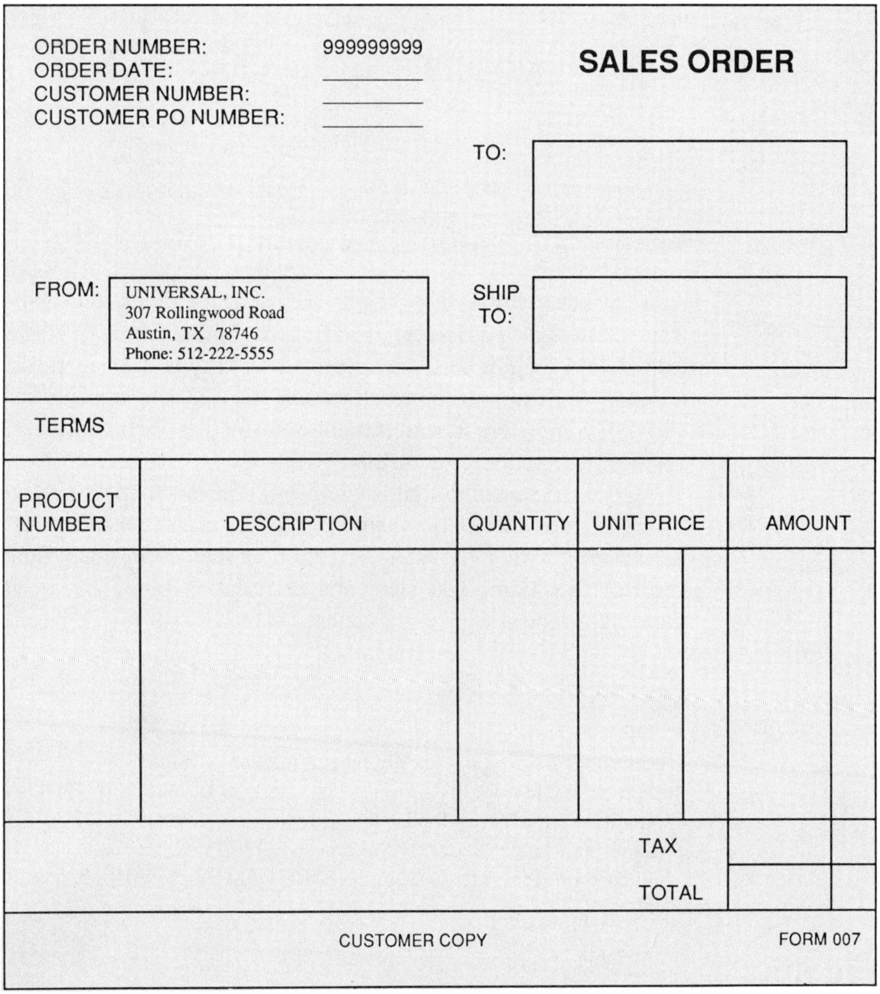
SALES ORDER

ORDER NUMBER: 999999999
ORDER DATE:
CUSTOMER NUMBER:
CUSTOMER PO NUMBER:

TO:

FROM: UNIVERSAL, INC.
307 Rollingwood Road
Austin, TX 78746
Phone: 512-222-5555

SHIP TO:

TERMS

PRODUCT NUMBER	DESCRIPTION	QUANTITY	UNIT PRICE	AMOUNT
			TAX	
			TOTAL	

CUSTOMER COPY FORM 007

Figure 16.19
Design for Customer Order Form

Figure 16.20
Flow of Data Entry

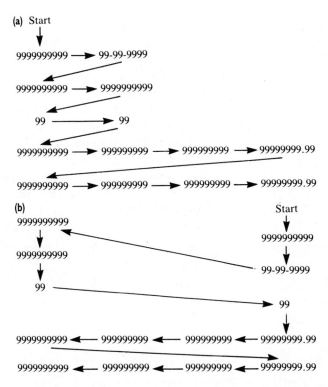

The key to improving the accuracy of data entry is feedback. Figure 16.21 lists several ways to check data accuracy. Specific techniques include editing entered data and echoing. Edit checks include tests for improper field type (alphabetic or numeric), unreasonable numbers (for example, a month greater than 12 or a monthly salary below $400 or above $8,000), completeness, and missing information. Echoing is re-displaying a field once it has been entered and requiring verification by the user.

Once the screen design is complete, a layout matrix is created to show headings and instructions as well as the main body of the screen with data definitions. Figure 16.22 is an example, with complete information on data definitions, function keys, and messages. Instead of including data element specifications on the layout, you can attach pages from the design repository.

Figure 16.21
Data Entry Checks
for Accuracy

1. Edit checks
   Improper field type (e.g., alphabetic instead of numeric)
   Unreasonable quantity
   Completeness (i.e., a field is not filled in)
   Limit and range (e.g., month exceeds 12)
   Record not found (e.g., value for CUSTOMER NUMBER does not exist in database)

2. Checking digits

3. Echoing

Figure 16.22
Example of a
Complete Screen
Layout Form

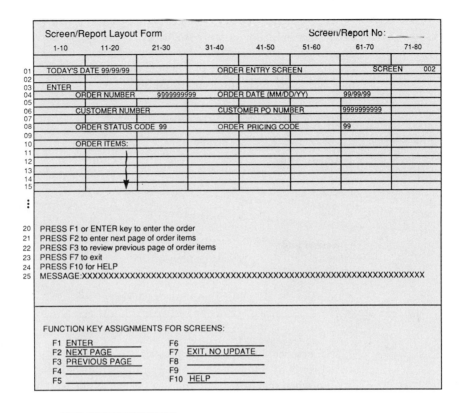

16.3.5 Human-Computer Dialogues

There are two issues in creating human-computer dialogues: (1) selecting the best dialogue type and (2) designing the dialogue. The main objective in selecting a dialogue type is to maximize the productivity of the users by making the dialogue both usable and learnable. If a frequent user of a system can reach his or her selection only by navigating through four layers of menu choices, the system is not very usable. The user's productivity will suffer. On the other hand, if an infrequent user is required to remember a complicated command language to access an application, the system is not very learnable. The user is likely to avoid the application, and frustration and decreased productivity will result. Obviously, the choice of a dialogue type depends greatly on how frequently users access the system.

The general guidelines for choosing a dialogue type (Figure 16.23) are based on a simple determination of usage frequency. Users who access a system infrequently should be provided with menus and/or question and answer dialogues to guide them in selecting options, and frequent users of a system should be provided with commands with which they can access their applications quickly.

Figure 16.23
Guidelines for Selecting a Dialogue Type

Dialogue Type	Usage Frequency		
	Low	Medium	High
Menu	Yes	Yes	No (Commands may be supplemented with menus when fast learning is important.)
Question and Answer (Prompt)	Yes (Answers should be limited to yes and no.)	Yes	Yes
Command	No	Yes	Yes

In practice, however, an application system is likely to be used both frequently and infrequently by different types of users. In addition, all users must go through a learning process when they first begin to use a system. While learning to use a system, users will need menus for guidance. Then, as they gain experience in using the system, they want quick access to the system via either commands or menus and commands. Thus an application system should generally provide both command and menu choices for the dialogue.

The guidelines in Figure 16.24 concern the design of the dialogues themselves. The important criteria for dialogues are simplicity, clarity, and consistency.

For the sake of simplicity, a menu should be limited to nine or fewer selections. People have difficulty understanding menus that have more than nine selections. Question and answer dialogues should call for yes or no answers when possible. For example, "Do you want to enter invoices (Y/N)"? is simpler than "What do you want to do next?" Commands should be composed of a minimal number of verbs and nouns. For example, ENTER INVOICES is a better command than RUN INVOICE ENTRY PROGRAM.

For the sake of clarity, menu selections should be specified as active verb-object phrases. The Universal menu in Figure 16.6 contains the selection ENTER INVOICES. If the selection were just INVOICES, the user would not know whether it meant PRINT invoices or ENTER invoices. By clearly specifying the selection, you can avoid frustrating the user of the menu. In addition, the paths between menu selections should be clear to the user. One way to make paths clear is to include a PREVIOUS SELECTION entry on the menu. This way a user can always reconstruct the path that led to the current menu selection. Clear question and answer dialogues state questions as complete sentences. "DO YOU WANT TO ENTER INVOICES? (Y/N)" is clearer than "INVOICES? (Y/N)." Finally, clear command syntax uses words that are meaningful to the user. The command ENTER INVOICES is clearer than RUN INVOICE ENTRY PROGRAM.

Figure 16.24

Guidelines for Designing a Dialogue Type

Dialogue Type	Criteria		
	Simplicity	**Clarity**	**Consistency**
Menu	Limit the number of selections to nine or less.	Use active verb-object phrases (for example, PRINT ORDER REGISTER REPORT). Make the paths between menus clear by providing a PREVIOUS SELECTION entry.	Place similar selections (for example, EXIT) in the same location on all menus. Make sure that the words used to specify similar selections do not change from one menu to another.
Question and Answer (Prompt)	Use questions that can be answered yes or no.	Use complete sentences.	Use similarly phrased questions. For example, do not use "WHAT IS YOUR NEXT SELECTION?" when most questions are to be answered yes or no.
Command	Use a minimal number of verbs and nouns.	Use verbs and nouns that are meaningful to the users of the system.	Never allow the same word to have more than one meaning.

For the sake of consistency, similar selections should always be in the same location on different menus. For example, EXIT should be the last selection on every menu. In addition, menu selections should never change meaning from one menu to the next. In the Universal system, for example, EXIT should always mean exiting the order tracking system. If EXIT were used on one menu to mean returning to the previous menu, then the menus would not be consistent. Consistent question and answer dialogues are composed of similarly phrased questions. In the midst of a yes/no type dialogue, a question such as "WHAT IS YOUR NEXT SELECTION?" is likely to confuse a user. Finally, having a consistent command syntax requires that the same word not have more than one meaning. For example, the word EXIT should not be used for two different purposes, as it is in the commands EXIT SYSTEM and EXIT TO MAIN MENU. Going to the menu should require a command such as RETURN TO MAIN MENU.

Dialogue charts should be created to show the relationships among menu options. These charts document how the user moves through menus, question and answer dialogues, data entry screens, and report selections. An example of a dialogue chart is shown in Figure 16.25, along with drawing conventions.

Figure 16.25
Conventions for
Dialogue Charts

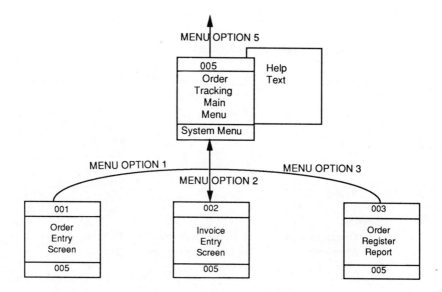

1. Rectangles represent menus or screens. For example, the Order Register Report is actually the screen used to request the printing of the report. Rectangles are divided into three sections:
The top section specifies the identification number for the screen.
The middle section specifies the name of the screen.
The lower section specifies the menus to which the user of the screen can exit.

2. A screen behind another screen specifies help text.

3. The arrows between screens specify the allowable selections between screens.

Source: J. L. Whitten, L. D. Bentley, and T. I. Ho, *Systems Analysis and Design Methods* (St. Louis, Mo.: Times Mirror/Mosby College Publishing, 1986), p. 542.

16.4 Designing Interfaces

The steps in designing the interface for a system are

1. Create the interface summary table for the system.

    1.1. Review the human-computer boundary in the data flow diagram.

    1.2. List the interfaces and review the design repository to define the data elements included in each output, input, and document.

2. Design the human-computer dialogue.

    2.1. Select the type(s) of dialogue.

    2.2. Design each dialogue.

3. Design input (data entry) screens.

4. Design reports.

    4.1. Select the output method for each report.

    4.2. Design internal reports.

    4.3. Design report screens.

  5. Design external documents.

These steps are shown in the form of a flowchart in Figure 16.26. Although the chart in Figure 16.26 implies a sequential design process, interface design is actually a cyclical process. The design for the user interface will undergo many iterations before it is com-

Figure 16.26
Steps in Interface
Design

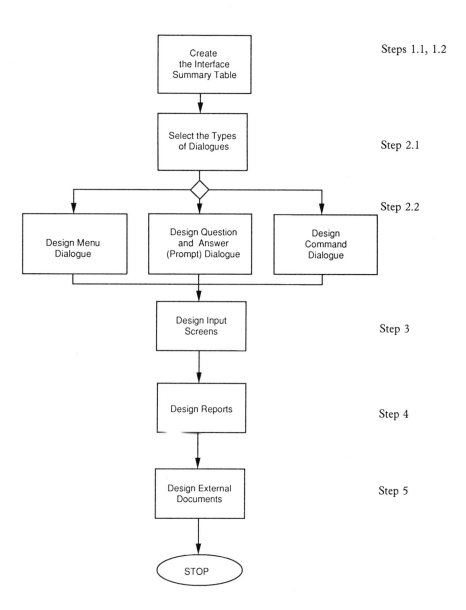

plete. As screens and reports are reviewed by users, the dialogue will often change. As the dialogue changes, reports and screens may be discarded or added.

When the design is complete, the deliverables will include the designs for documents, reports and screens, and the human-computer dialogue. A complete interface design will contain not only the general layout of documents, reports, and screens, but also detailed information such as whether a dollar sign should be displayed next to dollar amounts, whether leading zeros should be printed or displayed as blanks, the exact number of spaces between each column of a report, and the screens that can be accessed from a given menu. This detailed design information is needed by computer programmers to implement the interface.

There are two tools that are useful for capturing the detailed design information needed by programmers:

- Printer layout charts
- Display layout charts

The printer layout chart shows the exact locations of information presented in the heading and the main body of an external document or internal report and the editing masks (for example, spaces instead of leading zeros) for the information in the main body. The display layout chart shows the locations of information and editing masks, as well as information for the instruction window of a data entry or report screen (for example, that Function Key F7 is used to exit from the screen). In addition, a display layout chart like the one in Figure 16.22 shows the information presented in a menu or question and answer dialogue.

16.4.1 Interface Design from an Ordered Example

The following minicase uses the ordered example of the Meadows Pharmacy case to show how a user interface is developed. For this minicase we have expanded the development team. The team now includes Liisa Finn, a systems analyst who had previously worked for Universal, as well as the old members—Tito Hernandez, the assistant pharmacy manager; Fred Kahn, the programmer/analyst assigned to the project; Tracy Bell, the project leader; and Mary Henderson, the pharmacy manager and senior pharmacist.

MINICASE

Return to Meadows Hospital

Step 1—Identifying the Interfaces for the System

1.1 Review the human-computer boundary. Fred and Liisa started the interface design by reviewing the human-computer boundary for the pharmacy data flow diagram in Figure 16.27.

1.2 List interfaces and review the design repository for data elements in reports and screens. Fred and Liisa listed the interfaces needed by the pharmacy system in Figure 16.28. They gathered the information about data elements from the design repository.

Step 2—Designing the Human-Computer Dialogue

As the second step in the interface design, Liisa and Fred designed the dialogue for the pharmacy system.

Figure 16.27
Process
Prescriptions DFD

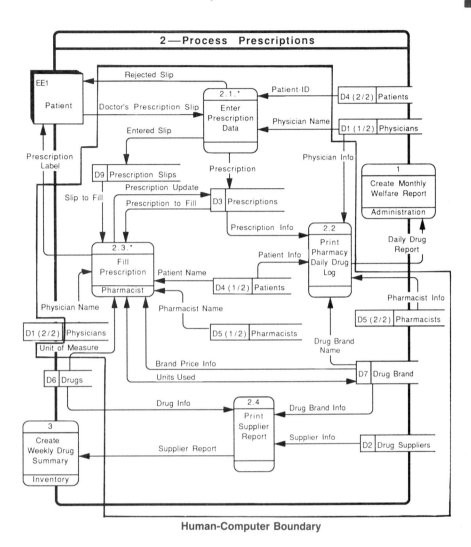

Human-Computer Boundary

They decided that a combination of menus and commands would best fit the diverse needs of users of the pharmacy system. Menus would be most helpful to pharmacists, who would use the system infrequently to update prescriptions via the Prescription Update screen. When pharmacists needed to access other screens, the menu would guide them through the selections available. Other users who used the system more frequently would be able to use commands to make selections quickly. Liisa and Fred created the dialogue chart in Figure 16.29 and reviewed it with Tito and Mary. The main pharmacy system menu is shown in Figure 16.30.

Step 3—Designing Data Entry Screens

Liisa and Fred started designing data entry screens by drawing rough layouts of the Prescription Entry and Prescription Update screens. To expedite data entry for the application, they designed the main body of the Prescription Entry screen to have a format similar to that of the doctors' prescription slip. They further increased the speed of data entry by designing the format so that data would be entered from left to right and top to bottom (see Figure 16.31). The information window was designed to be consistent with those of other screens used at Meadows Hospital. For example, all screens use function

Figure 16.28
Pharmacy System
Interface Summary
Table

No.	Name	Type	Data Elements
1	Daily Drug Log	Internal report	PRCT-ID-NBR, PAT-LAST-NAME, PAT-FIRST-NAME, PHY-LAST-NAME, PHY-MID-INIT-NAME, PHY-FIRST-NAME, DRUG-NAME, DRUGB-NAME
2	Prescription Entry Screen	Data entry	DRUG-NAME, PAT-ID-NBR, PAT-LAST-NAME, PHY-FIRST-NAME, PHY-MID-INIT-NAME, PHY-LAST-NAME, PRCT-DATE, PRCT-DRUG-QTY-NBR, PRCT-DOSE-IS-TEXT
3	Prescription Update Screen	Data entry	DRUG-NAME, PAT-ID-NBR, PHY-LAST-NAME, PRCT-DATE, PRCT-DRUG-QTY-NBR, PRCT-DOSE-IS-TEXT, PHAR-EMP-ID-NBR, DRUGB-NAME, DRUGB-UNIT-PR-AMT, DRUG-UNIT-AV-NBR, DRUG-UOM-CODE
4	Prescription Label (printed from Prescription Update screen)	External document	PRCT-ID-NBR, PHY-LAST-NAME, PHY-FIRST-NAME, PHY-MID-INIT-NAME, PAT-LAST-NAME, PAT-FIRST-NAME, PRCT-DOSE-IS-TEXT, DRUGB-NAME, PRCT-DRUG-QTY-NBR, PHAR-FIRST-NAME
5	Supplier Report	Internal report	DRUGSP-NAME, DRUGSP-VEN-ID-NBR, DRUG-NAME, DRUGB-NAME,-DRUG-UOM-CODE, DRUGB-YTD-USE-NBR, DRUGB-UNIT-AV-NBR

key F7 to exit a screen. In Figure 16.32 they defined function keys for scrolling, entering data, database inquiries, and getting help.

Liisa and Fred next designed controls to ensure the accuracy of the data entered via the Prescription Entry screen. The PAT-ID-NBR, PRCT-DATE, and PRCT-DRUG-QTY-NBR will be edit-checked to ensure that they are entered as numbers. Before prescription data is entered into files, a completeness check will be carried out to ensure that no field on the Prescription Entry screen was left blank. In addition, a range check will be made on PRCT-DATE to ensure that the date is not more than one day before the current date. Hospital policy requires that all prescriptions be filled on the same day that the doctor writes the prescription slip. Occasionally, however, a patient is not able to bring the prescription slip to the Pharmacy before it closes at 5:30 P.M. To ensure that patient numbers are entered correctly, the patient will be asked to write his or her name on the prescription slip, and the patient's name will be echoed back to the entry screen when the patient's number is entered. At the same time, the operator will be able to

Figure 16.29
Pharmacy System
Dialogue Chart

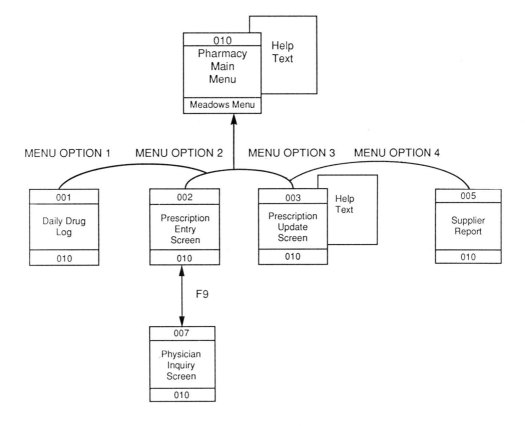

Figure 16.30
Pharmacy System Main
Menu

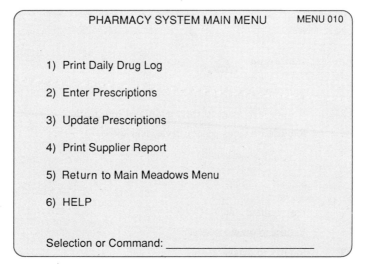

Figure 16.31
Doctors' Prescription
Slip and Prescription
Entry Screen

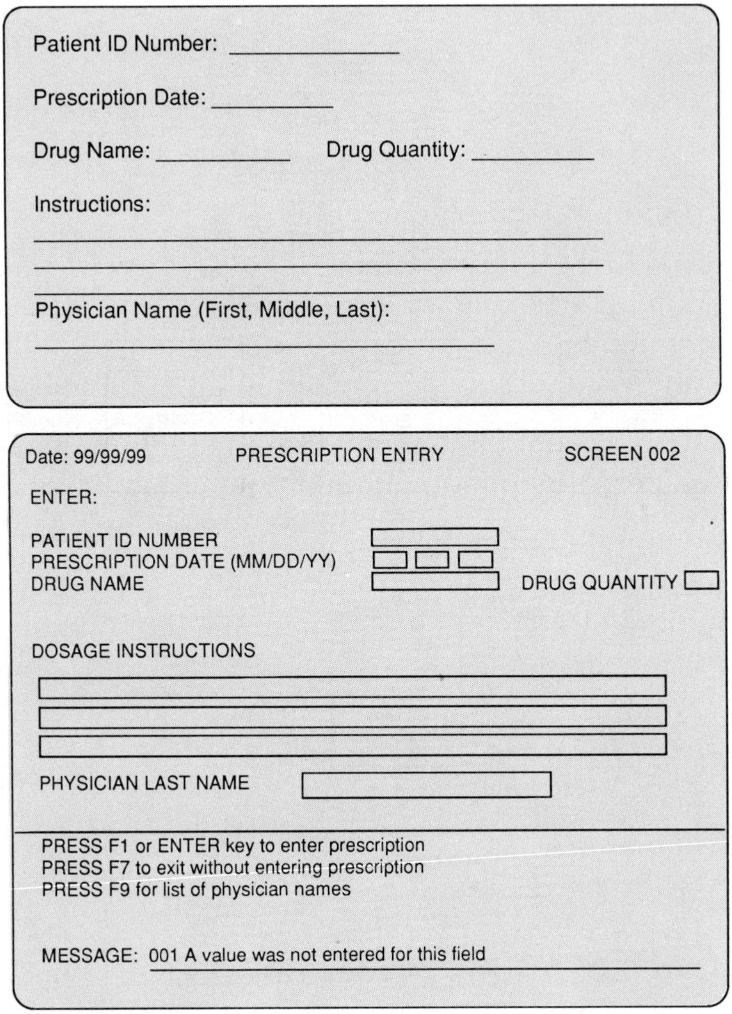

Patient ID Number: _____

Prescription Date: _____

Drug Name: _____   Drug Quantity: _____

Instructions:
_____
_____
_____

Physician Name (First, Middle, Last):
_____

Date: 99/99/99   PRESCRIPTION ENTRY   SCREEN 002

ENTER:

PATIENT ID NUMBER
PRESCRIPTION DATE (MM/DD/YY)
DRUG NAME   DRUG QUANTITY

DOSAGE INSTRUCTIONS

PHYSICIAN LAST NAME

PRESS F1 or ENTER key to enter prescription
PRESS F7 to exit without entering prescription
PRESS F9 for list of physician names

MESSAGE: 001 A value was not entered for this field

Figure 16.32
Function Keys for
Pharmacy Screens

Key	Command
F1	ENTER
F2	Request next page to enter additional information
F3	Request previous page to review/change
F4	
F5	
F6	
F7	Exit without update
F8	Return to previous screen
F9	Inquiry to database
F10	HELP

verify whether the number is a valid PAT-ID-NBR. As a final control, access to the Prescription Entry screen will be limited to users with a password.

As their last step in designing the pharmacy system screens, Liisa and Fred reviewed the screens with Tito and Mary. The Presciption Entry and Prescription Update screens were approved. The screen layout chart for the Prescription Entry screen is shown in Figure 16.33.

```
          10        20        30        40        50        60        70        80
          |         |         |         |         |         |         |         |
DATE: 99/99/99                PRESCRIPTION ENTRY            SCREEN 002

ENTER:

    PATIENT ID NUMBER              9999999999 XXXXXXXXXXXXXXXXXXX
    PRESCRIPTION DATE (MM/DD/YY)   99 99 99
    DRUG NAME                      XXXXXXXXXXXXXXXXXXXX              DRUG QUANTITY 999999

    DOSAGE INSTRUCTIONS

    XXXXXXXXXXXXXXXXXXXXXXXXXXXXXX
    XXXXXXXXXXXXXXXXXXXXXXXXXXXXXX
    XXXXXXXXXXXXXXXXXXXXXXXXXXXXXX

    PHYSICIAN LAST NAME            XXXXXXXXXXXXXX

    PRESS F1 or  ENTER key to enter prescription
    PRESS F7 to exit without entering prescription
    PRESS F9 for list of physician names


XXXXXXXXXXXXXXXXXXXXXXXXXXXXXXXXXXXXXXXXXXXXXXXXXXXXXXXXXXXXXXXXXXXXXXXXXXXXXXX

    FUNCTION KEY ASSIGNMENTS:

    F1  ENTER              F6  _____
    F2  _____              F7  EXIT
    F3   *                 F8  _____
    F4  _____              F9  LIST PHYS NAMES
    F5                     F10 _____
```

DATA DICTIONARY:

NO	SCREEN NAME	ELEMENT NAME	TYPE	SIZE	EDIT MASK	EDITING/VALIDATION
1	DATE	FROM SYSTEM	N	8	99/99/99	
2	PATIENT ID NUMBER	PAT-ID-NBR	N	10	9(10)	MUST CONTAIN VALID VALUE
3	ECHO FIELD	PAT-LAST-NAME	C	20	X(20)	DISPLAY ONLY
4	PRESCRIPTION DATE	PRCT-ID-NBR	N	8	99 99 99	MUST CONTAIN A VALUE
5	DRUG NAME	DRUG-NAME	C	20	X(20)	MUST CONTAIN A VALUE
6	DRUG QUANTITY	PRCT-DRUG-QTY-NBR	N	6	999999	MUST CONTAIN A VALUE
7	DOSAGE INSTRUCTIONS	PRCT-DOSE-IST-TEXT	C	90	X(30)	MUST CONTAIN A VALUE
8					X(30)	SPLIT INTO 3 FIELDS
9					X(30)	
10	PHYSICIAN LAST NAME	PHYS-LAST-NAME	C	15	X(15)	MUST CONTAIN VALID VALUE
11	MESSAGE LINE	from program	C	80	X(80)	ERROR

ERROR MESSAGES:

001   A value was not entered for this field.
002   Physician name does not exist in database - Press F9 for list of physicians.

Figure 16.33 Display Layout Chart for Prescription Entry Screen

Step 4—Designing Reports

4.1 Design internal reports. Fred and Liisa started report design by drawing a rough layout of the Daily Drug Log and Supplier report. They reviewed the manual reports currently being used by the Pharmacy department, as well as other computer-generated reports. Next, they went over the rough layouts with Tito Hernandez and Mary Henderson. Mary told them that the current Daily Drug Log was cluttered and difficult to read. They designed the main body of the format with two blank lines between each prescription to make the report easier to read. After Tito and Mary approved the documents and reports, Fred and Liisa created printer layout charts.

4.2 Design report screens. Fred and Liisa decided that none of the internal reports had to be CRT outputs. Both the Daily Drug Log and the Supplier report are needed by many users and must be kept available for an extended period of time. Thus, the reports would be printed in hard-copy form.

Step 5—Designing External Documents

As the final step in the design of the interface, Fred and Liisa designed the system's external documents. They started by drawing a rough layout of a prescription label,

and then they reviewed the layout with Tito Hernandez and Mary Henderson. Mary told them that the prescription label should contain the last name of the pharmacist because many patients felt uncomfortable using only the first name when they called with questions. They sent the layout chart for the prescription label, shown in Figure 16.34 to Meadow's custom forms supplier.

Figure 16.34
Prescription Label
Layout

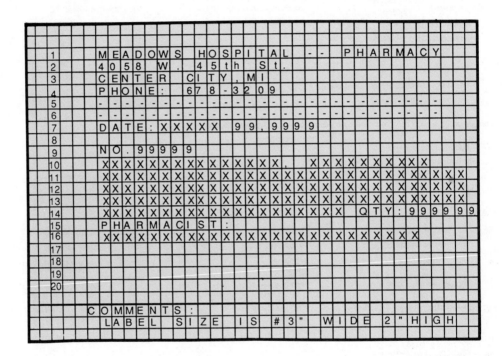

Summary

Interface design is the process of specifying how a system will look to a user. The data flow diagram is the input to the design process. The output of the design process is a description of the external documents, internal reports, report screens, data entry screens, and dialogues (menus, question and answers, and commands) that comprise the user interface.

The complex process of designing a user interface that is usable and learnable by all users of a system is managed by following general design guidelines. General guidelines are organized on the basis of five criteria used to evaluate the usability and learnability of the user interface. The five design criteria are quality, simplicity, clarity, consistency, and feedback.

Key Terms

(Section numbers are in parentheses.)

external document (16.2.1)   **human-computer dialogue (16.2.5)**
internal report (16.2.2)   **menu (16.2.5)**
report screen (16.2.3)   **question and answer (16.2.5)**
data entry screen (16.2.4)   **command (16.2.5)**

Exercises

(Answers to Exercises 16.1, 16.2, 16.3, and 16.5 are at the end of the book.)

16.1 Explain how the data flow diagram introduced in Chapter 10 is used in the user-interface design process.

16.2 List and describe the types of user interfaces.

16.3 Describe the three dialogue types. Indicate in which situations each type might be preferred over the others.

16.4 List and describe the five criteria used to evaluate the usability and learnability of the user interface.

16.5 Evaluate the layouts of the screens shown in Figures 16.35 and 16.36 on each of the following criteria:

a. quality

b. simplicity

c. clarity

d. consistency

Figure 16.35

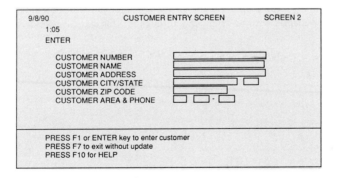

Figure 16.36

```
┌─────────────────────────────────────────────────────────────────┐
│  Sept. 8, 1990         Customer Orders and  DISCOUNTS    SCREEN 3 │
│     1:05                                                          │
│         CUSTOMER NUMBER           ┌──────────────────┐            │
│                                   └──────────────────┘            │
│         ORDER NUMBER              ┌──────────────────┐            │
│                                   └──────────────────┘            │
│       ITEM NO.              QUANTITY              PRICE           │
│                                                                   │
│    ┌──────────────┐     ┌──────────────┐     ┌──────────────┐     │
│    └──────────────┘     └──────────────┘     └──────────────┘     │
│    ┌──────────────┐     ┌──────────────┐     ┌──────────────┐     │
│    └──────────────┘     └──────────────┘     └──────────────┘     │
│    ┌──────────────┐     ┌──────────────┐     ┌──────────────┐     │
│    └──────────────┘     └──────────────┘     └──────────────┘     │
├───────────────────────────────────────────────────────────────────┤
│    PRESS ENTER key to enter order                                 │
│    PRESS F1 to display additional order lines                     │
│    PRESS F7 to exit without update                                │
│    PRESS F10 for HELP                                             │
│    PRESS F11 to enter customer discounts                          │
└───────────────────────────────────────────────────────────────────┘
```

16.6 Upon receiving an approved project request form, a clerk uses a CRT to establish the project information in the database. The approved project request form contains the following information (in order of appearance on the form): project ID number, project name, client ID number (the identifier for the owner of the project), employee ID number for the manager of the project, starting date for the project, estimated ending date for the project, and a project status code (1 = start up, 2 = design, 3 = construction phase, 4 = closing, 5 = closed).

a. Create a Project Entry screen layout for this situation.

b. Is your screen design simple? Justify your answer.

c. Is your screen design clear? Justify your answer.

16.7 Create a dialogue chart for the screens and reports in the project DFD in Figure 16.37. State any assumptions you feel are necessary.

Project

16.8 Read the article by Jonathan Grudin, "The Case Against User Interface Consistency," *Communications of the ACM*, vol. 32, no. 10, October 1989, pp. 1164–1173. Prepare a class presentation comparing Grudin's recommendations with the guidelines for interface design in this chapter and the arguments throughout this text for user-driven system development.

Figure 16.37
Project DFD

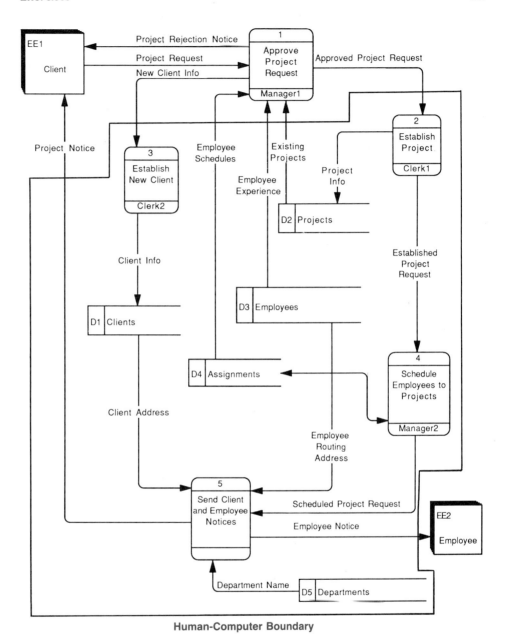

Human-Computer Boundary

Database Design

Overview

The conceptual data model introduced in Chapter 11 describes the data requirements of an information system. A conceptual data model, however, is an incomplete database description. The complete database description must conform to the rules of logical and physical data structures imposed by the database management system that will manage the database. Thus the conceptual data model must be supplemented with structures for logical and physical data. In this chapter we plan to

1. Provide an introduction to database design. (Section 17.1)

2. Explain the logical constructs used for database design. (Section 17.2)

3. Explain the physical constructs used for database design. (Section 17.3)

4. Introduce database management systems. (Section 17.4)

5. Provide guidelines for logical and physical database design. (Section 17.5)

6. Provide a step-by-step illustration of designing a database. (Section 17.6)

17.1 Introduction to Database Design

Figure 17.1 shows the inputs and outputs of database design. Database design can be viewed as a three-step process. The first step, conceptual data modeling, was introduced in Chapter 11. The second step, logical database design, transforms the conceptual data model into a logical description of data used by a database management system (DBMS). The third step, physical database design, tranforms the logical description into a physical

Figure 17.1
Database Design

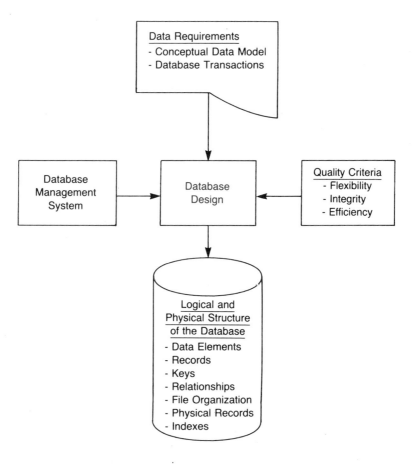

model that describes how the database will be organized and accessed on secondary storage devices.

If you think for a moment about how a library is organized, you will better understand conceptual, logical, and physical database design. Conceptually, a library includes entities such as books and periodicals, which are read and/or borrowed by library users. Logically, the books and periodicals are organized in card catalogs by subject and author. The logical organization helps library users to find the books and periodicals they need. The physical organization of the library books and periodicals determines their physical location within the library building—their room and shelf location. Library users find books by using two indexes. The first index is the Dewey Decimal number found on each card in the catalog. The second index is the general area within the library where books with Dewey Decimal numbers within a certain range can be found. Library materials are physically organized for the convenience of the librarians and the users of the library. For example, frequently used reference books are normally placed at a location on the ground floor near the main entrance to the library.

The challenge in organizing a library is to design the logical and physical organization of books and periodicals to be flexible (to meet the changing needs of borrowers), controlled (to guard against theft and misplaced materials), and efficient (to minimize the time users spend locating and borrowing books and periodicals). Database design involves similar challenges.

A complete database design is a description of logical and physical data structures that can be implemented on a DBMS. The quality criteria of flexibility, integrity, and efficiency* guide the process of transforming the conceptual data model into a database design. During logical and physical database design, you will consider

- the flexibility of the database with respect to future changes
- controls to guard the integrity of the data in the database
- the efficiency of data updates and retrievals
- the efficient utilization of space on external storage devices

Flexibility refers to the cost of making changes to the database when reports and screens are added or changed. Integrity refers to the cost of destroyed data, incorrect data, and violations of confidentiality. Efficiency refers to the storage costs for the database and the response times for the updates and retrievals that access the database.

Designing a database requires an understanding of (1) the logical and physical data structures, (2) the criteria that guide the transformation of a conceptual data model into the logical and physical data structures used by a DBMS, and (3) a method for designing the database using the structures and guidelines. We will use the Universal case to provide an overview of the structures, principles, and method of database design.

---

*These quality criteria are derived from the system quality criteria in Figure 2.3 of Chapter 2. Flexibility is determined by ease of maintenance and adaptability, and integrity corresponds to reliability.

Designing a Database for Universal, Inc.

Roy Johnson, the database administrator, and Jill Anderson, the data analyst for Universal, are designing the database for the Universal order tracking system. The process they will follow is depicted in Figure 17.2, starting with the top right bubble.

As the first step in database design, Jill and Roy translate the conceptual data model (Figure 17.3) into a logical data structure that conforms to the rules of the network DBMS (see Section 17.4.2) used to implement the database. During this step, entities are transformed into rec-

Figure 17.2
Overview of Database
Design Steps

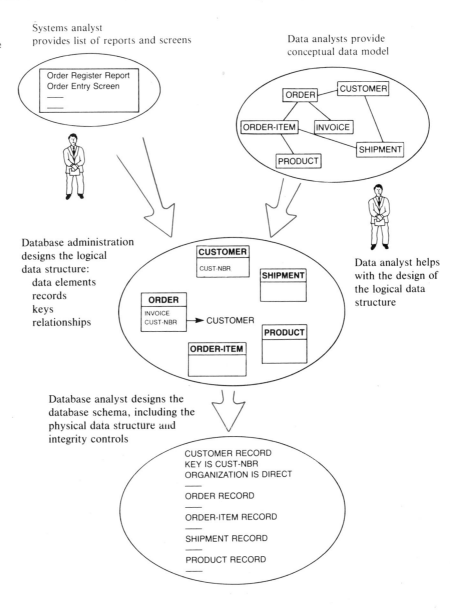

Systems analyst
provides list of reports and screens

Data analysts provide
conceptual data model

Database administration
designs the logical
data structure:
    data elements
    records
    keys
    relationships

Data analyst helps
with the design of
the logical data
structure

Database analyst designs the
database schema, including the
physical data structure and
integrity controls

Figure 17.3
Universal, Inc.
Conceptual
Data Model

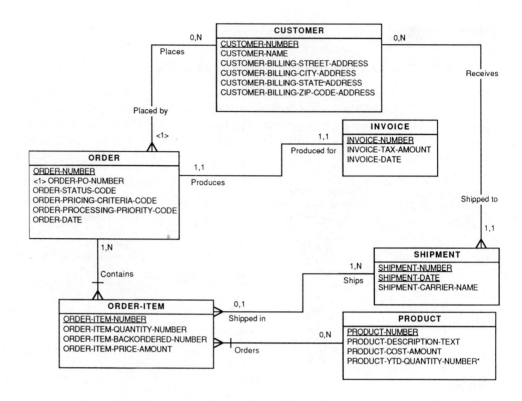

Transaction

Priority	Name	Action	Entities Accessed	Access Key	Cycle	Activity*
1	Order Register Report	Retrieve Retrieve Retrieve Retrieve Retrieve	INVOICE ORDER ORDER-ITEM CUSTOMER PRODUCT	INVOICE-NUMBER	Daily	100%
2	Order Entry Screen	Update Update Retrieve Retrieve	ORDER ORDER-ITEM PRODUCT CUSTOMER	ORDER-NUMBER	Daily	—
3	Invoice Entry Screen	Update Retrieve	INVOICE ORDER	INVOICE-NUMBER	Daily	—

*Percentage of record instances selected by the data access

Figure 17.4 Data Access Table for Universal's Order Tracking System

ords, attributes are transformed into data elements, identifiers are transformed into keys, and relationships between entities are transformed into relationships between records (for example, pointers and foreign keys are established). Following this step, Jill and Roy create a **data access table** (Figure 17.4), which documents the most critical updates and retrievals (that is, reports and screens that require quick response times) to and from the database. (Updates and retrievals are called **database transactions** because they involve exchanges of data to and from the database.) In addition, the expected number of instances for each record is doc-

umented. For example, based on the number of customers Universal has, Jill and Roy expect 10,000 instances of CUSTOMER. The information in the data access table helps the designer to determine the logical data structure that will make access to the database most efficient. The number of record instances is used to determine the number of records accessed by retrievals and updates and to calculate the space required by the database on external storage devices. Using the logical structure as a guide, Roy specifies physical data structures including records, file organization, and indexes, to further increase the efficiency of the database.

Figure 17.5
Universal, Inc. Database:
Logical Data Structure

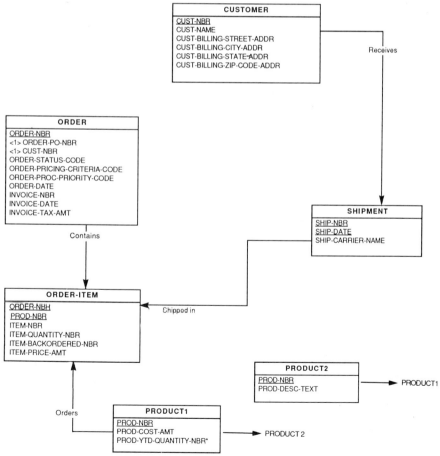

SCHEMA NAME IS UNIVERSAL.

RECORD NAME IS CUSTOMER
  LOCATION MODE IS CALC CUST-NBR.
  02 CUST-NBR   PIC IS INTEGER(10).
  02 CUST-NAME   PIC IS CHAR(40).
  02 CUST-BILLING-STREET-ADDR   PIC IS CHAR(40).
  02 CUST-BILLING-CITY-ADDR   PIC IS CHAR(15).
  02 CUST-BILLING-STATE-ADDR   PIC IS CHAR(2).
  02 CUST-BILLING-ZIP-CODE-ADDR PIC IS INTEGER(9).

RECORD NAME IS ORDER
  LOCATION MODE IS CALC ORDER-NBR.
  02 ORDER-NBR   PIC IS INTEGER(10).
  02 ORDER-PO-NBR   PIC IS INTEGER(10).
  02 CUST-NBR   PIC IS INTEGER(10).
  02 ORDER-STATUS-CODE   PIC IS INTEGER(2).
  02 ORDER-PRICING-CRITERIA-CODE PIC IS INTEGER(2).
  02 ORDER-PROC-PRIORITY-CODE   PIC IS INTEGER(2).
  02 ORDER-DATE   PIC IS INTEGER(8).
  02 INVOICE-NBR   PIC IS INTEGER(10).
  02 INVOICE-DATE   PIC IS INTEGER(8).
  02 INVOICE-TAX-AMT   PIC IS DECIMAL(10,2).

RECORD NAME IS ORDER-ITEM
  LOCATION MODE IS VIA, Contains SET.
  02 PROD-NBR   PIC IS INTEGER(10).
  02 ORDER-NBR   PIC IS INTEGER(10).
  02 ITEM-NBR   PIC IS INTEGER(4).
  02 ITEM-QUANTITY-NBR   PIC IS INTEGER(9).
  02 ITEM-BACKORDERED-NBR   PIC IS INTEGER(9).
  02 ITEM-PRICE-AMT   PIC IS DECIMAL(10,2).

RECORD NAME IS PRODUCT1
  WITHIN PRODUCT1
  LOCATION MODE IS CALC PROD-NBR.
  02 PROD-NBR   PIC IS INTEGER(10).
  02 PROD-COST-AMT   PIC IS DECIMAL(10,2).
  02 PROD-YTD-QUANTITY-NBR*   PIC IS INTEGER(10).

RECORD NAME IS PRODUCT2
  LOCATION MODE IS CALC PROD-NBR.
  02 PROD-NBR   PIC IS INTEGER(10).
  02 PROD-DESC-TEXT   PIC IS CHAR(40).

RECORD NAME IS SHIPMENT
  LOCATION MODE IS CALC SHIP-NBR, SHIP-DATE .
  02 SHIP-NBR   PIC IS INTEGER(10).
  02 SHIP-DATE   PIC IS INTEGER(8).
  02 SHIP-CARRIER-NAME   PIC IS CHAR(40).

SET NAME IS Receives
  MODE IS CHAIN
  ORDER IS NEXT
  OWNER IS CUSTOMER
  MEMBER IS SHIPMENT MANDATORY AUTOMATIC
  SET OCCURRENCE SELECTION IS THRU CURRENT OF:

SET NAME IS Contains
  MODE IS CHAIN
  ORDER IS NEXT
  OWNER IS ORDER
  MEMBER IS ORDER-ITEM FIXED AUTOMATIC
  SET OCCURRENCE SELECTION IS THRU CURRENT OF:

SET NAME IS Orders
  MODE IS CHAIN
  ORDER IS NEXT
  OWNER IS PRODUCT1
  MEMBER IS ORDER-ITEM FIXED AUTOMATIC
  SET OCCURRENCE SELECTION IS THRU CURRENT OF:

SET NAME IS Shipped in
  MODE IS CHAIN
  ORDER IS NEXT
  OWNER IS SHIPMENT
  MEMBER IS ORDER-ITEM OPTIONAL MANUAL
  SET OCCURRENCE SELECTION IS THRU CURRENT OF:

SET NAME IS INVOICE-INDEX
  MODE IS INDEX
  ORDER IS SORTED
  OWNER IS SYSTEM
  MEMBER IS ORDER
      INDEX DBKEY POSITION IS AUTO
      MANDATORY, AUTOMATIC
      ASCENDING KEY IS INVOICE-NBR
        DUPLICATES ARE NOT ALLOWED.

Figure 17.6   Universal, Inc. Database Schema

After the logical and physical structures have been specified, they are described in a schema written in the data description language of the DBMS. As a final step, controls such as passwords and backup and recovery files are added to ensure that the integrity of the data in the database is maintained.

Figure 17.5 contains the final logical data structure, and Figure 17.6 contains the database schema,* which specifies the logical and physical data structures for the Universal database.

*Note that some of the data element names in Figures 17.5 and 17.6 are abbreviations of the attribute names in Figure 17.3. Attribute names must often be shortened to satisfy the limits imposed by the DBMS on the length of data element names.

17.2 Logical Database Design Constructs

Design constructs describe the logical and physical data structures of a database. Four constructs make up a **logical data structure:** (1) data elements, (2) logical records, (3) keys, and (4) relationships. For each logical construct, we will

1. Introduce a symbol to represent the construct.
2. Define the construct.
3. Illustrate the construct with an example from the order tracking conceptual data model in Figure 17.3, logical data structure in Figure 17.5, schema and database in Figure 17.6.
4. Describe the decisions that are made in transforming a conceptual data model construct into a logical database structure.

17.2.1 Data Element

A name within a box denotes a data element (see Figure 17.7a). A **data element** represents the smallest unit of information defined for data. Data elements, often called fields,

Figure 17.7
Constructs of the Logical Data Structure

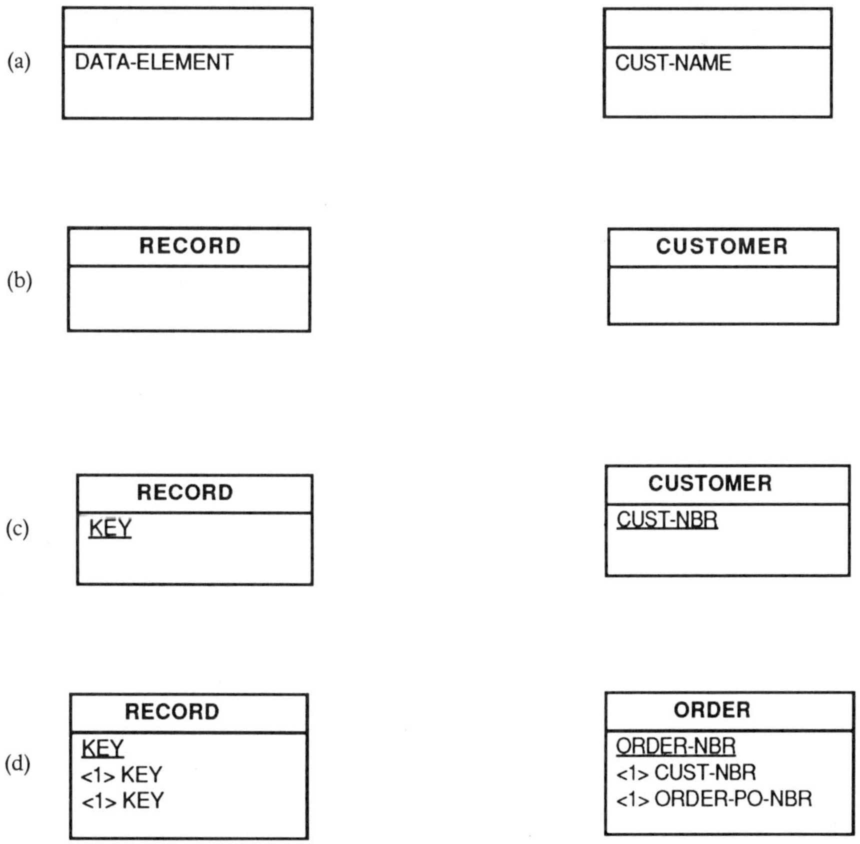

correspond to attributes, derived attributes, or identifiers in a conceptual data model. For example, in Figure 17.5, CUST-NAME, CUST-NBR, and PROD-YTD-QUANTITY-NBR* are data elements. Derived data elements are denoted by an asterisk placed after the element name.

A designer must make two decisions about the design of data elements:

1. Whether to store the derived attribute as a data element or to calculate it.
2. Whether or not to compress the space required by the attribute. Packing a numeric data element will reduce the space needed to store the element on disk by half.

17.2.2 Record

A box with a label denotes a record (see Figure 17.7b). A record is a named group of data elements. A **logical record** corresponds to an entity or to a collection of attributes from one or many entities.

During logical database design, the designer decides how to design logical records using the entities and attributes of a conceptual data model. Records are designed in three ways:

1. **Aggregation,** or combining attributes from different entities or relationships into one record.
2. **Segmentation,** or splitting attributes from one entity or relationship into different records.
3. Copying all the attributes from one entity or intersection entity into a record.

The ORDER record in Figure 17.5 is the aggregation of the ORDER and INVOICE entities. Records PRODUCT1 and PRODUCT2 are segments of the PRODUCT entity. The CUSTOMER record is copied directly from the CUSTOMER entity.

17.2.3 Key

An underlined data element denotes a key (see Figure 17.7c). A **key** uniquely identifies an instance of a record. The key corresponds to the identifier construct presented in Chapter 11.

When more than one identifier is defined for an entity, it is necessary to specify primary and alternative keys. For example, in Figure 17.5, ORDER can be identified either by the ORDER-NBR or by the combination of CUST-NBR and ORDER-PO-NBR. ORDER-NBR is the primary key, and CUST-NBR + ORDER-PO-NBR is an alternative key of the ORDER record. Alternative keys are assigned a number to distinguish them from primary keys. For example, the combination of <1>CUST-NBR and <1>ORDER-PO-NBR is the first alternative key of ORDER (see Figure 17.7d).

17.2.4 Relationship

A **relationship** is a correspondence between records (see Figure 17.8). Relationships correspond to relationships in a conceptual data model. In Figure 17.5, the element CUST-NBR in the ORDER record specifies a relationship between the CUSTOMER and ORDER records.

Figure 17.8
Relationship
Constructs

(a) Relationship using foreign key

(b) Relationship using aggregation with maximum cardinality of many

CUSTOMER
CUST-NBR
{0,N}
--SHIP-NBR
--SHIP-DATE

(c) Relationship using aggregation with maximum cardinality of 1

SHIPMENT
SHIP-NBR
SHIP-DATE
CUST-NBR
CUST-NAME

(d) Relationship using separate record

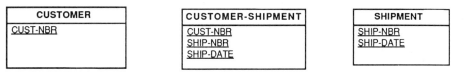

(e) Relationship using pointers

The major decision in logical database design is how to design relationships. Relationships between records can be designed in four ways:

1. The key of a related record can be included as a data element in the record. The data element is then called a **foreign key.** In Figure 17.8a, CUST-NBR is a foreign key that defines a relationship between SHIPMENT and CUSTOMER.

2. A related record can be aggregated, or absorbed, into another record. The new aggregated record may contain a repeating group, depending on the maximum cardinality of the relationship between the records. If the relationship between two records has a maximum cardinality of many and the record on the many side of the relationship is absorbed, the aggregated record will contain a repeating group. On the other hand, if the relationship between two records has a maximum cardinality of one, the new aggregated record will not contain a repeating group. In Figure 17.8b, the maximum cardinality of the relationship between CUSTOMER and SHIPMENT is many. Absorbing SHIPMENT into CUSTOMER results in a repeating group of SHIP-NBR and SHIP-DATE. The number of times that the group can repeat is denoted by a {minimum, maximum} symbol. SHIP-NBR and SHIP-DATE can repeat {0,N} times. In Figure 17.8c, absorbing CUSTOMER into SHIPMENT does not result in a repeating group because the maximum cardinality of the relationship between SHIPMENT and CUSTOMER is one.

3. A **relationship record** can be created that contains the keys of the two related records. In Figure 17.8d, the CUSTOMER-SHIPMENT record defines a relationship between CUSTOMER and SHIPMENT.

4. A **pointer** can link the two related records (see Figure 17.8e). A pointer is similar to an index (see Section 17.3.3).

17.3 Physical Database Design Constructs

Whereas the logical data structures of data elements, records, keys, and relationships describe how users view the database, the physical data structures describe how data is stored and accessed on external storage devices.

Before we discuss physical database structures, let us briefly consider external storage devices and how the data stored on them is accessed. External storage devices provide addressable locations for the storage of data. Figure 17.9 shows disk and diskette devices, the two most common types of external storage for a database. Disk devices are used for data storage because they hold large amounts of data at relatively little cost. Three actions are necessary to read and write data on a disk device. First, a read/write head is positioned over the track that contains the address of the data. The time required for this action is called the seek time. Then, the disk address of the data moves under the read/write head as the disk rotates. The time required for this operation is called the rotational delay. Finally, the data is transferred from the disk into main memory as the data rotates under the read/write head. The time required for this process is called the transfer time. Decisions about the physical structure of data will affect the time spent accessing data.

Three constructs make up a **physical data structure:** (1) physical records, (2) file organizations, and (3) indexes. For each physical construct, we will

1. Define the construct.

2. Illustrate the construct with examples from the order tracking database schema in Figure 17.6.

3. Describe the decisions that are made during design of a physical construct.

Figure 17.9
External Storage
Device

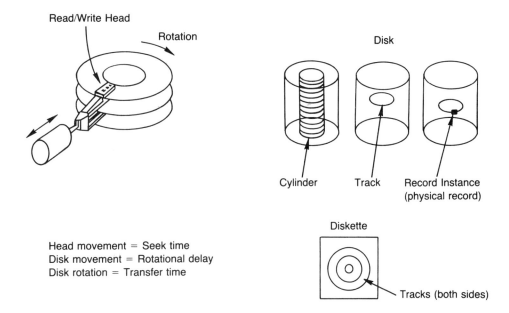

Head movement = Seek time
Disk movement = Rotational delay
Disk rotation = Transfer time

17.3.1 File Organization

A file is a named collection of record instances stored on disk (see Figure 17.10). The record instances are accessed by the values of key data elements. For example, the CUSTOMER file in Figure 17.10 allows the direct access of CUSTOMER records via the value of CUST-NBR. Entering the CUST-NBR value 145 will transfer from disk to memory the record instance

```
145  Don's Food  16 Wood Ave.  Austin  TX  78731
```

A file description is composed of a record name, key, and type of file organization (see Figure 17.10). The major decision in physical database design is how each file will be organized.

File organization refers to the physical layout of the file. There are three general types of file organization: sequential, direct, and indexed. In **sequential file organization,** the physical records are located next to each other on a disk device (see Figure 17.11). The records are in sequence according to key value or according to when the record was added (a serial type of sequential organization). The address of the first physical record in the file is known, and the remaining records are accessed by scanning the file sequentially.

In **direct file organization,** the physical records are located by the values of their key data elements (see Figure 17.11). Either the value of the key provides the exact disk address or the key value is applied a formula or function to determine the disk address of the physical record. The latter process is known as **hashing**.

In **indexed file organization,** physical records are stored in any order (sequential or random) and an index is used to locate single physical records (see Figure 17.11). An index is like a card catalog at a library. In a library, books are stored on shelves in sequential order according to book number. The book number is a key data element that allows

Figure 17.10
File Organization

CUST-NBR	CUST-NAME	CUST-BILLING-STREET-ADDR	CUST-BILLING-CITY-ADDR	CUST-BILLING-STATE-ADDR	CUST-BILLING-ZIP-CODE-ADDR
123	XYZ Inc.	PO Box 23	Austin	TX	78731
145	Don's Food	16 Wood Ave.	Austin	TX	78731
100	Computer Consultants	564 Maple Dr.	Westlake	TX	78746
198	The Daily News	115 Bedford St.	Austin	TX	78756
156	Mary's Enterprises	893 W 123 St.	Buda	TX	78610
783	Davey Jones Food	65 Meadow Dr.	Austin	TX	78746
531	Hearn's Manufacturing	5682 W 123 St.	Round Rock	TX	78664

Customer record instances

Locations on disk of Customer record instances

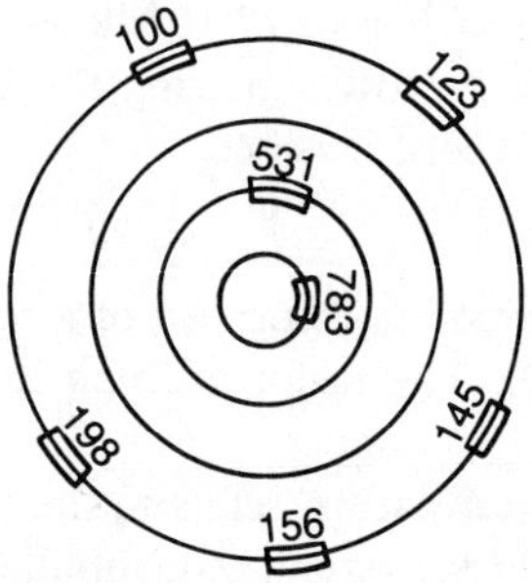

File Description
{
RECORD NAME IS CUSTOMER
KEY IS CUST-NBR
ORGANIZATION IS DIRECT USING CUST-NBR
}

instances of books (physical books, or records) to be accessed at the library. When we refer to a book, however, we use the author and/or the title. To find a specific book at the library, we could walk through each aisle and scan the author and title of every book on the shelves until we located the book. Alternatively, we could use the card catalog. The card catalog contains cards that provide book numbers by author name and subject. By looking up the name of the author or the subject of the book, it is possible to find the

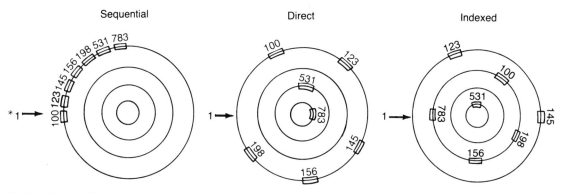

*Disk Address of Record 100 = 1

Customer Index	
Key Value	**Disk Address**
100	342
123	100
145	145
156	490
198	400
531	950
783	700

Figure 17.11 File Organization for the Customer File

book number and then the location of the book in the library. Thus, rather than searching sequentially through each book on the shelf, we can go directly to the shelf where the book is located. Similarly, in the ORDER file (see Figure 17.6), the index named INVOICE-INDEX provides access to order records via the INVOICE-NBR.

17.3.2 Physical Record

A **physical record** is the data that is located at the disk address and is transferred into main memory during data access. A physical record may correspond to one instance of a logical record, or it may be more than one instance of a logical record (that is, a block of logical records) if the file that contains the record instances is organized sequentially (see Figure 17.12). Because the unit of data transferred between an external storage device and main memory is a physical record, blocking can reduce the number of data accesses needed to satisfy a data request. The description of a physical record specifies the blocking factor (see Figure 17.12). A major decision in physical database design is how many logical records will be contained in a physical record.

Figure 17.12
Physical Records and
Blocking Factors

(a) Customer file organized sequentially with a blocking factor of 1. Seven accesses to the disk are necessary to read the entire Customer file.

Seven Physical
Records

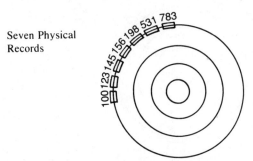

(b) Customer file organized sequentially with a blocking factor of 2. Four accesses to the disk are necessary to read the entire Customer file.

Four Physical Records,
Seven Logical
Records

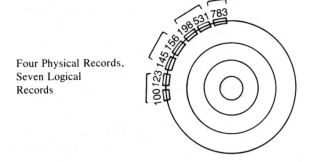

Blocking factor description: BLOCKING FACTOR IS 2.

17.3.3 Secondary Index

A **secondary index** provides access to physical records on a disk via the value of a data element that is not a primary key. Secondary indexes are used to speed up data access. For example, in Figure 17.6, the ORDER record is provided with an index for INVOICE-NBR to speed up the printing of the Order Register report (see Figure 17.13). The index is needed because the Order Register report (which is ordered by INVOICE-NBR) is a high-priority transaction in the data access table of Figure 17.4.

There are two common types of secondary indexes—inverted lists and linked lists (see Figure 17.14). An inverted list provides a cross-reference between the indexed data element and the value of the primary key for the record. The description of an index specifies the data element that is indexed. A linked list uses relative record numbers to provide links to the values of the indexed data element. The relative number of a record in a list gives the record's place relative to the beginning of the list. The link field specifies where to find the next value of the indexed element. For example, in the linked list in Figure 17.14, ORDER-NBR 25 has an ORDER-STATUS-CODE of 01 and is linked to

Report date: 8/28/90

INVOICE NUMBER	ORDER PO NUMBER	CUSTOMER NUMBER	NAME AND ADDRESS	TOTAL ORDER COST	------PRODUCT------ NO. DESCRIPTION		------QUANTITY------ ORDER BACK- TOTAL ORDERED		ITEM COST
1568	1234234	123	XYZ Inc. PO Box 23 Austin, TX	$60.00	4567	std. computer forms	3	0	$60.00
1569	345690	145	Don's Food 16 Wood Ave. Austin, TX	$225.00	4567 250	std. computer forms printer ribbons	10 5	0 0	$200.00 $25.00
1570	1234500	123	XYZ Inc. PO Box 23 Austin, TX	$475.00	4390 250 4567	special forms printer ribbons std. computer forms	4 3 15	1 0 0	$160.00 $15.00 $300.00
			TOTAL AMOUNT:	$760.00					

Figure 17.13 Order Register Report

the next record with the same ORDER-STATUS-CODE, which is relative record number 3, (ORDER-NBR 125). Linked lists are only useful for linking the values of keys that are not unique—for example, indexing ORDER-STATUS-CODE (the non-unique key) to ORDER-NBR. Kroenke and Dolan provide a good explanation of inverted and linked lists.[1]

An important decision in physical database design is which data elements in a record require indexes. The designer reviews the data access table to decide which elements require indexes.

17.4 Database Management Systems

Chapter 8 stressed that the objective of the data-oriented approach is to build databases that are shared by multiple application systems. The variety of possible logical and physical data structures, combined with the many possible application systems that may need to access data, creates a very difficult design problem. Every program in an application system that accesses the database must have a description of the logical and physical structures that define the data. If the structure of the shared data is maintained by the programs themselves, it is difficult to preserve consistency of the structures as programs are added and changed and new applications are developed. Database management systems provide a solution to this problem.

A **database management system (DBMS)** is a software system that maintains and controls the logical and physical structure of data independently of the programs that use

Figure 17.14
Secondary Index

Instances of Order Records

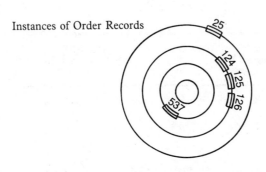

Secondary Index of INVOICE-NBR to ORDER-NBR **Inverted List**		Secondary Index of ORDER-STATUS-CODE to ORDER-NBR **Linked List**			
INVOICE-NBR	**ORDER-NBR**	**ORDER-NBR**	**ORDER-STATUS-CODE**	**LINK**	**Relative Record Number**
1568	25	25	01	3	1
1569	126	124	02	5	2
1570	537	125	01	4	3
1571	124	126	01	0	4
1582	125	537	02	0	5

Index Description: INDEXED ON INVOICE-NBR.
                     INDEXED ON ORDER-STATUS-CODE.

the data (see Figure 17.15). All access requests for data from programs and from users' queries go through the DBMS. To control the use of data for different programs and users, the DBMS imposes rules on how data is logically and physically defined.

When a DBMS is used to manage a database, the designer specifies a **database schema,** which describes the logical and physical data structure of the database (see Figure 17.6). The schema is specified using the data description language (DDL) of the DBMS. The DBMS schema describes

1. Components of the logical data structure, including data elements, logical records, keys, and relationships.

2. Components of the physical data structure, including physical records, file organizations, and indexes.

3. Integrity parameters such as validation criteria, access authorization, and backup and recovery policies.

Every commercial DBMS conforms to certain rules, or standards, for the definition

Figure 17.15
Overview of DBMS
Functions

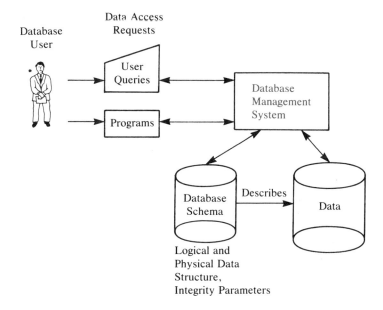

of the logical data structure. These rules are called the data structure class* of the DBMS. DBMSs also have rules that control the physical data structure, although these rules cannot be easily categorized by the type of DBMS. Figure 17.16 summarizes the rules for logical and physical data structures used by three broad categories of DBMSs: hierarchical, network, and relational. A detailed discussion of the three data structure classes can be found in Everest and Kroenke and Dolan.[2]

Figure 17.16
Rules for Logical and
Physical Data
Structures

	Hierarchical	Network	Relational
Records:			
Segmentation	yes	yes	yes
Aggregation	yes	yes	only for 0,1 or 1,1 relationships; no repeating groups allowed
Relationships:			
Foreign key	yes	yes	yes
Separate record	yes	yes	yes
Pointer	yes	yes	NA
Aggregation	yes	yes	only for 0,1 or 1,1 relationships; absorb M to 1 only
Secondary indexes	yes	yes	yes

*The data structure class is often referred to as the data structure or the underlying data model supported by the DBMS.

For the designer of an information system, the most important rules of a data structure class are those that govern how records and their relationships are established. This is because the design of records and relationships in a database influences the design of programs that access the database. As can be seen in Figure 17.16, both the hierarchical and network data structure classes allow record segmentation and aggregation, as well as the design of relationships using foreign keys, records, and pointers. The relational data structure class does not allow some forms of record aggregation* and limits the design of relationships to foreign keys and separate records. We will now discuss these three data structure classes in more detail.

17.4.1 Hierarchical DBMS

A hierarchical data structure class requires the use of hierarchical relationships between records. In a **hierarchical DBMS,** records are referred to as parents and children. Each record can have only one parent, but each parent can have many child records. When designing a hierarchical data structure, the designer must decide which records are parent records and which are child records. In mapping a conceptual data model into a hierarchical data structure, a general rule of thumb is to make the "1" side of a 1:M relationship the parent record and the "M" side the child record. Logical pointers are used to create a hierarchy when relationships in a conceptual data model are not hierarchical (for example, pointers would be used for the relationships between the ORDER, ORDER-ITEM, and PRODUCT entities in Figure 17.3.) Figure 17.17 illustrates the translation of the Universal conceptual data model into a hierarchical data structure class.

An important hierarchical DBMS is IBM's Information Management System (IMS). In IMS, records are called segments (SEGM). Sample DDL statements for an IMS database are shown in Figure 17.18.

17.4.2 Network DBMS

In a **network DBMS,** records can be related in any way. Network DBMSs are usually based on the CODASYL** database standard. Because hierarchies of records are not required, a conceptual data model developed using the rules from Chapter 11 can be transformed directly into a schema supported by a CODASYL-type DBMS. In network databases, relationships between records are typically implemented as pointers. The CODASYL construct for a pointer is called a SET. Figure 17.19 illustrates the transformation of the conceptual data model for the Universal database into a network data structure class.

---

*More accurately, the relational data structure class does not allow repeating groups of data elements. Therefore, any records that share a relationship with a maximum cardinality of many cannot be aggregated in the relational data structure class. For example, the aggregation of ORDER and ORDER-ITEM would not be allowed, as it would result in a repeating group of ORDER-ITEM within the ORDER record. The aggregation of ORDER and INVOICE, on the other hand, would be allowed because the two records share a relationship with a maximum cardinality of one. Therefore, the aggregated record would not have a repeating group.

**CODASYL, which stands for Conference on Data Systems Languages, is an organization that has developed standards for the network data structure class.

Figure 17.17
Translating the Universal, Inc. Data Model into a Hierarchical Structure

(a) Problem: Represent the conceptual data model in Figure 17.3 as a hierarchical data structure.
Solution:

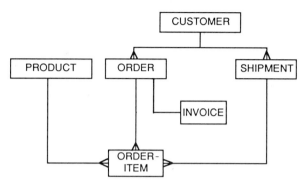

(b) Problem: Translate the hierarchical model from (a) so that ORDER-ITEM has three parent records: PRODUCT, ORDER, and SHIPMENT.
Solution: Duplicate ORDER-ITEM under each parent record.

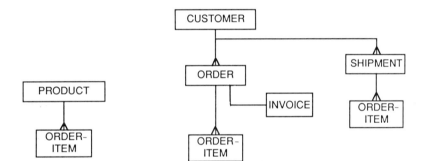

(c) Problem: There are three ORDER-ITEM records.
Solution: Use logical pointers to eliminate redundant ORDER-ITEM records. One ORDER-ITEM record with the parent ORDER is maintained, and PRODUCT and SHIPMENT records are provided with logical pointers to the ORDER-ITEM record.

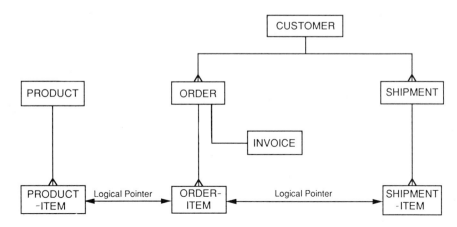

Figure 17.18
Sample IMS DDL for
the Universal, Inc.
Database

```
DBD       NAME = CUSTDB, ACCESS

SEGM      NAME = CUSTOMER, PARENT = 0, BYTES =
FIELD     NAME = CUST-NBR, BYTES = 10, START = 1
FIELD     NAME = CUST-NAME, BYTES = 40, START = 11
          ―――
          ―――
          ―――

SEGM      NAME = ORDER, PARENT = CUSTOMER, BYTES =
```

Important CODASYL-type network DBMSs include Cullinet's IDMS, Unisys's DMS II, and Software AG's ADABAS. Sample CODASYL DDL statements for the Universal database are shown in Figure 17.20.

Figure 17.19
Translating the
Universal, Inc.
Data Model
into a Network
Structure

Represent the conceptual model as a network, with relationships specified via pointers.

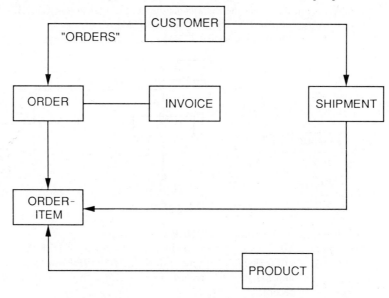

17.4.3 Relational DBMS

In a **relational DBMS,** records must be related using common data elements (that is, foreign keys), separate records or aggregation. Records are called relations or tables in a relational DBMS. Figure 17.21 illustrates the translation of the Universal conceptual data model into a relational data structure class.

Important relational DBMSs include IBM's DB2, Oracle's Oracle, Ashton-Tate's dBase IV, and Microrim's r:BASE System V. Sample DB2 DDL statements using Structured Query Language (SQL) are shown in Figure 17.22. Note that there is no DDL statement that directly specifies a key. It is the responsibility of the database user to know which data element is the primary key for the table.

Figure 17.20

Sample CODASYL DDL for the Universal, Inc. Database

```
SCHEMA NAME IS UNIVERSAL

RECORD NAME IS CUSTOMER
    LOCATION MODE IS CALC CUST-NBR
    CUST-NBR PIC IS INTEGER (10)
    CUST-NAME PIC IS CHAR (40);

    =====
    =====

RECORD NAME IS ORDER
    LOCATION MODE IS CALC ORDER-NBR
    ORDER-NBR PIC IS INTEGER (10)
    =====
    =====
    CUST-NBR PIC IS INTEGER (10)


SET NAME IS ORDERS
    MODE IS CHAIN
    ORDER IS NEXT
    OWNER IS PRODUCT1
    MEMBER IS ORDER-ITEM
    FIXED AUTOMATIC
    SET OCCURRENCE SELECTION
        IS THRU CURRENT OF SET


    =====
    =====
    =====

END SCHEMA
```

Figure 17.21

Translating the Universal, Inc. Data Model into a Relational Structure

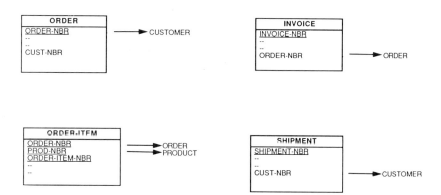

Figure 17.22
Sample DB2 DDL
Statements Using SQL
for the Universal, Inc.
Database

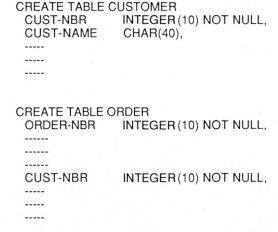

```
CREATE TABLE CUSTOMER
    CUST-NBR        INTEGER (10) NOT NULL,
    CUST-NAME       CHAR(40),
    -----
    -----
    -----


CREATE TABLE ORDER
    ORDER-NBR       INTEGER (10) NOT NULL,
    ------
    ------
    ------
    CUST-NBR        INTEGER (10) NOT NULL,
    -----
    -----
    -----
```

An important concept for record design in a relational DBMS is normalization. **Normalization** is a technique for minimizing redundancy by structuring data elements within records so that the elements are represented only once in the database. The primary benefit of a normalized data structure is a flexible database. That is, new records and data elements can be added to the database without extensive changes to the existing database and programs that access the database. We will discuss database flexibility in Section 17.5. A detailed discussion of normalization is beyond the scope of this text, but an illustration of normalization is provided in Appendix A. In addition, Kroenke and Dolan provide very detailed examples of normalization.[3]

17.5 Guidelines for Database Design

Because a DBMS is typically used by many systems, the database administrator (DBA) is usually the person who controls the design of databases managed by the DBMS. In this development environment, the systems analyst must still be aware of general principles of database design in order to help the DBA design a high-quality database for the application system.* The following guidelines for database design will help you to transform a conceptual data model into logical and physical data structures that will be implemented by a DBMS.

17.5.1 Criteria for Database Design Quality

Traditionally the quality of a database has been measured in terms of the amount of disk storage used by the database and the response time of the reports and screens that access the database. This narrow focus on efficiency during design, however, can lead to an inflexible database that cannot easily satisfy the requirements of new application systems. In addition to being efficient, a database must be flexible and maintain a high level of data integrity.

*Using the data-oriented approach discussed in Chapter 8 to design a database for an application system usually involves making changes to existing databases.

Database flexibility corresponds to the criteria of ease of maintenance and adaptability presented in Figure 2.3 of Chapter 2. An easy-to-maintain database is one that can readily accommodate new application systems or changes in the reports and screens of existing applications. A database is flexible if any new application requirements can be satisfied with only minor changes (such as adding a data element to a record) to the existing logical data structure. For example, if a new inventory application were developed at Universal, then the inventory reports and screens should be able to use production information in the order tracking database with only minor changes to the PRODUCT record.

Database integrity corresponds to the characteristic of reliability presented in Figure 2.3 of Chapter 2. Specifically, database integrity measures how successful the database is at withstanding threats to its existence, accuracy, and confidentiality. Maintaining the integrity of data is important in ensuring user confidence in the database.

The existence of a database is threatened by the accidental or intentional destruction of data. An entire database can be lost if a fire or natural disaster destroys the computer hardware. Hardware failures, such as a head crash, can also destroy a database. In a microcomputer environment, accidental (or intentional) erasure of floppy diskettes or even entire hard disks by users is possible. Partial destruction of data can occur whenever a program terminates abnormally. Abnormal termination may be caused by a power failure, a common problem with microcomputers.

The accuracy of a database is threatened by errors in input data. One error users commonly make is to forget to put the decimal point in an entry (for example, putting $10,000 instead of $100.00).

Confidentiality is threatened when the data is accessed by unauthorized users. Confidential data includes personal data, such as employee information, the credit ratings of customers, or medical histories of patients, and organizational data considered a competitive secret, such as names of customers or designs for new products.

Database efficiency is a function of the response times for reports and screens and the amount of disk space used by the database. The fact that a designer should not overemphasize efficiency during data base design does not mean that the efficiency is unimportant. The importance of designing a database for efficiency results from the two basic limitations of external storage devices: (1) slow data access and (2) limited storage space.

External storage devices need time to locate and transfer data into the memory before it can be processed. The three mechanical actions needed to locate and transfer data from a disk device to memory—head movement, disk movement, and disk rotation—result in seek time, rotational delay, and transfer time (see Figure 17.9). The most time consuming of these is seek time.

The storage capacity of a device depends on the number of tracks and the number of characters (8-bit bytes) per track. A double-sided $3\frac{1}{2}$ inch diskette with 80 tracks holds 46,800 characters per track and 720,000 characters per diskette.

Users will often demand database designs that emphasize efficiency. If the Order Register report in Figure 17.13 printed 1000 orders and the user wanted the response time for the report to be minimal, the designer would need to design a database that minimized the number of accesses to the disk required to generate the report. Alternatively, the designer could try to persuade the user to acquire a disk device that was very fast. In contrast, if the database was designed for a microcomputer with a 10-megabyte hard disk, and the disk had only 1 megabyte of usable space (the other 9 megabytes were being used by programs and other databases), the designer should probably place a premium on a design that conserved disk space. Alternatively, the designer might try to persuade the user to increase the size of the hard disk to 20 megabytes to lessen the severity of the constraint.

The three quality criteria of flexibility, integrity, and efficiency should guide the designer during the database design process. Considering each of these criteria during database design presents, however, an overwhelmingly complex design problem. In order to manage the complexity, it is necessary to divide database design into steps that focus on the design of logical and then physical data structures. During the first step, the data structures of data elements, records, keys, and relationships are designed within the data structure class supported by the DBMS used to implement the database. During the second step, the data structures of physical records, file organization, and secondary indexes are designed for the database. The next two sections provide guidelines for logical and physical database design.

17.5.2 Logical Database Design

Logical database design consists of designing the logical elements, records, and relationships of a database so as to maximize flexibility and efficiency. Integrity criteria are addressed during physical design, because data integrity refers to the actual physical data that resides in the database.

Flexibility   Figure 17.23 summarizes the guidelines for designing a flexible database. In general, a normalized data structure will produce the most flexible database (see Appendix A). The conceptual data model that is used for logical database design should already be normalized. Therefore, the most important guideline for record design is to change the conceptual data model as little as possible during the transformation to the logical data structure class of the DBMS.

Efficiency   Designing an efficient database requires an understanding of (1) the storage space currently available on disk devices, (2) the volumes of record instances, and (3) the characteristics of database retrievals and updates. Disk space availability is determined by

Figure 17.23
Guidelines for
Designing a Flexible
Database

Construct	Guidelines
Data elements	Do not store derived data elements. The values of derived data elements can easily become inconsistent with the values of elements used to calculate the derived elements; controls are needed to guard against inconsistencies.
Records	Normalize data elements. Simple, nonredundant structures are easier to change.
Relationships	Use separate records or foreign keys to implement relationships with a maximum cardinality of N. Aggregated records are less flexible.

analyzing the usage of existing disk devices. The volumes of record instances are determined by asking users (for example, asking the sales manager how many customers the company has) and/or by analyzing the files of existing systems (for example, checking how many records are in the customer file). The characteristics of critical database retrievals and updates are determined from report and screen specifications and/or from data flow diagrams. Using the data flow diagram for the Universal order tracking system (see Figure 17.24), the Universal designers documented three critical transactions in the data access table in Figure 17.4: the Order Register report (see Figure 17.13), Order Entry screen, and Invoice Entry Screen (see Figure 17.25).

Figure 17.24
DFD for Universal, Inc.
Order Tracking
System

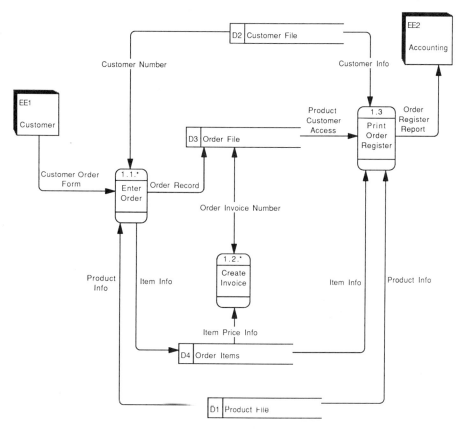

Figure 17.4 gives characteristics of data access that are needed to evaluate the response time of a report or screen: the action (retrieve/update), the entities that are selected by the access, the access keys used to order the retrieval or update, the cycle (frequency of execution of the retrieval), and the activity (percentage of record instances selected by the data access). When a data access table is constructed, each critical transaction is assigned a number based on its priority.

Using the data access table and the information about the space available on existing disk devices, the designer can change the logical data structure so as to efficiently satisfy

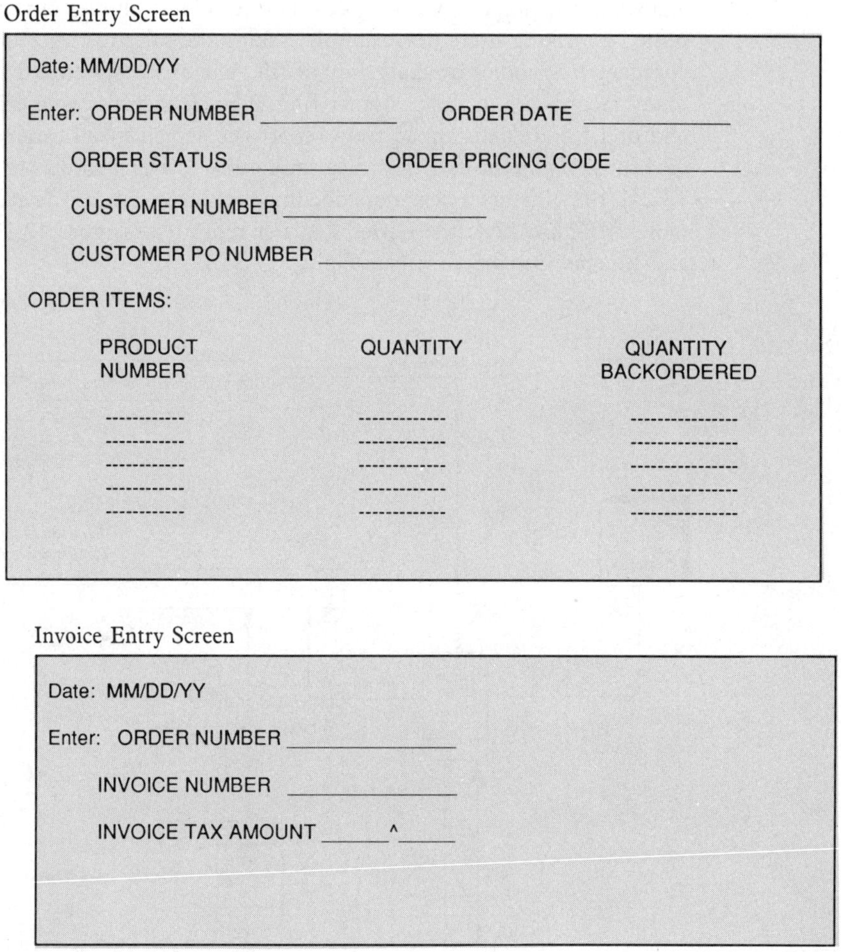

Figure 17.25
Order and Invoice
Entry Screens

Order Entry Screen

Invoice Entry Screen

storage and response time requirements. Figure 17.26 provides general guidelines for improving the efficiency of data storage and data access. Designing for efficiency of storage and response time involves the logical data structures of (1) data elements, (2) logical records, and (3) relationships.

1. *Data elements.* There are two decisions to be made concerning the logical design of data elements: (1) whether to store or calculate derived elements and (2) whether or not to pack numeric data elements. The decision as to whether to store or calculate derived data elements should be made on an element-by-element basis. When a derived element is not stored, less storage space is used by the database. Calculating a derived element can, however, dramatically increase access time for a record. This increase occurs because many accesses to disk may be necessary to calculate the element value. For example, calculating the value

Figure 17.26
Guidelines for
Efficiency of Data
Storage and Data
Access

Construct	Storage	Access	
		Update	**Retrieval**
Logical Design			
Data element	Do not store derived elements—they use storage space.	Do not store derived elements—updates will require calculation of new values for derived elements.	Store derived data elements—if derived elements are not stored, additional reads will be necessary to retrieve the elements.
Record	Not applicable	Segment and/or aggregate.*	Segment and/or aggregate.*
Relationship	No clear guideline is possible.	Aggregating related records will save one read/write per related record.	Aggregating related records will save one read per related record.
Physical Design			
File organization	Use sequential organization—less space is wasted between records on disk with sequential organization.	Depends on the characteristics of the updates.**	Depends on the characteristics of the retrievals.**
Physical record	A higher blocking factor saves space, because fewer gaps are needed between records.	Use a high blocking factor if the whole file or a high percentage of it is updated sequentially.	Use a high blocking factor if a high percentage of records in a file are retrieved sequentially.
Secondary index	Minimize the number of indexes—they use space.	No clear guideline is possible—indexes will speed retrievals, but the indexes must be updated when records are added or deleted—increasing the time required for an update.	Secondary indexes will speed retrievals of records.

*See Figure 17.27.
**See Figure 17.29.

of PROD-YTD-QUANTITY-NBR* in a report requires accessing many ORDER-ITEM records (the PROD-YTD-QUANTITY-NBR* is derived from the element ITEM-QUANTITY-NBR in the ORDER-ITEM record). Storing the value of PROD-YTD-QUANTITY-NBR*, however, requires an extra access to a PRODUCT record when an order is entered in the database. If the derived element is not stored, the PRODUCT file is only read to find the value of PROD-

COST-AMT. If the value is stored, however, the PRODUCT record must be updated (read and then written back with the new value of PROD-YTD-QUANTITY-NBR*). The decision as to whether or not to store derived data elements requires an analysis of all transactions that use the derived elements. Packing (compressing) a numeric data element that is used for calculations is always desirable, because packing will both save storage space and increase the speed of data access. Access speed is increased because less data must be transferred from disk to main memory. When a data element is defined as packed, the DBMS uses 4-bit rather than 8-bit characters to store the element. Hence, packed elements use about half the space of normal characters.*

2. *Logical records.* Logical records can be segmented or aggregated to speed up access time. Figure 17.27 provides guidelines for segmenting and aggregating records. In general, aggregation is considered if elements from multiple records occur together and are frequently retrieved or updated. For example, in Figure 17.5, the aggregation of the INVOICE record into the ORDER record reduces the time required to print the Order Register report by at least one access to disk for each order printed on the report. This is because a separate access to the database is not required for orders when an invoice is accessed.

Figure 17.27
Guidelines for Segmentation and Aggregation

	Speed of Response	
	Essential	**Not Essential**
Entities are frequently accessed together	Aggregate entities into one record	Leave entities as designed
Attributes within an entity are rarely used together by the same transaction	Segment attributes into separate records	Leave entities as designed

Adapted from: S. J. March and J. V. Carlis, "Query Processing in Data Base Systems," in W. Kim, D. Reiner and D. Batory, eds., *Physical Data Base Design: Techniques for Improved Data Base Performance* (New York: Springer-Verlag, 1984), pp. 19–37.

Segmentation of logical records can be used if some elements from a record are updated and retrieved infrequently and other elements from the same record are retrieved frequently. The PROD-NBR and PROD-DESC-TEXT are the only data elements of the PRODUCT record that are needed for the Order Register report. The other PRODUCT attributes, PROD-YTD-QUANTITY-NBR* and PROD-COST-AMT, are used only for the Order Entry screen. In Figure 17.5, the PRODUCT record is therefore segmented into two records to speed the printing of the Order Register report. Record PRODUCT2 is identified by PROD-NBR and has PROD-DESC-TEXT as its only element. Record PRODUCT1 is also identified by PROD-NBR, but its elements are PROD-COST-AMT and PROD-YTD-QUANTITY-NBR*. Of course, the Order Entry screen might have

*To calculate the storage space for packed data elements, add 1 to the number of digits, divide by 2, and round up to the nearest integer.

a slower response time, because it would have to access two PRODUCT records, rather than one.

3. *Relationships.* The design of relationships between records is dictated by the type of DBMS used to implement the database. A relationship in a relational database must be implemented as a foreign key an aggregated table or as a separate table (logical record) that contains the identifiers of the two related tables. Relationships that are implemented as foreign keys provide faster access to related records than do relationships implemented via separate tables. Access via separate tables is slower because a separate access to disk is necessary to read the relationship table. Network and hierarchical DBMSs can use pointers, foreign keys, or separate logical records for relationships. In network and hierarchical DBMSs, using pointers results in faster access to related records than does using foreign keys or related logical records.

17.5.3 Physical Database Design

Physical database design involves designing the physical structures of a database so as to maximize integrity and efficiency.

Integrity Figure 17.28 summarizes the controls used to protect the existence, accuracy, and confidentiality of data. The most common types of controls are (1) backup and recovery procedures to protect the existence of data, (2) data validation controls to protect the accuracy of data, and (3) passwords to protect the confidentiality of data. The detail with which these controls can be specified depends on the sophistication of the DBMS used to implement the system. All mainframe DBMSs, such as DB2 and IDMS, provide exten-

Figure 17.28 Guidelines for Integrity Controls	**Existence**	**Accuracy**	**Confidentiality**
	1. Backup and recovery controls: Periodically copy files onto tape or diskette. Write update transactions onto a log file. Record record image before and after update transactions. 2. Procedural controls: Remove commands, such as the MS-DOS FORMAT command, that can destroy data.	1. Validation controls: Use edit-checks on input screens. 2. Backup and recovery controls: Record record image before and after update transactions.	1. Access controls: Passwords 2. Isolation: Remove sensitive data from the disk and store it on diskette or tape when the data is not in use. 3. Monitoring: Write data access requests to an audit trail. 4. Encryption: Disguise the values of data elements.

sive backup, recovery, and password controls. On the other hand, microcomputer DBMSs such as dBASE IV and R:BASE System V do not provide extensive backup and recovery controls and have only limited password protection. For microcomputer DBMSs, the designer must be careful to provide users with manual procedures (for example, making two copies on diskette of important files) to control the integrity of the database.

Efficiency   Guidelines for efficiency are presented for (1) physical records, (2) file organization, and (3) index structures.

1. *Physical records.* The blocking of logical records into physical records is an important technique for improving the efficiency of a database. When physical records are stored sequentially, the speed of update and retrieval can be increased by reading blocks of more than one record instance at a time from external storage. When blocking is used, one access to disk will read more than one logical record into external storage. As a general rule, high blocking factors should be used for files that are organized and read sequentially.

2. *File organization.* Figure 17.29 provides general guidelines for designing file organizations. As Figure 17.29 shows, the selection of sequential, direct, or indexed sequential file organization depends on the number of records that are accessed by critical transactions. In general, if the most critical transactions access more than 10 percent of the records in a file, the file should be organized sequentially.

Figure 17.29
Guidelines for
Designing File
Organization

Quantity of Records Accessed by Critical Transactions	Speed of Response	
	Essential	**Not Essential**
One record	Direct	Indexed or sequential
Less than 10%	Indexed	Indexed or sequential
More than 10%	Sequential	Sequential

Source: D. G. Severence and J. V. Carlis, "A Practical Approach to Selecting Record Access Paths," *Computing Surveys,* vol. 9, no. 4, December 1977.

A sequential organization efficiently supports reports and screens that access a large percentage of physical records in a file. This is because only one access motion—that is, one seek of the disk read/write head—is needed to locate the first record. Accesses to the remaining records do not require movement of the read/write head. An efficient organization of the ORDER file for printing the Order Register report in Figure 17.13 would be sequentially by the value of INVOICE-NBR, because the Order Register report is ordered by INVOICE-NBR. A sequential file organization does not, however, support efficient generation of reports and screens that access a small percentage of physical records in a file. Delays in access occur because most of the file must be scanned to locate only one record.

A direct file organization provides efficient access to single physical records in a file, because only one access per record is required. In Figure 17.6, the CUSTOMER file is organized as a direct file on CUST-NBR because the Order Entry screen (see Figure 17.25) requires only single instances of customer records and the Order Register report must access single instances of the CUSTOMER file by CUST-NBR.* On the other hand, a direct organization does not provide efficient access for reports and screens requiring a large percentage of physical records, because a separate access is needed for each record.

An indexed organization provides both sequential and random access to physical records. An indexed sequential organization efficiently supports the data accesses of multiple reports and screens that require both large and small percentages of instances from different records.

3. *Secondary indexes.* Secondary indexes make access to record instances more efficient, but they also make the updating of those record instances less efficient. Indexes make transaction updates less efficient because the indexes must be updated when a record is deleted or added. In addition, indexes use disk space. In Figure 17.6, the INVOICE-NBR index for the ORDER file (the SET INVOICE-INDEX) will speed the printing of the Order Register report, which is the highest priority transaction for the Universal database. The index, however, will increase the time needed to enter an invoice using the Invoice Entry screen (see Figure 17.25), because an entry must be created for the index when the Order record is updated. Also, the INVOICE-NBR index will increase the storage space used by the Universal database by at least the number of ORDER records times the length of the INVOICE-NBR element and the length of the ORDER-NBR element. In general, indexes should be used only for data elements needed for the most critical transactions. Using the INVOICE-NBR index in Figure 17.6 makes sense, because the Order Register report is a critical transaction that requires fast response time.

17.6 Designing a Database

The logical and physical database structures guide the design of a database. The steps in designing a database for a system are as follows:

1. Design the logical database.

   1.1 Transform the conceptual data model into a logical database design that conforms to the data structure class of the DBMS.

   1.2 Evaluate and change the logical design for flexibility.

---

*The file organization is direct because the location of each record is calculated, or hashed, based on the value of CUST-NBR; the CODASYL schema statement is LOCATION MODE IS CALC CUST-NBR. For a discussion of the difference between LOCATION MODE IS CALC and LOCATION MODE IS VIA, see D. M. Kroenke and K. A. Dolan, *Database Processing: Fundamentals, Design, Implementation,* 3rd ed. (Chicago: Science Research Associates, 1988), pp. 529–530.

Figure 17.30
Method for Database
Design

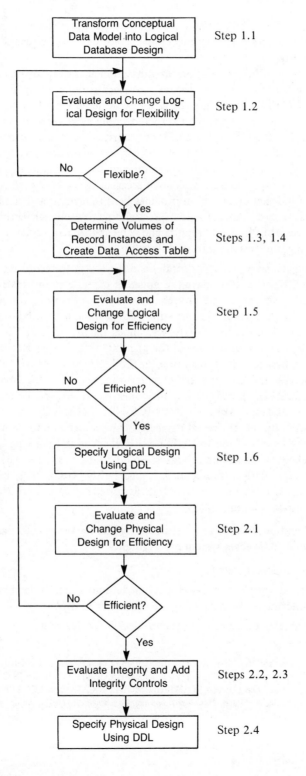

1.3 Determine volumes of record instances.

1.4 Create a data access table using a list of system interfaces.

1.5 Evaluate and change the logical design for efficiency.

1.6 Specify the logical design using the DDL of the DBMS.

2. Design the physical database.

2.1 Evaluate and change the physical design for efficiency.

2.2 Evaluate the database for integrity.

2.3 Add integrity controls to the database design.

2.4 Specify the physical design using the DDL of the DBMS.

When the design is complete, the deliverables will include the DDL for the logical and physical data structures of the database. The method for database design is shown in the form of a flowchart in Figure 17.30.

17.6.1 Database Design from an Ordered Example

The following minicase uses the ordered example of the Meadows Pharmacy case to show how a database design is developed. The development team consists of Jayne Ingerson, the data analyst, and John Kay, the database administrator.

Return to Meadows Hospital

1. Design the Logical Database

1.1 Transform the conceptual data model into a logical database design. The management of Meadows Hospital has decided that the pharmacy database should be implemented on the IBM DB2 database management system that was purchased last year. Because DB2 is a relational database, Jayne and John start the design process by transforming the conceptual data model in Figure 17.31 into a relational data structure class.

When transforming the attribute names to data element names, Jayne and John abbreviate them, because DB2 has a 17-character name limit. Keys are formed by combining the keys from dependent entities. For example, the key for DRUG-BRAND becomes the combination of DRUG-NAME and DRUGSP-VEN-ID-NBR, because the DRUG-BRAND entity is dependent on the DRUG-SUPPLIER and DRUG entities. Relationships from the conceptual model are implemented via foreign keys in the logical database design. For example, the relationship with a maximum cardinality of N between PRESCRIPTION and PHARMACIST is implemented by defining the foreign key PHAR-EMP-ID-NBR in the PRESCRIPTION record. The logical database design for the pharmacy system is shown in Figure 17.32.

1.2 Refine the logical design for flexibility. Next, Jayne and John refine the logical database design for flexibility. Only one derived data element, DRUGB-YTD-USE-NBR* is defined for the pharmacy database. John and Jayne decide to wait until the logical design is refined for efficiency to decide whether to store the derived element. Next, they must determine whether the relationships between the PRESCRIPTION record and the PATIENT, PHYSICIAN, and PHARMACIST records should

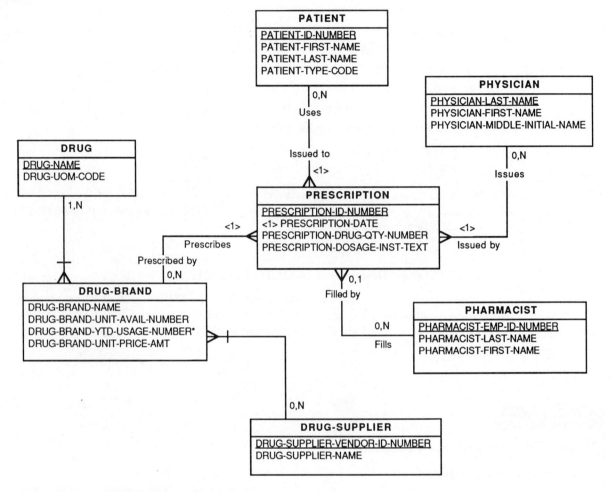

Figure 17.31   Pharmacy Conceptual Data Model

be changed from foreign keys to separate relationship tables. In the current logical design, the foreign keys reflect the cardinalities in the conceptual data model. To determine whether any of the cardinalities should be changed to "many to many," John and Jayne ask Mary Henderson, the pharmacy manager, if, in the future, it is possible that a prescription will ever be

- issued to more than one patient,
- issued by more than one physician, or
- filled by more than one pharmacist.

If so, then the relationships should be implemented as sep-

arate tables instead of foreign keys. A separate table would reflect a many-to-many relationship. Mary convinces Jayne and John that the cardinalities of the relationships should not be changed. Hence, no changes are made to the logical structures.

1.3 Determine record volumes. Jayne and John gather information on the expected number of instances for each record in the logical structure:

```
PRESCRIPTION = 30,000 (the pharmacy keeps
                      all prescriptions on file
                      for one year)
```

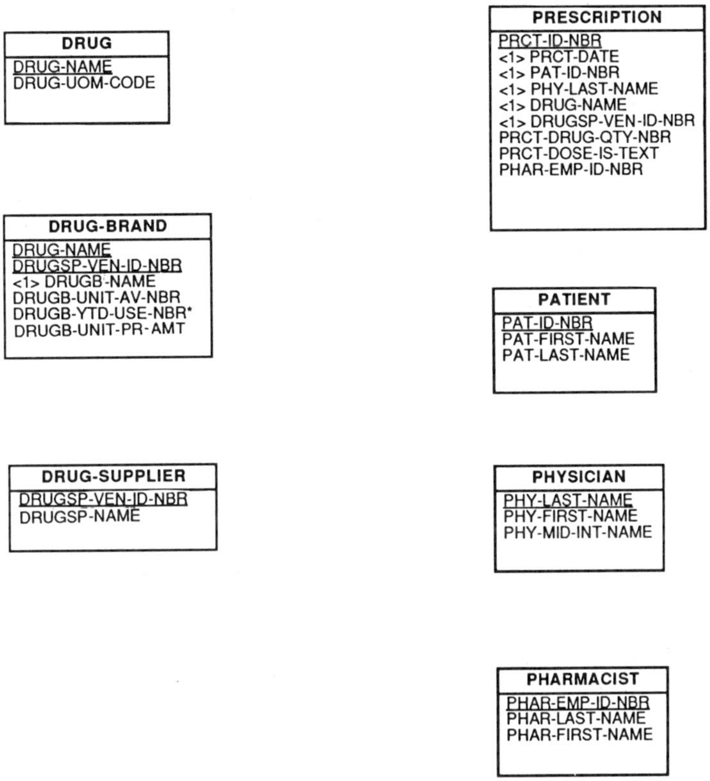

Figure 17.32

Preliminary Relational
Data Structure for
the Pharmacy
Database

```
          DRUG
   ┌───────────────────┐
   │ DRUG-NAME         │
   │ DRUG-UOM-CODE     │
   └───────────────────┘


       DRUG-BRAND
   ┌───────────────────────┐
   │ DRUG-NAME             │
   │ DRUGSP-VEN-ID-NBR     │
   │ <1> DRUGB-NAME        │
   │ DRUGB-UNIT-AV-NBR     │
   │ DRUGB-YTD-USE-NBR*    │
   │ DRUGB-UNIT-PR-AMT     │
   └───────────────────────┘


       DRUG-SUPPLIER
   ┌───────────────────────┐
   │ DRUGSP-VEN-ID-NBR     │
   │ DRUGSP-NAME           │
   └───────────────────────┘
```

```
          PRESCRIPTION
   ┌───────────────────────────┐
   │ PRCT-ID-NBR               │
   │ <1> PRCT-DATE             │
   │ <1> PAT-ID-NBR            │
   │ <1> PHY-LAST-NAME         │
   │ <1> DRUG-NAME             │
   │ <1> DRUGSP-VEN-ID-NBR     │
   │ PRCT-DRUG-QTY-NBR         │
   │ PRCT-DOSE-IS-TEXT         │
   │ PHAR-EMP-ID-NBR           │
   └───────────────────────────┘


           PATIENT
   ┌───────────────────────┐
   │ PAT-ID-NBR            │
   │ PAT-FIRST-NAME        │
   │ PAT-LAST-NAME         │
   └───────────────────────┘


          PHYSICIAN
   ┌───────────────────────┐
   │ PHY-LAST-NAME         │
   │ PHY-FIRST-NAME        │
   │ PHY-MID-INT-NAME      │
   └───────────────────────┘


          PHARMACIST
   ┌───────────────────────┐
   │ PHAR-EMP-ID-NBR       │
   │ PHAR-LAST-NAME        │
   │ PHAR-FIRST-NAME       │
   └───────────────────────┘
```

PHARMACIST	= 5
PATIENT	= 1000
PHYSICIAN	= 150
DRUG	= 1000
DRUG-BRAND	= 2000
SUPPLIER	= 25

John also determines that 100 megabytes of disk space is available for the pharmacy database.

1.4 Create a data access table. To evaluate the efficiency of the design, Jayne and John construct the data access table shown in Figure 17.33, using the list of pharmacy system interfaces in Figure 17.34. (The list was the created during interface design.) The Daily Drug report is given the highest priority, because it must be printed every day after the pharmacy closes at 5 P.M. and must be delivered to the Administration department before 7 P.M. The Prescription Update screen is given the second highest priority, because pharmacists will be using the screen frequently. The Supplier report is given the third highest priority, because it also must be printed every day after the pharmacy closes, but is not delivered to the Inventory department until the following morning. The Prescription Entry screen is given the lowest priority.

1.5 Evaluate and change the logical design for efficiency. Using the volumes of record instances and the data access table in Figure 17.33, Jayne and John first review the derived data element, DRUGB-YTD-USE-NBR*, to determine whether it should be stored or calculated. They review the definition of the derived attribute (from Chapter 11): for a given brand of drug (identified by DRUGB-NAME), find prescriptions that prescribe the DRUGB-NAME and that have a PRCT-DATE greater than or equal to the first day of the year; sum the value of PRCT-DRUG-QTY-NBR for each prescription found. Storing DRUGB-YTD-USE-NBR* would increase the data access time for the Prescription Update screen, because both a retrieval and an update of the DRUG-

Transaction Priority	Transaction Name	Action	Entities Accessed	Access Key	Cycle	Activity
1	Daily Drug Report	Retrieve	PRESCRIPTION	PRCT-DATE	daily	1% (= 100/day)
		Retrieve	PHYSICIAN			
		Retrieve	PATIENT			
		Retrieve	PHARMACIST			
		Retrieve	DRUG-BRAND			
2	Update Prescription Screen	Update/retrieve	PRESCRIPTION	PRCT-ID-NBR	daily	1% (= 100/day)
		Retrieve	PHYSICIAN			
		Retrieve	PATIENT			
		Retrieve	PHARMACIST			
		Retrieve/update	DRUG-BRAND			
		Retrieve	DRUG			
3	Supplier Report	Retrieve	SUPPLIER	DRUGSP-NAME	daily	100%
		Retrieve	DRUG-BRAND			
4	Prescription Entry Screen	Update	PRESCRIPTION	PRCT-ID-NBR	daily	1% (= 100/day)
		Retrieve	PHYSICIAN			

Figure 17.33   Data Access Table for the Pharmacy System

BRAND record would be required to store the value of DRUGB-YTD-USE-NBR*. They decide that the increase in access time would not be noticeable. On the other hand, not storing DRUGB-YTD-USE-NBR* would noticeably increase the time required to print the Supplier report, because a large number of PRESCRIPTION record instances would have to be retrieved to calculate the value of DRUGB-YTD-USE-NBR*. They decide, therefore, to store the derived data element.

Jayne and John next evaluate the records for efficiency. They know that aggregating is not possible, because all of the relationships in the pharmacy conceptional data model have maximum cardinalities of N. Any aggregated record would require a repeating group, and the relational data structure class does not allow repeating groups.

Next, John and Jayne review the relationships between the records to determine whether any improvements in efficiency are possible. No pointers are possible because of the rules of the relational data structure class. They consider absorbing the PHARMACIST record into PRESCRIPTION, but decide against it because the resulting database would be less flexible if more data about pharmacists were required in the future. They decide, therefore, that the current logical structure is efficient.

As a final step in efficiency design, they estimate the amount of space that will be required by the database (without any physical structures, such as indexes, yet defined). This information will help them make decisions regarding the design of physical structures for the database. The procedure they follow is simple:

1. Add the field lengths for each record together (any packed elements will be decreased by approximately one-half) to determine the size of each record.

2. Multiply the record size by the expected volume of record instances to determine the storage required by each record.

3. Sum the storage requirements for all records to determine the storage requirements for the database.

Their calculations are as follows:

No.	Name	Type	Data Elements
	Figure 17.34		
1	Daily Drug Log	Internal report	PRCT-ID-NBR, PAT-LAST-NAME, PAT-FIRST-NAME, PHY-LAST-NAME, PHY-MID-INIT-NAME, PHY-FIRST-NAME, DRUG-NAME, DRUGB-NAME
2	Prescription Entry Screen	Data entry	DRUG-NAME, PAT-ID-NBR, PAT-LAST-NAME, PHY-FIRST-NAME, PHY-MID-INIT-NAME, PHY-LAST-NAME, PRCT-DATE, PRCT-DRUG-QTY-NBR, PRCT-DOSE-IS-TEXT
3	Prescription Update Screen	Data entry	DRUG-NAME, PAT-ID-NBR, PHY-LAST-NAME, PRCT-DATE, PRCT-DRUG-QTY-NBR, PRCT-DOSE-IS-TEXT, PHAR-EMP-ID-NBR, DRUGB-NAME, DRUGB-UNIT-PRICE-AMT, DRUGB-UNIT-AV-NBR, DRUG-UOM-CODE
4	Prescription Label (printed from Prescription Update screen)	External document	PRCT-ID-NBR, PHY-LAST-NAME, PHY-FIRST-NAME, PHY-MID-INIT-NAME, PAT-LAST-NAME, PAT-FIRST-NAME, PRCT-DOSE-IS-TEXT, DRUGB-NAME, PRCT-DRUG-QTY-NBR, PHAR-FIRST-NAME
5	Supplier Report	Internal report	DRUGSP-NAME, DRUGSP-VEN-ID-NBR, DRUG-NAME, DRUGB-NAME, DRUG-UOM-CODE, DRUGB-YTD-USE-NBR, DRUGB-UNIT-AV-NBR

Figure 17.34
Pharmacy System Interface Summary Table

```
PRESCRIPTION:
  (record size = 182) × 30,000 records = 5,460,000 bytes

PHARMACIST:
  (record size = 45) × 5 records = 225 bytes

PATIENT:
  (record size = 45) × 1000 records = 45,000 bytes

PHYSICIAN:
  (record size = 37) × 150 records = 5550 bytes

DRUG:
  (record size = 24) × 1000 records = 24,000 bytes

DRUG-BRAND:
  (record size = 64) × 2000 records = 128,000 bytes
```

SUPPLIER:
(record size = 30) × 25 records = 750 bytes

Total Size of the Logical Database = 5,669,525 bytes

The total size of the database is well below the 100,000,000 bytes available.

1.6 Specify the logical design using the DDL. As the final step in logical design, John and Jayne transform the logical data model in Figure 17.32 into the DB2 DDL in Figure 17.35.

2. Design the Physical Database

Physical database design using a sophisticated DBMS like DB2 is a very complicated process. John will undertake the complexities of the physical design for the pharmacy database with the help of other analysts in the Database Administration department. Therefore, the only physical structure that Jayne and John will design is the indexes.

2.1 Evaluate and change the physical design for efficiency. Jayne and John begin the task of designing indexes by reviewing the data access table. The Daily Drug report requires the access of prescriptions based on the value of PRCT-DATE. That is, all prescriptions filled on the current date will be listed on the report. A good secondary

Figure 17.35
DB2 DDL for the
Pharmacy Database

```
CREATE TABLE DRUG
    (  DRUG-NAME              CHAR(20) NOT NULL,
       DRUG-UOM-CODE          CHAR(4) );

CREATE TABLE DRUG-BRAND
    (  DRUG-NAME              CHAR(20) NOT NULL,
       DRUGSP-VEN-ID-NBR      INTEGER (10) NOT NULL,
       DRUGBR-NAME            CHAR(20) NOT NULL,
       DRUGB-UNIT-AV-NBR      DECIMAL(7),
       DRUGB-YTD-USE-NBR *    DECIMAL(10),
       DRUGB-UNIT-PR-AMT      DECIMAL(9)  );

CREATE TABLE DRUG-SUPPLIER
    (  DRUGSP-VEN-ID-NBR      INTEGER(10) NOT NULL,
       DRUGSP-NAME            CHAR(20)  );

CREATE TABLE PATIENT
    (  PAT-ID-NBR             INTEGER(10) NOT NULL,
       PAT-FIRST-NAME         CHAR(15),
       PAT-LAST-NAME          CHAR(20)  );

CREATE TABLE PHARMACIST
    (  PHAR-EMP-ID-NBR        INTEGER(10) NOT NULL,
       PHAR-LAST-NAME         CHAR(20),
       PHAR-FIRST-NAME        CHAR(15)  );

CREATE TABLE PHYSICIAN
    (  PHY-LAST-NAME          CHAR(20) NOT NULL,
       PHY-FIRST-NAME         CHAR(15),
       PHY-MID-INIT-NAME      CHAR (2)  );

CREATE TABLE PRESCRIPTION
    (  PRCT-ID-NBR            INTEGER(10) NOT NULL,
       PRCT-DATE              INTEGER (8) NOT NULL,
       PAT-ID-NBR             INTEGER(10) NOT NULL,
       PHY-LAST-NAME          CHAR(20) NOT NULL,
       DRUG-NAME              CHAR(20) NOT NULL,
       DRUGSP-VEN-ID-NBR      INTEGER(10) NOT NULL,
       PRCT-DRUG-QTY-NBR      DECIMAL(6),
       PRCT-DOSE-IS-TEXT      CHAR(90),
       PHAR-EMP-ID-NBR        INTEGER(10)  );
```

index for the PRESCRIPTION table, therefore. is PRCT-DATE. They also decide to create indexes for

PAT-ID-NBR (to access the PATIENT table)

DRUGSP-VEN-ID-NBR, DRUG NAME (to access the DRUG-BRAND table)

PHY-LAST-NAME (to access the PHYSICIAN table)

PHAR-EMP-ID-NBR (to access the PHARMACIST table)

Other indexes are added to increase the response time of the Prescription Update screen and the Supplier report:

PRCT-ID-NBR (to access the PRESCRIPTION table)

DRUG-NAME (to access the DRUG table)

```
CREATE TABLE DRUG
  (   DRUG-NAME              CHAR (20) NOT NULL,
      DRUG-UOM-CODE          CHAR(4) );

CREATE TABLE DRUG-BRAND
  (   DRUG-NAME              CHAR(20) NOT NULL,
      DRUGSP-VEN-ID-NBR      INTEGER(10) NOT NULL,
      DRUGB-NAME             CHAR(20) NOT NULL,
      DRUGB-UNIT-PR-AMT      DECIMAL(7),
      DRUGB-UNIT-AV-NBR      DECIMAL(7),
      DRUGB-YTD-USE-NBR      DECIMAL(10) );

CREATE TABLE DRUG-SUPPLIER
  (   DRUGSP-VEN -ID-NBR     INTEGER(10) NOT NULL,
      DRUGSP-NAME            CHAR(20) );

CREATE TABLE PATIENT
  (   PAT-ID-NBR             INTEGER(10) NOT NULL,
      PAT-FIRST-NAME         CHAR(15),
      PAT-LAST-NAME          CHAR(20) );

CREATE TABLE PHARMACIST
  (   PHAR-EMP-ID-NBR        INTEGER(10) NOT NULL,
      PHAR-LAST-NAME         CHAR(20),
      PHAR-FIRST-NAME        CHAR(15) );

CREATE TABLE PHYSICIAN
  (   PHY-LAST-NAME          CHAR(20) NOT NULL,
      PHY-FIRST-NAME         CHAR(15),
      PHY-MID-INIT-NAME      CHAR(2) );

CREATE TABLE PRESCRIPTION
  (   PRCT-ID-NBR            INTEGER(10) NOT NULL,
      PRCT-DATE              INTEGER(8) NOT NULL,
      PAT-ID-NBR             INTEGER (10)' NOT NULL,
      PHY-LAST-NAME          CHAR(20) NOT NULL,
      DRUG-NAME              CHAR(20) NOT NULL,
      DRUGSP-VEN -ID-NBR     INTEGER(10) NOT NULL,
      PRCT-DRUG-QTY-NBR      DECIMAL (6),
      PRCT-DOSE-IS-TEXT      CHAR(90),
      PHAR-EMP-ID-NBR        INTEGER(10) );
```

```
GRANT ALL ON PRESCRIPTION TO PHARMACY
GRANT ALL ON PHYSICIAN TO PHARMACY
GRANT ALL ON PATIENT TO PHARMACY
GRANT ALL ON PHARMACIST TO PHARMACY
GRANT ALL ON DRUG-BRAND TO PHARMACY
GRANT ALL ON DRUG TO PHARMACY
GRANT ALL ON DRUG-SUPPLIER TO PHARMACY

GRANT SELECT ON PRESCRIPTION TO STAFF
GRANT SELECT ON PHYSICIAN TO STAFF
GRANT SELECT ON PATIENT TO STAFF
GRANT SELECT ON PHARMACIST TO STAFF
GRANT SELECT ON DRUG-BRAND TO STAFF
GRANT SELECT ON DRUG TO STAFF
GRANT SELECT ON DRUG-SUPPLIER TO STAFF
```

```
CREATE UNIQUE INDEX Primary_DRUG ON DRUG (DRUG-NAME);
CREATE UNIQUE INDEX Primary_DRUG-BRAND ON DRUG-BRAND
(DRUG-NAME, DRUGSP-VEN-ID-NBR);
CREATE UNIQUE INDEX Primary_DRUG-SUPPLIER ON DRUG
SUPPLIER (DRUGSP-VEN-ID-NBR);
CREATE UNIQUE INDEX Primary_PATIENT ON PATIENT (PAT-ID-NBR);
CREATE UNIQUE INDEX Primary_PHARMACIST ON PHARMACIST (PHAR-EMP-ID-NBR);
CREATE UNIQUE INDEX Primary_PHYSICIAN ON PHYSICIAN (PHY-LAST-NAME);
CREATE INDEX PRCT-DATE-INDEX ON PRESCRIPTION (PRCT-DATE);
CREATE UNIQUE INDEX Primary_PRESCRIPTION ON PRESCRIPTION (PRCT-ID-NBR);
```

Figure 17.36 DB2 DDL for the Pharmacy Database

DRUGSP-VEN-ID-NBR (to access the DRUG-SUP-PLIER table)

2.2 Evaluate the physical design for integrity. Next, Jayne and John evaluate the controls to protect the existence, accuracy, and confidentiality of the pharmacy database. Meadows Hospital must follow very strict laws and regulations concerning information about patients, drugs, and prescriptions. The necessary controls were determined during the requirements analysis for the pharmacy system.

To protect the existence of the database, the normal backup and recovery mechanisms of DB2, such as transaction logging, will be used.

2.3 Add controls. Protecting the accuracy of prescription data requires validation controls, including procedures and extensive edit-checking for the Prescription Entry and Prescription Update screens. John and Jayne work with Fred Kahn, the systems analyst for the project, to define the validation controls. One procedure that will be followed by pharmacists is to always fill the prescription from the original copy of the doctor's prescription slip. This will ensure that an input error during the entry of the prescription will never lead to an error in the medication provided.

Protecting the confidentiality of patient data requires access controls. John and Jayne define password protection so as to ensure that only pharmacists are authorized to retrieve and update data from the pharmacy database. Other pharmacy staff will be allowed only to retrieve data.

2.4 Specify the physical design using the DDL. The final DDL for the pharmacy database is shown in Figure 17.36.

Appendix A: Normalization

Normalization allows us to use the procedure for conceptual data modeling presented in Chapter 11 to construct entities that have the following simple structure: (1) a unique identifier and (2) attributes that are characteristics of only the entity that is identified by the unique identifier. The most important benefit of designing a database from simple entities is flexibility—the database will be easy to change as new application systems are developed.

Normalization is a procedure that complements conceptual data modeling. Normalization provides guidelines for verifying the simplicity of entities or the records that are created from the entities. The guidelines specify various levels of normalization, called normal forms. There are three practical normal forms, each of which specifies a simpler data structure: first, second, and third normal form.

To understand normalization, you must first understand the concept of functional dependency. Functional dependency is used to describe the relationship between data elements and the key of a record. A data element is functionally dependent on the key of a record if the value of the key determines a unique value for the data element. For example, in Figure 17.37a, a value for the key ORDER-NBR will always provide a unique value for ORDER-DATE, because an order is placed on only one date. Thus we say that ORDER-DATE is functionally dependent on ORDER-NBR. In contrast, many values of PROD-DESC-TEXT are possible for a value of ORDER-NBR (for example, "std. computer forms," "printer ribbons"). Thus, PROD-DESC-TEXT is not functionally dependent on ORDER-NBR; it is, however, functionally dependent on PROD-NBR.

We will now illustrate how the ORDER record in Figure 17.37a is normalized into first, second, and third normal form. A record is in first normal form (1NF) if there are no data elements that repeat a variable number of times. In Figure 17.37a, PROD-NBR, PROD-DESC-TEXT, and ITEM-QUAN-NBR all repeat a variable number of times. To

(a)

ORDER

ORDER-NBR	ORDER-DATE	INVOICE-NBR	INVOICE-DATE	PROD-NBR	PROD-DESC-TEXT	ITEM-QUAN-NBR
25	8/15/87	1568	8/28/87	4567	STD. COMPUTER FORMS	3
126	8/16/87	1569	8/28/87	4567	STD. COMPUTER FORMS	10
				250	PRINTER RIBBONS	5
537	8/18/87	1570	8/28/87	4390	SPECIAL FORMS	4
				250	PRINTER RIBBONS	3
				4567	STD. COMPUTER FORMS	15

(b) First Normal Form

ORDER

ORDER-NBR	ORDER-DATE	INVOICE-NBR	INVOICE-DATE
25	8/15/87	1568	8/28/87
126	8/16/87	1569	8/28/87
537	8/18/87	1570	8/28/87

ORDER-ITEM

ORDER-NBR	PROD-NBR	PROD-DESC-TEXT	ITEM-QUAN-NBR
25	4567	STD. COMPUTER FORMS	3
126	4567	STD. COMPUTER FORMS	10
126	250	PRINTER RIBBONS	5
537	4390	SPECIAL FORMS	4
537	250	PRINTER RIBBONS	3
537	4567	STD. COMPUTER FORMS	15

(c) Second Normal Form

ORDER

ORDER-NBR	ORDER-DATE	INVOICE-NBR	INVOICE-DATE
25	8/15/87	1568	8/28/87
126	8/16/87	1569	8/28/87
537	8/18/87	1570	8/28/87

ORDER-ITEM

ORDER-NBR	PROD-NBR	ITEM-QUAN-NBR
25	4567	3
126	4567	10
126	250	5
537	4390	4
537	250	3
537	4567	15

PRODUCT

PROD-NBR	PROD-DESC-TEXT
4567	STD. COMPUTER FORMS
250	PRINTER RIBBONS
4390	SPECIAL FORMS

(d) Third Normal Form

ORDER

ORDER-NBR	ORDER-DATE	INVOICE-NBR
25	8/15/87	1568
126	8/16/87	1569
537	8/18/87	1570

ORDER-ITEM

ORDER-NBR	PROD-NBR	ITEM-QUAN-NBR
25	4567	3
126	4567	10
126	250	5
537	4390	4
537	250	3
537	4567	15

PRODUCT

PROD-NBR	PROD-DESC-TEXT
4567	STD. COMPUTER FORMS
250	PRINTER RIBBONS
4390	SPECIAL FORMS

INVOICE

INVOICE-NBR	INVOICE-DATE
1568	8/28/87
1569	8/28/87
1570	8/28/87

Figure 17.37 Example of Normalization

convert ORDER into first normal form, we remove the three repeating elements and group them into a new ORDER-ITEM record, as shown in Figure 17.37b. To maintain the relationship with the ORDER record, we make ORDER-NBR part of the key for ORDER-ITEM.

A record is in second normal form (2NF) if it is in first normal form and every data element is functionally dependent on both elements of a compound key. Second normal form applies only to records that have compound keys. In Figure 17.37b, PROD-DESC-TEXT is not functionally dependent on the compound key of ORDER-NBR and PROD-NBR. (For example, order number 537 produces three values of PROD-DESC-TEXT.) Rather, PROD-DESC-TEXT is dependent only on PROD-NBR. To convert ORDER-ITEM into second normal form, we remove PROD-DESC-TEXT and group it into a new PRODUCT record with PROD-NBR as the key, as shown in Figure 17.37c.

A record is in the third normal form (3NF) if it is in first and second normal forms and every data element is functionally dependent on the key. If an element is also functionally dependent on a data element that is not the key of the record, the record is not in third normal form. In Figure 17.37c, INVOICE-DATE of the ORDER record is functionally dependent on both INVOICE-NBR and ORDER-NBR. To convert the ORDER record into third normal form, we remove INVOICE-DATE and group it into a new INVOICE record with INVOICE-NBR as the key, as shown in Figure 17.37d.

Summary

Database design is the process of specifying how the data requirements for a system will be implemented as a database. Inputs to the design process are the conceptual data model and database transactions. The output of the design process is a description of the logical and physical structure of the database. Seven constructs describe the logical and physical structure of a database: data elements, records, keys, relationships, file organizations, physical records, and indexes.

A database management system (DBMS) is a software system that maintains and controls the logical and physical structures of a database independently of the programs that use the database. Every DBMS conforms to a data structure class that provides rules for the definition of logical data structures. The three most common data structure classes are hierarchical, network (based on the CODASYL standard), and relational. The logical and physical description of a database is specified using the data description language (DDL) of the DBMS.

Transforming a conceptual data model into a description of a database is a complex process. Logical and physical design guidelines are necessary to manage this complexity. Guidelines help ensure that the database satisfies the three quality criteria of flexibility, integrity, and efficiency.

Key Terms

(Section numbers are in parentheses.)

data access table (17.1)	aggregation (17.2.2)
database transactions (17.1)	segmentation (17.2.2)
logical data structure (17.2)	key (17.2.3)
data element (17.2.1)	relationship (17.2.4)
logical record (17.2.2)	foreign key (17.2.4)

relationship record (17.2.4)   secondary index (17.3.3)
pointer (17.2.4)   database management system (DBMS) (17.4)
physical data structure (17.3)   database schema (17.4)
file organization (17.3.1)   hierarchical DBMS (17.4.1)
sequential file organization (17.3.1) network DBMS (17.4.2)
direct file organization (17.3.1)   relational DBMS (17.4.3)
hashing (17.3.1)   normalization (17.4.3)
indexed file organization (17.3.1)   logical database design (17.5.2)
physical record (17.3.2)   physical database design (17.5.3)

Notes

1. D. M. Kroenke and K. A. Dolan, *Database Processing: Fundamentals, Design, Implementation*, 3rd ed. (Chicago: Science Research Associates, 1988).

2. See G. C. Everest, *Database Management: Objectives, System Functions, and Administration* (New York: McGraw-Hill, 1986); and Kroenke and Dolan, *Database Processing*.

3. Kroenke and Dolan, *Database Processing*, pp. 133–156.

Exercises

(Answers to Exercises 17.1 and 17.7 are at the end of the book.

17.1 Explain how the conceptual data model introduced in Chapter 11 is used in the database design process.

17.2 List and explain the seven constructs used for database design.

17.3 Name and describe the actions necessary to read and write data on a disk device.

17.4 Explain how the three types of data structure classes for DBMSs differ.

17.5 Use the conceptual data model in Figure 17.38 to do the following:

a. Represent the conceptual data model as a hierarchical data structure.

b. Represent the conceptual data model as a network data structure.

c. Represent the conceptual data model as a relational data structure.

17.6 The relational schema in Figure 17.39 is the final database design for the conceptual data model in Figure 17.38. Use the schema to answer the following questions. State any assumptions you feel are necessary.

a. Is the design flexible? Explain your answer.

b. Is the design efficient? Explain your answer.

c. If the data stored in the database were confidential, what design features would you suggest to safeguard the integrity of the data?

17.7 Review the record layout in Figure 17.40, and then do the following. List any assumptions that you make.

a. Normalize the record into first normal form.

b. Normalize the record into second normal form.

c. Normalize the record into third normal form.

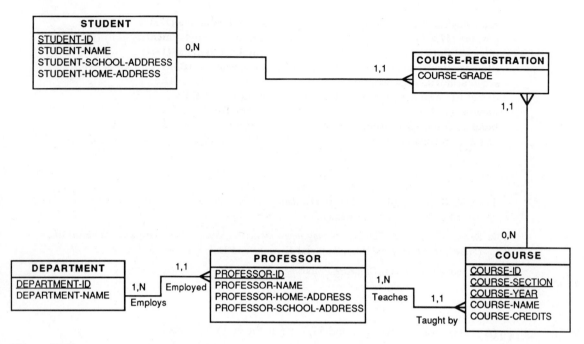

Figure 17.38

17.8 Review Arnie's situation at Special Transportation Services (Exercise 1.10). Should Wilma have recommended flat files or a DBMS?

    a. Justify your answer by referring to the information system goals and subgoals summarized in Figure 2.7.

    b. Justify your answer by referring to at least ten of the cells of the development process matrix in Figure 1.20.

    c. Justify your answer by referring to all of the criteria for database design listed in Section 17.5.

17.9 Review the situation at Stafford Plastics (Exercise 6.8). Should the Marketing Analysis System data storage component be flat files or a DBMS?

    a. Justify your answer by referring to the information system goals and subgoals in Figure 2.7.

    b. Justify your answer by referring to at least ten of the cells of the development process matrix in Figure 1.20.

    c. Justify your answer by referring to all of the criteria for database design listed in Section 17.5.

```
CREATE TABLE COURSE
  (  COURSE-ID                   INTEGER(10) NOT NULL,
     COURSE-SECTION              INTEGER(2) NOT NULL,
     COURSE-YEAR                 INTEGER(4) NOT NULL,
     COURSE-NAME                 CHAR(20),
     COURSE-CREDITS              INTEGER(1),
     COURSE-STUDENT-NUMBER*      INTEGER(3),
     PROFESSOR-ID                INTEGER(10));
```

* COURSE-STUDENT-NUMBER is the number of students enrolled in the course

```
CREATE TABLE COURSE-REGISTRATION
  (  COURSE-ID                   INTEGER(10) NOT NULL,
     COURSE-SECTION              INTEGER(2) NOT NULL,
     COURSE-YEAR                 INTEGER(4) NOT NULL,
     STUDENT-ID1                 INTEGER(10) NOT NULL,
     COURSE-GRADE                CHAR(1),
     COURSE-REGISTER-DATE        INTEGER(8),
     STUDENT-ID2                 INTEGER(10));
```

```
CREATE TABLE PROFESSOR
  (  PROFESSOR-ID                INTEGER(10) NOT NULL,
     PROFESSOR-NAME              CHAR(30),
     PROFESSOR-SCHOOL-ADDRESS    CHAR(30),
     PROFESSOR-HOME-ADDRESS      CHAR(50),
     DEPARMENT-ID                INTEGER(10),
     DEPARTMENT-NAME             CHAR(20));
```

```
CREATE TABLE STUDENT1
  (  STUDENT-ID                  INTEGER(10) NOT NULL,
     STUDENT-NAME                CHAR(30));
```

```
CREATE TABLE STUDENT2
  (  STUDENT-ID                  INTEGER(10) NOT NULL,
     STUDENT-NAME                CHAR(20),
     STUDENT-SCHOOL-ADDRESS      CHAR(50),
     STUDENT-HOME-ADDRESS        CHAR(50),
     STUDENT-GPA*                DECIMAL(2,1));
```

* STUDENT-GPA is the calculated GPA for all courses the student has completed

```
CREATE UNIQUE INDEX Primary_COURSE ON COURSE (COURSE-ID, COURSE-SECTION, COURSE-YEAR);
CREATE UNIQUE INDEX Primary_COURSE-REGISTRATION ON COURSE-REGISTRATION (COURSE-ID, STUDENT-ID);
CREATE UNIQUE INDEX Primary_PROFESSOR ON PROFESSOR (PROFESSOR-ID);
CREATE UNIQUE INDEX Primary_STUDENT1 ON STUDENT1 (STUDENT-ID);
CREATE UNIQUE INDEX Primary_STUDENT2 ON STUDENT2 (STUDENT-ID);
```

Figure 17.39

Project

Project-ID	Project-date	Client-ID	Client-name	Client-addr	Emp-ID	Emp-name	Dept-ID	Dept-name
01	07-01-88	103	Joseph James	Austin, TX	02	Fran Jones	01	Residential
02	08-01-88	150	Parker, Inc.	Austin, TX	06	Sue Post	02	Special Projects
					05	Pam Wright	01	Residential
03	08-15-88	150	Parker, Inc.	Austin, TX	02	Fran Jones	01	Residential

Figure 17.40

Program Design

Overview

During program design, specifications are created that will guide programmers in constructing the programs of a system during the implementation phase. Obviously, a good specification should result in a set of programs that satisfy user requirements for the system and that are easy to maintain. Considering that information systems departments typically spend about 50 to 70 percent of their budgets maintaining existing programs, the importance of good program specifications cannot be overemphasized. Fortunately, a structured design process can help us achieve these two objectives for program specifications. Chapter 10 introduced structured design techniques such as data flow diagrams and process specifications. In this chapter we discuss structured program design. Specifically, we plan to

1. Introduce structured program design and the role played by structure charts. (Section 18.1)

2. Explain the use of each structure chart symbol. (Section 18.2.1)

3. Explain the use of a program definition language (PDL) for specifying the modules of a structure chart. (Section 18.2.2)

4. Explain how to create a structure chart from a data flow diagram. (Section 18.3)

5. Explain how to refine the structure chart using the design guidelines of coupling and cohesion. (Section 18.4)

6. Explain how to package program specifications. (Section 18.4.4)

7. Provide a step-by-step illustration of designing a program. (Section 18.5)

8. Describe how CASE tools can aid program design. (Section 18.6)

18.1 Introduction to Structured Program Design

Structured program design is a set of techniques, guidelines, and a method for making program coding, testing, and maintenance easier by reducing the complexity of programs. Structured design reduces the complexity of programs by breaking the programs into small pieces called modules. Ideally, each module of a program should perform a distinctive function or activity and should perform this function independently of the other program modules. A system developed using structured design is characterized by small, relatively simple modules that are easier to code, test, and maintain than are the few large, complex programs of an unstructured system.

The techniques used for structured program design are the structure chart and program definition language (PDL). The structure chart allows us to create an outline of a program by specifying modules and how the modules are connected. PDL is used to specify the processing of each module. Program design guidelines are rules for evaluating the complexity of modules as the structure chart and PDL are being constructed. The design method provides a procedure for identifying programs and then constructing and refining the structure chart and PDL for each program.

You are undoubtedly familiar with the benefits of structured design from your own experience in writing reports and term papers. A good report is organized into sections, each of which is developed to express a distinct idea of the report. Sections are organized into paragraphs, and each paragraph expresses one sub-idea of a section. Once the organization of the paper has been defined by an outline, the actual writing is easy because the outline allows you to concentrate on developing clearly defined and simple ideas, one section at a time. In addition, adding new ideas to this type of structure is easy, because the new ideas require at most minor changes to the ideas already developed in the rest of the paper.

Figure 18.1 summarizes the program design process. The inputs to the design process are the data flow diagram (DFD), user procedures, interface and database specifications, and the design repository, or data dictionary. The outputs of the design process are the updated design repository, or data dictionary, and packaged program specifications, in-

Figure 18.1
Program Design

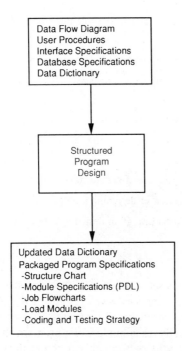

Data Flow Diagram
User Procedures
Interface Specifications
Database Specifications
Data Dictionary

Structured
Program
Design

Updated Data Dictionary
Packaged Program Specifications
 -Structure Chart
 -Module Specifications (PDL)
 -Job Flowcharts
 -Load Modules
 -Coding and Testing Strategy

cluding structure charts, PDL for each module, job flowcharts, load modules, and a coding and testing strategy for the program modules.

You might wonder why we don't code and test programs directly from the DFDs, thereby bypassing the structure chart and PDL. Recall from Chapter 10 that a DFD provides a system description that users can evaluate to determine whether their requirements have been adequately understood by systems developers. The DFD describes data that is input to the system, data that is output from the system, and how the processes of the system transform inputs into outputs. The description, however, does not include information that is essential to controlling the processing of computerized programs. Detailed design information such as database and screen accesses, error messages, and end-of-file conditions are not specified in a DFD. The structure chart and PDL provide a way to represent this information and therefore are used for program design. The Universal case will again be used to introduce program design.

MINICASE

Program Design at Universal, Inc.

Figure 18.2 shows the process that will be used by Rebecca Tovar, a programmer/analyst for Universal, to design the programs for the Universal order tracking system. You can follow the design process by starting at the top bubble in Figure 18.2.

As the first step in the design process, Rebecca identifies the programs that will be needed to implement the order tracking system. She decides to create the Create Invoice program first.

First, Rebecca identifies the processes on the Create Invoice DFD (see Figure 18.3) that define the Create Invoice program. She produces a first draft of the structure chart (Figure 18.4) by converting processes to modules. She then adds control, screen, and file access information

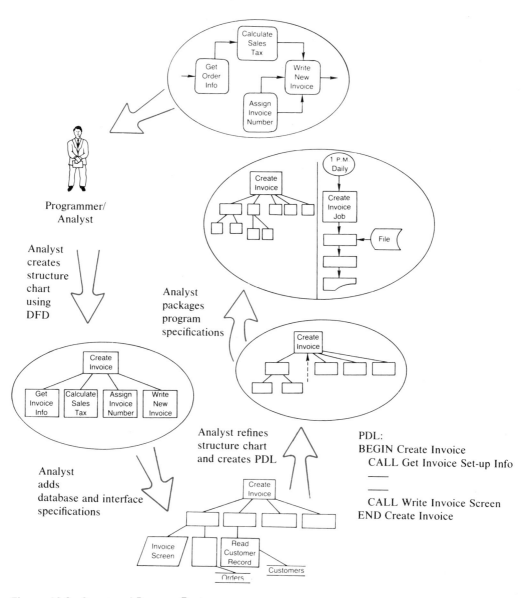

Figure 18.2 Structured Program Design

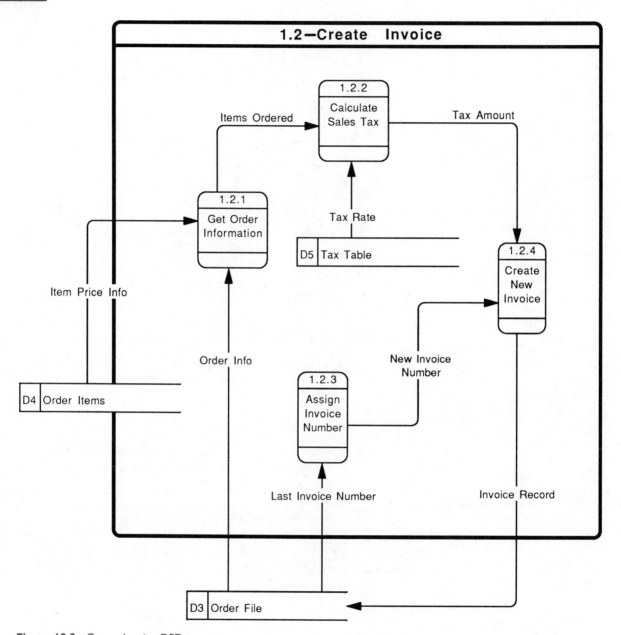

Figure 18.3   Create Invoice DFD

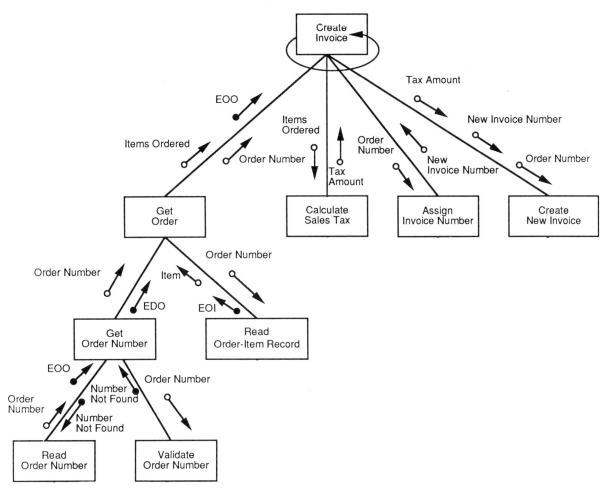

Figure 18.4 First Draft of Create Invoice Structure Chart

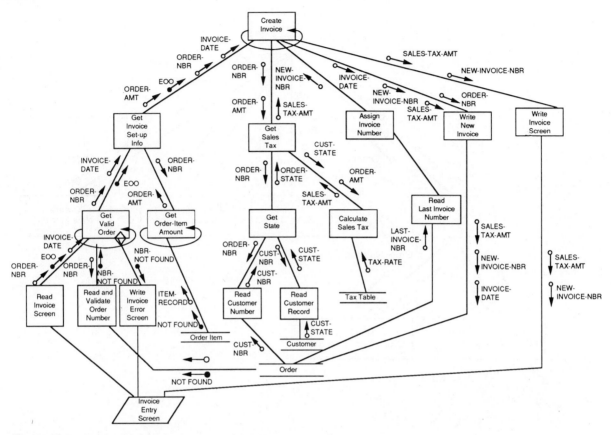

Figure 18.5 Completed Create Invoice Structure Chart

to the structure chart, based on the interface and database specifications. Rebecca converts the structured English of the DFD process descriptions into PDL that more formally describes the processing of each module. Next, she refines the structure chart, using structured design guidelines, until she is satisfied that the modules each perform a well-defined function and are independent of one another. Finally, Rebecca packages the program specifications. Figure 18.5 shows the completed structure chart for the Create Invoice program.

18.2 Techniques of Structured Program Design

The Create Invoice structure chart in Figure 18.5 reveals something important about structured techniques: an entire program, with perhaps hundreds of lines of program code, can be "understood" from a one-page graphic description. A designer can build, evaluate, and refine the structure chart until the design objective of simplicity is achieved. Then, when the designer is satisfied with the design, the detailed program specifications necessary for programming can be written in PDL. The benefit of structured techniques is that they allow us to design programs without getting bogged down in details. In this section we discuss the structured techniques of structure charts and PDL.

18.2.1 Structure Charts

A **structure chart** is a graphic description of program structure that depicts the modules of a program, the hierarchy and organization of module communication, and the information that is exchanged between modules. Only three symbols are required for a structure chart: (1) modules, (2) module connections, and (3) information flows. In addition to the required symbols, a fourth group of symbols is included to describe special processing, such as screen and file accesses. Structure chart symbols are illustrated in Figure 18.6.

Module A box with a name denotes a module (see Figure 18.6). A **module** is a group of statements, or instructions, that are executed to perform a function of the program. The name of the module describes its function or activity. In Figure 18.5, the function of Get Invoice Set-up Info is to retrieve information needed to create an invoice for the Create Invoice module. The information sent to Create Invoice includes the date of the invoice (INVOICE-DATE), the dollar amount of the order (ORDER-AMT), and the order number (ORDER-NBR).

A complete description of a module covers (1) function, (2) input, (3) output, (4) processing, and (5) internal data. The function of Calculate Sales Tax in Figure 18.5 is to calculate a sales tax amount, given an amount and a state code. The input to the module is the amount and the state code; the output is the sales tax amount. (Module inputs and outputs are discussed in the following paragraphs.) The processing and internal data describe how the Calculate Sales Tax module calculates a sales tax from the amount and the state code. (Module processing and internal data will be discussed in the next section on PDL.)

The program design objective of simplicity dictates an important rule for module design: each module will have only one entry and exit point. This means that a module is *always* executed in the same way—it uses the same statements and has the same inputs and outputs. For example, Calculate Sales Tax always expects to receive an amount and a state code and always returns a sales tax amount, regardless of which module executes it.

Module Connection The modules of a program are not isolated from one another—they must communicate to accomplish the overall function of the program. The structure chart actually describes a hierarchy of communicating modules. This hierarchy is referred to as the calling hierarchy. With a structure chart we represent the paths of communication and the types of communication between modules, or module inputs and outputs.

Communication paths, or module connections, are represented by lines between modules on the structure chart (see Figure 18.6). A connecting line represents a call in which one module requests the execution of the statements of the other module. In Figure 18.5, Get Sales Tax requests the calculation of a sales tax for a given amount by calling Calculate Sales Tax. We refer to the calling module as the boss and the called module as the worker or subordinate.

Figure 18.6
Structure Chart
Symbols

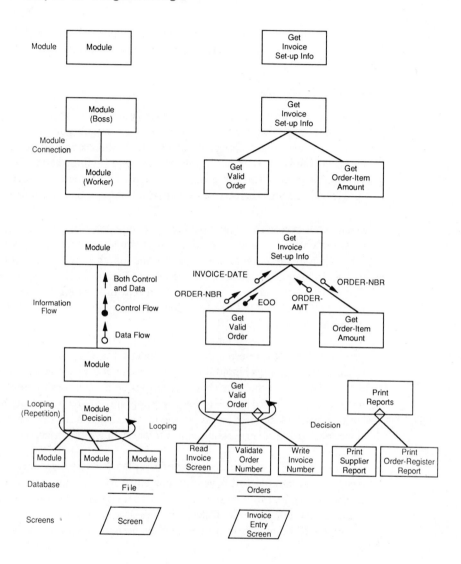

Information Flow   Two types of information are exchanged between modules: control and data (see Figure 18.6). A control flow is denoted by a closed-dot arrow that points in the direction of the flow. A **control flow** is a flag or indicator that directs the processing of a module or reports on the status of a condition. In Figure 18.5, when the EOO (end of orders) control flow is turned on, it reports to the Create Invoice module that the user has finished inputting order numbers. Create Invoice then stops calling the Get Invoice Set-up Info module.

A data flow is denoted by an open-dot arrow that points in the direction of the flow. A **data flow** contains one or more data values. The ORDER-NBR flow in Figure 18.5

contains a single data element. In contrast, the ITEM-RECORD flow contains an entire record with many data elements.

Supplements Supplements to the structure chart include symbols for looping (repetition), decisions, database files, and screens (see Figure 18.6). Looping is denoted by an arrow that loops around the connections to the modules that are called. In Figure 18.5 Create Invoice repeats the calling of Get Invoice Set-up Info, Get Sales Tax, Assign Invoice Number, Write New Invoice, and Write Invoice Screen. A decision is denoted by a diamond that contains the connections to the modules that are imbedded in the decision procedure. In Figure 18.5, a decision is made within Get Valid Order to call Write Invoice Error Screen. Files are denoted by two parallel lines. A screen is denoted by a parallelogram.

18.2.2 Program Definition Language

Program definition language (PDL) is a language that is used to specify the mechanics and internal data of a module. In other words, PDL specifies the processing statements of a module. PDL is similar to the structured English that is used to specify the lower level processes in a data flow diagram. DFD process specifications include all conditions that arise as data inputs are transformed into data outputs. The difference between PDL and structured English is that PDL includes statements to specify calls to other modules, parameters of data and control that flow between modules, user dialogues, error checks, database accesses, and definitions of data that are used in a module. These statements are needed by programmers in order to code the modules in a programming language. Although PDL does not follow the exact syntax of a programming language, it can be easily converted into programming code.

We will use the Calculate Sales Tax module in Figure 18.5 to compare PDL with structured English. In structured English, the specification of the Calculate Sales Tax process is

```
Input amount and state.
From the tax table, get the tax rate for the state.
Multiply amount by tax rate to derive tax amount.
Output tax amount.
```

The PDL equivalent of the structured English is

```
BEGIN Calculate Sales Tax (SALES-TAX-AMT;CUST-STATE,ORDER-AMT)
  FILE Tax Table
    STATE-ID,
    TAX-RATE
  SET SALES-TAX-AMT to zero
  READ Tax Table where STATE-ID = CUST-STATE
  CALCULATE SALES-TAX-AMT = ORDER-AMT * TAX-RATE
END Calculate Sales Tax
```

PDL includes syntax for the three basic constructs of program control: sequence, looping, and decision. In addition, syntax is provided for module calls and the passing of parameters (that is, data and control flows), module declarations, file access, and calculations. PDL syntax is described and illustrated in Figure 18.7. Figure 18.8 provides an example of PDL for the Create Invoice and Get Invoice Set-up Info modules in Figure 18.5.

18.3 Creating the Structure Chart

Structured design techniques can help us to build programs that are easy to maintain, but we must start the design from the DFD to ensure that programs are built according to user requirements. A necessary first step in structured design, therefore, is to convert DFDs into program structure charts. Two structured techniques are provided for this conversion: transform analysis and transaction analysis. Depending on the characteristics of the processes specified by the DFD, either or both techniques can be used to create a structure chart. After the initial structure chart has been created, database and user-interface information is added to the structure chart, and each module is specified using PDL.

Figure 18.7
PDL Syntax

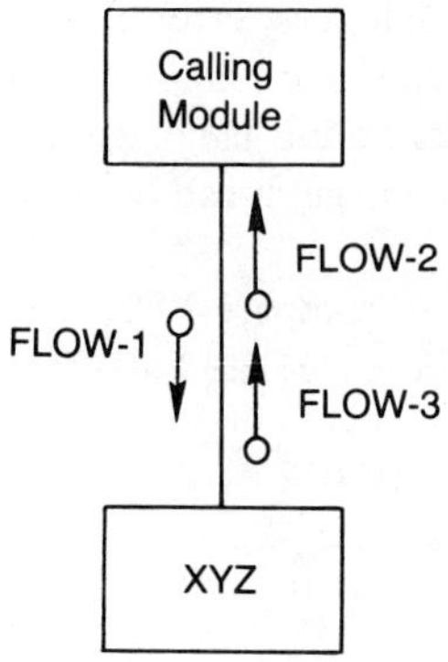

Module Call

A module call is specified using the verb CALL followed by the name of the called module and a list of parameters—the data and control flows to and from the called module. In the parameter list, flows sent to the called module are specified first, followed by flows returned from the called module. A semicolon separates input flows from output flows. If no flows are input to a module, the parameter list begins with a semicolon.

```
CALL XYZ (flow-1;flow-2,flow-3)
```

Module Declaration

A module declaration defines the start and end of the module statements. The BEGIN statement declares the module name and the flows sent to and from the module. The flows sent from the module are specified first, followed by the flows sent to the module. Note that the order of the flows here is opposite that in the parameter list in a module call. The END statement includes only the module name.

```
BEGIN XYZ (flow-2,flow-3;flow-1)
  --
  --
END XYZ
```

File Access

File access statements include

```
FILE--declares a file
READ, WRITE, DELETE, ADD, CHANGE,--file operations
```

Calculations

Calculations can be performed using the CALCULATE or other statements.

```
CALCULATE sum-tot = number 1 + number 2
means to add number 1 to number 2 to get sum-tot.
```

Figure 18.8

PDL for Create Invoice and Get Invoice Set-up Info

BEGIN Create Invoice

SET EOO to false

REPEAT UNTIL EOO is true
    CALL Get Invoice Set-up Info(;EOO,ORDER-AMT,ORDER-NBR,INVOICE-DATE)
    If EOO is false
    THEN
        CALL Get Sales Tax(ORDER-NBR,ORDER-AMT;SALES-TAX-AMT)
        CALL Assign Invoice Number (;NEW-INVOICE-NBR)
        CALL Write New Invoice(SALES-TAX-AMT,NEW-INVOICE-NBR,ORDER-NBR,INVOICE-DATE;)
        CALL Write Invoice Screen(SALES-TAX-AMT,NEW-INVOICE-NBR;)
    END-IF
ENDREPEAT

END Create Invoice

BEGIN Get Invoice Set-up Info(EOO,ORDER-AMT,ORDER-NBR,INVOICE-DATE;)

    CALL Get Valid Order(;ORDER-NBR,INVOICE-DATE,EOO)
    CALL Get Order-Item Amount(ORDER-NBR;ORDER-AMT)

END Get Invoice Set-up Info

18.3.1 Transform Analysis

Transform analysis is used to create a structure chart from a data flow diagram that contains sequential processes. Sequential processes transform data flows much as an assembly line transforms material. Raw materials, the inputs to the assembly line, are transformed through a step-by-step process into finished goods, the outputs of the assembly line. Enter Order in Figure 18.9 is a DFD with sequential processes. Enter Order transforms the customer order form into records in the ORDER and ORDER ITEMS files.

The objective of transform analysis is to create a structure chart that is arranged in a hierarchy, with the left-most modules converted from processes associated with inputs to the DFD (raw, unprocessed data) and the right-most modules converted from processes associated with the outputs of the DFD (processed data). The processes on the DFD that are between the inputs and outputs, called the area of central transform, become the modules in the center of the structure chart. A module is created at the top of the structure chart hierarchy to serve as the highest level boss. This module is assigned the name of the program. Figure 18.10 shows how transform analysis converts the Enter Order DFD into a structure chart. The top module for the Enter Order structure chart is Enter Order.

18.3.2 Transaction Analysis

Transaction analysis is used to create a structure chart from a data flow diagram that contains case-structured processes. A case-structured process is more like a custom job shop operation than a sequential, assembly-line type process. An order is received, evalu-

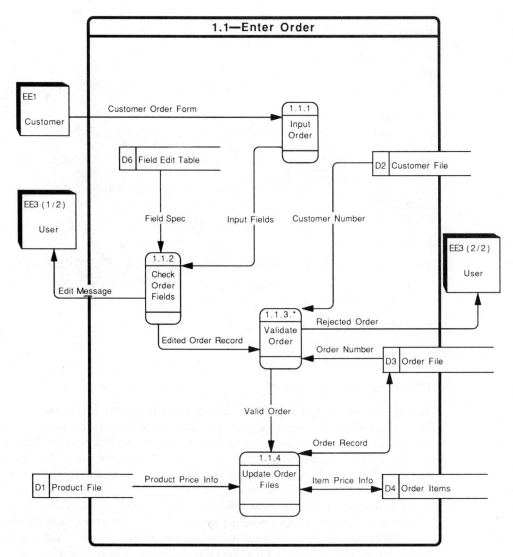

Figure 18.9 Sequential Processes: Enter Order DFD

ated, and then, depending on the nature of the order, routed to the appropriate processes necessary to complete the order. A menu is the classic example of a case-structured process. The Validate Order process in Figure 18.11 is a case-structured process. Within the Validate Order process, the Distribute Order process receives an edited order record, decides whether the record is new or an update to an existing record (change or delete), and then passes the record to the appropriate validation process.

The objective of transaction analysis is to identify the process that determines where to route the incoming data flow. This process is known as the transaction center. Then a

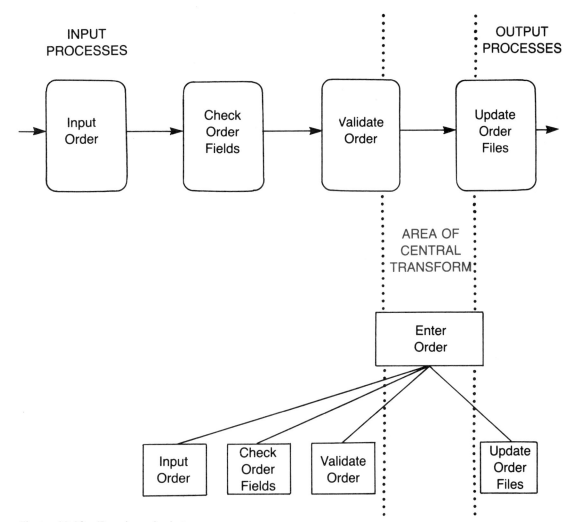

Figure 18.10   Transform Analysis

structure chart is formed, with the transaction center at the top of the hierarchy. Figure 18.12 shows how transaction analysis converts the Validate Order DFD into a structure chart.

Transform and transaction analysis are often used together on the same DFD. For example, for the Enter Order process, transform analysis created the initial Enter Order structure chart, and then transaction analysis created the structure chart for Validate Order, whose DFD is an explosion of the Validate Order process in the Enter Order DFD.

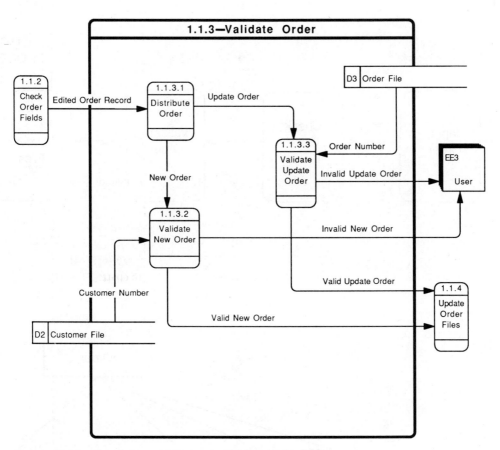

Figure 18.11 Case Structured Processes: Validate Order DFD

In practice, the order in which transform and transaction analysis are used is often the reverse of that of the previous example. It is more common to use transaction analysis first—for example, to specify the selections of a menu. Then transaction analysis is used to create the initial structure chart for each menu selection.

18.3.3 Adding Database and Interface Specifications to the Structure Chart

Programs interact in many ways with the database and user interface. Programs read and write database records, read from and write to screens, write report headings and detail lines, and issue and interpret control information such as error messages and end-of-file messages. For example, in Figure 18.5, to get valid order information for the Get Invoice Set-up Info module, the Get Valid Order module must read the order number from the Invoice screen, interpret whether the user wants to end the session (by sending the EOO control flag), validate the order number by reading the ORDER file, and so on. This detailed database

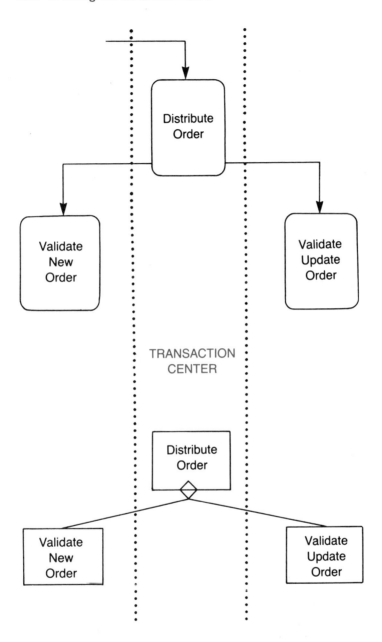

and user-interface information is essential to the structure chart. Figure 18.13 summarizes the special database and user-interface specifications that are included in the structure chart.

Because the DFD does not provide detailed information about interactions with the database and interface, this information is added to the structure chart after transform or transaction analysis. The program designer uses database and user-interface specifications such as DDL and screen layouts to help with this task. Database specifications provide

Figure 18.13
Database and User-In-
terface Enhancements
to the Structure
Chart

Database	Module or PDL for each type of access to each file:
	add
	delete
	change
	read (no update)
	Control flows for database errors (for example, DUPLICATE-KEY-VALUE,NOTFOUND)
	Looping control for file accesses (for example, Read Until END-OF-FILE = true)
Interface	One read module for a screen
	One write module for a screen or report
	Control flows for each type of error (for example, INVALID-CUSTOMER-NBR)

information about file access keys; interface specifications contain information about errors and the control of screen processing. For example, in order to specify the Get ORDER-ITEM AMOUNT Item Record module, we would review the Universal database specifications in Figure 18.14 to determine whether the ORDER-ITEM file had a secondary index defined on ORDER-NBR. In Figure 18.15, the screen layout for the Create Invoice screen describes the function keys available to the user, which, in turn, define the control flows that must be handled by the Read Invoice Screen module.

18.3.4 Specifying Modules Using PDL

Once the structure chart has been updated with database and interface information, it is necessary to use PDL to specify the processing of each module. In practice, the specification of modules is a continuous process that is finished only when the program specifications are packaged and delivered to the programmers of the system. As the structure chart is refined using the guidelines of coupling and cohesion (discussed in the next section), the PDL of modules can change dramatically, and much time can be consumed making changes to module specifications. Therefore, a good specification strategy is to incrementally write PDL for modules.

    With an **incremental strategy,** you start by specifying only the essential information needed to understand the function of the module and its interaction with other modules and then add detail as the structure chart is refined. The initial specification would include the module declaration (the parameters the module receives from and sends back to a calling module), any calls made to other modules, and a brief description (one or two sentences) of the module's function. During this first step, any data used by the module is described in the design repository. Then, as the structure chart is refined and the design of the module stabilizes, the complete PDL is written. For some modules, this last step occurs immediately before packaging. Figure 18.16 illustrates the specification of the Get Valid Order module using an incremental strategy.

SCHEMA NAME IS UNIVERSAL

RECORD NAME IS CUSTOMER
  LOCATION MODE IS CALC CUST-NBR.
  02 CUST-NBR   PIC IS INTEGER(10).
  02 CUST-NAME   PIC IS CHAR(40).
  02 CUST-BILLING-STREET-ADDR   PIC IS CHAR(40).
  02 CUST-BILLING-CITY-ADDR   PIC IS CHAR(15).
  02 CUST-BILLING-STATE-ADDR   PIC IS CHAR(2).
  02 CUST-BILLING-ZIP-CODE-ADDR   PIC IS INTEGER(9).

RECORD NAME IS ORDER
  LOCATION MODE IS CALC ORDER-NBR.
  02 ORDER-NBR   PIC IS INTEGER(10).
  02 ORDER-PO-NBR   PIC IS INTEGER(10).
  02 CUST-NBR   PIC IS INTEGER(10).
  02 ORDER-STATUS-CODE   PIC IS INTEGER(2).
  02 ORDER-PRICING-CRITERIA-CODE   PIC IS INTEGER(2).
  02 ORDER-PROC-PRIORITY-CODE   PIC IS INTEGER(2).
  02 ORDER-DATE   PIC IS INTEGER(8).
  02 INVOICE-NBR   PIC IS INTEGER(10).
  02 INVOICE-DATE   PIC IS INTEGER(8).
  02 INVOICE-TAX-AMT   PIC IS DECIMAL(10,2).

RECORD NAME IS ORDER-ITEM
  LOCATION MODE IS VIA, Contains SET.
  02 PROD-NBR   PIC IS INTEGER(10).
  02 ORDER-NBR   PIC IS INTEGER(10).
  02 ITEM-NBR   PIC IS INTEGER(4).
  02 ITEM-QUANTITY-NBR   PIC IS INTEGER(9).
  02 ITEM-BACKORDERED-NBR   PIC IS INTEGER(9).
  02 ITEM-PRICE-AMT   PIC IS DECIMAL(10,2).

RECORD NAME IS PRODUCT1
  WITHIN PRODUCT1
  LOCATION MODE IS CALC PROD-NBR.
  02 PROD-NBR   PIC IS INTEGER(10).
  02 PROD-COST-AMT   PIC IS DECIMAL(10,2).
  02 PROD-YTD-QUANTITY-NBR*   PIC IS INTEGER(10).

RECORD NAME IS PRODUCT2
  LOCATION MODE IS CALC PROD-NBR.
  02 PROD-NBR   PIC IS INTEGER(10).
  02 PROD-DESC-TEXT   PIC IS CHAR(40).

RECORD NAME IS SHIPMENT
  LOCATION MODE IS CALC SHIP-NBR, SHIP-DATE .
  02 SHIP-NBR   PIC IS INTEGER(10).
  02 SHIP-DATE   PIC IS INTEGER(8).
  02 SHIP-CARRIER-NAME   PIC IS CHAR(40).

SET NAME IS Receives
  MODE IS CHAIN
  ORDER IS NEXT
  OWNER IS CUSTOMER
  MEMBER IS SHIPMENT MANDATORY AUTOMATIC
  SET OCCURRENCE SELECTION IS THRU CURRENT OF:

SET NAME IS Contains
  MODE IS CHAIN
  ORDER IS NEXT
  OWNER IS ORDER
  MEMBER IS ORDER-ITEM FIXED AUTOMATIC
  SET OCCURRENCE SELECTION IS THRU CURRENT OF:

SET NAME IS Orders
  MODE IS CHAIN
  ORDER IS NEXT
  OWNER IS PRODUCT1
  MEMBER IS ORDER-ITEM FIXED AUTOMATIC
  SET OCCURRENCE SELECTION IS THRU CURRENT OF:

SET NAME IS Shipped in
  MODE IS CHAIN
  ORDER IS NEXT
  OWNER IS SHIPMENT
  MEMBER IS ORDER-ITEM OPTIONAL MANUAL
  SET OCCURRENCE SELECTION IS THRU CURRENT OF:

SET NAME IS INVOICE-INDEX
  MODE IS INDEX
  ORDER IS SORTED
  OWNER IS SYSTEM
  MEMBER IS ORDER
    INDEX DBKEY POSITION IS AUTO
    MANDATORY, AUTOMATIC
    ASCENDING KEY IS INVOICE-NBR
        DUPLICATES ARE NOT ALLOWED.

Figure 18.14 Universal, Inc. Database Schema

18.4 Refining the Program Design Specifications

Transform analysis and transaction analysis help us to get started with program design, but they do not provide any guidelines for reducing the complexity of the design, nor do they produce specifications that are very useful to the programmers who will code and test the programs. To help simplify program designs, structured techniques provide guidelines for reducing the coupling, or interdependence, between modules and increasing the cohesion, or the degree to which a module performs a well-defined function. Other guidelines, or design heuristics, for module size, fan-out, and fan-in aid in further evaluating

Figure 18.15
Invoice Entry Screen

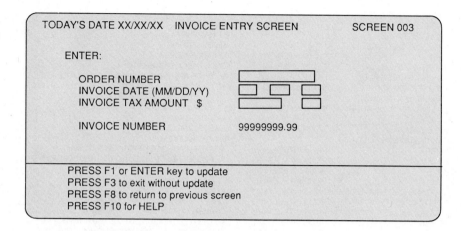

```
TODAY'S DATE XX/XX/XX    INVOICE ENTRY SCREEN              SCREEN 003

      ENTER:

           ORDER NUMBER              ┌──────────────┐
           INVOICE DATE (MM/DD/YY)   ┌───┐ ┌───┐ ┌───┐
           INVOICE TAX AMOUNT  $     ┌───────┐   ┌───┐

           INVOICE NUMBER            99999999.99


      ┌─────────────────────────────────────────────────────┐
        PRESS F1 or ENTER key to update
        PRESS F3 to exit without update
        PRESS F8 to return to previous screen
        PRESS F10 for HELP
```

Figure 18.16

Incremental Specification of the Get Valid Order Module

Brief Specification of the Get Valid Order Module

BEGIN Get Valid Order(EOO,ORDER-NBR,INVOICE-DATE;)

> *Function:* to retrieve screen input of validated order number and invoice date.

> Repeatedly calls Read Invoice Screen(;ORDER-NBR,EOO,INVOICE-DATE), then calls Read and Validate Order Number(ORDER-NBR;NBR-NOTFOUND) and Write Invoice Error
> Screen(NBR-NOTFOUND;) until NBR-NOTFOUND is false.

END Get Valid Order

PDL for the Get Valid Order Module

BEGIN Get Valid Order(EOO,ORDER-NBR,INVOICE-DATE;)

SET EOO to false
SET NBR-NOTFOUND to true
REPEAT UNTIL NBR-NOTFOUND is false or EOO is true
    CALL Read and Read Invoice Screen(;ORDER-NBR,EOO,INVOICE-DATE)
    IF EOO is false
    THEN
        CALL Validate Order Number(ORDER-NBR;NBR-NOTFOUND)
        IF NBR-NOTFOUND is true
        THEN
            CALL Write Invoice Error Screen(NBR-NOTFOUND;)
        END-IF
    END-IF
ENDREPEAT

END Get Valid Order

and reducing the complexity of the design. Finally, guidelines are available for "packaging" the specifications so that programmers can effectively code and test the programs. Figure 18.17 summarizes the guidelines for program design.

18.4.1 Coupling

Coupling is a measure of module independence. We say that modules are loosely coupled if they are independent, and tightly coupled if they are interdependent. The objective in refining the structure chart is to design independent, loosely coupled modules. Following are the five types of coupling, from loosest to tightest.

1. Data coupling
2. Stamp coupling   **loose coupling**
3. Control coupling
4. Common coupling   **tight coupling**
5. Content coupling

Data Coupling Two modules are data coupled if one module passes to the other only single data elements or data structures composed of similar data elements. The Calculate Sales Tax and Get Sales Tax modules in Figure 18.5 are data coupled because they communicate only via the SALES-TAX-AMT, STATE, and AMOUNT data elements.

Because modules must communicate to accomplish the function of the program, a certain amount of data coupling is usually necessary. Too many data flows, however, can complicate the connection between modules. In Figure 18.18a, for example, the large

Figure 18.17
Summary of Program
Design Guidelines

Measure	Objective	Guideline
Coupling	Design modules so as to minimize the number of parameters passed between modules.	Parameter name—specific and meaningful Number of parameters—reasonable Types of parameters—data or reporting
Cohesion	Design each module to perform one function.	Module name = verb + object
Module size	Design modules that can be understood without flipping through the pages of a printout.	Module size < 30–50 statements or one page
Fan-out (span of control)	Design boss modules to control a reasonable number of workers.	Number of worker modules reporting to a boss ≤ 7
Fan-in	Create generalized modules to maximize fan-in.	Modules must have strong or moderate cohesion.

Figure 18.18
Data Coupling

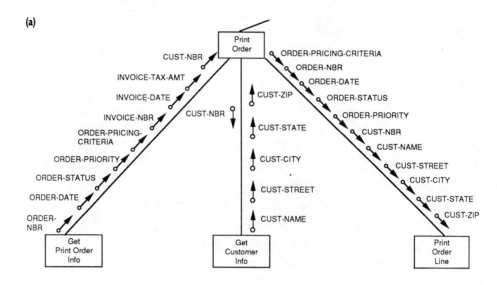

(a)

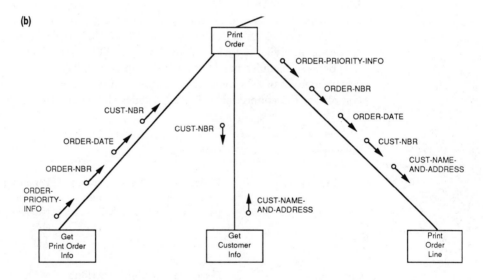

(b)

number of data elements flowing between Print Order and its subordinate modules makes the structure chart difficult to read. Undoubtedly the parameter lists of each module would be difficult to maintain.

Tight data coupling can be loosened by combining similar data elements into data structures and by ensuring that only essential data is passed to a module. A **data structure** is a collection of data elements or other data structures that are grouped together for some purpose (see Figure 18.19). In Figure 18.18b, the data coupling of the Print Order

Figure 18.19
Data Structures

The most common example of a data structure is a record. In the context of data flows and coupling, a good data structure is one that is composed of similar elements. Consider the following data structure:

```
ADDRESS
  (STREET-ADDRESS,
  CITY-ADDRESS,
  STATE,
  ZIP-CODE-ADDRESS)
```

ADDRESS is a well-defined data structure composed of similar elements. The elements of ADDRESS are similar because they all provide information about an address.

Now consider the INPUT-STUFF data structure:

```
INPUT-STUFF
  (STATE,
  CUSTOMER-NAME,
  TAX-AMOUNT,
  ORDER-NBR,
  PAYMENT-STATUS)
```

INPUT-STUFF is a poorly defined data structure because it provides information about many different things.

The name of the data structure is often a good indication of whether the structure is well or poorly defined. A vague or meaningless name usually indicates a structure that is composed of different types of data elements.

---

module has been greatly reduced by creating the ORDER-PRIORITY-INFO and CUST-NAME-AND-ADDRESS data structures and by removing the three invoice data flows from the structure chart.

The CUST-NAME-AND-ADDRESS data structure is composed of the data flows passed from Get Customer Info to Print Order. The INVOICE-TAX-AMT, INVOICE-DATE, and INVOICE-NBR flows were removed because they are not printed with the rest of the order and customer information. The design in Figure 18.18a required Print Order to remove the elements from its parameter list before calling Print Order Line. The design in Figure 18.18b achieves loose data coupling by making Get Print Order Info responsible for removing the invoice elements from the ORDER record before passing data back to Print Order Line.

Stamp Coupling Two modules are stamp coupled if one module passes to the other a data structure that contains unnecessary data elements. In Figure 18.20, Print Order and its subordinate modules are stamp coupled because they communicate via the CUSTOMER and ORDER records. As we know from Figure 18.18, these records contain many data elements that are not needed by the modules on the Print Order structure chart.

Stamp coupling adds unnecessary complexity to modules and module connections. Just think of all the work required of Print Order Line in Figure 18.20 to remove unnece-

Figure 18.20
Stamp Coupling

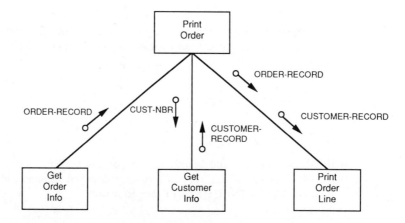

sary data elements from the ORDER and CUSTOMER records! Worse yet, if any changes were made to either the CUSTOMER or ORDER records, such as the addition of a new element to the CUSTOMER record, then the Print Order, Get Customer Info, and Print Order Line modules would have to be changed, whether or not the new element was used by these modules. The changes might not be necessary if only individual data elements or well-defined data structures were passed between the modules.

Vague data structure names or entire records passed between modules are an indication of stamp coupling. Stamp coupling can be changed to data coupling by refining data structures or records to include only necessary data elements. The stamp-coupled modules in Figure 18.20 were changed to data-coupled modules in Figure 18.18b by breaking down the ORDER and CUSTOMER records into data elements and data structures.

Control Coupling   Two modules are control coupled if one module controls the internal processing of the other via a control flow. In Figure 18.21a, Update Invoice Record controls the processing of Print Customer Notice through the PRINT-OVERPAYMENT-NOTICE control flow. If the PRINT-OVERPAYMENT-NOTICE control flow is received, Print Customer Notice calls Print Overpayment Notice. Otherwise, Print Customer Notice calls Print Normal Notice.

The problem with control coupling is that a change to the called module will often result in a change to the calling module. For example, adding a new module to the structure chart to print underpayment notices would require the creation of another control flow, the PRINT-UNDERPAYMENT-NOTICE control flow. Although the PRINT-UNDERPAYMENT-NOTICE flow would be used only by the new module, it would have to be added as a parameter to most of the modules in the Apply Invoice Payment structure chart.

Certain types of control flows do not result in control coupling. Control flows that report error and end-of-file conditions behave like data flows. For example, the NBR-NOTFOUND control flow in Figure 18.5 does not control the processing of Get Valid Order; it only reports that the ORDER-NBR provided by the user does not exist in the ORDER file. Reporting control flows, therefore, do not result in control coupling.

The name and direction of a control flow indicates whether the flow directs or re-

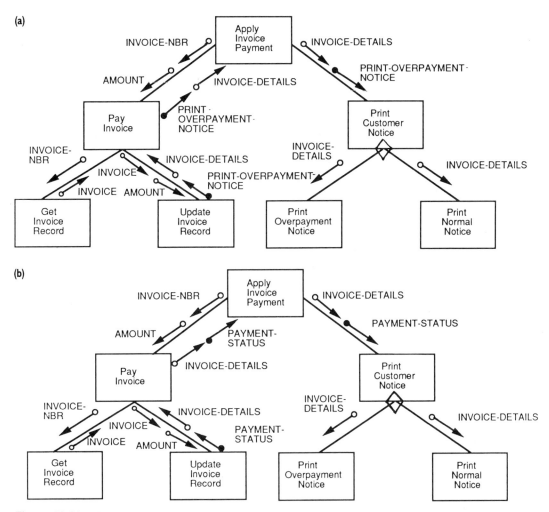

Figure 18.21 Control Coupling

ports. If the name of the control flow contains a verb, the modules that communicate through the flow are probably control coupled. PRINT-OVERPAYMENT-NOTICE contains the verb "print," which implies directive control. A control flow that moves from the calling to the called module (that is, down the module hierarchy) is another clue that modules are control coupled. Control coupling can be reduced by changing directive control flows into data flows or reporting control flows. In Figure 18.21b, the PRINT-OVERPAYMENT-NOTICE control flow has been changed into the PAYMENT-STATUS data flow that simply reports the status of the customer account.

Common Coupling Modules are common coupled if they communicate using data and control flows that are defined in a global data area. Figure 18.22 illustrates common coupling for the Apply Invoice Payment structure chart. Notice that the INVOICE and

Figure 18.22
Common Coupling

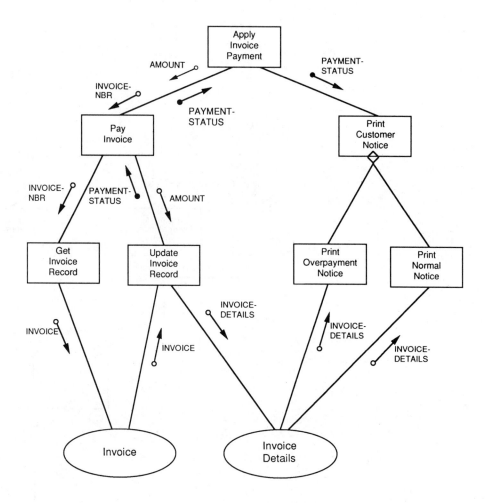

INVOICE-DETAILS data flows are defined in global data areas that are accessible to all modules of the structure chart.

Common coupling results in maintenance problems because a change to a global data element can necessitate changes to every module that accesses the global data area where the element is defined. In any case, each module in the program must be reviewed to determine whether it uses the common data element that has been changed. This added maintenance is time consuming and increases the probability of errors.

Defining data elements locally, within the boundaries of the modules that use them, avoids the problems of common coupling. In practice, however, defining data locally is not always possible because of the characteristics of some programming languages used to code the program modules. With most versions of COBOL, for example, the common Data Division makes local data definitions possible only if a separate program is created for each module on the structure chart. Because it is more convenient to code modules in COBOL as paragraphs or subroutines, common coupling is often tolerated in COBOL programs.

Content Coupling Modules are content coupled if one module refers to a statement within a second module without using a formal call. In Figure 18.23, Print Overpayment Notice branches to a statement in Update Invoice Record to change the PAYMENT-STATUS once an overpayment notice has been printed. In COBOL, this type of branch would be implemented using the GO TO statement.

Figure 18.23
Content Coupling

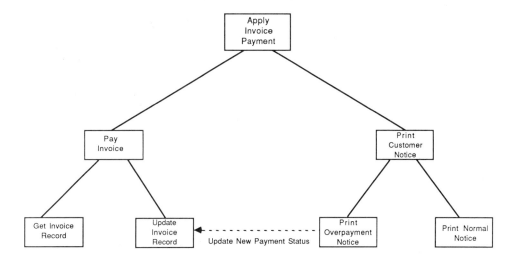

Content coupling is the worst type of coupling, because even a simple change to one module may necessitate changes to many other modules in a program. For example, the programmer making a change to Update Invoice Record might also have to change statements in Print Overpayment Notice. Unlike common coupling, content coupling is inexcusable. Content coupling can be alleviated by enforcing the use of module calls.

18.4.2 Cohesion

Cohesion is a measure of the strength of association between the processing statements in a module. We say that the statements (that is, PDL) in a module have strong, moderate, or weak cohesion depending on the functions or activities performed by the module. The objective in refining the structure chart is to design strong, highly cohesive modules. Following are the seven types of cohesion, from strongest to weakest.

1. Functional   **strong cohesion**
2. Sequential
3. Communicational
4. Procedural   **moderate cohesion**
5. Temporal
6. Logical   **weak cohesion**
7. Coincidental

Functional Cohesion   A module has functional cohesion if its statements all contribute to a single well-defined function or activity. Calculate Sales Tax in Figure 18.5 is a module with functional cohesion. Notice that the name "Calculate Sales Tax" is a precise verb-object pair. The name of a module is a good indication of module strength. Functionally cohesive modules are economical because they can be used easily in more than one program. For example, any program that needed to calculate a sales tax could use the Calculate Sales Tax module.

Sequential Cohesion   A module has sequential cohesion if its statements perform a sequence of activities in which the output from one activity becomes the input to the next activity—as in an assembly line. The module Assign Invoice Number and Write New Invoice in Figure 18.24a is a sequentially cohesive module. First the statements of the module establish an invoice number, and then the invoice number is used to create a new invoice. Sequentially cohesive modules have strong cohesion and therefore are easy to maintain. Because their activities will in general not be used together, however, sequen-

Process Description:
Find the last invoice number from the ORDER file. Add 1 to this number to get the new invoice number. Create a new invoice by updating the order record (identified by ORDER-NBR) with the new invoice number and sales tax amount.

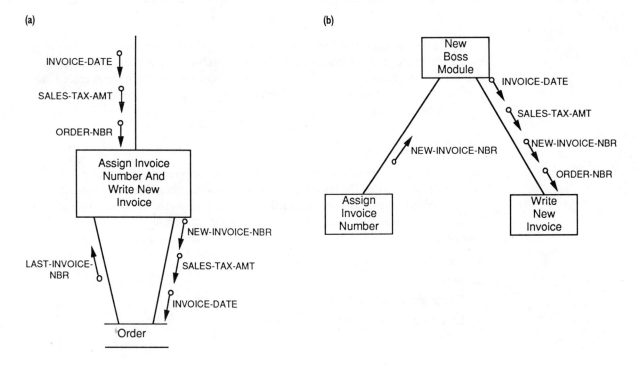

Figure 18.24   Sequential Cohesion

tially cohesive modules are not used as easily in other programs as are functionally cohesive modules.

The strength of sequentially cohesive modules can be improved by creating a separate module for each function or activity of the module. For example, in Figure 18.24b, Assign Invoice Number and Write New Invoice has been split into two modules: (1) Assign Invoice Number and (2) Write New Invoice. Although these two modules are more cohesive than the single module in Figure 18.24a, increased data coupling has added some complexity to the design.

Communicational Cohesion   A module has communicational cohesion if its statements perform activities that use the same input or output data. Calculate Sales and Excise Tax in Figure 18.25a is a communicationally cohesive module. Communicational cohesion is similar to sequential cohesion, except that the order of activities is not important. In Figure 18.25a, it is not important whether the sales or excise tax is calculated first. Communicationally cohesive modules are strongly cohesive and maintainable, but they make the sharing of modules difficult. For example, although other modules might need to calculate either a sales or an excise tax, they are not likely to want to calculate both.

The strength of communicationally cohesive modules can be improved by creating a separate module for each function or activity of the module. In Figure 18.25b, Calculate Sales and Excise Tax has been split into two modules: (1) Calculate Sales Tax and (2) Calculate Excise Tax.

Figure 18.25
Communicational
Cohesion

Process Description:
Using STATE as an access key, retrieve SALES-TAX-RATE from the Sales Tax Table. Calculate SALES-TAX-AMT as

`SALES-TAX-AMT = AMOUNT * SALES-TAX-RATE`

Using STATE as an access key, retrieve EXCISE-TAX-RATE from the Excise Tax Table. Calculate EXCISE-TAX-AMT as

`EXCISE-TAX-AMT = AMOUNT * EXCISE-TAX-RATE`

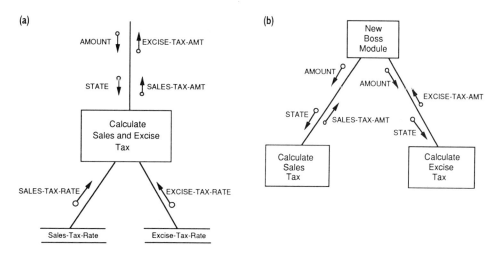

Procedural Cohesion   A module has procedural cohesion if its statements perform activities that are part of the same procedure but are not related sequentially or communicationally. The module Write New Invoice and Write Invoice Screen in Figure 18.26a is procedurally cohesive. The module creates an invoice and then displays on the Invoice screen information about the invoice that was just created.

The problem with procedural cohesion is that the activities within the module are often related to activities in other modules, which results in tight coupling and, consequently, difficult maintenance. Notice in Figure 18.5 that the Read Invoice Screen and Write Invoice Error Screen modules also perform activities using the Invoice screen. These modules, along with the Write New Invoice and Write Invoice Screen module, are coupled through the Invoice screen in Figure 18.26a. If, for example, a new display field is added to the Invoice screen, then a change will be required in each module that accesses the screen. The function of the module that writes the new invoice will be subject to errors from the change, even though it has nothing to do with the Invoice screen.

Processing Description:
Update the ORDER record identified by ORDER-NBR with invoice information. Then write NEW-INVOICE-NBR and SALES-TAX-AMT to the Invoice screen.

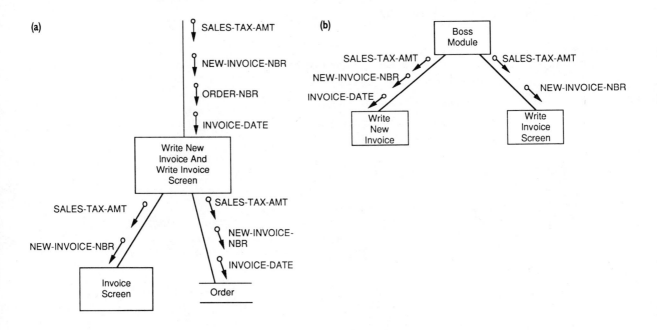

Figure 18.26 Procedural Cohesion

The strength of procedurally cohesive modules can be improved by creating a separate module for each function or activity of the module. In Figure 18.26b, Write New Invoice and Write Invoice Screen has been split into two modules: (1) Write New Invoice and (2) Write Invoice Screen.

Temporal Cohesion A module has temporal cohesion if its statements perform activities that are related because they can be accomplished at the same time. The Start-Up module in Figure 18.27a has temporal cohesion. Initializing end-of-file flags, clearing the Order screen, and setting amounts to zero are related only because they are conveniently performed as the first step in the Process Order program.

Temporally cohesive modules suffer from the same problems as do procedurally cohesive modules. The activities performed are usually more closely related to activities in other modules than to the activities in the temporally cohesive module. This results in tight coupling and difficult maintenance.

The remedy for temporal cohesion is to determine which modules are most closely related to the activities in the temporally cohesive module and then move the activities to those modules. To refine a structure chart for cohesion, you must review the PDL. In Figure 18.27b, the activities of the Start-Up module have been moved to the other modules of the Process Order structure chart. The clearing of the Invoice screen is now done within Read Order, EOO is initialized in Process Order, and ORDER-AMT is set to 0 in the Calculate Order Amount module.

Logical Cohesion A module has logical cohesion if its statements perform activities that are members of a general category but that are not performed at the same time. In addition, the activities are related neither by a flow of data nor by a flow of control. Get Info in Figure 18.28a is a logically cohesive module that is used for general-purpose file access. Because Get Info can access numerous files, a directive control flag (FILE-TO-READ) is required to tell it which file to access when it is called. The need for a directive control flag is a characteristic of logically cohesive modules. Notice that the name "Get Info" is vague in comparison to the names of modules with stronger cohesion. Vague, general-purpose names are characteristic of logically cohesive modules.

Logically cohesive modules suffer from a number of problems. They are difficult to understand and, hence, maintain. As with temporally cohesive modules, their activities are normally related more closely to activities performed in other modules. In addition, the need for a directive control flag means that a logically cohesive module is control coupled to its calling module.

The remedy for logical cohesion is to determine the functions performed by the module and then create separate modules based on those functions. In Figure 18.28b, Get Info has been split into the Get Customer Info, Get Order Info, and Get Shipment Info modules.

Figure 18.27
Temporal Cohesion

Process Description of Start-Up:
Set EOO to false
Clear Order screen
Set ORDER-AMT to 0

(a) Problem:

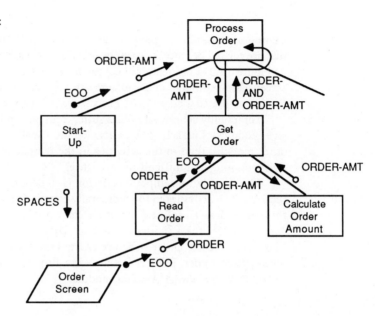

(b) Solution:

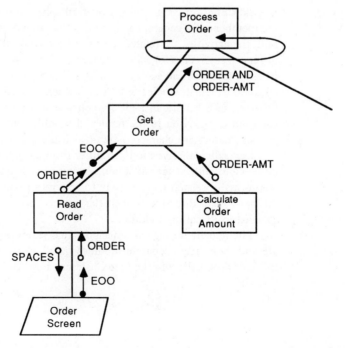

Figure 18.28
Logical Cohesion

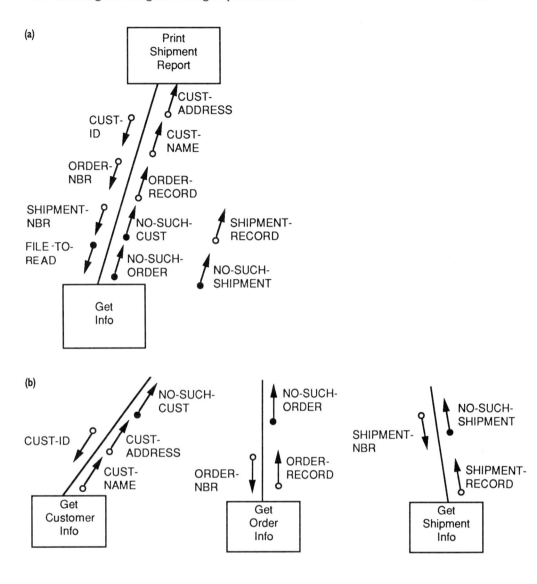

Coincidental Cohesion A module has coincidental cohesion if its statements perform functions or activities that have no apparent relationship to each other. Module XYZ in Figure 18.29a is a coincidentally cohesive module. Like the logically cohesive Get Info module, Module XYZ requires a control flag (FUNCTION-TO-PERFORM) to tell it which activities will be performed during a call. Directive control flags are also a characteristic of coincidentally cohesive modules. Whereas the name Get Info is vague, the name Module XYZ is meaningless. Meaningless names are another characteristic of coincidentally cohesive modules.

Coincidentally cohesive modules suffer from the same problems as do logically cohe-

Figure 18.29
Coincidental Cohesion

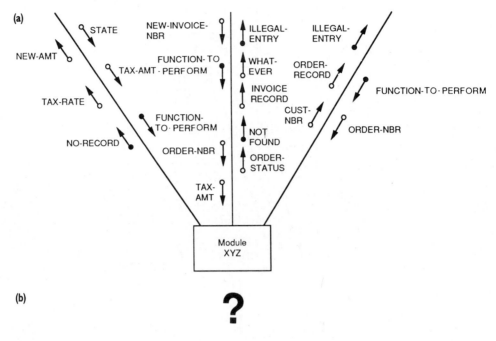

sive modules. Because there is no logical basis for the activities performed by their statements, coincidentally cohesive modules are the most difficult modules to understand and maintain.

The remedy for coincidental cohesion is to analyze the functions performed by the module and then create separate modules based on those functions. As Figure 18.29b illustrates, making sense out of a coincidentally cohesive module is not easy. Defining the directive control flag is a good way to start the analysis of the module.

It should be apparent from the above discussions of coupling and cohesion that the two guidelines are closely related. For example, a program designed as one large module would be loosely coupled but also weakly cohesive. The two criteria, therefore, must be considered together as the structure chart is refined.

18.4.3 Design Heuristics

In addition to coupling and cohesion, three other criteria are the subject of useful heuristics, or rules of thumb, for improving the quality of a program design. These criteria are (1) module size, (2) fan-out, and (3) fan-in.

Module Size   The **module size** is the number of PDL statements (or statements in the programming language used to code the module) needed to specify the activities that the module performs. In general, a module should have no more than thirty to fifty statements. Another way to phrase this rule of thumb is to say that the statements of a module should take up no more than one page of a computer listing.

Limiting the size of a module is important for two reasons. First, a large module probably has moderate or weak cohesion. Second, a large module with many statements is more difficult to understand, and hence maintain, than a module with few statements. You have probably experienced the frustration of reading a long paragraph in a book and wondering what the paragraph was about when you had finished! A paragraph is more difficult to read and understand when it spans two pages. The same holds true for program modules.

We must make an exception to the one-page limit for module size. A module that is functionally cohesive should never be reduced in size, even if it is larger than one page. For example, a functionally cohesive module that calculates the withholding amount for a state income tax should not be reduced in size, even if it contains 200 statements. (As we will discuss next, if many of the statements are calls to other modules, the module might be split to reduce fan-out.) A functionally cohesive module with 200 statements may not be easy to understand, but splitting it up into more than one module will not make understanding it any easier. In fact, the split modules will be more difficult to understand because of the complexity added by the module calls.

Fan-out   Also known as span of control, **fan-out** is the number of modules called by a module. In general, fan-out should be seven modules or less—that is, a boss module should call no more than seven subordinate modules. If a module calls more than seven modules, it is probably difficult to understand and maintain.

Seven modules is not an arbitrary limit; psychological studies have found that humans have difficulty working with more than seven concepts at the same time. Naturally, this principle applies to programmers trying to understand and maintain computer programs. In addition, a module that calls a large number of modules may suffer from weak cohesion.

Figure 18.30a provides an example of the complexity inherent in modules with high fan-out. Print Order Register in Figure 18.30a is difficult to understand (if you don't agree, just try to memorize the subordinates of Print Order Register). In Figure 18.30b, the fan-out has been reduced by creating the Print Order and Print Order Item modules as another level between Print Order Register and its former subordinates. Print Order and Print Order Item were identified by analyzing the subordinate modules for common functions. The modules that fell into one functional area were then grouped under the new boss module responsible for that function—printing an order or printing an order item. As you can see from Figure 18.30b, the new Print Order Register module with five module calls is much easier to understand than the old one in Figure 18.30a, which has ten calls.

Fan-in   **Fan-in** is the number of modules that call a module (that is, the number of bosses that a module has). Whereas we try to decrease fan-out, we want to increase the fan-in of a module as much as possible. High fan-in saves programming and maintenance effort because the same function does not have to be coded in more than one place. Print Page Heading in Figure 18.30b is an example of a module with high fan-in. The Print Page Heading module is called by three different modules.

An important restriction on the use of fan-in is that the called module must exhibit strong or moderate cohesion. The XYZ module in Figure 18.29 has very high fan-in, but

(a) Fan-out

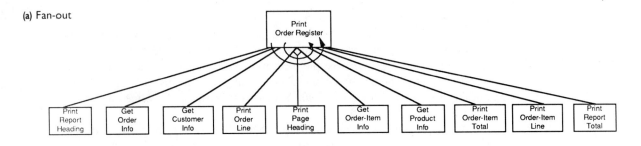

(b) Fan-in

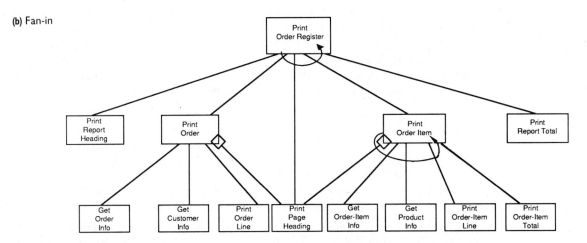

Figure 18.30   Fan-out/Fan-in

only coincidental cohesion. Any logically or coincidentally cohesive module can be made to have high fan-in, but such modules are difficult to understand and maintain.

18.4.4 Packaging, Coding, and Testing

Once the structure chart and PDL have been refined, we are at the end of the design stage and at the beginning of implementation. Before we can start implementation, however, we must combine the numerous design specifications created to this point—program, user, procedure, database, and interface—into a single, organized package that unambiguously specifies how the program specifications will be implemented as a computerized system. In addition, we must tailor the program specifications in the package so that the programs will run efficiently on the computer hardware once they are implemented. Finally, we must include in the package a strategy that programmers can follow to code and test the hierarchy of modules specified by the structure chart. Together, these activities are known as packaging the design specification.

If you have ever run into trouble assembling something because you failed to read the instructions or because the instructions were missing or unclear, you already know why packaging is such an important step. Like the do-it-yourself consumer, a programmer needs instructions for assembling the different design specifications into the programs that will become the system. If these instructions are missing or unclear, the programmer will have difficulty building the system and the quality of the system is likely to suffer.

Packaging is accomplished in two steps. The first step is adding interface and database specifications to program specifications, defining and specifying jobs, and tailoring program specifications into load modules. The second step is devising a coding and testing strategy for the programs.

Interface/Database, Jobs, and Load Modules The report and screen layouts developed during the interface design phase are the interface specifications that are added to program specifications. Interface and program specifications are combined by reviewing each structure chart and then attaching the report and/or screen layouts used by that structure chart. For example, the Invoice Entry screen specifications (see Figure 18.15) would be attached to the Create Invoice structure chart in Figure 18.5.

The database specifications added to program specifications are (1) the access paths, such as secondary indexes or keys, that modules use to retrieve or update records from files and (2) the schema for the database. File access paths are specified in the PDL of a module. During the packaging step, every module that accesses a file is reviewed to ensure that access paths have been specified.

It is important in packaging the design to document the access paths to files that are used by modules. This will ensure that programmers use the most efficient access paths when the programs are coded. In Figure 18.5, for example, Get Order-Item Amount must access the ORDER ITEM file using ORDER-NBR as a key. The designer decides the best way to access order items and then specifies the access path in the PDL for Get-Order-Item Amount. The Universal database schema in Figure 18.14 helps the designer specify access paths by supplying information about the structure of the database (for example, its indexes and keys).

The definition and specification of **jobs** is required for programs that are run at set times and in a particular sequence of steps. A job that you are probably familiar with is the balance checkbook job in Figure 18.31. Typical jobs in organizations include payroll, backup and recovery, the yearly printing of W2 income tax forms, and preparation of various internal reports such as an order register report. Notice that system flowcharts are used to specify jobs. Flowcharts are used because they are better than data flow diagrams at describing the sequence of job steps. The flow chart also can specify the time at which the job should start.

The timing of jobs is usually dictated by organizational policies or procedures. If the policy of an organization is to pay its employees every other Friday, the payroll must be run every two weeks—probably as the last job Thursday night or the first job Friday morning. The payroll checks can then be delivered to employees Friday afternoon. If the policy of an organization is to back up its computer files every night, the file backup procedure must be run every night.

The sequence of job steps is dictated by a number of factors, including established procedure, the order in which files must be updated to produce the output of the job,

Figure 18.31
Balance Checkbook
Job

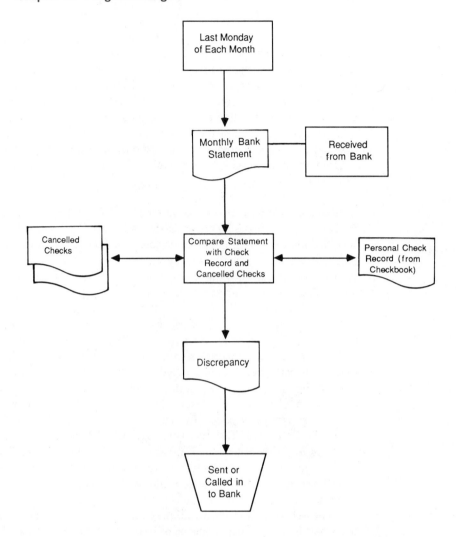

backup and recovery considerations, and whether the job is run in a batch or on-line mode. A description of the job for printing the Universal Order Register report is provided in the form of a flowchart in Figure 18.32.

The final activity of the first packaging step is defining load modules from the modules on the structure chart. A **load module** is a physical unit that is loaded into computer memory and executed. In many cases the modules of a program require more memory than the computer has available. The designer then must decide which modules will be loaded into memory at the same time and which modules will remain outside of memory.

Figure 18.33 illustrates the problem of defining load modules. In the example, the modules of the Create Invoice program require 1000 units of memory, but only 800 units of memory is available to run the program. Consequently, only part (that is, one or more modules) of the Create Invoice program can reside in memory at the same time. (The dashed lines show the memory units used by the modules.)

Figure 18.32
Job Flowchart for Universal Order Register Report

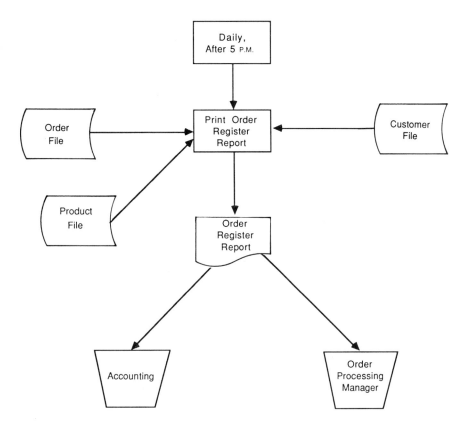

The definition of load modules is important for efficiency reasons. In general, the more modules of a program stored in memory at the same time, the faster the program will execute. Modules not in memory are swapped back and forth between disk and memory as they are needed. This process requires accesses to disk and, hence, takes more time than if all the modules of the program were loaded into memory at once.

Anyone who has swapped diskettes while using a personal computer with only one diskette drive will appreciate why the definition of load modules is so important. Typically the program and data files needed for an application are too large for a single diskette, and consequently the user is continually being interrupted by prompts from the computer's operating system to remove one diskette from the diskette drive and insert the other. This swapping action takes time and decreases the user's efficiency. This decrease in efficiency is similar to that encountered when a computer must execute a program that is too large to fit into memory in one piece.

The objective in defining load modules is to make programs run as fast as possible. A good rule of thumb is to combine into single load modules modules that frequently pass data back and forth. Figure 18.34 suggests load modules for the Create Invoice program. One load module is created for the Get Invoice Set-up Info hierarchy of modules because of the high frequency of interaction among these modules. We would definitely not want to separate the Read Invoice Screen, Read and Validate Order Number, and Write

Figure 18.33
Load Modules

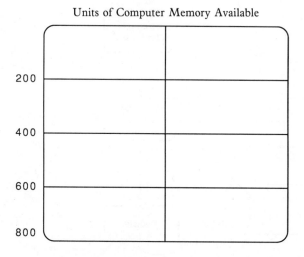

Units of Computer Memory Available

Units of Computer Memory Necessary

Invoice Error Screen modules into different load modules, because these modules can interact quite frequently—especially if the user inputs an invalid order number. Load modules are specified on the structure chart by drawing a line around the modules that will be contained in a single load module.

Coding and Testing   The second step in packaging is to devise a coding and testing strategy for the programs. Using the hierarchy of modules provided by the structure chart, we can employ one of three strategies for coding and testing: (1) top-down, (2) bottom-up, or (3) sandwich. We code and test top down by starting at the top-level modules and

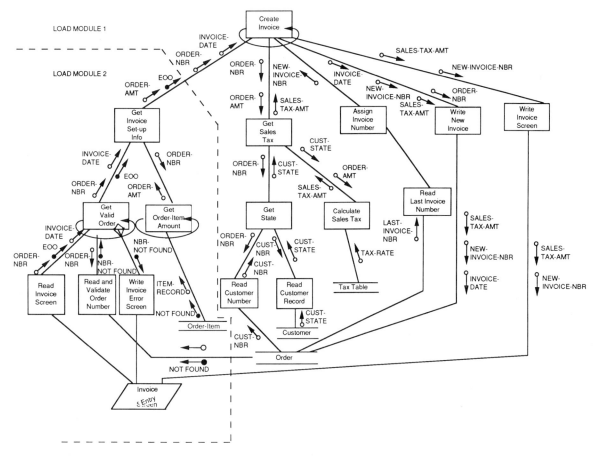

Figure 18.34 Load Modules and Create Invoice Structure Chart

working toward the bottom of the module hierarchy. Bottom-up coding and testing starts at the lowest level modules and works up through the hierarchy. Finally, coding and testing can take place top down for the top-level modules and bottom up for the lower-level modules. This strategy is known as the sandwich strategy. Each of these strategies will be discussed fully in Chapter 21.

18.5 Designing Programs

The creation and refinement of structure charts guides the design of programs. The steps in designing programs for a system are

1. Review the data flow diagram and interface specifications to identify programs.
2. Select a data flow diagram for one program.
3. Perform transform or transaction analysis:

Figure 18.35
Method for Program
Design

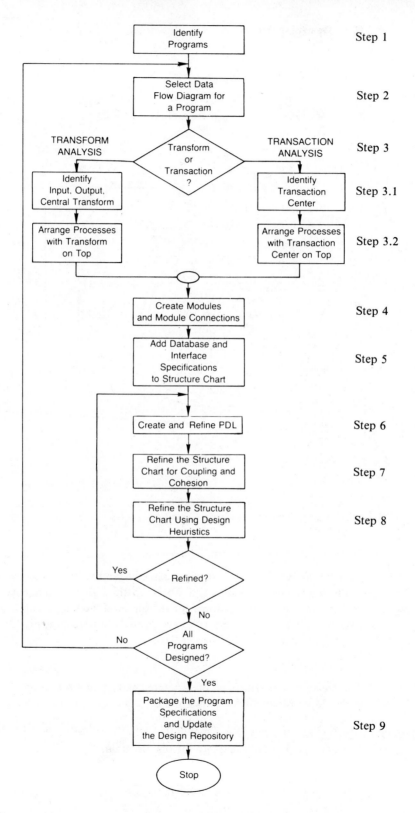

Step 1 — Identify Programs

Step 2 — Select Data Flow Diagram for a Program

Step 3 — Transform or Transaction ?

TRANSFORM ANALYSIS

TRANSACTION ANALYSIS

Step 3.1 — Identify Input, Output, Central Transform / Identify Transaction Center

Step 3.2 — Arrange Processes with Transform on Top / Arrange Processes with Transaction Center on Top

Step 4 — Create Modules and Module Connections

Step 5 — Add Database and Interface Specifications to Structure Chart

Step 6 — Create and Refine PDL

Step 7 — Refine the Structure Chart for Coupling and Cohesion

Step 8 — Refine the Structure Chart Using Design Heuristics

Refined? — Yes

All Programs Designed? — No

Step 9 — Package the Program Specifications and Update the Design Repository

Stop

If transform analysis:

3.1 Identify the input, output, and central transform processes.

3.2 On a sheet of paper, arrange the processes so that the central transform is at the top, the inputs are on the left, and the outputs are on the right.

If transaction analysis:

3.1 Identify the transaction center.

3.2 On a sheet of paper, arrange the processes so that the transaction center is at the top.

4. Change the processes into modules and the data flows into module connections.

5. Add database and interface specifications to the structure chart.

6. Convert the structured English for each process into PDL for each module.

7. Refine the program design for coupling and cohesion.

8. Refine the program design using design heuristics.

9. Package the program specifications once all the programs for the system have been specified. Update the design repository.

When the design is complete, the deliverables will include the packaged structure chart and PDL. The method for structured program design is shown in the form of a flowchart in Figure 18.35.

MINICASE

Return to Meadows Hospital

Fred Kahn, the programmer/analyst assigned to the project, and Tracy Bell, the project leader, have been charged with developing the programs for the Meadows Hospital pharmacy system.

I. Review the Data Flow Diagram and Interface Specifications to Identify Programs

Fred and Tracy begin by reviewing the pharmacy system data flow diagram in Figure 18.36 and the list of interfaces in Figure 18.37. They identify five programs to be designed: the Enter Prescription Data screen, Fill Prescription screen, Daily Drug Log report, Supplier report, and Prescription Label program.

2. Select a Data Flow Diagram for One Program

Fred and Tracy select the Enter Prescription Data screen as the first program to be designed. They start by analyzing the processes on the Enter Prescription DFD in Figure 18.38.

3 and 4. Perform Transform or Transaction Analysis and Change the Processes into Modules and the Data Flows into Module Connections

Because Enter Prescription Data is composed of sequential processes, they decide to use transform analysis to create the first-cut structure chart shown in Figure 18.39. There is no process in the Enter Prescription Data DFD that stands out as the central transform, so Fred and Tracy create an artificial "Enter Prescription Data" module to serve as the central transform.

5. Add Database and Interface Specifications to the Structure Chart

Fred and Tracy use the display layout chart for the Prescription Entry Screen (shown in Figure 18.40) and the schema for the pharmacy database (shown in Figure 18.41) to add database and interface specifications to the Enter Prescription Data structure chart. They add read modules to the structure chart for the Prescription Entry

Figure 18.36
Process Prescriptions
DFD

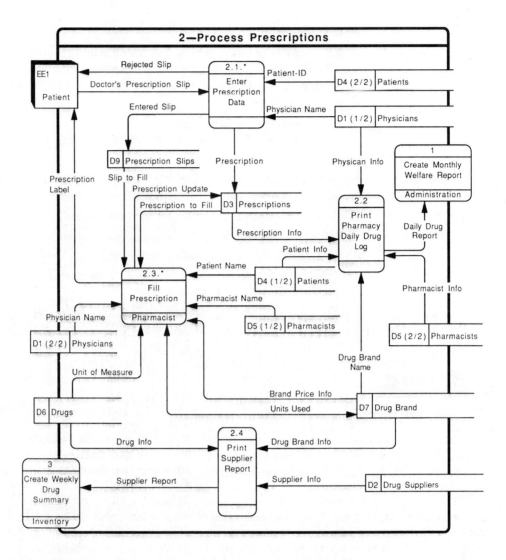

screen, Field Edit table, PHYSICIAN file, and PATIENT file. They add a write module to the structure chart for the PRESCRIPTION file and the Prescription Entry screen. The write module is needed for the screen to inform the user of errors or problems with the input data, such as a nonnumeric field or an invalid physician name. During this step, Fred and Tracy also add data and control flows to the structure chart. For example, the EXIT and PHYS-NAMES (display the physician names in the database) control flags were added from the Prescription Entry screen specifications (see Figure 18.40). Finally,

they add the Display Physician Names module to the structure chart. This module was not a process on the Enter Prescription Data DFD, but it was an option on the Prescription Entry screen. The second-cut structure chart is shown in Figure 18.42.

6. Convert the Structured English for Each Process into PDL for Each Module

Fred and Tracy create PDL specifications for every module on the structure chart except Enter Prescription Data. They do not specify PDL for Enter Prescription

No.	Name	Type	Data Elements
	Figure 18.37 Pharmacy System In- terface Table		
1	Daily Drug Log	Internal report	PRCT-ID-NBR, PAT-LAST-NAME, PAT-FIRST-NAME, PHY-LAST-NAME, PHY-MID-INIT-NAME, PHY-FIRST-NAME, DRUG-NAME, DRUGB-NAME
2	Prescription Entry Screen	Data entry	DRUG-NAME, PAT-ID-NBR, PAT-LAST-NAME, PHY-FIRST-NAME, PHY-MID-INIT-NAME, PHY-LAST-NAME, PRCT-DATE, PRCT-DRUG-QTY-NBR, PRCT-DOSE-IS-TEXT
3	Prescription Update Screen	Data entry	DRUG-NAME, PAT-ID-NBR, PHY-LAST-NAME, PRCT-DATE, PRCT-DRUG-QTY-NBR, PRCT-DOSE-IS-TEXT, PHAR-EMP-ID-NBR, DRUGB-NAME, DRUGB-UNIT-PR-AMT, DRUGB-UNIT-AV-NBR, DRUG-UOM-CODE
4	Prescription Label (printed from Prescription Update screen)	External document	PRCT-ID-NBR, PHY-LAST-NAME, PHY-FIRST-NAME, PHY-MID-INIT-NAME, PAT-LAST-NAME, PAT-FIRST-NAME, PRCT-DOSE-IS-TEXT, DRUGB-NAME, PRCT-DRUG-QTY-NBR, PHAR-FIRST-NAME
5	Supplier Report	Internal report	DRUGSP-NAME, DRUGSP-VEN-ID-NBR, DRUG-NAME, DRUGB-NAME, DRUG-UOM-CODE-DRUGB-YTD-USE-NBR, DRUGB-UNIT-AV-NBR

Data, because they know the module will change dramatically when the structure chart is refined.

7 and 8. Refine the Program Design for Coupling, Cohesion, Module Size, Fan-out, and Fan-in

Fred and Tracy notice that the modules on the Enter Prescription Data structure chart suffer from control and stamp coupling. The control coupling results from the REJECT-PRCT-PHYS-NAME (reject this prescription be-

cause the physician name is invalid) and REJECT-PRCT-PAT-ID control flows. These control flows direct the processing of the Enter Prescription Data and the Input Prescription Data modules. Fred and Tracy simply change the two directive control flows into reporting control flows to alleviate the control coupling. The names of the data flows are changed to NOTFOUND-PHYS-NAME (this physician's name was not found in the database) and NOTFOUND-PAT-ID.

The stamp coupling occurs between Enter Prescrip-

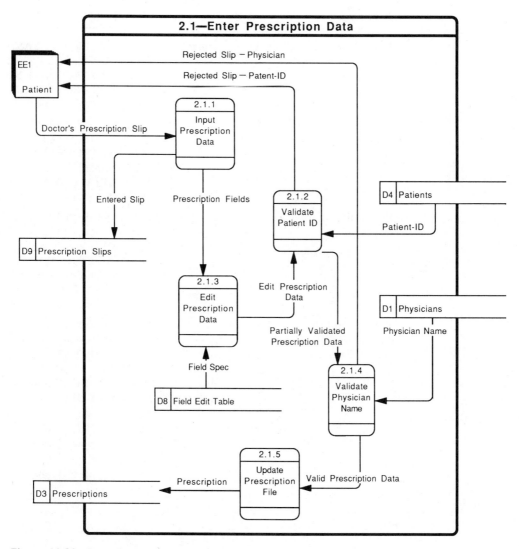

Figure 18.38 Enter Prescription Data DFD

tion Data and its subordinate modules. Fred and Tracy notice that various forms of the PRCT-RECORD data flow (for example, PRCT-FIELDS, EDITED-PRCT-REC-ORD, and PART-VALID-PRCT-RECORD) are passed through the entire structure chart when in fact only parts of the record are needed by most modules. For example, the entire Prescription record is passed to the Validate Physician Name module, but the modue validates only the PHYS-NAME element of the record.

The stamp coupling is alleviated by creating additional levels of modules and breaking down the all-purpose data flows for the Prescription record into specific data elements. Figure 18.43 is the final structure chart for the Enter Prescription Data program. The most important change made by Fred and Tracy to the program design is the creation of the Get Prescription Record module. The PDL for Get Prescription Record is shown in Figure 18.44.

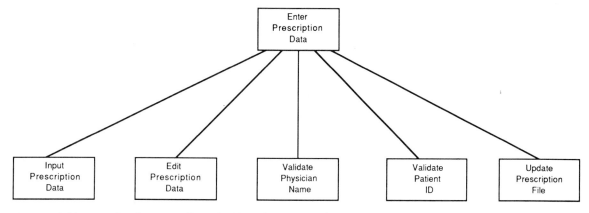

Figure 18.39 First-Cut Structure Chart for Enter Prescription Data

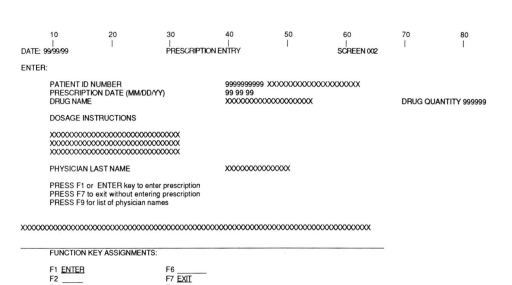

```
         10          20          30          40          50          60          70          80
         |           |           |           |           |           |           |           |
DATE: 99/99/99                    PRESCRIPTION ENTRY                  SCREEN 002

ENTER:

         PATIENT ID NUMBER                    9999999999  XXXXXXXXXXXXXXXXXXXX
         PRESCRIPTION DATE (MM/DD/YY)         99 99 99
         DRUG NAME                            XXXXXXXXXXXXXXXXXXX         DRUG QUANTITY 999999

         DOSAGE INSTRUCTIONS

         XXXXXXXXXXXXXXXXXXXXXXXXXXXXXX
         XXXXXXXXXXXXXXXXXXXXXXXXXXXXXX
         XXXXXXXXXXXXXXXXXXXXXXXXXXXXXX

         PHYSICIAN LAST NAME                  XXXXXXXXXXXXXX

         PRESS F1 or  ENTER key to enter prescription
         PRESS F7 to exit without entering prescription
         PRESS F9 for list of physician names


XXXXXXXXXXXXXXXXXXXXXXXXXXXXXXXXXXXXXXXXXXXXXXXXXXXXXXXXXXXXXXXXXXXXXXXXXXXXXXXXX
```

FUNCTION KEY ASSIGNMENTS:

F1 <u>ENTER</u>   F6 _____
F2 _____   F7 <u>EXIT</u>
F3 _____   F8 _____
F4 _____   F9 <u>LIST PHYS NAMES</u>
F5 _____   F10 _____

DATA DICTIONARY:

NO	SCREEN NAME	ELEMENT NAME	TYPE	SIZE	EDIT MASK	EDITING/VALIDATION
1	DATE	FROM SYSTEM	N	8	99/99/99	
2	PATIENT ID NUMBER	PAT-ID-NBR	N	10	9(10)	MUST CONTAIN VALID VALUE
3	ECHO FIELD	PAT-LAST-NAME	C	20	X(20)	DISPLAY ONLY
4	PRESCRIPTION DATE	PRCT-ID-NBR	N	8	99 99 99	MUST CONTAIN A VALUE
5	DRUG NAME	DRUG-NAME	C	20	X(20)	MUST CONTAIN A VALUE
6	DRUG QUANTITY	PRCT-DRUG-QTY-NBR	N	6	999999	MUST CONTAIN A VALUE
7	DOSAGE INSTRUCTIONS	PRCT-DOSE-IST-TEXT	C	90	X(30)	MUST CONTAIN A VALUE
8					X(30)	SPLIT INTO 3 FIELDS
9					X(30)	
10	PHYSICIAN LAST NAME	PHYS-LAST-NAME	C	15	X(15)	MUST CONTAIN VALID VALUE
11	MESSAGE LINE	from program	C	80	X(80)	ERROR

ERROR MESSAGES:

001   A value was not entered for this field.
002   Physician name does not exist in database - Press F9 for list of physicians.

Figure 18.40 Display Layout Chart for Prescription Entry Screen

Figure 18.41
DB2 DDL for the
Pharmacy Database

```
CREATE TABLE DRUG
  (   DRUG-NAME              CHAR (20) NOT NULL,
      DRUG-UOM-CODE          CHAR(4) );

CREATE TABLE DRUG-BRAND
  (   DRUG-NAME              CHAR(20) NOT NULL,
      DRUGSP-VEN-ID-NBR      INTEGER(10) NOT NULL,
      DRUGB -NAME            CHAR(20) NOT NULL,
      DRUGB-UNIT-PR-AMT      DECIMAL(7),
      DRUGB-UNIT-AV-NBR      DECIMAL(7),
      DRUGB-YTD-USE-NBR      DECIMAL(10) );

CREATE TABLE DRUG-SUPPLIER
  (   DRUGSP-VEN  -ID-NBR    INTEGER(10) NOT NULL,
      DRUGSP-NAME            CHAR(20) );

CREATE TABLE PATIENT
  (   PAT-ID-NBR             INTEGER(10) NOT NULL,
      PAT-FIRST-NAME         CHAR(15),
      PAT-LAST-NAME          CHAR(20) );

CREATE TABLE PHARMACIST
  (   PHAR-EMP-ID-NBR        INTEGER(10) NOT NULL,
      PHAR-LAST-NAME         CHAR(20),
      PHAR-FIRST-NAME        CHAR(15) );

CREATE TABLE PHYSICIAN
  (   PHY-LAST-NAME          CHAR(20) NOT NULL,
      PHY-FIRST-NAME         CHAR(15),
      PHY-MID-INIT-NAME      CHAR(2) );

CREATE TABLE PRESCRIPTION
  (   PRCT-ID-NBR            INTEGER(10) NOT NULL,
      PRCT-DATE              INTEGER(8) NOT NULL,
      PAT-ID-NBR             INTEGER (10) NOT NULL,
      PHY-LAST-NAME          CHAR(20) NOT NULL,
      DRUG-NAME              CHAR(20) NOT NULL,
      DRUGSP-VEN-ID-NBR      INTEGER(10) NOT NULL,
      PRCT-DRUG-QTY-NBR      DECIMAL(6),
      PRCT-DOSE-IS-TEXT      CHAR(90),
      PHAR-EMP-ID-NBR        INTEGER(10) );

CREATE UNIQUE INDEX Primary_DRUG ON DRUG (DRUG-NAME);
CREATE UNIQUE INDEX Primary_DRUG-BRAND ON DRUG-BRAND
(DRUG-NAME, DRUGSP-VEN-ID-NBR);
CREATE UNIQUE INDEX Primary_DRUG-SUPPLIER ON DRUG
SUPPLIER (DRUGSP-VEN-ID-NBR);
CREATE UNIQUE INDEX Primary_PATIENT ON PATIENT (PAT-ID-NBR);
CREATE UNIQUE INDEX Primary_PHARMACIST ON PHARMACIST (PHAR-EMP-ID-NBR);
CREATE UNIQUE INDEX Primary_PHYSICIAN ON PHYSICIAN (PHY-LAST-NAME);
CREATE INDEX PRCT-DATE-INDEX ON PRESCRIPTION (PRCT-DATE);
CREATE UNIQUE INDEX Primary_PRESCRIPTION ON PRESCRIPTION (PRCT-ID-NBR);
```

```
GRANT ALL ON PRESCRIPTION TO PHARMA
GRANT ALL ON PHYSICIAN TO PHARMACY
GRANT ALL ON PATIENT TO PHARMACY
GRANT ALL ON PHARMACIST TO PHARMAC
GRANT ALL ON DRUG-BRAND TO PHARMAC
GRANT ALL ON DRUG TO PHARMACY
GRANT ALL ON DRUG-SUPPLIER TO PHARM

GRANT SELECT ON PRESCRIPTION TO STA
GRANT SELECT ON PHYSICIAN TO STAFF
GRANT SELECT ON PATIENT TO STAFF
GRANT SELECT ON PHARMACIST TO STAF
GRANT SELECT ON DRUG-BRAND TO STAF
GRANT SELECT ON DRUG TO STAFF
GRANT SELECT ON DRUG-SUPPLIER TO ST
```

Get Prescription Record greatly reduces the coupling between Enter Prescription Data and its subordinate modules. With the new design, Enter Prescription Data only passes PRCT-FIELDS to the Update Prescription file, evaluates the EXIT control flow to determine whether the user wants to quit the session, and evaluates the PHYS-NAMES control flow to determine whether the

user wants to review a list of physician names. The Display Physician Names module represents a program that is specified by another structure chart, so it is not broken down into its subordinate modules on the Enter Prescription Data structure chart.

As Fred and Tracy evaluate and change the modules for coupling, they also evaluate the cohesion, module

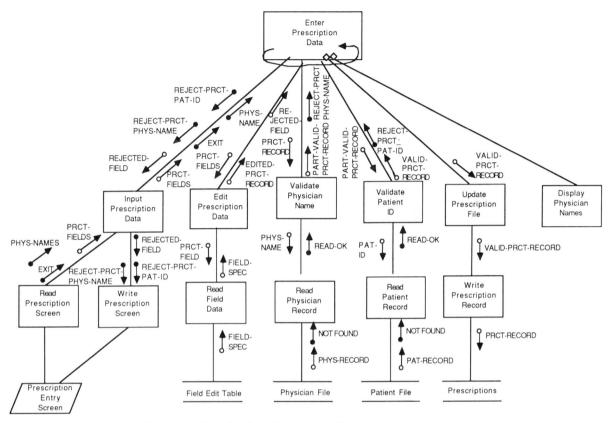

Figure 18.42 Second-Cut Structure Chart for Enter Prescription Data

size, fan-out, and fan-in of individual modules. All of the modules appear to be functionally cohesive. Each module performs a distinct function that is accurately named by a single verb-object pair. The size of each module is within the thirty-to-fifty-statement limit, and no module has a fan-out greater than seven modules.

9. Package the Program Specifications and Update the Design Repository

Fred and Tracy package the program specifications after they have finished all five structure charts for the pharmacy system. For the first packaging step, they attach report or screen specifications to each structure chart and review modules to ensure that file access paths are specified. They also include the pharmacy database schema in the package. Then they create a flowchart for the Daily Drug Log report. They determine that the report is a job because it must be produced and delivered on a daily schedule to the Administration department. The flowchart is shown in Figure 18.45. Finally, they determine that each program is small enough to be a single load module. This fact is noted on each structure chart.

For the second packaging step, Fred and Tracy suggest a top-down strategy for coding and testing the pharmacy system programs.

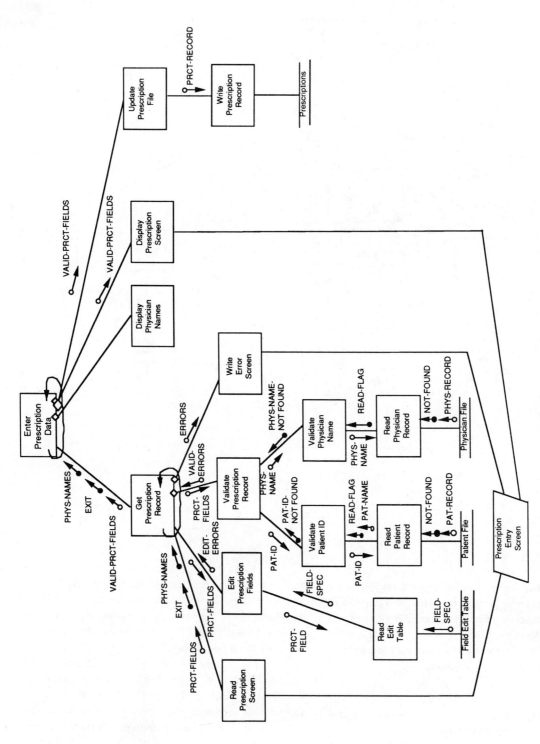

Figure 18.43 Final Structure Chart for Enter Prescription Module

Figure 18.44

PDL for Get
Prescription Record

```
BEGIN Get Prescription Record ( VALID-PRCT-FIELDS, EXIT, PHYS-NAMES;)
    SET GOOD-REC to false
    CLEAR EDIT-ERRORS, VALID-ERRORS, ERRORS arrays
    REPEAT UNTIL GOOD-REC is true
        CALL Read Prescription Screen (;PRCT-FIELDS, EXIT, PHYS-NAMES)
        IF EXIT or PHYS-NAMES is true
        THEN
            GO TO end-label
        END-IF
        CALL Edit Prescription Fields (PRCT-FIELDS; EDIT-ERRORS)
        IF EDIT-ERRORS is not blank
        THEN
            MOVE EDIT-ERRORS to ERRORS
        ELSE
            CALL Validate Prescription Record (PRCT-FIELDS; VALID-ERRORS)
            IF VALID-ERRORS is not blank
            THEN
                MOVE VALID-ERRORS to ERRORS
            END-IF
        END-IF
        IF ERRORS is blank
        THEN
            SET GOOD-REC to true
        ELSE
            CALL Write Error Screen (ERRORS;)
        END-IF
    END REPEAT
end-label
END Get Prescription Record
```

Figure 18.45

Job Flowchart for
Daily Drug Log

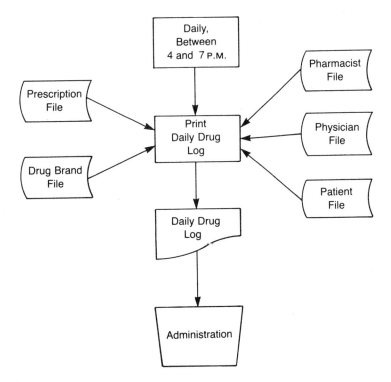

18.6 Design Tools for Program Generation

Computer Aided System Engineering (CASE) tools can reduce the tediousness of design, increase the productivity of developers, and improve the quality of design. CASE tools that generate program code can dramatically increase programmer productivity by eliminating program construction and reducing the time required for testing programs.

Figure 18.46 is a copy of a layout screen for MicroSTEP, a CASE tool that produces executable programs for the IBM/PC family of computers. A MicroSTEP flow diagram contains both data flow and procedural information—the two components required to complete a description of any working system. Inside the boundary of Figure 18.36 lies the same data flow information as in the Figure 18.46 diagram. Behind the MicroSTEP screen is a design repository that has been filled in with the details on data and program logic necessary to generate a complete system. Once the developer has designed the system, a MicroSTEP component checks the design for completeness and consistency. When all the design errors have been resolved, MicroSTEP produces an executable program for the design.

Figure 18.46
Layout Screen for
MicroSTEP CASE Tool

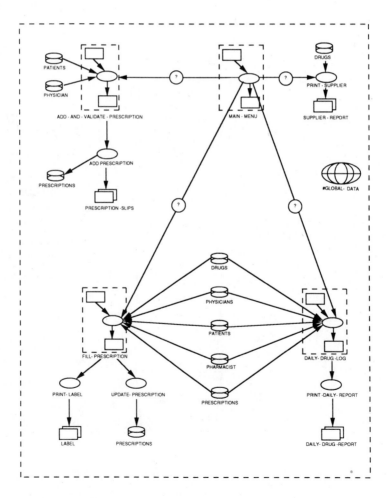

Summary

Program design is the process of creating specifications that will guide programmers in implementing a system. The objectives in creating program specifications are to ensure that programs (1) satisfy user information requirements and (2) are easy to maintain. Structured program design helps us achieve these two objectives by ensuring that the design process begins with the DFD, which was approved by the users, and by providing a set of techniques and guidelines that reduces the complexity of programs.

The main techniques of structured program design are the structure chart and PDL. A structure chart is a graphic representation of modules, module connections, and data and control flows along module connections. Program definition language (PDL) is a formal syntax for specifying the processing statements of modules.

We begin the structured design process by converting data flow diagrams into structure charts and process descriptions into PDL. Two strategies are available for converting a data flow diagram into a structure chart: transform and transaction analysis. Transform analysis is used if the data flow diagram contains sequential-type processes. Transaction analysis is used if the data flow diagram contains case-structured processes.

Once the structure chart has been created, it is refined using the guidelines of structured design. The two most important guidelines relate to coupling and cohesion. Coupling measures the independence of modules from other modules—the objective is to design loosely coupled, independent modules. Cohesion measures the strength of association between the statements of a module—the objective is to design strongly cohesive, functional modules. Other useful strategies for refining the structure chart include limiting the size of a module to less than fifty statements, limiting the fan-out of a module to seven modules, and maximizing the fan-in of a module.

Packaging is the important final step in structured program design. Packaging involves adding interface and database specifications to program specifications, defining and specifying jobs, tailoring program specifications into load modules, and devising a coding and testing strategy for the programs.

Key Terms

(Section numbers are in parentheses.)

structured program design (18.1)	**coupling (18.4.1)**
structure chart (18.2.1)	**data structure (18.4.1)**
module (18.2.1)	**cohesion (18.4.2)**
control flow (18.2.1)	**module size (18.4.3)**
data flow (18.2.1)	**fan-out (18.4.3)**
Program definition language (PDL) (18.2.2)	**fan-in (18.4.3)**
transform analysis (18.3.1)	**jobs (18.4.4)**
transaction analysis (18.3.2)	**load module (18.4.4)**
incremental strategy (18.3.4)	

Exercises

(Answers to Exercises 18.1, 18.2, 18.3, and 18.4, are at the end of the book.)

18.1 Explain how the data flow diagram is used in the program design process.

18.2 List and explain the symbols used in a structure chart.

18.3 Compare and contrast PDL and structured English.

18.4 Explain transform and transaction analysis.

18.5 Evaluate the structure chart in Figure 18.47 on each of the following characteristics:

    a. Coupling   **b.** Cohesion   **c.** Fan-out and fan-in

Figure 18.47

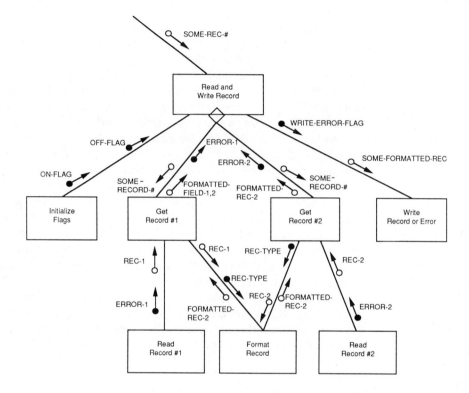

18.6 At the county courthouse, a sequential match process is run daily to create a summary file of pet stores in each county of the state. Each pet store record (from the pet store file) is matched with a county master record (from the county master file record). If no county master matching record is found for a pet store record, an error code of 1 is set. If a pet store record has fields that are invalid for particular county master fields, error codes are set. Errors are listed on an error summary and detail report.

    Totals from all valid pet store records are accumulated for each county. A County Analysis Summary report is created showing these totals. An Error report is also created. The other output is a new file: one record per county is created on the County Analysis Summary file. Each of these outputs has county description information from the county master file and totals accumulated from the valid pet store records. There is also a total line at the end of the County Analysis Summary report that gives statewide totals. This report goes to all regional offices and the state commissioner. The File DFD for this system is shown in Figure 18.48.

    Create a structure chart for the system, using the DFD and process description. You are not required to show data and control flows.

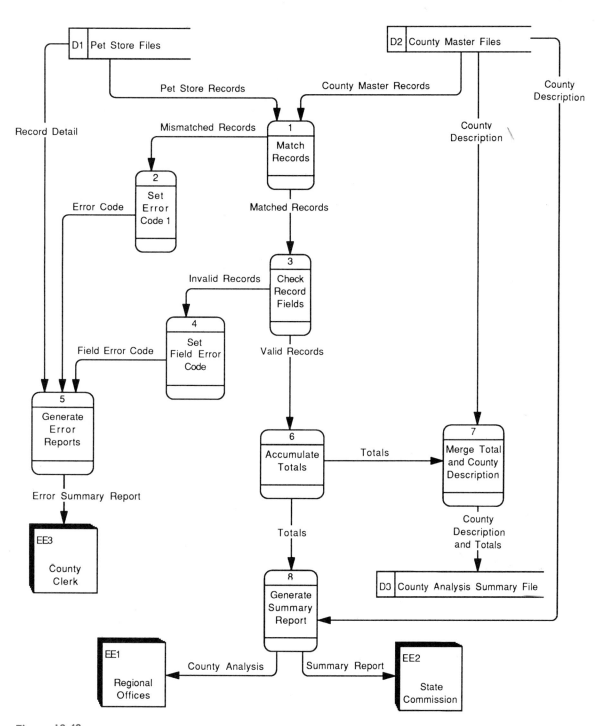

Figure 18.48

18.7 Use the structure chart created in Exercise 18.6 to answer the following questions. State any assumptions you feel are necessary.

   a. Does your design have minimal coupling? Explain your answer.

   b. Is your design cohesive? Explain your answer.

   c. Draw a job flowchart for the County Analysis Summary and File DFD.

6

Implementation Activities

Implementation Overview

Every day in committee rooms around the world, people propose ideas to solve problems or to take advantage of opportunities. When these ideas seem worthwhile and feasible, they are usually stated more formally in a proposal memo or report. This formal document outlines the problem or opportunity and presents a plan for addressing its requirements. Once this plan has been approved, someone—often the original proposer—is given the task of implementing the idea or putting the plan into practice. Often the toughest job is making what looks good on paper work in the real world.

So far we've focused on the ideas-on-paper stages of this scenario. You've learned how to respond to user-suggested problems and opportunities by identifying requirements, evaluating alternatives, and designing a system to meet the user's needs. Now you're ready to learn how to turn those plans on paper into systems that contribute to the organization's well-being and growth.

From our previous discussions of the systems development process, you know that implementing a system absorbs slightly more than half of the project effort and cost. Your goal as a systems developer is to minimize the percentage of resources absorbed during this fourth stage by completing the first three stages as carefully and thoughtfully as feasible. Putting more time and effort into the earlier ideas-on-paper stages should pay off now in an implementation that is efficient and orderly.

In Part 6 we will detail the implementation activities of the systems development process. Specifically, we plan to

1. Present an overview of these activities. (Chapter 19)

2. Discuss system construction, documentation, and training. (Chapter 20)

3. Explain the testing process. (Chapter 21)

4. Address installation changeover and post-installation activities and issues. (Chapter 22)

19.1 What Is Implementation?

Implementation is the completion stage of the systems development project. Its activities turn the design of the proposed system into a system for production use. The basic implementation activities for all five system components are summarized in Figure 19.1. Creating a functioning system from plans on paper requires three basic activities:

1. Construction

2. Testing

3. Installing

19.1.1 Implementation Activities

System construction is the process of building the five system components to meet the specifications developed during the design phase. Your role in constructing a system is

Figure 19.1
Summary of Implementation Activities

	People	Procedures	Data	Software	Hardware
Determine Requirements					
Evaluate Alternatives					
Specify Design					
Implement Design	Train users	Test and document procedures	Build test files and production files; test and install	Code if necessary; test and install software	Prepare site; install and test hardware

similar to that of a builder in constructing a house. Just as a builder works from an architect's blueprints, you work from the system design specifications to turn plans on paper into a tangible product. For example, through your efforts as a programmer, program specifications will become working software and data files. If your role is that of an end-user consultant, you may help the user purchase hardware and prepare the installation site. Or, using the knowledge you gained from observing procedures and interviewing users, you may write user manuals and create training materials. If yours is an administrative role, you may be responsible for writing a job description for a database specialist and then hiring someone to fill that position.

As this short list of construction roles and activities suggests, construction involves numerous and varied activities and often requires the combined skills and efforts of a large development team. Managing these efforts is vital to the success of the system; how closely the system constructed conforms to the system designed depends largely on the coordination of designers, programmers, and trainers—how well the five system components are integrated into a single, smoothly functioning system.

As the system is constructed, you will test the individual components to ensure that the users understand the procedures, that the hardware operates correctly, and that the software produces the correct output. You will build test data files to evaluate the reliability of the system; you will observe end-users and system operators to be sure that the procedures you've constructed are clear and that you've accurately represented the tasks to be performed. Testing is the process of ensuring that the system quality goals are met when the system is installed.

Remember that every system is tested eventually. You can test the system now, while its errors and inefficiencies can be corrected relatively easily and inexpensively. Or you can let the users test it after it is installed and risk frustrated users and expensive revisions. Testing after installation is analogous to leaving it to the home buyer to discover that there are no electrical outlets in the kitchen. A home builder should check such details as the house is built, so system omissions and errors are discovered *before* the wallboard goes up and the drywall is applied. Your success as a systems developer depends on your attention to detail and your awareness that, no matter how many times you've done something correctly in the past, there's always a chance that this time you've done it wrong. Avoid living dangerously: always test before you install.

Once you've tested all the system components, you're ready to install the system. Installation is the process of putting the system into production use. The transition from the old system to the new system can be achieved in several ways—the best approach depends on the nature of the system to be installed. Your goals here are to make the transition smoothly, to obtain management approval, and to turn control of the system over to the production staff. Achievement of these goals ends the implementation process and signals the end of a successful systems development cycle.

19.1.2 The Timing of Implementation Activities

In the standard life cycle approach, implementation activities are concentrated in the final stage of the project. A list of the activities commonly performed during implementation is given in Figure 19.2. Note that in this list, construction and test activities alternate. You should never build an entire system without repeatedly testing the hardware, soft-

Figure 19.2

Checklist of Implementation Activities

I.1 Preliminary construction

    I.1.1 Prepare site

    I.1.2 Install hardware

    I.1.3 Install (or code) software

    I.1.4 Build test files

    I.1.5 Prepare training materials and documentation

I.2 Preliminary test

    I.2.1 Test components

    I.2.2 Test system

I.3 Final construction

    I.3.1 Revise software

    I.3.2 Build production files

    I.3.3 Document procedures

    I.3.4 Hire and train personnel

I.4 Test

    I.4.1 Test subsystems

    I.4.2 Test system

I.5 Install system

I.6 Obtain management approval (of completion)

I.7 Changeover

ware, data, and procedures components as they are constructed. By building small, well-designed test files and then using these files to verify that each component works correctly, you can identify problems early and correct them before they mushroom into colossal headaches during production use.

If you follow the phased development approach, the preliminary construction and testing activities (I.1 and I.2 in Figure 19.2) will be interspersed with requirements determination, evaluation, and design activities. Nonetheless, the final construction and testing activities will follow the standard pattern outlined in I.3 and I.4 and will be succeeded in order by installation, approval, and changeover. Thus, steps I.1 and I.2 may vary depending on the development approach you adopt, but the final steps, I.3 through I.7, will be basically the same no matter what approach you follow.

Figures 19.3 and 19.4 present CPM models of these implementation activities. Figure 19.3 focuses on preliminary construction and testing details; Figure 19.4 focuses on final construction and testing details. These illustrations show that the activities may not proceed in exactly the order given in Figure 19.2 and that some activities are performed concurrently with others. Each implementation activity will be discussed fully in Chapters 20, 21, and 22.

Figure 19.3
Overview CPM Model
for Implementation
with Preliminary
Construction and
Testing Details
(Purchased or Existing
Software Component)

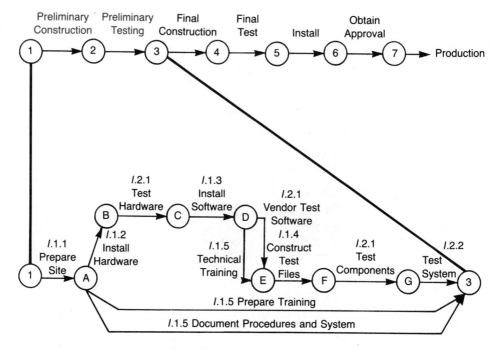

19.2 The Total Development Effort

We've already discussed the iterative nature of the system life cycle, so you know that a system is developed and put into production and then repeatedly revised and returned to production. In this section we will review how much effort implementation takes during the initial development phase, which encompasses the activities required to put a new system into production use. We will then discuss the relative amounts of effort spent on initial development and on ongoing development, which encompasses revisions to and maintenance of a system already in production use.

19.2.1 The Effort Implementation Consumes During Initial Development

When a system is first developed using third generation tools, implementation activities will consume over half of the development effort.[1] The top pie chart in Figure 19.5 summarizes the division of effort among stages and highlights the effort consumed by implementation using third generation tools. The bottom pie chart in Figure 19.5 segments the implementation effort into its three components: construction, testing, and installation. Notice that constructing the system consumes 36 percent of the total development effort; this percentage is consistent with the 3-times-programming rule that you learned in Chapter 6. Construction involves building test files, documenting procedures, coding programs, and training users, as well as coding programs.

When you develop a system using existing software or fourth generation tools, you

Figure 19.4
Overview CPM Model
for Implementation
with Final
Construction and
Testing Details

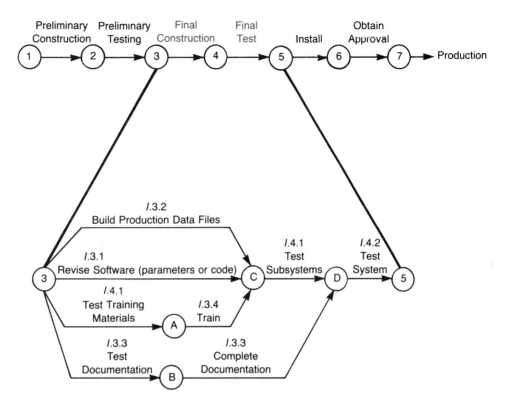

reduce construction effort, thereby reducing the percentage of the total development effort consumed by implementation. Building a system with purchased software eliminates the tremendous effort of coding programs and may reduce the effort required to develop user documentation and training materials. Using fourth generation tools will reduce the effort involved in coding programs (remember the adjustment in the 3-times-programming rule for 4GLs); however, the amount of effort involved in documenting procedures and preparing training materials will not be affected.

No matter how you construct the software component of a system—third or fourth generation language, purchased or custom-developed software—you will still need to build test files, document procedures, and train users and then test and install the system. Thus, using fourth generation tools or existing software *reduces but does not eliminate* the effort required to implement a system.

19.2.2 Development Effort Over the Full Life Cycle

The life cycle of a system is a series of development and production phases. These periods of development and production alternate, with total development costs accumulating over the life cycle of the system. Studies have shown that for ten-year-old systems, only 20 to

Figure 19.5
Distribution of Effort
for Systems
Development with
Third Generation
Tools—First-Time
Development

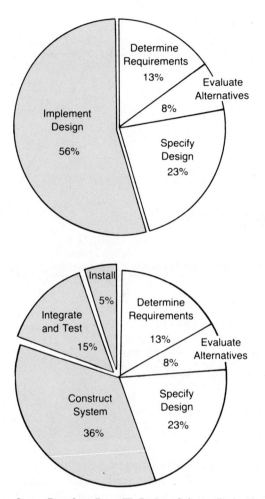

Source: Data from Barry W. Boehm, *Software Engineering Economics* (Englewood Cliffs, N.J.: Prentice-Hall, 1981), pp. 64–65.

40 percent of the total development costs were incurred during the initial development period.[2] The other 60 to 80 percent of the development costs resulted from revisions to the initial system.

The common term for system revisions is **maintenance.** An extensive study of 487 information systems divisions indicated that information systems staff spend almost half their time maintaining current systems,[3] as illustrated in the top pie chart in Figure 19.6. Careful readers may have noted a discrepancy between the findings of the two studies just cited. The first study attributed 60 to 80 percent of effort to maintenance; the second study found that 49 percent of the total effort was expended for maintenance. The higher figure is based only on systems that have lasted at least ten years and that have, therefore, been maintained for ten or more years. Systems that are discarded sooner contribute to

Figure 19.6

Time Spent on New-System Development and Maintenance

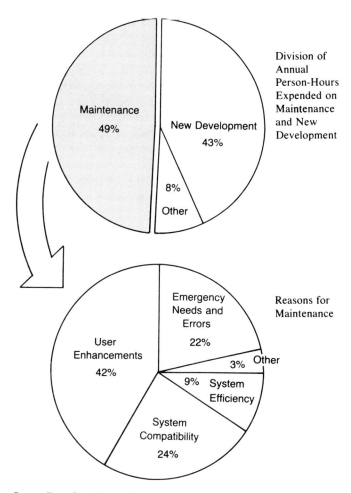

Division of Annual Person-Hours Expended on Maintenance and New Development

Reasons for Maintenance

Source: Data from Bennet P. Lientz and E. Burton Swanson, *Software Maintenance Management* (Reading, Mass.: Addison-Wesley, 1980), p. 24 and p. 73.

the lower average found in the second study, which examined overall information systems development efforts. Even 49 percent of total effort translates into a sizable expenditure for maintenance, however, so the reasons systems are revised are well worth examining further.

Note in the bottom pie chart of Figure 19.6 that system compatibility accounts for 24 percent of all maintenance. **System compatibility maintenance** is necessary any time the system is revised to include new hardware or data requirements—in other words, any time an old system must interface with a new system.

Improved system efficiency accounts for another 9 percent of the maintenance effort. **System efficiency maintenance,** like system compatibility maintenance, is not really maintenance in the sense of correcting errors. Instead, both efforts are geared toward improving the overall performance of production systems that are running correctly but inefficiently. Only the "emergency needs and errors" pie slice, which consumes 22 percent of all maintenance effort, is maintenance in the sense of repair work necessary because of normal deterioration. This type of maintenance is required by the hardware component; hardware will deteriorate if you don't maintain it. Software, on the other hand, deteriorates *with* maintenance. As revisions alter the original structure of the programs in a piecemeal fashion, the software's integrity deteriorates.

Enhancing the system for users is the single most frequent reason for maintenance. The bottom pie chart in Figure 19.7 details the types of **user enhancements,** which are user requests for system revisions to improve or augment the reports generated or to conform with new reporting requirements. New reports and revisions to current reports account for most user enhancements. Acting on requests for changes and learning about new requirements consume a tremendous amount of analysts' time over the system life cycle.

Figure 19.7
Breakdown of Types
of User
Enhancements

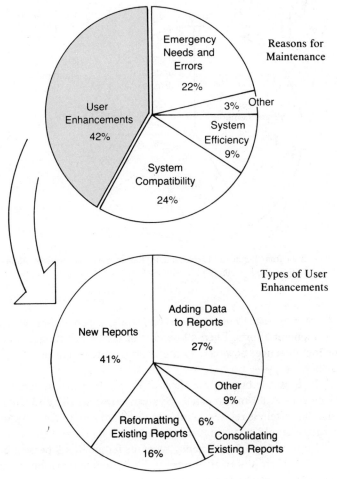

Source: Data from Bennet P. Lientz and E. Burton Swanson, *Software Maintenance Management* (Reading, Mass.: Addison-Wesley, 1980), pp. 73–74.

19.2.3 Strategies for Reducing System Maintenance

Since so much time and so many information services resources are spent on maintenance, improving productivity depends not only on reducing initial development effort but also on avoiding frequent revisions. The strategies presented here are designed to reduce system maintenance.

System compatibility maintenance can be reduced by designing and implementing systems that meet the system flexibility characteristics outlined in Figure 19.8. A flexible system functions well in various environments and with various devices. Its hardware architecture allows it to interface with a number of printers and storage media and to operate under a standard operating system. A flexible system is built in such a way as to

Figure 19.8
Criteria for Evaluating
System Quality

System Quality Subgoals	First-Level Characteristics	Second-Level Characteristics
1. Functionality: How well (reliably, clearly, efficiently) does the system function?	Reliability	Completeness Accuracy Robustness/integrity
	Clarity	Consistency Predictability
	Efficiency	Fast turnaround Low memory requirements Nonredundant procedures and processes
2. Ease of maintenance: How easy is it to maintain (understand, modify, and test) the system?	Understandability	Clear documentation Cohesiveness Consistency
	Modifiability	Modular structure Modular independence
	Testability	Clear documentation Modular structure
3. Flexibility: How flexible is the system with respect to changes in its components?	Portability	Site independence Device independence Language independence
	Adaptability	Program-data independence Procedural flexibility

Adapted from Boehm's software quality tree in Barry W. Boehm, J. R. Brown, and M. Lipow, "Quantitative Evaluation of Software Quality," *Proceedings and International Conference on Software Engineering* (San Francisco, October 1976), pp. 592–605.

ensure program-data independence, so that later changes in data requirements involve only minor alterations. A flexible system also is easily adapted to changes in security and user procedures.

The effort required for system efficiency and reliability maintenance can be reduced by employing structured techniques and conducting frequent tests as you develop the system. Structured walkthroughs at each stage of the development process will help you ensure that the system meets user requirements and that it does what it is supposed to do. Thorough testing of all system components during initial implementation will catch errors caused by both humans and machines—it will identify inconsistencies or omissions in both user procedures (for example, data entry) and program instructions (for example, data retrieval, manipulation, and reporting). Often improving the efficiency of a system is a simple matter of training users to follow the procedures closely and to take advantage of all that the software and hardware can do.

System enhancement maintenance can be reduced by ensuring that the original development of the system is user driven. By involving users in every phase—from determining requirements to evaluating alternatives to designing and implementing the system—you increase the likelihood that the system will meet user expectations. Some of the strategies for promoting user involvement include having users develop part (for example, procedures) or all of the system and using prototypes to acquaint users with system features before the system is fully implemented. You can also reduce the number of user enhancements if, early in the development process, you encourage users not only to identify their current needs but also to project their future needs. In Chapter 3, Tracy recommended that the pharmacy staff purchase a prescription package that also kept track of inventory. Although it's certainly not necessary to implement every conceivable feature users foresee needing, you should design the current system so that it can be easily enhanced to fulfill future needs.

Of course, any system will be easier to enhance and to maintain if it meets the ease-of-maintenance criteria outlined in Figure 19.8. Clear complete documentation, structured modules, and a consistent format will reduce the effort required to ensure compatibility, to improve efficiency, and to enhance the capability of the system.

19.3 The Goals of Implementation

Implementing a system is a time-consuming process, whether you're developing a new system or revising an existing one. This investment of time, money, and personnel must be managed so as to realize the goals of implementation:

1. Implement the design, meeting all specifications for all five components in a reasonable amount of time and at a reasonable cost.

2. Turn over control of the system to a well-trained, committed production staff.

To achieve these goals, you need to think in terms of the larger goals of organizational relevance, project management, and system quality emphasized throughout this text.

19.3.1 Implement the Design

The first goal of implementation may seem obvious and trivial. Of course you will implement the design—that's what implementation is! Yet, if you consider the full text of that goal statement, you'll see that it places three stipulations on implementing the design. The system implemented should

1. Meet all specifications for all components
2. Be completed in a reasonable amount of time
3. Be completed at a reasonable cost

The first stipulation relates to the system quality goals highlighted in Figure 19.8. These system quality goals become the criteria against which the system you develop is evaluated. As you test each system component, you need to keep these criteria in mind. Is the user interface transparent? Are the hardware and software reliable and efficient? Are the procedures clear and consistent? Are they well documented?

The second and third stipulations relate to project management goals. Because estimating the effort required to implement a system is extremely difficult, a project manager's estimated schedule often fails during implementation and a project that seemed to be on schedule falls seriously behind schedule. One way to avoid this problem is to prepare a detailed implementation schedule with lots of milestones to help you measure progress. These milestones should be product deliveries for each activity on the implementation checklist. Scheduling tangible product deliveries will allow you to obtain the feedback you need to keep track of the team's progress.

Also very important to meeting the project management goals is coordinating the divergent activities performed during implementation. You need to plan for contingencies in your schedule; finishing task A on time may be critical to starting and finishing task B as scheduled. As project leader of a large team, you'll need to manage the team's communication and resources to maximize team productivity. Because schedule overruns inevitably lead to cost overruns, your success as a project leader depends on your ability to manage the process as you produce a quality product.

19.3.2 Turn Over Control of the System

The second goal of implementation relates largely to the people and procedures components of the system. You want to be certain that changeover is a positive, orderly transition and that the production staff feels confident and positive about assuming responsibility for the system. To achieve a successful changeover, you must manage the implementation stage activities so that users don't become frustrated by delays, by confusing procedures, or by malfunctioning hardware or software. To maintain the users' commitment to the system, you need to involve them in the testing process—especially the testing of procedures. The people who will use the documentation are the best judges of how clear and complete your instructions for using the system are. Many elegantly designed systems have failed because the systems developers failed to secure user commitment. You can avoid the wasteful expenditure of time, effort, and money that such a failed system represents by continuing to involve the users as you test and install the system and by remembering that people are the component for which procedures, data, software, and hardware are designed.

Summary   Implementation is the process of executing the design specifications to create a system for production use. Implementation involves three major activities: construction, testing, and installation. Construction and testing activities are performed in two phases: (1) preliminary construction and testing, during which the hardware and software components are installed and tested, and (2) final construction and testing, during which the data, people, and procedures components are built and/or tested. The third major activity—installation—brings all the tested components together to create the final system. When management approves the installed system, the development team turns control of the system over to the production staff, signaling changeover and the beginning of the production phase of the system life cycle.

Key Terms   (Section numbers are in parentheses.)

maintenance (19.2.2)	**system efficiency maintenance (19.2.2)**
system compatibility maintenance (19.2.2)	**user enhancements (19.2.2)**

Notes

1. Barry W. Boehm, *Software Engineering Economics* (Englewood Cliffs, N.J.: Prentice-Hall, 1981), pp. 64–65.

2. Barry W. Boehm, "Software Engineering," *Computer*, December 1976, pp. 1226–1241.

3. Bennet P. Lientz and E. Burton Swanson, *Software Maintenance Management* (Reading, Mass.: Addison-Wesley, 1980), p. 24.

Exercises   (Answers to Exercises 19.1, 19.3, 19.7, 19.10, and 19.11 are at the end of the book.)

19.1 Explain how each of the following strategies could reduce system maintenance.

    a. creating test files to test all possible data conditions

    b. providing ongoing user education

    c. implementing the system with purchased software

    d. performing frequent walkthroughs

19.2 Explain how each of the following strategies could reduce system maintenance.

    a. having users generate their own reports

    b. using system documentation software

    c. considering all five system components during requirements determination and evaluation

    d. implementing the system with a fourth generation tool

    e. using structured techniques

    f. integrating data files under a DBMS

    g. maintaining program-data independence

    h. designing modules to be loosely coupled and cohesive

19.3 A project team at XYZ, Inc. has spent thirteen effort-months determining requirements, evaluating alternatives, and designing system specifications. According to the life cycle stage model (see Chapter 6 and Figure 19.5), how many more effort-months will the team require to implement the system?

19.4 A project leader had planned to implement a system in only four effort-months. The first three stages have consumed ten effort-months. According to the life cycle stage model, should the leader revise her implementation estimate? If so, how many effort-months should she allow?

19.5 The programs required for a new payroll system will total about 50,000 lines of code. Estimate the total number of effort-months required to develop this system. How many of those effort-months will implementation be likely to consume?

19.6 Review the CPM network show in Figure 5.16. Where are schedule breakdowns or over-runs likely to occur? Explain your answer.

19.7 Review the CPM network and Gantt chart given as the answers to Exercise 5.1, parts a and e. Where are schedule breakdowns or overruns likely to occur? Explain your answer.

19.8 Review the Gantt chart given as the answer to Exercise 6.7 at the end of the book. Where are schedule breakdowns or overruns likely to occur? Explain your answer.

19.9 Reread the Chapter 14 minicase Selecting a Database for *Outerspace* Magazine. Assume that management has chosen a database package to purchase. Identify at least five product deliveries Alex could use as milestones as he plans his implementation schedule.

19.10 Reread the Chapter 5 minicase Word Processing Systems for *Outerspace* Magazine. Assume that all the activities up to node 5 in Figure 5.16 have been completed on schedule and that *all* design activities have been completed. Prepare a Gantt chart planning your seven-week implementation schedule in detail.

    a. Identify at least fifteen implementation activities to be completed, assigning one or more team members to each activity.

    b. Include whatever project management activities are needed to coordinate, monitor, and review the project.

    c. Put an asterisk beside each activity that will produce a tangible product delivery.

    d. Allocate time to each activity, assuming that you're starting at week 8 on the project schedule. Changeover should be achieved during week 14.

    e. Is this implementation schedule realistic? Explain your answer.

19.11 Reread the case study in Exercise 6.8 Identify at least five product deliveries that could be used as milestones in planning the implementation stage of this project.

19.12 Reread the case study in Exercise 6.8. Assume that you're taking over as project leader at node 4 of the CPM network overview provided in the answers to Chapter 6 at the end of book. Prepare a Gantt chart planning your implementation schedule in detail.

    a. Identify at least fifteen implementation activities to be completed, assigning one or more team members to each activity.

    b. Include whatever project management activities are needed to coordinate, monitor, and review the project.

    c. Put an asterisk beside each activity that will produce a tangible product delivery.

    d. Allocate time to each activity, assuming that you're starting at node 4, which is the beginning of month 6 on the project schedule. Changeover should begin in month 18 and be achieved during month 21.

e. Is this implementation schedule realistic? Explain your answer.

19.13 The marketing analysis system developed in Exercise 19.12 was implemented using a third generation language, COBOL. Revise your detailed implementation schedule from Exercise 19.12, assuming that a 4GL will be used to create whatever programs are necessary.

a. Prepare a Gantt chart of the system implementation activities required if a 4GL is used.

b. Compare your revised plan to your original plan in Exercise 19.12 for 3GL implementation. How much time is saved? What activities are faster?

19.14 Tom A., project leader in the Exercise 6.8 case study, has just seen a demonstration of a marketing analysis software package that can do everything the Stafford Plastics VP wants done—and it can interface with the current sales analysis system data. Revise your detailed implementation schedule from Exercise 19.12, assuming that the VP has approved purchase of the marketing analysis package.

a. Prepare a Gantt chart of the system implementation activities required to complete the system using existing software.

b. Compare your revised plan to your original plan in Exercise 19.12 for 3GL implementation. How much time is saved? What activities are faster?

CHAPTER 20

Constructing Systems

Constructing the System Components
Preparing the Facility and Installing Hardware
Installing Purchased Software
Coding Custom-Written Software
Building Production Files
Minicase: Preliminary Construction of a Timekeeping System

Documenting the System
Documentation Standards
User Manuals
Technical Manuals

Training the Users and Technical Staff
Training Plans
Training Methods and Materials
Minicase: Training for the Timekeeping System
Ongoing Training

Summary
Key Terms ▪ Notes ▪ Exercises ▪ Projects

Overview

The implementation stage is a time of high activity and excitement. The system, which until now has been largely a paper construct, begins to take physical shape as software is coded, hardware installed, and users trained. This chapter discusses construction of the five system components. Specifically, we plan to

1. Describe the activities involved in constructing the data, software, and hardware components. (Section 20.1)

2. Examine the documentation of procedures, including user and technical manuals. (Section 20.2)

3. Discuss the methods and materials used to train the users and technical staff. (Section 20.3)

20.1 Constructing the System Components

Now that your design has been completed and approved, you are ready to begin constructing the system. But where do you start? You begin by preparing the facility, installing any new hardware, coding and/or installing the software, and building production data files.

20.1.1 Preparing the Facility and Installing Hardware

Constructing a system is similar to constructing a house. Both activities begin with the foundation. In system construction, the facility is the foundation, whether it is a large, specially constructed area with expensive mainframe equipment or just a revamped user area with microcomputer equipment. The construction of a large computer facility is a complex undertaking beyond the scope of this book. Usually projects will involve modifying an existing facility rather than constructing a new one.

Modification of an existing facility includes activities such as redesigning the physical layout to accommodate new equipment, installing a new environmental control system (with such characteristics as air conditioning, fire protection, power surge protection, and power backup), and altering the lighting and noise reduction features of the users' work area. As an example, let us consider modification of a facility to accommodate a new automated order processing system being developed by C'est Cheese, a telemarketing company specializing in cheese gifts. Previously, customers phoned in their orders to operators who manually completed an order form for each customer. The new system provides each operator with a terminal connected to a mini-computer (housed in another room). Preparing the facility for this new system involves running electrical and communication lines to each operator's workstation. One of the main concerns in preparing this facility is simply keeping all the wires out of the operators' way.

The hardware configuration and layout, determined during the design stage, can be installed when the facility is complete. Installing and configuring a large mainframe system requires specialized expertise. Usually the vendor will work with the operations staff to install mainframe computers, disk drives, tape drives, communications equipment, and high-speed printers. If the vendor does not provide installation support, computer consultants are available to assist with installation. The development team or operations staff installs and configures most microcomputer-based equipment.

20.1.2 Installing Purchased Software

When a system is based on purchased software, the development team's responsibilities are often reduced. The purchase agreement usually specifies that the vendor will help install mainframe software. Configuring parameters, such as the amount of main memory and the communication port settings used, and correcting bugs are then the vendor's job, not the development team's. In these situations, it is generally also the vendor's responsibility to test the software to determine whether it satisfies predefined functional criteria.

Software purchased for microcomputer systems will usually be installed by the development team, following the instructions provided in the software documentation. Exceptions are software custom-written by a third party and expensive integrated or networking software. Both of these will often be installed and tested by the third-party developer or the vendor.

20.1.3 Coding Custom-Written Software

Although building the software component from scratch requires more time and effort than installing purchased software, often the development team has no choice. In Chapter 2 we discussed the three sources of software and noted that if the organization has unique needs, purchasing software may be infeasible, in which case software must be coded from the specifications developed during the design stage.

Part of the evaluation stage is identifying who should write any custom-written software: end-users or IS professionals? Criteria for making this decision include

1. The availability of fourth generation tools
2. The complexity of the hardware component (for example, mainframe-based systems are more complex than microcomputer-based systems)
3. The relative importance of functionality versus efficiency
4. The frequency of changes and volume of exception reports anticipated

For a large, complicated system project, the specific requirements for all criteria except the first one above are likely to change during detailed design activities. Before construction begins, it is worthwhile to review the requirements and determine whether the earlier decisions about who will code the software still apply.

Software for a large mainframe system for which no 4GLs are available should be written by professional programmers. Similarly, if efficiency and transportability are vital requirements, software should be coded in a standard third generation language by the programming staff. But if the software will run on a microcomputer and end-users have developed similar applications using fourth generation tools, then having the end-users write the software should reduce the total system development cost.

When the development team codes the software, another question arises: What programming language should be used? Should the team use a standard third generation language, such as COBOL or Pascal, or opt for a 4GL? Generally the factors in this choice will be the same ones affecting the choice between end-user and programmer coding. The programmers' familiarity with the language, the degree of low-level machine control required (for light sensors or other special peripherals), portability, and efficiency are all factors to consider. In addition, the nature and frequency of changes in user requirements may make using a 4GL the only feasible choice. Figure 20.1 outlines the relative advantages and disadvantages of 3GLs and 4GLs.

For large systems, it is wise to mix 3GL and 4GL modules to take advantage of each language's strengths for specific functions. Using a data capability approach to phased development, as explained in Chapter 5, you might choose to have the main data entry and processing programs written in COBOL to take advantage of COBOL's superior run-time efficiency for high-volume work. Users could be trained to use a 4GL to generate their own exception reports, in order to reduce the development time devoted to satisfying frequent small requests. To take advantage of a mixture of software source codes, however, you must have a database management system that allows access by a 3GL and a 4GL, or the development team must construct interfaces to allow this flexibility.

Throughout this text we have emphasized the importance of building maintainable systems. Chapter 19 discussed the percentage of time spent maintaining—or, more accurately, enhancing—systems. Using 4GLs is one way to reduce the time required both to

Figure 20.1

Comparison of Third and Fourth Generation Languages

Feature	3GLs	4GLs
Ease of use	Difficult to learn; experience and expertise required.	Short learning curve; suitable for end-user development.
Development speed	Coding may consume a large percentage of development time; not amenable to frequent changes in user requirements.	Reduce time required to create and to modify code.
Efficiency	Quite efficient, even for heavy I/O applications.	Slow execution speeds; not suitable for low-level machine control.
Maintainability	Difficult to maintain, but less than in the past now that most versions support structured programming.	Brevity eases maintenance; do not support structured programming.
Compatibility/portability	More compatible than most 4GLs.	May be incompatible with standard database or file techniques.

Sources: Albert F. Case Jr., *Information Systems Development* (Englewood Cliffs, N.J.: Prentice-Hall, 1986), pp. 152–154; and Gary Elfring, "Choosing a Programming Language," *Byte,* vol. 10, no. 6, June 1985, pp. 235–240.

understand and to modify code. When execution efficiency is important, however, the development team cannot take advantage of 4GL's reduced development time. Instead they need to write 3GL code that is easy to maintain. Whether coding software in a 3GL or a 4GL, programmers must write code that is very flexible—that is, portable and adaptable. To achieve this goal, programmers need to follow standards.

Programming standards are the guidelines adopted by an organization's programming staff so as to produce maintainable and flexible systems. These standards specify conventions for naming data elements and documenting program code, as well as structured programming practices for formatting and organizing code. Many of these standards come into play before coding begins; the data modeling concepts in Chapter 11 and the structured design guidelines discussed in Chapters 17 and 18 set the stage for implementing good programming practices.

Figure 20.2 gives some simple guidelines for minimizing errors in spreadsheet development. Spreadsheets often include hard-to-detect errors.[1] Their support of "What if?" questions makes comparing figures under different scenarios easy, but sometimes the figures being compared are nonsensical. For example, when adding a row for overhead costs to an existing spreadsheet, a programmer could easily make the mistake of inserting the row outside the range of rows totaled to compute the final costs. Overhead costs would be in the spreadsheet, but they would not be included in the computation of total costs. Such mistakes can be prevented if developers follow simple standards such as those suggested in Figure 20.2.

Why should an organization adopt programming standards? Studies have shown that

Figure 20.2

Guidelines for Structured Spreadsheets

Know your problem.	Determine and summarize requirements before starting to build your spreadsheet.
Design modules top down.	Decompose the spreadsheet into smaller, less complex modules; for example, an overall construction bid spreadsheet would be linked to spreadsheets determining labor, material, and overhead costs.
Keep modules small.	Each spreadsheet should solve a single function (for example, overhead costs).
Document your work.	Label formula cells and rows with totals on the spreadsheet itself as well as in all user documentation.
Organize your spreadsheet.	Separate your spreadsheet into four sections, using blank lines for clarity: the introduction, the input section, the calculation section, and the report.

Source: Dan N. Stone and Robert L. Black, "Building Structured Spreadsheets," *The Journal of Accountancy,* vol. 168, no. 4, October 1989, pp. 131–142.

adopting and enforcing programming standards makes code easier to read and easier to maintain. In many cases, debugging time has been reduced by as much as 50 percent when structured programming practices were followed.[2]

20.1.4 Building Production Files

The success of a new system depends to a great degree on the integrity of its data. If the old system used manual files, the development team will choose a file organization and design the physical format of each file during the design stage, as discussed in Chapter 17. During construction, the manual files will be converted to tape or drive storage files through a process called **file conversion.** Converting even a small manual database of 5,000 or fewer records may consume as much as three to four effort-weeks, depending on how complicated the key entry process is. For example, keying a customer file will be much easier if all the data for each record is available from a one-page customer order form than if the data must be extracted from five different documents. If the old system was automated, some data conversion may still be required, especially if incompatible hardware or software is being installed or if requirements demand that data be organized in a new format.

Procedures must be followed to ensure the validity of the files prior to conversion. The development team or users make a preliminary review of each manual or computer file, purging unnecessary records and verifying that the file is accurate and current. Then a freeze date is set; after this date no further updates are made to the files awaiting conversion. Instead, updates are tracked separately so that files can be brought up to date after conversion is complete.

Measures must also be taken to ensure the integrity of data during conversion. One simple control technique involves grouping records in batches of 50 or 100 each and assigning each batch a unique number. A total is then calculated for one selected field by manually summing the values on the various records in the batch. This total is compared to the total accumulated as the records are converted. A discrepancy indicates a conversion error. For financial records, a batch total of a financial field such as account balance or total cost of order is used. For nonfinancial records, a hash total of a numeric field such as patient number or part number can be used.

As you can see, converting data is one of the more rigorous implementation activities. It requires both careful planning and attention to detail. Given its complexity, file conversion should be treated as a subproject and a team of users and developers should be assigned to plan, monitor, and perform its many tasks.

The following minicase, Preliminary Construction of a Timekeeping System, reviews the construction activities discussed in this section.

MINICASE

Preliminary Construction of a Timekeeping System

The Production department at King Industries requested a timekeeping system for its three shifts of assembly-line personnel, to record personnel data for payroll and production scheduling. Implementation of the system would require the purchase of handheld optical scanners and the construction of a room in the manufacturing area to protect the hardware from dust.

Sarah Turner, the project manager for the timekeeping system, planned the construction of the system during the design phase. Figure 20.3 shows the CPM model of her plan.

Facility preparation began as soon as the steering committee and production management approved the design. A convenient area in the factory—one that employees pass as they begin and end their shifts—was selected, and construction work began. The cables required to connect the terminals and printers to the computer room had to be installed without disrupting the assembly line's wiring and equipment. To meet this requirement, the new room was constructed with a raised floor and the cables were enclosed in a pipe that contained other wiring for the assembly line.

Next, the hardware was installed in the newly prepared user facility so that the network connections to the main computer could be tested. The company computer's main memory had to be upgraded before the new timekeeping software could be installed. Sarah assigned Bob Mattison from Technical Support to install the upgrade and configure the controller to accommodate the additional terminal. Bob also installed the terminal and the optical scanners in the systems area so that they could be tested while the user facility was being constructed. Meanwhile, the print shop prepared sample employee cards so that the hardware and software could be tested. The vendor installed the software on the main computer and verified that it met the specifications outlined in the purchase agreement. As soon as the user facility was ready, Sarah arranged for the hardware to be installed, thus completing the last of the activities required to reach node 6 on the CPM chart.

A special programming team was set up to code and test payroll's interface to the timekeeping system. Payroll personnel verified the preliminary test results. More extensive testing would be conducted during the test phase of the installation. The development team could now focus on completing the documentation, while Sarah implemented her plan for training the users and technical support staff.

Figure 20.3

CPM Model of Sarah's Preliminary Construction Plan

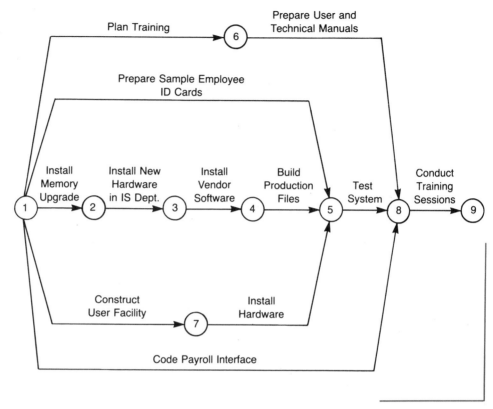

20.2 Documenting the System

The usability of a system is directly related to the quality of its documentation. Without clear, accurate, and easily accessible user and technical manuals, even the best designed system will be difficult to use. We recommend that, where feasible, users prepare their own user manuals. Having selected users work with an analyst to document procedures creates a pool of expert users and increases the likelihood that the user manual will be understood by its nontechnical audience.

The guidelines in Chapter 12 for documenting requirements apply equally well to creating user and technical manuals. Be sure to review these guidelines and to relate them to the more specific ones given here.

20.2.1 Documentation Standards

System documentation is seldom, if ever, read from front to back for pleasure. Instead, system documentation is read in sections as needed. Users appreciate effective documentation that allows them to find needed information quickly and easily. To ensure that documentation is effective, every organization should define guidelines for documenting systems. These guidelines, or **documentation standards,** set parameters for organization and format and specify the general content, order of presentation, and style of each document. Documentation standards promote consistency by assuring that a topic appears in approximately the same location under the same heading in every one of the organization's systems manuals.

Documentation standards address four major issues: content, organization, style, and format.[3] Content standards specify the maximum length of each manual, the number and type of illustrations recommended, and the level of detail appropriate to each manual (for example, technical manuals will include more hardware and operating system details than user manuals will). Content standards also indicate the chapters required in each manual, describe the kinds of instructions to be included, and suggest ways to present instructions effectively.

Organization standards specify how to maintain the logical flow and continuity of information. To some degree these standards strive to create a consistent user view of the documentation. By stipulating the order of presentation and the kinds of illustrations to be used, these standards capitalize on the users' experience with other manuals. Organization standards also describe the preferred method for separating chapters (for example, using tabs or colored sheets) and for distinguishing user actions from system responses (for example, using boldface or different type styles).

Style standards delineate the sentence length and word usage appropriate for different kinds of manuals. They describe the level of technical language allowed and indicate where technical terms are to be defined—in the text, in footnotes, or in a glossary. Style standards also enforce consistency by requiring that common system functions, such as add, change, delete, and insert, be described in a predefined way and that key entry requirements be shown consistently (for example, Ctrl–Z for the Control and Z double-strike command).

Format standards cover page design requirements (margins, line spacing, headings, indentations) and the placement of illustrations (before or after the text explanation). These standards also indicate the method for binding the manual; the size, quality, and color of the paper; and the style and size of the typeface.

Developing documentation standards helps to ensure the readability and consistency of system manuals. These standards help the development team, not only by providing guidelines but also by making available boilerplate descriptions of common functions.

20.2.2 User Manuals

User manuals provide information that nontechnical users need to use the system. Determining just what that information should include requires knowledge of the procedures the users will perform. For example, the user of a microcomputer system often performs the tasks of both a functional area user and an operator. If the user is expected to install software, load and run programs, and format diskettes, instructions for performing these technical procedures must be provided in the user manuals. In a large system built around a mainframe computer, these procedures will usually be performed by a computer operator; therefore, they need not be addressed in the user documentation.

User manuals focus on the data entry procedures that users commonly perform. They explain tasks such as transferring data from a source document to the computer via a data entry screen. They also describe the reports the system will generate and the steps the user must follow to produce the desired output. Figure 20.4 lists the topics most frequently included in a user manual.

Figure 20.4

Common Sections of
a User Manual

1. System overview
   Purpose of the system
   Narrative and graphical overview of system inputs, processing, and outputs

2. General procedures and information
   Sign-on and sign-off procedures (mainframe system or microcomputer network)
   Operating instructions (definition of function keys)
   Procedures for loading and running programs
   Explanation of standard error messages

3. Procedure documentation (repeat for each major procedure)
   a. Procedure overview
      Summary description of procedure
      Context diagram or data flow diagram
   b. Detailed procedure description
      Detailed procedure narrative or data flow diagram of work flow
      Screen formats, including sample formats and detailed explanations of screen options (add, insert, delete)
      Description of source documents and instructions for data entry, including all codes and uses of codes
      Output descriptions
      Sample output forms with detailed explanations and instructions for receiving and distributing output
   c. Data definitions
      Description of data used in procedure
      Data ownership and responsibility
      Data access security considerations
   d. Interface areas
      Data received from other procedures/user groups
      Information provided to other procedures/user groups

4. Glossary of terms

User manuals are often supplemented with quick reference guides and tutorials. A **quick reference guide** is a page or chart of frequently used commands and procedures, such as system log-on, data entry, report capabilities, and log-off. **Tutorials** are software-based lessons that introduce the user to the capabilities of the system. The user manual for a general ledger accounting system might include a tutorial with lessons on creating a ledger, processing transactions, and posting daily updates to the ledger—all with dummy data. The experience of using the system correctly to create and process dummy accounts builds the user's confidence and reduces the likelihood of errors later on.

Developing useful, usable manuals requires a good dose of common sense and consideration for the readers. Following the documentation guidelines discussed in Chapter 12 will help you to prepare user-friendly manuals. In addition, every user manual must be edited and proofread thoroughly. The development team and users should check its contents to ensure that all information is clear and correct. After the project manager verifies that the manual conforms to the organization's documentation standards, the user-sponsor approves the final version of the manual so that it can be copied for distribution to users.

20.2.3 Technical Manuals

Since user manuals usually take precedence, technical manuals are often forgotten in the rush to install a new system. Both are extremely important, however. There are three types of technical manuals:

1. Technical operations manuals
2. Installation manuals
3. System and program documentation

Technical operations manuals describe start-up, run control, and end-of-day procedures for the system hardware and software. These manuals also give instructions for running supervisory programs, performing hardware maintenance, logging errors, ensuring security, and recovering from a general system failure. Figure 20.5 lists the typical contents of a technical operations manual for a large computer system.

Installation manuals describe how to install hardware and software and how to configure the system for the current operating system and peripherals. These manuals also describe the main memory and peripherals required to use the hardware or software being installed. Software installation manuals also list and describe all program and data files. Often a separate installation manual is not prepared, in which case information about installation is given in the technical operations manual (for large systems) or the user manual (for small microcomputer systems, if the user is expected to install the system).

System documentation serves as a manual for maintaining the system and as a reference for future systems development. The system documentation gives an overview of any custom-written software and describes how each program module fits into the system. It provides program flowcharts and listings, input-output format samples, and data element definitions. The system documentation also describes and documents the procedures for requesting and implementing changes to the system after changeover. Figure 20.6 lists the topics usually discussed in system documentation.

20.3 Training the Users and Technical Staff

Training is one of the most people-intensive activities of systems development. It can also be one of the most costly activities, since it takes workers away from their daily tasks. System users and technical staff, already overburdened with daily responsibilities, must attend training sessions that they sometimes view as a waste of time. To overcome these negative perceptions, you must make training a worthwhile investment and solicit the support of user and strategic management to ensure full and active participation.

20.3.1 Training Plans

Planning training activities can be a complex task. Reserving rooms and equipment, preparing materials, and determining a feasible, convenient training schedule require a lot of

Figure 20.5

Contents of a Technical Operations Manual

1. Introduction
   Purpose of the manual
   Hardware configuration
   Computer room layout
   Emergency service numbers

2. Hardware operations
   Step-by-step powering-up instructions
   Hardware checks and restarts
   Log-in and log-out procedures
   Instructions for operating peripheral hardware
   Hardware switching (processor to processor, disk to disk, or printer to printer)
   Equipment failure recovery procedures
   Preventive maintenance cycle

3. Supervisory programs
   Start-of-day procedures, including on-line system start-up, operating system and communications network start-up, database start-up, file space allocation, and transaction log initialization
   Run control and error recovery procedures, including input control, authorization and special requests, output control, quality and distribution, and system utilities
   End-of-day procedures, including batch processing, security backup procedures, and shutdown procedures

4. Error logging and recovery
   Logging errors for hardware and software
   Hardware engineering liaison
   Software engineering liaison
   Recovery procedures

5. System security
   Computer room security
   Restricted access zones
   System security, access, and passwords
   Network security
   File security and backups
   Fire prevention procedures

6. Software library maintenance
   Cataloging procedures
   Version control, including simultaneous, current, and previous versions
   Update procedures
   Software backup procedures

7. Glossary of terms

Figure 20.6
Contents of System
Documentation

1. System overview
   Description of the application
   System flowchart
   Top-down system structure chart
   Brief module description and index
   Interfaces to other systems
   System operation procedures
   Database procedures
   Context diagram of user group
   System support group

2. Program modules (repeat for each program module)
   Date of most recent update
   Library location and name
   Program structure chart
   Program data flow diagrams
   Input description, samples, and user/module sources
   Output description, samples, and user/module destinations
   Error messages and error handling
   Program listing

3. Data files (repeat for each file)
   Data model
   Data element definitions
   Data access security

4. Change control documents
   Procedures for implementing requested changes
   Original request, specification, and authorization

5. Glossary of terms

effort and coordination. The development team's workload is reduced somewhat if the hardware and/or software vendors conduct some of the training sessions and provide some of the training materials. Hiring a consultant or a training specialist to handle these tasks may be a good idea if the organization lacks the resources to plan, prepare, and conduct its own training. Most of the time, however, the development team is extensively involved in training users and technical staff.

Figure 20.7 outlines the steps in planning a training schedule. Figure 20.8 gives a form that developers can use to plan and solicit approval for training activities. Two major concerns are determining effective training methods and identifying the room, equipment, and training materials required.

20.3.2 Training Methods and Materials

The most important training materials are the user and technical manuals. Since these are given their test run during training, they must be ready before training can begin.

Most people link training with classrooms and lots of handouts, but training has

Figure 20.7

Steps in Planning the
Training Schedule

1. Schedule training to occur during the two-week period before changeover.

2. Reserve classroom facilities, instructors, equipment, and training materials at least one month in advance of the training date.

3. Notify all trainees three times: one month, two weeks, and two days prior to their training session. Require that trainees confirm their ability to attend their scheduled sessions. Provide user management with a list of participants for each training session.

4. The day before training, check the classroom facility to make sure that the necessary hardware and software are available and functioning properly. Also ensure that adequate copies of any additional training materials are available.

5. Train the technical support and maintenance staff first.

6. Next train user-managers so that they can help train their operational staff.

7. Train users with similar functions or from similar functional areas together.

8. Schedule one or more make-up training sessions as needed.

9. Conduct a survey or informal review session to evaluate the effectiveness of the training provided.

moved into the computer age. Several methods have been developed for training users and technical staff. For computer-based training in common system operations, prepackaged courseware is available. In addition, several computer book publishers have prepared textbooks and training diskettes for many of the most popular business software packages. There are even software products, such as IBM's Personal Computer Instruction System and PC Pilot, that are designed to facilitate the development of organization-specific computer-based training materials. Whether purchased or developed in-house, computer-based training materials satisfy one of the criteria of good training: flexibility. The users can learn at their own pace and on their own schedule. Even if an organization's primary training method is instructor-led sessions, computer-based instruction can be used to refresh skills and to review procedures introduced in the sessions.

When training sessions are led by an instructor, a variety of methods and media should be used to capture and maintain the participant's interest. Studies have shown that people learn more effectively when several media are used. Thus, an effective training session might include

- Transparencies on which main ideas or steps are outlined
- Videotapes of procedures being performed
- Hands-on learning activities

The effectiveness of the training methods should be reviewed in a post-training evaluation session. During such a session, trainees are asked to comment on what worked, what didn't work, and why. Some developers prepare a questionnaire that asks trainees to evaluate the training methods, materials, and instructor at the end of each training session. Others evaluate training effectiveness by developing objective criteria for measuring whether the trainees achieved the desired skill level.

The minicase Training for the Timekeeping System returns to King Industries for a look at Sarah's training plan.

Figure 20.8
Training Plan Approval
Form

TRAINING PLAN APPROVAL PLAN		Page
System		Date

User Department	Project Manager	Signature

Describe Type of Training, Topics, and Instructor(s) for Each Topic:

Tentative Schedule:

Date	Time	Topic	# Hours	# Participants

Participants:

Requirements:
Room:
Equipment:

Training Materials:

Title	Quantity	Buy/Develop	Cost

Approved by:

Systems Group	Date	User-Sponsor	Date

Training for the Timekeeping System

As project manager for King Industries' Production department timekeeping system, Sarah Turner was responsible for planning the training of the technical staff and the user group. The Gantt chart in Figure 20.9 shows her training plan.

First, Sarah confirmed the dates of each training session with the participants. Training would take place in the newly constructed room in the Production area.

Sarah reserved the room and the equipment required for each session.

Next, Sarah identified the training materials required. The purchase agreement had specified that the vendor would provide comprehensive manuals and training documents, so the development team just augmented these documents with materials specific to King Industries: data management and hardware usage policies,

Figure 20.9
Sarah's Gantt Chart of Training Activities

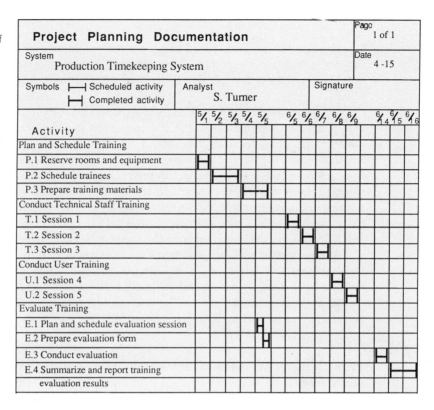

computer operations procedures, interfaces to other company information systems, and maintenance procedures. User training materials included the user and technical operations manuals.

Sarah prepared a topic outline and checklist for each training session. Each session would begin with an overview and would include exercises designed to build user confidence and independence. Sufficient time would be allowed for a question-and-answer period and for coffee breaks as needed.

At the first session, the Production senior analyst, maintenance programmers, technical support staff, and system operators were introduced to the new system and trained in its operations. At the second session, they learned about the new software's processing capabilities. Only the maintenance programmers attended the third

session, at which they learned to use the report writing and programming languages available with the package so that they could build additional interfaces and user-requested reports. The Production manager, John Buffington, attended both the first and the second training session. Participation in these early sessions enabled him to help train the shift supervisors later.

The shift supervisors were the first user group to be trained (Session 4). The senior analyst and John Buffington assisted Sarah during this training session. Then, the shift supervisors helped train the production-line workers (Session 5). The production-line workers arrived for their shifts an hour early so that their shift supervisors could explain the new system and orient them to the new timekeeping procedures.

20.3.3 Ongoing Training

The previous section concentrated on pre-changeover training for a new system. Although this type of training is important, the major training expense associated with a large-scale, multi-user system is the cost of training new users of the production system once it is "live."

One concern in training new users of a production system is access to training data. One possibility is to use the test data employed in the development of the system and during initial training. This data should be saved and documented for this purpose. Another option is to have data created specifically for training new users. For situations in which trainers are not available, tutorial packages with dummy data work well. In no situation, however, should production data or the production system itself be used for ongoing training. The production environment and the training environment should never overlap. Maintaining strict boundaries between production and training activities will help you to avoid compromising the integrity of the production system.

Another part of ongoing training is introducing new users to the environment. Initial training is usually developed for experienced users who know more about the job than the developer does, so introduction to the job environment itself is brief—the training focuses on changes in procedures. For new employees, a more extensive introduction is necessary, because this training may be their primary on-the-job training.

Summary

Preparing the facility and installing the hardware are the first activities in the construction of a new system. Usually preparing the facility will entail modifying the facility layout; however, complete construction is sometimes necessary. Once the layout is complete, hardware can be installed. Vendors and/or consultants often assist the operations staff with installation.

Software is installed next. If the software has been purchased for use on a mainframe, vendors are usually responsible for installation. Software purchased for microcomputer systems is usually installed by the development team or operations staff. If software is to be custom written, determining who should code the software, choosing a programming language, and establishing programming standards are some of the concerns of the development team in the construction phase.

Building the production files is an especially complex activity. During file conversion, a major concern is maintaining data integrity as the new files replace the old ones. One control technique is grouping records in batches and then comparing batch or hash totals for a selected numeric field.

The second major activity of preliminary construction is documenting the system. User and technical manuals should adhere to documentation standards, which fall into four categories: content standards, organization standards, style standards, and format standards. User manuals provide the nontechnical user with reference material for understanding and operating the system. These manuals are often supplemented with quick reference guides and tutorials. Technical manuals are divided into three types: (1) technical operations manuals for start-up, run control, and end-of-day procedures; (2) installation manuals for hardware and software installation; and (3) system documentation for system maintenance and reference.

Training is the third major activity in system construction. Training activities, methods, and materials must be carefully planned. Hiring a consultant or a training specialist may be a good approach. Other training methods include computer-based training and instructor-led training sessions with transparencies, handouts, videotapes, and hands-on learning activities. Training must be regarded as an ongoing process in order to achieve optimal usage of the new system.

Key Terms

(Section numbers are in parentheses.)

programming standards (20.1.3)   **tutorials (20.2.2)**
file conversion (20.1.4)   **technical operations manuals (20.2.3)**
documentation standards (20.2.1)   **installation manuals (20.2.3)**
user manuals (20.2.2)   **system documentation (20.2.3)**
quick reference guide (20.2.2)

Notes

1. Dan N. Stone and Robert L. Black, "Building Structured Spreadsheets," *The Journal of Accountancy*, vol. 168, no. 4, October 1989, pp. 131–142.

2. Edward Yourdon, *Managing the Structured Techniques*, 2nd ed. (Englewood Cliffs, N.J.: Prentice-Hall, 1979), p. 4.

3. Polly Perryman, "Standards and Documentation," *Information Center*, vol. 2, no. 8, August 1986, pp. 31–37.

Exercises

(Answers to Exercises 20.1 and 20.3 are at the end of the book.)

20.1 Complete a Gantt chart for the system construction activities for the Meadows Hospital case in Chapter 3. Use the following breakdown for activities:

```
C-construction
D-documentation
T-training
```

For example, the activity Install Hardware in Information Services would be written under the Construction section as

```
C.2. Install Hardware in Information Services
```

20.2 The Geological Research Center collects core samples, vials, cuttings, and other miscellaneous rock. The Center requires a system for identifying, categorizing, and numbering the different samples that its warehouse receives. Each sample is cut into two pieces. One piece is archived as a permanent geological reference. The other piece becomes part of a library for patrons of the Geological Research Center and can be checked out or viewed.

You have determined requirements, evaluated system alternatives, and completed the design. Now you are ready to begin constructing the system. You have selected a well-known package for geological core archiving, developed at a local university. The university department that wrote the software has modified the original package to include library checkout procedures. A preliminary tested version of the package has already been delivered. The center wants to install this package on a new personal computer network.

A total of five personal computers will be installed. One computer will be used by the librarian, one by the archivist, one by the manager of the center, and two by library patrons. Two printers will also be installed: one in the library area, for the librarian and patrons, and one in the archive office, for staff use. You have recruited a team of users, which includes the librarian, the archivist, the manager, and two patrons who have volunteered to test the library computing facility when it is ready.

a. Prepare a Gantt chart for the preliminary construction phase. Include the steps in preparing the facility, installing the hardware, installing the software, and building the production files.

b. List the documents you will need for this system, and provide a brief description of the contents of each document.

c. Prepare a training schedule for the users of this system.

d. Prepare a Gantt chart for the completion of the construction, documentation, and training activities.

20.3 Review the guidelines for building spreadsheets in Figure 20.2, and state how each guideline contributes to one or more of the first-level characteristics of system quality in Figure 19.8. Mention second-level characteristics where applicable.

Projects

20.4 Examine the manuals of two or three software packages designed for the same application (for example, word processing or spreadsheets). Prepare a short report in which you compare them with respect to

a. content   **b.** organization   **c.** style

d. format   **e.** quick reference guides and tutorials

Figure 20.10
Documentation Standards of XYZ Company

I. Content Standards
   A. Length
      1.
      2.
   B. Illustrations
      1.
      2.
   C. Level of Detail
      1.
      2.
   D. Chapters Required
      1.
      2.

II. Organization Standards
    .
    .
    .

20.5 Examine the manuals of two or three software packages produced by a single software manufacturer (for example, the MacDraw, MacWrite series). Identify the similarities among the manuals, and then create an outline of what you think the manufacturer's documentation standards might be. Use a format similar to the one in Figure 20.10.

20.6 Contact a large organization in your community to learn about its training methods and materials. Prepare a short oral or written report in which you discuss the following issues:

a. Who is responsible for training: the development team, the information services staff, or a consultant? Does responsibility shift depending on the nature of the development project?

b. What training methods are used?

c. What training materials are used? Are materials purchased or developed in-house?

d. Are different methods and materials used in different situations? For example, do the methods and materials used to train users of mainframe systems differ from those used to train users of microcomputer systems?

Testing the System

Overview

One of Murphy's laws states that anything that can go wrong will go wrong. This is especially true in systems development. Experienced developers know that only trivial systems are error-free on the first run. A system must be thoroughly tested to reveal its errors and misconceived functions before it goes into production. Failure to find these errors will cause problems with clients, customers, and users. Errors in a commercial product will ruin a product's chances of success; retailers will avoid selling a flawed product and industry media will review error-prone software unfavorably. Systems developed in-house and put into production without thorough testing are likely to so frustrate users that the users will reject the system, thus wasting all the resources invested in developing it. Testing all the components helps avoid the crises caused by these system deficiencies.

This chapter emphasizes the importance of testing and explains how to test a system thoroughly. Specifically, we plan to

1. Discuss the management activities of the testing phase. (Section 21.1)

2. Explain strategies for testing hardware and software. (Section 21.2)

3. Suggest techniques for testing procedures and data. (Section 21.3)

4. Discuss the system test. (Section 21.4)

5. Provide some guidelines on how much testing is enough. (Section 21.5)

21.1 Introduction to Testing

The goal of testing is to locate system errors before installation. These system errors can take several forms. They may be software coding errors that produce incorrect output or hardware design errors that reduce system efficiency. They may be in the form of faulty procedures documentation that causes the user to enter invalid data. Errors may appear in the master files, whose accuracy is vital to successful production runs. Or errors may take the form of omissions in design specifications that unacceptably limit system performance. The point is that you need to test for more than simple errors in coding—the bugs that plague programmers.

21.1.1 Potential Problem Areas in Testing

As one of the last activities in the life cycle approach to systems development, testing is the development activity most likely to get pushed beyond the scheduled completion date. To meet the completion date, developers may omit or do a haphazard job testing the system. A remedy for this tendency is the phased development approach. Early demonstrations to users are a good test of requirements determination, design, and system construction.

Another cause of inadequate testing is developer fixation. Systems analysts design test procedures for *expected* problems; they may not understand the production operations well enough to anticipate all the things that could go wrong. One solution to this problem is to have a user design the test data files. Another is to follow systematic testing procedures, covering even functions that you feel certain will work. Any systematic test data files built during initial development should be saved and made a permanent part of the testing environment. Systematic testing and user testing are particularly helpful if the development team members become weary of the project (yes, this happens) and are not as reliable as they were earlier in the project.

Developer fixation is an even greater problem in maintenance—"such a small fix couldn't have any errors"—so the existence of an easy-to-use testing environment is especially important for the ongoing maintenance part of the life cycle. When software is revised, the system may be tested quickly with the systematic test data files built and documented during initial development. During maintenance, a quick fix may introduce errors in unexpected ways, and these are likely to be discovered through systematic testing.

The particular problem areas that most need to be addressed in system testing are

1. All input, process, and output conditions

2. The coordination of coded modules

3. The system's compliance with user specifications, as well as the completeness and accuracy of the specifications

4. User/management confirmation of programming assumptions

5. The coordination of the five components of the system (people, procedures, data, software, hardware)

21.1.2 Creating a Test Plan

As project leader, you need to specify testing procedures as carefully as you planned the previous stages of the project. Your test plan should cover all of the following:

1. Personnel and supplies
2. Preliminary tests of each component
3. Final tests
4. Documentation of test plans, data, and results

Personnel and Supplies   To ensure that testing is carried out in an organized manner, it is necessary to form a **test group** responsible for developing the test data and for carrying out tests at each stage. The test group also evaluates adherence to standards and inspects system documentation. Large projects often are evaluated by an independent quality assurance group with permanent, experienced members. Smaller projects cannot afford this luxury; their test group is a changing team of people drawn from programming teams that have completed their modules.

Whenever possible, users should participate in tests. Users' participation increases their commitment to the system and gives developers insight into how well their requirements are being met. All of the time, effort, and resources consumed by development may be wasted if you fail to gain and maintain user confidence. When you encourage users to participate, warn them that errors and omissions *will emerge*. Explain that their role is to help identify the errors that must be eliminated before the system is put into production. Involving users in the testing process also educates them about the costs and benefits of system features and serves as training in the use of the system.

Planning the test phase requires that you identify all the supplies needed for the tests. If the project involves installing new hardware, you need to be sure that you have tapes, disk packs, floppy disks, printer paper, and so forth—not only the right kind but also a sufficient quantity. Keep in mind that supplies will be needed for the many backup files maintained during testing. If you're installing purchased software, be sure that you have enough copies of system and user documentation so that access to reference materials is not a problem. Planning for supply needs may seem a trivial concern, but remember that "for want of a nail the shoe was lost . . . for want of a nail the kingdom was lost." Don't let the little things foul up your project; plan for even these mundane needs.

Preliminary Tests   During preliminary tests, the components are tested individually to determine their ability to meet **acceptance criteria**—the functional requirements that have been identified as the basis for accepting the system. To plan for these activities, you need to specify the tests to be performed, the people responsible for performing them, and the paperwork required to document them. Preparing a Gantt chart of these activities will help you manage the process more effectively. The Gantt chart in Figure 21.1 delineates the preliminary test activities for testing the pharmacy system in Chapter 3.

Figure 21.1
Gantt Chart of
Preliminary Test
Activities

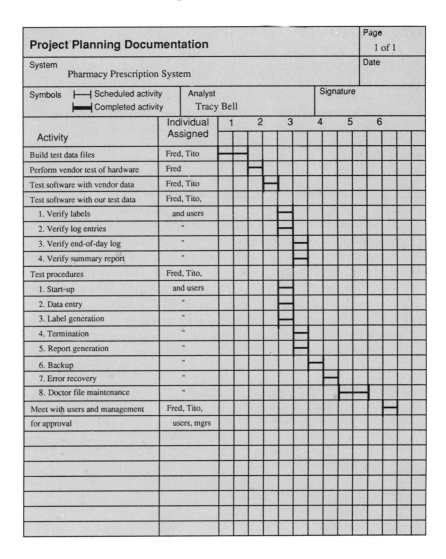

Project Planning Documentation								Page 1 of 1			
System Pharmacy Prescription System								Date			
Symbols ⊢——⊣ Scheduled activity ▬▬▬ Completed activity		Analyst Tracy Bell						Signature			
Activity	Individual Assigned	1	2	3	4	5	6				
Build test data files	Fred, Tito	▬▬									
Perform vendor test of hardware	Fred		▬								
Test software with vendor data	Fred, Tito		⊢⊣								
Test software with our test data	Fred, Tito,										
1. Verify labels	and users			⊢							
2. Verify log entries	"			⊢							
3. Verify end-of-day log	"				⊢						
4. Verify summary report	"				⊢						
Test procedures	Fred, Tito,										
1. Start-up	and users			⊢							
2. Data entry	"			⊢							
3. Label generation	"			⊢							
4. Termination	"				⊢						
5. Report generation	"				⊢						
6. Backup	"					⊢					
7. Error recovery	"					⊢					
8. Doctor file maintenance	"					⊢⊣					
Meet with users and management	Fred, Tito,						⊢⊣				
for approval	users, mgrs										

Activities likely to be performed during preliminary testing include the following:

1. Identify acceptance criteria (user and system requirements; system quality goals).

2. Build test files; identify users to test procedures.

3. Test each component.

4. Document test activities and results.

5. Discuss test results with users and/or management to determine priorities for repair. (Note: Ideally, acceptance criteria and repair priorities should be determined before testing begins.)

6. Fix each component in preparation for the system test. (Steps 3, 4, and 6 would be repeated as often as necessary and feasible.)

We will discuss preliminary testing in more detail as we explain how to test each component.

Final Tests   After all the individual components have been tested and shown to meet the acceptance criteria, they are brought together and tested as a unit. Depending on the size and complexity of the system being developed, the final tests may consume a few hours, a few days, or a few weeks. If the final testing process will be fairly involved, you would be wise to prepare a Gantt chart to help you plan tasks, personnel, supplies, and schedule. Your responsibility as a project leader is to bring all the facets of the system together, to coordinate the testing process, and to achieve user acceptance and management approval.

Documentation   Since testing is a planned process that is critical to the success of the system, it requires extensive documentation. The documentation should detail the entire test plan, including the specific tests to be conducted, the sequence in which they will be conducted, and the tentative test schedule. The test documentation should contain listings of the test data and the broad performance standards expected of the system. Results of test runs are also filed with the test documentation.

One standard documentation form used by many organizations is the **test specification,** shown in Figure 21.2. Notice that this form provides headings for the major details that need to be documented, including what will be tested, how it will be tested, what results will verify that the system passed the test, who will perform the test, and when.

Test Specification				Page
		Module		
Analyst				Date
Objectives				
Test Condition	Description of Condition	Test Steps	Expected Results	Executed by/ Date

Figure 21.2   Test Specification Form

21.2 Testing the Software and Hardware

Whether you use custom-written or existing software, whether you install new hardware or use the old hardware for a new purpose, you need to test the software and hardware components thoroughly.

21.2.1 Choosing an Approach to Testing

There are two approaches to testing system accuracy: black box and white box testing. Although both are designed to create accurate systems, one focuses on error-free functions and the other on error-free code.

Black box testing concentrates on the system's function—whether or not the system creates accurate output. It is based on the assumption that if what goes in and what comes out is correct, the system must be correct. Data is created and run through the system. If the output is correct, the system, a black box, is assumed to be correct. Users are ideal black box testers, as they have the best knowledge of the system's intended function.

In **white box testing,** each program module's code is checked by reviewing each line or by creating data to verify every line. The best white box testing is a code walk-through by the programmer and the analyst. Research indicates that more than twice as many errors are found when someone besides the author participates in the walkthrough.[1] The minicase A Full-Flex Grade Book System for State University provides examples of these testing approaches.

A Full-Flex Grade Book System for State University

Kerry Williams, a teaching assistant at State University, had been given the task of developing a grading system with all the features necessary to support a teacher's grading of any number of classes and any number of students. As a graduate student who had studied COBOL programming and systems development, Kerry knew the value of testing a system with the same care used in designing it. So, as she designed the grade book system, she conducted design walkthroughs with intended users and with fellow graduate students.

After Kerry had constructed the system, she tested the individual components, focusing primarily on verifying the COBOL programs she had written as the heart of the system. Kerry created a small sample of test cases (test data sets) and executed the programs with the test cases. She compared the output generated to her prepared table of expected output for each case. If the gen-

erated output agreed with the expected output and if the function being tested was fairly straightforward, she assumed that the function was correct. For example, the simple function Delete Student was tested as a black box because its program involved few loops or conditions. In contrast, Kerry tested more complex functions as white boxes— every program instruction and every path was executed at least once. For example, the Add Student function and the Add Class function were thoroughly tested because they involved complicated controls and conditions.

After all the modules had been tested individually, Kerry combined them so that she could test all the paths and the intersections between them. She was surprised at how simple testing these paths was; using structured techniques to design the grade book system made finding and correcting errors quite easy.

21.2.2 Building Test Data Files

In order to test the running of a system, you need data. **Test data** should force the system to traverse every possible path. Because each system being tested is unique, your judgment as an experienced systems developer will be the key to designing good test data. Nonetheless, here are some useful guidelines:

1. Test each function in the system separately.
2. Check the flow of control through the system to ensure that the desired paths exist.
3. Test valid, invalid, and boundary values.
4. Test data that is not supposed to change for consistency.
5. Verify error detection routines.
6. Have users test interactive systems.
7. Test the program interfaces.
8. Validate system backup and recovery procedures.

Rather than develop a single large data set to accomplish these purposes, you should build several small, well-designed subsets that will force errors, test boundary conditions, and check as many paths and data conditions as the testing schedule and budget permit. One of these subsets might be an extract from actual production data; another might be developed by the programmers to test error detection routines, menu selection routines, and data consistency. Another test data subset might be designed by a production user who is familiar with the kinds of incorrect data the system is likely to encounter. During preliminary testing, several short runs with small data sets generally produce more valuable insights than does a long, time-consuming test using a single, large set of test data. All of the test data files should be documented and stored as part of the testing environment for repeated use during the preliminary and final testing periods of initial development, as well as testing during the ongoing maintenance part of the life cycle.

In addition to creating input test files for the testing environment, you should save and document correct output files. One way to determine whether a system is performing correctly is to compare a test output file with a correct output file for a given set of inputs to the system. The two files can be compared using a simple program that prints discrepancies. If differences exist, the system is not executing as specified. This technique is especially useful where the volume of output data is high and a tedious manual procedure would otherwise be required to verify its accuracy.

Figure 21.3 shows three of the test data sets that Fred Kahn constructed to test the pharmacy system in Chapter 3. Notice that Fred developed several small data sets, each one designed to test a particular system function.

Test scripts may be created for interactive systems by saving keystrokes of an interactive session in which data is entered and reports are displayed and printed. The file of keystrokes can then be used to execute the revised system, after which the results produced by the revised system are compared with the documented past performance of the system. Each time a bug is found, keystrokes (commands and data) can be added to the script to

Test Data Set #1 (Doctor File)

Doctor #	Doctor Name
001	Bounous, P.S.
003	Gutierrez, R.T.
008	Miller, F.G.
012	Miller, S.Q.
019	Yudof, W.L.

Test Data Set #2 (Verify Labels & Log)

Doctor #	Patient Name	Charge Code	Drug
008	Alhadad, Hafez	H	Wyamycin
003	Grena, Emmett	W	Veracillin
019	Wimberly, Harry	H	Meprogesic
001	Moritz, Evelyn	H	Malatal

Test Data Set #3 (Error Recovery)

Test Condition #	Doctor #	Patient Name	Charge Code	Drug
031	010	Moritz, Evelyn	H	Malatal
032	008	Alhadad, Hafez	J	Wyamycin
033	003	Grena, Emmett	W	Veracillin
034	019	Wimberly, Harry	H	Meprogesic

Test Specification				Page 1
System Pharmacy Prescription System		Module Data Entry		
Prepared by Fred Kahn				Date
Objective To test data validation and error recovery procedures				
Test Con-dition	Description of Condition	Test Steps	Expected Results	Executed by / Date
031	Invalid doctor code	Enter doctor number "010" at "Enter Doctor #:" prompt	Error message: "Doctor number 010 does not exist."	
032	Invalid charge code	Enter charge code "J" at "Enter charge code:" prompt	Error message: "Invalid charge code; enter H or W only."	
033	Name and charge code entry error	Enter "Grena" <press ENTER> "Emmett" at "Enter Name:" prompt	Error message: "Invalid charge code; enter H or W only."	
034	Charge code and drug entry error	Enter "HMeprogesic" at "Enter charge code:" prompt	Error message: "Invalid charge code; enter H or W only."	

Figure 21.3 Examples of Test Data Sets for the Pharmacy Prescription System

test that particular bug and make sure no future change unintentionally re-creates the problem.

The test data sets used and the results generated should be documented and maintained as part of the testing environment. Test data is a valuable resource which can be used throughout the life cycle of the system. As the system is upgraded, this same test data can be used again to ensure that maintenance has not corrupted other system functions.

21.2.3 Testing the Software Component

The amount of testing needed for software depends on whether the software is custom-written or purchased.

Testing Custom-Written Software   Custom-written software is often tested as a white box—every line of code is verified against the requirements specification. This line-by-line or paragraph-by-paragraph process proceeds from the beginning of the program to the end.

There are three basic approaches to black box testing of custom-written software: top-down, bottom-up, and sandwich. These approaches are based on the hierarchy of modules in the structure chart. The approach you should use will be determined by the unique circumstances of your development project. Whichever strategy is employed, you will need to detail the processes you followed in your test documentation.

With the **top-down testing strategy,** higher-level, or control, modules are tested before the lower-level, or process, modules. Testing begins with the highest-level module and then proceeds down the levels of the structure chart. The advantage of this approach is that it allows you to begin testing even if lower-level, more detailed modules have not yet been constructed. If the lower-level modules accessed by the higher-level modules haven't been written, you will need to write stubs to run the tests. A **stub module** is a simulation module whose only purpose is to verify calls from higher-level modules. Its code is designed to display a message verifying that the call was successful.

With the **bottom-up testing strategy,** the lowest-level modules are tested first. You test each basic module individually and then test each module's interface to other modules at the same or higher levels. In essence this strategy allows you to test the software's details before you test its overview, or the glue that holds it together. To use this strategy, you will need to write a **driver module** to simulate the roles of the higher-level modules that normally would access data and control processing.

The **sandwich testing strategy** "burns the candle at both ends." You code and test the top-level modules by following the top-down strategy and the lower-level modules by following the bottom-up strategy. Eventually the two strategies meet in the middle. This approach requires that the development team be large enough that two or more members can be assigned to perform testing activities concurrently. Usually the person who coded the lower-level modules is also responsible for testing them. The person responsible for coordinating the modules will usually test the higher-level modules.

The final step in the preliminary testing of custom-written software is the **software component test.** In this test, all the software modules are tested as a single functioning unit. Here is where having designed cohesive, loosely coupled modules should pay off. Adherence to structured design techniques should reduce the likelihood of errors in the module interfaces and should facilitate identification of whatever errors do exist.

Testing Purchased or Existing Software Testing purchased or existing software usually requires less effort and consumes less time than does testing custom-written software. Generally, purchased or existing software is tested as a black box, with tests proceeding function by function instead of line by line, module by module. For example, if the software being tested is menu driven, you might begin by testing the capabilities of the first menu function, then move to the second menu function, and so on. If the software is command driven, you test each command-level function. You build and use test data subsets just as you do in custom-written software tests.

In testing existing software, the emphasis is on detecting errors common to that application. For example, data management software often requires that you specify the length and data type of each field; common errors to test include length and data type violations. Most data management packages allow you to sort records on a variety of keys and to limit access to records that meet a specified criterion (for example, you might want to print only the records of employees who had been with the company for ten or more years). These functions should be tested to verify the accuracy of their processing and output. The minicase on page 570, Testing an Expenditure Forecasting System for Meadows Hospital, provides an example of testing a system developed with spreadsheet software.

21.2.4 Testing the Hardware Component

Often systems are developed using an organization's existing hardware resources. In such situations, you will need to test the hardware to make sure that it can handle the added load your application will place on it. Sometimes hardware that performed adequately before a new application was added does not perform adequately afterward. The increased processing load, the expanded number of accesses to files, or the greater number of terminals active simultaneously may so degrade the hardware's performance that response time and turnaround time become unacceptable.

If you're installing new hardware, you'll need to test it to make sure that it meets specifications. When you solicited bids from vendors, you stated the **technical specifications,** or the capabilities the hardware would have to possess. These technical specifications include processing speed, communication ports supported, disk access speed, printer speed, and memory capacity. Before you purchased the hardware, you probably ran several benchmark tests at the vendor's site to determine the hardware's ability to meet these specifications. Now you need to test the hardware at your site with your data. These tests will assure you not only that the hardware runs properly but also that you've prepared

Testing an Expenditure Forecasting System for Meadows Hospital

Each year Meadows Hospital allocates a lump sum to each department to cover maintenance and operating expenses. In the past, the Pharmacy department has exceeded its allocation. Tito Hernandez, the assistant manager of the pharmacy, requested that Information Services develop an automated system to help the department forecast expenses. Programmer-analyst Fred Kahn was assigned the job.

First Fred needed to understand the Pharmacy department's expense process. He interviewed June Davis, the pharmacy accounts director, who gave him the department's spending data for the last five years. June also showed him the monthly expense summary she generated using a spreadsheet package (see Figure 21.4). This spreadsheet contained several puzzles for Fred, but by the end of the meeting, he understood how expenses were incurred.

After reviewing and evaluating the five years of expense data, Fred decided to develop the forecasting system using the same spreadsheet package June was cur-

Meadows Hospital
Pharmacy Division
Operating Expense Report
1990–1991

Category	September	October	November	December	January
Comp. Supply	$2,053.21	$1,679.90	$1,493.24	$2,146.53	$2,239.86
Duplicating	740.64	605.98	538.65	774.31	807.97
Equipment	1,529.85	1,251.69	1,112.62	1,599.39	1,668.92
Maintenance	1,632.40	1,335.60	1,187.20	1,706.60	1,780.80
Postage	299.49	245.03	217.81	313.10	326.71
Service	145.70	119.21	105.96	152.32	158.94
Supplies	890.73	728.78	647.80	931.21	971.70
Telephones	158.70	129.84	115.42	165.91	173.12
Other	383.90	314.10	279.20	401.35	418.80
Totals	$7,834.60	$6,410.12	$5,697.89	$8,190.71	$8,546.83
Encumbrances	41,563.71	34,006.67	30,228.15	43,452.97	45,342.23
Trans/Apro	(11,996.90)	(9,815.64)	(8,725.02)	(12,542.21)	(13,087.52)
Expenditures	$37,401.41	$30,601.15	$27,201.02	$39,101.47	$40,801.54
Balance	$137,598.59	$106,997.44	$79,796.42	$40,694.94	($106.59)
Original Budget	$175,000.00				

Figure 21.4 Pharmacy Division Operating Expense Spreadsheet

rently using. Therefore, no new software or hardware purchases would be needed. Fred planned to create a forecasting template for each of the nine line-item expenses on the present summary report. The forecast would be based on historical spending patterns over the last five years.

Adopting a top-down construction and testing strategy, Fred constructed and tested the major module (the actual forecast) first. Then he created all the template spreadsheets using a small test data set. He reviewed these basic templates with Tito and June and made all the corrections they suggested. For Fred's next review with

Figure 21.5
Fred's Forecasting
System Test
Specification

Spreadsheet Test Specification		
SYSTEM Expenditure Forecasting System		Page 1 of 1
PREPARED BY Fred Kahn Test Participants Tito Hernandez, June Davis		Date
Activity	Completion Date	Initials
1. Clear historical file names		
2. Clear column labels		
3. Protected formula cells		
4. Correct calculations		
5. Correct field validity checks		
6. Double-defined variables eliminated		
7. Cell formatting large enough (Add footnote if rounding possible in any row or column.)		
8. Correct crossfoot totals		
9. Average is protected against blank field counted as value.		
10. Automatic recalculation set to "on"		
11. Distribution list for all revisions		
12. Two backup copies		

Tito and June, he enlarged the test data base and proceeded through the standard Meadows Hospital test specification for spreadsheet developers. This checklist was created by the Meadows Hospital end-user computing support staff because of frequent problems with spreadsheet errors; it is shown in Figure 21.5.

After Tito and June approved his progress to date, Fred created two more sets of test data and checked the detailed logic carefully. Finally, he supervised the construction of the production data set, and then he, Tito, and June once again proceeded through the spreadsheet testing steps shown in Figure 21.5.

an appropriate facility to house it (for example, that the cabling, electrical supply, and temperature control are adequate).

Tests commonly performed on hardware are listed in Figure 21.6.

Figure 21.6
Common Hardware Tests

1. Test the access speed.	Are there enough communication channels to ensure an acceptable response time when a user logs onto a terminal? Can the user retrieve data from secondary storage without an unacceptable delay?
2. Test the processing speed.	Does the hardware meet the throughput or turnaround requirements of the users' production schedule—does it process transactions at an acceptable rate?
3. Test the storage capacity.	Do the disk or tape drives store the volume of data required? Do they store the record length stated in the technical specifications?
4. Test the peak load.	What happens when all terminals are active simultaneously? Does turnaround time, access speed, or response time decrease to an unacceptable level? Can the printer withstand the peak volume of printing activity expected?

21.3 Testing the Procedures and Data

In almost any systems development effort, at least minimal testing of hardware and software will be scheduled. Through the process of testing the software, some testing of data integrity is also likely to occur—possibly only as a side effect. The test activities most likely to be omitted are those that test the procedures and the data itself. Yet the success of the system is just as dependent on accurate, easy-to-understand procedures and valid data files as it is on properly functioning hardware and software. This section stresses the importance of testing data and procedures and offers some strategies for performing these testing activities.

Procedures   Several classes of tasks are covered by the blanket term *procedures*. Among these tasks are

1. Starting up the system terminating a system activity or run
2. Entering data and generating reports

3. Backing up the system's files

4. Recovering from system errors or failure

Systems based on computers don't run themselves. Human users and operators are very much a part of the system; these people require clearly written, accurate procedures to help them perform their tasks. They also require a system designed to accommodate their capabilities.

For instance, in an interactive environment, a user will be unable to perform a particular procedure if it involves immediately processing transactions that arrive at his or her workstation in rapid-fire succession. The user will feel like Charlie Chaplin in *Modern Times,* working on a too-fast assembly line. Clearly, the system needs to be adjusted to lengthen the span between transactions or, better yet, to let the user control the arrival rate.

One aspect of a systems developer's job is to prepare manuals to document the procedures for using a system. What makes this task difficult is the difference between the manual writer's knowledge of the system and the manual reader's knowledge of the system. Too often what is second nature to the writer is not at all obvious or is downright foreign to users. We've all had the experience of reading instructions and not understanding them. Usually our response is anger at the instruction manual author and reduced interest in the product. Thus, testing procedures for clarity is vital if the intended users are to understand and be committed to the system.

One of the best ways to test procedures is to involve users in the hardware and software component tests. For example, to test a data entry module, you could have a user follow the procedures necessary to enter the data and you could note any comments the user made about confusing or incomplete instructions. Similarly, as you test the hardware, you could have the users follow the system recovery procedures to restart the system. The main consideration here is selecting users who can offer useful comments but who won't be dismayed by the inevitable errors and failures of the test process.

Another strategy for testing procedures is to train a select group of users before the regular training sessions are conducted. Whenever developing a system will require training a large number of users, appoint several users to help prepare and test the procedures manuals and training materials. These users will then become responsible for maintaining the manuals and training new users hired after the system has been installed.[2] The first users can identify and correct errors in the manuals and training materials before the rest of the users are exposed to the system.

Don't think that testing procedures involves only testing the users' ability to use the software or to operate the hardware. Also vital is the users' ability to complete manual forms or to maintain a manual log. Any task procedures required as part of the system need to be verified. In addition, you need to consider ergonomic issues. **Ergonomics** is the study of environmental and human factors in the design of workplaces; its concern is increasing worker productivity and morale by providing a healthful, comfortable work space. You might recall that in Chapter 3 the pharmacy staff was very concerned about the placement of the new microcomputer and printer. Keyboards that are poorly placed, screens that reflect every light in the room, a printer whose clacking makes a telephone conversation impossible—all these are ergonomic issues that need to be addressed to ensure that the system is a positive addition to the users' workplace.

Your main concern as you test procedures should be *actively* involving the users in as many facets as feasible. Allowing the users to take a backseat role—to be passive observers—makes losers of both you and them. You lose the opportunity to put your system to its most strenuous test under the eyes of its most critical audience; as a result, errors in documentation and costly foul-ups may occur after changeover, jeopardizing the success of the system. The users lose the chance to be a guiding force in the systems development process, to have a say in how the system is operated and how the facility is arranged. They feel like "cogs in the wheel," when in fact they should see themselves as the wheel, and the hardware, software, data, and procedures as cogs designed to make their jobs easier and more rewarding. The users' active involvement in testing the procedures—and the other components of the system—provides the feedback and the sense of user control and commitment needed to make the system a success. A checklist of concerns in testing procedures is given in Figure 21.7.

Figure 21.7
A Checklist of Procedures Testing Concerns

.. Start-up procedures	Logging on
	Accessing the desired application
	Limiting access (security)
	Mounting tapes or loading disks
	Initializing the printer
2. Termination procedures	Closing files
	Logging out
	Shutting down appropriate hardware
3. Routine procedures	Executing all functions
	Overall: clear error messages referring the user to the manual or providing instructions on what to do next
4. Backup procedures	Making duplicate copies of disk files
	Maintaining transaction and audit files
	Storing backup files (for example, at another site)
5. Recovery procedures	Restarting the system
	Checking for data or transaction losses
6. User manuals	Clear documentation of all procedures
	Easy-to-use table of contents and index
	Terminology appropriate for nontechnical users
7. Ergonomics	Safe, healthful working environment
	Anti-glare screens/controlled lighting
	Noise-reducing enclosures for printers
	Unobstructed access to hardware

Data The data itself is to some extent verified when test data files are used to test procedures and software, since misunderstood rules for data field sizes and types will cause unexpected error messages in testing. However, the conversion of production files from one form to another for a new system is not verified by test data files. Thus the developer should create programs that compare new and old files field by field, printing any discrepancies for further investigation. The verification procedures explained in Section 20.1.4, using batch and hash totals, are also important, especially for the creation of computer files from hard-copy data.

21.4 Testing the Components as a System

After each component has been tested thoroughly, all five are brought together for the final test. The **system test** brings together the trained users (people), the reference and user manuals (procedures), several test data files (data), and the software and hardware, to determine how the components perform as a single functioning unit. System tests are often performed after hours—in the evening or over one or more weekends. The same test data files built to test the software and hardware are now used to test the system.

The system is put through several test runs. One test run may require the users to enter a small set of standard production data to verify that the data entry screens are easy to read, that the procedures for recovering from data entry errors are clear and correct, and that the system produces the expected output. Another more extensive test run might test the system's capacity. One or more of these tests should be a walkthrough with several users. How well does the system meet specifications for access speed, turnaround time, and so forth? Can it process the expected data volume as quickly as required? What are its storage, throughput, and output limits? When pressed past its limits, does the system degrade gracefully?

Yet another test run might introduce intentional hardware failures to test the backup and recovery procedures. Is the audit trail accurate? Have transactions been logged correctly? Do the users understand how to perform the necessary manual backup procedures? Can they restart the system without losing data or duplicating transactions? Once these controlled tests have been completed and the results meet user acceptance criteria, the system is ready for installation.

Even after the system is accepted by the users, testing is not usually complete until the system has been used for day-to-day production operations. Systems that have passed all the tests mentioned above have been known to collapse during their initial production runs. Such a breakdown is particularly disastrous in an on-line, real-time environment such as airline reservations or consumer banking. There are three methods of installation, two of which are designed to ward off potential disaster. These are explained in the next chapter on installation and changeover.

21.5 Economics of Testing

No chapter on testing would be complete if it didn't consider the economics of testing. Testing is a time-consuming, labor-intensive activity that can rapidly become very expensive. We've emphasized the importance of testing; now we need to give you some indication of how much testing is enough.

In his discussion of the value-of-information approach, Boehm identifies several fallacies about testing.[3] The two most relevant to our concerns are

1. Always build the software (or system) twice.
2. Every piece of code should be proved correct.

In some situations, these guidelines are appropriate; in others, they are not. For example, if the system being built is extremely important to the organization, if system failure would incapacitate the company or threaten human life, or if even a small failure or minor error would greatly diminish the system's integrity or security, then, by all means, build twice and test everything. Because prototyping and intensive testing are high-cost activities, however, this expense is justified only for high-risk systems. Thoroughly prototyping a routine system, such as a payroll or other common accounting application, or rigorously testing a purchased software package is wasteful; the value of the information provided (in the form of absolutely error-free runs, user satisfaction that the system operates correctly, and so forth) may be much lower than the cost of obtaining it.

Summary

Testing is an important systems development activity that is too often omitted or performed haphazardly. Testing uncovers design limitations, coding errors, unforeseen system requirements, faulty procedures, and more. The goal of testing is to reveal these deficiencies so that they can be corrected before the system is put into production. Careful testing requires careful planning of the test activities and resources. The result is an error-free system and a documented testing environment that can be used for testing in the ongoing maintenance phase of the life cycle.

Before the system can be tested, acceptance criteria for measuring the system's compliance with user requirements and technical specifications must be identified. Then the developers and/or users build several small sets of test data that will cause the system to perform all its functions and to traverse all its paths. The test data are designed to force likely error conditions, thus verifying error recovery procedures and data validation functions.

Each component of the system is tested individually before all the components are brought together for the system test. Testing the components may involve testing custom-written software using the top-down, bottom-up, or sandwich approach. Component testing also involves verifying procedures, such as error recovery, start-up, and backup procedures, and making sure that the hardware performs satisfactorily in the context of the particular application (that is, its turnaround time, processing speed, and so forth are acceptable). After each component is found to meet user requirements, all are tested together as a functioning system.

How thoroughly a system needs to be tested depends on the nature of the system. High-risk systems in which errors or failures could cost lives or incapacitate the organization should be tested more thoroughly than routine or low-risk systems. The concern for all systems is gaining user acceptance of and commitment to the system. Involving users in the test activities is one way to obtain this acceptance and commitment.

Key Terms

(Section numbers are in parentheses.)

test group (21.1.2)
acceptance criteria (21.1.2)
test specification (21.1.2)
black box testing (21.2.1)
white box testing (21.2.1)
test data (21.2.2)
top-down testing strategy (21.2.3)
stub module (21.2.3)

bottom-up testing strategy (21.2.3)
driver module (21.2.3)
sandwich testing strategy (21.2.3)
software component test (21.2.3)
technical specifications (21.2.4)
ergonomics (21.3)
system test (21.4)

Notes

1. Gerald M. Weinberg, *The Psychology of Computer Programming* (New York: Van Nostrand Reinhold, 1971), p. 57.

2. C. L. Biggs, E. G. Birks, and W. Atkins, *Managing the Systems Development Process* (Englewood Cliffs, N.J.: Prentice-Hall, 1980), p. 183.

3. Barry Boehm, *Software Engineering Economics* (Englewood Cliffs, N.J.: Prentice-Hall, 1981), pp. 299–300.

Exercises

(Answers to Exercises 21.4 and 21.6 are at the end of the book.)

21.1 Review the Chapter 18 minicase Return to Meadows Hospital, paying particular attention to the Enter Prescription Data structure chart shown in Figure 18.42.

    a. Choose a strategy (top-down, bottom-up, or sandwich) for testing this program. Explain your reasons for choosing this strategy, and discuss any stub or driver modules required.

    b. Number each module (highest level = 1.0; second level = 2.1, 2.2, . . . , 2.6; bottom level = 3.1, 3.2, . . . , 3.6), and indicate whether you would treat each module as a black box or a white box. Explain your choice for each module.

    c. Use a Gantt chart to plan the activities required to test this program.

21.2 Review the minicase Testing an Expenditure Forecasting System for Meadows Hospital.

    a. Did Fred follow a white box or black box testing strategy? Explain your answer.

    b. How could each of the five components be tested?

21.3 Review the minicase A Full-Flex Grade Book System for State University. Compare Kerry's testing strategies with your own testing of programming assignments. What are the major differences? The major similarities?

21.4 Assume that the Add Student module in Kerry's grade book system requires that the user enter the following data:

```
Student name: last name first, maximum 25 characters (alphabetic)
Student SSN: XXX-XX-XXXX (numeric)
Student number: XXX (numeric)
Student major: three-letter code (alphabetic)
```

    a. Identify at least five data entry errors that might arise as this data is entered.

    b. Create a small set of test data to test for these error conditions.

    c. Is this test a black box or a white box test? Explain your answer.

21.5 Review the Invoice Entry screen shown in Figure 18.15. Assume that the order number must not exceed nine characters.

    a. Identify at least five data entry errors that might arise as this data is entered.

    b. Create a small set of test data to test for these error conditions.

    c. Is this test a black box or a white box text? Explain your answer.

21.6 After reviewing the Chapter 11 minicase, prepare a test specification form to verify the output on the Supplier Report given in Figure 11.25. (Photocopy Figure 21.2 and fill in the appropriate details.)

21.7 After reviewing the Chapter 11 minicase Return to Meadows Hospital, prepare a test plan to verify the output on the Prescription Label shown in Figure 11.28, and the Pharmacy Daily Drug Log in Figure 11.33. (Photocopy Figure 21.2 and fill in the appropriate details.)

21.8 How could you involve users in the test activities described in your test plans for Exercises 21.6 and 21.7?

21.9 Review the Customer Order Form shown in Figure 16.19. Assume that instructions for manually completing this form will be provided as part of the user documentation.

   a. How could you test the procedures required to complete this form?

   b. The information written on this form will become input data for an automated order processing system. Given this purpose, explain why the procedures for completing this form must be accurate and easy to follow.

21.10 Figure 16.31 shows a prescription slip and the Prescription Entry Screen. Explain how you could validate the procedures for accurately entering the information from the prescription slip on the Prescription Entry screen.

21.11 Review the Chapter 18 minicase and the Process Prescriptions DFD shown in Figure 18.36.

   a. Prepare a Gantt chart detailing the activities required to perform the system test.

   b. What supplies would you need to run this test?

   c. How would you document the tests performed and the results generated?

Projects

21.12 Check your library's *Computer Literature Index* or another reference tool to locate two or three articles on testing mainframe hardware systems and their peripherals. Prepare a two- to three-page written report or a 10-minute oral report on some aspect of testing this hardware. Your audience is classmates who have very little knowledge of this subject.

21.13 In groups of three, investigate the testing activities performed when a local organization implements a new system. Have one member of your group interview a user of the system, a second member interview a programmer, and the third interview a systems analyst. Prepare a panel discussion in which you compare the perspectives of the user, programmer, and analyst on testing (for example, describe the activities they perform, the importance they assign to thorough testing, and their goals).

CHAPTER 22

Installation and Changeover

Overview

Finally we are at the end of the systems development cycle. The system has been constructed and tested; only installation activities have yet to be completed. Inexperienced developers and users may think that the system is ready to be handed over for production use. But several important activities remain. Just as we can't simply ask the users what they need during requirements determination, we can't just give the system to the users at installation. Installing the system, achieving changeover, and conducting the post-implementation evaluation are activities designed to smooth the transition from old system to new, from the development environment to the production environment.

Installation and changeover are exciting and demanding activities for both users and developers. At changeover, the users assume full ownership of the system, and the developers have the pleasure of seeing the system in production use. In this chapter we plan to

1. Explain three strategies for installation. (Section 22.1)

2. Describe installation and changeover activities. (Section 22.2)

3. Discuss the post-implementation evaluation. (Section 22.3)

22.1 Installation Strategies

The primary task of installation is coordinating the activation of the new system and the disconnection of the old system. Coordinating these installation activities can be difficult, even for simple systems. Each step must be verified and each unforeseen problem addressed as it arises. In this section we discuss three ways to install a new system:

1. Immediate replacement

2. Parallel operation

3. Phased installation

Each strategy incurs different installation costs and a different degree of risk, as illustrated in Figure 22.1. Yet each can be an effective strategy, depending on the nature of the system being installed.

Figure 22.1
Relative Cost and Risk of the Three Installation Strategies

	Factor	
Strategy	**Cost**	**Risk**
Immediate Replacement	Low	High
Parallel Operation	High	Low
Phased Installation	Medium	Medium

22.1.1 Immediate Replacement

Immediate replacement is the most direct installation strategy. With this strategy, the old system is dismantled and the new system is put into operation simultaneously. In other words, the old system is shut down and immediately replaced by the new system, with no transition period during which parts of both systems are live. As you might expect, this strategy incurs the lowest installation costs; it also incurs the greatest risk. Therefore, following the immediate replacement strategy requires careful consideration and planning.

Installing a system with the immediate replacement strategy is somewhat like performing a high-wire act without a safety net. If problems arise or errors are encountered, there is no net to fall into or old system to fall back on. Another factor making immediate replacement a risky strategy is that it does not allow you to verify the operations of the new system by comparing its output to the old system's output.

Nonetheless, the immediate replacement strategy is sometimes a good—even the *only*—choice. For example, installing a new communication network usually requires the disconnection of the old communication system. Since the new system can be tested thoroughly before changeover and since operating the two systems concurrently is not feasible, immediate replacement is an appropriate strategy. When installation is simple and straightforward or when any other installation strategy would be too costly or too complicated, immediate replacement may be the only feasible choice.

The risk of immediate replacement can be reduced by conducting a final test of the installed system during a slow period or after working hours. In the case of the communication system mentioned above, the network would probably be closed for several hours to all but a few users involved in the final test. This test would be conducted at night or on a weekend so that very few users would be inconvenienced. After the low-volume test, the network would be opened to all users. Similarly, a department store might make a final check of its installed point-of-sale system by conducting a rehearsal run while the store was closed to customers.

22.1.2 Parallel Operation

With the **parallel operation** strategy, the new system is run simultaneously with the old until the accuracy and reliability of the new system can be verified. The greatest advantage of this strategy is that it is very low risk; its greatest disadvantage is that it is very high cost and often requires complicated procedures.

Parallel operation reduces risk in several ways:

1. It allows you to verify the new system's outputs by comparing them to the old system's outputs.

2. It builds user confidence in and comfort with the new system by allowing users to verify and become accustomed to the new system in a production environment.

3. It provides a safety net—the still functioning old system—in case the new system fails. This feature is often called **fallback** because it allows you to fall back to the old system if necessary.

The high costs and complicated logistics associated with parallel operation may make it infeasible. Running both systems simultaneously strains the organization's resources; the same number of people who ran only the old system before must now oversee the operation of both systems. When a manual system is being replaced by an automated one, users must continue to perform all the old manual procedures while also performing all the new procedures of the automated system. The increased workload and mental strain of parallel operation can quickly take its toll. If both the old and the new system are automated, computer resources may be pushed beyond their limits, resulting in increased downtime and turnaround time. These complications increase the likelihood of errors, in effect increasing the risk of system failure while reducing the difficulty of coping with that failure (by providing the old system as fallback should a failure occur).

As you can see, several factors can make parallel operation prohibitively difficult:

1. Too many resources may be required.

2. Comparing the new system to the old may be too difficult.

3. The required procedures or logistics may be too complicated.

4. There may be no equivalent operation in the old system (for example, when a manual ticket reservation system is computerized).

The overall risk reduction achieved through the parallel operation strategy, however, may justify living with and planning for these complications. Figure 22.2 lists several techniques for managing parallel operation.

Figure 22.2
Techniques for Managing Parallel Operation

---

1. Phase the parallel operations if possible. That is, instead of running all aspects of the new system in parallel with the old, bring the new system on-line function by function or file by file.

2. Bring in temporary staff or reduce the workload of users during parallel operation.

3. Plan for additional computer resources. For example, order more supplies and ask other users to reduce their requirements or to reschedule their computer activities to avoid conflicts.

4. Prepare interim quick-reference procedure sheets by placing procedure summaries on placards and encasing them in plastic. These sheets should contain both old and new procedures—for example, the procedure sheet for creating a balance sheet would give the steps for the old manual system and then the steps for the new computerized system. These quick-reference sheets will guide users through complicated procedures and alleviate some of their stress.

5. Maintain user morale by recognizing their increased workload and showing your appreciation of their contribution. Schedule frequent morale-boosting activities.

Another way of dealing with these problems is to perform a variation of the parallel operation strategy. For example, the new system might be tested using old data to simulate a historical parallel run. That is, a new computerized accounting system might go live over a weekend, running old but genuine data from the old manual system. The output from the new system could be compared to that generated by the old system to verify the new system's operations. Furthermore, the users could operate the new system in a no-risk environment, thus avoiding not only the stress of running both systems simultaneously but also the anxiety of using the new system to produce output that affects the organization. Although this alternative is feasible only for small systems with few users, it deserves consideration when circumstances permit.

One question that must be addressed when the parallel operation strategy is adopted is how long to continue parallel operation before dismantling the old system. The length of the parallel operation period will vary depending on the complexity of the new system and the consequences of its failure. In the Chapter 3 case, the pharmacist's assistants used a variation of the parallel operation installation strategy for only a short time. This strategy and time frame were appropriate because the new system was fairly straightforward and errors in its functions would be neither critical nor life-threatening. In contrast, when a large organization installs a new accounting system, it may continue parallel operation through several accounting cycles because the validity of the system's data and reports is crucial to the organization's survival. The adage about ends justifying means comes to mind—the cost and complexity incurred by a more extended parallel operation period are justified by the peace of mind and risk reduction achieved.

22.1.3 Phased Installation

An installation strategy that achieves a happy medium on the cost and risk scales is **phased installation,** in which the system is installed in stages. We've discussed the phased development approach in previous chapters, so you're familiar with the benefits of performing complicated processes in stages. Phased installation differs from phased development in that the first is an *installation* strategy whereas the second is a *development* approach. A system being installed with a phased installation strategy may have been developed via the standard REDI life cycle approach.

System installation can be divided into phases by functional area, geographic area, or subsystem. For example, a new corporate database system could be installed in phases by functional area—first accounting data; then inventory, sales, and marketing data; and finally production and personnel data. Similarly, a new point-of-sale system for a national grocery chain could be installed in stores in the West Coast region first and then in other stores region by region.

The order of functions for phased installation by subsystem is usually determined either by the needs of the users or by the logical progression of functions. In the first case, system functions are installed one by one on the basis of user priorities. For example, when a new sales management system is being installed, users may determine that the order subsystem should be installed first, the software interface to the accounting system next, and so on, until the entire system has been installed. In the second case, system functions are installed successively to deliver capabilities in the order in which they can be used. For example, the data capability delivery of functions, discussed in Chapter 5, can become a strategy for phased installation.

The following minicase, Phased Installation of an Inventory Management System, provides an overview of the issues and concerns in phased installation.

Phased Installation of an Inventory Management System

Microcomputer Inc., a national wholesale distributor of microcomputers, maintains an inventory of microcomputers, components, and supplies for sale to small retail outlets. Ten months ago management decided to implement an inventory management system to keep track of inventory at all its branch locations.

Ted Alexander, project manager for the inventory management system, is pleased that development has progressed smoothly. Upper-level managers knew what they wanted and were quite helpful during the requirements determination, evaluation, and design stages. They chose a system based on a purchased inventory management package, to be installed on the main office's central computer; the branch offices will all use the system via a communication network. The implementation strategy is to install the system first at the main office and then at the other locations.

The main office's computer facility and the communication network have been upgraded, and testing for the inventory package has gone smoothly. Documentation is complete for both the users and the technical staff, and training is in progress. Ted is ready to prepare a plan for phased installation.

First, Ted asks strategic management to prioritize the branch offices for installation of the new system. Strategic management decides that the order of installation will be (1) East Coast offices, (2) Northwest offices, (3) West Coast offices, (4) South offices, and (5) Central offices.

Then Ted analyzes the installation requirements for the main office. Software interfaces to the inventory package have already been coded and debugged for bridging to existing software for the Accounting and Sales departments. Since the Inventory department will be the first to be affected by the new system, Ted decides to install the Inventory department subsystem first, followed by the Sales interface, and then the Accounting software interface. The inventory management package will be installed before any of the interfaces are installed. The package contains a data management component, which is activated by loading relevant data, and a procedure component, which is activated once the data has been loaded. The same subsystem installation phases will be repeated for each branch location until all branch offices are active. Ted's phased installation plan is shown in Figure 22.3.

Figure 22.3
Ted's Phased Installation Plan

Installation Plan for
Inventory Management System
Microcomputer Inc.

A. Geographical phased installation
   1. Main office
   2. East Coast offices
   3. Northwest offices
   4. West Coast offices
   5. South offices
   6. Central offices

B. Subsystem phases at each site
   1. Inventory department subsystem
   2. Sales interface
   3. Accounting interface
   4. Parallel operation (two months)
   5. Acceptance review
   6. Changeover
   7. Post-implementation evaluation (two months after changeover)

Management wants the old system and the new system to run in parallel for two months before changeover. Ted remembers to plan a post-implementation evaluation two months after changeover. At changeover, all parallel activities will cease and the old system will be discarded.

22.2 Installation and Changeover

In the introduction to this chapter we noted that the development team doesn't just *give* the system to the users. Instead, transferring production operations from the old system to the new system involves several activities. These activities are designed to manage this transition and to maintain the integrity of inputs, outputs, and files. The transition stage is composed of three major activities, or milestones: installation, acceptance review, and changeover.

22.2.1 Installation

Installation is the period during which production files and operations are transferred from the old system to the new. Installation requires that affected components of the old system be replaced or modified by the components of the new system. For example, additional personnel may join the user group or operations staff to oversee functions of the new system. At a minimum, the current users will begin to perform different procedures as they use new hardware or software to accomplish their job objectives. As we discussed in Chapter 20, building data files for the new system is a major task in installation.

Managing the installation process requires careful planning, attention to detail, and concern for security and control. The development team's installation plan will include the following:

1. The installation schedule, which identifies who will do what when (we suggest that you use a Gantt chart to document the installation schedule)

2. Installation procedures and controls to maintain data integrity and to cross-check the old and new systems

3. A contingency plan in case any aspect of the old or new system fails during conversion

4. A timetable for the systematic dismantling of the old system, including removing old hardware, software, and documentation and archiving final copies of reports, programs, and files from the old system

Figure 22.4 is a checklist of common installation activities categorized by system component. This form will help you to plan these tasks, to document their completion, and to secure approval as tasks are completed.

Many project managers feel that the number and complexity of these tasks warrant the formation of a special installation team. An **installation team** is composed of users and developers—perhaps some from the original development team—who begin planning for installation early in the project. Although a special installation team may not be necessary for small system projects, the need for extensive file conversion may justify appointment of an installation team.

22.2.2 Acceptance Review

Once all components have been installed, the system is subjected to a final test: the **acceptance review.** During the acceptance review, users test the system under routine and exceptional conditions to determine whether the system satisfies the acceptance criteria

Installation Plan Checklist		Date		Page	
System		Analyst			
Activity (Check all that apply)	Person Responsible	Start Date	Finish Date	Approved By	
I. People _____ A. Hiring of New Personnel _____ B. Training _____ C. Formation of Installation Team					
II. Procedures _____ A. User Manuals _____ B. Technical Manuals _____ C. Printing/Distribution of Paper Forms _____ D. User Acceptance Review _____ E. Removal of Out-of-Date Documentation					
III. Data _____ A. Control Procedures for File Conversion _____ B. Review of Current Files _____ C. Freeze Date and File Conversion _____ D. Update of Converted Files _____ E. User Acceptance Review _____ F. Archiving of Old Files					
IV. Software _____ A. Application Program Library _____ B. System Program Library _____ C. Backup Program Library _____ D. User Acceptance Review _____ E. Removal/Archiving of Old Software					

V. Hardware
 _____ A. Electrical Outlets, Cables, etc.
 _____ B. Supplies
 _____ C. Device Installation
     _____ CPU   _____ Communication
     _____ Printer(s)   _____ Terminals
     _____ Other _____
 _____ D. System Security
     _____ Power Backup
     _____ Off-Site Storage
     _____ Access Restriction
 _____ E. User Acceptance Review
 _____ F. Removal of Old Hardware					

Figure 22.4   Installation Plan Checklist

established during requirements determination. Users scrutinize documentation, measure system response and turnaround times, study input screens and reports, evaluate backup, recovery, and security procedures, and rate the system's usability and reliability. Any components or functions that fail to satisfy the acceptance criteria must be modified. In other words, the development team isn't off the hook until the users signal their acceptance of the system by signing off on each criterion. Figure 22.5 is an example of a user acceptance review form.

Figure 22.5
User Acceptance
Review Form

User Acceptance Review Form	Date	
System	Review Date	
Review Prepared by		
Acceptance Criteria	Approved by	Date
1.		
2.		
3.		
4.		
5.		
6.		
7.		
8.		
9.		
10.		

Acceptance Acknowledgement

The undersigned representatives agree that this project, identified above, has been completed in a satisfactory manner.

Information Systems Management   User Management

_____   _____   _____   _____
Authorized Signature   Date   Authorized Signature   Date

_____   _____
Title   Title

When the parallel operation or phased installation strategy is used, the acceptance review may be an ongoing process. With the parallel operation strategy, the users assess the system's acceptability throughout the latter portion of the parallel operation period. With the phased installation strategy, users perform an acceptance review as each phase or subsystem is installed. Whatever installation strategy is used, the development team's goal is to gain user acceptance and to achieve changeover.

22.2.3 Changeover

When the users have thoroughly checked the system and are satisfied that it meets their needs, a formal meeting is conducted with the development team, users, and information systems management. At this meeting, the installation and new system are officially assessed, and the users sign off on the acceptance criteria, thus accepting responsibility for the new system. Finally, the development team hands over the system to the users, thereby achieving changeover and beginning the production phase of the system life cycle.

Changeover is an exciting time both for the users, who gain full control of the system, and for the developers, who see months of labor finally brought to fruition. Although the development team is available to answer user questions during the first weeks after changeover, the system is turned over to the maintenance group for ongoing support and maintenance.

Changeover signals the end of the project, and it would not be complete without recognition of the outstanding contributions of key developers, users, and managers. Everyone will be refreshed by a celebration that alleviates the psychological letdown associated with the end of an intense activity. Although post-project recognition ceremonies or celebrations may seem frivolous, they are valuable motivational tools that formally mark the end of a project, revitalize users and developers, and restore some of the stamina needed to take on tomorrow's projects.

22.3 Post-Implementation Evaluation

After changeover has been achieved and the users have adjusted to the system, the final task is to evaluate the project and the system delivered.[1] By this time there should be measurable results. A **post-implementation evaluation** investigates the results of the project and alerts developers to ways in which future projects can be improved. It also provides feedback on how well the development team met the system objectives, stayed within the project constraints, and estimated the project schedule and budget. This feedback serves as a measure of team performance and helps analysts become better estimators.

The post-implementation evaluation report, generally prepared two to three months after changeover, addresses the three goals of systems development:

1. *System quality.* Does the system do what it is supposed to do? Does it function reliably and efficiently? Is it well documented to facilitate maintenance? Can the system adapt to changes in the organization? Is it compatible with other systems?

2. *Project management.* What project management approaches were used? Were they successful? Why or why not? Were management and users kept abreast of the status of the project schedule through reviews at major milestones? Was the system completed on time and within budget? What lessons were learned about managing a project such as this one? Should the organization adopt any new policies to take advantage of these lessons? Are the users satisfied with the system? Are they pleased with the way the project was conducted?

3. *Organizational relevance.* Does the system improve an operational task critical to the organization's objectives? Does it support management control or provide strategic value? Is it producing the benefits expected? Do the benefits the system provides justify its ongoing production costs?

As these questions indicate, the post-implementation evaluation relies on information gathered from the development team, the users, and management. This information, along with technical data about the system's functionality, will be used to evaluate project outcomes.

22.3.1 Review Project Documents

The first step in the evaluation process is to compare the old system, the promised system, and the delivered system. Reviewing earlier project documents, especially the requirements document and the cost/benefit analysis, will refresh your memory and help you identify the objectives and expected benefits of the development project. This review step is shown as activity 2.1 in the CPM model in Figure 22.6. The documentation review will also provide the technical information needed for a summary of the delivered system, such as the one shown in Figure 22.7.

Figure 22.6
CPM for Post-Implementation Review

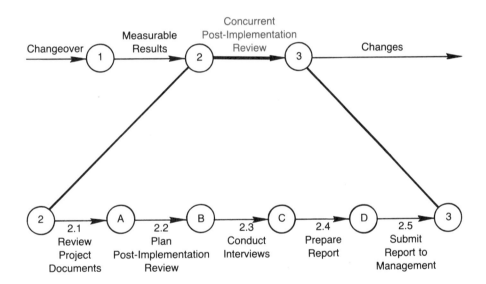

22.3.2 Plan Post-Implementation Review

The next step is to prepare a plan for the evaluation, which involves identifying individuals to be interviewed and assigning team members to the various tasks involved in gathering the data and evaluating the findings. The team leader for the post-implementation evaluation decides which users, team members, and managers are to be interviewed. The criteria for evaluation are those established through the review of the project documents.

Figure 22.7
Project Summary

Project Summary	Page
System	Date
Prepared by	

Schedule

Date implemented (Mo/Yr) _____

Duration of the project, in months
(from authorization to
implementation):

  Earliest estimate _____
  Authorized estimate _____
  Actual duration _____

Size

Size of the system:

  K lines of code _____
  K bytes of object code _____
  Number of programs _____
  Other _____

Was this an enhancement project?
[ ]Yes [ ]No
If yes: How much bigger is the new
system than the old system?_____ %
What portion of the old system was
replaced?_____ %

How many people and departments
receive data from the system?
  People _____
  Departments _____

Cost

Cost of the project, in $ thousands
(from authorization to implementation):

  Earliest estimate _____
  Authorized estimate _____
  Actual cost _____

Costs include (check all that apply)
[ ] Internal systems personnel
[ ] External systems personnel
[ ] User personnel
[ ] Computer resource charges
[ ] Purchased software
[ ] Purchased hardware
[ ] Other_____

Was the project cost justified? _____
  Using ROI? _____%
  Using Payback? _____years
  Using Present Value? $_____[thou]
  Other? _____
If the project was NOT cost justified: What
was the basis for proceeding?_____

_____

Technology
Hardware technology (check all that apply):
[ ] Mainframe or mini
[ ] On-line terminals
[ ] Personal computers

Principal language(s) _____

_____
   (ignore operating systems
   or small amounts of code)

22.3.3 Conduct Interviews

Except for the information gained from studying error logs and other documentation of the system in operation, most of the information on the success of the project will come from interviewing users, developers, and managers. The Chapter 9 guidelines for conducting interviews also apply here. Of critical importance in post-implementation interviews is gathering the interviewee's true feelings. Many users will hesitate to express negative comments about the project management or system quality, especially if the person conducting the interview is one of the developers! You can overcome this hesitancy by using a questionnaire such as the one shown in Figure 22.8 to elicit user responses. After the

Figure 22.8 User Evaluation Form

Page 1 of 2

User Evaluation					
System		Evaluator Date		Page	1 of 2
		Evaluator			

Please evaluate the project on the criteria listed by circling the response that best describes your viewpoint.

	Very Unsatisfactory						Very Satisfactory

Functionality

Reliability

1. Comprehensiveness of options on screens and menus (all necessary choices provided) 1 2 3 4 5 6 7
2. Sufficiency of help options 1 2 3 4 5 6 7
3. Integration of functions 1 2 3 4 5 6 7
4. Accuracy of data 1 2 3 4 5 6 7
5. Reliability of system 1 2 3 4 5 6 7
6. Security 1 2 3 4 5 6 7

Clarity

7. Consistency and predictability of system. 1 2 3 4 5 6 7
8. Ease of learning and use. 1 2 3 4 5 6 7
9. Clarity of instructions, prompts, error messages and help messages 1 2 3 4 5 6 7
10. Clarity of choices on screens and menus. 1 2 3 4 5 6 7
11. Clarity of report formats and labeling 1 2 3 4 5 6 7

Efficiency

12. Response time 1 2 3 4 5 6 7
13. Number of keystrokes. 1 2 3 4 5 6 7
14. Ease of movement between functions 1 2 3 4 5 6 7

Ease of Maintenance

Understandability

15. Clarity and completeness of user documentation 1 2 3 4 5 6 7
16. Clarity and adequacy of training materials. 1 2 3 4 5 6 7

Modifiability

17. Ability of screens and menus to continue to be used, even when changes are implemented 1 2 3 4 5 6 7
18. Frequency of requests for modifications. 1 2 3 4 5 6 7

Testability

19. Completeness and helpfulness of test plan 1 2 3 4 5 6 7

Page 2 of 2

User Evaluation			Page	2 of 2

	Very Unsatisfactory						Very Satisfactory

Flexibility

Portability

20. System can be used at other offices 1 2 3 4 5 6 7
21. System can be used on other hardware 1 2 3 4 5 6 7

Adaptability

22. System similar to other systems already in use. 1 2 3 4 5 6 7
23. System not dependent on other systems to be functional. 1 2 3 4 5 6 7

Team's Performance

24. Met agreed milestones 1 2 3 4 5 6 7
25. Interested in future needs. 1 2 3 4 5 6 7
26. Cooperative attitude 1 2 3 4 5 6 7
27. Used non-technical terms 1 2 3 4 5 6 7
28. Kept user informed on progress 1 2 3 4 5 6 7
29. Thorough training 1 2 3 4 5 6 7

Overall Project

30. Level of user involvement 1 2 3 4 5 6 7
31. Management commitment 1 2 3 4 5 6 7
32. Overall satisfaction. 1 2 3 4 5 6 7

Comments: _____

user has completed the form, a developer or a disinterested third party should follow up by asking the user about his/her expectations of the system and lessons learned.

The project development team and management will also need to be interviewed. Interviewing several team members and managers should provide a representative sample of assessments of the project and its outcomes. Figure 22.9 shows an interview form or questionnaire that can be used to gather team members' comments on a project. Figure 22.10 lists some questions that delve into management's assessment of the system and whether it satisfies organizational relevance goals.

Figure 22.9
Team Member Project
Evaluation Form

Team Member Project Evaluation	Date
System	Evaluator

Please evaluate the project on the criteria listed by circling the response that best describes your viewpoint.

System Quality	Very Unsatisfactory				Very Satisfactory		

Functionality
1. Error rate   1   2   3   4   5   6   7
2. Timeliness of reports delivered.   1   2   3   4   5   6   7
3. Completeness of reports delivered.   1   2   3   4   5   6   7

Maintainability
4. Quality of documentation (user and
   technical)   1   2   3   4   5   6   7
5. Quality of testing procedures documentation   1   2   3   4   5   6   7
6. Quality of programming standards   1   2   3   4   5   6   7
7. Clarity and functionality of modules   1   2   3   4   5   6   7

Flexibility
8. Ability of system to be used at other sites . .   1   2   3   4   5   6   7
9. Ability of system to be used on other
   hardware   1   2   3   4   5   6   7
10. Procedural flexibility   1   2   3   4   5   6   7

Project Management

Timeliness
11. Meeting of agreed-upon milestones   1   2   3   4   5   6   7

Cost
12. System cost   1   2   3   4   5   6   7

User Commitment
13. Involvement during development   1   3   4   5   6   7
14. Enthusiasm about completed system   1   3   4   5   6   7

Overall Project

15. Background of development team   1   2   3   4   5   6   7
16. Performance of development team   1   2   3   4   5   6   7
17. Priority assigned by management   1   2   3   4   5   6   7
18. Upper-management commitment   1   2   3   4   5   6   7
19. Overall benefits from the system   1   2   3   4   5   6   7
20. Overall rating.   1   2   3   4   5   6   7

Comments:_____

_____

Project Management Evaluation	Date
System	Evaluator

Please evaluate the project on the criteria listed by circling the response that best describes your viewpoint.

<u>System Quality</u>

	Very Unsatisfactory				Very Satisfactory		

1. Satisfaction of users
   a. Were user requirements met?.....................   1   2   3   4   5   6   7
   b. Is the data valid, integrated, and secure?..   1   2   3   4   5   6   7
   c. Is the system easy to use, responsive, and stable?...   1   2   3   4   5   6   7
   d. Were schedule and budget requirements met?...   1   2   3   4   5   6   7
2. Satisfaction of the IS group
   a. Does the system conform to IS data and architecture goals?..............................   1   2   3   4   5   6   7
   b. Is it easy to operate, audit, and maintain?.   1   2   3   4   5   6   7
   c. Does it operate within cost and schedule requirements?...   1   2   3   4   5   6   7

<u>Project Management</u>

3. Control of progress (Throughout the project, were the status of the project schedule, budget, and features to be delivered communicated clearly to all user managers?)........................   1   2   3   4   5   6   7
4. Tradeoff among cost, schedule, and features (particularly with respect to technical issues of development)..   1   2   3   4   5   6   7
5. Team leadership (Did team leadership enhance team productivity and provide members with the opportunity to develop and enhance their skills?)..............................   1   2   3   4   5   6   7

<u>Organizational Relevance</u>

6. Value added to the enterprise (Does the system improve efficiency or effectiveness, in tangible or intangible ways, in the short or long run?)..   1   2   3   4   5   6   7
7. Total cost and delivery dates for the system..   1   2   3   4   5   6   7
8. Overall rating   1   2   3   4   5   6   7

Comments:_____

Figure 22.10   Project Management Evaluation Form

22.3.4 Prepare the Evaluation Report

Chapter 12 provided numerous guidelines for documenting project activities; these guidelines also apply to documenting project outcomes. The emphasis in the post-implementation evaluation report is on (1) evaluating the project's satisfaction of the systems development goals and (2) recommending policies and strategies to facilitate future development projects.

A model for the post-implementation report is given in Figure 22.11. As with all formal business reports, the first part is a brief (one-page) executive summary that serves as a cover letter and highlights the two or three most important findings in the report. Next is the table of contents.

The first section of the text discusses conclusions and recommendations. What is the overall assessment of the system? What did the users, developers, and managers learn from this project that could be used to advantage in future projects? Here you recommend that policies be changed or that new policies be implemented. You also discuss any insights about investing in development tools or user training and about documenting for easier maintenance. In some cases your evaluation may lead you to recommend that the system be modified or (heaven forbid!) scrapped.

Figure 22.11

A Model for the Post-Implementation Evaluation Report

1. Executive summary
2. Table of contents
3. Conclusions and recommendations
   3.1 Major successes and failures
   3.2 Recommendations for future projects
4. Overview of the project
   4.1 Project objectives
   4.2 Project participants
       4.2.1 Development team
       4.2.2 User organization
       4.2.3 Vendors, consultants, etc.
5. Project summary
   5.1 Project characteristics
       5.1.1 Size and complexity
       5.1.2 Project management strategies
       5.1.3 Development tools used
6. Assessment of outcomes
   6.1 System quality
       6.1.1 Functionality
       6.1.2 Ease of maintenance
       6.1.3 Flexibility
   6.2 Project management
   6.3 Organizational relevance

The second section provides an overview of the project. This section states the project objectives and may include excerpts from the requirements document. Implicit and secondary objectives should be acknowledged here. For example, one objective for the Information Services department might be learning a fourth generation language with which to develop part of the system. Also included in this section are an organization chart showing the participants (the user-sponsor, the user-manager, and any user-liaisons) and, where appropriate, lists of vendors, consultants, and development team members.

The third section, the project summary, discusses project characteristics and events that may be important to assessing project outcomes. Topics discussed here include the size and complexity of the project, the project management strategies used, any special development tools used (for example, 4GLs or CASE tools), and any special problems encountered.

The fourth section, assessment of outcomes, evaluates the project and system in terms of the objectives stated in the first section. Here is where the information gathered from interviews and questionnaires is summarized. The three goals of systems development serve as an effective organizational device for this section—the objectives of each goal can be addressed in turn. Critical success factors for implementation, such as user involvement, design quality, project management, and resource adequacy,[2] are among the issues that should be discussed. Both successes and failures need to be pinpointed clearly and unequivocally. Although you will want to discuss any cause-effect relationships that explain why an objective was not achieved, you should *not* turn this section into a litany of excuses or an exercise in scapegoating. Remember that not meeting some of the objectives may not have made a difference. For example, the users may not have cared that the system was delivered six weeks late or that the interface lacked some of the features originally desired.

The post-implementation evaluation report is a reference for future systems development projects. It serves as a guidebook for estimating and managing projects, as a sourcebook for technical problem solutions, and as a handbook on user-developer relations. Thus the time required to compile and document its information is time well spent.

22.3.5 Submit the Report to Management

The team leader for the post-implementation evaluation should present a summary of the highlights of the report to appropriate representatives of upper management. Members of the post-implementation team, the original project manager, appropriate users, and IS managers should attend the presentation to answer questions, provide supplementary information, and express dissenting opinions. The systems development project is concluded when the report is accepted.

22.4 Change Management

System changes are inevitable. The post-implementation evaluation may identify change requests that need to be acted on immediately. If a system revision is required to meet the original project specifications, the work may be viewed as an extension of the original systems development. Otherwise you have come full circle, as shown in Figure 1.12 at the beginning of the book. Requests for changes are the first step in another development process. You are back to requirements determination. What are the objectives of this system revision? What are the constraints? Are the potential benefits of the revision worth the effort? You begin the development process again, to deliver a high-quality system of justifiable value to the organization, whose development is managed well.

Summary

Installation and changeover are periods of high emotion during which detailed procedures must be performed to finish the development project. Careful planning and attention to detail are critical to the successful management of installation activities.

We present three strategies for installing systems: (1) immediate replacement, (2) parallel operation, and (3) phased installation. Each strategy incurs different installation costs and a different level of risk. The immediate replacement strategy should be attempted only if both the other strategies are infeasible. The parallel operation strategy is expensive and requires complicated procedures for operating both the old and the new system simultaneously. The phased installation strategy is especially useful for large systems that can be installed in stages by subsystem or by geographic or functional area.

During installation, the components of the old system are replaced by those of the new. Following installation, a final test or acceptance review of the system is conducted to gain user sign-off on each of the acceptance criteria. A successful acceptance review culminates in changeover, at which point the system becomes the users' responsibility and the production phase begins.

The final task of the development team is conducting the post-implementation evaluation. Two or three months after changeover, user, developer, and management assessments of the development product (the system) and the development process (the project) are compiled. This information is documented in the post-implementation evaluation report, which points out successes and failures and suggests ways to improve future projects. If changes are required to the system, the development process is initiated again to create a revised system.

Key Terms

(Section numbers are in parentheses.)

immediate replacement (22.1.1)　　**installation team (22.2.1)**
parallel operation (22.1.2)　　**acceptance review (22.2.2)**
fallback (22.1.2)　　**post-implementation evaluation (22.3)**
phased installation (22.1.3)

Notes

1. See *A Management System for the Information Business* (White Plains, N.Y.: International Business Machines Corporation, 1983); or E. Burton Swanson, *Information System Implementation: Bridging the Gap between Design and Utilization* (Homewood, Ill.: Richard D. Irwin, 1988), pp. 74–75.

2. Swanson, *Information System Implementation,* pp. 2–8.

Exercises

(Answers to Exercises 22.1 and 22.3 are at the end of the book.)

22.1 Review the Chapter 9 minicase Using NGT for Systems Planning at Woods, Inc.

   a. What would be a good strategy for installing the system?

   b. Prepare a Gantt chart of the installation activities for the strategy you select, and justify your choice.

22.2 Review the Meadows Hospital case in Chapter 3.

   a. Describe the installation strategy and activities of the development team.

   b. What fallback provisions did the team make?

22.3 In the Chapter 8 minicase Lite's Production Management System, George made many mistakes during development. Discuss how using a different installation strategy might have permitted detection of some of these mistakes.

22.4 Review the Chapter 1 minicase Abby Clark and Her Turnkey System.

   a. Discuss Abby's installation strategy.

   b. Explain what steps Abby and Cecil should have followed to install the system and convert from a manual filing system to an automated filing system.

   c. Prepare an installation plan checklist to guide Abby and Cecil as they install the new system. Refer to Figure 22.4 for an example of an installation plan checklist.

Projects

22.5 Contact the information services director of an organization in your community to learn about its policies on installing systems. Prepare an oral or written report on the company's installation methods and its successes and failures with these methods.

22.6 Contact the information services director of an organization in your community to learn about its policies on post-implementation reviews. Prepare an oral or written report on the company's installation methods and its successes and failures with these methods.

22.7 Contact the information services director of an organization in your community and offer to conduct a post-implementation review of one or more production systems that have recently been installed. Conduct interviews with developers and users, using the forms provided in this chapter. Prepare a post-implementation review of each system you evaluate.

Glossary

Acceptance criteria   Functional requirements identified as the basis for accepting the system. (21.1.2)

Acceptance review   The final test of a new system, during which users test the system under routine and exceptional conditions to determine whether it meets the acceptance criteria. (22.2.2)

Aggregation   Combining attributes from different entities or relationships into one logical record during database design. (17.2.2)

Analyst   An information systems professional who works with users to determine requirements and to evaluate alternative systems, and then works with users and other IS professionals to design and implement the system. (1.1.1)

Analyzing strategy   A requirements determination strategy that involves studying the activities of a functional area to determine its inputs and outputs, objectives, critical success factors, procedures, and inter-organization interactions. (7.4.3)

Application software   Software that performs a specific task important in the user's functional area—e.g., general ledger accounting or statistical analysis. (1.1.4)

Asking strategy   A requirements determination strategy that involves interviewing the intended users of a system. (7.4.3)

Attribute   A characteristic or fact about an entity. (11.2.2)

Black box testing   A program testing technique that focuses on whether or not the system creates accurate output. (21.2.1)

Bottom-up testing strategy   A testing method in which process modules are tested before control modules. (21.2.3)

Capacity planning   Estimating the processing requirements of a proposed system. (12.3.5)

Cardinality   The number of instances of one entity that can describe one instance of another entity in a relationship—e.g., {1,1}, {1,N}. (11.2.3)

CASE tools   Computer-assisted software engineering tools used to automate some aspects of systems development. (7.2)

Changeover   The point at which a system switches from development to production. (1.2)

Checklist approach   A planning method used to identify activities for a development schedule. (5.1.1)

Child process   A process that combines with other processes to form a parent process. (10.2.3)

Clarity   The degree to which a system interacts with users in a consistent, easy-to-understand, and predictable manner. (2.1.1)

Cohesion   A measure of the strength of association between processing statements in a module. (18.4.2)

Command   A human-computer dialogue format that requires the user to type special commands or press specific keys in order to make a selection. (16.2.5)

Comment log   Documentation that can be used to validate a data model. (11.4)

Composite criteria   Combinations of two or more related criteria. (14.2.1)

Conceptual data model   A structured tool that describes the data objects and relationships required by a system. (7.2)

Concurrent multi-user system   A system that two or more users can access, seemingly at the same time. (1.1.2)

Construction   The implementation process of building the five system components to meet the specifications developed during the design stage. (1.2.4)

Context diagram   A structured technique that depicts an information system environment, including data flows into and out of the system. (7.2, 8.2)

Control flow   A flag or indicator that directs the processing of a module or reports on the status of a condition. (18.2.1)

Coordinating   The project management activity of forming a project team and managing the activities of its members and its resources. (2.2.3)

Coupling   A measure of module independence in structured program design. (18.4.1)

Critical path   The sequence of activities requiring the most time. (5.2.1)

Critical path method (CPM) network   A graphic tool that shows the sequence of systems development tasks as well as the time requirements for a project. (4.3.1, 5.2.1)

Critical success factors (CSF)   The few factors that are critical to the success of an organization. (8.1, 14.3.3)

Critical success factors method   A technique for identifying organizational information requirements by identifying the critical success factors. (8.1)

Data   Information; the critical component of an information system, made up of input data, data stores, and output data. (1.1.3)

Data access table   A summary of reports and screens that make the most critical database updates and retrievals. (17.1)

Data element   A representation of the smallest unit of information defined for data; also known as a field or attribute. (17.2.1)

Data entry controls   Standards for ensuring the accuracy, integrity, and confidentiality of the data that is entered and accessed through the interface. (15.2.1)

Data entry screen   An input format used to enter data from source documents and reports into computer files or to update data. (16.2.4)

Data flow   A transfer of data between two entities. (8.2.1, 18.2.1)

Data flow diagram (DFD)   A structured technique that depicts the movement of data between processes and storage areas within a system, as well as external sources and destinations. (7.2, 10.1)

Data store   Stored data, represented in a data flow diagram by an elongated rectangle. (10.1.3)

Data structure   A collection of data elements or structures that are grouped together. (18.4.1)

Data volume   The amount of data a system must be capable of processing and storing. (12.3.3)

Database design   The second step in system design, in which it is determined how the data requirements for a system will be implemented as a database. (15.2.2)

Database management system (DBMS)   A software system that maintains and controls the logical and physical structure of data independently of the applications that access the data. (17.4)

Database schema   A description of the logical and physical data structure of a database, stated in a data description language. (17.4)

Database specifications   A description of the logical and physical structures of a database. (15.2.2)

Database transaction An update or retrieval of data in a database. (17.1)

Derived attribute An attribute whose value is derived from the values of other attributes. (11.2.2)

Deriving strategy A requirements determination strategy that involves investigating current systems internal and external to the sponsoring organization. (7.4.3)

Design repository An automated storage facility for such system development information as report and screen definitions. (7.2)

Design specification The third stage of the REDI model, during which the design for the five system components—people, procedures, data, software, and hardware—is specified. (1.2.3)

Developer An information systems professional who works with users to create a system. The developer's tasks include building and integrating the five components of an information system in order to meet the users' needs. (1.1.1)

Development costs Expenses incurred during the systems development process. (13.4.2)

Development phase The period during which an information system is created or modified. (1.2)

Development process matrix A two-dimensional model of development activities, with the REDI model stages along the vertical axis and the five system components along the horizontal axis. (1.3)

Direct file organization A method of file organization in which physical records are located by the values of their key data elements. (17.3.1)

Documentation standards Guidelines adopted by an organization for documenting systems. (20.2.1)

Driver module A module used in testing to simulate the role of control modules that would normally access data and control processing. (21.2.3)

Ease of maintenance A qualitative measure of how simply modifications can be made to a system. (2.1.1)

Efficiency The degree to which a system's processing speed is maximized and its turnaround time and memory requirements are minimized. (2.1.1)

Effort-month A measure used in estimating how much time a project would require if all tasks were performed sequentially and only one person was assigned to the project. (5.2.2)

End-user A person who directly interacts with a system. (1.1.1)

Entity Any object, person, concept, or event about which data is collected and which is described in a data model. (11.2.1)

Entity-relationship (ER) notation A system of notation used for describing a data model. It includes symbols for entities, attributes, identifiers, relationships, and dependencies. (11.2.7)

Ergonomics The study of environmental and human factors in the design of workplaces. Its goal is to increase worker productivity and morale. (21.3)

Evaluation The second stage of the REDI model, during which alternatives for each system component are identified and evaluated and one alternative is selected. (1.2.2)

Evaluation grid A graphic summary of the ratings of alternatives on two criteria. (14.2.1)

Evaluation matrix A summary table showing the criteria, weights, and ratings for two or more alternatives being evaluated. (14.1.1)

Existence dependency A dependency arising when the instances of one entity exist as a result of instances of another entity within a relationship. (11.2.5)

Existing software Application software already available for purchase or from some free source, such as public-domain software or another part of the organization. The term does not apply to productivity software, like spreadsheets or database management systems, or system software, like COBOL compiler, that are development tools. (2.4.1)

External document   A document that provides information to or requests information from people outside of the system. (16.2.1)

External entity   An agency, business, or person outside the sponsoring organization. (8.2.1)

Fallback   An old system that an organization can fall back on if the new one fails. (22.1.2)

Fan-in   The number of boss modules that a module has. (18.4.3)

Fan-out   The number of modules called by a module; also known as span of control. (18.4.3)

Feasibility analysis   An evaluation of one alternative in order to decide whether to pursue, revise, or abandon it. (13.1.2)

File conversion   Changing manual files to tape or drive storage files during the construction phase of implementation. (20.1.4)

File organization   A description of the physical layout of a file. (17.3.1)

Flexibility   A qualitative measure of how portable and adaptable a system is. (2.1.1)

Flexibility criteria   Evaluation criteria that relate to the portability and adaptability of a system. (14.3.2)

Foreign key   A key of a related record used as a data element in another record to define a relationship between the two records. (17.2.4)

Fourth generation language (4GL)   A systems development tool that is suited to developing input/output-oriented systems. (2.4.2)

Function point model   An effort estimation technique in which the complexity of the functions a system must deliver is used to estimate the development effort. (6.5)

Functional area boundary   The scope of a system defined in terms of the major organizational divisions or subunits it affects. (7.3.1)

Functional criteria   Evaluation criteria that relate to system capabilities. (13.3.1)

Functional primitive   A process that cannot be subdivided any further through structured decomposition. (10.2.3)

Functional requirements   Requirements that state what actions the system must perform. (1.2.1, 7.3.3)

Functionality   A qualitative measure of a system's reliability, clarity, and efficiency. (2.1.1)

Gantt chart   A graphical tool for planning, monitoring, and coordinating systems development, on which are listed project activities, their start and completion times, and the person(s) assigned to each activity. (4.3.4, 5.3)

Geographical boundary   The scope of a system defined in terms of the physical area it encompasses. (7.3.1)

Hardware   The physical components of the computer system. (1.1.5)

Hashing   A technique for calculating a physical storage address from a key field(s). (17.3.1)

Hierarchical DBMS   A database structure in which records are related as parents and children. (17.4.1)

Human-computer dialogue   The method of interaction between a user and a computer. (16.2.5)

Identifier   An attribute or set of attributes that has a unique value for each instance of an entity. (11.2.4)

Identifier dependency   A dependency arising when the instances of an entity cannot be uniquely identified by the values of its attributes. (11.2.5)

Immediate replacement The most direct installation strategy, in which the old system is dismantled and simultaneously the new system is put into production. (22.1.1)

Implementation The fourth stage of the REDI model, during which the system is constructed, tested, and installed. (1.2.4)

Incremental strategy A method for specifying modules whereby the amount of detail in the PDL is increased as the corresponding structure chart is refined. (18.3.4)

Indexed file organization A method of file organization in which physical records are stored in any order, sequential or random, and an index is used to locate single physical records. (17.3.1)

Information system An integrated system, composed of people, procedures, data, software, and hardware, that produces information by accessing and processing data. (1.1)

Information system boundary The scope of a system defined in terms of the extent of the activities it will perform. (7.3.1)

Installation The implementation process during which production files and operations are transferred from the old system to the new. (1.2.4)

Installation manual Instructions that state how to install hardware and software as well as how to configure the system for the current operating system and peripherals. (20.2.3)

Installation team A group of users and developers who begin planning for installation early in the project life cycle. (22.2.1)

Instance A unique set of values for the attributes of an entity. (11.2.1)

Intangible benefits Benefits that cannot be quantified, such as improved company image. (13.4.2)

Interface specifications Outputs of the interface design process, such as design layouts for screens and reports as well as information about errors and the control of screen processing. (15.2.1)

Internal entity A functional area within the sponsoring organization. (8.2.1)

Internal report A document that provides information to personnel within an organization. (16.2.2)

Intersection entity An entity created when two entities stand in a N:M relationship with each other. (11.2.3)

Job The specification of processes required to run one or more programs at set times and in a particular sequence. (18.4.4)

Job level system flowchart The most detailed system flowchart, which shows commands for a job. (10.3.3)

Key A unique identifier used to denote an instance of a record. (17.2.3)

Leveling *See* Structured decomposition.

Life cycle model A systems development model that divides a system's life cycle into two phases: development and production. (1.2)

Life cycle stage model An effort estimation technique in which percentages of total effort are allocated among the stages of the project. (6.6)

Lines-of-code model An effort estimation technique in which the total number of effort-months required to complete a project is calculated from the formula $EM = 2.4 \, (KDSI)^{1.05}$, where EM = effort-months, and $KDSI$ = thousands (K) of delivered source instructions. (6.4)

Load module A physical unit that is loaded into computer memory and executed. (18.4.4)

Logical data flow diagram A data flow diagram that details the functions of a system without specifying the people, places, or equipment involved. (10.2.1)

Logical data structure The data elements, logical records, keys, and relationships of a database. (17.2)

Logical database design   Designing the logical elements, records, and relationships of a database so as to maximize flexibility and efficiency. (17.5.2)

Logical record   A combination of entities and attributes of a conceptual data model. (17.2.2)

Maintenance   Revisions to a system. (19.2.2)

Maintenance criteria   Evaluation criteria that relate to how easy software is to modify and maintain. (14.3.2)

Management constraints   Requirements stipulated by management to limit the resources consumed by a system. (7.3.2)

Management overhead   The amount of time necessary for coordinating, monitoring, planning, and reviewing. (6.7)

Management review   A formal meeting of users, the user-manager, the user-sponsor, and information systems personnel after each major milestone to gain user acceptance and to review the project schedule. (12.4.2)

Menu   A human-computer dialogue format in which alternative selections are listed. (16.2.5)

Milestone   A measurable activity scheduled to be completed at a designated time. (4.2)

Minimum criteria   Stated requirements used to narrow the range of products before evaluation; also called first-cut criteria. (13.7.2)

Minimum project schedule   The sum of the times required for the tasks on the critical path of a CPM network. (5.2.2)

Module   A group of statements or instructions that is executed in order to perform a function of a program. (18.2.1)

Module size   The number of statements, in PDL or programming language, needed to specify the activities that the module performs. (18.4.3)

Monitoring   The project management activity of tracking individual and team progress. (2.2.2)

Network DBMS   A database structure in which records may be related in any way. (17.4.2)

Nominal group technique   A group interviewing technique that maximizes individual contributions by minimizing inhibitions caused by peers or superiors. (9.1.3)

Normal procedures   Instructions for the normal use of an information system. (1.1.2)

Normalization   A technique for structuring data elements within records in order to minimize data redundancy. (17.4.3)

Observation instrument   A guidesheet for collecting observations. (9.2.2)

Operator   A person who manages, controls, services, and maintains computer equipment. (1.1.1)

Operator procedures   Instructions for operating a computer and other hardware—e.g., how to start the system, how to back up data. (1.1.2)

Organization chart   A graphic tool for representing the relationships among functional areas and managers. (8.1.2)

Organizational boundary   The scope of a system defined in terms of the entities outside the organization with which the system interacts. (7.3.1)

Organizational relevance   The systems development goal concerned with a project's contribution to organizational goals and profitability. (2.1.3)

Overview system flowchart   A global flowchart that depicts multiple jobs or tasks. (10.3.3)

Parallel operation   An installation strategy in which the new system is run simultaneously with the old system until the accuracy and reliability of the new system can be verified. (22.1.2)

Parent process   A process that is decomposed into more detailed processes. (10.2.3)

Payback analysis   An evaluation technique in which the costs and benefits of a system are compared by determining the time period required to recoup the costs. (13.4.2)

Payback point   The point in time when systems development costs are recovered. (13.4.2)

PERT (Program Evaluation and Review Technique) chart   An extension of a CPM network that includes estimates of the shortest possible time, most likely time, and longest possible time for system completion. (5.2.3)

Phased development   A development strategy in which the REDI stage activities are repeated in several iterations, allowing a series of small products to be presented to the user. (2.3, 4.2.1)

Phased installation   An installation strategy in which installation occurs in stages. (22.1.3)

Physical data structure   The file organization, physical records, and indexes of a database that describe how data is stored and accessed on external storage devices. (17.3)

Physical database design   Designing the physical structures of a database so as to maximize integrity and efficiency. (17.4.3)

Physical record   The data located at a disk address and transferred into main memory during data access. (17.3.2)

Planning   The project management activity of determining process activities, estimating their duration, allocating resources, and documenting the schedule. (2.2.1)

Pointer   A link, or index, between two related records. (17.2.4)

Post-implementation evaluation   The formal review of an installed system during which the results of the project are investigated and developers are alerted to ways to improve future projects. (22.3)

Procedure design   The fourth step of system design, during which the normal, recovery, and training procedures for a new system are described. (15.2.4)

Procedures   Instructions for people. (1.1.2)

Process box   The circle or rounded rectangle used in a data flow diagram to represent a performed action. (10.1.1)

Process specifications   A detailed definition of processes performed by a system. (7.2)

Product delivery approach   A phased development strategy in which a large system is partitioned into smaller subsystems or data capabilities, each of which is delivered to the user upon its completion. (5.1.3)

Product delivery point   A point at which a measurable activity is completed, producing a tangible system or process product. (4.2.2)

Production costs   Expenses incurred during the production phase of the system life cycle. (13.4.2)

Production phase   The operational period of an information system, during which it is used to perform ongoing business functions. (1.2)

Productivity software   Software that increases the user's power to create systems—e.g., spreadsheets and database management software. (1.1.4)

Program definition language (PDL)   A language used to specify the processing statements of a module. (18.2.2)

Program design   The third step of system design, whose main activity is packaging the interface, procedure, and database specifications into specifications for programs. (15.2.3)

Program specifications   Guides, such as program structure charts and test specifications, that are used by computer programmers during the implementation stage of the system life cycle. (15.2.3)

Programmer   An information systems professional who designs, codes, documents, tests, and maintains programs. (1.1.1)

Programming standards   Guidelines adopted by an organization in order to produce maintainable and flexible systems. (20.1.3)

Project authorization form A document that lists the acceptance criteria for system installation and that is signed by the project manager and the user-sponsor. (12.2.2)

Project management The systems development goal that focuses on coordination of the development process. (2.1.2)

Project risk measures Factors that determine the degree of risk associated with developing a system. (7.4.1)

Prototyping A development strategy in which a working model of the proposed system is shown to users for feedback purposes. (2.3)

Prototyping strategy A requirements determination strategy in which a system prototype is created to help users identify requirements. (7.4.3) (11.4.3)

Question and answer A human-computer dialogue format in which questions and alternative answers are presented; the user selects the alternative that best answers the question. (16.2.5)

Quick reference guide A page or chart of frequently used commands and procedures. (20.2.2)

Recovery procedures Instructions on what to do if the system fails—e.g., how to restore the system to operational status after a failure. (1.1.2)

REDI model A model in which the development phase of the life cycle is divided into four stages—requirements determination, evaluation of alternatives, design specifications, and implementation. (1.2)

Relational DBMS A database structure in which records, called relations, are related using shared data elements, such as foreign keys. (17.4.3)

Relationship In a conceptual data model, a correspondence or association between two or more entities in a data model; in database design, a correspondence between records. (11.2.3, 17.2.4)

Reliability A qualitative measure of a system's completeness, accuracy, and robustness. (2.1.1)

Report screen An output method in which a report is displayed on a CRT. (16.2.3)

Requirements determination The first stage of the REDI model, during which the system boundary is defined and the functional requirements are investigated and documented. (1.2.1)

Requirements document A formal written report that brings together findings about a current system and identifies the requirements for a proposed system. (12.1)

Reviewing The project management activity of developing presentations for and consulting with users and managers. (2.2.4)

Role A construct that associates similar entities by assigning each entity to a category—e.g., for the role CUSTOMER-TYPE, W = wholesale customer and R = retail customer. (11.2.6)

Rough first pass A preliminary evaluation of system solution alternatives. (13.4.1)

Sandwich testing strategy A testing method in which control modules are tested using the top-down strategy while process modules are tested using the bottom-up strategy. (21.2.3)

Schedule-month A measure used in estimating the number of months required to complete a project. (5.2.2)

Secondary index A data access method that uses the value of a data element that is not a primary key. (17.3.3)

Segmentation The splitting of attributes from one entity or relationship into different logical records during database design. (17.2.2)

Sequential file organization A method of file organization in which physical records are located in the file in sequence according to a key value or according to when the record was added. (17.3.1)

Sequential multi-user system A system that many users can access but that is used by only one person at a time. (1.1.2)

Sign-off The user-sponsor's approval of system development deliveries. (4.2.2)

Single-user system   A system that only one person uses. (1.1.2)

Slack time   The extra time available for completing an activity when one path or portion of a path in a CPM chart is shorter than a parallel path. (5.2.3)

Software   Instructions for hardware; often referred to as programs. (1.1.4) See also application software, existing software, productivity software, and system software.

Software component test   A testing method in which all the software modules are tested as a single functioning unit. (21.2.3)

Span of control   *See* Fan-out.

Structure chart   A graphic description of program structure that depicts the modules of a program, the hierarchy and organization of module communication, and the information that is exchanged between modules. (18.2.1)

Structured decomposition   A procedure for creating levels of data flow diagrams in a hierarchy so as to give increasingly detailed views of processes; also called leveling. (10.2.3)

Structured program design   A set of techniques and guidelines to facilitate program coding, testing, and maintenance. (18.1)

Stub module   A module with only a simple display statement to verify calls from higher-level modules. (21.2.3)

Sum-of-tasks method   An effort estimation technique in which the individual estimates for development activities are summed to estimate the total development effort. (6.2)

System boundary   The scope of a systems development effort. (1.2.1)

System compatibility maintenance   A system revision designed to make an old system interface with a new one. (19.2.2)

System constraints   Limits placed on resources available for systems development and production. (1.2.1, 7.1.2)

System documentation   Manuals that serve as guides for maintaining the system and as references for future systems development. (20.2.3)

System efficiency maintenance   Revisions to a system that are designed to increase system efficiency. (19.2.2)

System flowchart   A graphic technique for depicting hardware, programs, and data at the file level. (10.3)

System objectives   Goals or end results to be achieved through systems development. (1.2.1, 7.1.2)

System quality   The systems development goal concerned with the functionality, ease of maintenance, and flexibility of the system. (2.1.1)

System requirements   The features of each system component necessary to achieve the system objectives within the stated constraints. (7.3.3)

System test   The test that brings together the five components of a system in order to evaluate how the components perform as a single functioning unit. (21.4)

Systems software   Software that controls basic hardware functions or provides a general service—e.g., the computer's operating system, a network manager. (1.1.4)

Tangible benefits   Benefits that can be physically observed and quantified, such as increased sales or decreased response time. (13.4.2)

Technical operations manual   A description of start-up, run control, and end-of-day procedures for a system's hardware and software. (20.2.3)

Technical specifications   A detailed description of the capabilities a system should have, such as the processing speed and the memory capacity. (21.2.4)

Test data Data used to test the running of a system. (21.2.2)

Test group People responsible for developing test data as well as overseeing testing. (21.1.2)

Test specifications A document that specifies the who, what, when, where, why, and how of testing activities. (21.1.2)

Testing The implementation process of ensuring that the system works by examining all five of the system components. (1.2.4)

Third generation language (3GL) A procedure-oriented programming language such as CO-BOL or Pascal. (2.4.2)

3-times-programming rule An effort estimation technique in which the estimated coding time is multiplied by three in order to estimate the total effort required to complete all project activities. (6.3)

Top-down approach A requirements determination approach in which the desired information system is placed in the wider context of the organization so that the objectives, constraints, and requirements of both are aligned. (7.1.3)

Top-down testing strategy A testing method in which higher-level, or control modules are tested before the lower-level, or process modules. (21.2.3)

Total project effort The sum of the times required for all systems development tasks. (5.2.2)

Transaction analysis A structured technique used to create a structure chart from a data flow diagram that depicts case-structured processes. (18.3.2)

Transform analysis A structured technique used to create a structure chart from a data flow diagram that depicts sequential processes. (18.3.1)

Turnkey system A system that can be installed and used immediately with no development effort. (1.1.6)

Tutorial A software-based lesson that introduces the user to the capabilities of a system. (20.2.2)

User access mode The category within which a system falls with respect to the number of users and the timing of their access: single-user, sequential multi-user, or concurrent multi-user. (1.1.2)

User enhancements System revisions to improve or augment generated reports or to conform with new reporting requirements. (19.2.2)

User-interface design The first step in designing a system, during which the reports, screens, menus, and other control mechanisms that directly interact with users are specified. (15.2.1)

User-manager The person who supervises end-users; usually the manager of a department or division within the organization. (1.1.1)

User manual Instruction manual that provides information for nontechnical users of a system. (20.2.2)

User procedures Instructions on how to use system hardware and software—e.g., how to enter data or obtain reports. (1.1.2)

User-sponsor The person who approves development of the system. (1.1.1)

Walkthrough An informal review of progress designed to obtain user feedback, encourage communication between users and developers, and aid in requirements determination, design, and testing. (12.4.1)

White box testing A program testing technique in which each module's code is checked by reviewing each line or by creating data to verify every line. (21.2.1)

Work breakdown structure A hierarchical list of the activities required to complete a system. (5.1)

Answers to Selected Exercises

Chapter 1

1.1 Component Summary for: <u>Property Management System</u>

1. People
a. developer—Cecil
b. operator—Cecil (either Abby or the bookkeeper or both need to become operators)
c. end-user—Cecil (either Abby or the bookkeeper or both need to become end-users)
d. user-manager—Abby
e. user-sponsor—Abby

2. Procedures—none specified

3. Data
a. data stores—master file on properties (from two file cabinets)
b. input—rent, otherwise not identified
c. output—not identified

4. Software
a. operating system—Kaypro operating system
b. application software—INVESTMAN
c. productivity software—none used

5. Hardware
a. facility—Abby's office
b. computer—Kaypro 4
c. storage—floppy disks
d. input devices—keyboard to disk only
e. output devices—Okidata 82 printer

1.2
a. Best answer: sequential multi-user. The computer and software components are the same for Georgia and May. Plus there is some data overlap, since both are storing their files on the same hard disk. There is minimal user interaction in this case, but Georgia and May must coordinate their file naming procedures at the very least, or they might accidentally write over each other's files on the hard disk.

Acceptable answer: single user. If we assume that Georgia and May use a hard disk organizing package to keep their disk storage areas separate, this is a reasonable answer. In this case only the hardware would be the same

for the two systems, since Georgia and May would have their own separate data files and, possibly, software copies.
b. sequential multi-user. This is the only acceptable answer for this situation, since the data overlaps completely and Georgia and May are clearly alternative users of the same five-component system.

1.3
a. concurrent multi-user access mode. All the store checkers must be able to access the product files concurrently, each using the same data, software, and central hardware (but individual cash register-terminals and scanners).
b. Component Summary for: <u>Grocery Checkout System</u>

1) People
a. developer—not identified
b. operator—store checkers
c. end-user—store checkers
d. user-manager—none specified
e. user-sponsor—none specified

2) Procedures
a. user normal procedures—scan product code, give receipt to customer
b. user recovery procedures—none specified
c. operator normal procedures—none specified
d. operator recovery procedures—none specified

3) Data
a. data stores—master file of product codes, types, and prices
b. input—universal product bar code
c. output—voice output of price, printed output of product type and price

4) Software
a. operating system—microprocessor's operating system
b. application software—program to translate bar code, access and print product type and price, and generate voice output
c. productivity software—none specified

5) Hardware
a. facility—Big Bob's store

b. computer—microprocessor

c. storage—not specified

d. input devices—scanner, cash register–terminal

e. output devices—cash register–terminal

1.7

a. R.1   b. R.3   c. I.1   d. I.2

e. R.3 Note: R.3 is a better answer than I.2, since this is Sam's first specification of detailed requirements. Had he done it earlier, I.2 would be the best answer since his feedback would be part of Mary's testing process.

f. I.1   g. I.2   h. I.3   i. I.1

1.8

a. Mary Yu b. Mary Yu c. Sam Jones d. Sam Jones

1.9 I.2—a test after the revision to the system language

Chapter 2

2.1

a. SQ; ease of maintenance: (1) understandability; (2) all three of its second-level characteristics and (1) modifiability; (2) both second-level characteristics

b. OR; strategic (or operational level, by reducing costs)

c. SQ; functionality: (1) reliability; (2) accuracy

d. SQ; flexibility: (1) portability; (2) language independence

e. SQ; functionality: (1) clarity; (2) predictability

f. PM; timeliness and user commitment

g. SQ; functionality: (1) clarity; (2) consistency

h. OR; managerial   i. PM; user commitment

2.3

a. project management

b. see the list below:

1) Abby's idea of *system quality* was very limited. She asked for "something that works" more as a constraint for the store clerk than as a positive goal. She probably assumed that she needed little more explanation of functionality. She apparently assumed that ease of maintenance and flexibility were of no concern, as in buying a large appliance such as a stove, but she learned very quickly that the computer did not function in the environment of her office.

2) *Project management* was Abby's main goal because she stressed that she did not want "any big expensive computer system with all the frills"; she chose a "bargain with free software."

3) The immediate effect on the organization was negative. Not only was the $2,000 capital investment of no use for more than three months; it caused "bickering back and forth" between Abby and the bookkeeper and entailed hiring additional personnel.

2.8

a. ES. Existing software is easy to purchase for procedures as common as preparing legal documents, letters, and bills.

b. ES. Existing software would be the first choice, since valuable expertise could be purchased with well-tested programs. If no software existed for the current hardware, ISWS might be best, since the software required is complex and must operate efficiently.

c. UWS. User-written software would be the best choice if one of the users was an expert with existing spreadsheet software. If it was possible to purchase a compatible spreadsheet template or even more specific forecasting software, ES would be the recommended solution.

Chapter 3

3.1 *System quality.* The concern for functionality was visible throughout the process (observations of end-users, interviews with accountants and pharmacy staff to determine complete requirements, verification of ease of operation through on-site visits, check on label printing speed, etc.). Ease of maintenance and flexibility are dependent on the vendor's policy and plans for updates as needed. Although this did not seem to be a major consideration in the case, the chosen package (Rapid Pharmacy) did receive good points for vendor support and runs on three micros, which may mean that the company is strong and reliable and the software is adaptable to many environments.

Project management. Time, budget, and user involvement were consistent concerns throughout the process.

Organizational relevance. This system has a clear value at the operational level. Fred's recognition of the parallel activities in labeling and log keeping broadened the scope of the project, so its organizational effect at the operational level was even greater than originally intended.

Overall. The goals of the team seem nicely balanced; the team avoided the pitfall of focusing on one goal at the expense of the others.

3.2

a. Tracy's poor morale might make her a poor liaison with the users. She might fail to gain their commitment to the system. Also, she did not catch the procedures overlap that Fred saw, which would have been an unfortunate oversight.

b. Fred's inexperience would make him a risky choice as a single analyst. His greatest weakness would probably be in project management; he lacks the experience to see that money and time constraints are as important as system quality. Thus, he did not realize that having pharmacy staff members develop their own system was a poor idea because it would consume too much time. It seems that Tracy kept the team on track and considered the cost and time constraints as well as system quality.

Chapter 4

4.1

a. process product delivery of a CPM overview chart. This is a process delivery, since the CPM chart is not part of the actual system.

b. process product delivery. This milestone would be better if it specified "planning schedule."

c. system product delivery of user's manual

d. system product delivery of program module. This milestone would be better if it specified "compiled with no errors" or "tested with test data" or some other specific level of completion.

e. process activity with no measurable product

4.2

a. 4.3 weeks × 4 months = 17 weeks

6 team members × 17 weeks = 102 milestones

b. Plan the first 4 weeks in detail: 6 × 4 = 24 milestones. Plan 10 to 15 major milestones for the remaining 13 weeks.

```
Total milestones = 24 + 10 to 24 + 15
                 = 34 to 39 milestones
```

c. It is likely that for the first four weeks activities will correspond fairly closely to the detailed plan for monitoring progress. Past that point (give or take a week or so), details are likely to change. The major milestones allow you to keep track of general progress without risking wasting time on details that are very likely to change.

d. a graphic form with each chart containing five to nine activities

4.3

a. Demonstrate *user interface* to user-manager for sign-off.

b. Prepare *Gantt chart* for project.

c. Create *test files* and produce *test runs* using purchased software.

d. Develop *flowchart* of current operating procedures.

e. Prepare *presentation* for management on results of initial investigation.

Chapter 5

5.1

a. CPM chart:

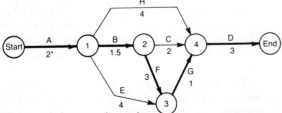

*Estimated times are in weeks.

b.

Possible Paths	Weeks Required	
A-H-D	2 + 4 + 3	= 9
A-B-C-D	2 + 1.5 + 2 + 3	= 8.5
A-B-F-G-D	2 + 1.5 + 3 + 1 + 3	= 10.5 (critical path)
A-E-G-D	2 + 4 + 1 + 3	= 10

c. 10.5 schedule-weeks   d. 20.5 effort-weeks

e. Gantt chart:

Activity	Week Ending										
	1/10	1/17	1/24	1/31	2/7	2/14	2/21	2/28	3/7	3/14	3/21
A	⊢——⊣										
B			⊢—⊣								
C					⊢——⊣						
D									⊢——⊣		
E				⊢————⊣							
F					⊢————⊣						
G							⊢—⊣				
H				⊢————⊣							

f. Total project time can be reduced by shifting resources to critical path tasks from other activities. In this problem, employees involved with activities C, E, or H could be shifted to activity F. Note that these shifts are possible because it was assumed that any employee could work on any activity. In general you can switch people from paths with slack time to critical path tasks, but not always. For example, switching H people to D would do no good, since G must be finished first.

5.2

a. CPM chart:

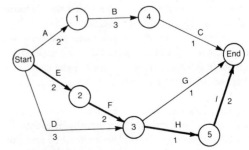

*Estimated times are in days.

b.

Possible Paths	Days Required		
A-B-C	2 + 3 + 1	= 6	
E-F-G	2 + 2 + 1	= 5	
E-F-H-I	2 + 2 + 1 + 2	= 7	(critical path)
D-G	3 + 1	= 4	
D-H-I	3 + 1 + 2	= 6	

c. 7 schedule-days

d. 17 effort-days

e. Gantt chart:

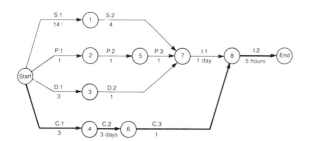

f. Total project time can be reduced by shifting employees to critical path tasks from other activities for which there is slack time. In this problem, employees could be shifted from activity D to F, or from activity C to I.

5.9

a. Point-of-sales system network:

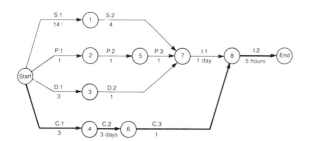

*Activity times are in weeks except as marked.

b.

Possible Paths	Effort Required
S.1-S.2-I.1-I.2	18 weeks + 1 day + 5 hours (critical path)
P.1-P.2-P.3-I.1-I.2	3 weeks + 1 day + 5 hours
D.1-D.2-I.1-I.2	4 weeks + 1 day + 5 hours
C.1-C.2-C.3-I.2	4 weeks + 3 days + 5 hours

c. The minimum project schedule is 18 schedule-weeks, 1 schedule-day, and 5 schedule-hours.

d. 29 effort-weeks, 4 days, 5 hours

e. Project time can be reduced by having personnel who are working on shorter paths switch over to working on the longer paths, provided they have the expertise to be helpful. For instance, the programming staff working on path D could switch over and work with the other programmers on path S. Similarly, the users working on path P could switch over and help the other users working on path C.

f. Gantt chart:

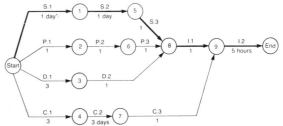

5.10

a.

*Activity times are in weeks except as marked.

b.

Possible Paths	Effort Required
S.1-S.2-S.3-I.1-I.2	1 week + 3 days + 5 hours
P.1-P.2-P.3-I.1-I.2	3 weeks + 1 day + 5 hours
D.1-D.2-I.1-I.2	4 weeks + 1 day + 5 hours
C.1-C.2-C.3-I.2	4 weeks + 3 days + 5 hours (critical path)

c. The minimum project schedule is 4 weeks, 3 days, and 5 hours.

d. The total project effort is 12 weeks, 6 days, and 5 hours.

Chapter 6

6.1

a. 10 months × 3 = 30 effort-months

b. 3-times-programming rule (Section 6.3 in text)

c. 20 schedule-months

d. The estimate of 20 schedule-months is based on several assumptions. First we assumed that programming would consume a little less than one-third of the effort and that the number of effort-months could be reduced by one-half to yield the programming schedule. We assumed that the remaining effort could be reduced by only one-third:

```
programming schedule = 10 × 0.50 =  5.0
remaining schedule   = 20 × 0.67 = 13.4
                       30          18.4
```

Finally, we added 1.6 months, for a total of 20 months. For a smaller project we might have just rounded up to the nearest whole number, but this is such a long project that there are likely to be many unavoidable complications.

6.2

a. $2.4(13)^{1.05} = 2.4(14.78) = 35.47 = 36$ effort-months

b. Boehm's lines-of-code model, rounded to the nearest month (Section 6.4 in text)

c. 16 schedule-months

d. The logic is the same as for 6.1d, but the beginning effort estimate is larger and we have three team members so the schedule can be reduced further:

```
programming schedule = 12 × 0.33 =  4.0
remaining schedule   = 24 × 0.50 = 12.0
                       36          16.0
```

We did not round this total up a full 12 months, since we have more knowledge about the new system than we did for Exercise 6.1 and the effort estimate was already rounded up. Note that our 0.50 reduction for the nonprogramming work is a very rough guess.

e. 27 effort-months

f. The reduction in the effort due to the 4GL will affect only the approximately one-third of the original effort allotted to programming the system in COBOL. This part of the effort is reduced by the predicted factor of 4, but the remaining portion stays the same:

```
programming effort = 12 × 0.25 =  3.0
remaining effort   = 24         = 24.0
                     36           27.0 effort-
                                       months
```

g. 13 schedule-months

h. The logic is the same as in 6.2d, but we begin with the reduced effort estimate for programming that was calculated in 6.2f:

```
programming schedule =  3 × 0.33 =  1.0
remaining schedule   = 24 × 0.50 = 12.0
                       27           13.0
                                    schedule-
                                    months
```

6.3

a. 13 effort-months, rounded up

```
Method 1:
  10 (months taken)  =    x (months left)
  44 (percent done)     56 (percent left)
     10(56)          = 12.72 or 13 months left
       44
Method 2:
    13%
     8%
    23%
    44%  = 10 effort-months (step 1)

  1% =  10 (months)  = 0.227  month
        44 (percent)           percent
                              (step 2)
0.227  month  × 56 (percent left) = 12.71
       percent                      effort-
                                    months
                                    (step 3)
```

b. Boehm's life cycle stage model (Section 6.6 in text)

c. 8 months

d. We assumed that programming would consume approximately one-third (or eight months) of the total 23 effort-months and that the two developers would have to do all or most of the work, rather than assigning users to write manuals or train other users. We further assumed that the programming effort could be reduced by one-half to yield the programming schedule and the remaining effort could be reduced by one-third. (See pg. 613.)

```
programming schedule  =  8 × 0.50 = 4.00
remaining schedule    =  5 × 0.67 = 3.35
                        13            7.35
```

Rounding up yields an estimate of 8 months.

e. 6 to 6.5 months

f. Following the rationale in 6.3d, we split the estimate into 8- and 5-month estimates for programming and remaining effort. We reduced the programming effort by a factor of 3 instead of a factor of 2 and assumed that three developers might be able to reduce the remaining effort by a factor of 2:

```
programming schedule  =  8 × 0.33 = 2.64
remaining schedule    =  5 × 0.50 = 2.50
                        13            5.14
```

To allow for additional management overhead, we rounded the 5.14 months up and added a safety range.

6.7 Sample answer: The chart below shows the main tasks to be completed, with frequent user meetings clearly indicated. Note that integrated testing starts with 25 percent of the six months left. Boehm's stage percentages indicate that at least 15 percent of the total time is required. Evaluation was omitted, since constraints stated in the problem led to a rather limited choice of general solutions.

6.8

a. 16 programs with an average of 1,000 lines each would come to 16,000 lines of code.

$$EM = 2.4(16)^{1.05} = 2.4(18.38)$$
$$= 44 \text{ effort-months}$$

This estimate is based on the lines-of-code mode. If many of the functions could be coded with the current query and report-generating capability of the DBMS, the effort might be reduced. However, requirements determination might take much longer than the lines-of-code model assumes, so effort might be much greater.

Assuming that 44 effort-months is a rough middle-range estimate of effort, the number of schedule-months should be between one-third (the unattainable ideal for a three-member team) and one-half of that:

```
programming   = 14 × 0.50 =  7.0 for 2 programmers
 schedule
remaining     = 30 × 0.40 = 12.0 for 3 team
 schedule       44                   members
                          19.0 schedule-months
```

Project Planning Documentation																	Page 1 of 1	
System Pet Store Licensing																	Date 4/29	
Symbols ⊢——⊣ Scheduled activity ▬▬ Completed activity		Analyst Sue Smith						Signature										
Activity	Individual Assigned	May		June		July		Aug.		Sept.		Oct.						
		15	31	15	30	15	31	15	31	15	30	15	31					
REQUIREMENTS STAGE																		
R.1 Form Team		⊢⊣																
R.2 Define Requirements			⊢→															
R.3 Define Spec. Req's				⊢														
DESIGN STAGE																		
D.1 Plan Project				⊢→														
D.2 Design Interfaces					⊢													
D.3 Specify Program Changes					⊢													
D.4 Specify I/O Storage					⊢													
D.5 Specify Procedures																		
D.6 Specify Training and																		
Documentation				⊢														
D.7 Organize Design Doc.					⊢→													
IMPLEMENTATION STAGE																		
I.1 Preliminary Construction							⊢——⊣											
I.2 Preliminary Tests							⊢——→											
I.3 Final Construction									⊢									
I.4 Final Tests										⊢——⊣								
I.5 Installation												⊢—→						

* User Checkpoints

b.

Information System Goal and Subgoal	Relevant Case Issue	Action Planned to Meet Goal
System Quality		
Functionality	Determining all the functions desired to meet Tom and the VP's goals is likely to be tricky, since this is a strategic system that cannot be based on any existing system at Stafford Plastics.	Allow time for interviews and as much research as possible to determine the functions required to meet the system objectives.
Maintainability	This system is likely to require frequent changing since it provides new functions for Stafford regional offices.	Develop the first phase of the system using the report generator and standard queries as such a system can be changed more easily than COBOL programs.
Flexibility	This system will run in 16 regional offices, and Tom specifically wants flexibility.	Train regional users to write report generation modules so that they can revise them for their site. Write clear user documentation to help with regional user staff changes.
Project Management		
Timeliness	There is no specific information here. A new system like this one is likely to take time.	Prepare careful planning documents and keep the VP and other user-managers informed about the time schedule.
Cost	There is no specific information here.	Benefits should be estimated as a first step in determining how much this system might be worth, and then funds should be budgeted accordingly.
User Commitment	The VP support is clear, but this seems to be a system dictated from the top.	Develop clear documentation on system benefits to sell the system to regional users. Enlist the VP in selling the system also.
Organizational Relevance		
Operational	The proposed strategic system is an extension of the operational level sales analysis system.	Make sure no operational functions are disrupted or made more difficult by the strategic system.
Managerial	The initial sales analysis system includes managerial level sales data.	Make sure managerial use is not disrupted. Interview regional managers to see what managerial functions could be incorporated into the new marketing analysis system.
Strategic	The clearly stated goal of this system is strategic: determine better strategies for product development and advertising.	Research company objectives, current product mix, and competitive market forces as part of requirements determination.

c.

	People	Procedures	Data	Software	Hardware
Determine Requirements	Interview key users in each region and corporate headquarters.	Determine basic procedures and flexibility needs.	Document sales system data. Research external sources of data.	Check available software, even if just for prototype.	Run capacity checks early.
Evaluate Alternatives	Identify alternative phases for delivery with varying amounts of coding by users.	Evaluate mix of corporate and regional office responsibilities.	Evaluate alternative I/O and storage designs.	Evaluate procedures and program boundaries and COBOL v. queries.	Identify any advantages of expansion.
Specify Design	Design training, including coding of DBMS queries and reports.	Specify and check all procedures.	Verify I/O designs with prototype.	Specify all modules. Conduct design walkthroughs.	Document details, especially any original site changes.
Implement Design	Regional users do report generation. Train in phases with pilot testing.	Complete documents. Train and test in phases.	Test storage design. Build final database.	Complete COBOL and DBMS coding and test all modules.	Test capacity early.

d.

Project Planning Documentation		Page	
System	Marketing Analysis System	Date	

Symbols ⊢⊣ Scheduled activity ▶──◀ Completed activity	Analyst Tom A.		Signature	

Activity	Individual Assigned	W	Th	F	M										
REQUIREMENTS DEFINITION															
R.1 Define Problem															
R.1.1 Existing System	Mo														
R.1.2 Proposed Changes	Tom														
R.1.3 Team Discussion	All														
R.2 Determine Rough															
Functional Requirements	All														
R.3 Assess Feasibility	Tom, Mo														
R.4 Technical Review															
R.4.1 Prepare CPM	Mo														
R.4.2 Prepare Visual Aids	May														
R.4.3 Prepare Cost-Benefit															
Summary	Tom														
R.4.4 Team Review	All														
R.4.5 Management Review	All														

e. Sample answer:

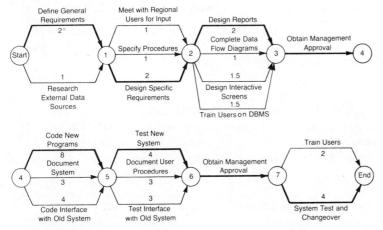

*Estimated times are in months.
Total effort: 44 effort-months.

Chapter 7

7.1

a. administrative staff of ERD. This is the immediate functional area of the users.

b. Engineering Research Division
   (Applied Research, Inc. should not be identified here since the corporate level is unlikely to be affected by this revision to an operational system at the division level.)

7.2

a. constraint (hardware)   b. objective

c. objective   d. requirement

7.5 Step 1: Evaluate project risk.

Factors Affecting Project Risk	Factor Rating (+1 = Yes, 0 = Maybe, −1 = No)
1) Characteristics of the system environment	
A. Are boundaries stable and well defined?	+1
B. Are procedures structured and clear?	0
2) Characteristics of the information system	
A. Is a model available or are requirements stable and readily specifiable?	+1
B. Are the procedures addressed routine and well structured?	+1
C. Is only one existing system affected by the proposed system?	+1
D. Can the project be completed within one year?	+1
3) Characteristics of the users	
A. Do users have functional expertise?	+1
B. Do users have experience developing system?	−1
C. Are users committed to the project?	+1
4) Characteristics of the development team	
A. Do analysts have experience developing similar systems?	−1
B. Are analysts skilled at eliciting requirements?	−1
Total points	4

Step 2: The total number of risk points is 4, so assume high risk.

Steps 3 and 4: Determine the mix of requirements determination strategies.

Strategy	Percent of Requirements Determination Investigation
Asking	10%
Deriving from an existing system	50%
Analyzing/researching	40%
Prototyping	
Total	100%

Chapter 8

8.1 Critical success factors:

- Provide high-quality specialty products to customers (competitive strategy).
- Ensure freshness by purchasing raw products from local growers (competitive strategy).
- Hold raw materials no more than one week prior to processing (industry/competitive strategy).
- Determine the amount of product to produce from the monthly sales forecast and actual orders placed (environment).
- Dispose of finished products that are not sold within two weeks (industry).

8.3

1) The diagram needs, at a minimum, the company name, the systems development project title, and the date the context diagram was prepared.
2) The data flow to the entity marked Mr. Talbot should be identified.
3) The entity labeled Marketing and Sales does not have any data flows. If the area is not part of the systems development project, it should not be shown on the diagram. If it is part of the systems development project, its data flows to other entities must be indicated.

4) There seems to be a data flow missing between the warehouse and accounting.

Chapter 9

9.1

a. The users need a system that will reduce the effort needed to produce the paperwork required by the Administrative division.

b. The new system will facilitate communication by allowing the assistants to record information immediately, thus eliminating the confusion caused by placing filled prescriptions aside for later recording and reducing the number of mistakes. The accuracy of the pharmacy reports will be improved.

9.2 The types of documents that Tracy and Fred could collect include

- Procedures manuals—overview of current procedures for data entry, processing, and report generation
- Hospital trade magazines—information about potential software
- Prescriptions—data to be transferred to labels and recorded in log
- Prescription labels—format of required output
- Pharmacy division daily drug log—data and format of required report
- Pharmacy division end-of-day report for administration—data and format of required report
- (Optional: software manual for any purchased software)

9.4 Possible interview schedule for Tracy and Fred:

1) Meet with Information Services supervisor and with pharmacy manager to clarify request for systems development.
2) Interview pharmacists' assistants—both individually and in a group—to discover current procedures and problems with the current system.
3) Interview pharmacists—both individually and in a group with pharmacists' assistants and pharmacy manager—to identify problems with the current system and verify requirements for the proposed system. (Because the proposed system involves a routine operational procedure, Tracy and Fred probably don't need to interview any higher level personnel.)

9.8

a.

A teller receives a completed request form for a cash withdrawal from a client. The teller enters the client's checking account number and the amount of the withdrawal into the computer system. The system verifies the account number. If the account number is correct, the system checks the account balance to ensure that there are sufficient funds. If there are sufficient funds, the amount is subtracted from the account balance and an account transaction is created and added to the daily transaction log. A cash withdrawal receipt is printed, which the teller hands to the client along with the requested cash.

b.

Actor and Action	Upon	Conditions and Action
Client completes	request form	
Teller enters	account number withdrawal amount	
System verifies	account number	If correct—proceed If not—not specified
System verifies	account balance funds	If sufficient—proceed If not—not specified
System subtracts	withdrawal amount from balance	
System creates	account transaction	
System adds	transaction to daily transaction log	
System prints	receipt	
Teller returns	receipt cash	

Chapter 10

10.1

1) Processes are missing between:
   (a) the Customer external entity and the D1 data store; and
   (b) the D2 data store and the three hardware output symbols.

2) The process 2 label should be in verb and object format.

3) The three hardware symbols for the output data Payments, Daily Reports, and charges are incorrect. The data should be shown in flow lines.

10.2

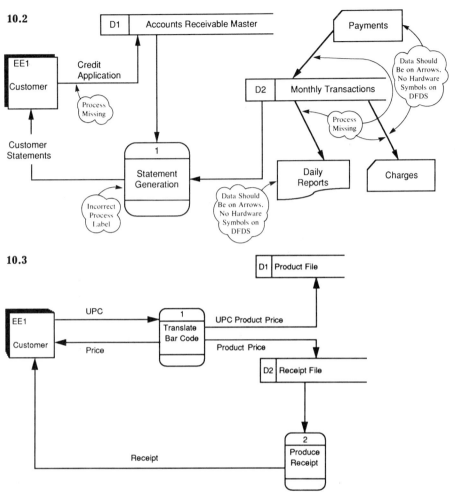

10.3

10.4 Version 1 (overview version acceptable for exercise; better for presentation than more detailed version 2):

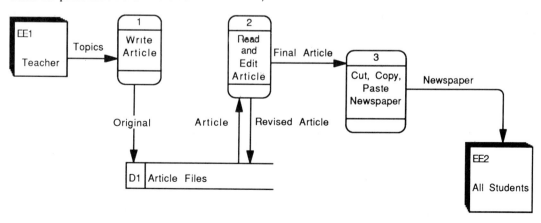

Version 2 (more detailed, leveled version of teacher part of process; separate process boxes are better if the last three processes are performed by different people):

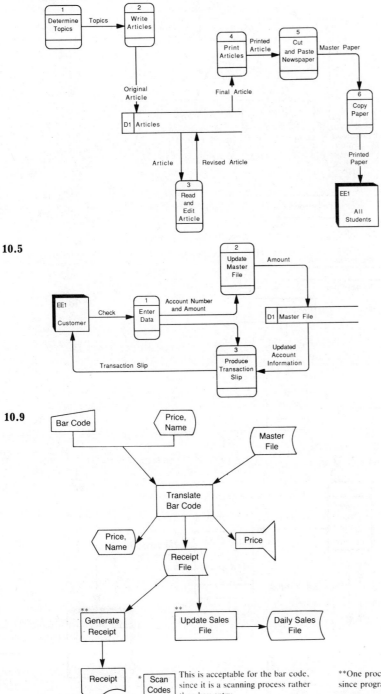

10.5

10.9

* | Scan Codes | This is acceptable for the bar code, since it is a scanning process rather than key entry.

**One process rectangle is acceptable, since program partitioning is not known.

Chapter 11

11.1

a. PRESCRIPTION-ID-NUMBER, PRESCRIPTION-DATE, PRESCRIPTION-DRUG-QTY-NUMBER, PRESCRIPTION-DOSAGE-INST-TEXT

b. PRESCRIPTION-ID-NUMBER, DRUG-SUPP-VENDOR-ID-NBR, PATIENT-ID-NUMBER, PRESCRIPTION-DATE, DRUG-BRAND-NAME, PHYSICIAN-LAST-NAME

c. PHARMACIST: PRESCRIPTION, 0,N and 0,1

d. DRUG-BRAND is an intersection entity. It is the result of the many-to-many relationship between DRUG and DRUG-SUPPLIER.

e. Sample answer: Wyamycin or Malatal

f. Sample answer: Sept 15, 1990 or 09/15/90

11.2

a. Entities: STUDENT, COURSE-REGISTRATION, COURSE, PROFESSOR

b. Attributes: STUDENT-NUMBER, STUDENT-NAME, STUDENT-ADDRESS, COURSE-GRADE, COURSE-NUMBER, COURSE-DESCRIPTION, PROFESSOR-NUMBER, PROFESSOR-NAME

c. Identifiers: STUDENT-NUMBER, COURSE-NUMBER, PROFESSOR-NUMBER

d. Relationships: PROFESSOR:COURSE, 1,N and 1,1; STUDENT: COURSE, many-to-many
STUDENT: COURSE-REGISTRATION, 1,N and 1,1;
COURSE: COURSE-REGISTRATION, 1,N and 1,1

e. Dependencies: COURSE-REGISTRATION is dependent on STUDENT and COURSE. COURSE is dependent on PROFESSOR.

11.3

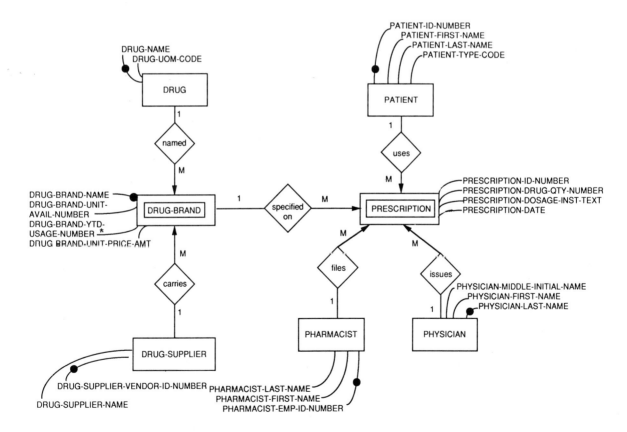

11.4

1) CRIME entity has no identifier.

2) The attribute NAME for VICTIM should be VICTIM-NAME.

3) The attribute NAME for CRIMINAL should be CRIMINAL-NAME.

4) There should be an intersection entity between the entities CRIME and CRIMINAL.

5) No relationships are labeled.

11.5 There are no errors. Each path has a unique meaning. WORK-ASSIGNMENT is a three-way relationship among WORKER, MACHINE, and SHIFT. A work assignment is a worker assigned to a machine on a given shift. Only WORKER and SHIFT are needed to identify a WORK-ASSIGNMENT, however.

11.6 Victims are identified by victim-number. Other data such as name and phone number is maintained for each victim. Criminals are identified by criminal-number. The criminal's name is also maintained. A crime is assigned a crime-number. The date and description of the crime are maintained. A criminal may commit many crimes, and a crime may be committed by several criminals. Each crime may have many victims, but each victim is a part of only one crime. A victimless crime is possible, but a victim cannot exist without a crime.

Chapter 12

12.1

a. team strategy. Tracy completed the problem definition form and a formal summary at an early meeting (Section 3.2.2). Fred presented a list of current procedures at the same meeting. Otherwise it is not clear who actually created documents or charts, but in Section 3.2.5 it states that "the project team presented the objectives and functional requirements of the new system. . . ."

b. Examples of reviews conducted by Tracy and Fred:

- Initial meeting of entire project team—formal, group
- Tracy's interviews with pharmacist and assistants—informal, individual
- Fred's interview with accountant—informal, individual
- Project meeting on the third day to discuss findings—formal, group
- Management review of functional specifications—formal, group
- Further investigation with pharmacist's assistants and pharmacists—informal, individual
- Evaluation of microcomputer software—formal, individual, and group

- Tracy's talk with accountants about the acceptability of software—formal, individual, perhaps group
- Management review—formal, group

12.9

a.

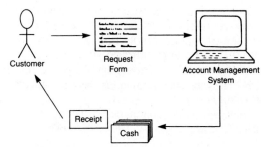

b.

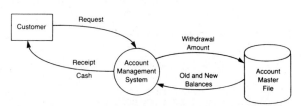

Note: By using the disk symbol for the master file we are mixing system flowchart symbols with data flow diagram symbols. The parallel lines or open rectangle symbolizing a data store may be used instead if you are more familar with that symbol.

c.

Manual	Automated
Client completes request form	①
Teller enters account number and amount	②
	③ Check account number and balance
	④ Update account master balance
	⑤ Create transaction and add to daily log file
	⑥ Print receipt
Teller gives receipt and cash to client	⑦

Chapter 13

13.1

a. poor. This criterion is so general it is meaningless.

b. improper. This is a design specification.

c. improper. This is a constraint. (When the $10,000 cost is a preference rather than an absolute limit, it would be a project management criteria.)

d. improper. This is a condition of the marketplace. The potential success of a system depends on the specific needs of the company, not on its competitors.

13.2 Suggested solutions:

Criteria. Usage and user satisfaction are similar, so we can combine them to read "User satisfaction and frequent usage." This criterion includes both the bookkeeper's acceptance of the system and subsequent usage. If the two were not combined, we would indirectly be putting too much emphasis on similar criteria, as it would be difficult to distinguish between them. Operational efficiency is a good criterion because it will force the decision maker to think of storage capacity, speed, smoothness of operation, and so forth. An additional criterion is needed, however, to evaluate whether the system does what Abby wants it to do and whether it does it well. This criterion will force the decision maker to think of the needs the system is supposed to fulfill. The decision maker will have to write down a list of wants, such as daily cash flow reports, monthly generated profit and loss statements, monthly generated balance sheets, and quarterly generated renter account balances printed on Abby Clark stationery. After the needs list has been completed, each potential system can be evaluated. As an insurance policy, in case the system doesn't really do what it says it does, Abby should have a trial period for testing the system, with the option of returning it if she is dissatisfied.

Constraints. Cecil's parameters are properly related to budget and time parameters, but the cost restriction on hardware and software purchases may be a bit too low, since the inadequate Kaypro 4 cost over $3,100.

13.3

a. Rough estimates:

	Development Costs	Production Costs	Development Time
Phone Plan	$16,000	$30,000	4–6 weeks
Patch Plan	200	$20,800	4–6 weeks (includes training time)
Motivate Plan	0	$18,750	Immediate

b. Comparison table:

Rank	Cost	Time
1	Motivate Plan	Motivate Plan
2	Patch Plan	Patch or Phone
3	Phone Plan	——

c. The Phone Plan exceeds the production costs limit of $22,000.

d. If sales increased by more than $14,000 per year because of increased time for selling, the Phone Plan could be feasible.

13.4

a. Step 1: Determine benefits.

Benefit = savings of annual clerical costs attributable to the new system

```
No. of clerks                     55
Hourly cost             ×          8
Hours per register      ×         40
Semesters per year      ×          3
Current cost            $52,800
Fractional Savings      ×        2/3
   Total Savings        $35,200
```

Step 2: Determine costs. We must carefully distinguish between development costs and ongoing production costs.

```
Cost of software                $20,000
Training costs
  (1,000 × 5)                      5,000
Conversion costs                   3,000
  Total development costs        $28,000
No. of data entry operators            5
Hourly cost             ×          $12
Hours per semester      ×           80
Semesters per/year      ×            3
  Data entry cost                $14,400
Additional supply
  costs (2,000 × 3)                6,000
  Total annual cost              $20,400
```

Step 3: Compute the payback period.
Diagram of the cash flow is shown on page 624.

Development Period	Year 1	Year 2	Year 3	Year 4	Year 5
	35,200	35,200	35,200	35,200	35,200
<28,000>	<20,400>	<20,400>	<20,400>	<20,400>	<20,400>
<28,000>	14,800	14,800	14,800	14,800	14,800

The payback point is just prior to the end of the second year.

b. Based on the payback period, it is likely the university would build the new system, particularly given the intangible benefits cited.

c. Other information to consider:

- Importance of other projects that demand analyst time
- Risk of the project—What is the likelihood that a system meeting the specified requirements could be completed on time?
- Expected and reasonable life of the system
- The rank and importance of the individual who wants to see this system created

Chapter 14

14.1 Worksheet for grid:

	Functional Capabilities		Support	
Criteria	ACCM	TAX	ACCM	TAX
Reporting requirements	20	25		
Job costing capability	8	4		
Vendor support/ service			20	12
Installation/ training	—	—	25	15
Total	28	29	45	27

Walker and Sons
Accounting Package Selection
02/10/1989

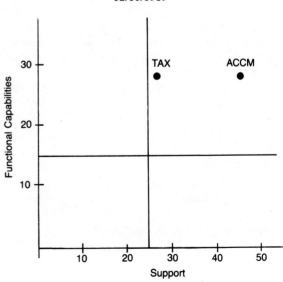

14.2 Worksheet for grid:

Criteria	WP	MW	VW	WS	MM
Manuscript capabilities:					
Footnotes	4	4	2	4	2
Index	4	4	1	1	1
Bibliography	1	1	1	1	1
Outline	4	4	1	1	1
Total	13	13	5	7	5
Support:					
Show commands	3	5	3	4	3
Smart help	4	3	3	4	3
Tutorial manual	4	4	2	3	3
Total	11	12	8	11	9

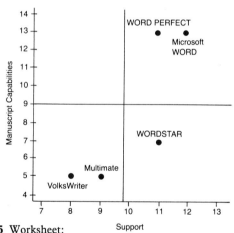

Electronic Learning Magazine
Survey of Word Processing Packages
March 1987

14.5 Worksheet:

	CL	TL	IA	PP	TR	CT	LR
Functional (vertical axis)							
1. Text control	40	40	40	40	40	30	40
2. Graphics/type control	60	80	100	100	100	60	40
3. Screen control	60	80	90	100	84	60	100
4. Sound control	50	0	45	45	0	0	45
5. Access levels/reports	45	68	66	53	68	75	53
Total	255	268	341	338	292	225	278
Support (horizontal axis)							
6. Help and error messages	40	30	30	30	30	40	30
7. Peripheral support	15	23	23	23	25	20	20
8. Documentation	40	38	35	45	50	38	45
Total	95	91	88	98	105	98	95

Grid:

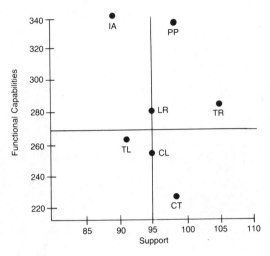

Chapter 15

15.1 The DFD and design repository are used throughout the design phase to identify design features and to coordinate the efforts of individual designers. For example, the DFD is used during interface design to identify reports and screens and during procedure design to identify manual procedures that are needed to control the use of screens and reports. The design repository can help coordinate the efforts of program and database designers by providing a single storage location for the documentation of data elements.

15.2 *System quality* is measured by the functionality, ease of maintenance, and adaptability of the system. System quality is the goal most visible to the user of the system. The goal of *project management* is to complete the design activities on time and within budget and in a way that keeps the users committed to the project. *Organizational relevance* is measured by how well the system designed supports the objectives of the organization.

15.3

1) Interface design specifies how the system will appear to the users. The interface specification describes external documents, internal reports, report screens, data entry screens, and dialogues (menus, questions and answers, and commands). It also specifies controls to ensure the accuracy, integrity, and confidentiality of the data that is entered and accessed through the interface.

2) Database design specifies how the data requirements for a system will be implemented as a database. Database specifications describe the logical and

physical structures of the database. These structures include data elements, records, keys, relationships, file organizations, physical records, and indexes of the database.

3) Program design specifies how interface, procedure, and database specifications are packaged into programs. The program specifications include program structure charts and a test plan.

4) Procedure design specifies how the flow of work for the new system will be controlled. Procedure specifications include procedures, manual controls, and the training materials for the system.

5) Negotiating hardware and software contracts involves negotiating with vendors for any additional hardware and purchased software required for the new system. The negotiations center on delivery schedules and prices.

6) The review and approval of the design involves the re-evaluation of the feasibility of the project and the schedule in light of economic, technical, operational, and human factors. If approved, the design specifications become the input for the implementation stage.

15.4 User access is either multiple or single. The software source is either existing (packaged) or custom-written software.

Design specification usually addresses all five components of an information system: people, procedures, data, software, and hardware. Often, however, one or more of these components will be emphasized, depending on the type of user access and the software source. Greater attention to procedures and data is required for multiple-user systems than for most single-user systems. Designing systems using custom-written software requires the completion of all six design steps. Designing systems that use existing software requires emphasis on three design steps: (1) designing procedures, (2) negotiating hardware and software contracts, and (3) reviewing design specifications.

15.5

1) Procedure design should not be scheduled before the interface, database, and programs are designed. Procedures specify the flow of work for the new system. The flow of work includes the use of reports, screens, and files. For example, the flow of work to run a daily production report should include the name of the report, the names of the programs that create the report, and the files that are accessed to create the report. If the interface, programs, and database have not been designed when the daily

reporting procedure is written, the designer cannot accurately specify the procedure.

2) Training design should not be scheduled before the interface, database, and programs are designed. Training must be designed for the user who will use the interface and the operators who will use the interface and control jobs that interact with programs and files. Thus, training cannot be accurately specified if the interface, program, and database designs are not yet completed.

3) Program design starts too early. Program design specifications include information about how programs will access data in the database. If the database has not been even partially designed, how can even the initial program specifications be written? Although program structure charts may be begun before the database design is complete, program and database design should not begin simultaneously.

Chapter 16

16.1 The human-computer boundary of the DFD identifies the interfaces of a system. The data dictionary for the DFD is used to identify the data elements used by each interface (external documents, internal reports, report screens, data entry screens, and dialogues).

16.2

- *External document*—provides information to, or requests an action from, people outside of the system. Example: an invoice.
- *Internal report*—supplies information to personnel within the organization. Example: an order register.
- *Report screen*—a report displayed via a CRT.
- *Data entry screen*—used to enter or update data in computer files.
- *Human-computer dialogue*—defines how the interaction between the user and the computer takes place. The three types of dialogue are menu, question and answer, and command.

16.3

- *Menu*—displays a list of alternative selections to a user. Menu dialogues are the most learnable type of dialogue and are preferred when the usage frequency of the dialogue is low.
- *Question and answer*—presents questions and alternative answers. The user selects the alternative that best answers the question. Question and answer dialogues are appropriate for any level of usage frequency. If usage frequency is low and learnability

is important, questions that require yes or no answers are effective. If usage frequency is medium or high, open-ended questions are effective.

- *Command*—requires the typing of special commands or pressing of specific keys to make selections. Command dialogues provide the quickest way for an experienced user to access the applications of a system. Commands are preferred when the usage frequency of the dialogue is high.

16.5

a. Screen 2 is aesthetically pleasing. Screen 3 uses a mixture of upper and lower case for the title; this lowers the quality of the screen.

b. Screen 2 is simple; it supports only one function. Screen 3 is more complex; it supports two functions: order entry and the set-up of customer discounts.

c. Both screens have some problems with clarity. Neither screen has labels for the DATE and TIME fields in the upper left-hand corner. Screen 2 does not specify whether "STATE" is a two-character state code or any common abbreviation. The field label "CUSTOMER AREA + PHONE" is not clear. It should be changed to "CUSTOMER AREA CODE-PHONE NUMBER."

d. The screens are not consistent. Screen 2 uses a MM/DD/YY format for the date. Screen 3 abbreviates the month and uses a four-digit year. Screen 2 allows either F1 or "ENTER" for entering data, whereas Screen 3 allows only "ENTER." Screen 3 uses F1 for displaying additional order lines, which is a very risky double use of a function key.

Chapter 17

17.1 The conceptual data model introduced in Chapter 11 is used to understand the data needed by users of a system. This model is the major input to the database design process. In the logical phase of database design, the entities, relationships, and attributes of the conceptual data model are transformed into records, relationships, and data elements according to the constraints imposed by the data structure class of the DBMS.

17.6

a. The schema is flexible, except for the PROFESSOR table. The PROFESSOR table is an aggregation of the PROFESSOR and DEPARTMENT entities. This table, therefore, implicitly includes the 1:M relationship between the PROFESSOR and DEPARTMENT entities. In addition, the design assumes that a department cannot exist without at least one professor. If the relationship changed (for example, if a professor could belong to two or more departments or if a department could exist without a professor), the database would require substantial changes. Creating separate tables for the PROFESSOR and DEPARTMENT entities would make the design more flexible.

b. Apparently the efficiency of data retrieval was the primary criterion used in designing the schema. If the database is used in a typical university environment, data retrieval may be the most important efficiency criterion. Updates and changes to records should be infrequent (only at the beginning and end of semesters or quarters), and the volumes of data (e.g., the number of students) should be relatively stable.

Chapter 18

18.1 The DFD is used to understand the processes and data needed by users of a system. The DFD is the major input to the program design process. In the first step of program design, the processes and data flows of the DFD are transformed into the modules, module connections, and data and control flows of a structure chart. Then, the structure chart is refined for coupling and cohesion, and PDL is added to specify each module. The PDL is derived from the structured English specifications of the DFD processes.

18.2

- *Module*—a group of statements, or instructions, that is executed to perform a function of the program. Modules are the fundamental building blocks of the structure chart.
- *Module connection*—a communication path between modules.
- *Data flow*—one or more data values that are passed between two modules. A data flow is passed only between modules with an established connection.
- *Control flow*—a flag or indicator that controls the processing of a module or reports on the status of a condition. A control flow is passed only between modules with an established connection.
- *Supplements*—structure chart symbols that show looping, decisions, files, and screens.

18.3 PDL is an acronym for Program Definition Language. PDL specifies the processing statements of a module, whereas structured English specifies the transformation of data inputs into data outputs for a process. The difference between PDL and structured English is that PDL includes statements to specify calls to other modules, parameters of data and control that flow between modules, user dialogues, error processing, accesses of data from the database, and definitions of data used in a module. PDL is used to communicate with programmers, whereas structured English is used to communicate with users.

18.4 Transform analysis and transaction analysis are two techniques used to convert a DFD into a structure chart. Transform analysis is used for a DFD that has processes arranged sequentially. The objective of transform analysis is to create a structure chart that is arranged in a hierarchy, with the left-most modules converted from processes associated with inputs to the DFD (raw, unprocessed data) and the right-most modules converted from processes associated with the outputs of the DFD (processed data). The processes on the DFD that are between the inputs and outputs, called the area of central transform, become the modules in the center of the structure chart.

Transaction analysis is used for a DFD that has case-structured processes. The objective of transaction analysis is to identify the process that determines where to route incoming data flows. This process is known as the transaction center. A structure chart is formed with the transaction center at the top of the hierarchy.

Chapter 19

19.1

a. Thoroughly testing the programs using test files increases the likelihood that any bugs will be eliminated before the system goes into production, thus reducing system reliability maintenance. This testing under all possible data error conditions may also help you develop a better user interface, because you may identify errors that the system can be programmed to correct, errors that require clear messages to the users, and errors whose recovery procedures need to be documented fully in the users manual. Making these changes now will reduce the need for system efficiency and user enhancement maintenance later.

b. Maintaining a well-educated staff of users increases the likelihood that the system will be used fully and correctly, thus reducing system reliability and efficiency maintenance. Knowledgeable users are better able to understand the costs of maintenance and thus less likely to request trivial enhancements. Also, especially when 4GLs are used, these users may be able to perform some of the maintenance for their own systems. Finally, users who understand systems and the development/maintenance process may provide better input during the requirements determination stage, thus ensuring that the system implemented is indeed the one they need and reducing the number of user enhancements requested.

c. Using purchased software effectively transfers many maintenance responsibilities to the vendor: any bugs or updates are the vendor's concern, not yours.

d. Performing frequent walkthroughs as the system is developed reduces the need for system reliability and efficiency maintenance and user enhancements. Involving users in these walkthroughs acquaints them with the system's capabilities and design specifications at an early stage—and ideas on paper are much easier to revise than fully implemented ideas. Walkthroughs also can reduce the need for system compatibility maintenance if points where the new system interfaces with the old are identified and thoroughly tested as a result of these walkthroughs.

19.3

$$\frac{13 \text{ months}}{13 + 8 + 23\%} = \frac{x \text{ months}}{56\%}$$

$$\frac{13 \text{ months} \times 56\%}{44\%} = x \text{ months}$$

$$\frac{728}{44} = 16.55 \text{ or about 17 effort-months}$$

19.7 Breakdowns are likely to occur wherever beginning one task is contingent on having completed another. Thus, all the activities on the critical path A-B-F-G-D are susceptible to schedule overruns. Activities E, H, and C are less susceptible because of the slack time on their paths.

19.10
a–d.

Project Planning Documentation										Page 1				
System Word Processing System										Date				
Symbols ⊢—⊣ Scheduled activity ⊨—⊨ Completed activity		Analyst Grayson Parker				Signature								
Activity	Individual Assigned		Weeks											
		8	9	10	11	12	13	14						
1.1 Implement Editorial WP														
1.1.1 Prepare site for computer and printer	Grayson, Cindy	⊢												
1.1.2 Test hardware components	Grayson	⊢⊣												
1.1.3 Build form letter files	Sheila, Cindy		⊢⊣											
1.1.4 Test files *			⊢											
1.1.5 Document procedures*	Cindy, Grayson			⊢										
1.1.6 Test procedures	Cindy				⊢									
1.1.7 Install	Grayson, Cindy				⊢									
1.1.8 Train users	Grayson, Cindy				⊢——⊣									
1.1.9 Mgmt approval/changeover						⊦⊦								
1.2 Implement Marketing WP														
1.2.1 Build form letter files*	Grayson						⊢							
1.2.2 Test files	Grayson						⊢							
1.2.3 Install	Grayson							⊢						
1.2.4 Mgmt approval/changeover								⊢						
1.3 Implement Circulation WP														
1.3.1 Build form letter files	Cindy						⊢							
1.3.2 Test files	Cindy							⊢						
1.3.3 Build subscription file	Ed							⊢						
1.3.4 Test file	Ed							⊢						
1.3.5 Document procedures	Cindy, Ed							⊢⊣						
1.3.6 Test procedures	Cindy							⊢						
1.3.7 Install	Ed, Cindy								⊢⊣					
1.3.8 Train users	Cindy								⊢⊣					
1.3.9 Mgmt approval/changeover									⊢⊣					

* Tangible product delivery

Assumptions Answered in the Gantt chart in the left column for Gantt chart planning:

1) The secretaries are the primary users of the system, which consists of a microcomputer, a printer, and WP software.
2) The individual departments have designed boilerplate, or form, letters to be used as the foundation of most correspondence.
3) The circulation system needs to be capable of merging form letters with a subscriber address file.
4) The secretaries' training on the marketing and circulation systems will be completed concurrently, and it will require less time because the secretaries will be familiar with the system from their editorial system training.
5) The procedures for using the systems will be basically the same, since all use the same software and are centered on form letters and mail merge capabilities.
6) Assigning more than two people to an activity is counterproductive (too many cooks spoil the broth!).

e. The original CPM network in Figure 5.16 allotted three weeks for implementing the marketing system and only two weeks for implementing the circulation and editorial systems. These allotments have been reversed in the Gantt chart here, given the assumptions stated above. Since the project team members and the second secretary will need to perform their usual daily duties as they build, test, and are trained to use the system, it seems that the goal of achieving changeover on all three systems in just seven weeks may be optimistic. The likelihood of meeting this schedule is dependent largely on the size of the workload these people must carry as they implement the system.

19.11 Sample answers for product deliveries:

- User documentation (normal and error recovery procedures)
- Construction and testing of control menus
- Construction and testing of each program
- Construction of test and master files
- Construction and testing of interface to old system
- Sign-off on sample reports
- Sign-off on data query screens

Chapter 20

20.1 The Gantt chart below shows detailed activities that conform to Fred's two-week plan in Figure 3.10. The two-week plan seems overly optimistic, since testing also has to be completed during these two weeks. In fact, we know from the end of the Meadows Hospital case that a third week was required for the actual work. Completing a detailed Gantt chart like the one below, one might have led Fred to revise his plans, rather than learn in the second week that implementation would take twice as long as planned. (Note that post-installation construction activities are also shown here, since those are part of construction planning.)

20.3

1) Know your problem. This increases the chances of developing a system that is complete and accurate and therefore is more reliable and functions better.
2) Design modules top down. Modular structure makes a system easier to understand and modify and therefore easier to understand and maintain.
3) Keep modules small. Cohesive (single-function) modules make a system easier to understand and therefore easier to maintain.
4) Document your work. Clear documentation makes a system easier to understand and therefore easier to maintain.
5) Organize your spreadsheet. Clear software documentation makes a system easier to understand and test and therefore easier to maintain.

Chapter 21

21.4
a. Possible data entry errors:

1) Name too long
2) Name contains nonalphabetic characters
3) SSN too long or contains nonnumeric characters
4) Student number too long or contains nonnumeric characters
5) Student major code too long or contains nonalphabetic characters or is not one of the predefined valid entries
6) SSN, student number, or student major code entries too short
7) Trying to add a student who already is listed
8) Assigning a student number that was already assigned to another student
9) Duplicate SSNs—two students listed as having the same SSN

Project Planning Documentation

		Page	

System: Pharmacy Record Keeping System (Implementation) — Date

Symbols ⊢⊣ Scheduled activity ▬ Completed activity — Analyst Fred Kahn — Signature

Activity	Individual Assigned	PRE-INSTALLATION CONSTRUCTION											POST-I	
		M	T	W	Th	F	M	T	W	Th	F	S	S	WK 1	WK 2
C. CONSTRUCTION														
C.1 Install Hdw in Info. Serv.	Vendor, Fred			⊢⊣										
C.2 Install Rapid Pharmacy	Vendor, Fred			⊢⊣										
C.3 Build Test Files	Fred								⊢⊣					
C.4 Build Production Files	Fred									⊢⊣				
C.5 Build Printer Shelf	Maint. Div.			⊢⊣										
C.6 Add Electric Outlet	Maint. Div									⊢⊣				
C.7 Clean up Files	Fred													⊢⊣
D. DOCUMENTATION														
D.1 Write Quick Reference	Fred		⊢⊣											
D.2 Create Doctor List	Fred			⊢⊣										
D.3 Write Daily Backup Procedure	Fred, Tito				⊢⊣									
D.4 Revise Documents	Fred, Tito									⊢⊣				
D.5 Evaluate Documents	Fred, Tito												⊢⊣	
D.6 Revise Documents	Fred, Tito													⊢⊣
T. TRAINING														
T.1 Self-Training (Info. Serv.)	Fred						⊢⊣							
T.2 Vendor Training # 1 (Sales Office)	Tito, 3 staff members							⊢⊣						
T.3 Customize Training Materials	Tito, 1 staff member								⊢⊣					
T.4 Vendor Training # 2	1/2 remaining staff									⊢⊣				
T.5 Vendor Training # 3	1/2 staff										⊢⊣			
T.6 Evaluate Training	Tito												⊢⊣	
T.7 Create New Staff Training	Tito													⊢⊣

b. Sample test data (error codes from 21.4a):

Error Code	Name	SSN	S-Number	S-Major
E1	Klintzenmueller, Alexandreena	381561987	133	MAN
E2	Li, Chung-Hsing	455098869	131	MIS
E3	Montreaux, William	987A35496	134	ENG
E4	Peters, Roxanne	459178369	MKT	MIS
E9	Hintz, Robert	381561987	136	ACC
E5	Anderson, Paul	519304612	137	NAN
no error	Garcia, Christina	459109182	138	DPA

c. This is a black box test, since it is a test of correct output based on input designed to test for specific logic.

21.6

Test Specification					Page 1 of 1
System	Pharmacy	Module	Supplier Report		
Prepared by	Fred Kahn				Date
Objective	Verify supplier report				
Test Condition	Description of Condition	Test Steps	Expected Results		Executed By / Date
010	Verify order #s	Compare to numbers in test file	Report results should be identical to test data with one entry for each supplier number.		
011	Verify supplier	Compare to suppliers in test file	Report results should match test data with one supplier name for each supplier number.		
012	Verify drug name / brand	Compare to test data for drugs and brands	This should be all available drugs for every supplier. Order in number and supplier name should not repeat.		
013	Verify UOM (unit of measure), usage, and quantity available	Compare to test data	This reflects stored data. Should repeat for every drug.		

Chapter 22

22.1

a. The plan at Woods, Inc. is to implement the communication network and sales reporting system in phases. For this problem we will assume that installation will be divided into three phases: (1) installation of the communication network, (2) installation of high-priority sales reports, and (3) installation of the remaining sales reports. The best installation strategy varies for the different phases.

The best installation strategy for the communication network is immediate replacement, since the same lines will be used for the old and new systems. (In the installation plan for 22.1b, the risks of immediate replacement are minimized by thoroughly testing the system at headquarters and the second-priority site before installing and checking it at the remaining sites.)

Parallel installation can be used at each site for both phases of the sales reporting system, although the parallel runs should be made over the weekend so as not to overload the hardware. Having staff alternate working the weekend shift will minimize personnel problems. If the installation runs go well, there will be just one weekend when the new sales reporting system will be run in parallel with the old at headquarters. If the first-weekend results are perfectly matched or have only minor errors, the new system will become the production system. For the next two weekends, the old system will be run in parallel with the new. After perfect test results are obtained at headquarters, at the remaining sites the new system will be run in parallel with the old for just one weekend, unless difficulties or errors are encountered. Then the new system will be installed at the remaining sites and the old system will become the parallel system for one weekend before end-of-year reports are tested in a "quasi-parallel" (short-year) run.

b. These three installation plans could be set up as Gantt charts, but information about dates and team members is not available.

Installation Plan for Woods, Inc. Communication Network and Sales Reporting System

Communications Installation

CI.1 Install new software at headquarters (HQ) and Aurora, 1 A.M., and prevent access from other sites

CI.2 Test at HQ and Aurora (1 A.M. to 4 A.M.)

CI.3 Reinstall current software at HQ and Aurora (4 A.M.)

CI.4 Evaluate installation test

CI.5 Repeat CI.1–CI.4 at HQ and Aurora (1 A.M. to 4 A.M.)

CI.6 Repeat CI.1–CI.4 at HQ and Aurora (1 A.M. to 4 A.M.), if needed

CI.7 Install new software at remaining sites (1 A.M.)

CI.8 Test at remaining sites (1 A.M. to 4 A.M.)

CI.9 Reinstall current software at remaining sites, if needed, and repeat CI.7 and CI.8 until successful at remaining sites

Sales System Phase A Installation
  Headquarters Installation

SA.1 Parallel test new software (weekend)

SA.2 Compare old and new results (during week)

SA.3 Repeat SA.1 and SA.2, if needed

SA.4 Install new software for production

SA.5 Parallel test old software (weekend)

SA.6 Compare old and new results (during week)

SA.7 Repeat SA.5 and SA.6

SA.8 Run end-of-year sales reports (as if end)

SA.9 Compare results for end of year

SA.10 Repeat SA.5, SA.6, SA.8, and SA.9, as needed

  Site Installation
Repeat SA.1–SA.6, SA.8–SA.9 for Aurora
Repeat SA.1–SA.6, SA.8–SA.9 for Millworks and Woods Service
Repeat SA.1–SA.6 for remaining sites

Sales System Phase B Installation
Follow same activities as for phase A

22.3 At a minimum, George should have used a phased installation strategy, installing just one system function at a time. At least then he would have had a small review disaster rather than a major one. It would have been even better to phase development. Defining, evaluating, designing, and implementing just a small portion of the system would have resulted in his getting the attention of the busy production and information systems managers much earlier than he did.

Index

Acceptance review, 585–587
Access, *see* Data access
Accuracy, database integrity and, 447
Adaptability, database design and, 447
ADBAS, 444
Address, file organization and, 435
Aggregation
  of attributes, 432
  of records, 434
Alternatives
  documentation of, 323
  evaluation of, 23, 76, 322–324, 354–373
  generation of, 323
  identification of, 22–23, 75
  management review of, 76–78
Analyst, *see* Systems analyst
Analyzing strategy, 179, 181, 220–222
Appendixes, requirements document and, 307
Application software, 12
  custom-written by end-users, 57–59
  custom-written by professionals, 59–61
  sources of, 56–61
Application systems
  databases shared by, 439
  frequency of use, 410
Approvals, design stage and, 387
Asking strategy, 179, 181, 211–218
Attributes
  aggregation of, 432
  data models and, 267–268
  defining, 289–292
  derived, 268, 280, 432
  grouping, 289–292
  identifiers and, 273–274
  role discriminator and, 276
  segmentation of, 432
  technical characteristics of, 268
  validating, 292–294
Audit trail, 39

Backup, 7, 83
Batch processing systems, 252

Benchmark tests, 569
Benefits
  cost/benefit analysis and, 23, 589
  intangible, 334
  payback analysis and, 334–336
  requirements determination and, 168
  tangible, 334
Black box testing, 565
Blinking fields, 406
Blocking, 437, 453
Bottom-up testing strategy, 509, 568
Boundaries, system, 19, 199, 205, 393, 415, 422
  constraints and, 175
  requirements determination and, 172–173
  site and, 174
  testing conditions, 566
Brainstorming
  CPM networks and, 116
  creativity and, 324–325
  Nominal Group Technique and, 215
Budget
  completion within, 41
  estimating, *see* Estimation
  evaluation process and, 331–332
  See also Cost(s)
Business report writing, 303–304

Calling hierarchy, 477
Calling module, 486
Capacity planning, 311
Cardinality, 271, 277
Case-structured processes, data flows and, 481–484
CASE (Computer Aided System Engineering) tools, 61, 171–172, 230, 520
Change management, 595–596
Changeover, 18, 25, 537, 588
  out-of-date systems and, 90
  user approval of, 95
  user commitment and, 42
Change requests, 170

The Development Process Matrix for Development with Existing Software

	People	Procedures	Data	Software	Hardware
Determine Requirements	Form development team Determine possible users	Determine procedural requirements	Determine I/O and volume requirements	Determine functional requirements	Determine facility and equipment requirements
Evaluate Alternatives	Identify and select users	Identify and select procedures	Identify alternative I/O and storage solutions	Identify and select software	Identify and select hardware
Specify Design	Specify and organize users	Specify procedures and documentation	Specify and organize data	Negotiate contract and order software	Negotiate contract and order hardware
Implement Design	Train people	Test and document procedures	Build test files and production files	Test and install software	Prepare site Install and test hardware